The Visualization Toolkit

An Object-Oriented Approach to 3D Graphics

To Susan and Z,
*   - Will*

To Michelle and my parents,
*   - Ken*

To Terri.
*   - Bill*

The Visualization Toolkit

An Object-Oriented Approach To 3D Graphics

Will Schroeder, Ken Martin, Bill Lorensen

For book and bookstore information

http://www.prenhall.com

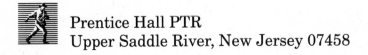

Prentice Hall PTR
Upper Saddle River, New Jersey 07458

Library of Congress Cataloging-in-Publication Data

Schroeder, Will.
   The visualization toolkit : an object-oriented approach to 3D graphics
Will Schroeder, Ken Martin, Bill Lorensen.
      p. cm.
   Includes bibliographical references and index.
   ISBN 0-13-199837-4
   1. Object-oriented programming (Computer science) 2. Computer graphics.
   I. Martin, Kenneth W. II. Lorensen, Bill. III. Title.
QA76.64.kS37 1996
 001.4'225'028566--dc20   95-49177
                                                              CIP

Editorial/production supervision: *Ann Sullivan*
Manufacturing manager: *Alexis R. Heydt*
Acquisitions editor: *Mary Franz*
Editorial assistant: *Noreen Regina*
Cover manager: *Jerry Votta*

© 1996 by Prentice Hall PTR
Prentice-Hall, Inc.
A Simon & Schuster Company
Upper Saddle River, New Jersey 07458

The publisher offers discounts on this book when ordered in bulk quantities.
For more information, contact:

Corporate Sales Department
PTR Prentice Hall
One Lake Street
Upper Saddle River, NJ 07458

Phone: 800-382-3419, Fax: 201-236-7141
E-mail: corpsales@prenhall.com

Printed in the United States of America
10 9 8 7 6 5 4 3 2 1

ISBN: 0-13-199837-4

Prentice-Hall International (UK) Limited, *London*
Prentice-Hall of Australia Pty. Limited, *Sydney*
Prentice-Hall Canada Inc., *Toronto*
Prentice-Hall Hispanoamericana, S.A., *Mexico*
Prentice-Hall of India Private Limited, *New Delhi*
Prentice-Hall of Japan, Inc., *Tokyo*
Simon & Schuster Asia Pte. Ltd., *Singapore*
Editora Prentice-Hall do Brasil, Ltda., *Rio de Janeiro*

Contents

Chapter 4 The Visualization Pipeline 75

Chapter 9   Algorithms II   269

Chapter 10   Interpreters   331

Preface

Visualization is a great field to work in these days. Advances in computer hardware and software have brought this technology into the reach of nearly every computer system. Even the ubiquitous personal computer now offers specialized 3D graphics hardware. And with the release of Windows95 and OpenGL, there is an API for 3D graphics as well.

We view visualization and visual computing as nothing less than a new form of communication. All of us have long known the power of images to convey information, ideas, and even feelings. Recent trends have brought us 2D images and graphics as evidenced by the variety of graphical user interfaces and business plotting software. But 3D images have been used sparingly, and often by specialists using specialized systems. Now this is changing. We believe we are entering a new era where 3D images, visualizations, and animations will begin to extend, and in some cases, replace the current communication paradigm based on words, mathematical symbols, and 2D images. Our hope is that along the way the human imagination will be freed like never before.

This text and companion software offers one view of visualization. The field is broad, including elements of computer graphics, imaging, computer science, computational geometry, numerical analysis, statistical methods, data analysis, and studies in human perception. We certainly do not pretend to cover the field in its entirety. However, we feel that this text does offer you a great opportunity to learn about the fundamentals of visualization. Not only can you learn from the written word and companion images, but the included software will allow you to *practice* visualization. You can start by using the sample data we have provided here, and then move on to your own data and applications. We believe that you will soon appreciate visualization as much as we do.

We hope you enjoy the experience.

Acknowledgments

*D*uring the creation of the *Visualization Toolkit* we were fortunate to have the help of many people. Without their aid this book and the associated educational software might never have existed. Their contributions included performing book reviews, discussing software ideas, creating a supportive environment, and providing key suggestions for some of our algorithms and software implementations.

We would like to first thank our management at the General Electric Corporate R&D Center who allowed us to pursue this project and utilize company facilities: Peter Meenan, Manager of the Computer Graphics and Systems Program, and Kirby Vosburgh, Manager of the Electronic Systems Laboratory.

We thank our co-workers at the R&D Center who have all been supportive: Majeid Alyassin, Rick Avila, Jeanette Bruno, Shane Chang, Nelson Corby, Rich Hammond, Margaret Kelliher, Tim Kelliher, Joyce Langan, Charles Law, Paul Miller, Chris Nafis, Lisa Sobierajski, Bob Tatar, Chris Volpe, Boris Yamrom, Bill Hoffman, Harvey Cline and Siegwalt Ludke. We thank former co-workers Skip Montanaro, Dan McLachlan and Michelle Barry. Many ideas and helpful hints came from this delightful and talented group of people.

A special thanks to the software and text reviewers who spent their own time to track down some nasty bugs, provide examples, and offer suggestions and improvements. Thank you Tom Citriniti, Mark Miller, George Petras, Hansong Zhang, Penny Rheingans, Paul Hinker, Richard Ellson, and Roger Crawfis. We'd also like to mention that Tom Citriniti at RPI, and Penny Rheingans at the

University of Mississippi were the first faculty members to teach from early versions of this text. Thank you Penny and Tom for your feedback and extra effort.

We'd especially like to thank Mary Franz, Noreen Regina, Ann Sullivan, and the rest of the folks at Prentice Hall who helped turn our dreams into reality. These are some of the most enthusiastic people we've ever worked with, an invaluable quality when it seems as if things will never end.

Most importantly we would like to thank our friends and loved ones who supported us patiently during this project. We know that you shouldered extra load for us. You certainly saw a lot less of us! But we're happy to say that we're back. Thank you.

Introduction

Visualization - "2: the act or process of interpreting in visual terms or of putting into visual form," *Webster's Ninth New Collegiate Dictionary.*

1.1 What Is Visualization?

Visualization is a part of our everyday life. From weather maps to the exciting computer graphics of the entertainment industry, examples of visualization abound. But what is visualization? Informally, visualization is the transformation of data or information into pictures. Visualization engages the primary human sensory apparatus, *vision,* as well as the processing power of the human mind. The result is a simple and effective medium for communicating complex and/or voluminous information.

Terminology

Different terminology is used to describe visualization. *Scientific visualization* is the formal name given to the field in computer science that encompasses user interface, data representation and processing algorithms, visual representations, and other sensory presentation such as sound or touch [McCormick87]. The term *data visualization* is another phrase used to describe visualization.

Data visualization is generally interpreted to be more general than scientific visualization, since it implies treatment of data sources beyond the sciences and engineering. Such data sources include financial, marketing, or business data. In addition, the term data visualization is broad enough to include application of statistical methods and other standard data analysis techniques [Rosenblum94]. Another recently emerging term is *information visualization*. This field endeavors to visualize abstract information such as hyper-text documents on the World Wide Web, directory/file structures on a computer, or abstract data structures [InfoVis95]. A major challenge facing information visualization researchers is to develop coordinate systems, transformation methods, or structures that meaningfully organize and represent data.

In this text we use the term data visualization instead of the more specific terms scientific visualization or information visualization. We feel that scientific visualization is too narrow a description of the field, since visualization techniques have moved beyond the scientific domain and into areas of business, social science, demographics, and information management in general. We also feel that the term data visualization is broad enough to encompass the term information visualization.

Examples of Visualization

Perhaps the best definition of visualization is offered by example. In many cases visualization is influencing peoples' lives and performing feats that a few years ago would have been unimaginable. A prime example of this is its application to modern medicine.

Computer imaging techniques have become an important diagnostic tool in the practice of modern medicine. These include techniques such as X-ray *Computed Tomography* (CT) and *Magnetic Resonance Imaging* (MRI). These techniques use a sampling or data acquisition process to capture information about the internal anatomy of a living patient. This information is in the form of *slice-planes* or cross-sectional images of a patient, similar to conventional photographic X-rays. CT imaging uses many pencil thin X-rays to acquire the data, while MRI combines large magnetic fields with pulsed radio waves. Sophisticated mathematical techniques are used to reconstruct the slice-planes. Typically, many such closely spaced slices are gathered together into a *volume* of data to complete the study.

As acquired from the imaging system, a slice is a series of numbers representing the attenuation of X-rays (CT) or the relaxation of nuclear spin magnetization (MRI) [Krestel90]. On any given slice these numbers are arranged in a matrix, or regular array. The amount of data is large, so large that it is not possible to understand the data in its raw form. However, by assigning to these numbers a gray scale value, and then displaying the data on a computer screen, structure emerges. This structure results from the interaction of the human visual system with the spatial organization of the data and the gray-scale values we have chosen. What the computer represents as a series of numbers, we see as a cross section through the human body: skin, bone, and muscle. Even more impressive results are possible when we extend these techniques into three-dimensions. Image slices can be gathered into volumes and the volumes can be processed to reveal complete anatomical structures. Using modern techniques we can view the entire brain, skeletal system and vascular system on a living patient without interventional surgery. Such capability has revolutionized modern medical diagnostics, and will increase in importance as imaging and visualization technology matures.

Another everyday application of visualization is in the entertainment industry. Movie and television producers routinely use computer graphics and visualization to create entire worlds that we could never visit in our physical bodies. In these cases we are visualizing other worlds as we imagine them, or past worlds we suppose existed. It's hard to watch the movies like *Jurassic Park* and *Toy Story* and not gain a deeper appreciation for the awesome Tyrannosaurus Rex, or to be charmed by *Toy Story*'s heroic Buzz Lightyear.

Morphing is another popular visualization technique widely used in the entertainment industry. Morphing is a smooth blending of one object into another. One common application is to morph between two faces. Morphing has also been used effectively to illustrate car design changes from one year to the next. While this may seem like an esoteric application, visualization techniques are used routinely to present the daily weather report. The use of isovalue, or contour, lines to display areas of constant temperature, rainfall, and barometric pressure has become a standard tool in the daily weather report.

Many early uses of visualization were in the engineering and scientific community. From its inception the computer has been used as a tool to simulate physical processes such as ballistic trajectories, fluid flow, and structural mechanics. As the size of the computer simulations grew, it became necessary to transform the resulting calculations into pictures. The amount of data overwhelmed the ability of the human to assimilate and understand it. In fact, pictures were so important that early visualizations were created by manually transcribing numbers into pictures. Today we can take advantage of advances in computer graphics and computer hardware. But, whatever the technology, the application of visualization is the same: to display the results of simulations, experiments, measured data, and fantasy; and to use these pictures to communicate, understand, and entertain.

1.2 Why Visualize?

Visualization is a necessary tool to make sense of the flood of information in today's world of computers. Satellites, supercomputers, laser digitizing systems, and digital data acquisition systems acquire, generate, and transmit data at prodigious rates. The Earth-Orbiting Satellite (EOS) transmits terabytes of data every day. Laser scanning systems generate over 500,000 points in a fifteen second scan [Waters91]. Supercomputers model weather patterns over the entire earth [Chen93]. In the first four months of 1995, the New York Stock Exchange processed, on average, 333 million transactions per day [NYTimes]. Without visualization, most of this data would sit unseen on computer disks and tapes. Visualization offers some hope that we can extract the important information hidden within the data.

There is another important element to visualization: it takes advantage of the natural abilities of the human vision system. Our vision system is a complex and powerful part of our bodies. We use it and rely on it in almost everything we do. Given the environment in which our ancestors lived, it is not surprising that certain senses developed to help them survive. As we described earlier in the example of a 2D MRI scan, visual representations are easier to work with. Not only do we have strong 2D visual abilities, but also we are adept at integrating different viewpoints and other visual clues into a mental image of a 3D object or plot. This leads to interactive visualization, where we can manipulate our viewpoint. Rotating about the object helps to achieve a better understanding. Likewise, we have a talent for recognizing temporal changes in an image. Given an animation consisting of hundreds of frames, we have an uncanny ability to recognize trends and spot areas of rapid change.

With the introduction of computers and the ability to generate enormous amounts of data, visualization offers the technology to make the best use of our highly developed visual senses. Certainly other technologies such as statistical analysis, artificial intelligence, mathematical filtering and sampling theory will play a role in large scale data processing. However, because visualization directly engages the vision system and human brain, it remains an unequalled technology for understanding and communicating data.

Visualization offers significant financial advantages as well. In today's competitive markets, computer simulation teamed with visualization can reduce product cost and improve time to market. A large cost of product design has been the expense and time required to create and test design prototypes. Current design methods strive to eliminate these physical prototypes, and replace them with digital equivalents. This digital prototyping requires the ability to create and manipulate product geometry, simulate the design under a variety of operating conditions, develop manufacturing techniques, demonstrate product maintenance and service procedures, and even train operators on the proper use of the product before it is built. Visualization plays a role in each case. Already CAD systems are used routinely to model product geometry and design manufacturing procedures. Visualization enables us to view the geometry, and see special characteristics such as surface curvature. Analysis techniques such as finite element, finite difference, and boundary element techniques are used to simulate product performance and visualization is used to view the results. Recently, human ergonomics and anthropometry are being analyzed using computer techniques in combination with visualization [MDHMS]. Three-dimensional graphics and visualization are being used to create training sequences. Often these are incorporated into a hypertext document or World Wide Web (WWW) pages. Another practical use of graphics and visualization has been in flight simulators. This has been shown to be a significant cost savings as compared to flying real airplanes, and is an effective training method.

1.3 Imaging, Computer Graphics and Visualization

There is confusion surrounding the difference between imaging, computer graphics, and visualization. We offer these definitions.

- *Imaging*, or image processing, is the study of 2D pictures, or images. This includes techniques to transform (e.g., rotate, scale, shear), extract information from, analyze and enhance images.

- *Computer graphics* is the process of creating images using a computer. This includes both 2D paint and draw techniques as well as more sophisticated 3D drawing (or rendering) techniques.

- *Visualization* is the process of exploring, transforming, and viewing data as images (or other sensory forms) to gain understanding and insight into the data.

Based on these definitions we see that there is overlap between these fields. The output of computer graphics is an image, while the output of visualization is often produced using computer graphics. Sometimes visualization data is in the form of an image, or we wish to visualize object geometry using realistic rendering techniques from computer graphics.

Generally speaking we distinguish visualization from computer graphics and image processing in three ways.

1. The dimensionality of data is three dimensions or greater. Many well-known methods are available for data of two dimensions or less; visualization serves best when applied to data of higher dimension.

2. Visualization concerns itself with data transformation. That is, information is repeatedly created and modified to enhance the meaning of the data.

3. Visualization is naturally interactive, including the human directly in the process of creating, transforming, and viewing data.

Another perspective is that visualization is an activity that encompasses the process of exploring and understanding data. This includes both imaging and computer graphics as well as data processing and filtering, user interface methodology, computational techniques, and software design. Figure **1–1** depicts this process.

As this figure illustrates we see that the visualization process focuses on data. In the first step data is acquired from some source. Next, the data is transformed by various methods, and then mapped to a form appropriate for presentation to the user. Finally, the data is rendered or displayed, completing the process. Often, the process repeats as the data is better understood or new models are developed. Sometimes the results of the visualization can directly control the generation of the data. This is often referred to as *analysis steering*. Analysis steering is an important goal of visualization because it enhances the interactivity of the overall process.

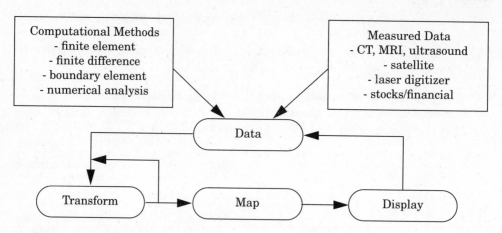

Figure 1–1 The visualization process. Data from various sources is repeatedly transformed to extract, derive, and enhance information. The resulting data is mapped to a graphics system for display.

1.4 Origins of Data Visualization

The origin of visualization as a formal discipline dates to the 1987 NSF report *Visualization in Scientific Computing* [McCormick87]. That report coined the term *scientific visualization*. Since then the field has grown rapidly with major conferences, such as IEEE Visualization, becoming well established. Many large computer graphics conferences, such as ACM SIGGRAPH, devote large portions of their program to visualization technology.

Of course, data visualization technology had existed for many years before the 1987 report referenced [Tufte83]. The first practitioners recognized the value of presenting data as images. Early pictorial data representations were created during the eighteenth century with the arrival of statistical graphics. It was only with the arrival of the digital computer and the development of the field of computer graphics, that visualization became a practicable discipline.

The future of data visualization and graphics appears to be explosive. Just a few decades ago, the field of data visualization did not exist and computer graphics was viewed as a offshoot of the more formal discipline of computer science. As techniques were created and computer power increased, engineers, scientists, and other researchers began to use graphics to understand and communicate data. At the same time, user interface tools were being developed. These forces have now converged to the point where we expect computers to adapt to humans rather than the other way around. As such, computer graphics and data visualization serve as the window into the computer, and more importantly, into the data that computers manipulate. Now, with the visualization window, we can extract information from data and analyze, understand, and manage more complex systems than ever before.

Dr. Fred Brooks, Kenan Professor of Computer Science at the University of North Carolina at Chapel Hill and recipient of the first John von Neumann Medal of the IEEE, puts it another way. At the award presentation at the ACM SIGGRAPH '94, Dr. Brooks stated that computer graphics and visualization offer "intelligence amplification" (IA) as compared to artificial intelligence (AI). Besides the deeper philosophical issues surrounding this issue (e.g., human before computer), it is a pragmatic observation. While the long-term goal of AI has been to develop computer systems that could replace humans in certain applications, the lack of real progress in this area has lead some researchers to view the role of computers as amplifiers and assistants to humans. In this view, computer graphics and visualization play a significant role, since arguably the most effective human/computer interface is visual. Recent gains in computer power and memory are only accelerating this trend, since it is the interface between the human and the computer that often is the obstacle to the effective application of the computer.

1.5 Purpose of This Book

There currently exist texts that define and describe data visualization, many of them using case studies to illustrate techniques and typical applications. Some provide high-level descriptions of algorithms or visualization system architectures. Detailed descriptions are left to academic journals or conference proceedings. What these texts lack is a way to *practice* visualization. Our aim in this text is to go beyond descriptions and provide tools to learn about and apply visualization to your own application area. In short, the purpose of the book is fourfold.

1. Describe visualization algorithms and architectures in detail.

2. Demonstrate the application of data visualization to a broad selection of case studies.

3. Provide a working architecture and software design for application of data visualization to real-world problems.

4. Provide effective software tools packaged in a C++ class library. We also provide a prototyping library in the interpreted language Tcl.

Taken together, we refer to the text and software as the *Visualization Toolkit*, or **vtk** for short. Our hope is that you can use the text to learn about the fundamental concepts of visualization, and then apply the computer code to your own applications and data.

1.6 What This Book Is Not

The purpose of this book is not to provide a rigorous academic treatise on data visualization. Nor do we intend to include an exhaustive survey of visualization technology. Our goal is to bridge the formal discipline of data visualization with practical application, and to provide a solid technical overview of this emerging technology. In many cases we refer you to the included software to understand implementation details. You may also wish to refer to the appropriate references for further information.

1.7 Intended Audience

Our primary audience is computer users who create, analyze, quantify, and/or process data. We assume a minimal level of programming skill. If you can write simple computer code to import data and know how to run a computer program, you can practice data visualization with the software accompanying this book.

As we wrote this book we also had in mind educators and students of introductory computer graphics and visualization courses. In more advanced courses this text may not be rigorous enough to serve as sole reference. In these instances this book will serve well as a companion text, and the software is well suited as a foundation for programming projects and class exercises.

Educators and students in other disciplines may also find the text and software to be valuable tools for presenting results. Courses in numerical analysis, computer science, business simulation, chemistry, dynamic systems, and engineering simulations, to name a few, often require large scale programming projects that create large amounts of data. The software tools provided here are easy to learn and readily adapted to different data sources. Students can incorporate this software into their work to display and analyze their results.

1.8 How to Use This Book

There are a number of approaches you can take to make effective use of this book. The particular approach depends on your skill level and goals. Three likely paths are as follows:

> *Novice.* You're a novice if you lack basic knowledge of graphics, visualization, or object-oriented principles. Start by reading Chapter 2 if you are unfamiliar with object-oriented principles, Chapter 3 if you are unfamiliar with computer graphics, and Chapter 4 if you are unfamiliar with visualization. Continue by reading the case studies in Chapter 9. You can then move on to the CD-ROM and try out some programming examples. Leave the more detailed treatment of algorithms and data representation until you are familiar with the basics, and plan to develop your own applications.

Hacker. You're a hacker if you are comfortable writing your own code and editing other's. Review the examples in Chapters 3, 4 and 9. Read the "Software Conventions" in Appendix A to get an understanding of how we have organized the software. Then retrieve the examples from the CD-ROM and start practicing.

Researcher/Educator. You're a researcher if you develop computer graphics and/or visualization algorithms or if you are actively involved in using and evaluating such systems. You're an educator if you cover aspects of computer graphics and/or visualization within your courses. Start by reading Chapters 2, 3 and 4. Select appropriate algorithms from the text and examine the associated source code. If you wish to extend the system, you will need to read the "Software Conventions" and "Development Guide" in Appendix A.

1.9 Software Considerations

In writing this book we have attempted to strike a balance between practice and theory. We did not want the book to become a user manual, yet we did want a strong correspondence between algorithmic presentation and software implementation. As a result, we have adopted the following approach:

Application versus Design. The book's focus is the application of visualization techniques to real-world problems. We devote less attention to software design issues. Some of these important design issues include memory management, deriving new classes, shallow versus deep object copy, single versus multiple inheritance, and interfaces to other graphics libraries. While Appendix A covers some of these design issues in detail, we did not want to distract you from the focus of this book.

Theory versus Implementation. Whenever possible, we separate the theory of data visualization from our implementation of it. We felt that the book would serve best as a reference tool if the theory sections were independent of software issues and terminology. Toward the end of each chapter there are separate implementation or example sections that are implementation specific. Earlier sections are implementation free.

Documentation. Appendix A contains documentation considered essential to understanding the software architecture. This includes object diagrams and condensed object descriptions. More extensive documentation of object methods and data members is embedded in the software and as help documentation and manual pages on the CD-ROM. You should also check out the reference pages in the latter half of this book. Appendix A also describes conventions used during implementation of the software.

We use a number of conventions in this text. Computer code including variable, class, and method names is denoted with a typewriter font. For example

`Foo`, `vtkObject`, and `Execute()` are examples of a variable, class name, and method. To avoid conflict with other C++ class libraries, all class names in **vtk** begin with the "`vtk`" prefix. Methods are differentiated from variables with the addition of the "`()`" postfix. (Other conventions are listed in Appendix A.)

All images in this text have been created using the *Visualization Toolkit* software and data on the CD-ROM. In addition, every image has source code (sometimes in C++ and sometimes a Tcl script). We decided against using images from other researchers because we wanted you to be able to practice visualization with every example we present. Each computer generated image indicates the originating file. Files ending in `.cc` are C++ code, files ending in `.tcl` are Tcl scripts. (See Chapter 10 for more information on Tcl.) Hopefully these examples can serve as a starting point for you to create your own applications.

1.10 Chapter-by-Chapter Overview

Object-Oriented Design

This chapter discusses some of the problems with developing large and/or complex software systems and describes how object-oriented design addresses many of these problems. This chapter defines the key terms used in object-oriented modelling and design and works through a real world example. The chapter concludes with a brief look at some object-oriented languages and some of the issues associated with object-oriented visualization.

Computer Graphics I

Computer graphics is the means by which our visualizations are created. This chapter covers the fundamental concepts of computer graphics from an application viewpoint. Common graphical entities such as cameras, lights, and geometric primitives are described along with some of the underlying physical equations that govern lighting and image generation. Issues related to currently available graphics hardware are presented, as they affect how and what we choose to render.

The Visualization Pipeline

This chapter explains our methodology for transforming raw data into a meaningful representation that the graphics engine can then render. We introduce the notion of a visualization pipeline, which is similar to a data flow diagram from software engineering. The differences between process objects and data objects are covered, as well as how we resolved issues between performance and memory usage. We explain the advantages to a pipeline network topology regarding execution ordering, result caching, and reference counting.

Data Representation I

There are many types of data produced by the variety of fields that apply visualization. This chapter describes the data objects that we use to represent and access such data. A flexible design is introduced where the programmer can interact with most any type of data using one consistent interface. The three high level components of data (structure, cells, and data attributes) are introduced, and their specific subclasses and components are discussed.

Algorithms I

Where the preceding chapter deals with data objects, this one introduces process objects. These objects encompass the algorithms that transform and manipulate our data. This chapter looks at commonly used techniques for isocontour extraction, scalar generation, color mapping, and vector field display, among others. The emphasis of this chapter is to provide the reader with a basic understanding of the more common and important visualization algorithms.

Computer Graphics II

This chapter covers advanced topics in computer graphics. We first introduce a variety of stereoscopic rendering techniques and then look at some of the issues and applications of transparency and texture mapping. We describe a number of effects that can be achieved through camera manipulation, including anti-aliasing and motion blur. We then conclude the chapter with an introduction to volume rendering, including object-order and image-order rendering techniques.

Data Representation II

Part of the function of a data object is to store the data. The first chapter on data representation discusses this aspect of data objects. This chapter focuses on basic geometric and topological access methods, and computational operations implemented by the various data objects. The chapter covers such methods as coordinate transformations for data sets, interpolation functions, derivative calculations, topological adjacency operations, and geometric operations such as line intersection and searching.

Algorithms II

This chapter is a continuation of Algorithms I and covers algorithms that are either more complex or less widely used. Scalar algorithms such as dividing cubes are covered along with vector algorithms such as stream ribbons. A large collection of modelling algorithms is discussed, including triangle strip generation, polygon decimation, feature extraction, and implicit modelling. We conclude with a look at some visualization algorithms that utilize texture mapping.

Interpreters

Most of this book assumes that you will be doing development in C++, a compiled language. There are some advantages to using an interpreted language for data visualization. This chapter discusses some of these trade-offs and describes an implementation of **vtk** that is integrated with the Tcl interpreted language. The basic syntax of Tcl is described along with some sample programs.

Applications

In this chapter we tie the previous chapters together by working through a series of case studies from a variety of application areas. For each case, we briefly describe the application and what information we expect to obtain through the use of visualization. Then, we walk through the design and resulting source code to demonstrate the use of the tools described earlier in the text.

1.11 Legal Considerations

We make no warranties, express or implied, that the computer code contained in this text is free of error or will meet your requirements for any particular application. Do not use this code in any application where coding errors could result in injury to a person or loss of property. If you do use the code in this way, it is at your own risk. The authors and publisher disclaim all liability for direct or consequential damages resulting from your use of this code.

The computer code contained in this text is copyrighted. We grant permission for you to use, copy, and distribute this software for any purpose. However, you may not modify and then redistribute the software. Some of the algorithms presented here are implementations of patented software. If you plan to use this software for commercial purposes, please insure that applicable patent laws are observed.

Some of the data on the CD-ROM may be freely distributed or used (with appropriate acknowledgment). Please refer to the local README files or other documentation for details.

Several registered trademarks are used in this text. UNIX is a trademark of UNIX System Laboratories. Sun Workstation and XGL are trademarks of Sun Microsystems, Inc. Microsoft, MS, MS-DOS, and Windows are trademarks of Microsoft Corporation. The X Window System is a trademark of the Massachusetts Institute of Technology. Starbase and HP are trademarks of Hewlett-Packard Inc. Silicon Graphics and OpenGL, are trademarks of Silicon Graphics, Inc. Macintosh is a trademark of Apple Computer.

1.12 Bibliographic Notes

A number of visualization texts are available. The first six texts listed in the reference section are good general references ([Nielson90], [Patrikalakis91], [Brodlie92], [Wolff93], [Rosenblum94], and [Gallagher95]). Gallagher [Gallagher95] is particularly valuable if you are from a computational background. Wolff and Yaeger [Wolff93] contains many beautiful images and is oriented towards Apple Macintosh users. The text includes a CD-ROM with images and software.

You may also wish to learn more about computer graphics and imaging. Foley and van Dam [FoleyVanDam90] is the basic reference for computer graphics. Suggested reference books on computer imaging are [Pavlidis82] and [Wolberg90].

Two texts by Tufte [Tufte83], [Tufte90] are particularly impressive. Not only are the graphics superbly done, but the fundamental philosophy of data visualization is articulated. He also describes the essence of good and bad visualization techniques.

Another interesting text is available from Siemens, a large company offering medical imaging systems [Krestel90]. This text describes the basic concepts of imaging technology, including MRI and CT. This text is only for those users with a strong mathematical background. A less mathematical overview of MRI is available from [SmithRanallo89].

1.13 References

[Brodlie92]
    K. W. Brodlie et al. *Scientific Visualization Techniques and Applications*. Springer-Verlag, Berlin. 1992.

[Chen93]
    P. C. Chen. "A Climate Simulation Case Study." In *Proceedings of Visualization '93*, pp. 397-401, IEEE Computer Society Press, Los Alamitos, CA, 1993.

[FoleyVanDam90]
    J. D. Foley, A. van Dam, S. K. Feiner, and J. F. Hughes. *Computer Graphics Principles and Practice (Second Ed)*. Addison-Wesley, Reading, MA, 1990.

[Gallagher95]
    R. S. Gallagher (ed). *Computer Visualization Graphics Techniques for Scientific and Engineering Analysis*. CRC Press, Boca Raton, FL, 1995.

[Krestel90]
    E. Krestel (ed). *Imaging Systems for Medical Diagnostics*. Siemens-Aktienges, Munich, 1990.

[InfoVis95]
    The First Information Visualization Symposium. IEEE Computer Society Press, Los Alamitos, CA, 1995.

[McCormick87]

   B. H. McCormick, T. A. DeFanti, and M. D. Brown. "Visualization in Scientific Computing." Report of the *NSF Advisory Panel on Graphics, Image Processing and Workstations.* 1987.

[MDHMS]

   McDonnell Douglas Human Modeling System Reference Manual. Report MDC 93K0281. McDonnell Douglas Corporation, Human Factors Technology. Version 2.1, July 1993.

[Nielson90]

   G. M. Nielson and B. Shriver (eds). *Visualization in Scientific Computing.* IEEE Computer Society Press, Los Alamitos, CA, 1990.

[NYTimes]

   The New York Times Business Day, Tuesday, May 2, 1995.

[Patrikalakis91]

   N. M. Patrikalakis (ed). *Scientific Visualization of Physical Phenomena.* Springer-Verlag, Berlin, 1991.

[Pavlidis82]

   T. Pavlidis. *Graphics and Image Processing.* Computer Science Press, Rockville, MD, 1982.

[Rosenblum94]

   L. Rosenblum et al. *Scientific Visualization Advances and Challenges.* Harcourt Brace & Company, London, 1994.

[SmithRanallo89]

   H. J. Smith and F. N. Ranallo. *A Non-Mathematical Approach to Basic MRI.* Medical Physics Publishing Corporation, Madison, WI, 1989.

[Tufte83]

   E. R. Tufte. *The Visual Display of Quantitative Information.* Graphics Press, Cheshire, CT, 1990.

[Tufte90]

   E. R. Tufte. *Envisioning Information.* Graphics Press, Cheshire, CT, 1990.

[Waters91]

   K. Waters and D. Terzopoulos. "Modeling and Animating Faces Using Scanned Data." *Visualization and Computer Animation,* 2:123-128, 1991.

[Wolberg90]

   G. Wolberg. *Digital Image Warping.* IEEE Computer Society Press, Los Alamitos, CA, 1990.

[Wolff93]

   R. S. Wolff and L. Yaeger. *Visualization of Natural Phenomena.* TELOS, Springer-Verlag, Santa Clara, CA, 1993.

## CHAPTER 2

Object-Oriented Design

*O*bject-oriented systems are becoming wide-spread in the computer industry for good reason. Object-oriented systems are more modular, easier to maintain, and easier to describe than traditional procedural systems. Since the *Visualization Toolkit* has been designed and implemented using object-oriented design, we devote this chapter to summarizing the concepts and practice of object-oriented design and implementation.

2.1 Introduction

Today's software systems try to solve complex, real world problems. A rigorous software design and implementation methodology can ease the burden of this complexity. Without such a methodology, software developers can find it difficult to meet a system's specifications. Furthermore, as specifications change and grow, a software system that does not have a solid, underlying architecture and design will have difficulty adapting to these expanding requirements.

Our visualization system is a good example of complex software that needs to be designed with extensibility in mind. Data visualization is a rapidly expanding field, with visualization techniques being introduced each year. Any system that hopes to incorporate future innovations must have an underlying design that supports the addition of new material without a significant impact on the existing system.

Object-oriented design is a software engineering methodology that deals comfortably with complexity and provides a framework for later changes and additions. The object-oriented design process attempts to divide a complex task into small and simple pieces called objects. The objects are computer abstractions that model physical or abstract pieces of the system being simulated. Object-oriented design methodologies provide mechanisms to identify the abstractions that exist within a system and to model the behavior of the objects.

2.2 Goals of Good Software Design

The quality of a software design is difficult to measure, but some qualitative aspects can guide us. A good software design should be robust, understandable, extendable, modular, maintainable, and reusable.

A robust system handles exceptional conditions gracefully and behaves consistently. Robustness gives software developers confidence that the underlying components of the system will behave as expected, even when the system is used under different circumstances than the original implementor intended.

An understandable system can be used by someone other than the original implementor. The use of the system should seem logical and sensible. The names of the components of the system should be derived from the problem domain.

Extendable systems accept new tasks while still doing the tasks they were originally intended to perform. A system should accept new forms of data and new algorithms without disrupting existing software. Adding a new primitive to the system should not cause large portions of the system to be modified. Experience shows that the more existing code that is modified in a system, the more likely errors will be introduced.

Modular software systems minimize the number of relationships that exist between components of a system. System components that are tightly coupled should be grouped together logically and obey common naming conventions and protocols.

Software maintenance is often ignored during system design. But the total cost of a system includes maintenance as well as the original development. A software system is maintainable if problems are easily isolated and the repair of one problem does not introduce problems in unrelated parts of the system.

Finally, the economics of software development require that we leverage as much of our past work as possible. In an ideal world, the implementation of a new technique in an existing system should be a simple task. This is seldom the case in software systems. Creation of reusable software components can reduce duplication of effort and promote consistent interfaces within a system. However, as we see throughout this book, creating software that can be reused often takes extra effort. A short-term view of productivity by one individual conflicts with the long-term view of the productivity of a software development organization.

2.3 Object-Oriented Concepts

Objects are the dominating concepts in object-oriented systems. Objects are abstractions that encapsulate the properties and behavior of the entities within a system. Each object has an identity that distinguishes it from other objects in the system. Often, the distinguishable aspects of an object are obvious. For example, a difference in color, location on a screen, size or contents distinguishes one window from another on a computer desktop. But, appearances can be deceiving, and even two objects that share all the same characteristics may still have different identities. Two automobiles may have the same manufacturer, model, options and colors, but remain two different cars. The real world distinguishes the two cars by a vehicle identification number. Likewise, programming systems that deal with multiple entities need an identity mechanism. A pointer to allocated memory or a variable name in a system-managed symbol table are often used to distinguish objects in a system. In a database system, a set of identifier keys (called an n-tuple) identifies an entity in a system.

But, how do object-oriented systems differ from conventional, procedural programming systems? The major difference is in the way the two approaches treat data abstraction. Conventional systems limit abstraction to data typing, while object-oriented systems create abstractions for both the data and the operations that can be applied to the data. In fact, an object-oriented system keeps the data and operations together in one programming construct called an object. Together, the data and operations comprise an object's *properties*. When an operation is applied to an object, the programming language's dynamic-binding mechanism executes the procedure that is appropriate for that object. This is not the case in procedure-oriented systems. The programmer must supply logic to decide which procedure to call. Systems that handle multiple types are often littered with case statements to select the appropriate procedure for an operation. As new types are added to these systems, the code that dispatches operations based on data type must be extended to handle the new type. For example, in a program to display different types of primitives, the following pseudo code shows how a procedure-oriented system differs from an object-oriented system.

Procedure oriented (in C):

```
Primitive *aPrim;
...
DrawPrimitive (aPrim)
...
procedure DrawPrimitive (aPrim)
{
  if (aPrim->type == TRIANGLE) then DrawTriangle (aPrim)
  else if (aPrim->type == SQUARE) then DrawSquare (aPrim)
  else if (aPrim->type == CIRCLE) then DrawCircle (aPrim)
  ...
}
```

Object-oriented (in C++):

```
...
aPrim->Draw ();
...
```

Later in this project's existence, someone may want to add a new primitive, let's say a quadratic. The person assigned with such a formidable task must search the existing system for all occurrences of the `if` statements in the first example and add a test for the new quadratic type. Of course, a good programmer will have isolated the code in one location, as we have done here, so the task is easier. Nevertheless, that programmer must first realize that the original programmer was skilled enough to modularize the drawing code, then find the code (without necessarily knowing the procedure name) and modify the code. To complicate matters, a system built by more than one programmer will undoubtedly be under a configuration management system, requiring a check-out, edit and check-in cycle.

The object-oriented programmer has an easier task. Consulting the design document that defines the object properties for a primitive, this programmer adds a draw operation to the quadratic object. The new primitive is available to the system without changing any existing code! Of course, this is an over simplified example. But think about past programs you have written and remember how hard it was to add a new data type. Were your changes isolated to the new code you added? Did you have to edit code that you did not write and maybe did not understand? Keep this example in mind as you read our object-oriented implementation of a data visualization library.

Before describing object-oriented design and programming in more detail, we provide an observation and prediction. Over the several years that we have designed and implemented software using an object-oriented methodology, we have observed that newcomers to the technique will say, "But this is how I already write programs. My systems are modular, they're robust, I can easily add to them." If you still feel that way after reading this book, do not fault the object-oriented approach. Rather, we have failed as authors. However, such a negative response is unlikely. In our experience, users become comfortable with this approach in a short time. Especially when they are introduced to objects through an existing, well-designed object-oriented system. You will reach the "aha" stage, after which it will be difficult to begin a software project without looking for the objects in the problem.

2.4 Object-Oriented Terminology

As with any software engineering design methodology, object-oriented design has its own terminology. Unfortunately, not everyone agrees on what that is. We adopt much of our terminology from Rumbaugh [Rumbaugh91] and, since the *Visualization Toolkit* is written in C++, from Stroustrup [Stroustrup84]. For the

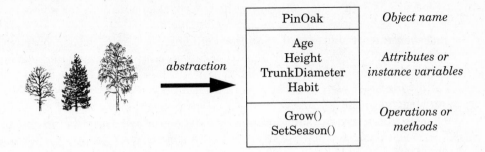

Figure 2–1 Mapping a real world object into an object abstraction. The real world objects are various types of trees. One of these objects (a pin oak tree) is mapped into the computer object we call PinOak.

most part, Rumbaugh's terminology is independent of programming language, while Stroustrup is specific to implementation in C++. The transition from design to programming will be painless though, and the mappings between the two terminologies are mostly obvious. Where we think there might be confusion, we will point out the correspondences.

What Is an Object?

An *object* is an abstraction that models the state and behavior of entities in a system. Abstraction is a mental process that extracts the essential aspects of a situation for a particular purpose. Entities are things in the system that have identity. Chairs, airplanes, and cameras are objects that correspond to physical entities in the real world. Binary trees, symbol tables, and ordered collections are objects that exist only within the world of computer science.

Figure **2–1** is an example of the abstraction that occurs when we map the state and behavior of a system component to an object. Here, the object is a particular type of tree: a pin oak. In this application we desire to simulate the growth of various types of trees over the course of a season. For our purpose we have decided that the important state variables are the tree's age, trunk diameter, height, and habit (i.e., growing form). To capture the behavior of the pin oak we have methods to simulate growth and seasonal effects corresponding to spring, summer, fall, and winter. There are also methods (not shown) for setting and getting current state variables.

We call the state of an object its *attributes* (also called *instance variables*) and define its behavior by the *operations* that can be applied to it. Attributes have a name, a data type, and a data value. The data type of an attribute may be a primitive type in the programming language (such as a char or float in C++), or another object. For example, the vtkTransform object in our visualization system has an attribute of type vtkMatrix4x4, another object. vtkMatrix4x4 in turn has attributes that are an array of primitive values declared as float values in C++.

Operations are functions or transformations that can be applied to an object. Operations define the behavior of the object. The operations for a particular object are implemented in procedures we call *methods*.

Together, the attributes and operations of an object comprise its *properties*. A two-dimensional line graph could have attributes that include an x and y axis, a legend, and a connected set of points. This graph has methods that draw the graph in a window. It also has methods that let a user specify the axes, data to draw, and legend to use.

Objects that share the same properties can be grouped using the process of *classification*. An object class, usually just called a class, specifies the properties that all objects in the class have. The class only specifies the names of the properties, not their specific values. Different classes can (and usually do) have properties with names that exist in other classes. Many classes in our visualization system have an attribute named `Position`. Although both a camera and actor in our visualization system have this attribute, the effect on each is different because they are different classes. Attribute names are shared by all objects in a given class, but separate storage is allocated for each object's attribute values.

When an operation with the same name is applied to objects of different classes we call the operation *polymorphic*. For example, our visualization system has an operation named `Render()` that can be applied to many different objects in the system. The implementation of an operation for a particular class is called a method. The print operation for a `vtkMatrix4x4` object is implemented in its print method. That is, there exists code that knows how to print objects of class `vtkMatrix4x4` and not objects of other classes. Objects know which method to use because they are kept within each object's data structure. In most systems the code for the methods is shared by all objects in the same class. Some programming languages, including C++, define a method by combining an operation name with its argument types. This process is called overloading an operation and is a powerful technique that permits the same name to be used for logically similar operations. For example, the class definition below defines three methods for calculating the square of a number. Even though these methods have the same operation name, they are unique because C++ uses both the operation name and the operations argument types.

```
class math
{
float square(float x);
int square(int x);
double square(double x);
}
```

To use a member of a class for some purpose, we create an instance of the class (the process of *instantiation*). Instance creation establishes the identity of the instance including specifying its initial state. The instance's class serves as a template for the instance during creation, defining the names of each of its attributes and operations. Creation establishes the similarities and differences between this instance and other instances of the same class. The similarities are the names and type of its attributes and the methods that implement its operations. The differences are the specific values of the attributes. The details of how one creates an instance of a class vary from programming language to programming language. In C++, a program creates an instance using a declarative form such as

```
vtkActor aBall;
```

which creates an object from the program stack, or by applying the new operation

```
vtkActor *aBall = new vtkActor;
```

which creates the object from the program heap.

Inheritance

Inheritance is a programming mechanism that simplifies adding new classes to a system when they differ in small ways from currently existing classes. The notion of inheritance is adopted from the observation that most systems can be specified using a hierarchical classification system. A fine example of a classification system is the phyla of life on earth.

Earlier we created an object corresponding to a pin oak tree. The properties of the tree can be more thoroughly described using inheritance (Figure **2–2**). The classification shown here is based on the five kingdom system of Margulis and Schwartz [Margulis88]. In this system, biota is classified as belonging to one of the five kingdoms Prokaryotae (bacteria), Protoctista (algae, protozoans and slime molds), Fungi (mushrooms, molds, lichens), Plantae (mosses, ferns, cone-bearing, and flowering plants), and Animalia (animals with and without backbones). Below this level we have the classifications named divisions, classes, orders, families, genus, and species. The figure shows the kingdom, division, class, genus, and species of the pin oak.

Organizing objects into an inheritance hierarchy provides many benefits. Properties of a general classification are also properties of its subclassification. For example, we know that all species of genus *Quercus* form acorns. From the software point of view this means any instance variables and methods of a *superclass* are automatically inherited by its *subclass*. This allows us to make changes to a number of objects simultaneously by modifying their superclass. Furthermore, if we desire to add a new class (say a red oak tree) to the hierarchy we can do so without duplicating existing functionality. We need only differentiate the new class from the others by adding new instance variables or overloading existing methods.

The ability to quickly add new classes that are slightly different from currently existing classes promotes the extensibility of a system. Inheritance can be derived top down using a process called *specialization* or it can be created bottom

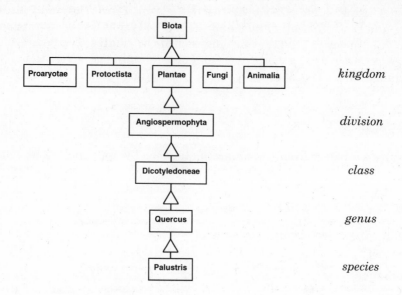

Figure 2–2 Inheritance hierarchy for pin oak tree.

up, combining similar classes during a process called *generalization*. The use of inheritance implies a class hierarchy with one or more classes being the superclasses of one or more subclasses. A subclass inherits the operations and attributes of its superclasses. In C++, subclasses are called *derived* classes and superclasses are called *base* classes. A subclass can add additional operations and attributes that modify the properties it inherited from its superclasses. Through this inheritance, an object can exhibit its superclass' behavior plus any additional behavior it wishes. It can also restrict, or override, operations implemented by its superclass.

Classes that exist only to act as superclasses for their subclasses are called *abstract* classes. Instance creation of an abstract class is generally prohibited. Abstract classes are useful for gathering attributes and methods that all subclasses will use. They can also define protocols for behavior for their subclasses. This is a powerful use of inheritance that will show up in the design of our visualization system. Abstract classes can enforce complex sequence and control protocols and ensure uniform behavior. They remove the responsibility of complex protocols from the individual subclasses and isolate the protocol in the superclass.

An example of a simple plotting package illustrates the power of abstract classes. Consider a data presentation application that allows for a variety of two-dimensional plotting. This application must support line charts and horizontal and vertical bar charts. The design process identifies properties common to all plots including title, axes, and legend. We then create an abstract class called

TwoDPlot to contain these common attributes. Common behavior can also be captured in TwoDPlot within its plot method:

```
Method Plot
{
Draw the border
Scale the data
Draw the axes
Draw the data
Draw the title
Draw the legend
}
```

An abstract class may or may not provide default behavior for each operation. In this example, default behavior for border and title drawing might be provided. Then subclasses of TwoDPlot would define their own functions for the other methods. The protocol specification explicitly spells out what methods a subclass of TwoDPlot should respond to. In the above example, subclasses will need to define their own methods for drawing the axis, data, and legend. Some subclasses might use TwoDPlot's methods for drawing the border, others might require their own version of this method. The abstract interface defined in TwoDPlot makes it easier to add new classes of 2D plots and the resulting subclasses tend to be more uniform and consistent.

Another mechanism, *delegation*, is useful for isolating and reusing behavior. Using delegation, an object applies operations to one of its attributes that is an object. As an example, in the *Visualization Toolkit* the vtkTransform object delegates its Identity() operation to its vtkMatrix4x4 attribute. This instance of vtkMatrix4x4 then performs the operation. There are many more useful object-oriented concepts, but for the time being we have enough information to describe how we can use objects to design a system.

2.5 Object-Oriented Modelling and Design

The design of any large software system is a formidable task and the first steps in system design are often the most challenging. No matter what design technique we choose, we must have a thorough understanding of the system's application domain. It would be difficult to see how one could design a fly-by-wire airplane control system without a detailed knowledge of the underlying hardware control systems. Of course, all flight system software is not designed by aeronautical engineers, so some form of system specification must exist. The depth of information in the specifications varies from application to application.

Object-oriented system design begins with a modelling step that extracts objects and their relationships with other objects from a problem statement or software requirement specification. First, the designer must completely understand the problem being solved. This often requires an in-depth knowledge of the problem domain or access to detailed specifications of the problem being solved.

Then, major abstractions must be identified within the system. The abstractions will become, at this high level of design, the first set of objects. For example, a system that keeps track of an investment portfolio will need objects such as stocks, bonds, and mutual funds. In a computer animation system we might need actors, cameras, and lights. A medical computed tomography system will have a table, X-ray source, detectors, and gantry. Our visualization system will have models, isosurfaces, streamlines, and cut planes. During this modelling step, we search the problem domain for objects, properties, and relationships. Later, during multiple passes through the design, the model will be expanded.

Modelling is a step in most design processes regardless of whether we are designing a ship, house, electronics system or software. Each discipline follows a methodology that uses techniques specifically created to make the design process efficient and worthwhile. These techniques are so-called "tools of the trade." An electrical engineer uses schematics and logic diagrams, an architect uses drawings and mock-ups, and a ship builder uses scale models. Likewise, software designers need tools that can help create a model of the system. The software tools should have enough expressive power to help the software designer evaluate a design against a specification and help communicate that design to others on the software team.

We use the Object Modeling Technique (OMT) developed at GE by Jim Rumbaugh and his colleagues [Rumbaugh91]. OMT uses three models to specify an object-oriented design: an object model, a dynamic model, and a functional model. Each model describes a different aspect of the system and each has a corresponding diagramming technique that helps us analyze, design, and implement software systems.

The Object Model

The object model identifies each object in the system, its properties, and its relationships to other objects in the system. For most software systems, the object model dominates the design. The OMT graphical technique uses rectangles to depict object classes, and a variety of connectors to depict inheritance and other object-object relations. Object classes are represented as solid rectangles. Instances are represented as dotted rectangles. The name of the class or instance occupies the top of the rectangle. A line separates the class name from the next section that contains the attributes. A third section describes the methods. Relationships between objects are shown with line segments connecting the two related objects. In OMT, relationships are called associations and they can have various cardinalities: one-to-one, one-to-many, and many-to-many. Special associations that represent containers of other objects are called aggregations. Associations can be labeled with roles. (Roles are names given to associations and are used to further describe the nature of the association.) OMT represents inheritance with a triangle, with the superclass attached to the apex and subclasses attached to the base of the triangle. Figure **2–3** shows an object model for locator devices in a virtual reality system.

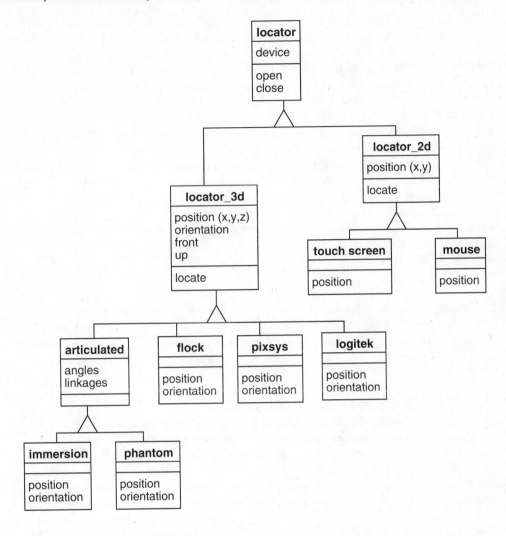

Figure 2–3 Object model for locator devices.

The first object in the class hierarchy is locator. This abstract class specifies common attributes and methods for all locators. The subclasses of locator are locator_2d and locator_3d. In the current rendition of this object model, the locator only has one attribute, a device and two methods, open() and close(). The two subclasses of locator, locator_2d and locator_3d are also abstract classes, containing attributes and methods that distinguish them from each other based on their spatial dimensionality. For example, locator_3d has an *x, y, z* position while locator_2d has an *x, y* position. Both locators have a locate() method that updates the current position. In the 3D locator class, locate() also updates the orientation. The subclasses of locator_3d include hardware from three different manufacturers: flock, pixsys and logitek, as well as an articulated positioner abstract class. The three object classes for the hardware contain methods specific to each device. Each method knows how to convert the hardware specific codes returned by the device. They know that to be considered a locator_3d subclass, they must implement a position and orientation operation that will provide x, y, z coordinates and three angular rotations that can be composed into a transformation matrix. The object model also shows us that the articulated locator has angles and linkages. Two specific articulated locators are immersion and phantom. An object model diagrammed in this fashion serves as a starting point for design and discussion. It reveals common methods and attributes as well as the distinguishing characteristics of each class.

Later, during implementation, we will convert these object models into software objects. The particular computer language we choose for implementation will dictate the details of the conversion.

The Dynamic Model

The object model describes the static portion of a system while the dynamic model details the sequences of events and time dependencies of the system. OMT uses state diagrams to model system dynamics. Dynamic models are frequently used to design control systems and user interfaces. Our visualization system has limited sequence and control aspects, so we will not dwell on state diagrams. But, if we were designing a user-friendly interface for a digital wrist watch, the state diagram in Figure **2–4** would be useful.

The ovals in the diagram show a state, the arrows show a transition from one state to another and the labels on the arrows show an event that causes the state transition. This example shows three display states and multiple setting states. The event b1 means button one is pressed. This watch has three buttons. The diagram shows what happens in each state when any of the three buttons is pressed. The diagram clearly shows that b1 is used to move between display modes for time, date and alarm. B2 changes from display mode into setting mode or selects the field to change in a given mode. B3 increments the selected field by one unit. The state diagram also shows what happens when illegal buttons are pressed. If the watch is displaying time and button 3 is pressed, nothing happens. If button 3 is pressed when the watch is displaying the alarm, the alarm on/off is toggled.

The Functional Model

The functional model shows how data flows through the system and how processes and algorithms transform the data. It also shows functional dependencies between processes. Exposing these relationships will affect the associations in the object model. The major components of a data flow diagram (DFD) are data sources, data sinks, and processes. Data sources and sinks are represented as rectangles. Ellipses show processes. Data stores are shown within two horizontal

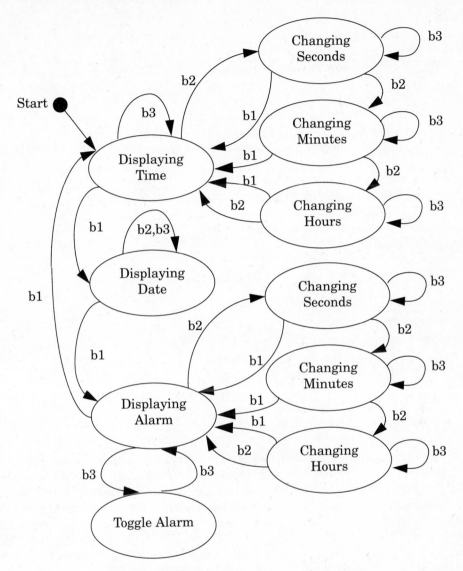

Figure 2–4 State diagram for a wrist watch.

lines. DFDs are useful to describe the overall flow in the system. They can also be used to describe any process that transforms one data representation into another. Processes identified in the DFD during function modelling may turn up as operations or objects in the object model.

Figure **2–5** shows a data flow diagram for a 3D medical imaging system. The diagram shows the data acquisition on the computed tomography (CT) or magnetic resonance imaging (MRI) scanner. The series of cross-sectional slices provided by the scanner is first processed by image processing filters to enhance

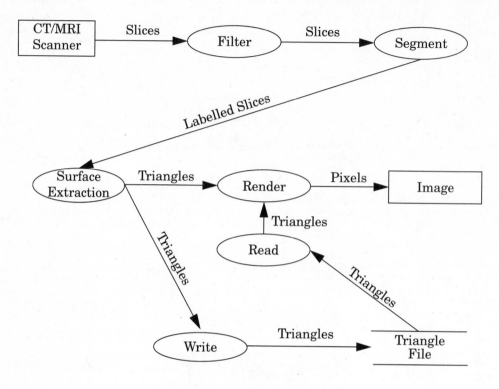

Figure 2–5 Data flow diagram.

features in the gray scale slices. A segment process identifies tissues and produces labels for the various tissues present in the slices. These labelled slices are then passed through a surface extraction process to create triangles that lie on the surfaces of each tissue. The render process transforms the geometry into an image. Alternatively, the write process stores the triangles in a file. Later, the triangles can be read and rendered into an image. We defer the decision whether to make the processes objects or operations until later. Chapter 4 uses DFDs to model the visualization pipeline.

2.6 Object-Oriented Programming Languages

Language choice is a religious issue. Every computer language has its evangelists and followers. Most of our experience in object-oriented languages is with C and C++. C itself does not have object-oriented facilities, but an object-oriented methodology and strict coding guidelines permit the development of object-oriented code. We chose C++ for the *Visualization Toolkit* because it has built in support for the notion of classes, dynamic binding of methods to objects, and inheritance. C++ is also widely available on many UNIX platforms and personal computers.

Simula [Birtwistle79] is usually acknowledged as the first object-oriented language, but Smalltalk [Goldberg83] is probably the best known language. Smalltalk was developed at the Xerox Palo Alto Research Center (PARC) in the seventies and eighties. Well before its time, Smalltalk provided not just a language, but also an operating system and programming environment built with objects. When you use Smalltalk, you live and breathe objects. For the object-oriented purist, there is no substitute. Smalltalk spin-offs include window systems, workstations and the desktop paradigm. Both Apple Computer and Microsoft acknowledge the influence that Smalltalk and Xerox PARC had on the Macintosh and Windows. Smalltalk was probably conceived ten years too early for widespread commercial acceptance. During Smalltalk's infancy and adolescence, the complexity of software was much lower than today's systems. FORTRAN served the scientific and engineering community, COBOL was the choice for business applications and the computer science community embraced C. The use of abstractions was limited to mathematicians. Programming was considered an art form and programmers concentrated on clever implementations of algorithms. Each new task often required a new program. Technical programmers did use numerical libraries for common mathematical operations, but any notions of common abstractions at a higher level were absent.

2.7 Object-Oriented Visualization

Don't underestimate the investment required to design a system. Although object-oriented technologies have tremendous potential to produce good software designs, these techniques do not guarantee a good design. The visualization system we present in this text has its roots in an animation [Lorensen89] and visualization system [Schroeder92] that we developed over a ten-year period. The initial design, which identified twenty-five classes for computer animation of industrial applications, took four software professionals ten months (almost 3.5 person years) to complete. During this design stage the developers produced zero (!) lines of code. The subsequent implementation took one month, or ten percent of the effort. This system still serves our visualization group even after twenty other software developers have added over 500 classes to the system. The original twenty-five classes still exist in the system today.

As a reader, we hope that you can benefit from our experience in visualization system design. We have tried to assist you by describing the properties (attributes and methods) of many of the *Visualization Toolkit* classes in each chapter's *"Putting It All Together"* section. We also include a series of object diagrams in Appendix A that will give you a quick overview of object relationships such as superclass and subclass. And of course, it will be helpful if you supplement this information with the examples in the text/code and on CD-ROM. In the next chapter we will also explain the decisions we made to design our object-oriented toolkit.

2.8 Chapter Summary

This chapter introduced object-oriented concepts and terminology. The emphasis was on dealing with complexity and how object-oriented technology provides mechanisms to reduce the complexity of software.

Model building is an important part of any design methodology. We introduced three models and notations. The object model describes the objects in a system and their static relationships, attributes, and methods. Object diagrams succinctly present this static information. The dynamic model focuses on the time dependent aspects of the system. State transition diagrams are used to model the sequence and control portions of the system. The functional model shows how objects in the system transform data or other objects. The data flow diagram is a convenient notation for showing functional dependencies.

There are several choices available today for object-oriented implementations. Although it is possible to implement an object-oriented system in a non-object-oriented language such as C, the methodology is best served by an object-oriented language. We have chosen C++ to implement the *Visualization Toolkit*.

The emphasis in this book is on architecture, data structure design, and algorithms. The object-oriented aspects of the system are important, but what the system does is far more important.

2.9 Bibliographic Notes

There are several excellent textbooks on object-oriented design. Both [Rumbaugh91] and [Birtwistle79] present language independent design methodologies. Both books emphasize modelling and diagramming as key aspects of design. [Meyer88] also describes the OO design process in the context of Eiffel, an OO language. Another popular book has been authored by Booch [Booch91].

Anyone who wants to be a serious user of object-oriented design and implementation should read the books on Smalltalk [Goldberg83][Goldberg84] by the developers of Smalltalk at Xerox Parc. In another early object-oriented programming book, [Cox86] describes OO techniques and the programming language Objective-C. Objective-C is a mix of C and Smalltalk and was used by Next Computer in the implementation of their operating system and user interface.

There are many texts on object-oriented languages. CLOS [Keene89] describes the Common List Object System. Eiffel, a strongly typed OO language is described by [Meyer88]. Objective-C [Cox86] is a weakly typed language.

Although C++ has become a popular programming language, there are few class libraries available for use in applications. [Gorlen90] describes an extensive class library for collections and arrays modeled after the Smalltalk classes described in [Goldberg83]. [Stepanov94] and [Musser94] describe the Standard Template Library, a framework of data structures and algorithms that will be part of the ANSI C++ standard.

C++ texts abound. The original description by the author of C++ [Stroustrup84] is a must for any serious C++ programmer. Another book

[Ellis90] describes standard extensions to the language. Check with your colleagues for their favorite C++ book.

To keep in touch with new developments there are conferences, journals and Web Sites. The strongest technical conference on object-oriented topics is the annual Object-Oriented Programming Systems, Languages and Applications (*OOPSLA*) conference. This is where researchers in the field describe, teach and debate the latest techniques in object-oriented technology. The bi-monthly *Journal of Object-Oriented Programming* (JOOP) published by SIGS Publications, NY, presents technical papers, columns and tutorials on the field. Resources on the world wide web include the Usenet newsgroups *comp.object* and *comp.lang.c++*.

2.10 References

[Birtwistle79]
> G. M. Birtwistle, O. Dahl, B. Myhrhaug, and K. Nygaard. *Simula Begin*. Chartwell-Bratt Ltd, England, 1979.

[Booch91]
> G. Booch. *Object-Oriented Design with Applications*. Benjamin/Cummings Publishing Co., Redwood City, CA, 1991.

[Cox86]
> B. J. Cox. *Object-Oriented Programming: An Evolutionary Approach*. Addison-Wesley, Reading, MA, 1986.

[Ellis90]
> M. Ellis and B. Stroustrup. *The Annotated C++ Reference Manual*. Addison-Wesley, Reading, MA, 1990.

[Goldberg83]
> A. Goldberg, D. Robson. *Smalltalk-80: The Language and its Implementation*. Addison-Wesley, Reading, MA, 1983.

[Goldberg84]
> A. Goldberg. *Smalltalk-80: The Interactive Programming Environment*. Addison-Wesley, Reading, MA, 1984.

[Gorlen90]
> K. Gorlen, S. Orlow, and P. Plexico. *Data Abstraction and Object-Oriented Programming*. John Wiley & Sons Ltd., Chichester, England, 1990.

[Keene89]
> S. Keene. *Object-Oriented Programming in Common Lisp: A Programmer's Guide to CLOS*. Addison-Wesley, Reading, MA, 1989.

[Lorensen89]
> W. E. Lorensen, B. Yamrom. "Object-Oriented Computer Animation." *Proceedings of IEEE NAECON*, 2:588-595, Dayton, Ohio, May 1989.

[Margulis88]
> L. Margulis and K. V. Schwartz. *Five Kingdoms An Illustrated Guide to the Phyla of Life On Earth*. W. H. Freeman & Co. New York, 1988.

[Meyer88]
  B. Meyer. *Object-Oriented Software Construction*. Prentice Hall International, Hertfordshire, England, 1988.

[Musser94]
  D. Musser and A. Stepanov. "Algorithm-Oriented Generic Libraries." *Software Practice and Experience*, 24(7):623-642, July 1994.

[Rumbaugh91]
  J. Rumbaugh, M. Blaha, W. Premerlani, F. Eddy, and W. Lorensen. *Object-Oriented Modeling and Design.* Prentice-Hall, Englewood Cliffs, NJ, 1991.

[Schroeder92]
  W. J. Schroeder, W. E. Lorensen, G. Montanaro, and C. Volpe. "Visage: An Object-Oriented Scientific Visualization System." In *Proceedings of Visualization '92*, pp. 219-226, IEEE Computer Society Press, Los Alamitos, CA, October 1992.

[Stepanov94]
  A. Stepanov and M. Lee. *The Standard Template Library*. ISO Programming Language C++ Project. Doc. No. X3J16/94-0095, WG21/N0482, May 1994.

[Stroustrup84]
  B. Stroustrup. *The C++ Programming Language*. Addison-Wesley, Reading, MA, 1986.

2.11 Exercises

2.1 Answer the following questions about a program you have written.
  a) How much time did you spend on design and implementation?
  b) What methodology, if any, did you use?
  c) Could you easily extend the system?
  d) Could anyone extend the system?

2.2 Identify the major objects and operations for the following applications.
  a) An airline reservation system.
  b) An adventure game.
  c) A 2D plotting package.
  d) An automatic teller machine.

2.3 Draw an object diagram for each example in Exercise 2.2.

2.4 Computer animation uses concepts from graphics and movie making. Identify the major objects and operations in a computer animation system.

2.5 For the animation system in Exercise 2.4, design control and looping objects that will allow flexible control of the properties of the actors in the system. If we call these control and looping objects scenes and cues, how would you expect them to look?

2.6 Draw a state diagram for your wrist watch using Figure 2–4 as an example.

2.7 Draw a data flow diagram for calculating the surface area and volume of a sphere and cylinder.

Computer Graphics I

Computer graphics is the foundation of data visualization. Practically speaking, we can say that visualization is the process that transforms data into a set of graphics primitives. The methods of computer graphics are then used to convert these primitives into pictures or animations. This chapter discusses basic computer graphics principles. We begin by describing how lights and physical objects interact to form what we see. Then we examine how to simulate these interactions using computer graphics techniques. Hardware issues play an important role here since modern computers have built-in hardware support for graphics. The chapter concludes with a series of examples that illustrate our object-oriented model for 3D computer graphics.

3.1 Introduction

Computer graphics is the process of generating images using computers. We call this process *rendering*. There are many types of rendering processes, ranging from 2D paint programs to sophisticated 3D techniques. In this chapter we focus on basic 3D techniques for visualization.

We can view rendering as the process of converting graphical data into an image. In data visualization our goal is to transform data into graphical data, or *graphics primitives*, that are then rendered. The goal of our rendering is not so much image realism as it is information content. We also strive for interactive

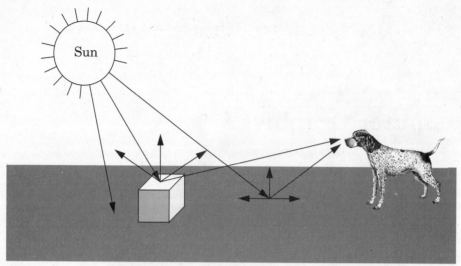

Figure 3–1 Physical generation of an image.

graphical displays so we can interact with the data. This chapter explains the process of rendering an image from graphical data. To begin, we look at the way lights and objects interact in the world around us. From this foundation we explain how to simulate this process on a computer.

A Physical Description of Rendering

Figure **3–1** presents a simplified view of what happens when we look at an object. Rays of light are emitted from a light source in all directions. (In this example we assume that the light source is the sun.) Some of these rays happen to strike the cube that we are viewing. The cube absorbs some of the light that hits it and the rest is reflected off of its surface. Some of this reflected light may head towards us and enter our eyes. If this happens, then we "see" the object. Likewise, some of the light from the sun will strike the ground and some small percentage of it will be reflected into our eyes.

As you can imagine, the chances of a ray of light from the sun travelling through space to hit a small object on a relatively small planet are low. This is compounded by the slim odds of the ray of light reflecting off the object and into our eyes. The only reason we can see is that the sun produces such an enormous amount of light that it overwhelms the odds. While this may work in real life, trying to simulate it with a computer can be difficult. Fortunately there are other ways to look at this problem.

A common and effective technique for 3D computer graphics is called *ray-tracing* or *ray-casting*. Ray-tracing simulates the interaction of light with objects by following the path of each light ray. Typically, we follow the ray backwards from the viewer's eyes and into the world to determine what the ray strikes. The direction of the ray is in the direction we are looking (i.e., the view direction) including effects of perspective (if desired). When a ray intersects an object, we can determine if that point is being lit by our light source. This is done by tracing a ray from the point of intersection towards the light. If the ray intersects the light, then the point is being lit. If the ray intersects something else before it gets to the light, then that light will not contribute to illuminating the point. For multiple light sources we just repeat this process for each light source. The total contributions from all the light sources, plus any ambient scattered light, will determine the total lighting or shadow for that point. By following the light's path backwards, ray-tracing only looks at rays that end up entering the viewer's eyes. This dramatically reduces the number of rays that must be computed by a simulation program.

Having described ray-tracing as a rendering process, it may be surprising that many members of the graphics community do not use it. This is because ray-tracing is a relatively slow image generation method since it is typically implemented in software. Other graphics techniques have been developed that generate images using dedicated computer hardware. To understand why this situation has emerged, it is instructive to briefly examine the taxonomy and history of computer graphics.

Image-Order and Object-Order Methods

Rendering processes can be broken into two categories: *image-order* and *object-order*. Ray-tracing is an image-order process. It works by determining what happens to each ray of light, one at a time. An object-order process works by rendering each object, one at a time. In the above example, an object-order technique would proceed by first rendering the ground and then the cube.

To look at it another way consider painting a picture of a barn. Using an image-order algorithm you would start at the upper left corner of the canvas and put down a drop of the correct color paint. (Each paint drop is called a picture element or *pixel*.) Then you would move a little to the right and put down another drop of paint. You would continue until you reached the right edge of the canvas, then you would move down a little and start on the next row. Each time you put down a drop of paint you make certain it is the correct color for each pixel on the canvas. When you are done you will have a painting of a barn.

An alternative approach is based on the more natural (at least for most of us) object-order process. We work by painting the different objects in our scene, independent of where the objects actually are located on the scene. We may paint from back-to-front, front-to-back, or in arbitrary order. For example, we could start by painting the sky and then add in the ground. After these two objects were painted we would then add in the barn. In the image-order process we worked on the canvas in a very orderly fashion; left to right, top to bottom. With an object-order process we tend to jump from one part of the canvas to another, depending on what object we are drawing.

The field of computer graphics started out using object-order processes. Much of the early work was closely tied to the hardware display device, initially a vector display. This was little more than an oscilloscope, but it encouraged graphical data to be drawn as a series of line segments. As the original vector displays gave way to the currently ubiquitous raster displays, the notion of representing graphical data as a series of objects to be drawn was preserved. Much of the early work pioneered by Bresenham [Bresenham65] at IBM focused on how to properly convert line segments into a form that would be suitable for line plotters. The same work was applied to the task of rendering lines onto the raster displays that replaced the oscilloscope. Since then the hardware has become more powerful and capable of displaying much more complex primitives than lines.

It wasn't until the early 1980's that a paper by Turner Whitted [Whitted80] prompted many people to look at rendering from a more physical perspective. Eventually ray-tracing became a serious competitor to the traditional object-order rendering techniques, due in part to the highly realistic images it can produce. Object-order rendering has maintained its popularity because there is a wealth of graphics hardware designed to quickly render objects. Ray-tracing tends to be done without any specialized hardware and therefore is a time consuming process.

Surface versus Volume Rendering

The discussion to this point in the text has tacitly assumed that when we render an object, we are viewing the surfaces of objects and their interactions with light. However, common objects such as clouds, water, and fog, are translucent, or scatter light that passes through them. Such objects cannot be rendered using a model based exclusively on surface interactions. Instead, we need to consider the changing properties inside the object to properly render them. We refer to these two rendering models as *surface rendering* (i.e., render the surfaces of an object) and *volume rendering* (i.e., render the surface and interior of an object).

Generally speaking, when we render an object using surface rendering techniques, we mathematically model the object with a surface description such as points, lines, triangles, polygons, or surface splines. The interior of the object is not described, or only implicitly represented from the surface representation (i.e., surface is the boundary of the volume). Although techniques do exist that allow us to make the surface transparent or translucent, there are still many phenomena that cannot be simulated using surface rendering techniques alone (e.g., scattering or light emission). This is particularly true if we are trying to render data interior to an object, such as X-ray intensity from a CT scan.

Volume rendering techniques allow us to see the inhomogeneity inside objects. In the prior CT example, we can realistically reproduce X-ray images by considering the intensity values from both the surface and interior of the data. Although it is premature to describe this process at this point in the text, you can imagine extending our ray-tracing example from the previous section. Thus rays not only interact with the surface of an object, they also interact with the interior.

In this chapter we focus on surface rendering techniques. While not as powerful as volume rendering, surface rendering is widely used because it is relatively fast compared to volume rendering, and allows us to create images for a wide variety of data and objects. Chapter 7 describes volume rendering in more detail.

Visualization Not Graphics

Although the authors would enjoy providing a thorough treatise on computer graphics, such a discourse is beyond the scope of this text. Instead we make the distinction between visualization (exploring, transforming, and mapping data) and computer graphics (mapping and rendering). The focus will be on the principles and practice of visualization, and not on 3D computer graphics. In this chapter and Chapter 7 we introduce basic concepts and provide a working knowledge of 3D computer graphics. For those more interested in this field, we refer you to the texts recommended in the "Bibliographic Notes" on page 72 at the end of this chapter.

One of the regrets we have regarding this posture is that certain rendering techniques are essentially visualization techniques. We see this hinted at in the previous paragraph, where we use the term "mapping" to describe both visualization and computer graphics. There is not currently and will likely never be a firm distinction between visualization and graphics. For example, many researchers consider volume rendering to be squarely in the field of visualization because it addresses one of the most important forms of visualization data. Our distinction is mostly for our own convenience, and offers us the opportunity to finish this text. We recommend that a serious student of visualization supplement the material presented here with deeper books on computer graphics and volume rendering.

In the next few pages we describe the rendering process in more detail. We start by defining colors. Then we examine the primary components of the rendering process. There are light sources such as the sun, there are objects we wish to render such as the cube (we refer to these as *actors*), and there is a camera which looks out into the world. These terms are taken from the movie industry and tend to be familiar to most people. Lights are self explanatory, actors represent graphical data or graphical objects, and the camera determines how we look at these actors. We call the combination of lights, camera, and actors the *scene*, and refer to the rendering process as rendering the scene.

3.2 Color

The visible spectrum for humans contains wavelengths ranging from about 400 to 700 nanometers. The light that enters our eyes consists of different *intensities* of these wavelengths, an example of which is shown in Figure **3–2**. This intensity

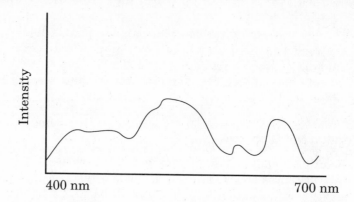

Figure 3–2 Wavelength intensity plot.

plot defines the color of the light, a different plot results in a different color. Unfortunately, we may not notice the difference since the human eye throws out most of this information. There are three types of color receptors in the human eye. Each type responds to a subset of the 400 to 700 nanometer wavelength range as in Figure **3–3**. Any color we see gets coded by our eyes into these three overlapping responses. This is a great reduction from the amount of information that actually comes into our eyes. As a result, the human eye is incapable of recognizing differences in any colors whose intensity curves, when applied to the human eye's response curves, result in the same triplet of responses. This also implies that we can store and represent colors in a computer using a simplified form without the human eye being able to recognize the difference.

The two simplified component systems that we use to describe colors are RGB and HSV color systems. The RGB system represents colors based on their red, green, and blue intensities. This can be thought of as a three dimensional space with the axes being red, green, and blue. Some common colors and their RGB components are shown in Figure **3–4**.

The HSV system represents colors based on their hue, saturation, and value. The value component is also known as the brightness or intensity component, and represents how much light is in the color. A value of 0.0 will always give you black and a value of 1.0 will give you something bright. The hue represents the dominant wavelength of the color. Hue is often illustrated using a circle as in Figure **3–5**. Each location on the circumference of this circle represents a different hue and can be specified using an angle. When we specify a hue we use the range from zero to one, where zero corresponds to zero degrees on the hue circle and one corresponds to 360 degrees. The saturation indicates how much of the hue is mixed into the color. For example, we can set the value to one, which gives us a bright color, and the hue to 0.66, to give us a dominant wavelength of blue. Now if we set the saturation to one, the color will be a bright primary blue. If we set the saturation to 0.5, the color will be sky blue, a blue with more white

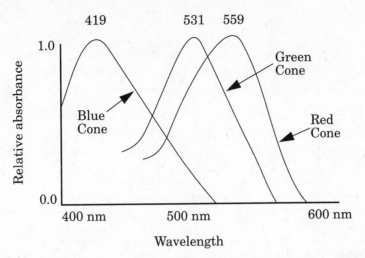

Figure 3–3 Relative absorbance of light by the three types of cones in the human retina [Dartnall83].

Color	RGB	HSV
Black	0,0,0	*,*,0
White	1,1,1	*,0,1
Red	1,0,0	0,1,1
Green	0,1,0	1/3,1,1
Blue	0,0,1	2/3,1,1
Yellow	1,1,0	1/6,1,1
Cyan	0,1,1	1/2,1,1
Magenta	1,0,1	5/6,1,1
Sky Blue	1/2,1/2,1	2/3,1/2,1

Figure 3–4 Common colors in RGB and HSV space.

mixed in. If we set the saturation to zero, this indicates that there is no more of the dominant wavelength (hue) in the color than any other wavelength. As a result, the final color will be white (regardless of hue value). Figure **3–4** lists HSV values for some common colors.

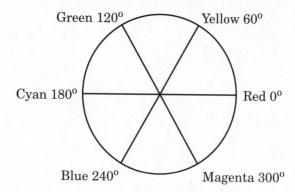

Figure 3–5 Circular representation of hue. (See Color Plate 11.)

3.3 Lights

Now we return to rendering our scene. From a physical perspective this starts with the light sources. If there are no lights, the resulting image will be black and rather uninformative. The reason that lights are so important is that the interaction between the emitted light and the surfaces of the actors defines what we see. Once rays of light intersect these surfaces, we have something for our camera to view.

Of the many different types of lights used in computer graphics, we will discuss the simplest, the infinitely distant point light source. This is a simplification of the typical incandescent light used at home and work. The physical lights that we are accustomed to, radiate from a volume of space such as that of the filament. The point source lighting model assumes that the light is emitted in all directions from a single point in space. For an infinite light source, we assume that it is positioned infinitely far away from what it is illuminating. This is significant because it implies that the incoming rays from such a source will be parallel to each other. The emissions of a local light source, such as a lamp in a room, are not parallel. Figure **3–6** illustrates the differences between a local light source with a finite volume, versus an infinite point light source. The intensity of the light emitted by our infinite light sources remains constant as it travels, in contrast to the actual $1/distance^2$ relationship physical lights obey. As you can see this is a great simplification, which later will allow us to use less complex lighting equations.

3.4 Surface Properties

As rays of light travel through space, some of them intersect our actors. When this happens, the rays of light interact with surface properties of the actor to produce a color. Part of this resulting color is actually not due to direct light, but

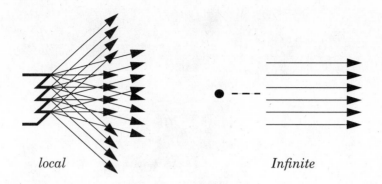

local　　　　　　　　　　　　*Infinite*

Figure 3–6 Local light source with a finite volume versus an infinite point light source.

rather from *ambient* light that is being reflected or scattered from other objects. An ambient lighting model accounts for this. It applies the intensity curve of the light source to the color of the object, also expressed as an intensity curve. The result is the color of the light we see when we look at that object. With such a model, it is important to realize that a white light shining on a blue ball is indistinguishable from a blue light shining on a white ball. The ambient lighting equation is

$$R_c = L_c \cdot O_c \qquad \textbf{(3-1)}$$

where R_c is the resulting intensity curve, L_c is the intensity curve of the light, and O_c is the color curve of the object. To help keep the equations simple we assume that all of the direction vectors are normalized (i.e., have a magnitude of one).

Two components of the resulting color depend on direct lighting. *Diffuse lighting*, which is also known as Lambertian reflection, takes into account the angle of incidence of the light onto an object. Figure **3–7** shows the image of a cylinder that becomes darker as you move laterally from its center. The cylinder's color is constant; the amount of light hitting the surface of the cylinder changes. At the center, where the incoming light is nearly perpendicular to the surface of the cylinder, it receives more rays of light per surface area. As we move towards the side, this drops until finally the incoming light is parallel to the side of the cylinder and the resulting intensity is zero. The contribution from diffuse lighting is expressed in equation Equation **3-2** and illustrated in Figure **3–9**.

$$R_c = L_c O_c\left(\vec{O}_n \cdot \left(-\vec{L}_n\right)\right) \qquad \textbf{(3-2)}$$

where R_c is the resulting intensity curve, L_c is the intensity curve for the light, and O_c is the color curve for the object. Notice that the diffuse light is a function

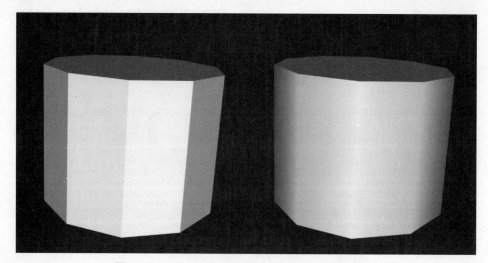

Figure 3–7 Flat and Gouraud shaded cylinders.

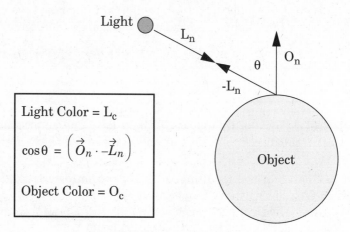

Light Color = L_c

$\cos\theta = \left(\vec{O}_n \cdot -\vec{L}_n \right)$

Object Color = O_c

Figure 3–8 Diffuse lighting.

of the relative angle between incident light vector $\vec{L}_n$ and the surface normal of the object $\vec{O}_n$. As a result diffuse lighting is independent of viewer position.

Specular lighting represents direct reflections of a light source off a shiny object. Figure **3–10** shows a diffusely lit ball with increasing amounts of specular reflection. There is an additional factor, O_{sp}, the specular power. This indicates how shiny an object is, more specifically it indicates how quickly specular reflections diminish as the reflection angles deviate from a perfect reflection. Higher values indicate a faster dropoff, and therefore a shinier surface. Figure **3–11**

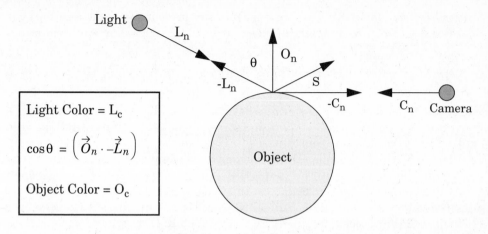

Figure 3–9 Specular lighting.

Light

L_n

$-L_n$

θ

O_n

S

$-C_n$

C_n Camera

Object

Light Color = L_c

$\cos\theta = \left(\vec{O}_n \cdot -\vec{L}_n\right)$

Object Color = O_c

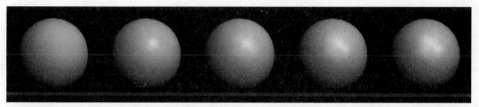

Figure 3–10 A diffuse lit ball with increasing amounts of specular reflection.

Figure 3–11 Effects of specular power, O_{sp} = (5,10,20,80,200).

shows the effects of the specular power. Referring to Figure **3–9**, the equation for specular lighting is

$$R_c = L_c O_c \left(\vec{S} \cdot \left(-\vec{C}_n\right)\right)^{O_{sp}}$$

$$\vec{S} = 2\left(\vec{O}_n \cdot \left(-\vec{L}_n\right)\right)\vec{O}_n + \vec{L}_n$$

(3-3)

where $\vec{C}_n$ is the direction of projection for the camera and $\vec{S}$ is the direction of specular reflection.

We have presented the equations for the different lighting models independently. We can apply all lighting models simultaneously or in combination. Equation **3-4** combines ambient, diffuse and specular lighting into one equation.

$$R_c = O_{ai}O_{ac}L_c - O_{di}O_{dc}L_c\left(\vec{O}_n \cdot \vec{L}_n\right) + O_{si}O_{sc}L_c\left(\vec{S} \cdot \left(-\vec{C}_n\right)\right)^{O_{sp}} \qquad \textbf{(3-4)}$$

The result is a color at a point on the surface of the object. The constants O_{ai}, O_{di}, and O_{si} control the relative amounts of ambient, diffuse and specular lighting for an object. The constants O_{ac}, O_{dc}, and O_{sc} specify the colors to be used for each type of lighting. These six constants along with the specular power are part of the surface material properties. (Other properties such as transparency will be covered in later sections of the text.) Different combinations of these property values can simulate dull plastic and polished metal. The equation assumes an infinite point light source as described in "Lights" on page 40. However the equation can be easily modified to incorporate other types of directional lighting.

3.5 Cameras

We have light sources that are emitting rays of light and actors with surface properties. At every point on the surface of our actors this interaction results in some composite color (i.e., combined color from light, object surface, specular, and ambient effects). All we need now to render the scene is a camera. There are a number of important factors that determine how a 3D scene gets projected onto a plane to form a 2D image (see Figure **3–12**). These are the position, orientation, and focal point of the camera, the method of camera *projection*, and the location of the camera *clipping planes*.

The position and focal point of the camera define the location of the camera and where it points. The vector defined from the camera position to the focal point is called the *direction of projection*. The camera image plane is located at the focal point and is typically perpendicular to the projection vector. The camera orientation is controlled by the position and focal point plus the camera *view-up* vector. Together these completely define the camera view.

The method of projection controls how the actors are mapped to the image plane. *Orthographic projection* is a parallel mapping process. In orthographic projection (or parallel projection) all rays of light entering the camera are parallel to the projection vector. *Perspective projection* occurs when all light rays go through a common point (i.e., the viewpoint or center of projection). To apply perspective projection we must specify a perspective angle or camera view angle.

The front and back *clipping planes* intersect the projection vector, and are usually perpendicular to it. The clipping planes are used to eliminate data either too close to the camera or too far away. As a result only actors or portions of actors within the clipping planes are (potentially) visible.

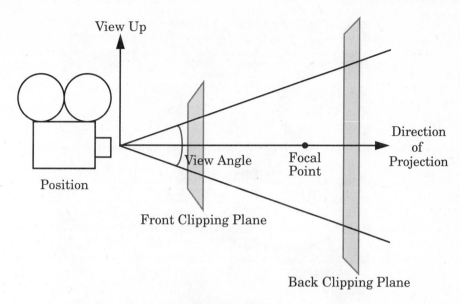

Figure 3–12 Camera attributes.

Taken together these camera parameters define a rectangular pyramid, with its apex at the camera's position and extending along the direction of projection. The pyramid is truncated at the top with the front clipping plane and at the bottom by the back clipping plane. The resulting frustum defines the region of 3D space visible to the camera.

In the *Visualization Toolkit*, clipping planes are typically perpendicular to the direction of projection. Their locations can be set using the cameras clipping range. The location of the planes are measured from the camera's position along the direction of projection. The front clipping plane is at the minimum range value, and the back clipping plane is at the maximum range value. Later on in Chapter 7, when we discuss stereo rendering, we will see examples of clipping planes that are not perpendicular to the direction of projection.

While a camera can be manipulated by directly setting the attributes mentioned above, there are some common operations that make the job easier. Figure **3–13** and Figure **3–14** will help illustrate these operations. Changing the *azimuth* of a camera rotates its position around its view up vector, centered at the focal point. Think of this as moving the camera to the left or right while always keeping the distance to the focal point constant. Changing a camera's *elevation* rotates its position around the cross product of its direction of projection and view up centered at the focal point. This corresponds to moving the camera up and down. To *roll* the camera, we rotate the view up vector about the view plane normal. Roll is sometimes also called twist.

The next two motions keep the camera's position constant and instead modify the focal point. Changing the *yaw* rotates the focal point about the view up centered at the camera's position. This is like an azimuth, except that the focal

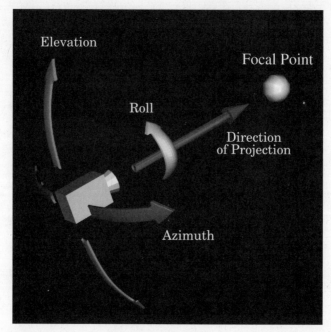

Figure 3–13 Camera movements around focal point (`camera.tcl`).

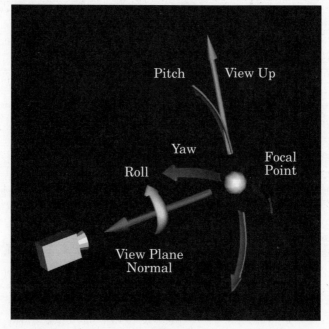

Figure 3–14 Camera movements centered at camera position (`camera2.tcl`).

point moves instead of the position. Changes in *pitch* rotate the focal point about the cross product of the direction of projection and view up centered at the camera's position. *Dollying* in and out moves the camera's position along the direction of projection, either closer or farther from the focal point. This operation is specified as the ratio of its current distance to its new distance. A value greater than one will dolly in, while a value less than one will dolly out. Finally, *zooming* changes the camera's view angle, so that more or less of the scene falls within the view frustum.

Once we have the camera situated, we can generate our 2D image. Some of the rays of light traveling through our 3D space will pass through the lens on the camera. These rays then strike a flat surface to produce an image. This effectively projects our 3D scene into a 2D image. The camera's position and other properties determine which rays of light get captured and projected. More specifically, only rays of light that intersect the camera's position, and are within its viewing frustum, will affect the resulting 2D image.

This concludes our brief rendering overview. The light has traveled from its sources to the actors, where it is reflected and scattered. Some of this light gets captured by the camera and produces a 2D image. Now we will look at some of the details of this process.

3.6 Coordinate Systems

There are four coordinate systems commonly used in computer graphics and two different ways of representing points within them (Figure **3–15**). While this may seem excessive, each one serves a purpose. The four coordinate systems we use are: *model*, *world*, *view*, and *display*.

The model coordinate system is the coordinate system in which the model is defined in, typically a local Cartesian coordinate system. If one of our actors represents a football, it will be based on a coordinate system natural to the football geometry (e.g., a cylindrical system). This model has an inherent coordinate system determined by the decisions of whoever generated it. They may have used inches or meters as their units, and the football may have been modeled with any arbitrary axis as its major axis.

The world coordinate system is the 3D space in which the actors are positioned. One of the actor's responsibilities is to convert from the model's coordinates into world coordinates. Each model may have its own coordinate system but there is only one world coordinate system. Each actor must scale, rotate, and translate its model into the world coordinate system. (It may also be necessary for the modeller to transform from its natural coordinate system into a local Cartesian system. This is because actors typically assume that the model coordinate system is a local Cartesian system.) The world coordinate system is also the system in which the position and orientation of cameras and lights are specified.

The view coordinate system represents what is visible to the camera. This consists of a pair of x and y values, ranging between (-1,1), and a z depth coordinate. The x, y values specify location in the image plane, while the z coordinate

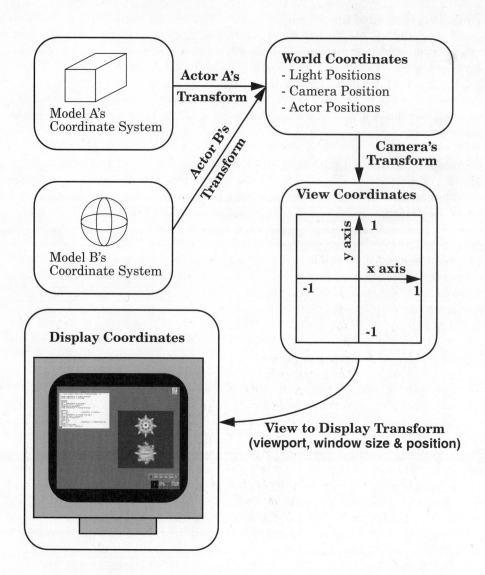

Figure 3–15 Modelling, world, view, and display coordinate systems.

represents the distance, or range, from the camera. The camera's properties are represented by a four by four transformation matrix (to be described shortly), which is used to convert from world coordinates into view coordinates. This is where the perspective effects of a camera are introduced.

The display coordinate system uses the same basis as the view coordinate system, but instead of using negative one to one as the range, the coordinates are actual *x, y* pixel locations on the image plane. Factors such as the window's size on the display determine how the view coordinate range of (-1,1) is mapped into pixel locations. This is also where the *viewport* comes into effect. You may want to render two different scenes, but display them in the same window. This can be done by dividing the window into rectangular viewports. Then, each renderer can be told what portion of the window it should use for rendering. The viewport ranges from (0,1) in both the x and y axis. Similar to the view coordinate system, the z-value in the display coordinate system also represents depth into the window. The meaning of this z-value will be further described in the section titled "Z-Buffer" on page 59.

3.7 Coordinate Transformation

When we create images with computer graphics, we project objects defined in three dimensions onto a two-dimensional image plane. As we saw earlier, this projection naturally includes perspective. To include projection effects such as vanishing points we use a special coordinate system called *homogeneous coordinates*.

The usual way of representing a point in 3D is the three element Cartesian vector (x, y, z). Homogeneous coordinates are represented by a four element vector (x_h, y_h, z_h, w_h). The conversion between Cartesian coordinates and homogeneous coordinates is given by:

$$x = \frac{x_h}{w_h} \qquad y = \frac{y_h}{w_h} \qquad z = \frac{z_h}{w_h} \qquad \text{(3-5)}$$

Using homogeneous coordinates we can represent an infinite point by setting w_h to zero. This capability is used by the camera for perspective transformations. The transformations are applied by using a 4×4 *transformation matrix*. Transformation matrices are widely used in computer graphics because they allow us to perform translation, scaling, and rotation of objects by repeated matrix multiplication. Such operations are not easily performed using a 3×3 matrix.

For example, suppose we wanted to create a transformation matrix that translates a point (x, y, z) in Cartesian space by the vector (t_x, t_y, t_z). We need only construct the translation matrix given by

$$T_T = \begin{bmatrix} 1 & 0 & 0 & t_x \\ 0 & 1 & 0 & t_y \\ 0 & 0 & 1 & t_z \\ 0 & 0 & 0 & 1 \end{bmatrix} \qquad \text{(3-6)}$$

and then post-multiply it with the homogeneous coordinate (x_h, y_h, z_h, w_h). To carry this example through, we construct the homogeneous coordinate from the Cartesian coordinate (x, y, z) by setting $w_h = 1$ to yield $(x, y, z, 1)$. Then, to determine the translated point (x', y', z') we pre-multiply the current position by the transformation matrix T_T to yield the translated coordinate. Substituting into Equation **3-6** we have the result

$$\begin{bmatrix} x' \\ y' \\ z' \\ w' \end{bmatrix} = \begin{bmatrix} 1 & 0 & 0 & t_x \\ 0 & 1 & 0 & t_y \\ 0 & 0 & 1 & t_z \\ 0 & 0 & 0 & 1 \end{bmatrix} \cdot \begin{bmatrix} x \\ y \\ z \\ 1 \end{bmatrix} \qquad \textbf{(3-7)}$$

Converting back to Cartesian coordinates via Equation **3-5** we have the expected solution

$$x' = x + t_x$$
$$y' = y + t_y \qquad \textbf{(3-8)}$$
$$z' = z + t_z$$

The same procedure is used to scale or rotate an object. To scale an object we use the transformation matrix

$$T_S = \begin{bmatrix} s_x & 0 & 0 & 0 \\ 0 & s_y & 0 & 0 \\ 0 & 0 & s_z & 0 \\ 0 & 0 & 0 & 1 \end{bmatrix} \qquad \textbf{(3-9)}$$

where the parameters s_x, s_y, and s_z are scale factors along the x, y and z axes. Similarly, we can rotate an object around the x axes by angle θ using the matrix

$$T_{R_x} = \begin{bmatrix} 1 & 0 & 0 & 0 \\ 0 & \cos\theta & \sin\theta & 0 \\ 0 & -\sin\theta & \cos\theta & 0 \\ 0 & 0 & 0 & 1 \end{bmatrix} \qquad \textbf{(3-10)}$$

Around the y axis we use

$$T_{R_y} = \begin{bmatrix} \cos\theta & 0 & -\sin\theta & 0 \\ 0 & 1 & 0 & 0 \\ \sin\theta & 0 & \cos\theta & 0 \\ 0 & 0 & 0 & 1 \end{bmatrix} \qquad \textbf{(3-11)}$$

and around the z axis we use

$$T_{R_z} = \begin{bmatrix} \cos\theta & \sin\theta & 0 & 0 \\ -\sin\theta & \cos\theta & 0 & 0 \\ 0 & 0 & 1 & 0 \\ 0 & 0 & 0 & 1 \end{bmatrix} \qquad (3\text{-}12)$$

Another useful rotation matrix is used to transform one coordinate axes $x - y - z$ to another coordinate axes $x' - y' - z'$. To derive the transformation matrix we assume that the unit x' axis makes the angles $(\theta_{x'x}, \theta_{x'y}, \theta_{x'z})$ around the $x - y - z$ axes (these are called direction cosines). Similarly, the unit y' axis makes the angles $(\theta_{y'x}, \theta_{y'y}, \theta_{y'z})$ and the unit z' axis makes the angles $(\theta_{z'x}, \theta_{z'y}, \theta_{z'z})$. The resulting rotation matrix is formed by placing the direction cosines along the rows of the transformation matrix as follows

$$T_R = \begin{bmatrix} \cos\theta_{x'x} & \cos\theta_{x'y} & \cos\theta_{x'z} & 0 \\ \cos\theta_{y'x} & \cos\theta_{y'y} & \cos\theta_{y'z} & 0 \\ \cos\theta_{z'x} & \cos\theta_{z'y} & \cos\theta_{z'z} & 0 \\ 0 & 0 & 0 & 1 \end{bmatrix} \qquad (3\text{-}13)$$

Rotations occur about the coordinate origin. It is often more convenient to rotate around the center of the object (or a user-specified point). Assume that we call this point the object's center O_c. To rotate around O_c we must first translate the object from O_c to the origin, apply rotations, and then translate the object back to O_c.

Transformation matrices can be combined by matrix multiplication to achieve combinations of translation, rotation, and scaling. It is possible for a single transformation matrix to represent all types of transformation simultaneously. This matrix is the result of repeated matrix multiplications. A word of warning: the order of the multiplication is important. For example, multiplying a translation matrix by a rotation matrix will not yield the same result as multiplying the rotation matrix by the translation matrix.

3.8 Actor Geometry

We have seen how lighting properties control the appearance of an actor, and how the camera in combination with transformation matrices is used to project an actor to the image plane. What is left to define is the geometry of the actor, and how we position it in the world coordinate system.

Modelling

A major topic in the study of computer graphics is modelling or representing the geometry of physical objects. Various mathematical techniques have been applied including combinations of points, lines, polygons, curves, and splines of various forms, and even implicit mathematical functions. This topic is beyond the scope of the text. The important point here is that there is an underlying geometric model that specifies where an object is located in the model coordinate system.

In data visualization, modelling takes a different role. Instead of directly creating geometry to represent our object, visualization algorithms *compute* these forms. Often the geometry is abstract (like a contour line) and has little bearing on real world geometry. We will see how these models are computed when we describe visualization algorithms in Chapters 6 and 9.

The representation of geometry for data visualization tends to be simple, even though computing the representations is not. These forms are most often primitives like points, lines, and polygons, or visualization data such as volume data. We use simple forms because we desire high performance and interactive systems. Thus we take advantage of computer hardware (to be covered in "Graphics Hardware" on page 53) or special rendering techniques like volume rendering (see "Volume Rendering" on page 209).

Actor Location

Every actor has a transformation matrix that controls its location and scaling in world space. The actor's geometry is defined by a model in model coordinates. We specify the actor's location using orientation, position, and scale factors along the coordinate axes. In addition, we can define an origin around which the actor rotates. This feature is useful because we can rotate the actor around its center or some other meaningful point.

The orientation of an actor is determined by rotations stored in an orientation vector (O_x, O_y, O_z). This vector defines a series of rotational transformation matrices. As we saw in the previous section on transformation matrices, the order of application of the transformations is not arbitrary. We have chosen a fixed order based on what we think is natural to users. The order of transformation is a rotation by O_y around the y axis, then by O_x around the x axis, and finally by O_z around the z axis. This ordering is arbitrary and is based on the standard camera operations. These operations (in order) are a camera azimuth, followed by an elevation, and then a roll (Figure **3–16**).

All of these rotations take place around the origin of the actor. Typically this is set to the center of its bounding box, but it can be set to any convenient point. There are many different methods for changing an actor's orientation. `RotateX()`, `RotateY()` and `RotateZ()` are common methods that rotate about their respective axes. Many systems also include a method to rotate about a user-defined axis.

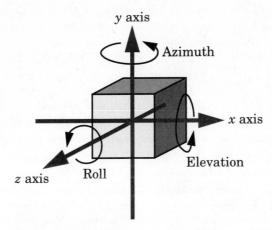

Figure 3–16 Actor coordinate system.

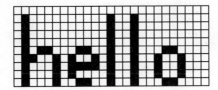

Figure 3–17 A pixel array for the word hello.

3.9 Graphics Hardware

Earlier we mentioned that advances in graphics hardware have had a large impact on how rendering is performed. Now that we have covered the fundamentals of rendering a scene, we look at some of the hardware issues. First, we discuss raster devices that have replaced vector displays as the primary output device. Then, we look at how our programs communicate to the graphics hardware. We also examine the different coordinate systems used in computer graphics, hidden line/surface removal, and z-buffering.

Raster Devices

Usually we see computer graphics in a printed picture or displayed on a computer monitor. Occasionally we see something on TV or in a movie. All of these mediums are raster devices. A raster device represents an image using a two dimensional array of picture elements called pixels. For example, the word "hello" can be represented as an array of pixels.

In Figure **3–17**, the word "hello" is written within a pixel array that is twenty-five pixels wide and ten pixels high. Each pixel stores one bit of information, whether it is black or white. This is how a black and white laser printer works, for each point on the paper it either prints a black dot, or leaves it the color of the paper. Due to hardware limitations, raster devices such as laser printers and computer monitors do not actually draw accurate square pixels like those in Figure **3–17**, instead they tend to be slightly blurred and overlapping. Another hardware limitation of raster devices is their resolution. This is what causes a 300 dpi (dots per inch) laser printer to produce more detailed output than a nine pin dot matrix printer. A 300 dpi laser printer has a resolution of 300 pixels per inch compared to roughly 50 dpi for the dot matrix printer.

Color computer monitors typically have a resolution of about 80 pixels per inch, making the screen a pixel array roughly one thousand pixels in width and height. This results in over one million pixels, each with a value that indicates what color it should be. Since the hardware in color monitors uses the RGB system, it makes sense to use that to describe the colors in the pixels. Unfortunately, having over one million pixels, each with a red, green and blue component, can take up a lot of memory. This is part of what differentiates the variety of graphics hardware on the market. Some companies use twenty-four bits of storage per pixel, others use eight, some advanced systems use more than 100 bits of storage per pixel. Typically, the more bits per pixel the more accurate the colors will be.

One way to work around color limitations in the graphics hardware is by using a technique called *dithering*. Say, for example, that you want to use some different shades of gray, but your graphics hardware only supports black and white. Dithering lets you approximate shades of gray by using a mixture of both black and white pixels. In Figure **3–18**, seven gray squares are drawn using a mixture of black and white pixels. From a distance the seven squares look like different shades of gray even though up close, it's clear that they are just different mixtures of black and white pixels. This same technique works just as well for other colors. For example, if your graphics hardware supports primary blue, primary green and white but not a pastel sea green, you can approximate this color by dithering the green, blue, and white that the hardware does support.

Interfacing to the Hardware

Now that we have covered the basics of display hardware, the good news is that you rarely need to worry about them. Most graphics programming is done using higher level primitives than individual pixels. Figure **3–19** shows a typical arrangement for a visualization program. At the bottom of the hierarchy is the display hardware that we already discussed; chances are your programs will not interact directly with it. The top three layers above the hardware are the layers you may need to be concerned with.

Many programs take advantage of application libraries as a high level interface to the graphics capabilities of a system. The *Visualization Toolkit* accompanying this book is a prime example of this. It allows you to display a complex object or graph using just a few commands. It also can interface to a

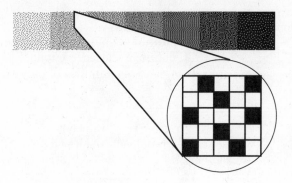

Figure 3–18 Black and white dithering.

number of different graphics libraries, since different libraries are supported on different hardware platforms.

The graphics library and graphics hardware layers both perform similar functions. They are responsible for taking high level commands from an application library or program, and executing them. This makes programming much easier by providing more complex primitives to work with. Instead of drawing pixels one at a time, we can draw primitives like polygons, triangles, and lines, without worrying about the details of which pixels are being set to which colors. Figure **3–20** illustrates some high level primitives that all mainstream graphics libraries support.

This functionality is broken into two different layers because different machines may have vastly different graphics hardware. If you write a program that draws a red polygon, either the graphics library or the graphics hardware must be able to execute that command. On high-end systems, this may be done

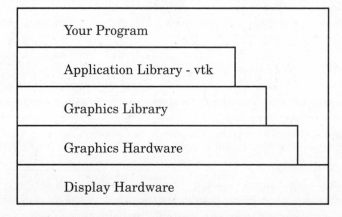

Figure 3–19 Typical graphics interface hierarchy.

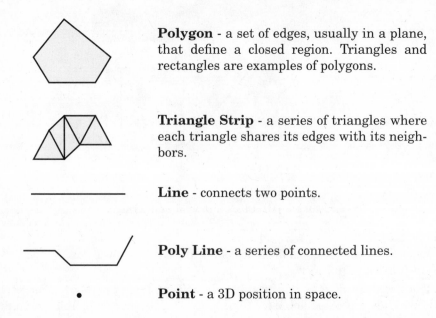

Polygon - a set of edges, usually in a plane, that define a closed region. Triangles and rectangles are examples of polygons.

Triangle Strip - a series of triangles where each triangle shares its edges with its neighbors.

Line - connects two points.

Poly Line - a series of connected lines.

Point - a 3D position in space.

Figure 3–20 Graphics primitives.

in the graphics hardware, on others it will be done by the graphics library in software. So the same commands can be used with a wide variety of machines, without worrying about the underlying graphics hardware.

The fundamental building block of the primitives in Figure **3–20** is a point (or vertex). A vertex has a position, normal, and color, each of which is a three element vector. The position specifies where the vertex is located, its normal specifies which direction the vertex is facing, and its color specifies the vertex's red, green and blue components. A polygon is built by connecting a series of points or vertices as shown in Figure **3–21**. You may be wondering why each vertex has a normal, instead of having just one normal for the entire polygon. A planar polygon can only be facing one direction regardless of what the normals of its vertices indicate. The reason is that sometimes a polygon is used as an approximation of something else, like a curve. Figure **3–22** shows a top down view of a cylinder. As you can see, it's not really a cylinder but rather a polygonal approximation of the cylinder drawn in gray. Each vertex is shared by two polygons and the correct normal for the vertex is not the same as the normal for the polygon. Similar logic explains why each vertex has a color instead of just having one color for an entire polygon.

When you limit yourself to the types of primitives described above, there are some additional properties that many graphics systems support. Edge color and edge visibility can be used to highlight the polygon primitives that make up an actor. Another way to do this is by adjusting the representation from *surface*

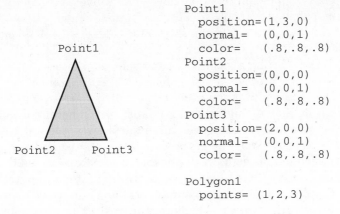

```
Point1
  position=(1,3,0)
  normal=  (0,0,1)
  color=   (.8,.8,.8)
Point2
  position=(0,0,0)
  normal=  (0,0,1)
  color=   (.8,.8,.8)
Point3
  position=(2,0,0)
  normal=  (0,0,1)
  color=   (.8,.8,.8)

Polygon1
  points= (1,2,3)
```

Figure 3–21 An example polygon.

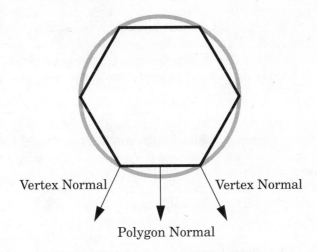

Figure 3–22 Vertex and polygon normals.

to *wireframe* or *points*. This replaces surfaces such as polygons with either their boundary edges or points respectively. While this may not make much sense from a physical perspective, it can help in some illustrations. Using edge visibility when rendering a CAD model can help to show the different pieces that comprise the model.

Rasterization

At this point in the text we have described how to represent graphics data using rendering primitives, and we have described how to represent images using raster display devices. The question remains, how do we convert graphics primitives into a raster image? This is the topic we address in this section. Although a thorough treatise on this topic is beyond the scope of this text, we will do our best to provide a high-level overview.

The process of converting a geometric representation into a raster image is called *rasterization*. This process is also called *scan conversion*. In the description that follows we assume that the graphics primitives are triangle polygons. This is not as limiting as you might think, because any general polygon can be converted into a set of polygons. Moreover, other surface representations such as splines are usually tessellated by the graphics system into triangles or polygons. (The method described here is actually applicable to convex polygons.)

Most of today's hardware is based on object-order rasterization techniques. As we saw earlier in this chapter, this means processing our actors in order. And since our actors are represented by polygon primitives, we process polygons one at a time. So although we describe the processing of one polygon, bear in mind that many polygons and possibly many actors are processed.

The first step is to transform the polygon using the appropriate transformation matrix. We also project the polygon to the image plane using either parallel or orthographic projection. Part of this process involves clipping the polygons. Not only do we use the front and back clipping planes to clip polygons too close or too far, but we must also clip polygons crossing the boundaries of the image plane. Clipping polygons that cross the boundary of the view frustum means we have to generate new polygon boundaries.

With the polygon clipped and projected to the image plane, we can begin scan-line processing (Figure **3–23**). The first step identifies the initial scan-line intersected by the projected polygon. This is found by sorting the vertex's y values. We then find the two edges joining the vertex on the left and right sides. Using the slopes of the edges along with the data values we compute delta data values. These data are typically the R, G, and B color components. Other data values include transparency values and z depth values. (The z values are necessary if we are using a z-buffer, described in the next section.) The row of pixels within the polygon (i.e., starting at the left and right edges) is called a *span*. Data values are interpolated from the edges on either side of the span to compute the internal pixel values. This process continues span-by-span, until the entire polygon is filled. Note that as new vertices are encountered, it is necessary to recompute the delta data values.

The shading of the polygon (i.e., color interpolation across the polygon) varies depending on the actor's interpolation attribute. There are three possibilities: *flat*, *Gouraud*, or *Phong shading*. Figure **3–7** illustrates the difference between flat and Gouraud interpolation. Flat shading calculates the color of a polygon by applying the lighting equations to just one normal (typically the surface normal) of the polygon. Gouraud shading calculates the color of a polygon at all of its vertices using the vertices' normals and the standard lighting equations. The interior and edges of the polygon are then filled in by applying the scan-line interpolation process. Phong shading is the most realistic of the three. It calculates a normal at every location on the polygon by interpolating the vertex nor-

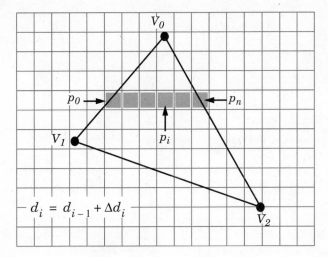

Figure 3–23 Rasterizing a convex polygon. Pixels are processed in horizontal spans (or scan-lines) in the image plane. Data values d_i at point p_i are interpolated along the edges and then along the scan-line using delta values. Typical data values are RGB components of color.

mals. These are then used in the lighting equations to determine the resulting pixel colors. Both flat and Gouraud shading are commonly used methods. The complexity of Phong shading has prevented it from being widely supported in hardware.

Z-Buffer

In our earlier description of the rendering process, we followed rays of light from our eye through a pixel in the image plane to the actors and back to the light source. A nice side effect of ray tracing is that viewing rays strike the first actor they encounter and ignore any actors that are hidden behind it. When rendering actors using the polygonal methods described above, we have no such method of computing which polygons are hidden and which are not. We cannot generally count on the polygons being ordered correctly. Instead, we can use a number of hidden-line methods for polygon rendering.

One method is to sort all of our polygons from back to front and then render them in that order. This is called the painter's algorithm or painter's sort, and has one major weakness illustrated in Figure **3–24**. Regardless of the order in which we draw these three triangles, we cannot obtain the desired result, since each triangle is both in front of, and behind, another triangle. There are algorithms that sort and split polygons as necessary to treat such a situation [Carlson85]. This requires more initial processing to perform the sorting and splitting. If the geometric primitives change between images, or the camera view changes, then this processing must be performed before each render.

Figure 3–24 Painter's algorithm flaw.

Another hidden surface algorithm, z-buffering, takes care of this problem and does not require sorting. Z-buffering takes advantage of the z-value (i.e., depth value along direction of projection) in the view coordinate system. Before a new pixel is drawn, its z-value is compared against the current z-value for that pixel location. If the new pixel would be in front of the current pixel, then it is drawn and the z-value for that pixel location is updated. Otherwise the current pixel remains and the new pixel is ignored.

Z-buffering has been widely implemented in hardware because of its simplicity and robustness. The down side to z-buffering is that it requires a large amount of memory, called a z-buffer, to store a z-value of every pixel. Most systems use a z-buffer with a depth of 24 or 32 bits. For a 1000 by 1000 display that translates into three to four megabytes just for the z-buffer. Another problem with z-buffering is that its accuracy is limited depending on its depth. A 24-bit z-buffer yields a precision of one part in 16,777,216 over the height of the viewing frustum. This resolution is often insufficient if objects are close together. If you do run into situations with z-buffering accuracy, make sure that the front and back clipping planes are as close to the visible geometry as possible.

3.10 Putting It All Together

This section provides an overview of the graphics objects and how to use them in the *Visualization Toolkit*.

The Graphics Model

We have discussed many of the objects that play a part in the rendering of a scene. Now it's time to put them together into a comprehensive object model for graphics and visualization.

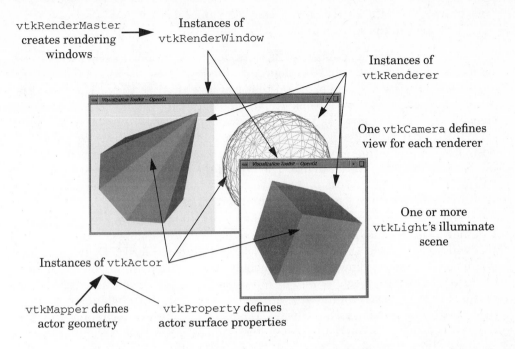

Figure 3–25 Illustrative diagram of graphics objects (`Model.cc`).

In the *Visualization Toolkit* there are eight basic objects that we use to render a scene. There are many more objects behind the scenes, but these eight are the ones we use most frequently. The objects are listed in the following and illustrated in Figure **3–25**.

- `vtkRenderMaster` - coordinates device-independent methods; use to create a rendering window.

- `vtkRenderWindow` - manages a window on the display device; one or more renderers draw into an instance of `vtkRenderWindow`.

- `vtkRenderer` - coordinates the rendering process involving lights, cameras, and actors.

- `vtkLight` - a source of light to illuminate the scene.

- `vtkCamera` - defines the view position, focal point, and other viewing properties of the scene.

- `vtkActor` - represents an object rendered in the scene, both its properties and position in the world coordinate system.

- `vtkProperty` - defines the appearance properties of an actor including color, transparency, and lighting properties such as specular and diffuse. Also representational properties like wireframe and solid surface.

- vtkMapper - the geometric representation for an actor. More than one actor may refer to the same mapper.

The first object is vtkRenderMaster. As we mentioned earlier, there are many different graphics libraries being used today. An application programmer would like to write just one program that works with all of them. The vtkRenderMaster class facilitates this. It has one method, MakeRenderWindow(), that returns an instance of the vtkRenderWindow class supported by your machine. If more than one graphics library is supported, it will try to select the best one. The environment variable VTK_RENDERER can be set to explicitly determine which graphics library to use. The type of the returned object, such as vtkStarbaseRenderWindow, is typecast to a generic vtkRenderWindow, allowing the same source code to work with different graphics libraries.

The vtkRenderWindow is the second object that ties the rendering process together. It is responsible for managing a window on the display device. For PCs this will probably be a window within Microsoft Windows, for UNIX systems this will be an X window. Characteristics such as size, position, and name are stored by instances of this object, as well as more graphics specific characteristics such as the window's depth and *double buffering*. The depth of a window indicates how many bits are allocated per pixel. Double buffering is a technique where a window is logically divided into two buffers. At any given time one buffer is currently visible to the user. Meanwhile, the second buffer can be used to draw the next image in an animation. Once the rendering is complete, the two buffers can be swapped so that the new image is visible. This common technique allows animations to be displayed without the user seeing the actual rendering of the primitives. High end graphics systems perform double buffering in hardware. A typical system would have a rendering window with a depth of 72 bits. The first 24 bits are used to store the red, green and blue (RGB) pixel components for the front buffer. The next 24 bits store the RGB values for the back buffer. The last 24 bits are used as a z-buffer.

In addition to window management, vtkRenderWindow objects create renderers. The renderers (instances of class vtkRenderer) draw into the rendering window and are device independent, just like the rendering window objects. This supports multiple graphics libraries without having to modify your source code.

The class vtkRenderer is responsible for coordinating its lights, camera, and actors to produce an image. Each instance maintains a list of the actors, lights, and an active camera in a particular scene. At least one actor must be defined, but if lights and a camera are not defined, they will be automatically created by the renderer. In such a case the actors are centered in the image and the default camera view is down the z-axis. Instances of the class vtkRenderer also provide methods to specify the background and ambient lighting colors. Methods are also available to convert to and from world, view, and display coordinate systems.

One unusual aspect of the renderers is that they are constructed from an instance of the vtkRenderWindow class. This associates the renderer with the window into which it is to draw. By default, the renderer draws into the full extent of the window (viewpoint coordinates (0,0,1,1)). It is possible to specify a particular rectangular region in which to render by specifying a smaller viewport.

Instances of the class `vtkLight` illuminate the scene. Various instance variables for orienting and positioning the light are available. It is also possible to turn on/off lights and set the color of the light. Normally at least one light is "on" to illuminate the scene. If no lights are defined and turned on, the renderer constructs a light automatically. Lights in **vtk** can be either positional or infinite. Positional lights have an associated cone angle and attenuation factors. Infinite lights project light rays parallel to one another.

Cameras are constructed by the class `vtkCamera`. Important parameters include camera position, focal point, location of front and back clipping planes, view up vector, and field of view. Cameras also have special methods to simplify manipulation. These include elevation, azimuth, zoom, and roll. Similar to `vtkLight`, an instance of `vtkCamera` will be automatically created by the renderer if none is defined.

Instances of the class `vtkActor` represent objects in the scene. In particular, `vtkActor` combines object properties (color, shading type, etc.), geometric definition, and orientation in the world coordinate system. This is implemented behind the scenes by maintaining instance variables that refer to instances of `vtkProperty`, `vtkMapper`, and `vtkTransform`. Normally you need not create properties or transformations explicitly, since these are automatically created and manipulated using `vtkActor`'s methods. You do need to create an instance of `vtkMapper` (or one of its subclasses). The mapper ties the data visualization pipeline to the graphics device.

There are other classes of actors with specialized behavior, implemented as subclasses of `vtkActor`. One example is `vtkFollower`. Instances of this class always face the active camera. This is useful when designing signs or text that must be readable from any camera position in the scene.

Instances of the class `vtkProperty` are used to affect the rendered appearance of an actor. When actors are created, a property instance is automatically created with them. Actor methods such as `SetColor()` are implemented by delegating the message to this property object. It is also possible to create property objects directly and then associate the property object with one or more actors. In this way actors can share common properties.

Finally, `vtkMapper` (and its subclasses) defines object geometry and, optionally, vertex colors. We will examine the mapping process in more detail in "Mapper Design" on page 178. For now assume that `vtkMapper` is an object that represents geometry and other types of visualization data. In addition, `vtkMapper` refers to a table of colors (i.e., `vtkLookupTable`) that are used to color vertices. (We discuss mapping of data to colors in "Color Mapping" on page 143.)

There is another important object, `vtkRenderWindowInteractor`, that captures events for a renderer in the rendering window. `vtkRenderWindowInteractor` captures these events and then triggers certain operations like camera dolly, pan, and rotate, actor picking, into/out of stereo mode, and so on.

Examples

This section works through some simple graphics applications implemented using the **vtk** graphics objects. The focus is on the basics: how to create renderers, lights, cameras, and actors. Later chapters tie together these basic principles to create applications for data visualization.

Render a Cone

The following C++ code uses most of the objects introduced in this section to create an image of a cone. The vtkConeSource generates a polygonal representation of a cone and vtkPolyMapper maps the geometry (in conjunction with the actor) to the graphics library. (The source code to this example can be found in Cone.cc.)

```
#include "vtk.hh"
main ()
{
  char a;
  vtkRenderMaster renMaster;     // our required RenderMaster
  vtkRenderWindow *renWindow;    // a RenderWindow to draw in
  vtkRenderer *ren;              // a Renderer to do the drawing
  vtkActor *coneActor;           // an actor to be drawn
  vtkConeSource *cone;           // the model data for the actor
  vtkPolyMapper *coneMapper;

  // create a rendering window and renderer
  renWindow = renMaster.MakeRenderWindow();
  ren = renWindow->MakeRenderer();
  // create an actor and give it cone geometry
  cone = new vtkConeSource;
    cone->SetResolution(8);
  coneMapper = new vtkPolyMapper;
    coneMapper->SetInput(cone->GetOutput());
  coneActor = new vtkActor;
    coneActor->SetMapper(coneMapper);
  // assign our actor to the renderer
  ren->AddActors(coneActor);
  // draw the resulting scene
  renWindow->Render();
  // wait until key is pressed
  cout << "Press any key followed by <Enter> to exit>> ";
  cin >> a;
}
```

Some words about this example. The include file vtk.hh includes class definitions for all objects in **vtk**. (This is a convenience to the user, you may want to include only the particular classes you're interested in to speed up compilation.) The beginning of the program contains type declarations for the objects. The

MakeRenderWindow() and MakeRenderer() methods create an instance of
vtkRenderWindow and vtkRenderer respectively. Next we create a polygonal
representation of the cone, and using the SetMapper() method we associate the
mapper's data with the coneActor. The next line adds coneActor to our renderer's list of actors. And finally we tell the renWindow to render itself. This in
turn causes the renderer instance ren to render itself. We conclude this example
by waiting for a keyboard stroke before exiting. Since there are no cameras or
lights defined in the above example, **vtk** automatically generates a default light
and default camera as a convenience to the user.

Creating Multiple Renderers

The next example is a little more complex and uses multiple renderers that
share a single rendering window. We use viewports to define where the renderers
should draw. (This C++ code can be found in Cone2.cc.)

```cpp
#include "vtk.hh"
main ()
{
  int i;
  vtkRenderMaster renMaster;      // our required RenderMaster
  vtkRenderWindow *renWindow;     // a RenderWindow to draw in
  vtkRenderer *ren1, *ren2;       // two Renderers this time
  vtkActor *coneActor;            // an actor to be drawn
  vtkConeSource *cone;            // the model data for the actor
  vtkPolyMapper *coneMapper;

  // create a rendering window and both renderers
  renWindow = renMaster.MakeRenderWindow();
  ren1 = renWindow->MakeRenderer();
  ren2 = renWindow->MakeRenderer();
  // create an actor and give it cone geometry
  cone = new vtkConeSource;
    cone->SetResolution(8);
  coneMapper = new vtkPolyMapper;
    coneMapper->SetInput(cone->GetOutput());
  coneActor = new vtkActor;
    coneActor->SetMapper(coneMapper);
  // assign our actor to both renderers
  ren1->AddActors(coneActor);
  ren2->AddActors(coneActor);
  // set the size of our window
  renWindow->SetSize(400,200);
  // set the viewports and background of the renderers
  ren1->SetViewport(0,0,0.5,1);
  ren1->SetBackground(0.2,0.3,0.5);
  ren2->SetViewport(0.5,0,1,1);
  ren2->SetBackground(0.2,0.5,0.3);
  // draw the resulting scene
```

Figure 3–26 Four frames of output from Cone2.cc.

```
renWindow->Render();
// make one view 90 degrees from the other
ren1->GetActiveCamera()->Azimuth(90);
// do a azimuth of the cameras 9 degrees per iteration
for (i = 0; i < 360; i += 9)
  {
  ren1->GetActiveCamera()->Azimuth(9);
  ren2->GetActiveCamera()->Azimuth(9);
  renWindow->Render();
  }
}
```

As you can see, much of the code is the same as the previous example. The first difference is that we create two renderers instead of one. We assign the same actor to both renderers, but set each renderer's background to a different color. We set the viewport of the two renderers so that one is on the left half of the rendering window and the other is on the right. The rendering window's size is specified as 400 by 200 pixels, which results in each renderer drawing into a viewport of 200 by 200 pixels.

A good application of multiple renderers is to display different views of the same world. In this example we send the first renderer's camera a 90 degree azimuth. We then start a loop that rotates the two cameras around the cone. Figure **3–26** shows four frames from this animation.

Introducing vtkRenderWindowInteractor

The previous examples are limited in that it is not possible to directly interact with the data without modifying and recompiling the C++ code. One common type of interaction is to change camera position so that we can view our scene from different vantage points. In the *Visualization Toolkit* we have provided a convenient object to do this: vtkRenderWindowInteractor.

Instances of the class vtkRenderWindowInteractor capture mouse and keyboard events in the rendering window, and perform operations depending on the particular event. For example, we can perform camera dolly, pan, and rotation with `vtkRenderWindowInteractor`. The following example shows how to instantiate and use this object. The example is the same as our first example with the addition of the interactor. The example C++ code is in `Cone3.cc`.

```
#include "vtk.hh"
main ()
{
  vtkRenderMaster renMaster;      // our required RenderMaster
  vtkRenderWindow *renWindow;     // a RenderWindow to draw in
  vtkRenderer *ren;               // a Renderer to do the drawing
  vtkActor *coneActor;            // an actor to be drawn
  vtkConeSource *cone;            // the model data for the actor
  vtkPolyMapper *coneMapper;
  vtkRenderWindowInteractor *iren; // interactor

  // create a rendering window and renderer
  renWindow = renMaster.MakeRenderWindow();
  ren = renWindow->MakeRenderer();
  iren = renWindow->MakeRenderWindowInteractor();
  // create an actor and give it cone geometry
  cone = new vtkConeSource;
    cone->SetResolution(8);
  coneMapper = new vtkPolyMapper;
    coneMapper->SetInput(cone->GetOutput());
  coneActor = new vtkActor;
    coneActor->SetMapper(coneMapper);
  // assign our actor to the renderer
  ren->AddActors(coneActor);
  // draw the resulting scene
  renWindow->Render();
  //  Begin mouse interaction
  iren->Start();
}
```

The interactor is created by using the special method `MakeRenderWindow-Interactor()` shown in the example. In order to use the interactor we have to execute its `Start()` method, which works with the event loop of the windowing system to begin to catch events. Some of the more useful events include the "w" key, which draws all actors in wireframe; the "s" key, which draws the actors in surface form; the "3" key, which toggles in and out of 3D stereo for those systems that support this; the "r" key, which resets camera view; and the "e" key, which exits the application. In addition, the mouse buttons rotate, pan, and dolly about the camera's focal point. Two advanced features are the "u" key, which executes a user defined function; and the "p" key, which picks the actor under the mouse pointer.

Properties and Transformations

The previous examples did not explicitly create property or transformation
objects or apply actor methods that affect these objects. Instead, we accepted
default instance variable values. This procedure is typical of **vtk** applications.
Most instance variables have been preset to generate acceptable results, but
methods are always available for you to override the default values.

This example creates an image of two cones of different colors and specular
properties. In addition, we transform one of the objects to lie next to the other.
The C++ source code for this example can be found in Cone4.cc.

```cpp
#include "vtk.hh"
main ()
{
  char a;
  vtkRenderMaster renMaster;       // our required RenderMaster
  vtkRenderWindow *renWindow;      // a RenderWindow to draw in
  vtkRenderer *ren;                // a Renderer to do the drawing
  vtkActor *cone1, *cone2;         // actors to be drawn
  vtkProperty *prop;               // property object
  vtkConeSource *cone;             // the model data for the actor
  vtkPolyMapper *coneMapper;
  vtkRenderWindowInteractor *iren; // interactor

  // create a rendering window and renderer
  renWindow = renMaster.MakeRenderWindow();
  ren = renWindow->MakeRenderer();
  iren = renWindow->MakeRenderWindowInteractor();
  // create an actor and give it cone geometry
  cone = new vtkConeSource;
    cone->SetResolution(8);
  coneMapper = new vtkPolyMapper;
    coneMapper->SetInput(cone->GetOutput());
  cone1 = new vtkActor;
    cone1->SetMapper(coneMapper);
    cone1->GetProperty()->SetColor(0.2000,0.6300,0.7900);
    cone1->GetProperty()->SetDiffuse(0.7);
    cone1->GetProperty()->SetSpecular(0.4);
    cone1->GetProperty()->SetSpecularPower(20);

  prop = new vtkProperty;
    prop->SetColor(1.0000, 0.3882, 0.2784);
    prop->SetDiffuse(0.7);
    prop->SetSpecular(0.4);
    prop->SetSpecularPower(20);
  cone2 = new vtkActor;
    cone2->SetMapper(coneMapper);
    cone2->SetProperty(prop);
    cone2->SetPosition(0,2,0);
```

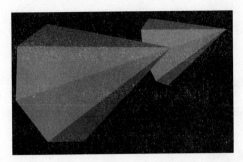

Figure 3–27 Modifying properties and transformation matrix (`Cone4.cc`).

```
// assign our actor to the renderer
ren->AddActors(cone1);
ren->AddActors(cone2);
// draw the resulting scene
renWindow->Render();
//  Begin mouse interaction
iren->Start();
}
```

We set the actor `cone1` properties by modifying the property object automatically created by the actor. This differs from actor `cone2`, where we create a property directly and then assign it to the actor. `Cone2` is moved from its default position by applying the `SetPosition()` method. This method affects the transformation matrix that is an instance variable of the actor. The resulting image is shown in Figure **3–27**.

Interpreted Code

In the previous example we saw how to create an interactor object that allows us to manipulate the camera (among other things). Although this provides flexibility and interactivity for a large number of applications, there are examples throughout this text where we want to modify other parameters. These parameters range from actor properties, such as color, to the name of an input file. Of course we can always write or modify C++ code to do this, but in many cases the turn around time between change and result is too long. To improve overall interactivity we use an interpreted system. Interpreted systems allow us to modify objects and immediately see the result, without the need to recompile and relink source code. Chapter 10 discusses interpreters in more depth.

The *Visualization Toolkit* uses the Tcl language as its interpreted language. There is a one-to-one mapping between C++ methods and Tcl functions for most objects in the system. The following example repeats our third example but is implemented using a Tcl script. (The script can be found in `Cone.tcl`.)

Figure 3–28 Using Tcl and Tk to build an interpreted application (`Cone.tcl`).

```
# user interface command widget
source vtkInt.tcl

# create a rendering window and renderer
vtkRenderMaster rm;
set renWin [rm MakeRenderWindow];
set ren [$renWin MakeRenderer];
set iren [$renWin MakeRenderWindowInteractor];

# create an actor and give it cone geometry
vtkConeSource cone;
  cone SetResolution 8;
vtkPolyMapper coneMapper;
  coneMapper SetInput [cone GetOutput];
vtkActor coneActor;
  coneActor SetMapper coneMapper;

# assign our actor to the renderer
$ren AddActors coneActor;

# enable user interface interactor
$iren SetUserMethod {wm deiconify .vtkInteract};
$iren Initialize;

# prevent the tk window from showing up then start the event loop
wm withdraw .
```

As we can see from this example, the number of lines of code is less for the Tcl example than for equivalent C++ code. Also, many of the complexities of C++ are hidden using the interpreted language. Most importantly, we extend the interactor so that when a "u" keystroke is entered into the window (i.e., the user function key), a Tcl/Tk command widget appears (Figure **3–28**). (Tk is a computer independent graphical user interface widget set that is part of Tcl.) Using this user interface tool we can create, modify, and delete objects, and modify their instance variables. The resulting changes appear as soon as a `Render()` method is applied or mouse events in the rendering window cause a render to occur. We encourage you to use Tcl for rapid creation of graphics and visualization examples. C++ is best used when you desire higher performing applications.

Transformation Matrices

Transformation matrices are used throughout *Visualization Toolkit*. Actors use them to position and orient themselves. Various filters, including `vtkGlyph3D` and `vtkTransformFilter`, use transformation matrices to implement their own functionality. As a user you may never use transformation matrices directly, but understanding them is important to successful use of many **vtk** classes.

The most important aspect to applying transformation matrices is to understand the order in which the transformations are applied. If you break down a complex series of transformations into simple combinations of translation, scaling, and rotation, and keep careful track of the order of application, you will have gone a long way to mastering their use.

A good demonstration example of transformation matrices is to examine how `vtkActor` uses its internal matrix. `vtkActor` has an internal instance variable `Transform` to which it delegates many of its methods or uses the matrix to implement its methods. For example, the `RotateX()`, `RotateY()`, and `RotateZ()` methods are all delegated to `Transform`. The method `SetOrientation()` uses `Transform` to orient the actor.

The `vtkActor` class applies transformations in an order that we feel is natural to most users. Instances of this class have an instance variable `Origin`. This is a point around which the actor rotates. Thus, to translate the actor to a specified position (p_x, p_y, p_z), scale it according to specified scale factors (s_x, s_y, s_z), and rotate around its origin (o_x, o_y, o_z), we use the following sequence of transformations (see Equation **3-6**, Equation **3-9**, and Equation **3-13**).

$$T = T_T(p_x + o_x, p_y + o_y, p_z + o_z) \, T_{R_z} T_{R_x} T_{R_y} T_S T_T(-o_x, -o_y, -o_z) \qquad \textbf{(3-14)}$$

(The term $T_T(x, y, z)$ denotes the translations in the x, y, and z directions.) Recall that we premultiply the transformation matrix times the position vector. This means the transformations are read from right to left. We begin the process with a negative translation from the actor's origin because subsequent rotations occur around this point. This initial translation is countered by a final translation that consists of the origin offset plus the position. The rotations are ordered to what is natural in most cases. We recommend that you spend some time with the software to learn how these transformations work with your own data.

3.11 Chapter Summary

The process of generating an image using a computer is called rendering. Computer graphics is the field of study that encompasses rendering techniques. Computer graphics forms the foundation of data visualization.

Three-dimensional rendering techniques simulate the interaction of objects, or actors, with lights and cameras to generate images. A scene consists of a combination of lights, cameras, and actors. Object-order rendering techniques generate images by rendering actors in a scene in order. Image-order techniques render the image one pixel at a time. Polygon-based graphics hardware is based on object-order techniques. Ray-tracing or ray-casting is an image-order technique.

Lighting models require a specification of color. We saw both the RGB (red-green-blue) and HSV (hue-saturation-value) color models. The HSV model is a more natural model than the RGB model for most users. Lighting models also include effects due to ambient, diffuse, and specular lighting.

There are four important coordinate systems in computer graphics. The model system is the 3D coordinate system where our geometry is defined. The world system is the global Cartesian system. All modeled data is eventually transformed into the world system. The view coordinate system represents what is visible to the camera. It is a 2D system scaled from (-1,1). The display coordinate system uses actual pixel locations on the computer display.

Homogeneous coordinates are a 4D coordinate system in which we can include the effects of perspective transformation. Transformation matrices are 4×4 matrices that operate on homogeneous coordinates. Transformation matrices can represent the combined effects of translation, scaling, and rotation of an actor.

Graphics programming is usually implemented using higher-level graphics libraries or hardware systems. These dedicated systems offer better performance and easier implementation of graphics applications. Common techniques implemented in these systems include dithering and z-buffering. Dithering is a technique to simulate additional colors by mixing combinations of available colors. Z-buffering is a technique to perform hidden-line and hidden-surface removal.

The *Visualization Toolkit* uses a graphics model based on lights, cameras, actors, and renderers. The renderers draw into rendering windows. Actor properties are represented by a property object and their geometry by a mapper object.

3.12 Bibliographic Notes

This chapter provides the reader with enough information to understand the basic issues and terms used in computer graphics. There are a number of good textbooks that cover computer graphics in much more detail and can be used by readers who would like a more thorough understanding. The bible of computer graphics is [FoleyVanDam90]. For those wishing for less intimidating books

[BurgerGillies89] and [Watt93] are useful references. You also may wish to peruse proceedings of the ACM SIGGRAPH conferences. These include papers and references to other papers for some of the most important work in computer graphics. [Carlson85] provides a good introduction for those who wish to learn more about the human vision system.

3.13 References

[Bresenham65]
> J.E. Bresenham."Algorithm for Computer Control of a Digital Plotter." *IBM Systems Journal*, 4(1): 25-30, January 1965.

[BurgerGillies89]
> P. Burger and D. Gillies. *Interactive Compute Graphics Functional, Procedural and Device-Level Methods*. Addison-Wesley, Reading, MA, 1989.

[Carlson85]
> N. R. Carlson. *Physiology of Behaviour (Third Edition)*. Allyn and Bacon Inc., Newton, MA, 1985.

[Dartnall85]
> H. J. A. Dartnall, J. K. Bowmaker, and J. D. Mollon. "Human Visual Pigments: Microspectrophotometric Results from the Eyes of Seven Persons." *Proceedings of the Royal Society,* London, 1983.

[FoleyVanDam90]
> J. D. Foley, A. van Dam, S. K. Feiner, and J. F. Hughes. *Computer Graphics Principles and Practice (Second Edition)*. Addison-Wesley, Reading, MA, 1990.

[Fuchs80]
> H. Fuchs, Z. M. Kedem, and B. F. Naylor. "On Visible Surface Generation By A Priori Tree Structure." *Computer Graphics (SIGGRAPH '80)*, 14(3):124-133, 1980.

[Watt93]
> A. Watt. *3D Computer Graphics (Second Edition)*. Addison-Wesley, Reading, MA, 1993.

[Whitted80]
> T. Whitted."An Improved Illumination Model for Shaded Display." *Communications of the ACM*, 23(6):343-349, 1980.

3.14 Exercises

3.1 Estimate the odds of a ray of light being emitted from the sun, travelling to earth and hitting a one meter square picnic blanket. You can assume that the sun is a point light source that emits light uniformly in all directions. The approximate distance from the sun to the earth is 150,000,000 km.

a) What are the odds when the sun is directly overhead?

b) What are the odds when the sun is inclined 45 degrees relative to the surface normal of the picnic blanket?

c) What assumptions or approximations did you make?

3.2 Proceeding from your result of Exercise 3.1, what are the difficulties in determining the odds of a ray of light travelling from the sun to hit the picnic blanket, and then entering a viewer's eye?

3.3 The color cyan can be represented in both the HSV and RGB color spaces as shown in Figure **3–4**. These two representations for cyan do not yield the same wavelength intensity plots. How do they differ?

3.4 The `vtkSphereSource` class generates a polygonal model of a sphere. Using the examples at the end of this chapter as starting points, create a program to display a white sphere. Set the ambient and diffuse intensities to 0.5. Then add a `for`-loop to this program that adjusts the ambient and diffuse color of this sphere so that as the loop progresses, the diffuse color goes from red to blue, and the ambient color goes from blue to green. You might also try adjusting other lighting parameters such as specular color, ambient, diffuse and specular intensity.

3.5 Using the `vtkSphereSource` as described in Exercise 3.4, create a program to display the sphere with a light source positioned at (1,1,1). Then extend this program by adding a `for`-loop that will adjust the active camera's clipping range so that increasing portions of the interior of the sphere can be seen. By increasing the first value of the clipping range you will be adjusting the position of the front clipping plane. Once the front clipping plane starts intersecting the sphere, you should be able to see inside of it. The default radius of the `vtkSphereSource` is 0.5, so make sure that you adjust the clipping range in increments less than 1.0.

3.6 Modify the program presented in "Render a Cone" on page 64 so that the user can enter in a world coordinate in homogenous coordinates and the program will print out the resulting display coordinate. Refer to the reference page for `vtkRenderer` for some useful methods.
a) Are there any world coordinates that you would expect to be undefined in display coordinates?
b) What happens when the world coordinates are behind the camera?

3.7 Consider rasterizing a ten by ten pixel square. Contrast the approximate difference in the number of arithmetic operations that would need to be done for the cases where it is flat, Gouraud, or Phong shaded.

3.8 When using a z-buffer, we must also interpolate the z-values (or depth) when rasterizing a primitive. Working from Exercise 3.7, what is the additional burden of computing z-buffer values while rasterizing our square?

The Visualization Pipeline

*I*n the previous chapter we created graphical images using simple mathematical models for lighting, viewing, and geometry. Geometry was defined as a static collection of graphics primitives such as points and polygons. To describe the process of visualization we need to extend our understanding of geometry to include more complex forms. We will see that the visualization process transforms data into graphics primitives. This chapter examines the process of data transformation and develops a model of data flow for visualization systems.

4.1 Overview

Visualization transforms data into images that efficiently and accurately represent information about the data. Hence, visualization deals with the issues of *transformation* and *representation*.

Transformation is the process of converting data from its original form into graphics primitives, and eventually into computer images. This is our working definition of the visualization process. An example of such a transformation is the process of extracting stock prices, and creating an *x-y* plot depicting stock price as a function of time.

Representation includes both the internal data structures used to depict the data, and the graphics primitives used to display the data. In the previous example, an array of stock prices and an array of times are the computational representation of the data, while the x-y plot is the graphical representation. Visualization transforms a computational form into a graphical form.

From an object-oriented viewpoint, transformations are processes in the functional model, while representations are the objects in the object model. Therefore we characterize the visualization model with both functional models and object models.

A Data Visualization Example

A simple mathematical function for a quadric will clarify these concepts. The function

$$F(x, y, z)) = a_0 x^2 + a_1 y^2 + a_2 z^2 + a_3 xy + a_4 yz + a_5 xz + a_6 x + a_7 y + a_8 z + a_9 \text{ (4-1)}$$

is the mathematical representation of a quadric. Figure **4–1**(a) shows a visualization of Equation **4-1** in the region $-1 \le x, y, z \le 1$. The visualization process is as follows. We sample the data on a regular grid at a resolution of $50 \times 50 \times 50$. Three different visualization techniques are then used. On the left, we generate 3D surfaces corresponding to constant function value $F(x, y, z) = c$. In the center, we show three different planes that cut through the data and are colored by function value. On the right we show the same three planes that have been contoured with constant valued lines. Around each we place a wireframe outline.

The Functional Model

The functional model in Figure **4–1**(b) illustrates the steps to create the visualization. The oval blocks indicate operations (processes) we performed on the data, and the rectangular blocks represent data stores (objects) that represent and provide access to data. Arrows indicate the direction of data movement. Arrows that point into a block are inputs, data flowing out of a block indicate outputs. The blocks also may have local parameters that serve as additional input. Processes that create data with no input are called data *source* objects, or simply sources. Processes that consume data with no output are called *sinks*. Processes with both an input and an output are called *filters*.

The functional model shows how data flows through the system. It also describes the dependency of the various parts upon one another. For any given process to execute correctly, all the inputs must be up-to-date. This suggests that functional models require a synchronization mechanism to insure correct behavior.

The Visualization Model

In the examples that follow we will frequently use a simplified representation of the functional model to describe visualization processes (Figure **4–1**(c)). We will not explicitly distinguish between sources, sinks, data stores, and process

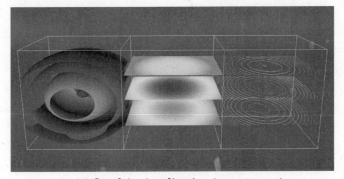

(a) Quadric visualization (`Sample.cc`)

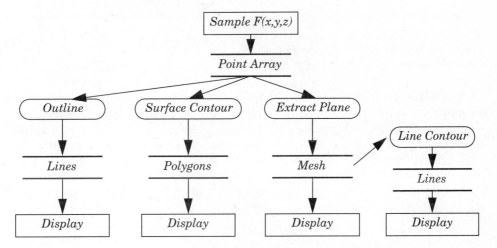

(b) Functional model

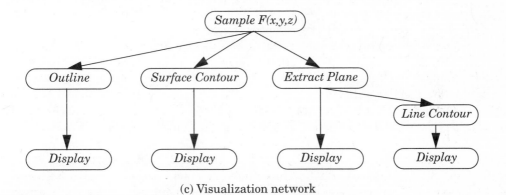

(c) Visualization network

Figure 4–1 Visualizing a quadric function $F(x,y,z) = c$.

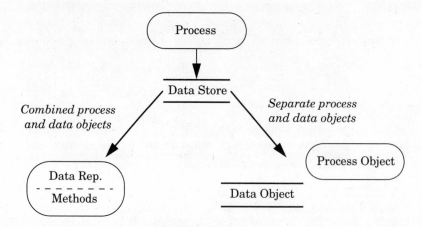

Figure 4–2 Object model design choices. One basic choice is to combine processes and data stores into a single object. This is the usual object-oriented choice. Another choice creates separate data objects and process objects.

objects. Sources and sinks are implied based on the number of inputs or outputs. Sinks will be process objects with no output. Sources will be process objects with no input. Filters will be process objects with at least one input and one output. Intermediate data stores will not be represented. Instead we will assume that they exist as necessary to support the data flow. Thus, as Figure **4–1**(c) shows, the *Lines* data store that the *Outline* object generates (Figure **4–1**(b)) are combined into the single object *Outline*. We use oval shapes to represent objects in the visualization model.

The Object Model

The functional model describes the flow of data in our visualization, the object model describes which modules operate on it. But what *are* the objects in the system? At first glance, we have two choices (Figure **4–2**).

The first choice combines data stores (object attributes) with processes (object methods) into a single object. In the second choice we use separate objects for data stores and processes. There is actually a third alternative: a hybrid combination of these two choices.

The conventional object-oriented approach (our first choice above) combines data stores and processes into a single object. This view follows the standard definition that objects contain a data representation combined with procedures to operate on the data. One advantage of this approach is that the processes, which are the data visualization algorithms, have complete access to the data structures, resulting in good computational performance. But this choice suffers from several drawbacks.

- From a user's perspective, processes are often viewed as independent of data representation. In other words, processes are naturally viewed as objects in the system. For example, we often say we want to "contour" data, meaning creating lines or surfaces corresponding to a constant data value. Hence, to the user it is convenient to have a single contour object to operate on different data representations.

- We must duplicate algorithm implementation. As in the previous contouring example, if we bind data stores and processes into a single object, the contour operation must be re-created for each data type. This results in duplicating code even though the implementations of an algorithm may be functionally and structurally similar. Modifying such algorithms also means modifying many different objects, since they are implemented across many objects.

- Binding data stores and algorithms together results in complex, data dependent code. Some algorithms may be much more complex than the data they operate on, with large numbers of instance variables and elaborate data structures. By combining many such algorithms with a data store, the complexity of the object greatly increases, and the simple meaning of the object becomes lost.

The second choice separates the data stores and processes. That is, one set of objects represents and provides access to the data, while another set of objects implements all operations on the data. Our experience shows that this is natural to users, although it may be considered unconventional to the object-oriented purist. We also have found that the resulting code is simple and modular, and easy for developers to understand, maintain, and extend.

One disadvantage to the second choice is that the interface between data representation and process is more formal. Thus the interface must be carefully designed to insure good performance and flexibility. Another disadvantage is that strong separation of data and process results in duplicate code. That is, we may implement operations that duplicate algorithms that cannot be considered strictly data access methods. One example of such a situation is computing data derivatives. This operation is more than simple data access, so strictly speaking it doesn't belong in the data object methods. So to compute derivatives we would have to duplicate the code each time we needed derivatives computed. (Or create a procedural library of functions or macros!)

As a result of these concerns we use the hybrid approach in the *Visualization Toolkit*. Our approach is closest to the second choice described above, but we have selected a small set of critical operations that we implement within the data objects. These operations have been identified based on our experience implementing visualization algorithms. This effectively combines the first two choices to receive the maximum benefit and fewest disadvantages of each.

4.2 The Visualization Pipeline

In the context of data visualization, the functional model of Figure **4–1**(c) is referred to it as the *visualization pipeline* or *visualization network*. The pipeline consists of objects to represent data (data objects), objects to operate on data (process objects), and an indicated direction of data flow (arrow connections between objects). In the text that follows, we will frequently use visualization networks to describe the implementation of a particular visualization technique.

Data Objects

Data objects represent information. Data objects also provide methods to create, access, and delete this information. Direct modification of the data represented by the data objects is not allowed except through formal object methods. This capability is reserved for process objects. Additional methods are also available to obtain characteristic features of the data. This includes determining the minimum and maximum data values, or determining the size or the number of data values in the object.

Data objects differ depending upon their internal representation. The internal representation has significant impact on the access methods to the data, as well as on the storage efficiency or computational performance of process objects that interact with the data object. Hence, different data objects may be used to represent the same data depending on demands for efficiency and process generality.

Process Objects

Process objects operate on input data to generate output data. A process object either derives new data from its inputs, or transforms the input data into a new form. For example, a process object might derive pressure gradient data from a pressure field or transform the pressure field into constant value pressure contours. The input to a process object includes both one or more data objects as well as local parameters to control its operation. Local parameters include both instance variables or associations, and references to other objects. For example, the center and radius are local parameters to control the generation of sphere primitives.

Process objects are further characterized as *source objects*, *filter objects*, or *mapper objects*. This categorization is based on whether the objects initiate, maintain, or terminate visualization data flow.

Source objects interface to external data sources, or generate data from local parameters. Source objects that generate data from local parameters are called *procedural* objects. The previous example of Figure **4–1** uses a procedural object to generate function values for the quadric function of Equation **4-1**. Source objects that interface to external data are called *reader* objects since the external file must be read and converted to an internal form. Source objects may also interface to external data communication ports and devices. Possible examples include simulation or modelling programs, or data acquisition systems to measure temperature, pressure, or other similar physical attributes.

Filter objects require one or more input data objects and generate one or more output data objects. Local parameters control the operation of the process object. Computing weekly stock market averages, representing a data value as a scaled icon, or performing union set operations on two input data sources are typical example processes of filter objects.

Mapper objects correspond to the sinks in the functional model. Mapper objects require one or more input data objects and terminate the visualization pipeline data flow. Usually mapper objects are used to convert data into graphical primitives, but they may write out data to a file or interface with another software system or devices. Mapper objects that write data to a computer file are termed *writer* objects.

4.3 Pipeline Topology

In this section we describe how to connect data and process objects to form visualization networks.

Pipeline Connections

The elements of the pipeline (sources, filters, and mappers) can be connected in a variety of ways to create visualization networks. However, there are two important issues that arise when we try to assemble these networks: *type* and *multiplicity*.

Type means the form or type of data that process objects take as input or generate as output. For example, a sphere source object may generate as output a polygonal or faceted representation, an implicit representation (e.g., parameters of a conic equation), or a set of occupancy values in a discretized representation of 3D space. Mapper objects might take as input polygonal, triangle strip, line, or point geometric representations. The input to a process object must be specified correctly for successful operation.

There are two general approaches to maintain proper input type. One approach is to design with type-less or single-type systems. That is, create a single type of data object and create filters that operate only on this one type (Figure **4–3**(a)). For example, we could design a general *DataSet* that represents any form of data that we're interested in, and the process objects would only input *DataSets* and generate *DataSets*. This approach is simple and elegant, but inflexible. Often, particularly useful algorithms (i.e., process objects) will operate only on specific types of data, and to generalize them results in large inefficiencies in representation or data access. A typical example is a data object that represents structured data such as pixmaps or 3D volumes. Because the data is structured it can easily be accessed as planes or lines. However a general representation will not include this capability because in the general case data is not structured.

Another approach to maintain proper input type is to design typed systems (Figure **4–3**(b)). In typed systems only objects of compatible type are allowed to be connected together. That is, more than one type is designed, but type checking is performed on the input to insure proper connection. Depending on the particu-

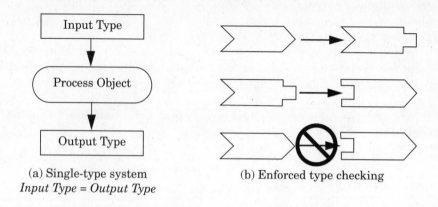

(a) Single-type system
Input Type = Output Type

(b) Enforced type checking

Figure 4–3 Maintaining compatible data type. a) Single-type systems require no type checking. b) In multiple-type systems only compatible types can be connected together.

lar computer language, type checking can be performed at compile, link, or run-time. Although type checking does insure correct input type, this approach often suffers from an explosion of types. If not careful, the designers of a visualization system may create too many types, resulting in a fragmented, hard to use and understand system. In addition, the system may require a large number of *type-converter* filters. (Type-converter filters serve only to transform data from one form to another.) Carried to extremes, excessive type conversion results in computationally and memory wasteful systems.

The issue of multiplicity deals with the number of input data objects allowed, and the number of output data objects created during the operation of a process object (Figure **4–4**). We know that all filter and mapper objects require at minimum one input data object, but in general these filters can operate sequentially across a list of input. Some filters may naturally require a specific number of inputs. A filter implementing boolean operations is one example. Boolean operations such as union or intersection are implemented on data values two at a time. However, even here more than two inputs may be defined as a recursive application of the operation to each input.

We need to distinguish what is meant by multiplicity of output. Most sources and filters generate a single output. *Multiple fan-out* occurs when an object generates an output that is used for input by more than one object. This would occur, for example, when a source object is used to read a data file, and the resulting data is used to generate a wireframe outline of the data, plus contours of the data (e.g., Figure **4–1**(a)). *Multiple output* occurs when an object generates two or more output data objects. An example of multiple output is generating x, y, and z components of a gradient function as distinct data objects. Combinations of multiple fan-out and multiple output are possible.

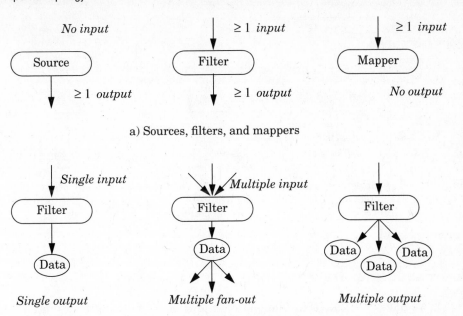

a) Sources, filters, and mappers

b) Multiplicity of input and output

Figure 4–4 Multiplicity of input and output. a) Definition of source, filter, and mapper objects. b) Various types of input and output.

Loops

In the examples described so far, the visualization networks have been free of cycles. In graph theory these are termed directed, acyclic graphs. However, in some cases it is desirable to introduce feedback loops into our visualization networks. Feedback loops in a visualization network allow us to direct the output of a process object upstream to affect its input.

Figure **4–5** shows an example of a feedback loop in a visualization network. We seed a velocity field with an initial set of random points. A probe filter is used to determine the velocity (and possibly other data) at each point. Each point is then repositioned in the direction of its associated vector value, possibly using a scale factor to control the magnitude of motion. The process continues until the points exit the data set or until a maximum iteration count is exceeded.

We will discuss the control and execution of visualization networks in the next section. However, loops pose no special problem in visualization networks. We need only make sure that the combined operation of the filters in the loop does not enter an infinite loop or non-terminating recursive state. Typically, we limit the number of executions of the loop in order to view intermediate results. However, it is possible to execute the loop repeatedly to process data as required.

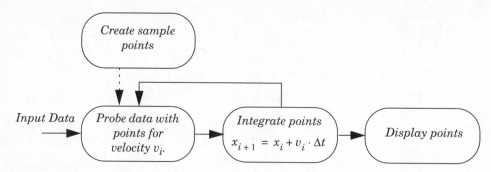

Figure 4–5 Looping in a visualization network. This example implements linear integration. The sample points are created to initialize the looping process. The output of the integration filter is used in place of the sample points once the process begins.

4.4 Executing the Pipeline

So far we have seen the basic elements of the visualization network, and ways to connect these elements together. In this section we discuss how to control the execution of the network.

To be useful, a visualization network must process data to generate a desired result. The complete process of causing each process object to operate is called the *execution* of the network.

Most often the visualization network is executed more than once. For example, we may change the parameters of, or the input to a process object. This is typically due to user interaction: the user may be exploring or methodically varying input to observe results. After one or more changes to the process object or its input, we must execute the network to generate up-to-date results.

For highest performance, the process objects in the visualization network must execute *only* if a change occurs to their input. In some networks, as shown in Figure **4–6**, we may have parallel branches that need not execute if objects are modified local to a particular branch. In this figure, we see that object D and the downstream objects E and F must execute because D's input parameter is changed, and objects E and F depend on D for their input. The other objects need not execute because there is no change to their input.

We can control the execution of the network using either a *demand-driven* or *event-driven* approach. In the demand-driven approach, we execute the network only when output is requested, and only that portion of the network affecting the result. In the event-driven approach, every change to a process object or its input causes the network to re-execute. The advantage of the event-driven approach is that the output is always up-to-date (except during short periods of computation). The advantage of the demand driven approach is that large numbers of changes can be accumulated without intermediate computation. The demand-driven approach minimizes computation and results in a more interactive visualization networks.

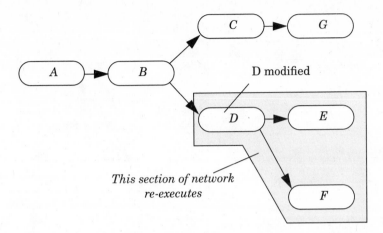

Figure 4–6 Network execution. Parallel branches need not execute if changes are local to a particular branch.

The execution of the network requires synchronization between process objects. We want to execute a process object only when all of its input objects are up-to-date. There are generally two ways to synchronize network execution: explicit or implicit control (Figure **4–7**).

Explicit Execution

Explicit control means directly tracking the changes to the network, and then directly controlling the execution of the process objects based on an explicit dependency analysis. The major characteristic of this approach is that a central-ized *executive* is used to coordinate network execution. This executive must track changes to the parameters and inputs of each object, including subsequent changes to the network topology (Figure **4–7**(a)).

The advantage of this approach is that synchronization analysis and update methods are local to the single executive object. In addition, we can cre-ate dependency graphs and perform analysis of data flow each time output is requested. This capability is particularly important if we wish to decompose the network for parallel computing, or to distribute execution across a network of computers.

The disadvantage of the explicit approach is that each process object becomes dependent upon the executive, since the executive must be notified of any change. Also, the executive cannot easily control execution if the network execution is conditional, since whether to execute or not depends on the local results of one or more process objects.

The explicit approach may be either demand-driven or event-driven. In the event-driven approach, the executive is notified whenever a change to an object occurs (typically in response to a user-interface event), and the network is imme-

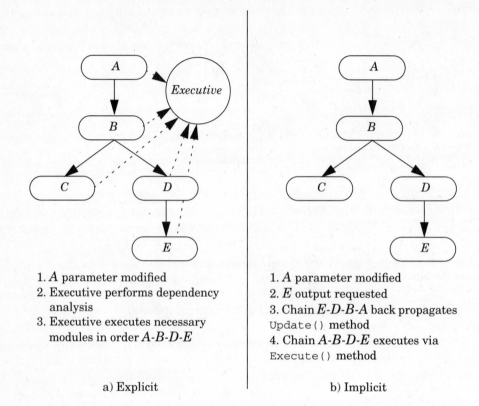

1. *A* parameter modified
2. Executive performs dependency
   analysis
3. Executive executes necessary
   modules in order *A-B-D-E*

1. *A* parameter modified
2. *E* output requested
3. Chain *E-D-B-A* back propagates
   `Update()` method
4. Chain *A-B-D-E* executes via
   `Execute()` method

a) Explicit

b) Implicit

Figure 4–7 Explicit and implicit network execution.

diately executed. In the demand-driven approach, the executive accumulates changes to object inputs and executes the network based on explicit user demand.

The explicit approach with a central executive is typical of many commercial visualization systems such as AVS, Irix Explorer, and IBM Data Explorer. Typically these systems use a visual-programming interface to construct the visualization network. Often these systems are implemented on parallel computers, and the ability to distribute computation is essential.

Implicit Execution

Implicit control means that a process object executes only if its local input or parameters change (Figure **4–7**(b)). Implicit control is implemented using a two pass process. First, when output is requested from a particular object, that object requests input from its input objects. This process is recursively repeated until source objects are encountered. The source objects then execute if they have changed or their external inputs have changed. Then the recursion unwinds as

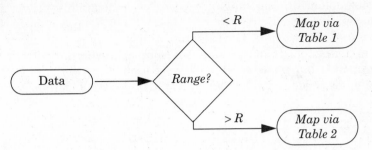

Figure 4–8 Examples of conditional execution. Depending upon range, data is mapped through different color lookup tables.

each process object examines its inputs and determines whether to execute. This procedure repeats until the initial requesting object executes and terminates the process. These two steps are called the *update* and *execution* passes.

Implicit network execution is naturally implemented using *demand-driven* control. Here network execution occurs only when output data is requested. Implicit network execution may also be event-driven if we simply request output each time an appropriate event is encountered (such as change to object parameter).

The primary advantage of the implicit control scheme is its simplicity. Each object only need keep track of its internal modification time. When output is requested, the object compares its modification time with that of its inputs, and executes if out of date. Furthermore, process objects need only know about their direct input, so no global knowledge of other objects (such as a network executive) is required.

The disadvantage of implicit control is that it is harder to distribute network execution across computers, or to implement sophisticated execution strategies. One simple approach is to create a queue that executes process objects in order of network execution (possibly in a distributed fashion). Of course, once a central object is introduced back into the system, the lines between implicit and explicit control are blurred.

Conditional Execution

Another important capability of visualization networks is conditional execution. For example, we may wish to map data through different color lookup tables depending upon the variation of range in the data. Small variations can be amplified by assigning more colors within the data range, while we may compress our color display by assigning a small number of colors to the data range (Figure **4–8**).

The conditional execution of visualization models (such as that shown Figure **4–1**(c)) can be realized in principle. However, in practice we must supplement the visualization network with a conditional language to express the rules for network execution. Hence, conditional execution of visualization networks is

a function of implementation language. Many visualization systems are pro-
grammed using the visual programming style. This approach is basically a
visual editor to construct data flow diagrams directly. It is difficult to express
conditional execution of networks using this approach. Alternatively, in a procedural programming language, conditional execution of networks is straightforward. We defer discussion of this topic until "Putting It All Together" on page 91.

4.5 Memory and Computation Trade-off

Visualization is a demanding application, both in terms of computer memory and
computational requirement. Data streams on the order of 1 to 100 megabytes are
not uncommon. Many visualization algorithms are computationally expensive,
in part due to input size, but also due to the inherent algorithm complexity. In
order to create applications that have reasonable performance, most visualization systems have various mechanisms to trade off memory and computation
costs.

Static and Dynamic Memory Models

Memory and computation trade-offs are important performance issues when executing visualization networks. In the networks presented thus far, the output of
a process object is assumed to be available to downstream process objects at all
times. Thus, network computation is minimized. However, the computer memory
requirement to preserve object output can be huge. Networks of only a few
objects can tie up extensive computer memory resources.

An alternative approach is to save intermediate results only as long as they
are needed by other objects. Once these objects finish processing, the intermediate result can be discarded. This approach results in extra computation each
time output is requested. The memory resources required are greatly reduced at
the expense of increased computation. Like all trade-offs, the proper solution
depends upon the particular application and the nature of the computer system
executing the visualization network.

We term these two approaches as *static* and *dynamic* memory models. In
the static model intermediate data is saved to reduce overall computation. In the
dynamic model intermediate data is discarded when it is no longer needed. The
static model serves best when small, variable portions of the network re-execute,
and when the data sizes are manageable by the computer system. The dynamic
model serves best when the data flows are large, or the same part of the network
executes each time. Often, it is desirable to combine both the static and dynamic
models into the same network. If an entire leg of the network must execute each
time, it makes no sense to store intermediate results, since they are never used.
On the other hand, we may wish to save an intermediate result at a branch point
in the network, since the data will be more likely to be reused. A comparison of
the static and dynamic memory model for a specific network is shown in
Figure **4–9**.

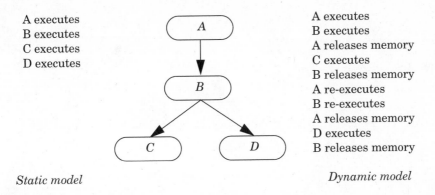

A executes
B executes
C executes
D executes

Static model

A executes
B executes
A releases memory
C executes
B releases memory
A re-executes
B re-executes
A releases memory
D executes
B releases memory

Dynamic model

Figure 4–9 Comparison of static versus dynamic memory models for typical network. Execution begins when output is requested from objects *C* and *D*. In more complex dynamic models, we can prevent *B* from executing twice by performing a more thorough dependency analysis.

As this figure shows, the static model executes each process object only once, storing intermediate results. In the dynamic model, each process object releases memory after downstream objects complete execution. Depending upon the implementation of the dynamic model, process object B may execute once or twice. If a thorough dependency analysis is performed, process B will release memory only after both objects C and D execute. In a simpler implementation, object B will release memory after C and then D executes.

Reference Counting

Another valuable tool to minimize memory cost is to share storage using reference counting. To use reference counting, we allow more than one process object to refer to the same data object. For example, assume that we have three objects *A, B, C* that form a portion of a visualization network as shown in Figure **4–10**. Also assume that these objects modify only part of their input data, leaving the data object that specifies *x-y-z* coordinate position unchanged. Then to conserve memory resources we can allow the output of each process object to refer to the single data object representing these points. Data that is changed remains local to each filter and is not shared.

4.6 Programming Models

Visualization systems are by their very nature designed for human interaction. As a result they must be easy to use. On the other hand, visualization systems must readily adapt to new data, and must be flexible enough to allow rapid exploration. To meet these demands, a variety of programming models have been developed.

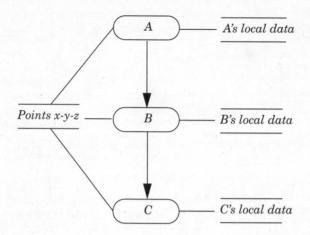

Figure 4–10 Reference counting to conserve memory resource. Each filter A, B, and C shares a common point representation. Other data is local to each object.

At the highest level are applications. Visualization applications have finely tailored user interfaces that are specific to an application area, e.g., stock market or fluid flow visualization. Applications are the easiest to use, but are the least flexible. It is very difficult or impossible for the user to extend applications into a new domain because of inherent logistical issues. Commercial turn-key visualization software is generally considered to be application software.

At the opposite end of the spectrum are programming libraries. A conventional programming library is a collection of procedures that operate on a library-specific data structure. Often these libraries are written in conventional programming languages such as C or FORTRAN. These offer great flexibility and can be easily combined with other programming tools and techniques. Programming libraries can be extended or modified by the addition of user-written code. Unfortunately, the effective use of programming libraries requires skilled programmers. Furthermore, non-graphics/visualization experts cannot easily use programming libraries because there is no notion of how to fit (or order) the procedures together correctly. These libraries also require extensive synchronization schemes to control execution as input parameters are varied.

Most commercial systems lie between these two extremes. These typically use a visual programming approach to construct visualization networks. The basic idea is to provide graphical tools and libraries of modules, or process objects. Modules may be connected subject to input/output type constraints, using simple graphical layout tools. In addition, user interface tools allow association of interface widgets with object input parameters. System execution is generally transparent to the user by way of an internal execution executive.

Another recently introduced technique for visual programming is the spreadsheet technique of Levoy [Levoy94]. In the spreadsheet model, we arrange operations on a regular grid similar to the common electronic accounting spreadsheets. The grid consists of rows and columns of cells, where each cell is expressed as a computational combination of other cells. The combination is expressed for each cell by using a simple programming language to add, subtract, or perform other more complex operations. The result of the computation (i.e., a visual output) is displayed in the cell.

Although visual programming systems are widely successful, they suffer two drawbacks. First, they are not as tailored as an application, and require extensive programming, albeit visual, to be so. Second, visual programming is too limited for detailed control, so constructing complex low-level algorithms and user interfaces is not feasible. What is required is a visualization system that provides the "modularity" and automatic execution control of a visual system, and the low-level programming capability of a programming library. Object oriented systems have the potential to provide these capabilities. Carefully crafted object libraries provide the ease of use of visual systems with the control of programming libraries. That is a major goal of the *Visualization Toolkit (**vtk**)* described in this text.

4.7 Putting It All Together

In the previous sections we have treated a variety of topics relating to the visualization model. In this section we describe the particular implementation details that we have adopted in the *Visualization Toolkit*.

Procedural Language Implementation

The *Visualization Toolkit* is implemented in the procedural language C++. A class library containing data and process objects facilitates visualization application building. Supporting abstract objects are available to derive new objects. The visualization pipeline is designed to connect directly to the graphics sub-system described in the previous chapter.

A visual programming interface could be implemented using the class library provided. However, for real-world applications the procedural language implementation provides several advantages. This includes straightforward implementation of conditional network execution and looping, and simple interfacing to other systems such as graphical user interfaces.

Strongly Typed

With the choice of C++ as the implementation language, strong type checking is mandatory. Most type checking is performed at compile time by the C++ compiler. There is one case where the type checking occurs at run-time. This occurs when there is one or more special requirements on input data type.

In this case we find that there are certain filters that operate on a special part of their input data. An example of such a case is the tube filter `vtkTube-Filter`. This filter creates a tube around any lines found in its input data. Lines are represented using the type vtkPolyData, which represents the graphics primitives we saw in the previous chapter (i.e., points, lines, polygons, and triangle strips). Sometimes the input data will not contain lines. At run-time vtk-TubeFilter will detect this and issue an error. So even though the compiler is satisfied, there are additional run-time checks that are not.

We would like to mention that one solution to this case is to create more data types. Instead of creating a single type that consists of points, lines, polygons, and triangle strips, we could create four different types of points, lines, polygons, and triangle strips. This certainly is a viable solution, but in our opinion the result is that too many data types are introduced into the system. The result is that the system is harder to understand and use, and is less efficient.

Implicit Control of Execution

We have implemented implicit control of visualization network execution. Execution of the network occurs when output is requested from an object (i.e., demand-driven). This approach is simple to implement, is nearly transparent to the user of the system, and accommodates conditional execution and looping. On parallel computers or other special hardware, implicit control can be used in conjunction with an explicit load balancing scheme by breaking the network into smaller sub-networks.

Our implementation is based on two key methods: Update() and Execute(). If you understand these methods, then you understand the basis for the implicit execution techniques found in **vtk**.

The Update() method is generally initiated when the user requests the system to render a scene. As part of the process the actors send a Render() method to their mappers. At this point network execution begins. The mapper invokes the Update() method on its input(s). These in turn recursively invoke the Update() method on their input(s). This process continues until a source object is encountered. At this point the source object compares its modified time to the last time it executed. If it has been modified more recently than executed, it re-executes via the Execute() method. The recursion then unwinds with each filter comparing its input time to its execution time. Execute() is called where appropriate. The process terminates when control is returned to the mapper.

This process is extremely simple, but depends upon keeping track of modified time and execution time properly. If you create a filter or source and fail to keep track of modification time correctly, you will encounter cases where your pipeline does not execute properly.

Multiple Input / Output

The *Visualization Toolkit* pipeline architecture has been designed to support multiple inputs and multiple outputs. In practice, you will find that most filters and sources actually generate a single output and filters accept a single input. This is because most algorithms (which sources and filters represent) tend to be

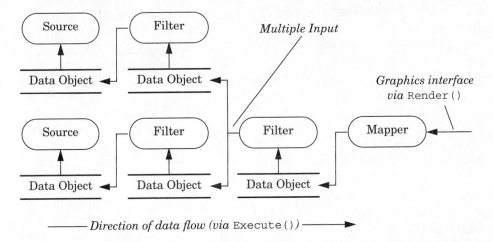

Figure 4–11 Description of implicit execution process implemented in **vtk**. The `Update()` method is initiated via the `Render()` method from the actor. Data flows back to mapper via `Execute()` method. Arrows connecting objects indicate direction of `Update()` process.

single input/output in nature. There are exceptions and we will describe some of these shortly.

The visualization pipeline architecture is depicted in Figure **4–11**. This figure shows how filters and data objects are connected together to form a visualization network. For the case shown here (i.e., objects with single input/output) the input data is represented by the `Input` instance variable and is set using the `SetInput()` method. The output data is represented by the `Output` instance variable and is accessed using the `GetOutput()` method. To connect filters together we generally use the C++ statement

```
filter2->SetInput(filter1->GetOutput());
```

where `filter1` and `filter2` are filter objects of compatible type. (The C++ compiler will enforce proper type).

The trick to this architecture is that data objects know which filters "own" them. That is, if a filter creates an output data object, the data object knows which filter created it. This allows us to delegate certain messages from a filter through the data object to the connected filter. For example, if `filter2` receives an `Update()` method, it forwards it to its input data object, which in turn forwards it to its owning filter (if any). In this case `filter1` is the owning filter of the data object. This process continues until a source object is reached, where the propagation of the `Update()` method terminates.

You probably already have seen how this approach can be extended to multiple inputs and multiple outputs. The difference is that when a filter receives a message to be forwarded (e.g., Update()), it sends them to all its inputs. Also, when a filter executes, it must update all its outputs. Let's look at some concrete examples.

vtkGlyph3D is an example of a filter that accepts multiple inputs and generates a single output. The inputs to vtkGlyph3D are represented by the Input and Source instance variables. The purpose of vtkGlyph3D is to copy the geometry defined by the data in Source to each point defined by Input. The geometry is modified according to the Source data values (e.g., scalars and vectors). (For more information about glyphs see "Glyphs" on page 173.) If you study the source code for this object carefully, you will see that the object implements its own Update() method (overloading its superclass method). To use the vtkGlyph3D object in C++ code you would do something like

```
glyph = new vtkGlyph3D;
   glyph->SetInput(foo->GetOutput());
   glyph->SetSource(bar->GetOutput());
   ...
```

where foo and bar are filters returning the appropriate type of output.

The class vtkExtractVectorComponents is an example of a filter with a single input and multiple outputs. This filter extracts the three components of a 3D vector into separate scalar components. Its three outputs are named VxComponent, VyComponent, and VzComponent. To use the filter you would use code similar to

```
vz = new vtkExtractVectorComponents;
foo = new vtkDataSetMapper;
   foo->SetInput(vz->GetVzComponent());
   ...
```

Several other special objects having multiple inputs or outputs are also available. Some of the more notable classes are vtkMergeFilter, vtkAppend-Filter, vtkAppendPolyData. These filters combine multiple pipeline streams and generate a single output. The class vtkProbeFilter takes two inputs. The first input is the data we wish to probe. The second input supplies a set of points that are used as probe points. Some process objects take a list of input data. The vtkBooleanStructuredPoints object performs set operations on volume datasets. The first data item in the list is used to initialize the set operation. Each subsequent item in the list is combined with the result of previous operations using a boolean operation specified by the user.

For more details regarding the object design of filters and data objects, please see Chapters 5 and 6.

Support of Looping and Conditional Execution

Our implementation supports network looping and conditional execution. Each loop executes only once each time the network is updated. Multiple loop executions can be effected by updating the network multiple times.

Conditional execution is implemented by using the conditional constructs of the C++ language in conjunction with a local update method available to each process object.

Flexible Computation / Memory Trade-off

By default, networks constructed using the *Visualization Toolkit* store intermediate computational results (i.e., favor computation). However, a single class variable can be set to discard intermediate data when they are no longer needed (i.e., favor memory). In addition, a local parameter can be set within each process object to control this trade-off at object level.

The global variable is set as follows. Given the process or data object O, invoke `O->SetGlobalReleaseDataFlagOn()` to enable data release. To enable data release for a particular object use `O->SetReleaseDataFlagOn()`. Appropriate methods exist to disable memory release as well.

High-Level Object Design

At this point in the text it is premature to describe design details. However, there are two important classes that affect many of the objects in the text. These are the classes `vtkObject` and `vtkRefCount`.

`vtkObject` is the base object for many inheritance hierarchies. It provides methods and instance variables to control run-time debugging and printing, and maintains internal object modification time. In particular, the method `Modified()` is used to update the modification time, and the method `GetMTime()` is used to retrieve it.

`vtkRefCount` implements data object reference counting (See "Reference Counting" on page 89.) Subclasses of `vtkRefCount` may be shared by other objects, without duplicating memory.

Note that we do not always include `vtkObject` and `vtkRefCount` in object diagrams to conserve space. Refer to the source code for a definitive statement.

Examples

We will now demonstrate some of the features of the visualization pipeline with four examples. Some of the objects used here will be unfamiliar to you. Please overlook missing details until we cover the information later in the book. The goal here is to provide a flavor and familiarity with the software architecture and its use.

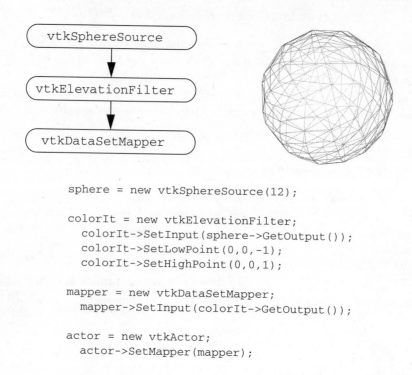

```
sphere = new vtkSphereSource(12);

colorIt = new vtkElevationFilter;
  colorIt->SetInput(sphere->GetOutput());
  colorIt->SetLowPoint(0,0,-1);
  colorIt->SetHighPoint(0,0,1);

mapper = new vtkDataSetMapper;
  mapper->SetInput(colorIt->GetOutput());

actor = new vtkActor;
  actor->SetMapper(mapper);
```

Figure 4–12 A simple sphere example (`ColorSph.cc`).

Simple Sphere

The first example demonstrates a simple visualization pipeline. A polygonal representation of a sphere is created with the source object (`vtkSphereSource`). The sphere is passed through a filter (`vtkElevationFilter`) that computes the height of each point of the sphere above a plane. The plane is perpendicular to the z-axis, and passes through the point (0,0,-1). The data is finally mapped (`vtkDataSetMapper`) through a lookup table. The mapping process converts height value into colors, and interfaces the sphere geometry to the rendering library. The mapper is assigned to an actor, and then the actor is displayed. The visualization network, a portion of code, and output image are shown in Figure **4–12**.

The execution of the pipeline occurs implicitly when we render the actor. Each actor asks its mapper to update itself. The mapper in turn asks its input to update itself. This process continues until a source object is encountered. Then the source will execute if modified since the last render. Then the system walks through the network and executes each object if its input or instance variables are out of date. When completed, the actor's mapper is up-to-date and an image is generated.

Now let's re-examine the same process of pipeline execution by following method invocation. The process begins when the actor receives a `Render()` message from a renderer. The actor in turn sends a `Render()` message to its mapper. The mapper begins network execution by asking its input to update itself via the `Update()` operation. This causes a cascade of `Update()` methods as each filter in turn asks its input to update itself. If branching in the pipeline is present, the update method will branch as well. Finally, the cascade terminates when a source object is encountered. If the source object is out of date, it will send itself an `Execute()` command. Each filter will send itself an `Execute()` as necessary to bring itself up-to-date. Finally, the mapper will perform operations to transform its input data into rendering primitives.

In the *Visualization Toolkit*, the `Update()` method is public while the `Execute()` method is protected. Thus, you can manually cause network execution to occur by invoking the `Update()` operation. This can be useful when you want to set instance variables in the network based on the results of upstream execution. The `Execute()` method is protected because it requires a certain object state to exist. The `Update()` method insures that this state exists.

One final note. The indentation of the code serves to indicate where objects are instantiated and modified. The first line (i.e., the `new` operator) is where the object is created. The indented lines that follow indicate that various operations are being performed on the object. We encourage you to use a similar indenting scheme in your own work.

Warped Sphere

This example extends the pipeline of the previous example, and shows the effects of type checking on the connectivity of process objects. We add a transform filter (`vtkTransformFilter`) to non-uniformly scale the sphere in the *x-y-z* directions.

The transform filter only operates on objects with explicit point coordinate representation (i.e., a subclass of `vtkPointSet`). However, the elevation filter generates the more general form `vtkDataSet` as output. Hence we cannot connect the transform filter to the elevation filter. But we can connect the transform filter to the sphere source, and then the elevation filter to the transform filter. The result is shown in Figure **4–13**.

The C++ compiler enforces the proper connections of sources, filters, and mappers. To decide which objects are compatible, we check the type specification of the `SetInput()` method. If the input object returns an output object of that type, or a subclass of that type, the two objects are compatible and may be connected.

Generating Oriented Glyphs

This example demonstrates the use of an object with multiple inputs. `vtkGlyph3D` places 3D icons or glyphs (i.e., any polygonal geometry) at every input point. The icon geometry is specified with the instance variable `Source`, and the input points are obtained from the `Input` instance variable. Each glyph

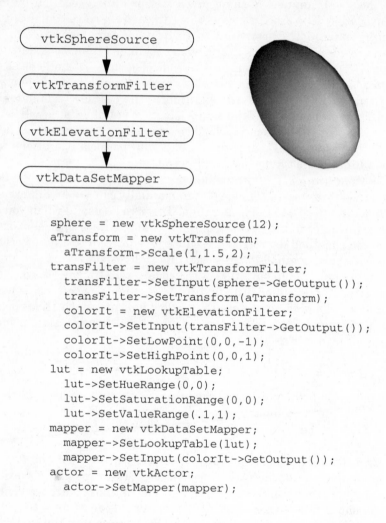

```
sphere = new vtkSphereSource(12);
aTransform = new vtkTransform;
  aTransform->Scale(1,1.5,2);
transFilter = new vtkTransformFilter;
  transFilter->SetInput(sphere->GetOutput());
  transFilter->SetTransform(aTransform);
  colorIt = new vtkElevationFilter;
  colorIt->SetInput(transFilter->GetOutput());
  colorIt->SetLowPoint(0,0,-1);
  colorIt->SetHighPoint(0,0,1);
lut = new vtkLookupTable;
  lut->SetHueRange(0,0);
  lut->SetSaturationRange(0,0);
  lut->SetValueRange(.1,1);
mapper = new vtkDataSetMapper;
  mapper->SetLookupTable(lut);
  mapper->SetInput(colorIt->GetOutput());
actor = new vtkActor;
  actor->SetMapper(mapper);
```

Figure 4–13 The addition of a transform filter to the previous example (StrSph.cc).

may be oriented and scaled in a variety of ways, depending upon the input and instance variables. In our example we place cones oriented in the direction of the point normals (Figure **4–13**).

The visualization network branches at vtkGlyph3D. If either branch is modified, then this filter will re-execute. Network updates must branch in both directions, and both branches must be up-to-date when vtkGlyph3D executes. These requirements are enforced by the Update() method, and pose no problem to the implicit execution method.

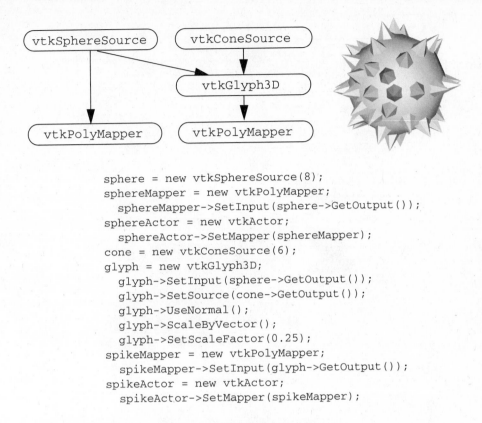

```
sphere = new vtkSphereSource(8);
sphereMapper = new vtkPolyMapper;
   sphereMapper->SetInput(sphere->GetOutput());
sphereActor = new vtkActor;
   sphereActor->SetMapper(sphereMapper);
cone = new vtkConeSource(6);
glyph = new vtkGlyph3D;
   glyph->SetInput(sphere->GetOutput());
   glyph->SetSource(cone->GetOutput());
   glyph->UseNormal();
   glyph->ScaleByVector();
   glyph->SetScaleFactor(0.25);
spikeMapper = new vtkPolyMapper;
   spikeMapper->SetInput(glyph->GetOutput());
spikeActor = new vtkActor;
   spikeActor->SetMapper(spikeMapper);
```

Figure 4–14 An example of multiple inputs and outputs (Mace.cc).

Disappearing Sphere

In our last example we construct a visualization network with a feedback loop, and show how we can use procedural programming to change the topology of the network. The network consists of four objects: vtkSphereSource to create an initial polygonal geometry, vtkShrinkFilter to shrink the polygons and create a gap or space between neighbors, vtkElevationFilter to color the geometry according to height above the *x-y* plane, and vtkDataSetMapper to map the data through a lookup table and interface to the rendering library. The network topology, a portion of the C++ code, and output are shown in Figure **4–13**.

After vtkSphereSource generates an initial geometry (in response to a render request), the input of vtkShrinkFilter is changed to the output of the vtkElevationFilter. Because of the feedback loop, vtkShrinkFilter will always re-execute. Thus, the behavior of the network is to re-execute each time a render is performed. Because the shrink filter is reapplied to the same data, the polygons become smaller and smaller and eventually disappear.

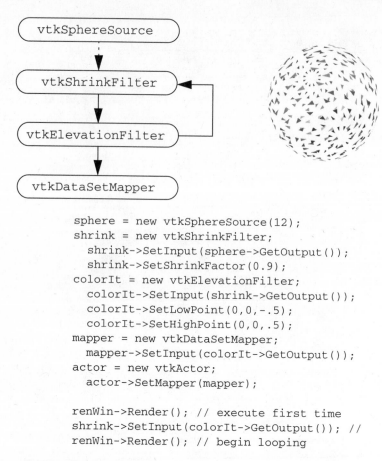

```
sphere = new vtkSphereSource(12);
shrink = new vtkShrinkFilter;
  shrink->SetInput(sphere->GetOutput());
  shrink->SetShrinkFactor(0.9);
colorIt = new vtkElevationFilter;
  colorIt->SetInput(shrink->GetOutput());
  colorIt->SetLowPoint(0,0,-.5);
  colorIt->SetHighPoint(0,0,.5);
mapper = new vtkDataSetMapper;
  mapper->SetInput(colorIt->GetOutput());
actor = new vtkActor;
  actor->SetMapper(mapper);


renWin->Render(); // execute first time
shrink->SetInput(colorIt->GetOutput()); //
renWin->Render(); // begin looping
```

Figure 4–15 A network with a loop (LoopShrk.cc).

4.8 Chapter Summary

The visualization process is naturally modelled using a combination of functional and object models. The functional model can be simplified and used to describe visualization networks. The object model specifies the components of the visualization network.

Visualization networks consist of process objects and data objects. Data objects represent information, process objects transform the data from one form to another. There are three types of process objects. Sources have no input and at least one output. Filters have at least one input and output. Sinks, or mappers, terminate the visualization network.

The execution of the network can be controlled implicitly or explicitly. Implicit control means that each object must insure its input is up-to-date, thereby distributing the control mechanism. Explicit control means that there is a centralized executive to coordinate the execution of each object.

Many techniques are available to program visualization networks. Direct visual programming is most common in commercial systems. At a higher level, applications provide tailored but more rigid interfaces to visualize information. At the lowest level, subroutine or object libraries provide the greatest flexibility. The *Visualization Toolkit* contains an object library implemented in C++ for constructing visualization networks.

4.9 Bibliographic Notes

The practical way to learn about the visualization process is to study commercially available systems. These systems can be categorized as either direct visual programming environments or as applications. Common visual programming systems include AVS [AVS89], Iris Explorer [IrisExplorer], IBM Data Explorer [DataExplorer], aPE [aPE90], and Khoros [Rasure91]. Application systems generally provide less flexibility than visual programming systems, but are better tailored to particular problem domains. PLOT3D [PLOT3D] is an early example of a tool for CFD visualization. This has since been superseded by FAST [FAST90]. FieldView is another popular CFD visualizer [FieldView91]. VISUAL3 [VISUAL3] is a general tool for unstructured or structured grid visualization. PV-WAVE [Charal90] can be considered a hybrid system, since it has both simple visual programming techniques to interface to data files, as well as a more structured user interface than the visual programming environments. Wavefront's DataVisualizer [DataVisualizer] is a general purpose visualization tool. It is unique in that it is part of a powerful rendering and animation package.

Although many visualization systems claim to be object-oriented, this is often more in appearance than implementation. Little has been written on object-oriented design issues for visualization. VISAGE [VISAGE92] presents an architecture similar to that described in this chapter. Favre [Favre94] describes a more conventional object-oriented approach. His dataset classes are based on topological dimension and both data and methods are combined into classes.

4.10 References

[aPE90]
D. S. Dyer. "A Dataflow Toolkit For Visualization." *IEEE Computer Graphics and Applications,* 10(4):60-69, July, 1990.

[AVS89]
C. Upson, T. Faulhaber Jr., D. Kamins and others. "The Application Visualization System: A Computational Environment for Scientific Visualization." *IEEE Computer Graphics and Applications,* 9(4):30-42, July, 1989.

[Charal90]

S. Charalamides. "New Wave Technical Graphics Is Welcome." *DEC USER*, Aug. 1990.

[DataExplorer]

Data Explorer Reference Manual. IBM Corp, Armonk, NY, 1991.

[DataVisualizer]

Data Visualizer User Manual. Wavefront Technologies, Santa Barbara, CA, 1990.

[FAST90]

G. V. Bancroft, F. J. Merritt, T. C. Plessell, P.G. Kelaita, R. K. McCabe, and A. Globus. "FAST: A Multi-Processed Environment for Visualization." In *Proceedings of Visualization `90*, pp. 14-27, IEEE Computer Society Press, Los Alamitos, CA, 1990.

[Favre94]

J. M. Favre and J. Hahn. "An Object Oriented Design for the Visualization of Multi-Variate Data Objects." In *Proceedings of Visualization '94*, pp. 319-325, IEEE Computer Society Press, Los Alamitos, CA, 1994.

[FieldView91]

S. M. Legensky. "Advanced Visualization on Desktop Workstations." In *Proceedings of Visualization `91*, pp. 372-378, IEEE Computer Society Press, Los Alamitos, CA, 1991.

[Haeberli88]

P. E. Haeberli. "ConMan: A Visual Programming Language for Interactive Graphics." *Computer Graphics (SIGGRAPH '88)*, 22(4):103-11, 1988.

[IrisExplorer]

Iris Explorer User's Guide. Silicon Graphics Inc., Mountain View, CA, 1991.

[Levoy94]

M. Levoy. "Spreadsheets for Images." In *Proceedings of SIGGRAPH '94*, pp. 139-146, 1994.

[PLOT3D]

P. P. Walatka and P. G. Buning. *PLOT3D User's Manual*. NASA Fluid Dynamics Division,1988.

[Rasure91]

J. Rasure, D. Argiro, T. Sauer, and C. Williams. "A Visual Language and Software Development Environment for Image Processing." *International Journal of Imaging Systems and Technology*, 1991.

[VISAGE92]

W. J. Schroeder, W. E. Lorensen, G.D. Montanaro, and C. R. Volpe. "VISAGE: An Object-Oriented Visualization System." In *Proceedings of Visualization '92*, pp. 219-226, IEEE Computer Society Press, Los Alamitos, CA, 1992.

[VISUAL3]

R. Haimes and M. Giles. "VISUAL3: Interactive Unsteady Unstructured 3D Visualization." AIAA Report No. AIAA-91-0794. January, 1991.

4.11 Exercises

4.1 Consider the following 2D visualization techniques: x-y plotting, bar charts, and pie charts. For each technique:
a) Construct functional models.
b) Construct object models.

4.2 A *height field* is a regular array of 2D points $h = f(x, y)$ where h is an altitude above the point (x,y). Height fields are often used to represent terrain data. Design an object-oriented system to visualize height fields.
a) How would you represent the height field?
b) What methods would you use to access this data?
c) Develop one process object (i.e., visualization technique) to visualize a height field. Describe the methods used by the object to access and manipulate the height field.

4.3 Describe how you would implement an explicit control mechanism for network execution.
a) How do process objects register their input data with the executive?
b) How is the executive notified of object modification?
c) By what method is the executive notified that network execution is necessary?
d) Describe an approach for network dependency analysis. How does the executive invoke execution of the process objects?

4.4 Visual programming environments enable the user to construct visualization applications by graphically connecting process objects.
a) Design a graphical notation to represent process objects, their input and output, and data flow direction.
b) How would you modify instance variables of process objects (using a graphical technique)?
c) By what mechanism would network execution be initiated?
d) How would you control conditional execution and looping in your network?
e) How would you take advantage of parallel computing?
f) How would you distribute network execution across two or more computers sharing a network connection?

4.5 Place oriented cylinders (instead of cones) on the mace in Figure **4–13**. (*Hint:* use vtkCylinderSource.)

4.6 The implicit update method for the visualization network used by **vtk** is simple to implement and understand. However, it is prone to a common programming error. What is this error?

4.7 Experiment with the transformation object in Figure **4–13**.
a) Translate the actor with vtkTransform's Translate() method.
b) Rotate the actor with the RotateX(), RotateY(), and RotateZ() methods.

c) Scale the actor with the `Scale()` method.

d) Try combinations of these methods. Does the actor transform in ways that you expect?

4.8 Visualize the following functions. (*Hint:* use `vtkSampleFunction` and refer to Figure **4–1**.)

a) $F(x, y, z) = x^2$

b) $F(x, y, z) = x + 2y + 3z + 1$

c) $F(x, y, z) = x^2 + y^2 - (\cos z + 1)$

Data Representation I

*I*n Chapter 4 we developed a working definition of the visualization process: mapping information into graphics primitives. We saw how this mapping proceeds through one or more steps, each step transforming data from one form, or data representation, into another. In this chapter we examine common data forms for visualization. The goal is to familiarize you with these forms, so that you can visualize your own data using the tools and techniques provided in this text.

5.1 Introduction

To design representational schemes for data we need to know something about the data we might encounter. We also need to keep in mind design goals, so that we can design good data representation schemes. The next two sections address these issues.

Characterizing Visualization Data

Since our aim is to visualize data, clearly we need to know something about the character of the data. This knowledge will help us create useful data models and powerful visualization systems. Without a clear understanding of the data, we risk designing inflexible and limited visualization systems. In the following we describe important characteristics of data. These characteristics are the discrete nature of data, whether it is regular or irregular, and its topological dimension.

First, visualization data is *discrete*. This is not so much because data is inherently in this form, but because we use digital computers to acquire, analyze, and represent our data. Hence, all information is necessarily represented in discrete form.

Consider visualizing the simple continuous function $y = x^2$. If we are using a conventional digital computer, we must discretize this equation to operate on the data it represents (we are ignoring symbolic/analog computers and methods). For example, to plot this equation we would sample the function in some interval, say (-1,1), and then compute the value y of the function at a series of discrete points $x = x_i$ in this interval. The resulting points $((x_0,y_0), (x_1,y_1), (x_2,y_2), \dots (x_n,y_n))$ connect the points with straight line segments. Thus, our (continuous) data is represented by a discrete sampling.

There is an important implication because of this characteristic of the data: we only know data values at discrete points. In-between these points we cannot claim to know anything. In our previous example, we know that data is generated from the function $y = x^2$, but, generally speaking, when we measure and even compute data, we do not know the character of the data between discrete points. This poses a serious problem, because an important visualization activity is to determine data values at arbitrary positions. For example, we might probe our data and desire data values even though the probe position does not fall on a known point.

There is an obvious solution to this problem: interpolation. We presume a relationship between neighboring data values. Often this is a linear function, but we can use quadratic, cubic, spline, or other interpolation functions. Chapter 8 discusses interpolation functions in greater detail, but for now suffice it to say that interpolation functions generate data values in-between known points.

Second, data is *regular* or *irregular* (alternatively, *structured* or *unstructured*). Regular data has an inherent relationship between data points. For example, if we sample on an evenly spaced set of points, we do not need to store all the point coordinates, only the beginning position of the interval, the spacing between points, and the total number of points. The point positions are then known implicitly, which we can take advantage of to save computer memory.

Irregular data is data that is not regular. The advantage of irregular data is that we can represent information more densely where it changes quickly, and less densely where the change is not so great. Thus, irregular data allows us to create adaptive representational forms, which can be beneficial given limited computing resources.

Characterizing data as regular or irregular allows us to make useful assumptions about the data. As we saw a moment ago, we can store regular data more compactly. Typically, we can also compute with regular data more efficiently relative to irregular data. On the other hand, irregular data gives us more freedom in representing data, and can represent data that has no regular patterns.

Finally, data has a topological *dimension*. In our example $y = x^2$, the dimension of the data is one, since we have the single independent variable x. Data is potentially of any dimension from 0D points, to 1D curves, 2D surfaces, 3D volumes, and even higher dimensional regions.

The dimension of the data is important because it implies appropriate methods for visualization and data representation. For example, in 1D we naturally use x-y plots, bar charts, or pie charts, and store the data as a 1D list of values. For 2D data we might store the data in a matrix, and visualize it with a deformed surface plot (i.e., a *height field* - see Exercise 4.2).

In this chapter and Chapter 8, we show how these characteristics: discrete, regular/irregular, and data dimension, shape our model of visualization data. Keep these features in mind as you read these chapters.

Design Criterion

Visualizing data involves interfacing to external data, mapping into internal form, processing the data, and generating images on a computer display device. We pose the question: what form or forms should we use to represent data? Certainly many choices are available to us. The choice of representation is important because it affects the ability to interface to external data and the performance of the overall visualization system. To decide this issue we use the following design criteria:

Compact. Visualization data tends to be large, so we need compact storage schemes to minimize computer memory requirements.

Efficient. Data must be computationally accessible. We want to retrieve and store data in constant time (i.e., independent of data size). This requirement offers us the opportunity to develop algorithms that are linear, or $O(n)$, in time complexity.

Mappable. There are two types of mappings. First, data representations need to efficiently map into graphics primitives. This insures fast, interactive display of our data. Second, we must be able to easily convert external data into internal visualization data structures. Otherwise we suffer the burden of complex conversion processes, or inflexible software.

Minimal Coverage. A single data representation cannot efficiently describe all possible data types. Nor do we want different data representations for every data type we encounter. Therefore we need a minimal set of data representations that balances efficiency against the number of data types.

Simple. A major lesson of applied computation is that simple designs are preferable to complex designs. Simple designs are easier to understand, and therefore optimize. The value of simplicity cannot be overemphasized. Many of the algorithms and data representations in this text assign high priority to this design criterion.

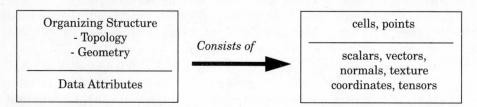

Figure 5–1 The architecture of a dataset. A dataset consists of an organizing structure, with both topological and geometric properties, and attribute data associated with the structure.

The remainder of this chapter describes common visualization data forms based on these design criteria. Our basic abstraction is the *dataset*, a general term for the various concrete visualization data types.

5.2 The Dataset

Data objects in the visualization pipeline are called *datasets*. The dataset is an abstract form; we leave the representation and implementation to its concrete subclasses.

A dataset consists of two pieces: an organizing *structure* and supplemental data *attributes* associated with the structure (Figure **5–1**).

The structure has two parts: *topology* and *geometry*. Topology is the set of properties invariant under certain geometric transformations [Weiler86]. Here we consider the transformations: rotation, translation, and non-uniform scaling. Geometry is the instantiation of the topology, the specification of position in 3D space. For example, saying that a polygon is a "triangle", specifies topology. By providing point coordinates, we specify geometry.

Dataset attributes are supplemental information associated with geometry and/or topology. This information might be a temperature value at a point, or the inertial mass of a cell.

Our model of a dataset assumes that the structure consists of *cells* and *points*. The cells specify the topology, while the points specify the geometry. The attributes are scalars, vectors, normals, texture coordinates, tensors, and user defined data.

The definition of the structure of a dataset as a collection of cells and points is a direct consequence of the discrete nature of our data. Points are located where data is known and the cells allow us to interpolate between points. We give detailed descriptions of dataset structure and attributes in the following sections.

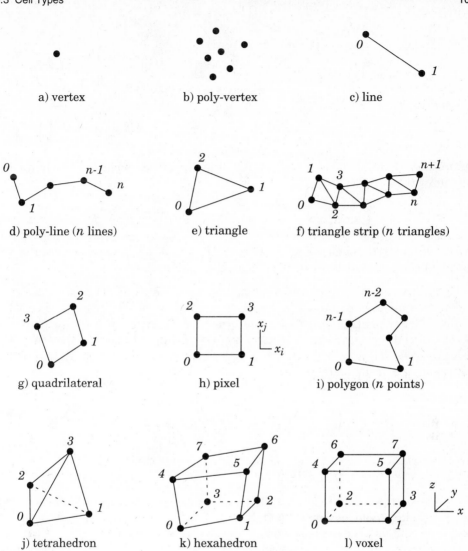

Figure 5–2 Cell types. Numbers define ordering of the defining points.

5.3 Cell Types

A dataset consists of one or more cells (Figure **5–2**). Cells are the fundamental building blocks of visualization systems. Cells are defined by specifying a *type* in combination with an ordered list of points. The ordered list, often referred to as the *connectivity list,* combined with the type specification, implicitly defines the topology of the cell. The *x-y-z* point coordinates define the cell geometry.

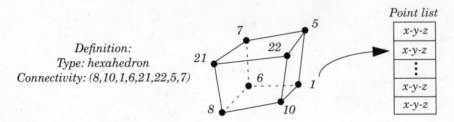

Figure 5–3 Example of a hexahedron cell. The topology is implicitly defined by the ordering of the point list.

Figure **5–3** shows one cell type, a hexahedron. The ordered list is a sequence of point ids that index into a point coordinate list. The topology of this cell is implicitly known: we know that (8,10) is one of the twelve edges of the hexahedron, and that (8,10,22,21) is one of its six faces.

Mathematically, we represent a cell by the symbol C_i. Then the cell is an ordered sequence of points $C_i = \{p_1, p_2, ..., p_n\}$ with $p_i \in P$, where P is a set of n-dimensional points (here $n=3$). The type of cell determines the sequence of points, or cell topology. The number of points n defining the cell is the *size* of the cell. A cell C_i "uses" a point p_i when $p_i \in C_i$. Hence the "use set" $U(p_i)$ is the collection of all cells using p_i:

$$U(p_i) = \{C_i : p_i \in C_i\} \qquad \textbf{(5-1)}$$

The importance of "uses" and "use sets" will become evident in Chapter 8 when we explore the topology of datasets.

Although we define points in three dimensions, cells may vary in topological dimension. Vertices, lines, triangles, and tetrahedron are examples of 0, 1, 2, and three-dimensional cells embedded in three-dimensional space. Cells can also be primary or composite. Composite cells consist of one or more primary cells, while primary cells cannot be decomposed into combinations of other primary cell types. A triangle strip, for example, consists of one or more triangles arranged in compact form. The triangle strip is a composite cell because it can be broken down into triangles, which are primary cells.

Certainly there are an infinite variety of possible cell types. In the *Visualization Toolkit* each cell type has been chosen based on application need. We have seen how some cell types: vertex, line, polygon, and triangle strip (Figure **3–20**) are used to represent geometry to the graphics subsystem or library. Other cell types such as the tetrahedron and hexahedron are common in numerical simulation. The utility of each cell type will become evident through the practice of visualization throughout this book. A description of the cell types found in the *Visualization Toolkit* is given in the following sections.

Vertex

The vertex is a primary zero-dimensional cell. It is defined by a single point.

Poly-Vertex

The poly-vertex is a composite zero-dimensional cell. The poly-vertex is defined by an arbitrarily ordered list of points.

Line

The line is a primary one-dimensional cell. It is defined by two points. The direction along the line is from the first point to the second point.

Poly-Line

The poly-line is a composite one-dimensional cell consisting of one or more connected lines. The poly-line is defined by an ordered list of $n+1$ points, where n is the number of lines in the poly-line. Each pair of points $(i, i+1)$ defines a line.

Triangle

The triangle is a primary two-dimensional cell. The triangle is defined by a counter-clockwise ordered list of three points. The order of the points specifies the direction of the surface normal using the right-hand rule.

Triangle Strip

The triangle strip is a composite two-dimensional cell consisting of one or more triangles. The points defining the triangle strip need not lie in a plane. The triangle strip is defined by an ordered list of $n+2$ points, where n is the number of triangles. The ordering of the points is such that each set of three points $(i, i+1, i+2)$ with $0 \le i \le n$ defines a triangle.

Quadrilateral

The quadrilateral is a primary two-dimensional cell. It is defined by an ordered list of four points lying in a plane. The quadrilateral is convex and its edges must not intersect. The points are ordered counterclockwise around the quadrilateral, defining a surface normal using the right-hand rule.

Pixel

The pixel is a primary two-dimensional cell defined by an ordered list of four points. The cell is topologically equivalent to the quadrilateral with the addition of geometric constraints. Each edge of the pixel is perpendicular to its adjacent edges, and lies parallel to one of the coordinate axes x-y-z. Hence, the normal to the pixel is also parallel to one of the coordinate axes.

The ordering of the points defining the pixel is different from the quadrilateral cell. The points are ordered in the direction of increasing axis coordinate, starting with x, then y, then z. The pixel is a special case of the quadrilateral and is used to improve computational performance.

One important note is that the definition of the pixel cell given here is different from the usual definition for a pixel. Normally pixels are thought of as constant-valued "picture-elements" in an image (see "Graphics Hardware" on page 53). The definition given here implies that four picture-elements form the four corner points of the pixel cell. We normally use the term pixel to describe a pixel cell, but the meaning of the term will vary depending on context.

Polygon

The polygon is a primary two-dimensional cell. The polygon is defined by an ordered list of three or more points lying in a plane. The polygon normal is implicitly defined by a counterclockwise ordering of its points using the right-hand rule.

The polygon may be non-convex, but may not have internal loops, and it cannot self-intersect. The polygon has n edges, where n is the number of points in the polygon.

Tetrahedron

The tetrahedron is a primary three-dimensional cell. The tetrahedron is defined by a list of four non-planar points. The tetrahedron has six edges and four triangular faces.

Hexahedron

The hexahedron is a primary three-dimensional cell consisting of six quadrilateral faces, twelve edges, and eight vertices. The hexahedron is defined by an ordered list of eight points as shown in Figure **5–2**. The faces and edges must not intersect any other faces and edges, and the hexahedron must be convex.

Voxel

The voxel is a primary three-dimensional cell. The voxel is topologically equivalent to the hexahedron with additional geometric constraints. Each face of the voxel is perpendicular to one of the coordinate x-y-z axes. The defining point list is ordered in the direction of increasing coordinate value as shown in Figure 5–2. The voxel is a special case of the hexahedron and is used to improve computational performance.

Similar to pixels, our definition of a voxel cell differs from the conventional definition of the term voxel. Typically, a voxel is referred to as a constant-valued

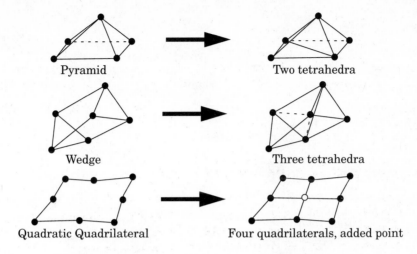

Figure 5–4 Decomposing cells into simpler forms.

"volume element". Using our definition, eight volume elements form the eight corner points of the voxel cell. We normally use the term voxel to describe a voxel cell, but the meaning of the term will vary depending on the context.

Other Types

We have implemented the previous twelve cell types in the *Visualization Toolkit*, but many other potential types exist. You may add new types to the library (Appendix A), but an alternative is to decompose your cell type into combinations of the twelve described earlier. For example, the cell types pyramid, wedge, and quadratic quadrilateral can be decomposed as follows (Figure **5–4**).

- Pyramid - decompose into two tetrahedra.
- Wedge - decompose into three tetrahedra.
- Quadratic quadrilateral (e.g., higher order finite element) - decompose into four quadrilaterals by introducing a midpoint vertex.

There are many problems when decomposing cells. Interpolation errors arise when artificial cell boundaries (vertices, edges, and faces) are introduced. Also, the internal cell variation (interpolation functions) of the decomposed cells may be markedly different from those of the original cell. To avoid these difficulties we recommend that you derive your own cell type. (See Appendix A.)

5.4 Attribute Data

Attribute data is information associated with the structure of the dataset. This structure includes both the dataset geometry and topology. Most often, attribute

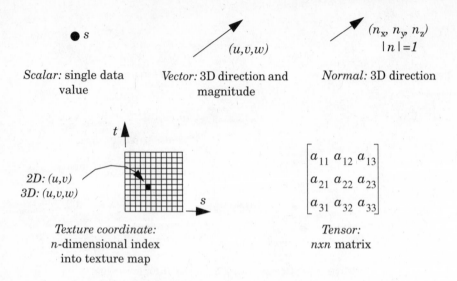

Figure 5–5 Attribute data.

data is associated with dataset points or cells, but sometimes attribute data may be assigned to cell components such as edges or faces. Attribute data may also be assigned across the entire dataset, or across a group of cells or points. We refer to this information as attribute data because it is an attribute to the structure of the dataset. Typical examples include temperature or velocity at a point, mass of a cell, or heat flux into and out of a cell face.

Attribute data is often categorized into specific types of data. These categories have been created in response to common data forms. Visualization algorithms are also categorized according to the type of data they operate on.

Single-valued functions, such as temperature or pressure, are examples of scalar data, which is one attribute type. More generally, attribute data can be treated as n-dimensional data arrays. For example, the single-valued function temperature can be treated as a 1×1 array, while velocity can be treated as a 3×1 array of components in the x, y, and z directions. This abstract model for data attribute can be extended throughout the visualization system. Some systems extend this model to include the structure of the data. For example, a structured point set (i.e., a volume) can be represented as a 3D array of $l \times m \times n$ data values. Unstructured data can be represented as a 3D vector of position, plus an array of connectivity. We refer to this general approach as the hyperdata model for visualization data (see "Other Data Abstractions" on page 120).

In the following sections we describe data attributes using the simpler type-specific model (Figure **5–5**). We also limit ourselves to three-dimensional structure, since the dataset structure and graphics are assumed to be three-dimensional.

Scalars

Scalar data is data that is single valued at each location in a dataset. Examples of scalar data are temperature, pressure, density, elevation, and stock price. Scalar data is the simplest and most common form of visualization data.

Vectors

Vector data is data with a magnitude and direction. In three dimensions this is represented as a triplet of values (u, v, w). Examples of vector data include flow velocity, particle trajectory, wind motion, and gradient function.

Normals

Normals are direction vectors: that is, they are vectors of magnitude $|n|=1$. Normals are often used by the graphics system to control the shading of objects. Normals also may be used by some algorithms to control the orientation or generation of cell primitives, such as creating ribbons from oriented lines.

Texture Coordinates

Texture coordinates are used to map a point from Cartesian space into a 1-, 2-, or 3-dimensional texture space. The texture space is usually referred to a *texture map*. Texture maps are regular arrays of color, intensity, and/or transparency values that provide extra detail to rendered objects. One application of texturing in two dimensions is to "paste" a photograph onto a single polygon, yielding a detailed image without a large number of graphics primitives. (Texture mapping is covered in more detail in Chapter 7.)

Tensors

Tensors are complex mathematical generalizations of vectors and matrices. A tensor of rank k can be considered a k-dimensional table. A tensor of rank 0 is a scalar, rank 1 is a vector, rank 2 is a matrix, and a tensor of rank 3 is a three-dimensional rectangular array. Tensors of higher rank are k-dimensional rectangular arrays.

General tensor visualization is an area of current research. Efforts thus far have been focused on two-dimensional rank 2 tensors, which are 3×3 matrices. The most common form of such tensors are the stress and strain tensors, which represent the stress and strain at a point in an object under load. **vtk** only treats real-valued, symmetric 3×3 tensors.

User Defined

Most visualization data can be mapped into the attribute data described previously. However, you may develop visualization techniques for a special application. In that case, you will have to develop your own representational form. We refer to such data as *user defined* data.

5.5 Types of Datasets

A dataset consists of an organizing structure plus associated attribute data. The structure has both topological and geometric properties, and is composed of one or more points and cells. The type of a dataset is derived from the organizing structure, and specifies the relationship that the cells and points have with one another. Common dataset types are shown in Figure **5–6**.

A dataset is characterized according to whether its structure is regular or irregular. A dataset is regular if there is a single mathematical relationship within the composing points and cells. If the points are regular, then the geometry of the dataset is regular. If the topological relationship of cells is regular, then the topology of the dataset is regular. Regular (or structured) data can be implicitly represented, at great savings in memory and computation. Irregular (or unstructured) data must be explicitly represented, since there is no inherent pattern that can be compactly described. Unstructured data tends to be more general, but requires greater memory and computational resources.

Polygonal Data

We have already seen how graphics libraries are designed to render such geometric primitives as lines and polygons. These primitives also are frequently generated or consumed by computational geometry and visualization algorithms. In the *Visualization Toolkit*, we call this collection of graphics primitives *polygonal data*. The polygonal dataset consists of vertices, poly-vertices, lines, polylines, polygons, and triangle strips. The topology and geometry of polygonal data is unstructured, and the cells that compose that dataset vary in topological dimension. The polygonal dataset forms a bridge between data, algorithms, and high-speed computer graphics.

Vertices, lines, and polygons form a minimal set of primitives to represent 0-, 1-, and 2-dimensional geometry. We have included poly-vertex, poly-line, and triangle strip cells for convenience, compactness, and performance. Triangle strips in particular are high-performing primitives. To represent n triangles with a triangle strip requires just $n+2$ points, compared to the $3n$ points for conventional representations. In addition, many graphics libraries can render triangle strips at higher speeds than triangle polygons.

Our selection of cells is based on common application and performance, representing a subset of the cells available in some graphics libraries. Other types include quadrilateral meshes, Bezier curves and surfaces, and other spline types such as NURBS (Non-Uniform Rational B-Splines) [Mortenson85]. Spline surfaces are generally used to accurately model and visualize geometry. Few visualization algorithms (other than geometry visualization) have been developed that require spline surfaces.

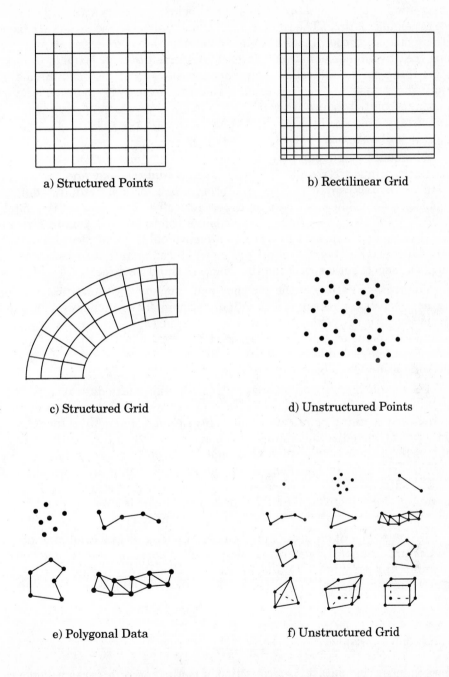

a) Structured Points

b) Rectilinear Grid

c) Structured Grid

d) Unstructured Points

e) Polygonal Data

f) Unstructured Grid

Figure 5–6 Dataset types. The unstructured grid consists of all cell types.

Structured Points

A structured points dataset is a collection of points and cells arranged on a regular, rectangular lattice. The rows, columns, and planes of the lattice are parallel to the global x-y-z coordinate system. If the points and cells are arranged on a plane (i.e., two-dimensional) the dataset is referred to as a pixmap, bitmap, or image. If the points and cells are arranged as stacked planes (i.e., three-dimensional) the dataset is referred to as a volume. We use the more general term structured points because we can refer to images, volumes, or one-dimensional point arrays collectively. Note that some authors have referred to structured points as uniform grids.

Structured points consist of line elements (1D), pixels (2D), or voxels (3D). Structured points are regular in both geometry and topology and can be represented completely implicitly. The representational scheme requires only data dimensions, an origin point, and an aspect ratio. The dimension of the data is a 3-vector (n_x, n_y, n_z), specifying the number of points in the x, y, and z directions. The origin point is the position in three-dimensional space of the minimum x-y-z point. Each pixel (2D) or voxel (3D) in a structured point dataset is identical in shape, the aspect ratio specifying the length in the x-y-z directions.

The regular nature of the topology and geometry of the structured points dataset suggests a natural i-j-k coordinate system. The number of points in the dataset is $n_x \times n_y \times n_z$ while the number of cells is $(n_x - 1) \times (n_y - 1) \times (n_z - 1)$. A particular point or cell can be selected by specifying the three indices i-j-k. Similarly, a line is defined by specifying two out of three indices, and a plane by specifying a single index.

The simplicity and compactness of representation are desirable features of structured points. It is an efficient structure to traverse and compute with. For this reason structured points are rivaled only by polygonal data as the most common form of visualization dataset. The major disadvantage with structured points is the so called "curse of dimensionality". To obtain greater data resolution we must increase the dimensions of the dataset. Increasing the dimensions of an image results in an $O(n^2)$ increase in memory requirement, while volumes require an $O(n^3)$ increase. Hence, to resolve a small feature using structured points may require more disk space or computer memory than is available.

Structured point datasets are often used in imaging and computer graphics. Volumes are frequently generated from medical imaging technologies such as Computed Tomography (CT) and Magnetic Resonance Imaging (MRI). Sometimes volumes are used to sample mathematical functions or numerical solutions.

Rectilinear Grid

The rectilinear grid dataset is a collection of points and cells arranged on a regular lattice. The rows, columns, and planes of the lattice are parallel to the global x-y-z coordinate system. While the topology of the dataset is regular, the geometry is only partially regular. That is, the points are aligned along the coordinate axis, but the spacing between points may vary.

Like the structured points dataset, rectilinear grids consist of pixels (2D) or voxels (3D). The topology is represented implicitly by specifying grid dimensions. The geometry is represented by maintaining a list of separate x, y, and z coordinates. To obtain the coordinates of a particular point, values from each of the three lists must be appropriately combined.

Structured Grid

A structured grid is a dataset with regular topology and irregular geometry. The grid may be warped into any configuration in which the cells do not overlap or self-intersect.

The topology of the structured grid is represented implicitly by specifying a 3-vector of dimensions (n_x, n_y, n_z). The geometry is explicitly represented by maintaining an array of point coordinates. The composing cells of a structured grid are quadrilaterals (2D) or hexahedron (3D). Like structured points, the structured grid has a natural coordinate system that allows us to refer to a particular point or cell using topological i-j-k coordinates.

Structured points are commonly found in finite difference analysis. Finite difference is a numerical analysis technique to approximate the solution to partial differential equations. Typical applications include fluid flow, heat transfer, and combustion.

Unstructured Points

Unstructured points are points irregularly located in space. There is no topology in an unstructured point dataset, and the geometry is completely unstructured. The vertex and poly-vertex cells are used to represent unstructured points.

Unstructured points are a simple but important type of dataset. Often data has no inherent structure, and part of the visualization task is to discover or create it. For example, consider a piston in a car instrumented with temperature gages. The number of gages and their location is chosen at a finite set of points, resulting in temperature values at "unrelated" (at least in terms of visualization topology) positions on the surface of the piston. To visualize the surface temperature, we have to create an interpolation surface and scheme to fill in intermediate values.

Unstructured points serve to represent such unstructured data. Typically, this data form is transformed into another more structured form for the purposes of visualization. Algorithms for transforming unstructured points into other forms are described in "Visualizing Unstructured Points" on page 300.

Unstructured Grid

The most general form of dataset is the unstructured grid. Both the topology and geometry are completely unstructured. Any cell type can be combined in arbitrary combinations in an unstructured grid. Hence the topology of the cells ranges from 0D (vertex, poly-vertex) to 3D (tetrahedron, hexahedron, voxel). In the *Visualization Toolkit* any dataset type can be expressed as an unstructured grid. We typically use unstructured grids to represent data only when absolutely necessary, because this dataset type requires the most memory and computational resources to represent and operate on.

Unstructured grids are found in fields such as finite element analysis, computational geometry, and geometric modelling. Finite element analysis is a numerical solution technique for partial differential equations (PDEs). Applications of finite element analysis include structural design, vibration, dynamics, and heat transfer. (This compares to finite difference analysis for PDEs. One advantage of finite element analysis is that the constraint on regular topology is removed. Hence complex domains can be more easily meshed.)

5.6 Other Data Abstractions

Other data models have been proposed besides the dataset model presented here. We briefly examine two other models that have been applied successfully. These are the AVS field model and the model of Haber, Lucas, and Collins, adapted in modified form by the commercial IBM Data Explorer system. The section concludes with a brief comparison between these two models and **vtk**'s data model.

The Application Visualization System

AVS (the Application Visualization System) was the first large-scale, commercial visualization system [AVS89]. Much of the early growth, visibility, and successful application of visualization technology was achieved because of the direct application of AVS or the influence of AVS on other researchers. AVS is a data-flow visualization system with a crisp user interface to create, edit, and manipulate visualization networks. Using an explicit executive to control execution of networks, AVS can run distributed and parallel visualization applications. Since the AVS architecture is open, researchers and developers can and have donated filters for use by others.

The AVS data model consists of primitive data and aggregate data. Primitive data are fundamental representations of data such as byte, integer, real, and string. Aggregate types are complex organizations of primitive types and include fields, colormaps, geometries, and pixel maps. Fields can be considered AVS' fundamental data type, and will be described in detail shortly. Colormaps are used to map functional values (i.e., scalar values) into color and transparency values. Geometries consist of graphics primitives such as points, lines, and polygons, and are used by the geometric renderer to display objects. A pixel map is the rendered image, or output, of a visualization.

The field is the most interesting part of the AVS data model. In general, it is an n-dimensional array with scalar or vector data at each point. A scalar is a single value, while a vector is two or more values (not necessarily three). The field array can have any number of dimensions, and the dimensions can be of any size. There is no implicit structure to the field, instead, a *mapping* function is defined. That is, either an implicit or explicit relationship from data elements to coordinate points is specified. Thus a field is a mapping between two kinds of space: the *computational space* of the field data and the *coordinate* space, which is typically the global coordinate system. AVS supports three types of mappings: uniform (i.e., structured), rectilinear, and irregular (i.e., unstructured).

The Data Explorer

The data model of Haber, Lucas, and Collins [Haber91] is based on the mathematics of fiber bundles. The goal of their work is to create a general model for piecewise representations of fields on regular and irregular grids. They refer to their model as the *field data model*, but their definition of the word *field* is different from the AVS model. A field is an object composed of a *base* and *dependent data*. Informally, the base is a manifold whose coordinates are the independent variables for the field, and the dependent data relate the values of dependent variables to the independent variables of the base. Visualization data consists of *field elements* that describe the base and dependent variables over a local region.

The Visualization Toolkit

There are similarities and differences between these data models and **vtk**'s dataset model. The greatest difference is that these other models are more abstract. They are capable of representing a wider range of data and are more flexible. In particular, the AVS field model is capable of representing arbitrary streams of numbers in a simple and elegant manner. The field data model of Haber *et al.* is also powerful: the authors show how this data representation can be used to exploit regularity in data to obtain compact representations. On the other hand, all these models (including **vtk**'s) share the notion of structure versus data. The AVS field model introduces structure by using a mapping function. The field data of the Haber *et al.* model resembles **vtk**'s dataset model, in that the base is equivalent to **vtk**'s cells, and the field data model's dependent data is analogous to **vtk**'s attribute data.

The difference in level of abstraction raises important issues in the design of visualization systems. In the following discussion we will refer to data models as abstract or concrete, where the relative level of abstraction is lower in concrete models. In general we can compare abstract and concrete classes as follows;

- Abstract models are more flexible and capable of representing a wider range of data forms than concrete models.

- Abstract models lend themselves to compact computer code.

- Concrete models are easier to describe, interface, and implement than abstract models.

- The level of abstraction influences the computer code and/or database interface to the data model. Abstract models result in abstract code and data representations; concrete models result in concrete code and data representations.

- The complexity of abstract models can be hidden by creating simpler, application-specific interfaces. However, this requires extra effort. Concrete models, on the other hand, cannot be made more abstract by modifying interfaces.

The design of computer systems demands careful attention to the balance between abstract and concrete systems. Visualization systems, in particular, must be carefully designed because they interface to other systems and data models. Models that are too abstract can result in confusing computer code and interfaces, and can be misused because of user misunderstanding. On the other hand, concrete models are limited in flexibility and capability.

In the design of the *Visualization Toolkit*, we chose to use a data model more concrete relative to the AVS and field data models. Our decision was based on the premise that the system was to be informative as well as functional, and we wanted to clearly demonstrate basic concepts. On the other hand, **vtk**'s data model is general enough to support our practice of visualization. Our experience with users also has shown us that **vtk**'s data model is easier for the casual visualization user to understand than the more abstract models. If you decide to design your own system, we recommend that you examine other data models. However, we feel that the clarity of code manifested in the *Visualization Toolkit* is an example of a well-balanced trade-off between design abstraction and simplicity.

5.7 Putting It All Together

In this section we will describe the implementation details of the dataset types covered previously. We will also show you how to create these datasets through a variety of C++ examples.

Memory Allocation

Because of the size and scope of data, memory must be carefully managed to create efficient visualization systems. In the *Visualization Toolkit*, we use contiguous data arrays for most data structures. Contiguous arrays can be created, deleted, and traversed faster than alternative data structures, such as linked lists or arrays of pointers to structures.

Contiguous arrays also can be easily transported across a network, particularly if the information in the array is independent of computer memory address. Memory independence avoids the overhead of mapping information from one memory location to another. Therefore, in **vtk** we access information based on an "id", an integer index into an array-like object. Data arrays are 0-offset just like C++ arrays. That is, given n data values, we successively access these values using the ids $(0, 1, 2, ..., n-1)$.

An important design decision was not to represent data using arrays of objects (e.g., cells or points). Our experience has shown that such designs severely impact performance. Instead, we focus on designing objects at a higher level of abstraction. From the perspective of performance, the object-oriented approach serves best at the application level, not at the level of implementation.

The class `vtkFloatArray` is an example of a contiguous array. We will use this class to describe how contiguous arrays are implemented in **vtk**. As shown in Figure **5–7**, the instance variable `Array` is a pointer to memory of type float. The allocated length of the array is given by `Size`. The array is dynamic, so an

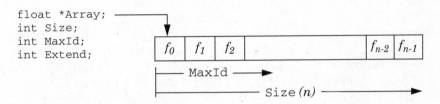

Figure 5–7 Implementation of contiguous array. This example is a fragment of the class definition `vtkFloatArray`.

attempt to insert data beyond the allocated size automatically generates a `Resize()` operation. The `Extend` field specifies the amount of additional memory that is requested during a resize operation. The `MaxId` field is an integer offset defining the end of inserted data. If no data has been inserted, then `MaxId` is equal to -1. Otherwise, `MaxId` is an integer value where $0 \leq \text{MaxId} < \text{Size}$.

Abstract/Concrete Data Array Objects

Visualization data comes in many forms: floating point, integer, byte, and double precision, to name a few simple types. More complex types such as character strings or multi-dimensional identifiers also are possible. Given this variety of types, how do we represent and manipulate such data using the representation model presented in this chapter? The answer is to use abstract data objects.

Abstract data objects are objects that provide uniform methods to create, manipulate, and delete data using dynamic binding. In C++ we use the `virtual` keyword to declare methods as dynamically bound. Dynamic binding allows us to execute a method belonging to a concrete object by manipulating that object's abstract superclass.

Consider the abstract class `vtkScalars`. We can access the scalar value at point id 129 by executing the method `float s = GetScalar(129)`. Since the virtual `GetScalar()` method returns a floating point scalar value, each sub-

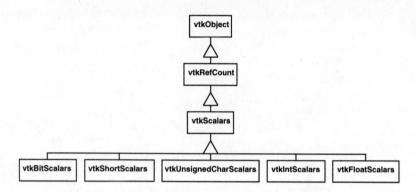

Figure 5–8 Scalar object diagram. `vtkScalar` is an abstract base class. Subclasses of `vtkScalar` implement type specific representation and operations.

class of `vtkScalars` must also return a floating point value. Although the subclass is free to represent data in any possible form, it must transform its data representation into a floating point value. This process may be as simple as a cast from a built-in type to floating point value, or it may be a complex mapping of data. For example, if our scalar data consists of character strings, we could create an alphabetical list and map the string into a location in the list.

vtk uses abstract data array objects for point coordinates, scalars, vectors, normals, texture coordinates, and tensors. Typically, we provide concrete subclasses based on the built-in types `char`, `short`, `int`, and `float`, but other types may be easily added.

Figure **5–8** shows the object diagram for scalar data. Similar object models exist for points, vectors, normals, texture coordinates, and tensors. The abstract class `vtkScalars` is a subclass of `vtkRefCount` and `vtkObject`, while the concrete classes `vtkBitScalars`, `vtkUnsignedCharScalars`, `vtkIntScalars`, `vtkShortScalars`, and `vtkFloatScalars` are subclasses of `vtkScalars`. These classes represent scalars of type packed bit (0/1 values), `unsigned char`, `int`, `short`, and `float`, respectively.

Dataset Representation

Four datasets are implemented in **vtk**: `vtkPolyData`, `vtkStructuredPoints`, `vtkStructuredGrid`, and `vtkUnstructuredGrid`. The unstructured points and rectilinear grid types are not implemented, but can be represented using one of the four types. Unstructured points can be represented using either `vtkPolyData` or `vtkUnstructuredGrid`. Rectilinear grids can be represented using `vtkStructuredGrid`, at additional memory cost.

We use a different representation for each dataset. By using different representations we minimize data structure memory requirements and implement efficient access methods. It would have been possible to use `vtkUnstruc-`

turedGrid to represent all dataset types, but the memory and computational overhead are unacceptable for large data.

vtkStructuredPoints

The simplest and most compact representation is vtkStructuredPoints. Both the dataset points and cells are represented implicitly by specifying the dimensions, aspect ratio, and origin. The dimensions define the topology of the dataset, while the origin and aspect ratio specify the geometry.

There is an implicit ordering of both the points and cells composing vtkStructuredPoints. Both the cells and points are numbered in the direction of increasing x, then y, then z. The total number of points is $n_x \times n_y \times n_z$ where n_x, n_y, and n_z are the dimensions of vtkStructuredPoints. The total number of cells is $(n_x - 1) \times (n_y - 1) \times (n_z - 1)$.

vtkStructuredGrid

Like vtkStructuredPoints, the topology of vtkStructuredGrid is regular and is defined by specifying dimensions in the topological *i-j-k* coordinate system. However, the geometry of vtkStructuredGrid is realized by specifying point coordinates in the global *x-y-z* coordinate system.

The abstract data class vtkPoints and its concrete subclasses (e.g., vtkFloatPoints) are used to represent the point coordinates. These are implemented as arrays. A particular point coordinate may be retrieved or set by specifying a particular point id. The numbering of the points and cells are implicit in the same fashion as vtkStructuredPoints. Care must be taken to insure that the number of points in the data array is the same as that implied by the dimensions of the grid.

vtkPolyData

Unlike vtkStructuredPoints and vtkStructuredGrid, the topology of vtkPolyData is not regular. Hence, both the topology and geometry of the dataset must be explicitly represented. The point data in vtkPolyData is represented using the vtkPoints class (and subclasses), just the same as in vtkStructuredGrid.

The *Visualization Toolkit* uses the class vtkCellArray to explicitly represent cell topology. This class is a list of connectivity for each cell. The structure of the list is a sequence of integer numbers (Figure **5–9**). The first number in the

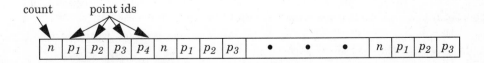

Figure 5–9 vtkCellArray structure to represent cell topology.

list is a count (the number of points in the cell connectivity), and the next series of numbers is the cell connectivity. (Each number in the connectivity list is an index into a point list.) Sequences of count followed by connectivity list are repeated until each cell is enumerated. Additional information such as the number of cells in the list and current position is also maintained by vtkCellArray.

Notice that type information is not directly represented in this structure. Instead, vtkPolyData maintains four separate lists to vertices, lines, polygons, and triangle strips. The vertex list represents cells of type vtkVertex and vtk-PolyVertex. The lines list represents cells of type vtkLine and vtkPolyLine. The polygon list represents cells of type vtkTriangle, vtkQuad, and vtkPoly-gon. The triangle strip list represents cells of the single type vtkTrian-gleStrip. As a result, the cell type is known from the particular list the cell is defined in, plus the number of points that define the cell.

Our design of the vtkPolyData class is based on two important requirements. First, we want an efficient interface to external graphics libraries. Second, we wish to aggregate cells according to topology. The four separate lists provide efficient interface because graphics libraries have separate vertex, line, polygon, and triangle strip primitives. As a result, in **vtk** no run-time checking is required to match the different cell types with the appropriate "load primitive" function, since the type is known from the list in which the primitive resides. The four lists also separate cells into 0-, 1-, and 2-dimensional types. This is useful because visualization algorithms often treat data of varying topological order differently.

vtkUnstructuredGrid

The dataset type vtkUnstructuredGrid is the most general in terms of its ability to represent topological and geometric structure. Both points and cells are explicitly represented using derived classes of vtkPoints and vtkCellArray. The class vtkUnstructuredGrid is similar to vtkPolyData except that vtkUnstructuredGrid must be capable of representing all cell types, not just the limited graphics types (i.e., vertices, lines, polygons, and triangle strips) of vtkPolyData.

Another distinguishing characteristic of vtkUnstructuredGrid is that we represent type information differently. In vtkPolyData we categorized cells into four separate lists, thereby representing cell type indirectly. In vtkUnstruc-turedGrid we add the additional class vtkCellList to represent cell type explicitly.

The vtkCellList is an array of supplemental information. For each cell, a flag defines the cell type. Another variable is used to record the location of the cell definition in the corresponding vtkCellArray (Figure **5–10**).

Besides representing cell type, this design also enables random access to cells. Because the length of a cell connectivity list varies, the vtkCellArray class cannot locate a particular cell without traversing its data structure from the origin. With the added class vtkCellList, however, it is possible to directly access a cell with a single dereference (i.e., using the offset value).

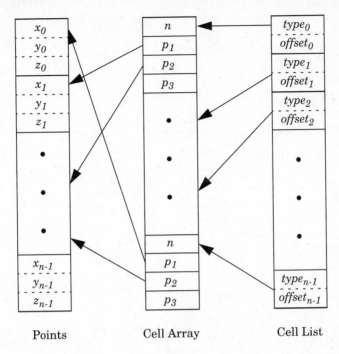

Points   Cell Array   Cell List

Figure 5–10 The `vtkUnstructuredGrid` data structure. (This is a portion of the complete structure. See Chapter 8 for complete representation.)

The `vtkCellList` may also be added to the `vtkPolyData` data representation – and indeed it has. However, our reasons for this addition are not to represent type explicitly, but rather to provide random access to the cells and enable many topological operations. We will expand on this idea in Chapter 8.

Object Model

The four datasets are implemented as shown in Figure **5–11**. As this object diagram illustrates, these concrete datasets are subclasses of the abstract class `vtkDataSet`. Two additional classes are introduced as well. The class `vtkStructuredData` contributes instance variables and methods for structured data. Subclasses of the class `vtkPointSet` represent their points explicitly, that is, through an instance of `vtkPoints` or its subclasses. `vtkPointSet` provides methods and instance variables to manipulate the point data, as well as a general searching capability to find points and cells. (See "Searching" on page 247.)

Cell Representation

In the *Visualization Toolkit* each cell type has been realized by creating specific classes. Each cell is a subclass of the abstract type `vtkCell`. Cell topology is rep-

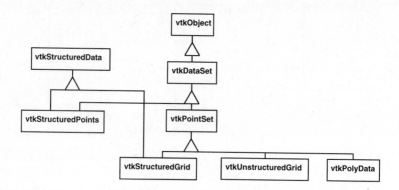

Figure 5–11 Dataset object diagram. These four datasets are implemented in **vtk**.

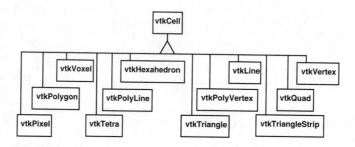

Figure 5–12 Object diagram for twelve cell types in **vtk**.

resented by a list of ordered point ids, and cell geometry is represented by a list of point coordinates. The object diagram for vtkCell and its subclasses is shown in Figure **5–12**.

The abstract class vtkCell specifies methods that each cell must implement. These methods provide a defined interface to the cell's geometry and topology. Additional methods perform computation on the cell. These methods will be discussed in detail in Chapter 8.

Data Attributes

Data attributes are associated with the structure of a dataset. The dataset model is built on points and cells, so it is natural to associate data attributes with points and cells as well. Intermediate structure features, such as cell edges or faces, are not explicitly represented so we cannot easily associate data attributes with them.

In **vtk** we have chosen to associate data attributes with the points. There is no association of data attributes to cells. (Here we refer to data attributes associated with points as *point attributes*, and data attributes associated with cells as *cell attributes*.) Our design choice is based on the following rationale.

- Point attributes are representationally complete. We can represent cell attributes by assigning cell values to each of the cell's points. Sometimes this may require duplication of points. For example, to represent a cell with constant data value, we need to duplicate each point and assign each point the cell data value.

- Point attributes are more common than cell attributes. Of course, this varies by application, but our experience suggests this to be generally true.

- Coding and implementation is greatly simplified. There is no need to introduce further complexity to maintain dual data representation.

- Inconsistencies in the data are avoided. If both point and cell attributes coexist, data values may not be consistent. For example, if a cell's scalar value is 0.5, and its points have scalar values other than 0.5, which is the correct value? Priority schemes can be devised to resolve such situations. However, we feel that this capability is not worth the additional complexity.

To represent point attributes we use the organizing class `vtkPointData` and the data specific classes `vtkScalars`, `vtkVectors`, `vtkNormals`, `vtkTCoords`, `vtkTensors`, and `vtkUserDefined`. `vtkPointData` serves to coordinate the movement of data from one process object to the next. It provides methods for copying, interpolating, and moving data between input and output. The data-specific classes represent and provide access to data. As with `vtkPoints`, the data-specific classes are abstract and depend on concrete subclasses to represent specific types of data (e.g., `float`, `char`, `int`).

There is a one-to-one correspondence between each dataset point and its attribute data. Point attributes are accessed by way of the point id. For example, to access the scalar value of point id 129 in the dataset instance `aDataSet`, we use

```
aDataSet->GetPointData()->GetScalars()->GetScalar(129);
```

This statement assumes that the scalar data has been defined for this dataset and is non-`NULL`.

The class `vtkPointData` provides important capabilities. When a filter object executes, attribute data from its input is operated on and passed on to its output. These operations are typically copying input data from one point to an output point, interpolating input data to generate output data, or passing entire data objects from input to output. When we perform these operations, the filters are designed to be as independent of the attribute data as possible. That is, we would like the filters to operate on the point data generically, without knowledge of the types of data associated with each point. Such capabilities simplify the coding of filters, and avoid the need to recode them if the representation of the point data changes.

Examples

In the examples that follow we show manual creation and manipulation of datasets. Typically, these operations are not performed directly by users of **vtk**. Instead, source objects are used to read data files or generate data. This is more convenient than the manual techniques shown here and should be used whenever possible.

Creation of datasets is a two step process. First the geometry and topology of the dataset must be defined. Depending on the type of dataset the geometry and topology definition will proceed differently. Then the point attribute data is created and associated with the dataset. Remember that there is a one-to-one relationship between the attribute data and the points in the dataset.

Create a Polygonal Dataset

In our first example we create a polygonal representation of a cube. The cube is defined by eight points and six quadrilateral faces. We also create eight scalar values associated with the eight vertices of the cube. Figure **5–13** shows the key C++ code fragments used to create the data, and the resulting image.

The geometry of the cube is defined using an instance of the class `vtk-FloatPoints`. The topology of the cube (i.e., polygons) is defined with an instance of the class `vtkCellArray`. These define the points and polygons of the cube, respectively. Scalar data is represented by an instance of the class `vtkIntScalars`.

As this example shows polygonal data is created by constructing pieces (e.g., points, cells, and point attribute data), and then assembling the pieces to form the complete dataset. If the name of the instance of `vtkPolyData` is `cube`, we can summarize these three steps as follows.

1. Create instance of subclass of `vtkPoints` to define geometry. Use the operator `cube->SetPoints()` to associate the points with the dataset.

2. Create instances of `vtkCellArray` to define topology for vertices, lines, polygons, and triangle strips. Use the operators `cube->SetVerts()`, `cube->SetLines()`, `cube->SetPolys()`, and `cube->SetStrips()` to associate the cells with the dataset.

3. Create point attribute data. Every dataset has an attribute that is an instance of `vtkPointData`. Use the operator `pd=cube->GetPointData()` to retrieve the pointer to the point attribute data. Associate the attribute data with the dataset using the operators `pd->SetScalars()`, `pd->Set-Vectors()`, `pd->SetNormals()`, `pd->SetTensors()`, `pd->SetTCoords()`, and `pd->SetUserDefined()`.

Polygonal data supports the cell types vertices, poly-vertices, lines, poly-lines, triangles, quadrilaterals, polygons, and triangle strips. Point attribute data does not need to be defined – you can create none, some, or all of the point attributes in any combination.

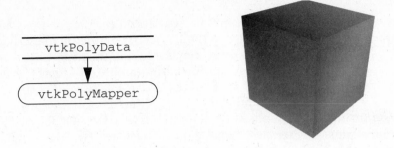

```
cube = new vtkPolyData;
points = new vtkFloatPoints(8);
polys = new vtkCellArray;
scalars = new vtkIntScalars(8);

for (i=0; i<8; i++) points->InsertPoint(i,x[i]);
for (i=0; i<6; i++) polys->InsertNextCell(4,pts[i]);
for (i=0; i<8; i++) scalars->InsertScalar(i,i);

cube->SetPoints(points);
points->Delete();
cube->SetPolys(polys);
polys->Delete();
cube->GetPointData()->SetScalars(scalars);
scalars->Delete();
```

Figure 5–13 Creation of polygonal cube (Cube.cc).

The most confusing aspect of this example is the Delete() method. To prevent memory leaks we must use a Delete() method (**vtk**'s destructor) after every new method. It is apparent from the example that the instances points, polys, and scalars are referred to by another object (e.g., cube). So doesn't invocation of the Delete() method pose a problem?

The answer is no. Certain data objects in **vtk** are reference counted to conserve memory resources (i.e., subclasses of vtkRefCount). That means they can be shared between objects. For most objects the Delete() will invoke the destructor. Reference counted objects act a little differently. The Delete() method simply decrements the reference count. This may or may not destroy the object depending on whether it is being used by another object. In this example the points, polys, and scalars are used by the polygonal dataset cube, so they are not deleted when Delete() is invoked. They will be freed once we free the dataset cube, that is, when their reference count drops to zero. (See "Special Objects" on page 391 of Appendix A.)

Create a Structured Points Dataset

In this example we create a structured points dataset (i.e., an instance of vtk-StructuredPoints). The topology of the dataset is defined by specifying the data dimensions. The geometry is defined by specifying the aspect ratio and origin. The aspect ratio specifies the length, width, and height of each voxel. The origin specifies the position in 3D space of the "lower-left" corner of the data. In our example we set the origin and aspect ratio of the dataset so that its center lies at the origin, and the bounds of the dataset are (-0.5,0.5, -0.5,0.5, -0.5,0.5).

In this example we create scalar data along with the structured points dataset. The scalar values are computed from the implicit function for a sphere

$$F(x, y, z) = \left(x^2 + y^2 + z^2 \right) - R^2 \tag{5-2}$$

with the radius $R = 0.4$. The scalar data is stored in an instance of vtk-FloatScalars and assigned to the point attribute data of the dataset.

To complete this example, a contour filter is used to generate a surface of scalar value $F(x, y, z) = 0$. Note that this functionality (in a more general form) is available from the source object vtkSampleFunction in combination with vtkSphere. Figure **5–14** shows the key C++ code fragment used to create the data and contour the scalar field, and the resulting image.

Structured points datasets are easy to construct because both the geometry and topology are implicitly defined. If the name of the instance of vtkStructuredPoints is vol, we can summarize the steps to create the dataset as follows.

1. Define the topology of the dataset using the operator vol->SetDimensions().

2. Define the geometry of the dataset using the operators vol->SetOrigin() and vol->SetAspectRatio().

3. Create point attribute data and associate it with the dataset.

You do not need to specify origin and aspect ratio. By default the aspect ratio is (1,1,1) in the x-y-z directions, and the origin is (0,0,0). Thus if the dimensions of the dataset are $n_x \times n_y \times n_z$, the default length, width, and height of the dataset will be $(n_x - 1, n_y - 1, n_z - 1)$.

The topological dimension of the dataset is implicitly known from its instance variables. For example, if any of the dimensions (n_x, n_y, n_z) is equal to one (and the other two are greater than one), the topological dimension of the dataset is two.

Create Structured Grid Dataset

In the next example we create a vtkStructuredGrid dataset. Topology is implicitly defined from the dimensions of the dataset. The geometry is explicitly defined by providing an object to represent the point coordinates. In this example

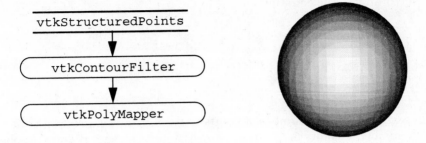

```
vol = new vtkStructuredPoints;
  vol->SetDimensions(26,26,26);
  vol->SetOrigin(-0.5,-0.5,-0.5);
  ar = 1.0/25.0;
  vol->SetAspectRatio(ar, ar, ar);

scalars = new vtkFloatScalars(26*26*26);
for (k=0; k<26; k++)
   {
   z = -0.5 + k*ar;
   kOffset = k * 26 * 26;
   for (j=0; j<26; j++)
      {
      y = -0.5 + j*ar;
      jOffset = j * 26;
      for (i=0; i<26; i++)
        {
        x = -0.5 + i*ar;
        s = x*x + y*y + z*z - (0.4*0.4);
        offset = i + jOffset + kOffset;
        scalars->InsertScalar(offset,s);
        }
      }
   }
  vol->GetPointData()->SetScalars(scalars);
  scalars->Delete();
```

Figure 5–14 Creating a structured points dataset. Scalar data is generated from the equation for a sphere. Volume dimensions are 26^3 (Vol.cc).

we use an instance of vtkFloatPoints and assume that the structured grid is warped according to the equation for a cylinder

$$x = r_i \cos\theta$$

$$y = r_i \sin\theta \qquad\qquad\qquad \textbf{(5-3)}$$

$$z = z_i$$

We arbitrarily choose the number of points in the tangential direction to be thirteen, the number of points in the radial direction to be eleven, and the number of points in the axis direction to be eleven (i.e., dimensions are $13 \times 11 \times 11$).

Vectors are generated tangential to the cylinder and of magnitude proportional to the radius. To display the data we draw small, oriented lines at each point as shown in Figure **5–13**. (This technique is called a *hedgehog*. See "Hedgehogs and Oriented Glyphs" on page 155.)

The creation of a structured grid dataset is partially explicit and partially implicit. Geometry is created explicitly be creating an instance of vtkPoints, while the topology is created implicitly by specifying dataset dimensions. If the name of the instance of vtkStructuredGrid is sgrid, the following three steps are used to create it.

1. Specify the dataset geometry by creating an instance of vtkPoints. Use the operator sgrid->SetPoints() to associate the points with the dataset.

2. The dataset topology is specified using the operator sgrid->SetDimensions(). Make sure the number of points created in item #1 above is equal to the implied number of points $n_x \cdot n_y \cdot n_z$

3. Create point attribute data and associate it with the dataset.

The topological dimension of the dataset is implied by the specified dimensions. For example, if any of the dimensions (n_x, n_y, n_z) is equal to one, the topological dimension of the dataset is two. If two of the three dimensions (n_x, n_y, n_z) are equal to one, the topological dimension of the dataset is one.

Create Unstructured Grid Dataset

Unstructured grid datasets are the most general dataset type in both topology and geometry. In this example we "artificially" create an unstructured grid using an instance of vtkUnstructuredGrid (Figure **5–16**). The grid contains examples of each cell type except for pixels and voxels. (Pixels and voxels are generally used internally to process structured points datasets. They can be explicitly created and manipulated as long as the required relationship of point geometry is observed.) Creating the dataset structure requires creating points to define the geometry and various cells to define the topology. (Note that in the finite element world we would refer to these as *nodes* and *elements*.)

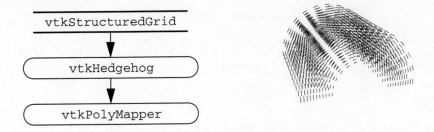

```
sgrid = new vtkStructuredGrid;
  sgrid->SetDimensions(dims);

vectors = new vtkFloatVectors(dims[0]*dims[1]*dims[2]);
points = new vtkFloatPoints(dims[0]*dims[1]*dims[2]);
deltaZ = 2.0 / (dims[2]-1);
deltaRad = (rMax-rMin) / (dims[1]-1);
v[2]=0.0;
for (k=0; k<dims[2]; k++){
  x[2] = -1.0 + k*deltaZ;
  kOffset = k * dims[0] * dims[1];
  for (j=0; j<dims[1]; j++)
    {
    radius = rMin + j*deltaRad;
    jOffset = j * dims[0];
    for (i=0; i<dims[0]; i++)
      {
      theta = i * 15.0 * math.DegreesToRadians();
      x[0] = radius * cos(theta);
      x[1] = radius * sin(theta);
      v[0] = -x[1];
      v[1] = x[0];
      offset = i + jOffset + kOffset;
      points->InsertPoint(offset,x);
      vectors->InsertVector(offset,v);
      }}}
sgrid->SetPoints(points);
points->Delete();
sgrid->GetPointData()->SetVectors(vectors);
vectors->Delete();
```

Figure 5–15 Creating a structured grid dataset of a semi-cylinder. Vectors are created whose magnitude is proportional to radius, and oriented in tangential direction (SGrid.cc).

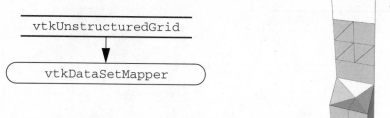

```
points = new vtkFloatPoints(8);
for (i=0; i<27; i++) points->InsertPoint(i,x[i]);

ugrid = new vtkUnstructuredGrid;
ugrid->Allocate(100);
ugrid->InsertNextCell(VTK_HEXAHEDRON, 8, pts[0]);
ugrid->InsertNextCell(VTK_HEXAHEDRON, 8, pts[1]);
ugrid->InsertNextCell(VTK_TETRA, 4, pts[2]);
ugrid->InsertNextCell(VTK_TETRA, 4, pts[3]);
ugrid->InsertNextCell(VTK_POLYGON, 6, pts[4]);
ugrid->InsertNextCell(VTK_TRIANGLE_STRIP, 6, pts[5]);
ugrid->InsertNextCell(VTK_QUAD, 4, pts[6]);
ugrid->InsertNextCell(VTK_TRIANGLE, 3, pts[7]);
ugrid->InsertNextCell(VTK_TRIANGLE, 3, pts[8]);
ugrid->InsertNextCell(VTK_LINE, 2, pts[9]);
ugrid->InsertNextCell(VTK_LINE, 2, pts[10]);
ugrid->InsertNextCell(VTK_VERTEX, 1, pts[11]);

ugrid->SetPoints(points);
points->Delete();
```

Figure 5–16 Creation of an unstructured grid (UGrid.cc).

To summarize the process of creating an instance of vtkUnstructuredGrid, we follow five steps. We assume the name of vtkUnstructuredGrid instance is ugrid.

1. Allocate memory for the dataset. Use the operator ugrid->Allocate(). This operator takes two optional parameters related to the size of the data. The first is the size of the connectivity list, and the second is the amount to extend storage (if necessary). As a rule of thumb, use the number of cells times the average number of points defining each cell for both parameters. Exact values for these parameters are not important, although the choice may affect performance. If you fail to execute this operation before inserting data, the software will break.

2. Create an instance of a subclass of `vtkPoints` to define the dataset geometry. Use the operator `ugrid->SetPoints()` to associate the points with the dataset.

3. Create dataset topology by using the cell insertion operator `ugrid->InsertNextCell()`. There are various flavors of this operator, use the appropriate one.

4. Create point attribute data and associate it with the dataset.

5. Complete the creation process by executing the `ugrid->Squeeze()` operator. This operator reclaims any extra memory consumed by the data structures. Although this step is not required, it will return memory resource back to the computer system.

The creation of unstructured grid datasets is somewhat different from the creation of the other dataset types. This is because of the unstructured nature of the data, and the complex nature of the internal data structures.

5.8 Chapter Summary

A dataset represents visualization data. The dataset has an organizing structure, with topological and geometric components, and associated attribute data. The structure of a dataset consists of cells (topology) and points (geometry). An important characteristic of the structure is whether its geometry and topology are regular or irregular (or equivalently, structured or unstructured). Regular data is more compact and often more computationally efficient than irregular data. Irregular data is more flexible in representation capability than regular data.

Important dataset types include polygonal data, structured points, structured grids, and unstructured grids. The polygonal dataset type is used to represent graphics data, as well as many kinds of visualization data. The unstructured grid is the most general type, consisting of arbitrary combinations of all possible cell types.

Attribute data consists of scalars, vectors, tensors, texture coordinates, normals, and user defined data. In the *Visualization Toolkit*, attribute data is associated with the dataset points.

5.9 Bibliographic Notes

A variety of representation schemes have been proposed for each dataset type described here. These schemes vary depending on design goals. For example, even the simple volume representation has been implemented with other more complex schemes such as run-length encoding and octrees [Bloomenthal88]. A description of more general representation schemes is available in [Haber91], the AVS field model [AVS89], and the compact cell structure [Schroeder94]. An overview of dataset types can be found in [Gelberg90]. Some structures for those mathematically oriented can be found in [Brisson90] and [Poluzzi93]. Haimes [VISUAL3] describes an efficient data structure for unstructured grid visualization.

If you are interested in more details on finite element methods see the classic Zienkiewicz [Zienkiewicz87] or [Gallagher75]. Information about both finite difference and finite element methods is available in [Lapidus82].

5.10 References

[AVS89]

C. Upson, T. Faulhaber Jr., D. Kamins and others. "The Application Visualization System: A Computational Environment for Scientific Visualization." *IEEE Computer Graphics and Applications,* 9(4):30-42, July, 1989.

[Bloomenthal88]

J. Bloomenthal. "Polygonization of Implicit Surfaces." *Computer Aided Geometric Design,* 5(4):341-355, November 1988.

[Brisson90]

E. Brisson. "Representing Geometric Structures in *d*-Dimensions: Topology and Order." *ACM Symposium on Computational Geometry.* ACM Press, NY, 1989.

[Gallagher75]

R. H. Gallagher. *Finite Element Analysis: Fundamentals.* Prentice Hall, Upper Saddle River, NJ, 1975.

[Gelberg90]

L. Gelberg, D. Kamins, D. Parker, and J. Stacks. "Visualization Techniques for Structured and Unstructured Scientific Data." *SIGGRAPH `90 Course Notes for State of the Art Data Visualization,* August, 1990.

[Haber91]

R. B. Haber, B. Lucas, N. Collins. "A Data Model for Scientific Visualization with Provisions for Regular and Irregular Grids." In *Proceedings of Visualization '91,* pp. 298-395, IEEE Computer Society Press, Los Alamitos, CA, 1991.

[Lapidus82]

L. Lapidus and G. F. Pinder. *Numerical Solution of Partial Differential Equations in Science and Engineering.* John-Wiley and Sons, New York, 1987.

[Mortenson85]

M. E. Mortenson. *Geometric Modeling.* John Wiley and Sons, New York, 1985.

[Poluzzi93]

A. Paoluzzi, F. Bernardini, C. Cattani, and V. Ferrucci. "Dimension-Independent Modeling with Simplicial Complexes." *ACM Transactions on Graphics,* 12(1):56-102, 1993.

[Schroeder94]

W. J. Schroeder and B. Yamrom. "A Compact Cell Structure for Scientific Visualization." *SIGGRAPH '93 and '94 Course Notes for Advanced Techniques for Scientific Visualization.*

[VISUAL3]
R. Haimes and M. Giles. "VISUAL3: Interactive Unsteady Unstructured 3D Visualization." AIAA Report No. AIAA-91-0794, January, 1991.

[Weiler86]
K. J. Weiler. *Topological Structures for Geometric Modeling*. PhD thesis, Rensselaer Polytechnic Institute, Troy, NY, May 1986.

[Zienkiewicz87]
O. C. Zienkiewicz and R. L. Taylor. *The Finite Element Method - Volume 1*. McGraw Hill Book Co., New York, 4th edition, 1987.

5.11 Exercises

5.1 Consider a pixmap of dimensions 100^2. Compare the memory requirements to represent this data using:
a) a structured point dataset,
b) a structured grid dataset,
c) a polygonal mesh of quadrilaterals,
d) an unstructured grid of quadrilateral cells,
e) and a triangle strip mesh of 100 strips of 200 triangles each.

5.2 Consider a volume of dimensions 100^3. Compare the memory requirements to represent this data using:
a) a structured point dataset,
b) a structured grid dataset,
c) and an unstructured grid of hexahedral cells.

5.3 Develop a representational scheme for a rectilinear grid. How does this compare (in memory requirement) to a structured grid?

5.4 Consider a volume of dimensions 100^3. Compute the memory requirements for the following point attribute types:
a) unsigned character scalars (1 byte per scalar),
b) float scalars (4 bytes per scalar),
c) float vectors,
d) and double precision tensors (3x3 tensors).

5.5 List three examples of scalar data.

5.6 List three examples of vector data.

5.7 List three examples of tensor data.

5.8 List three examples of user defined data.

5.9 A common method to represent cell connectivity is to list point ids with the last id negated. For example, triangle (8,7,3) would be represented (8,7,-3). The negative index represents end of cell definition. What are the advantages and disadvantages of this scheme as compared to the **vtk** cell array structure?

5.10 How many different ways can a hexahedral cell be decomposed into tetra-hedron? Are there compatibility issues between neighboring hexahedra?

5.11 Write a program to create and display a structured grid in the form of a hollow cylinder (i.e., cylinder with a hole through it).

5.12 Write a program to create and display an unstructured grid in the form of a hollow cylinder.

5.13 Write a program to create and display a polygonal octahedron.

Algorithms I

We have seen how to represent basic types of visualization data such as structured points and grids, unstructured grids, and polygonal data. This chapter explores methods to transform this data from one form to another and finally into images. These methods are called *algorithms*, and are of special interest to those working in the visualization world. Algorithms are the verbs that allow us to express our data in visual form. By combining these verbs appropriately, we can reduce complex data into simple, readily comprehensible sentences that are the power of data visualization.

6.1 Introduction

The algorithms that transform data are the heart of data visualization. To describe the various transformations available, we need to categorize algorithms according to the *structure* and *type* of transformation. By structure we mean the effects that transformation has on the topology and geometry of the dataset. By type we mean the type of dataset that the algorithm operates on.

Structural transformations can be classified in four ways, depending on how they effect the geometry, topology, and attributes of a dataset.

- *Geometric transformations* alter input geometry but do not change the topology of the dataset. For example, if we translate, rotate, and/or scale the points of a polygonal dataset, the topology does not change, but the point coordinates, and therefore the geometry, does.

- *Topological transformations* alter input topology but do not change geometry and attribute data. Converting a dataset type from polygonal data to unstructured grid data, or from structured points to unstructured grid, changes the topology but not the geometry. More often, however, the geometry changes whenever the topology does, so topological transformation is uncommon.

- *Attribute transformations* convert data attributes from one form to another, or create new attributes from the input data. The structure of the dataset remains unaffected. Computing vector magnitude or creating scalars based on elevation are data attribute transformations.

- *Combined transformations* change both dataset structure and attribute data. For example, computing contour lines or surfaces is a combined transformation.

We also may classify algorithms according to the type of data they operate on, or the type of data they generate. By type, we most often mean the type of attribute data, such as scalars or vectors. Typical categories include:

- *Scalar algorithms* operate on scalar data. For example, the generation of contour lines of temperature on a weather map.

- *Vector algorithms* operate on vector data. Showing oriented arrows of airflow (direction and magnitude) is an example of vector visualization.

- *Tensor algorithms* operate on tensor matrices. An example of a tensor algorithm is to show the components of stress or strain in a material using oriented icons.

- *Modelling algorithms* generate dataset topology or geometry, or surface normals or texture data. Modelling algorithms tend to be the catch-all category for many algorithms, since some do not fit neatly into any single category mentioned above. For example, generating glyphs oriented according to the vector direction, and then scaled according to the scalar value, is a combined scalar/vector algorithm. For convenience we classify such an algorithm as a modelling algorithm, because it does not fit squarely into any other category.

Algorithms also can be classified according to the type of data they process. This is the most common scheme found in the visualization literature. However, this scheme is not without its problems. Often the categories overlap, resulting in confusion. For example, a category (not mentioned above) is *volume visualization*, which refers to the visualization of volume data (or in our terminology, structured points). This category was initially created to describe the visualization of scalar data arranged on a volume, but more recently, vector (and even tensor) data has been visualized on a volume. Hence, we have to qualify our techniques to *volume vector visualization*, or other potentially confusing combinations.

In the text that follows, we will use the type classification scheme: scalar, vector, tensor, and modelling. In cases where the algorithms operate on a particular dataset type, we place them in the appropriate category according to our best judgement. Be forewarned, though, that alternative classification schemes do exist, and may be better suited to describing the true nature of the algorithm.

Generality Versus Efficiency

Most algorithms can be written specifically for a particular dataset type, or more generally, treating any dataset type. The advantage of a specific algorithm is that it is usually faster than a comparable general algorithm. (See "Other Data Abstractions" on page 120 where we discussed the trade-off between abstract and concrete forms.) An implementation of a specific algorithm also may be more memory efficient and its implementation may better reflect the relationship between the algorithm and the dataset type it operates on.

One example of this is contour surface creation. Algorithms for extracting contour surfaces were originally developed for volume data, mainly for medical applications. The regularity of volumes lends itself to efficient algorithms. However, the specialization of volume-based algorithms precludes their use for more general datasets such as structured or unstructured grids. Although the contour algorithms can be adapted to these other dataset types, they are less efficient than those for volume datasets.

Our presentation of algorithms favors the more general implementations. In some special cases we will describe performance improving techniques for particular dataset types. Refer to the bibliography at the end of each chapter for detailed descriptions of specialized algorithms.

6.2 Scalar Algorithms

Scalars are single data values associated with each point and/or cell of a dataset. (Recall that in the *Visualization Toolkit* we associate data with points.) Because scalar data is commonly found in real world applications, and because scalar data is so easy to work with, there are many different algorithms to visualize it.

Color Mapping

Color mapping is a common scalar visualization technique that maps scalar data to colors, and displays the colors on the computer system. The scalar mapping is implemented by indexing into a *color lookup table*. Scalar values serve as indices into the lookup table.

The mapping proceeds as follows. The lookup table holds an array of colors (e.g., red, green, blue components or other comparable representations). Associated with the table is a minimum and maximum *scalar range (min, max)* into

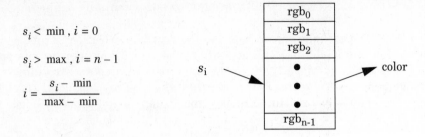

$$s_i < \min \, , \, i = 0$$

$$s_i > \max \, , \, i = n - 1$$

$$i = \frac{s_i - \min}{\max - \min}$$

Figure 6–1 Mapping scalars to colors via lookup table.

which the scalar values are mapped. Scalar values greater than the maximum range are clamped to the maximum color, scalar values less than the minimum range are clamped to the minimum color value. Then, for each scalar value s_i, the index i into the color table with n entries (and 0-offset) is given by Figure **6–1**.

A more general form of the lookup table is called a *transfer function*. A transfer function is any expression that maps scalar value into a color specification. For example, Figure **6–2** maps scalar values into separate intensity values for the red, green, and blue color components. We can also use transfer functions to map scalar data into other information such as local transparency. (Transfer functions are discussed in more detail in "Transparency and Alpha Values" on page 199 and "Volume Rendering" on page 209.) A lookup table is a discrete sampling of a transfer function. We can create a lookup table from any transfer function by sampling the transfer function at a set of discrete points.

Color maps are a one-dimensional visualization technique. They map one piece of information (i.e., a scalar value) into a color specification. However, the display of color information is not limited to one-dimensional displays. Often we use color information mapped onto 1D, 2D, or 3D objects. This is a simple way to increase the information content of our visualizations.

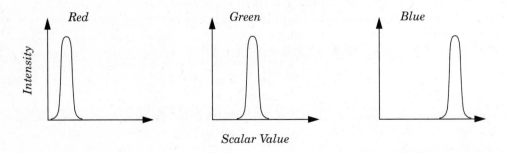

Figure 6–2 Transfer function for color components red, green, and blue as a function of scalar value.

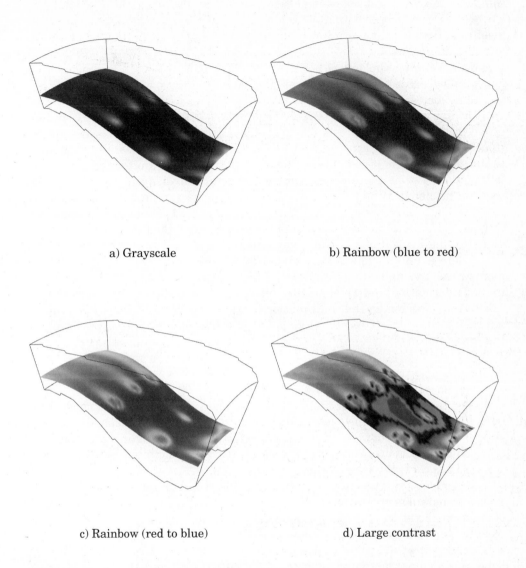

a) Grayscale   b) Rainbow (blue to red)

c) Rainbow (red to blue)   d) Large contrast

Figure 6–3 Flow density colored with different lookup tables a) Grayscale. b) Rainbow (blue to red). c) Rainbow (red to blue). d) Large contrast (`rainbow.tcl`).

The key to color mapping for scalar visualization is to choose the lookup table entries carefully. Figure **6–3** shows four different lookup tables used to visualize gas density as fluid flows through a combustion chamber. The first lookup table is grayscale. Grayscale tables often provide better structural detail to the eye. The other three images in Figure **6–3** use different color lookup tables. The second uses rainbow hues from blue to red. The third uses rainbow hues arranged from red to blue. The last table uses a table designed to enhance contrast. Careful use of colors can often enhance important features of a dataset. However, any type of lookup table can exaggerate unimportant details, or create visual artifacts because of unforeseen interactions between data, color choice, and human physiology.

Designing lookup tables is as much art as it is science. From a practical point of view, tables should accentuate important features, while minimizing less important or extraneous details. It is also desirable to use palettes that inherently contain scaling information. For example, a color rainbow scale from blue to red is often used to represent temperature scale, since many people associate "blue" with cold temperatures, and "red" with hot temperatures. However, even this scale is problematic: a physicist would say that blue is hotter than red, since hotter objects emit more blue light (i.e., shorter wavelength) than red. Also, there is no need to limit ourselves to "linear" lookup tables. Even though the mapping of scalars into colors has been presented as a linear operation (Figure **6–1**), the table itself need not be linear. That is, tables can be designed to enhance small variations in scalar value using logarithmic or other schemes.

There is another element to visualization that is the artistic, or aesthetic quality. Good visualizations represent a balance between effective communication of information and aesthetically pleasing presentation. While it is true in this day of mass media that information is often sacrificed for the sake of image, improving the comfort level and engaging the human observer more deeply in the presentation of data improves the effectiveness of communication.

Contouring

A natural extension to color mapping is *contouring*. When we see a surface colored with data values, the eye can separate similarly colored areas into distinct regions. When we contour data, we are effectively constructing the boundary between these regions. These boundaries correspond to contour lines (2D) or surfaces (3D) of constant scalar value.

Examples of 2D contour displays include weather maps annotated with lines of constant temperature (isotherms), or topological maps drawn with lines of constant elevation. Three-dimensional contours are called *isosurfaces*, and can be approximated by many polygonal primitives. Examples of isosurfaces include constant medical image intensity corresponding to body tissues such as skin, bone, or other organs. Other abstract isosurfaces such as surfaces of constant pressure or temperature in fluid flow also may be created.

The *marching cubes* [Lorensen87] algorithm is a simple, elegant technique for creating 3D isosurfaces. To explain this technique we introduce the *marching squares* algorithm, an analogous 2D technique.

Consider the 2D structured grid shown in Figure **6–4**. Scalar values are shown next to the points that define the grid. Contouring always begins by selecting a scalar value, or contour value, that corresponds to the contour lines or surfaces generated. To generate the contours, some form of interpolation must be used. This is because we have scalar values at a finite set of points in the dataset, and our contour value may lie between the point values. Since the most

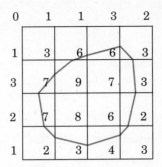

Figure 6–4 Contouring a 2D structured grid with contour line value = 5.

common interpolation technique is linear, we generate points on the contour surface by linear interpolation along the edges. If an edge has scalar values 10 and 0 at its two endpoints, and if we are trying to generate a contour line of value 5, then edge interpolation computes that the contour passes through the midpoint of the edge.

Once the points on cell edges are generated, we can connect these points into contours using a few different approaches. One approach detects an edge intersection (i.e., the contour passes through an edge) and then "tracks" this contour as it moves across cell boundaries. We know that if a contour edge enters a cell, it must exit a cell as well. The contour is tracked until it closes back on itself, or exits a dataset boundary. If it is known that only a single contour exists, then the process stops. Otherwise, every edge in the dataset must be checked to see whether other contour lines exist.

Another approach uses a divide and conquer technique, treating cells independently. This is the "marching squares" technique. The basic assumption of this technique, and its higher dimension counterparts, is that a contour can only pass through a cell in a finite number of ways. A case table is constructed that enumerates all possible topological *states* of a cell, given combinations of scalar values at the cell points. The number of topological states depends on the number of cell vertices, and the number of inside / outside relationships a vertex can have with respect to the contour value. A vertex is considered inside a contour if its scalar value is larger than the scalar value of the contour line. Vertices with scalar values less than the contour value are said to be outside the contour. For example, if a cell has four vertices and each vertex can be either inside or outside the contour, there are $2^4 = 16$ possible ways that contour lines can pass through the cell. In the case table we are not interested in where the contour passes through the cell, just whether it passes through the cell.

Figure **6–5** shows the sixteen combinations for a square cell. An index into the case table can be computed by encoding the state of each vertex as a binary digit. For 2D data represented on a rectangular grid, we can represent the 16 cases with 4 bit index. Once the proper case is selected, the location of the contour line / cell edge intersection can be calculated using interpolation. The algorithm processes a cell and then moves, or *marches to* the next cell. After all cells are visited, the contour will be completed. In summary, the marching algorithms proceeds as follows:

1. Select a cell.

2. Calculate the inside / outside state of each vertex of the cell.

3. Create an index by storing the binary state of each vertex in a separate bit.

4. Use the index to look up the topological state of the cell in a case table.

5. Calculate the contour locations for each edge in the case table.

Variations on how to select the next cell and interpolation schemes are possible.

There are advantages and disadvantages to both the edge tracking and marching cubes approaches. The marching squares algorithm is easy to implement. This is particularly important when we extend the technique into three dimensions, where isosurface tracking becomes much more difficult. On the other hand, the algorithm creates disconnected line segments and points, and a special hashing operation is required to remove duplicate points and join the separate line segments into a single polyline. If implemented properly, the tracking algorithm will generate a single polyline per contour line, avoiding the need to merge coincident points.

The 3D analogy of marching squares is *marching cubes*. Here, there are 256 different combinations of scalar value, given that there are eight points in a cubical cell (i.e., 2^8 combinations). Figure **6–6** shows these combinations reduced to 15 cases by using arguments of symmetry. We use combinations of rotation and mirroring to produce topologically equivalent cases.

An important issue is *contouring ambiguity*. Careful observation of marching squares cases numbered 5 and 10 and marching cubes cases numbered 3, 6, 7, 10, 12, and 13 shows that there are configurations where a cell can be contoured in more than one way. (This ambiguity also exists when using an edge tracking approach to contouring.) Contouring ambiguity arises on a 2D square or

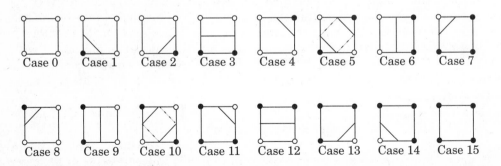

Figure 6–5 Sixteen different marching squares cases. Dark vertices indicate scalar value is above contour value. Cases 5 and 10 are ambiguous.

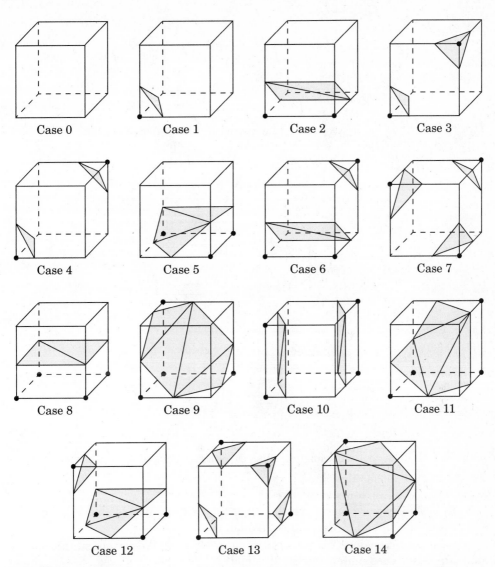

Figure 6–6 Marching cubes cases for 3D isosurface generation. The 256 possible cases have been reduced to 15 cases using symmetry. Dark vertices are greater than the selected isosurface value.

the face of a 3D cube when adjacent edge points are in different states, but diagonal vertices are in the same state.

In two dimensions, contour ambiguity is simple to treat: for each ambiguous case we implement one of the two possible cases. The choice for a particular case is independent of all other choices. Depending on the choice, the contour may either extend or break the current contour as illustrated in Figure **6–7**.

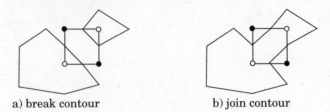

a) break contour   b) join contour

Figure 6–7 Choosing a particular contour case will break (a) or join (b) the current contour. Case shown is marching squares case 10.

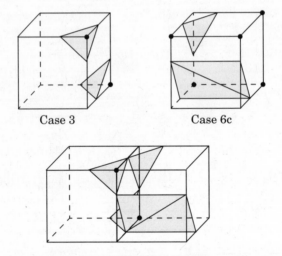

Case 3   Case 6c

Figure 6–8 Arbitrarily choosing marching cubes cases leads to holes in the isosurface.

Either choice is acceptable since the resulting contour lines will be continuous and closed (or will end at the dataset boundary).

In three dimensions the problem is more complex. We cannot simply choose an ambiguous case independent of all other ambiguous cases. For example Figure **6–8** shows what happens if we carelessly implement two cases independent of one another. In this figure we have used the usual case 3 but replaced case 6 with its *complementary* case. Complementary cases are formed by exchanging the "dark" vertices with "light" vertices. (This is equivalent to swapping vertex scalar value from above the isosurface value to below the isosurface value, and vice-versa.) The result of pairing these two cases is that a hole is left in the isosurface.

Several different approaches have been taken to remedy this problem. One approach tessellates the cubes with tetrahedron, and uses a *marching tetrahedra* technique. This works because the marching tetrahedra exhibit no ambigu-

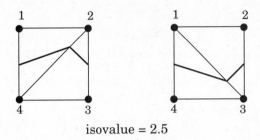

isovalue = 2.5

Figure 6–9 Using marching triangles or marching tetrahedra to resolve ambiguous cases on rectangular lattice (only face of cube is shown). Choice of diagonal orientation may result in "bumps" in contour surface. In 2D, diagonal orientation can be chosen arbitrarily, but in 3D diagonal is constrained by neighbor.

ous cases. Unfortunately, the marching tetrahedra algorithm generates isosurfaces consisting of more triangles, and the tessellation of a cube with tetrahedra requires making a choice regarding the orientation of the tetrahedra. This choice may result in artificial "bumps" in the isosurface because of interpolation along the face diagonals as shown in Figure **6–9**. Another approach evaluates the asymptotic behavior of the surface, and then chooses the cases to either join or break the contour. Nielson and Hamann [Nielson91] have developed a technique based on this approach they call the *asymptotic decider*. It is based on an analysis of the variation of the scalar variable across an ambiguous face. The analysis determines how the edges of isosurface polygons should be connected.

A simple and effective solution extends the original 15 marching cubes cases by adding additional complementary cases. These cases are designed to be compatible with neighboring cases and prevent the creation of holes in the isosurface. There are 6 complementary cases required, corresponding to the marching cubes cases 3, 6, 7, 10, 12, and 13. The complementary marching cubes cases are shown in Figure **6–10**.

We can extend the general approach of marching squares and marching cubes to other topological types. In **vtk** we use marching lines, triangles, and tetrahedra to contour cells of these types (or composite cells that are composed of these types). In addition, although we speak of regular types such as squares and cubes, marching cubes can be applied to any cell type topologically equivalent to a cube (e.g., hexahedron or non-cubical voxel).

Figure **6–11** shows four applications of contouring. In Figure **6–11**(a) we see 2D contour lines of CT density value corresponding to different tissue types. These lines were generated using marching squares. Figure **6–11**(b) through Figure **6–11**(d) are isosurfaces created by marching cubes. Figure **6–11**(b) is a surface of constant image intensity from a computed tomography (CT) X-ray imaging system. (Figure **6–11**(a) is a 2D subset of this data.) The intensity level corresponds to human bone. Figure **6–11**(c) is an isosurface of constant flow density. Figure **6–11**(d) is an isosurface of electron potential of a iron protein molecule. The image shown in Figure **6–11**(b) is immediately recognizable because of

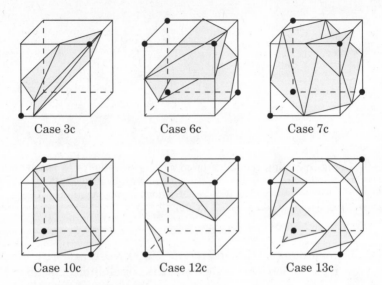

Figure 6–10 Marching cubes complementary cases.

our familiarity with human anatomy. However, for those practitioners in the fields of computational fluid dynamics and molecular biology, Figure **6–11**(c) and Figure **6–11**(d) are equally familiar. Methods for contouring are powerful but general techniques for visualizing data from a variety of fields.

Scalar Generation

The two visualization techniques presented thus far, color mapping and contouring, are simple, effective methods to display scalar information. It is natural to turn to these techniques first when visualizing data. However, often our data is not in a form convenient to these techniques. The data may not be single-valued (i.e., a scalar), or it may be a mathematical or other complex relationship. That is part of the fun and creative challenge of visualization: we must tap our creative resources to convert data into a form we can visualize.

For example, consider terrain data. We assume that the data is x-y-z coordinates, where x and y represent the coordinates in the plane, and z represents the elevation above sea level. Our desired visualization is to color the terrain according to elevation. This requires creating a colormap: possibly using white for high altitudes, blue for sea level and below, and various shades of green and brown corresponding to elevation between sea level and high altitude. We also need scalars to index into the colormap. The obvious choice here is to extract the z coordinate. That is, scalars are simply the z-coordinate value.

This example can be made more interesting by generalizing the problem. Although we could easily create a filter to extract the z-coordinate, we can create a filter that produces elevation scalar values where the elevation is measured

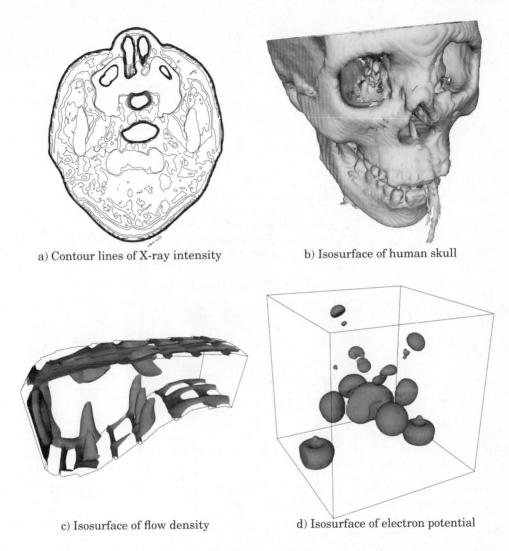

a) Contour lines of X-ray intensity

b) Isosurface of human skull

c) Isosurface of flow density

d) Isosurface of electron potential

Figure 6–11 Contouring examples. a) Marching squares used to generate contour lines (`headSlic.tcl`). b) Marching cubes surface of human bone (`headBone.tcl`). c) Marching cubes surface of flow density (`combIso.tcl`). d) Marching cubes surface of iron-protein (`ironPIso.tcl`).

along any axis. Given an oriented line starting at the point p_l (e.g., sea level) and ending at the point p_h (e.g., mountain top), we compute the elevation scalar s_i at point $p_i = (x_i, y_i, z_i)$ using the dot product as shown in Figure **6–12**. The scalar is normalized using the magnitude of the oriented line, and may be clamped between minimum and maximum scalar values (if necessary). The bottom half of this figure shows the results of applying this technique to a terrain model of

$$s_i = \frac{(p_i - p_0) \cdot (p_h - p_l)}{|p_h - p_l|^2}$$

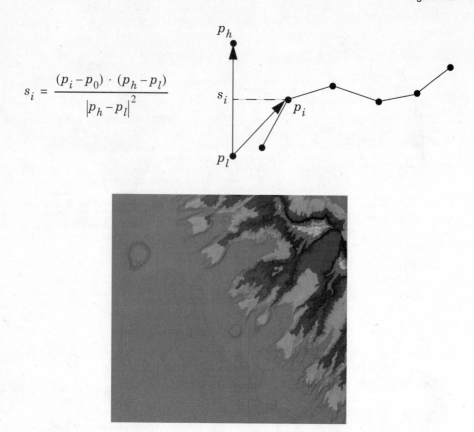

Figure 6–12 Computing scalars using normalized dot product. Bottom half of figure illustrates technique applied to terrain data from Honolulu, Hawaii (`hawaii.tcl`).

Honolulu, Hawaii. A lookup table of 256 ranging from deep blue (water) to yellow-white (mountain top) is used to color map this figure.

Part of the creative practice of visualization is selecting the best technique for given data from the palette of available techniques. Often this requires creative mapping by the user of the visualization system. In particular, to use scalar visualization techniques we need only to create a relationship to generate a unique scalar value. Other examples of scalar mapping include using data to index into a list of data, computing vector magnitude or matrix determinate, evaluating surface curvature, or determining distance between points. Scalar generation, when coupled with color mapping or contouring, is a simple yet effective technique for visualizing many types of data.

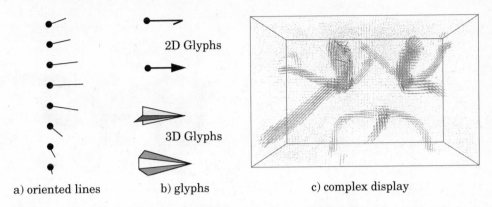

a) oriented lines   b) glyphs   c) complex display

Figure 6–13 Vector visualization techniques a) oriented lines b) using oriented glyphs c) complex vector visualization (complexV.tcl).

6.3 Vector Algorithms

Vector data is a three-dimensional representation of direction and magnitude. Vector data often results from the study of fluid flow, or when examining derivatives (i.e., rate of change) of some quantity.

Hedgehogs and Oriented Glyphs

A natural vector visualization technique is to draw an oriented, scaled line for each vector (Figure **6–13**(a)). The line begins at the point with which the vector is associated, and is oriented in the direction of the vector components (v_x, v_y, v_z). Typically, the resulting line must be scaled up or down to control the size of its visual representation. This technique is often referred to as a *hedgehog* because of the bristly result.

There are many variations of this technique (Figure **6–13**(b)). Arrows may be added to indicate the direction of the line. The lines may be colored according to vector magnitude, or some other scalar quantity (e.g., pressure or temperature). Also, instead of using a line, oriented "glyphs" can be used. By glyph we mean any 2D or 3D geometric representation such as an oriented triangle or cone.

Care should be used in applying these techniques. In 3D it is often difficult to understand the position and orientation of a vector because of its projection into a 2D image. Also, using large numbers of vectors can clutter the display to the point where the visualization becomes meaningless. Figure **6–13**(c) shows 167,000 3D vectors (using oriented and scaled lines) in the region of the human carotid artery. The larger vectors lie inside the arteries, the smaller vectors lie outside the arteries and are randomly oriented (measurement error) but small in

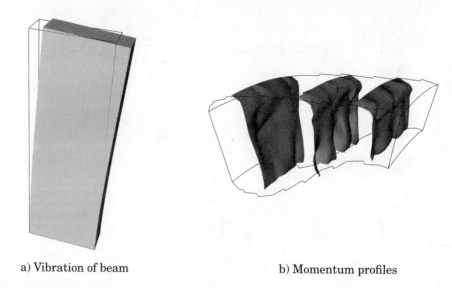

a) Vibration of beam   b) Momentum profiles

Figure 6–14 Warping geometry to show vector field. a) Beam displacement (`vib.tcl`). b) Flow momentum (`velProf.tcl`).

magnitude. Clearly the details of the vector field are not discernible from this image.

Scaling glyphs also poses interesting problems. In what Tufte has termed a "visualization lie," [Tufte83] scaling a 2D or 3D glyph results in non-linear differences in appearance. The surface area of an object increases with the square of its scale factor, so two vectors differing by a factor two in magnitude may appear up to four times different based on surface area. Such scaling issues are common in data visualization, and great care must be taken to avoiding misleading viewers.

Warping

Vector data is often associated with "motion." The motion is in the form of velocity or displacement. An effective technique for displaying such vector data is to "warp" or deform geometry according to the vector field. For example, imagine representing the displacement of a structure under load by deforming the structure. Or if we are visualizing the flow of fluid, we can create a flow profile by distorting a straight line inserted perpendicular to the flow.

Figure **6–14** shows two examples of vector warping. In the first example the motion of a vibrating beam is shown. The original undeformed outline is shown in wireframe. The second example shows warped planes in a structured grid dataset. The planes are warped according to flow momentum. The relative back and forward flow are clearly visible in the deformation of the planes.

Typically we must scale the vector field to control geometric distortion. Too small a distortion may not be visible, while too large a distortion can cause the structure to turn inside out. In such a case the viewer of the visualization is likely to lose context, and the visualization will become ineffective.

Displacement Plots

Vector displacement on the surface of an object can be visualized with displacement plots. A displacement plot shows the motion of an object in the direction perpendicular to its surface. The object motion is caused by an applied vector field. In a typical application the vector field is a displacement or strain field.

Vector displacement plots draw on the ideas in "Scalar Generation" on page 152. Vectors are converted to scalars by computing the dot product between the surface normal and vector at each point (Figure **6–15**(a)). If positive values result, the motion at the point is in the direction of the surface normal (i.e., positive displacement). Negative values indicate that the motion is opposite the surface normal (i.e., negative displacement).

A useful application of this technique is the study of vibration. In vibration analysis, we are interested in the eigenvalues (i.e., natural resonant frequencies) and eigenvectors (i.e., mode shapes) of a structure. To understand mode shapes we can use displacement plots to indicate regions of motion. There are special regions in the structure where positive displacement changes to negative displacement. These are regions of zero displacement. When plotted on the surface of the structure, these regions appear as the so-called *modal* lines of vibration. The study of modal lines has long been an important visualization tool for understanding mode shapes.

Figure **6–15**(b) shows modal lines for a vibrating plate. The vibration mode in this figure is the second torsional mode, clearly indicated by the crossing modal lines. (The aliasing in the figure is because of the coarseness of the analysis mesh.) To create the figure we combined the procedure of Figure **6–15**(a) with a special lookup table. The lookup table was arranged with dark areas in the center (i.e., corresponds to zero dot product) and bright areas at the beginning and end of the table (corresponds to 1 or -1 dot product). As a result, regions of large normal displacement are bright and regions near the modal lines are dark.

Time Animation

Some of the techniques described so far can be thought of as moving a point or object over a small time step. The hedgehog line is an approximation of a point's motion over a time period whose duration is given by the scale factor. In other words, if velocity $\vec{V} = dx/dt$, then the displacement of a point is

$$dx = \vec{V} \, dt \qquad \qquad \textbf{(6-1)}$$

This suggests an extension to our previous techniques: repeatedly displace points over many time steps. Figure **6–16** shows such an approach. Beginning with a sphere S centered about some point C, we move S repeatedly to generate the bubbles shown. The eye tends to trace out a path by connecting the bubbles,

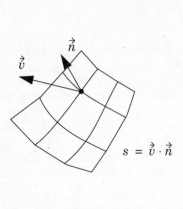

a) Scalar computation   b) Displacement plot

Figure 6–15 Vector displacement plots. a) Vector converted to scalar via dot product computation. b) Surface plot of vibrating plate. Dark areas show nodal lines. Bright areas show maximum motion (dispPlot.tcl).

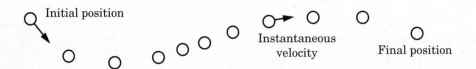

Figure 6–16 Time animation of a point C. Although the spacing between points varies, the time increment between each point is constant.

giving the observer a qualitative understanding of the fluid flow in that area. The bubbles may be displayed as an animation over time (giving the illusion of motion) or as a multiple exposure sequence (giving the appearance of a path).

Such an approach can be misused. For one thing, the velocity at a point is instantaneous. Once we move away from the point the velocity is likely to change. Using Equation **6-1** above assumes that the velocity is constant over the entire step. By taking large steps we are likely to jump over changes in the velocity. Using smaller steps we will end in a different position. Thus the choice of step size is a critical parameter in constructing accurate visualization of particle paths in a vector field.

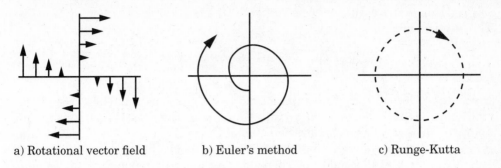

a) Rotational vector field   b) Euler's method   c) Runge-Kutta

Figure 6–17 Euler's integration (b) and Runge-Kutta integration of order 2 (c) applied to uniform rotational vector field (a). Euler's method will always diverge.

To evaluate Equation **6-1** we can express it as an integral:

$$\vec{x}(t) = \int_t \vec{V} dt \qquad\qquad \text{(6-2)}$$

Although this form cannot be solved analytically for most real world data, its solution can be approximated using numerical integration techniques. Accurate numerical integration is a topic beyond the scope of this book, but it is known that the accuracy of the integration is a function of the step size dt. Since the path is an integration throughout the dataset, the accuracy of the cell interpolation functions, as well as the accuracy of the original vector data, plays an important role in realizing accurate solutions. No definitive study is yet available that relates cell size or interpolation function characteristics to visualization error. But the lesson is clear: the result of numerical integration must be examined carefully, especially in regions of large vector field gradient. However, as with many other visualization algorithms, the insight gained by using vector integration techniques is qualitatively beneficial, despite the unavoidable numerical errors.

The simplest form of numerical integration is Euler's method,

$$\vec{x}_{i+1} = \vec{x}_i + \vec{V}_i \Delta t \qquad\qquad \text{(6-3)}$$

where the position at time $\vec{x}_{i+1}$ is the vector sum of the previous position plus the instantaneous velocity times the incremental time step Δt.

Euler's method has error on order of $O(\Delta t^2)$, which is not accurate enough for some applications. One such example is shown in Figure **6–17**. The velocity field describes perfect rotation about a central point. Using Euler's method we find that we will always diverge and instead of generating circles, will generate spirals instead.

In this text we will use the Runge-Kutta technique of order 2 [Conte72]. This is given by the expression

$$\vec{x}_{i+1} = \vec{x}_i + \frac{\Delta t}{2}\left(\vec{V}_i + \vec{V}_{i+1}\right)$$ (6-4)

where the velocity $\vec{V}_{i+1}$ is computed using Euler's method. The error of this method is $O(\Delta t^3)$. Compared to Euler's method, the Runge-Kutta technique allows us to take a larger integration step at the expense of one additional function evaluation. Generally this trade-off is beneficial, but like any numerical technique, the best method to use depends on the particular nature of the data. Higher-order techniques are also available, but generally not necessary, because the higher accuracy is countered by error in interpolation function or inherent in the data values. If you are interested in other integration formulas, please check the references at the end of the chapter.

One final note about accuracy concerns. The errors involved in either perception or computation of visualizations is an open research area. The discussion in the proceeding paragraph is a good example of this. There we characterized the error in streamline integration using conventional numerical integration arguments. But there is a problem with this argument. In visualization applications, we are integrating across cells whose function values are continuous, but whose derivatives are not. As the streamline crosses the cell boundary, subtle effects may occur that are not treated by the standard numerical analysis. Thus the standard arguments need to be extended for visualization applications.

Integration formulas require repeated transformation from global to local coordinates. Consider moving a point through a dataset under the influence of a vector field. The first step is to identify the cell that contains the point. This operation is a search (see "Searching" on page 241), plus a conversion to local coordinates. Once the cell is found, then the next step is to compute the velocity at that point by interpolating the velocity from the cell points. The point is then incrementally repositioned (using the integration formula Equation **6-4**). The process is then repeated until the point exits the dataset, or the distance or time traversed exceeds some specified value.

This process can be computationally demanding. There are two important steps we can take to improve performance.

- *Improving search procedures*. There are two distinct types of searches. Initially the starting location of the particle must be determined by a global search procedure. Once the initial location of the point is determined in the dataset, an incremental search procedure can then be used. Incremental searching is efficient because the motion of the point is limited within a single cell, or at most across a cell boundary. Thus, the search space is greatly limited, and the incremental search is faster relative to the global search.

- *Coordinate transformation*. The cost of a coordinate transformation from global to local coordinates can be reduced if either of the following conditions are true: the local and global coordinate systems are identical with one another (or vary by x-y-z translation), or if the vector field is transformed from global space to local coordinate space. The structured point coordinate system is an example of parallel coordinates, and global to local coordinate transformation can be greatly accelerated. If the vector field is transformed into local coordinates (either as a pre-processing step or on a cell-by-cell basis), then the integration can proceed completely in local space. Once the integration path is computed, selected points along the path can be transformed into global space for the sake of visualization.

Streamlines

A natural extension of the previous time animation techniques is to connect the point position $\vec{x}(t)$ over many time steps. The result is a numerical approximation to a particle trace represented as a line.

Borrowing terminology from the study of fluid flow, we can define three related line representation schemes for vector fields.

- *Particle traces* are trajectories traced by fluid particles over time.

- *Streaklines* are the set of particle traces at a particular time t_i that have previously passed through a specified point x_i.

- *Streamlines* are integral curves along a curve s satisfying the equation

$$s = \int_t \vec{V} ds, \text{ with } s = s(x, \bar{t}) \tag{6-5}$$

for a particular time $\bar{t}$.

Streamlines, streaklines, and particle traces are equivalent to one another if the flow is steady. In time-varying flow, a given streamline exists only at one moment in time. Visualization systems generally provide facilities to compute particle traces. However, if time is fixed, the same facility can be used to compute streamlines. In general, we will use the term streamline to refer to the method of tracing trajectories in a vector field. Please bear in mind the differences in these representations if the flow is time-varying.

Figure **6–18** shows forty streamlines in a small kitchen. The room has two windows, a door (with air leakage) and a cooking area with a hot stove. The air leakage and temperature variation combine to produce air convection currents throughout the kitchen. The starting positions of the streamlines were defined by creating a *rake*, or curve (and its associated points). Here the rake was a straight line. These streamlines clearly show features of the flow field. By releasing many streamlines simultaneously we obtain even more information, as the eye tends to assemble nearby streamlines into a "global" understanding of flow field features.

Many enhancements of streamline visualization exist. Lines can be colored according to velocity magnitude to indicate speed of flow. Other scalar quantities such as temperature or pressure also may be used to color the lines. We also may

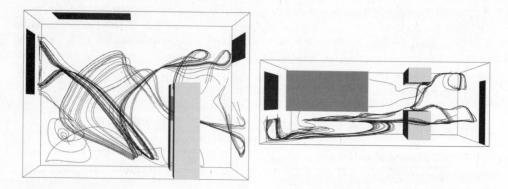

Figure 6–18   Flow velocity computed for a small kitchen (top and side view). Forty streamlines start along the rake positioned under the window. Some eventually travel over the hot stove and are convected upwards (`Kitchen.cc`).

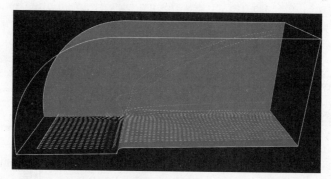

Figure 6–19   Dashed streamlines around a blunt fin. Each dash is a constant time increment. Fast moving particles create longer dashes than slower moving particles. The streamlines also are colored by flow density scalar (`bluntStr.cc`).

create constant time dashed lines. Each dash represents a constant time increment. Thus, in areas of high velocity, the length of the dash will be greater relative to regions of lower velocity. These techniques are illustrated in Figure **6–19** for airflow around a bluntfin. This example consists of a wall with half a rounded fin projecting into the fluid flow. (Using arguments of symmetry only half of the domain was modelled.) Twenty-five streamlines are released upstream of the fin. The boundary layer effects near the junction of the fin and wall are clearly evident from the streamlines. In this area flow recirculation is apparent, as well as the reduced flow speed.

$$
\begin{bmatrix}
\sigma_x & \tau_{xy} & \tau_{xz} \\
\tau_{yx} & \sigma_y & \tau_{yz} \\
\tau_{zx} & \tau_{zy} & \sigma_z
\end{bmatrix}
\qquad
\begin{bmatrix}
\dfrac{\partial u}{\partial x} & \left(\dfrac{\partial u}{\partial y}+\dfrac{\partial v}{\partial z}\right) & \left(\dfrac{\partial u}{\partial z}+\dfrac{\partial w}{\partial x}\right) \\
\left(\dfrac{\partial u}{\partial y}+\dfrac{\partial v}{\partial z}\right) & \dfrac{\partial v}{\partial y} & \left(\dfrac{\partial v}{\partial z}+\dfrac{\partial w}{\partial y}\right) \\
\left(\dfrac{\partial u}{\partial z}+\dfrac{\partial w}{\partial x}\right) & \left(\dfrac{\partial v}{\partial z}+\dfrac{\partial w}{\partial y}\right) & \dfrac{\partial w}{\partial z}
\end{bmatrix}
$$

a) Stress tensor   b) Strain tensor

Figure 6–20 Stress and strain tensors. Normal stresses in the x-y-z coordinate direc tions indicated as $\sigma_x, \sigma_y, \sigma_z$, shear stresses indicated as τ_{ij}. Material displacement rep resented by u, v, w components.

6.4 Tensor Algorithms

As we mentioned earlier, tensor visualization is an active area of research. How-ever there are a few simple techniques that we can use to visualize 3×3 real symmetric tensors. Such tensors are used to describe the state of displacement or stress in a 3D material. The stress and strain tensors for an elastic material are shown in Figure **6–20**.

In these tensors the diagonal coefficients are the so-called normal stresses and strains, and the off-diagonal terms are the shear stresses and strains. Nor-mal stresses and strains act perpendicular to a specified surface, while shear stresses and strains act tangentially to the surface. Normal stress is either com-pression or tension, depending on the sign of the coefficient.

A 3×3 real symmetric matrix can be characterized by three vectors in 3D called the eigenvectors, and three numbers called the eigenvalues of the matrix. The eigenvectors form a 3D coordinate system whose axes are mutually perpen-dicular. In some applications, particularly the study of materials, these axes also are referred to as the principle axes of the tensor and are physically significant. For example, if the tensor is a stress tensor, then the principle axes are the direc-tions of normal stress and no shear stress. Associated with each eigenvector is an eigenvalue. The eigenvalues are often physically significant as well. In the study of vibration, eigenvalues correspond to the resonant frequencies of a structure, and the eigenvectors are the associated mode shapes.

Mathematically we can represent eigenvalues and eigenvectors as follows. Given a matrix **A**, the eigenvector $\vec{x}$ and eigenvalue λ must satisfy the relation

$$A \cdot \vec{x} = \lambda \vec{x} \qquad \text{(6-6)}$$

For Equation **6-6** to hold, the matrix determinate must satisfy

$$\det|A - \lambda I| = 0 \qquad \text{(6-7)}$$

Expanding this equation yields a nth degree polynomial in λ whose roots are the eigenvalues. Thus, there are always n eigenvalues, although they may not be distinct. In general, Equation **6-7** is not solved using polynomial root searching because of poor computational performance. (For matrices of order 3 root searching is acceptable because we can solve for the eigenvalues analytically.) Once we determine the eigenvalues, we can substitute each into Equation **6-7** to solve for the associated eigenvectors.

We can express the eigenvectors of the 3×3 system as

$$\vec{v}_i = \lambda_i \vec{e}_i, \text{ with } i = 1, 2, 3 \tag{6-8}$$

with $\vec{e}_i$ a unit vector in the direction of the eigenvalue, and λ_i the eigenvalues of the system. If we order eigenvalues such that

$$\lambda_1 \geq \lambda_2 \geq \lambda_3 \tag{6-9}$$

then we refer to the corresponding eigenvectors $\vec{v}_1$, $\vec{v}_2$, and $\vec{v}_3$ as the *major*, *medium*, and *minor* eigenvectors.

Tensor Ellipsoids

This leads us to the tensor ellipsoid technique for the visualization of real, symmetric 3×3 matrices. The first step is to extract eigenvalues and eigenvectors as described in the previous section. Since eigenvectors are known to be orthogonal, the eigenvectors form a local coordinate system. These axes can be taken as the *minor*, *medium*, and *major* axes of an ellipsoid. Thus, the shape and orientation of the ellipsoid represent the relative size of the eigenvalues and the orientation of the eigenvectors.

To form the ellipsoid we begin by positioning a sphere at the tensor location. The sphere is then rotated around its origin using the eigenvectors, which in the form of Equation **6-8** are direction cosines. The eigenvalues are used to scale the sphere. Using 4×4 transformation matrices and referring to Equation **3-6**, Equation **3-9**, and Equation **3-13**, we form the ellipsoid by transforming the sphere centered at the origin using the matrix T

$$T = T_T \cdot T_R \cdot T_S \tag{6-10}$$

(remember to read right-to-left). The eigenvectors can be directly plugged in to create the rotation matrix, while the point coordinates x-y-z and eigenvalues $\lambda_1 \geq \lambda_2 \geq \lambda_3$ are inserted into the translation and scaling matrices. A concatenation of these matrices forms the final transformation matrix T.

Figure **6–21**(a) depicts the tensor ellipsoid technique. In Figure **6–21**(b) we show this technique to visualize material stress near a point load on the surface of a semi-infinite domain. (This is the so-called Boussinesq's problem.) From Saada [Saada74] we have the analytic expression for the stress components in Cartesian coordinates shown in Figure **6–21**(c). Note that the z-direction is defined as the axis originating at the point of application of the force P. The vari-

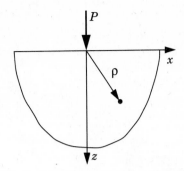

a) Tensor ellipsoid

b) Point load on semi-infinite domain

$$\sigma_x = -\frac{P}{2\pi\rho^2}\left(\frac{3zx^2}{\rho^3} - (1-2v)\left(\frac{z}{\rho} - \frac{\rho}{\rho+z} + \frac{x^2(2\rho+z)}{\rho(\rho+z)^2}\right)\right)$$

$$\sigma_y = -\frac{P}{2\pi\rho^2}\left(\frac{3zy^2}{\rho^3} - (1-2v)\left(\frac{z}{\rho} - \frac{\rho}{\rho+z} + \frac{y^2(2\rho+z)}{\rho(\rho+z)^2}\right)\right)$$

$$\sigma_z = -\frac{3Pz^3}{2\pi\rho^5}$$

$$\tau_{xy} = \tau_{yx} = -\frac{P}{2\pi\rho^2}\left(\frac{3xyz}{\rho^3} - (1-2v)\left(\frac{xy(2\rho+z)}{\rho(\rho+z)^2}\right)\right)$$

$$\tau_{xz} = \tau_{zx} = -\frac{3Pxz^2}{2\pi\rho^5}$$

$$\tau_{yz} = \tau_{zy} = -\frac{3Pyz^2}{2\pi\rho^5}$$

c) Analytic solution

Figure 6–21 Tensor ellipsoids. a) Ellipsoid oriented along eigenvalues (i.e., principle aces) of tensor. b) Pictorial description of Boussinesq's problem. c) Analytic results according to Saada.

able ρ is the distance from the point of load application to a point x-y-z. The orientation of the x and y axes are in the plane perpendicular to the z axis. (The rotation in the plane of these axes is unimportant since the solution is symmetric around the z axis). (The parameter v is Poisson's ratio which is a property of the material. Poisson's ratio relates the lateral contraction of a material to axial elongation under a uniaxial stress condition. See [Saada74] or [Timoshenko70] for more information.)

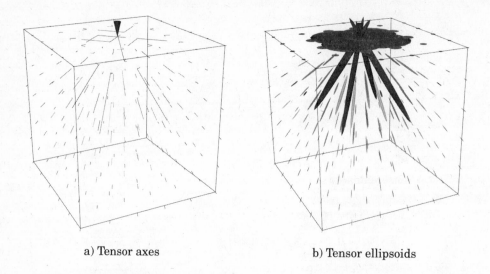

a) Tensor axes   b) Tensor ellipsoids

Figure 6–22 Tensor visualization techniques. a) Tensor axes (`TenAxes.tcl`). b) Tensor ellipsoids (`TenEllip.tcl`).

In Figure **6–22** we visualize the analytical results of Boussinesq's problem from Saada. The left hand portion of the figure shows the results by displaying the scaled and oriented principal axes of the stress tensor. (These are called *tensor axes*.) In the right hand portion we use tensor ellipsoids to show the same result. Tensor ellipsoids and tensor axes are a form of *glyph* (see "Glyphs" on page 173) specialized to tensor visualization.

A certain amount of care must be taken to visualize this result since there is a stress singularity at the point of contact of the load. In a real application loads are applied over a small area, and not at a single point. Also, plastic behavior prevents stress levels from exceeding a certain point. The results of the visualization, as with any computer process, are only as good as the underlying model.

6.5 Modelling Algorithms

Modelling algorithms are the catch-all category for our taxonomy of visualization techniques. Modelling algorithms have one thing in common: they create or change dataset geometry or topology.

Source Objects

As we have seen in previous examples, source objects begin the visualization pipeline. Source objects are used to create geometry such as spheres, cones, or cubes to support visualization context, or are used to read in data files. Source objects also may be used to create dataset attributes. Some examples of source objects and their use are as follows.

Modelling Simple Geometry

Spheres, cones, cubes, and other simple geometric objects can be used alone or in combination to model geometry. Often we visualize real-world applications such as air flow in a room, and need to show real world objects such as furniture, windows, or doors. Real-world objects often can be represented using these simple geometric representations. These source objects generate their data procedurally. Alternatively, we may use reader objects to access geometric data defined in data files. These data files may contain more complex geometry such as that produced by a 3D CAD (Computer-Aided Design) system.

Supporting Geometry

During the visualization process we may use source objects to create supporting geometry. This may be as simple as three lines to represent a coordinate axis, or as complex as tubes wrapped around line segments to thicken and enhance their appearance. Another common use is as supplemental input to objects such as streamlines or probe filters. These filters take a second input that defines a set of points. For streamlines, the points determine the initial positions for generating the streamlines. The probe filter uses the points as the position to compute attribute values such as scalars, vectors, or tensors.

Data Attribute Creation

Source objects can be used as procedures to create data attributes. For example, we can procedurally create textures and texture coordinates. Another use is to create scalar values over a uniform grid. If the scalar values are generated from a mathematical function, then we can use the visualization techniques described here to visualize the function. In fact, this leads us to a very important class of source objects: implicit functions.

Implicit Functions

Implicit functions are functions of the form

$$F(x, y, z) = c \qquad \text{(6-11)}$$

where c is an arbitrary constant. Implicit functions have three important properties.

- *Simple geometric description.* Implicit functions are convenient tools to describe common geometric shapes. This includes planes, spheres, cylinders, cones, ellipsoids, and quadrics.

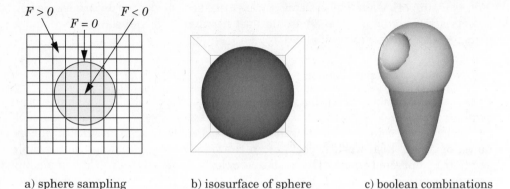

a) sphere sampling   b) isosurface of sphere   c) boolean combinations

Figure 6–23 Sampling functions a) 2D depiction of sphere sampling, b) Isosurface of sampled sphere. c) Boolean combination of two spheres, a cone, and two planes. (One sphere intersects the other, the planes clip the cone). (Refer to `sphere.tcl` and `iceCream.tcl`.)

- *Region separation.* Implicit functions separate 3D Euclidean space into three distinct regions. These regions are inside, on, and outside the implicit function. These regions are defined as $F(x, y, z) < 0$, $F(x, y, z) = 0$, and $F(x, y, z) > 0$, respectively.

- *Scalar generation.* Implicit functions convert a position in space into a scalar value. That is, given an implicit function we can sample it at a point (x_i, y_i, z_i) to generate a scalar value c_i.

An example of an implicit function is the equation for a sphere of radius R

$$F(x, y, z) = x^2 + y^2 + z^2 - R^2 \qquad \textbf{(6-12)}$$

This simple relationship defines the three regions $F(x, y, z) = 0$ (on the surface of the sphere), $F(x, y, z) < 0$ (inside the sphere), and $F(x, y, z) > 0$ (outside the sphere). Any point may be classified inside, on, or outside the sphere simply by evaluating Equation **6-12**.

Implicit functions have a variety of uses. This includes geometric modelling, selecting data, and visualizing complex mathematical descriptions.

Modelling Objects

Implicit functions can be used alone or in combination to model geometric objects. For example, to model a surface described by an implicit function, we sample F on a dataset and generate an isosurface at a contour value c_i. The result is a polygonal representation of the function. Figure **6–23**(b) shows an isosurface for a sphere of radius=1 sampled on a volume. Note that we can choose non-zero contour values to generate a family of offset surfaces. This is useful for creating blending functions and other special effects.

Implicit functions can be combined to create complex objects using the boolean operators union, intersection, and difference. The union operation $F \cup G$ between two functions $F(x, y, z)$ and $G(x, y, z)$ at a point (x_0, y_0, z_0) is the minimum value

$$F \cup G = min\,(F(x_0, y_0, z_0), G(x_0, y_0, z_0))$$ **(6-13)**

The intersection between two implicit functions is given by

$$F \cap G = max\,(F(x_0, y_0, z_0), G(x_0, y_0, z_0))$$ **(6-14)**

The difference of two implicit functions is given by

$$F - G = max\,(F(x_0, y_0, z_0), -G(x_0, y_0, z_0))$$ **(6-15)**

Figure **6–23**(c) shows a combination of simple implicit functions to create an ice-cream cone. The cone is created by clipping the (infinite) cone function with two planes. The ice cream is constructed by performing a difference operation on a larger sphere with a smaller offset sphere to create the "bite." The resulting surface was extracted using surface contouring with isosurface value 0.0.

Selecting Data

We can take advantage of the properties of implicit functions to select and cut data. In particular we will use the region separation property to select data. (We will discuss data cutting in "Cutting" on page 175.)

Selecting or extracting data with an implicit function means choosing cells and points (and associated attribute data) that lie within a particular region of the function. To determine whether a point x-y-z lies within a region, we simply evaluate the point and examine the sign of the result. A cell lies in a region if all its points lie in the region.

Figure **6–24**(a) shows a 2D implicit function, here an ellipse, used to select the data (i.e., points, cells, and data attributes) contained within it. Boolean combinations also can be used to create complex selection regions as illustrated in Figure **6–24**(b). Here, two ellipses are used in combination to select voxels within a volume dataset. Note that extracting data often changes the structure of the dataset. In Figure **6–24** the input type is a structured points dataset, while the output type is an unstructured grid dataset.

Visualizing Mathematical Descriptions

Some functions, often discrete or probabilistic in nature, cannot be cast into the form of Equation **6-11**. However, by applying some creative thinking we can often generate scalar values that can be visualized. An interesting example of this is the so-called *strange attractor*.

Strange attractors arise in the study of nonlinear dynamics and chaotic systems. In these systems, the usual types of dynamic motion – equilibrium, periodic motion, or quasi-periodic motion – are not present. Instead, the system

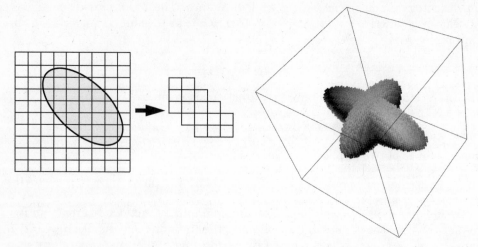

a) Selecting data with implicit function   b) Selecting data with boolean combination

Figure 6–24 Implicit functions used to select data. a) 2D cells lying in ellipse are selected. b) Two ellipsoids combined using the union operation used to select voxels from a volume. Voxels shrunk 50% (`extractD.tcl`).

exhibits chaotic motion. The resulting behavior of the system can change radically as a result of small perturbations in its initial conditions.

A classical strange attractor was developed by Lorenz in 1963 [Lorenz63]. Lorenz developed a simple model for thermally induced fluid convection in the atmosphere. Convection causes rings of rotating fluid and can be developed from the general Navier-Stokes partial differential equations for fluid flow. The Lorenz equations can be expressed in non-dimensional form as

$$\frac{dx}{dt} = \sigma\,(y - x)$$

$$\frac{dy}{dt} = \rho x - y - xz \qquad\qquad \textbf{(6-16)}$$

$$\frac{dz}{dt} = xy - \beta z$$

where x is proportional to the fluid velocity in the fluid ring, y and z measure the fluid temperature in the plane of the ring, the parameters σ and ρ are related to the Prandtl number and Raleigh number, respectively, and β is a geometric factor.

Certainly these equations are not in the implicit form of Equation **6-11**, so how do we visualize them? Our solution is to treat the variables x, y, and z as the

Figure 6–25 Visualizing a Lorenz strange attractor by integrating the Lorenz equations in a volume. The number of visits in each voxel is recorded as a scalar function. The surface is extracted via marching cubes using a visit value of 50. The number of integration steps is 10 million, in a volume of dimensions 200^3. The surface roughness is caused by the discrete nature of the evaluation function (`Lorenz.cc`).

coordinates of a three-dimensional space, and integrate Equation **6-16** to generate the system "trajectory", that is, the state of the system through time. The integration is carried out within a volume and scalars are created by counting the number of times each voxel is visited. By integrating long enough, we can create a volume representing the "surface" of the strange attractor, Figure **6–25**. The surface of the strange attractor is extracted by using marching cubes and a scalar value specifying the number of visits in a voxel.

Implicit Modelling

In the previous section we saw how implicit functions, or boolean combinations of implicit functions, could be used to model geometric objects. The basic approach is to evaluate these functions on a regular array of points, or volume, and then to generate scalar values at each point in the volume. Then either volume rendering (see "Volume Rendering" on page 209), or isosurface generation in combination with surface rendering, is used to display the model.

An extension of this approach, called implicit modelling, is similar to modelling with implicit functions. The difference lies in the fact that scalars are generated using a distance function instead of the usual implicit function. The distance function is computed as a Euclidean distance to a set of generating primitives such as points, lines, or polygons. For example, Figure **6–26** shows the distance functions to a point, line, and triangle. Because distance functions are well-behaved monotonic functions, we can define a series of offset surfaces by

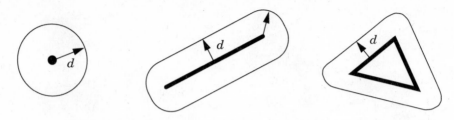

Figure 6–26 Distance functions to a point, line, and triangle.

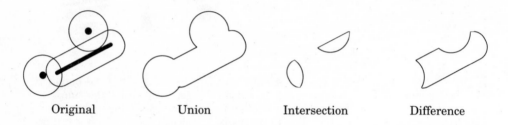

Original   Union   Intersection   Difference

Figure 6–27 Boolean operations using points and lines as generating primitives.

specifying different isosurface values, where the value is the distance to the generating primitive. The isosurfaces form approximations to the true offset surfaces, but using high volume resolution we can achieve satisfactory results.

Used alone the generating primitives are limited in their ability to model complex geometry. By using boolean combinations of the primitives, however, complex geometry can be easily modelled. The boolean operations union, intersection, and difference (Equation **6-13**, Equation **6-14**, and Equation **6-15**, respectively) are illustrated in Figure **6–27**. Figure **6–28** shows the application of implicit modelling to "thicken" the line segments in the text symbol "HELLO". The isosurface is generated on a $110 \times 40 \times 20$ volume at a distance offset of 0.25 units. The generating primitives were combined using the boolean union operator. Although Euclidean distance is always a non-negative value, it is possible to use a signed distance function for objects that have an outside and an inside. A negative distance is the negated distance of a point inside the object to the surface of the object. Using a signed distance function allows us to create offset surfaces that are contained within the actual surface.

Another interesting feature of implicit modelling is that when isosurfaces are generated, more than one connected surface can result. These situations occur when the generating primitives form concave features. Figure **6–29** illustrates this situation. If desired, multiple surfaces can be separated by using the connectivity algorithm described in "Connectivity" on page 287.

Figure 6–28 Implicit modelling used to thicken a stroked font. Original lines can be seen within the translucent implicit surface (`hello.tcl`).

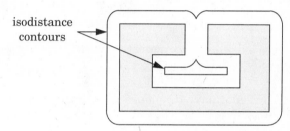

Figure 6–29 Concave features can result in multiple contour lines/surfaces.

Glyphs

Glyphs, sometimes referred to as icons, are a versatile technique to visualize data of every type. A glyph is an "object" that is affected by its input data. This object may be geometry, a dataset, or a graphical image. The glyph may orient, scale, translate, deform, or somehow alter the appearance of the object in response to data. We have already seen a simple form of glyph: hedgehogs are lines that are oriented, translated and scaled according to the position and vector value of a point. A variation of this is to use oriented cones or arrows. (See "Hedgehogs and Oriented Glyphs" on page 155.)

More elaborate glyphs are possible. In one creative visualization technique Chernoff [Chernoff73] tied data values to an iconic representation of the human face. Eyebrows, nose, mouth, and other features were modified according to financial data values. This interesting technique built on the human capability to recognize facial expression. By tying appropriate data values to facial characteristics, rapid identification of important data points is possible.

In a sense, glyphs represent the fundamental result of the visualization process. Moreover, all the visualization techniques we present can be treated as concrete representations of an abstract glyph class. For example, while hedgehogs are an obvious manifestation of a vector glyph, isosurfaces can be considered a topologically two-dimensional glyph for scalar data. Delmarcelle and

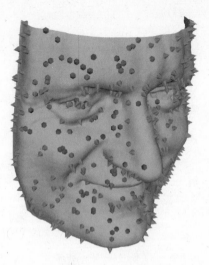

Figure 6–30 Glyphs indicate surface normals on model of human face. Glyphs positions are randomly selected (`spikeF.tcl`).

Hesselink [Delmarcelle95] have developed a unified framework for flow visualization based on types of glyphs. They classify glyphs according to one of three categories.

- *Elementary icons* represent their data across the extent of their spatial domain. For example, an oriented arrow can be used to represent surface normal.

- *Local icons* represent elementary information plus a local distribution of the values around the spatial domain. A surface normal vector colored by local curvature is one example of a local icon, since local data beyond the elementary information is encoded.

- *Global icons* show the structure of the complete dataset. An isosurface is an example of a global icon.

This classification scheme can be extended to other visualization techniques such as vector and tensor data, or even to non-visual forms such as sound or tactile feedback. We have found this classification scheme to be helpful when designing visualizations or creating visualization techniques. Often it gives insight into ways of representing data that can be overlooked.

Figure **6–30** is an example of glyphing. Small 3D cones are oriented on a surface to indicate the direction of the surface normal. A similar approach could be used to show other surface properties such as curvature or anatomical keypoints.

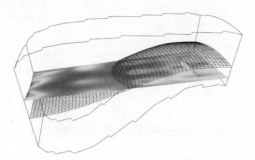

Figure 6–31 Cut through structured grid with plane. The cut plane is shown solid shaded. A computational plane of constant k value is shown in wireframe for comparison (`cut.tcl`).

Cutting

Often we want to cut through a dataset with a surface and then display the interpolated data values on the surface. We refer to this technique as *data cutting* or simply *cutting*. The data cutting operation requires two pieces of information: a definition for the surface, and a dataset to cut. We will assume that the cutting surface is defined by an implicit function. A typical application of cutting is to slice through a dataset with a plane, and color map the scalar data and/or warp the plane according to vector value.

A property of implicit functions is to convert a position into a scalar value (see "Implicit Functions" on page 167). We can use this property in combination with a contouring algorithm (e.g., marching cubes) to generate cut surfaces. The basic idea is to generate scalars for each point of each cell of a dataset, and then contour the surface value $F(x, y, z) = 0$.

The cutting algorithm proceeds as follows. For each cell, function values are generated by evaluating $F(x, y, z)$ for each cell point. If all the points evaluate positive or negative, then the surface does not cut the cell. However, if the points evaluate positive and negative, then the surface passes through the cell. We can use the cell contouring operation to generate the isosurface $F(x, y, z) = 0$. Data attribute values can then be computed by interpolating along cut edges.

Figure **6–31** illustrates a plane cut through a structured grid dataset. The plane passes through the center of the dataset with normal (-0.287, 0, 0.9579). For comparison purposes a portion of the grid geometry is also shown. The grid geometry is the grid surface $k=9$ (shown in wireframe). A benefit of cut surfaces is that we can view data on (nearly) arbitrary surfaces. Thus, the structure of the dataset does not constrain how we view the data.

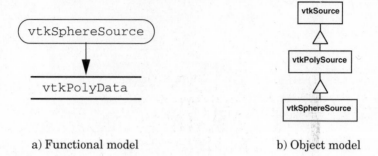

a) Functional model   b) Object model

Figure 6–32 Source object design. Example shown is a source object that creates a polygonal representation of a sphere.

6.6 Putting It All Together

Process Object Design

Algorithms are implemented in the *Visualization Toolkit* as process objects. These objects may be either sources, filters, or mappers (See "The Visualization Pipeline" on page 79.) In this section we will describe how these objects are implemented.

Source Design

Source objects have no visualization data for input and one or more outputs, Figure **6–32**. To create a source object, inheritance is used to specify the type of dataset that the process object creates for output. Figure **6–32** illustrates this for the concrete source object vtkSphereSource. This class inherits from vtk-Source, indicating that it is a source object, and vtkPolyData, indicating that it creates polygonal data on output.

The convenience object vtkPolySource has been created to simplify subclass derivation. For example, vtkBYUReader is also of type vtkPolySource. The major difference between vtkSphereSource and vtkBYUReader is the implementation of the virtual method Execute(). This method actually creates its output data. If you derive a source object you do not need to make it a subclass of any convenience object (e.g., vtkPolySource) but you should derive it from vtkSource. This is especially true when multiple-output objects are created, since no convenience classes exist expressly for derivation in this case.

Filter Design

Filter objects have one or more inputs and one or more outputs as shown in Figure **6–33**. (You may also refer to "Multiple Input / Output" on page 92.) To create a filter object, inheritance is used to specify the type of input and output data

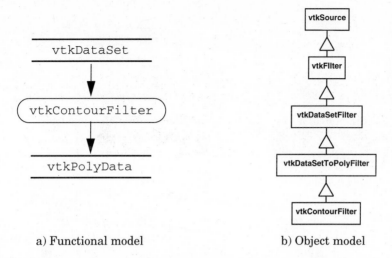

a) Functional model   b) Object model

Figure 6–33 Filter object design. Example shown is for an object that receives a general dataset as input, and creates polygonal data on output.

objects. Figure **6–33** illustrates this for the concrete source object vtkContourFilter (which implements marching cubes and other contouring techniques). It is worth examining this object diagram in detail since it is the basis for the architecture of the visualization pipeline.

The superclasses of vtkContourFilter are vtkSource, vtkFilter, vtkDataSetFilter, and vtkDataSetToPolyFilter. Although the inheritance of vtkContourFilter from vtkSource may be confusing at first glance, the meaning is this: the filter is a source of visualization data. Similarly, inheritance from vtkFilter means that vtkContourFilter has at least one input. The class vtkDataSetFilter specifies the type of data vtkContourFilter takes as input (i.e., a dataset), while vtkDataSetToPolyFilter specifies the type of output (i.e., polygonal data). Note that inheritance from vtkDataSetFilter and vtkDataSetToPolyFilter is optional – this functionality could be implemented directly in vtkContourFilter. These optional objects are simply convenience objects to make class derivation a little easier.

What is left for vtkContourFilter to implement is its Execute() method (as well as constructor, print method, and any other methods special to this class). Thus the primary difference between classes with equivalent inheritance hierarchies is the implementation of the Execute() method.

As we mentioned a moment ago, the class vtkDataSetFilter enforces filter input type with the type checking features of the C++ compiler. It accepts type vtkDataSet (or subclasses). Since vtkDataSet is a base class for all data types, this filter will accept any type as input. Specialized filters are derived from other classes. For example, filters that accept polygonal data are derived from vtkPolyFilter, and filters that accept structured point datasets are derived from vtkStructuredPointsFilter.

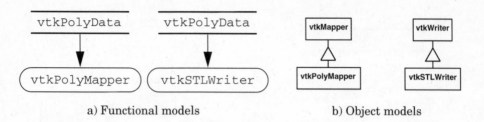

a) Functional models   b) Object models

Figure 6–34   Mapper object design. Graphics mapper shown (e.g., vtkPolyMapper) maps polygonal data through graphics library primitives. Writer shown (e.g., vtkSTL-Writer) writes polygonal data to stereo lithography format.

We encourage you to examine the source code carefully (included on CD-ROM) for a few filter and source objects. The architecture is simple enough that you can grasp it quickly.

Mapper Design

Mapper objects have one or more inputs and no visualization data output, Figure **6–34**. Two different types of mappers are available in the *Visualization Toolkit*: graphics mappers and writers. Graphics mappers interface geometric structure and data attributes to the graphics library. Writers write datasets to disk or other I/O devices.

Since mappers take datasets as input, type enforcement is required. Each mapper implements this functionality directly. For example, class vtkPolyMapper and vtkSTLWriter both implement a SetInput() method to enforce the input to be of type vtkPolyData. Other mappers and writers enforce input type as appropriate.

Although writers and mappers do not create visualization data, they both have methods similar to the Execute() method of the sources and filters. Each subclass of vtkMapper must implement the Render() method. This method is exchanged by the graphics system actors and its associated mappers during the rendering process. The effect of the method is to map its input dataset to the appropriate rendering library/system. Subclasses of the class vtkWriter must implement the WriteData() method. This method causes the writer to write its input dataset to disk (or other I/O device).

Color Maps

Color maps are created in the *Visualization Toolkit* using instances of the class vtkLookupTable. This class allows you to create a lookup table using HSVA (e.g., hue, saturation, value, and alpha transparency value) specification. Although we discussed the HSV color system in Chapter 3, we haven't yet defined alpha transparency. We shall do so in Chapter 7, but until then consider the alpha value to be the opacity of an object. Alpha values of one indicate that the object is opaque, while alpha values of zero indicate that the object is transparent.

`vtkLookupTable` also enables you to load colors directly into the table. Thus, you build custom tables that cannot be simply expressed as linear ramps of HSVA values.

To create a lookup table we specify a starting and ending value for each of the components of HSVA, and the number of table entries. For example, to create a rainbow lookup table from blue to red we can use the following C++ code.

```
vtkLookupTable *lut=new vtkLookupTable;
    lut->SetHueRange(0.6667, 0.0);
    lut->SetSaturationRange(1.0, 1.0);
    lut->SetValueRange(1.0, 1.0);
    lut->SetAlphaRange(1.0, 1.0);
    lut->SetNumberOfColors(256);
    lut->Build();
```

Since the default values for `SaturationRange`, `ValueRange`, `AlphaRange`, and the number of lookup table colors are (1,1), (1,1), (1,1), and 256, respectively, we can simplify this process to the following

```
vtkLookupTable *lut=new vtkLookupTable;
    lut->SetHueRange(0.6667, 0.0);
    lut->Build();
```

(The default values for `HueRange` are (0.0, 0.6667) - a red to blue color table). To build a black and white lookup table of 256 entries we use

```
vtkLookupTable *lut=new vtkLookupTable;
    lut->SetHueRange(0.0, 0.0);
    lut->SetSaturationRange(0.0, 0.0);
    lut->SetValueRange(0.0, 1.0);
```

In some cases you may want to specify colors directly. You can do this by specifying the number of colors, building the table, and then inserting new colors. When you insert colors, the RGBA color description system is used. For example, to create a lookup table of the three colors red, green, and blue, use the following C++ code.

```
vtkLookupTable *lut=new vtkLookupTable;
    lut->SetNumberOfColors(3);
    lut->Build();
    lut->SetTableValue(0, 1.0, 0.0, 0.0, 1.0);
    lut->SetTableValue(0, 0.0, 1.0, 0.0, 1.0);
    lut->SetTableValue(0, 0.0, 0.0, 1.0, 1.0);
```

Lookup tables in the *Visualization Toolkit* are associated with the graphics mappers. Mappers will automatically create a red to blue lookup table if no table

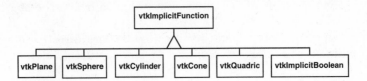

Figure 6–35 Inheritance hierarchy of vtkImplicitFunction and subclasses.

is specified, but if you want to create your own use the mapper->SetLookupT-able(lut) operation, where mapper is an instance of vtkMapper or its sub-classes.

A few final notes on using lookup tables.

- Mappers use their lookup table to map scalar values to colors. If no scalars are present, the mappers and their lookup tables do not control the color of the object. Instead the vtkProperty object associated with the vtkActor class does. Use the method actor->GetProperty()->SetColor(r,g,b) where r, g, and b are floating point values specifying color.

- If you want to prevent scalars from coloring your object, use the method mapper->ScalarsVisibleOff() to turn off color mapping. Then the actor's color will control the color of the object.

- The scalar range (i.e., the range into which the colors are mapped) is speci-fied with the mapper. Use the method mapper->SetScalarRange(min, max).

You can also derive your own lookup table types. Look at vtkLogLookupT-able for an example. This particular lookup table inherits from vtkLookupT-able. It performs logarithmic mapping of scalar value to table entry. This capability is useful when scalar values span many orders of magnitude.

Implicit Functions

As we have seen, implicit functions can be used for visualizing functions, creat-ing geometry, and cutting or selecting datasets. **vtk** includes several implicit functions including planes (vtkPlane), spheres (vtkSphere), cones (vtkCone), cylinders (vtkCylinder), and the general quadric (vtkQuadric). The class vtkImplicitBoolean allows you to create boolean combinations of these implicit function primitives. Other implicit functions can be added to **vtk** by deriving from the abstract base class vtkImplicitFunction.

The existing inheritance hierarchy for implicit functions is shown in Figure **6–35**. Subclasses of vtkImplicitFunction must implement the two methods Evaluate() and Gradient(). The method Evaluate() returns the value of the function at point (x,y,z), while the method Gradient() returns the gradient vector to the function at point (x,y,z).

Contouring

Scalar contouring is implemented in the *Visualization Toolkit* with `vtkCon-`
`tourFilter`. This filter object accepts as input any dataset type. Thus `vtkCon-`
`tourFilter` treats every cell type, and each cell type must provide a method for
contouring itself.

Contouring in **vtk** is implemented using variations of the marching cubes
algorithm presented earlier. That is, a contour case table is associated with each
cell type, so each cell will generate contouring primitives as appropriate. For
example, the tetrahedron cell type implements "marching tetrahedron" and creates triangle primitives, while the triangle cell type implements "marching triangles" and generates lines segments.

The implication of this arrangement is that `vtkContourFilter` will generate point, line, and surface contouring primitives depending on the combination of input cell types. Thus `vtkContourFilter` is completely general. We
have created another contour filter, `vtkMarchingCubes`, that is specific to the
dataset type structured points (in particular, 3D volumes). These two filters
allow us to compare (at least for this one algorithm) the cost of generality.

Recall from "Generality Versus Efficiency" on page 143 the issues regarding
the trade-offs between general and specific algorithms. Figure **6–36** show a comparison of CPU times for a volume dataset at $64 \times 64 \times 93$, $128 \times 128 \times 93$, and
$256 \times 256 \times 93$ resolution. The volume is a CT dataset of a human head. Three
cases were run. In the first case the `vtkMarchingCubes` object was used. The
output of this filter is triangles plus point normals. In the second case `vtkCon-`
`tourFilter` was run. The output of this filter is just triangles. In the last case
`vtkContourFilter` was combined with `vtkCleanPolyData` (to merge duplicate points) and `vtkPolyNormals` (to generate point normals). The output of
these filters is triangles plus point normals.

The execution times are normalized to the smallest dataset using the `vtk-`
`MarchingCubes` object. The results are clear: the specific object out-performs
the general object by a factor of 1.4 to 7, depending on data size and whether normals are computed. The larger differences occur on the smaller datasets. This is
because the ratio of voxel cells containing the isosurface, to the total number of
voxels is larger for smaller datasets. (Generally the total number of voxels
increases as resolution cubed, while the voxels containing the isosurface increase
as resolution squared.) As a result, more voxels are processed in the smaller
datasets relative to the total number of voxels than in the larger datasets. When
the datasets become larger, more voxels are "empty", and are not processed.

Although these results do not represent all implementations or the behavior of other algorithms, they do point to the cost of generality. Of course, there is
a cost to specialization as well. This cost is typically in programmer time, since
the programmer must rewrite code to adapt to new circumstances and data. Like
all trade-offs, resolution of this issue requires knowledge of the application.

An example use of `vtkContourFilter` is shown in Figure **6–37**. This
example is taken from Figure **4–1**, which is a visualization of a quadric function.
The class `vtkSampleFunction` samples the implicit quadric function using the

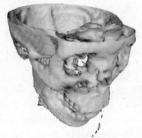 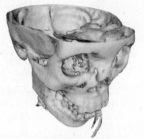 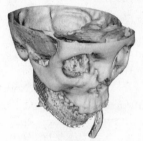

a) Quarter resolution   b) Half resolution   c) Full resolution

Resolution	Specific (w/ normals)	General (no normals)	Factor	General (w/ normals)	Factor
64 x 64 x 93	1.000	2.889	2.889	7.131	7.131
128 x 128 x 93	5.058	11.81	2.330	23.26	4.600
256 x256 x 93	37.169	51.62	1.390	87.23	2.350

Figure 6–36 The cost of generality. Isosurface generation of three volumes of different size are compared. The results show normalized execution times for two different implementations of the marching-cubes isosurface algorithm. The specialized filter is vtk-MarchingCubes. The general algorithms is vtkContourFilter in combination with vtkCleanPolyData and vtkPolyNormals.

vtkQuadric class. Although vtkQuadric does not participate in the pipeline in terms of data flow, it is used to define and evaluate the quadric function. It is possible to generate one or more isolines/isosurfaces simultaneously using vtk-ContourFilter. As Figure **6–37** shows, we use the GenerateValues() method to specify a scalar range, and the number of contours within this range (including the initial and final scalar values). vtkContourFilter generates duplicate vertices, so we can use vtkCleanPolyData to remove them. To improve the rendered appearance of the isosurface, we use vtkPolyNormals to create surface normals. (We describe surface normal generation in Chapter 8.)

Glyphs

The vtkGlyph3D class provides a simple, yet powerful glyph capability in the *Visualization Toolkit*. vtkGlyph3D is an example of an object that takes multiple inputs (Figure **6–38**). One input, specified with the SetInput() method, defines a set of points and possible attribute data at those points. The second input, specified with the SetSource() method, defines a geometry to be copied to every point in the input dataset. The source is of type vtkPolyData. Hence, any

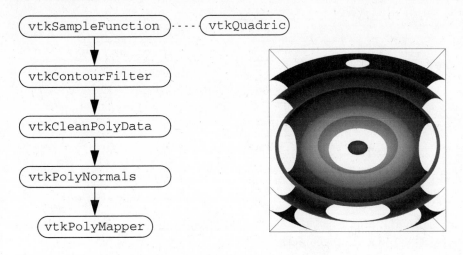

```
                // Sample quadric function
                quadric = new vtkQuadric;
                    quadric->SetCoefficients(.5,1,.2,0,.1,0,0,.2,0,0);
                sample = new vtkSampleFunction;
                    sample->SetSampleDimensions(50,50,50);
                    sample->SetImplicitFunction(quadric);
                contour = new vtkContourFilter;
                    contour->SetInput (sample->GetOutput());
                    contour->GenerateValues(5,0,1.2);
                clean = new vtkCleanPolyData;
                    clean->SetInput(contour->GetOutput());
                normals = new vtkPolyNormals;
                    normals->SetInput(clean->GetOutput());
                    normals->SetFeatureAngle(60);
                contourMapper = new vtkPolyMapper;
                    contourMapper->SetInput(normals->GetOutput());
                    contourMapper->SetScalarRange(0,1.2);
                contourActor = new vtkActor;
                    contourActor->SetMapper(contourMapper);

                // Create outline
                outline = new vtkOutlineFilter;
                    outline->SetInput(sample->GetOutput());
                outlineMapper = new vtkPolyMapper;
                    outlineMapper->SetInput(outline->GetOutput());
                outlineActor = new vtkActor;
                    outlineActor->SetMapper(outlineMapper);
                    outlineActor->GetProperty()->SetColor(0,0,0);
```

Figure 6–37 Contouring quadric function. Pipeline topology, C++ code, and resulting image are shown (contQuad.cc).

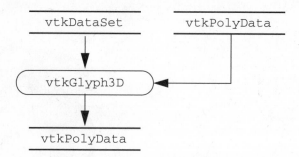

Figure 6–38 Data flow into and out of vtkGlyph3D class.

filter, sequence of filters creating polygonal data, or a polygonal dataset may be used to describe the glyph's geometry.

The behavior of an instance of vtkGlyph3D depends on the nature of the input data and the value of its instance variables. Generally the input Source geometry will be copied to each point of the Input dataset. The geometry will be aligned along the input vector data, and scaled according to the magnitude of the vector or the scalar value. In some cases, the point normal is used rather than the vector. Also, scaling can be turned on or off.

We saw how to use vtkGlyph3D in the example given in Figure **4–13**. Cones were used as the glyph and were located at each point on the sphere, oriented along the sphere's surface normal.

Streamlines

Streamlines and particle motion require numerical integration to guide a point through the vector field. Vector visualization algorithms that we will see in later chapters also require numerical integration. As a result, we designed an object hierarchy that isolates the numerical integration process into a single base class. The base class is vtkStreamer and it is responsible for generating a particle path through a vector field of specified length (expressed as elapsed time). Each derived class of vtkStreamer takes advantage of this capability to move through the vector field, but implements its own particular representational technique to depict particle motion. Streamlines (vtkStreamLine) draw connected lines while particle motion is shown by combining the output of vtk-StreamPoints with the vtkGlyph3D object. Using vtkGlyph3D we can place spheres or oriented objects such as cones or arrows at points on the particle path created by vtkStreamPoints. The inheritance hierarchy for vtkStreamer and subclasses is shown in Figure **6–39**.

The integration method in vtkStreamer is implemented as a virtual function. Thus it can be overloaded as necessary. Possible reasons for overloading include implementing an integration technique of higher or lower accuracy, or creating a technique specialized to a particular dataset type. For example, the

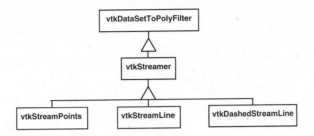

Figure 6–39 Inheritance hierarchy for vtkStreamer and subclasses.

search process in a volume is much faster than it is for other dataset types, so highly efficient vector integration techniques can be constructed.

The vector integration technique in **vtk** will accommodate any cell type. Thus, integration through cells of any topological dimension is possible. If the cells are of topological dimension 2 or less, the integration process constrains particle motion to the surface (2D) or line (1D). The particle may only leave a cell by passing through the cell boundary and travelling to a neighboring cell, or exiting the dataset.

Attribute Modification and General Output Type

Attribute transformations create or modify data attributes without changing the topology or geometry of a dataset. Hence filters that implement attribute transformation (e.g., vtkElevationFilter) can accept any dataset type as input, and may generate any dataset type on output. Unfortunately, because filters must specialize the particular type of data they output, at first glance it appears that filters that create general dataset types on output are not feasible. This is because the type vtkDataSet is an abstract type, and must be specialized to allow instantiation.

Fortunately there is a a solution to this dilemma. The solution is to use the "virtual constructor" MakeObject(). Although C++ does not allow virtual constructors, we can simulate it by creating a special virtual function that constructs a copy of the object that it is invoked on. For example, if this function is applied to a dataset instance of type vtkPolyData, the result will be a copy of that instance (Figure **6–40**). (Note that we use reference counting to make copies and avoid duplicating memory.) The virtual constructor function MakeObject() is implemented in a number of **vtk** classes including datasets and cells.

Using the virtual constructor we can construct filters that output abstract data types like vtkDataSet. We simply apply MakeObject() to the input of the filter. This will then return a pointer to a concrete object that is the output of the filter. The result is a general filter object that can accept any dataset type for input and creates the general vtkDataSet type as output. In **vtk**, this function-

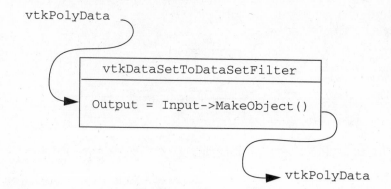

Figure 6–40 Depiction of delegation technique for generalized filter output. Certain data queries are forwarded to internal objects.

ality has been implemented in the abstract class `vtkDataSetToDataSetFilter`.

There are other filters that implement variations of this delegation technique. The class `vtkPointSetToPointSetFilter` is similar to `vtkDataSetToDataSetFilter`. This class takes as input any dataset whose geometry is explicitly defined via an instance of `vtkPoints` (or subclass), and generates on output an object of the same type (i.e., `vtkPointSet`). The class `vtkMergeFilter` combines dataset structure and point attributes from one or more input datasets. For example, you can read multiple files and combine the geometry/topology from one file with different scalars, vectors, and normals from other files.

Visualizing Blood Flow

In this example we'll combine a few different techniques to visualize blood flow in the human carotid arteries. Our data contains both vectors that represent the velocity of blood, and scalars that are proportional to the magnitude of the velocity (i.e., speed).

We can provide context for the visualization by creating an isosurface of speed. This isosurface shows regions of fastest blood flow, and is similar to (but not the same as) the actual surface of the arteries. But it provides us with a visual cue to the structure of the arteries.

The first vector visualization technique we'll use is to generate vector glyphs (Figure **6–41**). Unfortunately, we cannot just create glyphs at each point because of the number of points (over 167,000 points). To do so would result in a confusing mess, and the interactive speed would be poor. Instead, we'll use two filters to select a subset of the available points. These filters are `vtkThresholdPoints` and `vtkMaskPoints`.

`vtkThresholdPoints` allows us to extract points that satisfy a certain threshold criterion. In our example we choose points whose speed is greater than

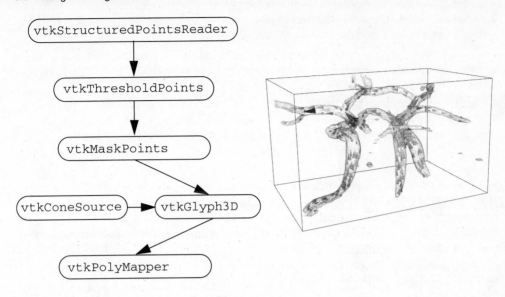

```
vtkStructuredPointsReader reader;
    reader SetFilename "../../data/carotid.vtk"
    reader DebugOn;
vtkThresholdPoints threshold;
    threshold SetInput [reader GetOutput];
    threshold ThresholdByUpper 200;
vtkMaskPoints mask;
    mask SetInput [Threshold GetOutput];
    mask SetOnRatio 10;
vtkConeSource cone;
    cone SetResolution 3;
    cone SetHeight 1;
    cone SetRadius 0.25;
vtkGlyph3D cones;
    cones SetInput [mask GetOutput];
    cones SetSource [cone GetOutput];
    cones SetScaleFactor 0.005;
    cones ScaleByVector;
vtkPolyMapper vecMapper;
    vecMapper SetInput [cones GetOutput];
    vecMapper SetScalarRange 2 10;
```

Figure 6–41 Visualizing blood flow in human carotid arteries. Cone glyphs indicate flow direction and magnitude. The code fragment shown is from the Tcl script `thrshldV.tcl` and shows creation of vector glyphs.

a specified value. This eliminates a large number of points, since most points lie outside the arteries and have a small speed value.

The filter `vtkMaskPoints` allows us to select a subset of the available points. We specify the subset with the `OnRatio` instance variable. This instance variable indicates that every `OnRatio` point is to be selected. Thus, if the `OnRatio` is equal to one, all points will be selected, and if the `OnRatio` is equal to ten, every tenth point will be selected. This selection can be either uniform or random. Random point selection is set using the `RandomModeOn()` and `RandomModeOff()` methods.

After selecting a subset of the original points, we can use the `vtkGlyph3D` filter in the usual way. A cone's orientation indicates blood flow direction, and its size and color correspond to the velocity magnitude. Figure **6–41** shows the pipeline, sample code, and a resulting image from this visualization. Note that we've implemented the example using the interpreted language Tcl. See chapter 10 if you want more information about Tcl.

In the next part of this example we'll generate streamtubes of blood velocity. Again we use an isosurface of speed to provide us with context. The starting positions for the streamtubes were determined by experimenting with the data. Because of the way the data was measured and the resolution of the velocity field, many streamers travel outside the artery. This is because the boundary layer of the blood flow is not captured due to limitations in data resolution. Consequently, as the blood flows around curves, there is a component of the velocity field that directs the streamtube outside the artery. As a result it is hard to find starting positions for the streamtubes that yield interesting results. We use the source object `vtkPointSource` in combination with `vtkThresholdPoints` to work around this problem. `vtkPointSource` generates random points centered around a sphere of a specified radius. We need only find an approximate position for the starting points of the streamtubes, and then generate a cloud of random seed points. `vtkThresholdPoints` is used to cull points that may be generated outside the regions of high flow velocity.

Figure **6–42** shows the pipeline, sample Tcl code, and a resulting image from the visualization. Notice that the isosurface is shown in wireframe. This provides context, yet allows us to see the streamtubes within the isosurface.

6.7 Chapter Summary

Visualization algorithms transform data from one form to another. These transformations can change the structure or attributes of a dataset. Structural transformations change either the topology or geometry of a dataset. Attribute transformations change dataset attributes such as scalars, vectors, normals, or texture coordinates.

Algorithms are classified according to the type of data they operate on. Scalar, vector, and tensor algorithms operate on scalar, vector, and tensor data, respectively. Modelling algorithms operate on dataset geometry or topology, tex-

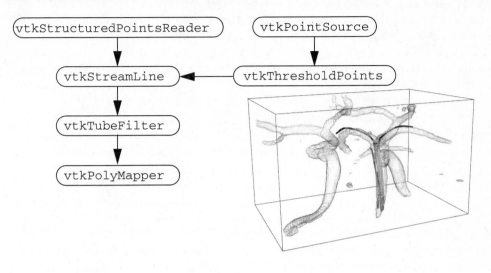

```
vtkStructuredPointsReader reader;
    reader SetFilename "../../data/carotid.vtk"
vtkPointSource source;
    source SetNumberOfPoints 25;
    source SetCenter 133.1 116.3 5.0;
    source SetRadius 2.0;
vtkThresholdPoints threshold;
    threshold SetInput [reader GetOutput];
    threshold ThresholdByUpper 275;
vtkStreamLine streamers;
    streamers SetInput [reader GetOutput];
    streamers SetSource [source GetOutput];
    streamers SetMaximumPropagationTime 100.0;
    streamers SetIntegrationStepLength 0.2;
    streamers SpeedScalarsOn;
    streamers SetTerminalSpeed .1;
vtkTubeFilter tubes;
    tubes SetInput [streamers GetOutput];
    tubes SetRadius 0.3;
    tubes SetNumberOfSides 6;
    tubes VaryRadiusOff;
vtkPolyMapper streamerMapper;
    streamerMapper SetInput [tubes GetOutput];
    streamerMapper SetScalarRange 2 10;
```

Figure 6–42 Visualizing blood flow in the human carotid arteries. Streamtubes of flow vectors (streamV.tcl).

ture coordinates, or normals. Modelling algorithms also may include complex techniques that may represent combinations of different data types.

Algorithms can be designed and implemented for general types of data or specialized for a specific type. General algorithms are typically less efficient than their specialized counterparts. Conversely, general algorithms are more flexible and do not require rewriting as new dataset types are introduced.

Important scalar algorithms include color mapping and contouring. Color maps are used to map scalar values to color values. Contouring algorithms create isosurfaces or isolines to indicate areas of constant scalar value.

Glyphs such as hedgehogs are useful for visualizing vector data. These techniques are limited by the number of glyphs that can be displayed at one time. Particle traces or streamlines are another important algorithm for vector field visualization. Collections of particle traces can convey something of the structure of a vector field.

Real, symmetric 3×3 tensors can be characterized by their eigenvalues and eigenvectors. Tensors can be visualized using tensor ellipsoids or oriented axes.

Implicit functions and sampling techniques can be used to make geometry, cut data, and visualize complex mathematical descriptions. Glyphs are objects whose appearance is associated with a particular data value. Glyphs are flexible and can be created to visualize a variety of data.

6.8 Bibliographic Notes

Color mapping is a widely studied topic in imaging, computer graphics, visualization, and human factors. References [Durrett87] [Ware88] [Rheingans92] provide samples of the available literature. You also may want to learn about the physiological and psychological effects of color on perception. The text by Wyszecki and Stiles [Wyszecki82] serves as an introductory reference.

Contouring is a widely studied technique in visualization because of its importance and popularity. Early techniques were developed for 2D data [Watson92]. Three dimensional techniques were developed initially as contour connecting methods [Fuchs77]. That is, given a series of 2D contours on evenly spaced planes, connect the contours to create a closed surface. Since the introduction of marching cubes, many other techniques have been implemented (a few of these include [Nielson91] [Montani94] and [Durst88]). A particularly interesting reference is given by Livnat et al. [Livnat95]. They show a contouring method with the addition of a preprocessing step that generates isocontours in near optimal time.

Although we barely touched the topic, the study of chaos and chaotic vibrations is a delightfully interesting topic. Besides the original paper by Lorenz [Lorenz63], the book by Moon [Moon87] is a good place to start.

Two and three dimensional vector plots have been used by computer analysts for many years [Fuller80]. Streamlines and streamribbons also have been applied to the visualization of complex flows [Volpe89]. Good general references on vector visualization techniques are given in [Helman90] and [Richter90].

Tensor visualization techniques are relatively few in number. Most techniques are glyph oriented [Haber90] [deLeeuw93]. We will see a few more techniques in Chapter 9.

Blinn [Blinn82], Bloomental [Bloomenthal88] and Wyvill [Wyvill86] have been important contributors to implicit modelling. Implicit modelling is currently popular in computer graphics for modelling "soft" or "blobby" objects. These techniques are simple, powerful, and are becoming widely used for advanced computer graphics modelling.

6.9 References

[Abraham85]
R. H. Abraham and Christopher D. Shaw. *Dynamics The Geometry of Behavior.* Aerial Press, Santa Cruz, CA, 1985.

[Blinn82]
J. F. Blinn. "A Generalization of Algebraic Surface Drawing." *ACM Transactions on Graphics*, 1(3):235-256, July 1982.

[Bloomenthal88]
J. Bloomenthal. "Polygonization of Implicit Surfaces." *Computer Aided Geometric Design,* 5(4):341-355, November 1982.

[Chernoff73]
H. Chernoff. "Using Faces to Represent Pints in *K*- Dimensional Space Graphically." *J. American Statistical Association,* 68:361-368, 1973.

[Cline93]
H. Cline, W. Lorensen, and W. Schroeder. "3D Phase Contrast MRI of Cerebral Blood FLow and Surface Anatomy." *Journal of Computer Assisted Tomography,* 17(2):173-177, March/April 1993.

[Conte72]
S. D. Conte and C. de Boor. *Elementary Numerical Analysis*. McGraw-Hill Book Company, 1972.

[deLeeuw93]
W. C. de Leeuw and J. J. van Wijk. "A Probe for Local Flow Field Visualization." In *Proceedings of Visualization '93*, pp. 39-45, IEEE Computer Society Press, Los Alamitos, CA, 1993.

[Delmarcelle95]
T. Delmarcelle and L. Hesselink. "A Unified Framework for Flow Visualization." In *Computer Visualization Graphics Techniques for Scientific and Engineering Analysis*, R. S. Gallagher (ed), CRC Press, Boca Raton, FL, 1995.

[Durrett87]
H. J. Durrett, editor. *Color and the Computer.* Academic Press, Boston, MA, 1987.

[Durst88]
M. J. Durst. "Additional Reference to Marching Cubes." *Computer Graphics,* 22(2):72-73, 1988.

[Fuchs77]

    H. Fuchs, Z. M. Kedem, and S. P. Uselton. "Optimal Surface Reconstruction from Planar Contours." *Communications of the ACM*, 20(10):693-702, 1977.

[Fuller80]

    A. J. Fuller and M.L.X. dosSantos. "Computer Generated Display of 3D Vector Fields." *Computer Aided Design*, 12(2):61-66, 1980.

[Haber90]

    R. B. Haber and D. A. McNabb. "Visualization Idioms: A Conceptual Model to Scientific Visualization Systems." *Visualization in Scientific Computing,* G. M. Nielson, B. Shriver, L. J. Rosenblum, editors. IEEE Computer Society Press, pp. 61-73, 1990.

[Helman90]

    J. Helman and L. Hesselink. "Representation and Display of Vector Field Topology in Fluid Flow Data Sets." *Visualization in Scientific Computing,* G. M. Nielson, B. Shriver, L. J. Rosenblum, editors. IEEE Computer Society Press, pp. 61-73, 1990.

[Livnat95]

    Y. Livnat, H. W. Shen, C. R. Johnson. "A Near Optimal Isosurface Extraction Algorithm for Structured and Unstructured Grids." *IEEE Transactions on Visualization and Computer Graphics*, (Submitted).

[Lorensen87]

    W. E. Lorensen and H. E. Cline. "Marching Cubes: A High Resolution 3D Surface Construction Algorithm." *Computer Graphics*, 21(3):163-169, July 1987.

[Lorenz63]

    E. N. Lorenz. "Deterministic Non-Periodic Flow." *Journal of Atmospheric Science*, 20:130-141, 1963.

[Montani94]

    C. Montani, R. Scateni, and R. Scopigno. "A Modified Look-Up Table for Implicit Disambiguation of Marching Cubes." *Visual Computer,* (10):353-355, 1994.

[Moon87]

    F. C. Moon. *Chaotic Vibrations.* Wiley-Interscience, New York, NY, 1987.

[Nielson91]

    G. M. Nielson and B. Hamann. "The Asymptotic Decider: Resolving the Ambiguity in Marching Cubes." In *Proceedings of Visualization '91*, pp. 83-91, IEEE Computer Society Press, Los Alamitos, CA, 1991.

[Rheingans92]

    P. Rheingans. "Color, Change, and Control for Quantitative Data Display." In *Proceedings of Visualization '92*, pp. 252-259, IEEE Computer Society Press, Los Alamitos, CA, 1992.

[Richter90]

    R. Richter, J. B. Vos, A. Bottaro, and S. Gavrilakis. "Visualization of Flow Simulations." *Scientific Visualization and Graphics Simulation*, D. Thalmann editor, pp. 161-171, John Wiley and Sons, 1990.

[Saada74]

    A. S. Saada. *Elasticity Theory and Applications.* Pergamon Press Inc., New York, NY, 1974.

[Timoshenko70]
>   S. P. Timoshenko and J. N. Goodier. *Theory of Elasticity, Third Edition.* McGraw-Hill Book Company, New York, NY, 1970.

[Tufte83]
>   E. R. Tufte. *The Visual Display of Quantitative Information.* Graphics Press, Cheshire, CT, 1990.

[Volpe89]
>   G. Volpe. "Streamlines and Streamribbons in Aerodynamics." Technical Report AIAA-89-0140, 27th Aerospace Sciences Meeting, 1989.

[Ware88]
>   C. Ware. "Color Sequences for Univariate Maps: Theory, Experiments and Principles." *IEEE Computer Graphics and Applications*, 8(5):41-49, 1988.

[Watson92]
>   D. F. Watson. *CONTOURING: A Guide to the Analysis and Display of Spatial Data*, Pergamon Press, 1992.

[Wyszecki82]
>   G. Wyszecki and W. Stiles. *Color Science: Concepts and Methods, Quantitative Data and Formulae*, John Wiley and Sons, 1982.

[Wyvill86]
>   G. Wyvill, C. McPheeters, B. Wyvill. "Data Structure for Soft Objects." *Visual Computer*, 2(4):227-234, 1986.

6.10 Exercises

6.1 Sketch contour cases for marching triangles. How many cases are there?

6.2 Sketch contour cases for marching tetrahedron. How many cases are there?

6.3 A common visualization technique is to animate isosurface value. The procedure is to smoothly vary isosurface value over a specified range.
a) Create an animation sequence for the quadric example (Figure **4–1**).
b) Create an animation sequence for the head sequence (Figure **6–11**(b)).

6.4 Marching cubes visits each cell during algorithm execution. Many of these cells do not contain the isosurface. Describe a technique to improve the performance of isosurface extraction by eliminating visits to cells not containing isosurface. (*Hint:* use a preprocessing step to analyze data. Assume that many isosurfaces will be extracted and that the preprocessing step will not count against execution time.)

6.5 Scan-line rasterization proceeds along horizontal spans in graphics hardware (see "Rasterization" on page 57). Interpolation of color occurs along horizontal spans as well.
a) Show how the orientation of a polygon affects interpolated color.
b) Discuss potential problems caused by orientation dependent viewing of visualizations.

6.6 Write a program to simulate beam vibration. Use the code associated with Figure **6–14**(a) as your starting point.

6.7 Using the filters `vtkStreamLine`, `vtkMaskPoints` and `vtkGlyph3D`, create a visualization consisting of oriented glyphs along a streamline.

6.8 Visualize the following functions.
a) Scalar $S(x, y, z) = \sin(xy)$, for x,y between 0 and π.
b) The effective stress field (a scalar field) from Figure **6–21**.
c) The vector field described in the combustor data (i.e., `compq.bin` and `compxyz.bin`).

6.9 Tensor ellipsoids are based on an ellipsoidal glyph. Describe two other glyphs that you might use.

6.10 Write a source object to generate a polygonal representation of a torus.

6.11 Design a glyph to convey airplane heading, speed, and altitude, and proximity (i.e., distance) to other planes.

6.12 Morphing is a process to smoothly blend images (2D) or geometry (3D) between two known images or geometry. Using an implicit modelling approach, how would you morph a torus into a cube?

6.13 Describe a technique to visualize vector information by animating a color map. (*Hint:* by choosing map carefully you can give the illusion of motion across a surface.)

6.14 Isoline contours of different values are typically shown together in one image.
a) Describe the advantages and disadvantages of displaying isosurfaces simultaneously.
b) What two graphics properties might you adjust to improve the display of multiple isosurfaces?

6.15 Describe a parallel algorithm for marching cubes. Use a parallel architecture of your choice.

Computer Graphics II

*C*hapter 3 introduced many of the fundamental concepts of computer graphics. This chapter extends those fundamentals to improve the realism, usefulness and flexibility of our work. We explore several techniques starting with stereo rendering to produce stereoscopic images. We also look at methods for simulating transparency using simple blending functions, and the problems involved with this approach. As with transparency, texture mapping is becoming more common because of the realism it can add to an image. There are a variety of issues regarding the use of two and three dimension texture maps, as well as procedural texture maps.

A frequent complaint regarding computer-generated images concerns the jagged edges introduced during rasterization. Later in this chapter we will cover three methods for overcoming these artifacts by producing antialiased images. This chapter concludes by looking at some advanced camera techniques, including motion blur and focal depth, followed by a summary section on volume rendering.

7.1 Stereo Rendering

Up to this point in the text, our discussion of computer graphics has neglected to take into account binocular parallax. Binocular parallax is a result of viewing a 3D objects with our two eyes. Since each eye sees a slightly different picture, our

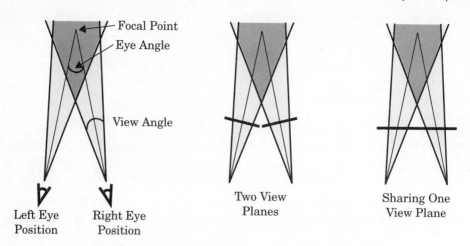

Left Eye   Right Eye   Two View   Sharing One
Position   Position   Planes   View Plane

Figure 7–1 Stereo rendering and binocular parallax.

mind interprets these differences to determine the depth of objects in our view. There have been a number of "3D" movies produced that take advantage of our binocular parallax. Typically these involve wearing a set of special glasses while watching the movie.

This effect can be valuable in our efforts to visualize complex datasets and CAD models. The additional depth cues provided by stereo viewing aid us in determining the relative positions of scene geometry, as well as forming a mental image of the scene. There are several different methods for introducing binocular parallax into renderings. We will refer to the overall process as *stereo rendering*, since at some point in the process a stereo pair of images is involved.

To generate correct left and right eye images, we need information beyond the camera parameters that we introduced in Chapter 3. The first piece of information we need is the separation distance between the eyes. The amount of parallax generated can be controlled by adjusting this distance. We also need to know if the resulting images will be viewed on one or two displays. For systems that use two displays (and hence two view planes), the parallax can be correctly produced by performing camera azimuths to reach the left and right eye positions. Head mounted displays and booms are examples of two display systems. Unfortunately, this doesn't work as well for systems that have only one view plane. If you try to display both the left and right views on a single display, they are forced to share the same view plane as in Figure **7–1**. Our earlier camera model assumed that the view plane was perpendicular to the direction of projection. To handle this non-perpendicular case, we must translate and shear the camera's viewing frustum. Hodges provides some of the details of this operation as well as a good overview on stereo rendering [Hodges92].

Now let's look at some of the different methods for presenting stereoscopic images to the user. Most methods are based on one of two main categories: *time multiplexed* and *time parallel* techniques. Time multiplexed methods work by alternating between the left and right eye images. Time parallel methods display both images at once in combination with a process to extract left and right eye views. Some methods can be implemented as either a time multiplexed or a time parallel technique.

Time multiplexed techniques are most commonly found in single display systems, since they rely on alternating images. Typically this is combined with a method for also alternating which eye views the image. One cost-effective time multiplexed technique takes advantage of existing television standards such as NTSC and PAL. Both of these standards use interlacing, which means that first the even lines are drawn on the screen, and then the odd. By rendering the left eye image to the even lines of the screen and the right eye image to the odd, we can generate a stereo video stream that is suitable for display on a standard television. When this is viewed with both eyes, it appears as one image that keeps jumping from left to right. A special set of glasses must be worn so that when the left eye image is being displayed, the user's left eye can see out and respectively for the right eye. The glasses are designed so that each lens consists of a liquid crystal shutter that can either be transparent or opaque, depending on what voltage is applied to it. By shuttering the glasses at the same rate as the television is interlacing, we can assure that the correct eye is viewing the correct image.

There are a couple of disadvantages to this system. The resolutions of NTSC and PAL are both low compared to a computer monitor. The refresh rate of NTSC (60 Hz) and PAL (50 Hz) produces a fair amount of flicker, especially when you consider that each eye is updated at half this rate. Also, this method requires viewing your images on a television, not the monitor connected to your computer.

To overcome these difficulties, some computer manufacturers offer stereo ready graphics cards. These systems use liquid crystal shuttered glasses to directly view the computer monitor. To obtain the alternating stereo images, the left eye image is rendered to the top half of the screen and the right eye image to the bottom. Then the graphics card enters a special stereo mode where it doubles the refresh rate of the monitor. So a monitor that initially displays both images at 60Hz begins to alternate between the left and right eye at a rate of 120Hz. This results in each eye getting updated at 60Hz, with its original horizontal resolution and half of its original vertical resolution. For this process to work, your application must take up the entire screen while rendering.

Some more recent graphics cards have a left image buffer and a right image buffer for stereo rendering. While this requires either more memory or a lower resolution, it does provide for stereo rendering without having to take over the entire screen. For such a card, double buffering combined with stereo rendering results in quad buffering, which can result in a large number of bits per pixel. For example: 24 bits for an RGB color, another 24 bits for the back buffer's color, plus 24 bits for the z-buffer results in 72 bits per pixel. Now double that for the two different views and you have 144 bits per pixel or 18 megabytes for a 1K by 1K display.

Figure 7–2 Single image random dot stereogram of a tetrahedron.

Time parallel techniques display both images at the same time. Head-mounted displays and booms have two separate screens, one for each eye. To generate the two video streams requires either two graphics cards or one that can generate two separate outputs. The rendering process then involves just rendering each eye to the correct graphics card or output. Currently, the biggest disadvantage to this approach is the cost of the hardware required.

In contrast, SIRDS (Single Image Random Dot Stereograms) require no special hardware. Both views are displayed in a single image, as in Figure **7–2**. To view such an image the user must focus either in front of, or behind the image. When the user's focal point is correct, the two triangular cutouts in the top of the image will appear as one and the image should appear focused. This works because dot patterns repeat at certain intervals. Here, only the depth information is present in the resulting image. This is incorporated by changing the interval between patterns just as our ocular disparity changes with depth.

The next two techniques for stereo rendering can be implemented using either the time parallel or time multiplexed methods. The distinction is slightly blurred because most of the time parallel methods can be multiplexed, though typically there is no advantage to it. Both of these methods have been used by the movie industry to produce "3D" movies. The first is commonly called red-blue (or red-green or red-cyan) stereo and requires the user to wear a pair of glasses that filter entering light. The left eye can only see the image through a red filter, the right through a blue filter. The rendering process typically involves generating images for the two views, converting their RGB values into intensity, and then creating a resulting image. This image's red values are taken from the left eye image intensities. Likewise the blue values (a mixture of blue and green) are taken from the right eye image intensities. The resulting image has none of the original hue or saturation, but it does contain both original images' intensities. (An additional note: red-green methods are also used because the human eye is more sensitive to green than blue.) The benefits of this technique are that the resulting images can be displayed on a monitor, paper or film, and all one needs to view them is an inexpensive pair of glasses.

The second technique is similar to the first but it preserves all the color information from the original images. It separates the different views by using polarized light. Normally the light we see has a mixture of polarization angles, but there are lenses that can filter out a subset of these angles. If we project a color image through a vertical polarizing filter, and then view it through another vertical filter, we will see the original image, just slightly dimmer because we've filtered out all the horizontally polarized light. If we placed a horizontal filter and a vertical filter together it blocks all the light. Polarized stereo rendering typically projects one eye's image through a vertical filter and the other through a horizontal filter. The user wears a pair of glasses containing a vertical filter over one eye and a horizontal filter over the other. This way each eye views the correct image.

All the methods we have discussed for stereo rendering have their advantages and disadvantages, typically revolving around cost and image quality. At the end of this chapter we will look at an example program that renders stereo images using the red-blue technique.

7.2 Transparency and Alpha Values

If you examine Color Plate 46 you will see an excellent and straightforward use of transparency. By making the skin semi-transparent, it becomes possible to see the internal organs and their relationship to the torso. This is just one of many applications that take advantage of transparency to either increase realism or lucidity. Transparency and its compliment, opacity, are often referred to as *alpha* in computer graphics. For example, a polygon that is 50% opaque will have an alpha value of 0.5 on a scale of zero to one. An alpha value of one represents an opaque object and zero represents a completely transparent object. Frequently, alpha is specified as a property for the entire actor, but it also can be done on a

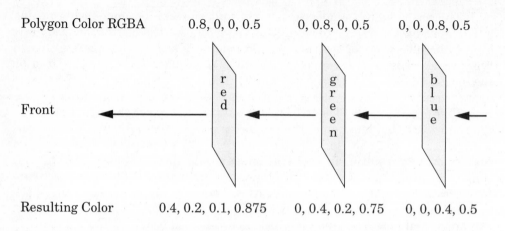

Figure 7–3 Alpha compositing.

vertex basis just like colors. In such cases, the RGB specification of a color is extended to RGBA where A represents the alpha component. On many graphics cards the framebuffer will store the alpha value along with the RGB values.

Unfortunately, having transparent actors introduces some complications into the rendering process. If you think back to the process of ray tracing, viewing rays are projected from the camera out into the world, where they intersect the first actor they come to. With an opaque actor, the lighting equations are applied and the resulting color is drawn to the screen. With a semi-transparent actor we must solve the lighting equations for this actor, and then continue projecting the ray farther to see if it intersects any other actors. The resulting color is a composite of all the actors it has intersected. For each surface intersection this can be expressed as Equation **7-1**.

$$R = A_s R_s + (1 - A_s) R_b$$
$$G = A_s G_s + (1 - A_s) G_b$$
$$B = A_s B_s + (1 - A_s) B_b \qquad \textbf{(7-1)}$$
$$A = A_s + (1 - A_s) A_b$$

In this equation subscript s refers to the surface of the actor, while subscript b refers to what is behind the actor. The term $1 - A_s$ is called the transmissivity, and represents the amount of light that is transmitted from behind the actor. As an example, consider starting with three polygons colored red, green and blue each with a transparency of 0.5. If the red polygon is in the front and the background is black, the resulting RGBA color will be (0.4, 0.2, 0.1, 0.875) on a scale of zero to one (Figure **7–3**).

It is important to note that if we switch the ordering of the polygons, the resulting color will change. This underlies a major technical problem in using transparency. If we ray trace a scene, we will intersect the surfaces in a well-defined manner – from front to back. Using this knowledge we can trace a ray back to the last surface it intersects, and then composite the color by applying Equation **7-1** to all the surfaces in reverse order (i.e., from back to front). In object-order rendering methods this compositing is commonly supported in hardware, but unfortunately we are not guaranteed to render the polygons in any specific order. Even though our polygons are situated as in Figure **7–3**, the order in which the polygons are rendered might be the blue polygon, followed by the red and finally the green polygon. Consequently the resulting color is incorrect.

If we look at the RGBA value for one pixel we can see the problem. When the blue polygon is rendered, the frame buffer and z-buffer are empty, so the RGBA quad (0,0,0.8,0.5) is stored along with the its z-buffer value. When the red polygon is rendered, a comparison of its z-value and the current z-buffer indicates that it is in front of the previous pixel entry. So, Equation **7-1** is applied using the frame buffer's RGBA value. This results in the RGBA value (0.4,0,0.2,0.75) being written to the buffer. Now, the green polygon is rendered and the z comparison indicates that it is behind the current pixel's value. Again this equation is applied, this time using the frame buffer's RGBA value for the surface and the polygon's values from behind. This results in a final pixel color of (0.3,0.2, 0.175,0.875), which is different from what we previously calculated. Once the red and blue polygons have been composited and written to the frame buffer, there is no way to insert the final green polygon into the middle where it belongs.

One solution to this problem is to sort the polygons from back to front and then render them in this order. Typically this must be done in software, requiring additional computational overhead. Sorting also interferes with actor properties (such as specular power), which are typically sent to the graphics engine just before rendering the actor's polygons. Once we start mixing up the polygons of different actors, we must make sure that the correct actor properties are set for each polygon rendered.

Another solution is to store more than one set of RGBAZ values in the frame buffer. This is costly because of the additional memory requirements, and is still limited by the number of RGBAZ values you can store. Some new techniques use a combination of multiple RGBAZ value storage and multipass rendering to yield correct results with a minimum performance hit [Kelly94].

The second technical problem with rendering transparent objects occurs less frequently, but can still have disastrous effects. In certain applications, such as volume rendering, it is desirable to have thousands of polygons with small alpha values. If the RGBA quad is stored in the frame buffer as four eight-bit values, then the round-off can accumulate over many polygons, resulting in gross errors in the output image. Some of the newer systems solve this by using more bits for storing the RGBA values.

7.3 Texture Mapping

Texture mapping is a technique to add detail to an image without requiring modelling detail. Texture mapping can be thought of as pasting a picture to the surface of an object. The use of texture mapping requires two pieces of information: a *texture map* and *texture coordinates*. The texture map is the picture we paste, and the texture coordinates specify the location where the picture is pasted. More generally, texture mapping is a table lookup for color, intensity, and/or transparency that is applied to an object as it is rendered. Textures maps and coordinates are most often two-dimensional, but three-dimensional texture maps and coordinates are becoming more common.

The value of texture mapping can be shown through the simple example of rendering a wooden table. The basic geometry of a table can be easily created, but achieving the woodgrain details is difficult. Coloring the table brown is a good start, but the image is still unrealistic. To simulate the woodgrain we need to have many small color changes across the surface of the table. Using vertex colors would require us to have millions of extra vertices just to get the small color changes. The solution to this is to apply a woodgrain texture map to the original polygons. This is like applying an oak veneer onto inexpensive particleboard.

There are several ways in which we can apply texture data. For each pixel in the texture map (commonly called a *texel* for texture element), there may be one to four components that affect how the texture map is pasted onto the surface of the underlying geometry. A texture map with one component is called an *intensity map*. Applying an intensity map results in changes to the intensity (or value in HSV) of the resulting pixels. If we took a grey scale image of wood grain, and then texture mapped it onto a brown polygon, we would have a reasonable looking table. The hue and saturation of the polygon would still be determined by the brown color, but the intensity would be determined from the texture map. A better looking table could be obtained by using a color image of the wood. This is a three component texture map, where each texel is represented as a RGB triplet. Using an RGB map allows us to obtain more realistic images, since we would have more than just the intensity changes of the wood.

By adding alpha values to an intensity map we get two components. We can do the same to an RGB texture map to get an RGBA texture map. In these cases, the alpha value can be used to make parts of the underlying geometry transparent. A common trick in computer graphics is to use RGBA textures to render trees. Instead of trying to model the complex geometry of a tree, we just render a rectangle with a RGBA texture map applied to it. Where there are leaves or branches, the alpha is one, where there are gaps and open space, the alpha is zero. As a result, we can see through portions of the rectangle, giving the illusion of viewing through the branches and leaves of a tree.

Besides the different ways in which a texture map can be defined, there are options in how it interacts with the original color of the object. A common option for RGB and RGBA maps is to ignore the original color; that is, just apply the

3D Polygonal Model   2D Texture Map

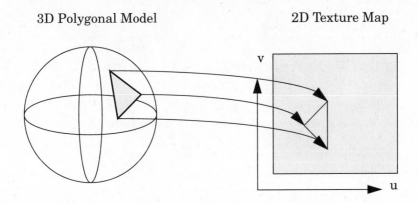

Figure 7–4 Vertex texture coordinates.

texture color as specified. Another option is to modulate the original color by the texture map color (or intensity) to produce the final color.

While we have been focusing on 2D texture maps, they can be of any dimension, though the most common are 2D and 3D. Three-dimensional texture maps are used for textures that are a function of 3D space, such as wood grain, stone, or X-ray intensity (i.e., CT scan). In fact, a structured point dataset is essentially a 3D texture. We can perform high-speed pseudo volume rendering (to be discussed shortly) by passing planes through a 3D texture and compositing them using translucent alpha values in the correct order. This is a recent development in computer graphics hardware and requires large amounts of texture memory to process large structured point datasets.

A fundamental step in the texture mapping process is determining how to map the texture onto the geometry. To accomplish this, each vertex has an associated texture coordinate in addition to its position, normal, color, and other point attributes. The texture coordinate maps the vertex into the texture map as shown in Figure **7–4**. The texture coordinate system uses the parameters (u,v) and (u,v,t) or equivalently (r,s) or (r,s,t) for specifying 2D and 3D texture values. Points between the vertices are linearly interpolated to determine texture map values.

Another approach to texture mapping uses procedural texture definitions instead of a texture map. In this approach, as geometry is rendered, a procedure is called for each pixel to calculate a texel value. Instead of using the (u,v,t) texture coordinates to index into an image, they are passed as arguments to the procedural texture that uses them to calculate its result. This method provides almost limitless flexibility in the design of a texture, therefore it is almost impossible to implement in dedicated hardware. Most commonly, procedural textures are used with software rendering systems that do not make heavy use of existing graphics hardware.

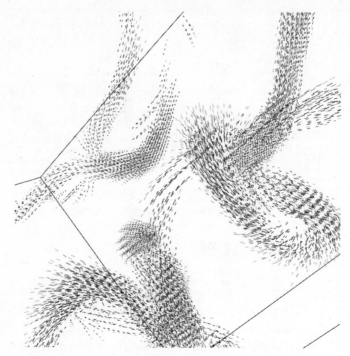

Figure 7–5 One frame from a vector field animation using texture maps.

While texture maps are generally used to add detail to rendered images, there are important visualization applications.

- Texture maps can be generated procedurally as a function of data. One example is to change the appearance of a surface based on local data value.

- Texture coordinates can be generated procedurally as a function of data. For example, we can *threshold* geometry by creating a special texture map, and then setting texture coordinates based on local data value. The texture map consists of two entries: fully transparent ($\alpha = 0$) and fully opaque ($\alpha = 1$). The texture coordinate is then set to index into the transparent portion of the map if the scalar value is less than some threshold, or into the opaque portion otherwise.

- Texture maps can be animated as a function of time. By choosing a texture map whose intensity varies monotonically from dark to light, and then "moving" the texture along an object, the object appears to crawl in the direction of the texture map motion. We can use this technique to add apparent motion to things like hedegehogs to show vector magnitude. Figure **7–5** is an example of a texture map animation used to simulate vector field motion.

These techniques will be covered in greater detail in Chapter 9. (See "Texture Algorithms" on page 308.)

Figure 7–6 Wireframe image and antialiased equivalent.

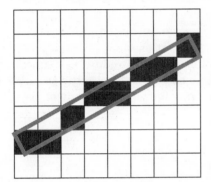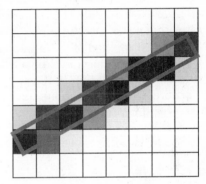

Figure 7–7 A one pixel wide line (outlined in grey) draw using a winner take all approach (left) and a coverage approach (right).

7.4 Aliasing

At one point or another most computer users have run into aliasing problems. This "stair-stepping" occurs because we represent continuous surface geometry with discrete pixels. In computer graphics the most common aliasing problem is jagged edges when rendering lines or surface boundaries, as in Figure **7–6**.

The aliasing problem stems from the rasterization process as the graphics system converts primitives, such as line segments, into pixels on the screen. For example, the quickest way to rasterize a line is to use an all or nothing strategy. If the line passes through the pixel, then the pixel is set to the line's color, otherwise it is not altered. As can be seen in Figure **7–7**, this results in the stair-stepped appearance.

There are several techniques for handling aliasing problems, and they are collectively known as *antialiasing* techniques. One approach to antialiasing is to change how the graphics system rasterizes primitives. Instead of rasterizing a line using an all or nothing approach, we look at how much of the pixel the line occupies. The resulting color for that pixel is a mixture of its original color and the line's color. The ratio of these two colors is determined by the line's occupancy. This works especially well when working primarily with wireframe models. A similar approach breaks each pixel down into smaller subpixels. Primitives are rendered using an all or nothing strategy, but at subpixel resolutions. Then the subpixels are averaged to determine the resulting pixel's color. This tends to require much more memory.

Good results can be obtained by breaking each pixel into ten subpixels, which requires about ten times the memory and rendering time. If you don't have access to hardware subpixel rendering, you can approximate it by rendering a large image and then scaling it down. Using a program such as pnmscale, which does bilinear interpolation, you can take a 1000 by 1000 pixel image and scale it down to a 500 by 500 antialiased image. If you have a graphics library that can render into memory instead of the screen, large images such as 6000 by 6000 pixels can be scaled down into high quality results, still at high resolutions such as 2000 by 2000. This may seem like overkill, but on a good 300dpi color printer this would result in a picture roughly seven inches on a side.

The last method of antialiasing we will look at uses an accumulation buffer to average a few possibly aliased images together, to produce one antialiased result. An accumulation buffer is just a segment of memory that is set aside for performing image operations and storage. The following fragment of C++ code illustrates this process.

```
for (imageNum = 0; imageNum < imageTotal; imageNum++)
  {
  // Jitter the camera and focal point by less than one pixel
  // Render an image
  // add the image to the accumulation buffer
  }
// Divide the accumulation buffer by imageTotal
// Display the resulting antialiased image
```

Instead of using one image with eight subpixels per pixel, we can use eight images without subpixels. The antialiasing is achieved by slightly translating the camera's position and focal point between each image. The amount of translation should be within one pixel of magnitude and perpendicular to the direction of projection. Of course, the camera's position is specified in world coordinates not pixels, but Equation **7-2** will do the trick. We calculate the new camera position and focal point (i.e., p_{new} and f_{new}) from the offset to avoid difficulties surrounding the transformation matrix at the camera's position.

$$f_{new} = (fM_{WD} + O_p) M_{DW}$$
$$O_w = f_{new} - f$$
$$p_{new} = p + O_w$$

(7-2)

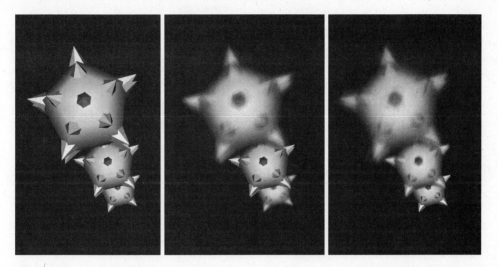

Figure 7–8 Three images showing focal depth. The first has no focal depth, the second is focused on the center object, the third image is focused on the farthest object.

In this equation O_p is the offset in pixel coordinates, O_w is the offset in world coordinates, f is the camera focal point, p is the camera position, and the transformation matrices M_{WD} and M_{DW} transform from world coordinates to display coordinates and from display coordinates to world coordinates, respectively.

7.5 Camera Tricks

In the previous section we saw how to combine an accumulation buffer and small camera translations to produce an antialiased image. In this section we will cover a few other camera techniques of interest. You may have noticed that with computer generated images all actors are in focus. With a real camera you have to set the focal depth to match the distance of the object you are photographing. Anything that is closer or father than your focal depth will appear out of focus. This is because a real camera has a lens that lets light pass through a finite area. The camera model we have introduced has a point lens, where all the light travels through at exactly the same point. (See Figure 7–8 for a comparison.)

We can simulate a finite camera lens by rendering many images, each with a slightly different camera position but the same focal point. Then we accumulate these images and take the average. The resulting image simulates a camera lens with focal depth. The different camera positions are determined by selecting random points from the lens you are trying to simulate. Larger diameter lenses will produce more distortion and vice-versa. Increasing the number of random points will improve the precision of your result. Typically ten to thirty samples is desirable. The images in Figure 7–8 were created using thirty sample points.

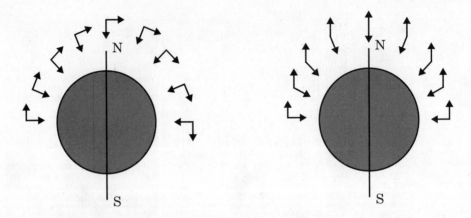

Figure 7–9 Rotations using an orthogonalized view-up vector (left) and a constant view-up vector (right).

Another difference between a real camera and a computer camera is in the shutter speed. Our model generates an image for a single moment in time; in contrast, a photograph captures what the camera views while its shutter is open. Fast moving objects appear blurred because of changes in their position during the small time that the shutter is open. This effect, known as *motion blur*, can also be simulated with our camera model. Instead of rendering one image and displaying it, we render a few subframes that are accumulated, averaged and finally displayed. This is similar to the antialiasing and focal depth techniques we just discussed. In both of those techniques, the camera is jittered while the actors remain fixed in time. To implement motion blur we don't jitter the camera, we increment the scene's time between each subframe. Moving objects or camera movements will result in differences between each subframe. The resulting image approximates the effects of photographing moving objects over a finite time.

7.6 Mouse Based Interaction

There's no doubt that being able to interactively view an object aids in understanding and recognizing its important features. Using a pointing device (e.g. a mouse or trackball) is certainly the most common method for controlling such movements. The software that accompanies this book contains the vtkRender-WindowInteractor object that translates mouse and keyboard events into modifications to the camera and actors. For example, while the user holds the left mouse button down, the vtkRenderWindowInteractor rotates the camera towards the current pointer position. The farther the pointer is from the center of the window, the faster the camera rotates.

Most of these interactions are straightforward, but there are a few issues associated with rotations. When rotating around an object, one must decide what to do with the view-up vector. We can keep it perpendicular to the direction of projection as we rotate, or we can leave it unchanged. This results in two different types of rotations. If we keep our view-up vector orthogonal to the direction of projection, we will rotate all around the object much like a plane flying around the globe. This is shown in the left-half of Figure **7–9**. If we leave the view-up vector unchanged, our plane will start flying backwards at the north and south poles, as shown in the right-half of Figure **7–9**.

The advantage of a constant view-up vector is that some objects have a natural sense of up and down (e.g., terrain). Elevation and azimuth operations remain consistent as we move around the object. On the other hand, there are singular points where the view-up vector and direction of projection become parallel. In these cases the camera viewing transformation matrix is undefined. Then we have to modify the view-up vector, or use the perpendicular view-up / direction of projection method to handle this situation. If the data you are working with has a well-defined up and down, then it probably makes sense to leave the view-up constant during rotations, otherwise it makes sense to keep it orthogonal to the direction of projection.

7.7 Volume Rendering

In Chapter 3 we categorized rendering techniques as either surface or volume rendering. In this section we will introduce volume rendering concepts.

In applying surface rendering techniques, the rendering primitives we use are of two or less dimensions, i.e., surface primitives. This includes points, lines, polygons, triangle strips, and spline surfaces. When we are faced with visualizing a 3D dataset using surface rendering, we have to generate isosurfaces, streamlines, or some other structure consisting of these surface primitives. Volume rendering is a technique that allows us to render 3D datasets directly, without having to generate intermediate 2D surface primitives. Moreover, volume rendering allows us to "see inside" or "see through" our data. This capability allows us to visualize more information as compared to standard surface rendering techniques.

There are two basic approaches for volume rendering. These are the object-order and image-order approaches we described in Chapter 3. In object-order volume rendering techniques, a forward mapping scheme is used to project volume data (i.e., voxels) onto the image plane. This is often referred to as splatting. In image-order volume techniques, a backward mapping scheme is used, where rays are cast from each pixel in the image plane through the volume to determine the resulting pixel value. This method is an extension of the ray casting techniques we saw in Chapter 3. Hybrid methods that combine image-order and object-order techniques also exist.

Volume rendering is inherently different from surface rendering because we are trying to view the interior structure of a 3D object (or data). To see inside these objects, our transfer functions naturally include translucent alpha values (see "Color Mapping" on page 143). In both object-order and image-order tech-

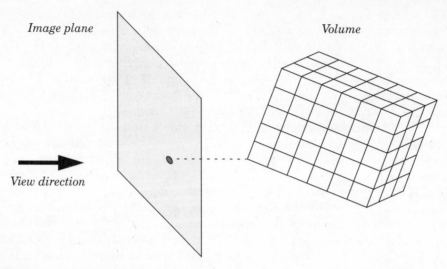

Figure 7–10 Object-order volume rendering. Voxels are composited in order.

niques the transfer function allows us to blend or composite data from the 3D object onto a 2D image plane. Thus, proper construction of transfer functions (or RGBA colormaps) is critical to constructing high quality volume visualizations. It is possible to render object surfaces with volume rendering techniques by using opaque transfer functions. In fact, one of the nice features of volume rendering is that its generality encompasses surface rendering.

Some of the important issues in volume rendering are the techniques we use for compositing the data, dealing with lighting/shading calculations, and performance issues. Compositing describes how to accumulate the 3D data onto the 2D image plane. We will see how various techniques treat this problem. Lighting and shading calculations are problematic because we need to simulate how the interior of an object is lit. That means considering how the light reaches a particular point (the light is affected by the material it passes through), and then how the light travels from the point to the observer's eye. Finally, we wish to do these computations as fast as possible. Many of the modern volume rendering techniques build on the basic methods presented here, but perform elaborate computations to speed up the overall process.

Object-Order Techniques

In object-order techniques we map the data (i.e., voxels) to the image plane directly (Figure **7–10**). Thus, we determine the pixels that are affected by each data sample. This is done using a variation of alpha compositing as illustrated in Figure **7–3**. As we saw in this figure the compositing process must be properly ordered. Thus object-order techniques require an ordered compositing to achieve the correct result.

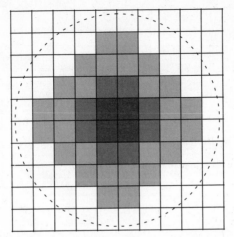

Figure 7–11 A splat footprint shown in black/white. Dark areas indicate regions of higher intensity.

We can use two different ordering schemes: a back-to-front and front-to-back order. (The front of the volume is closest to the viewer's eye with the image plane between the viewer and volume as shown in Figure **7–3**). To apply these techniques we do not need to sort all voxels into strict order. Instead we only need to project voxels in such a way that if two voxels v_i and v_j map to the same image plane pixel, they map in the correct order. So if v_j is closer to the image plane than v_i, v_i will be mapped before v_j if we are using a back-to-front order; and v_j will be mapped before v_i if we are using a front-to-back order.

We can order voxels by traversing the volume plane-by-plane and row-by-row within each plane. The result is that we have three nested loops indexing on x, y, and z. The loops may occur in either increasing or decreasing order along each axes, and the order of nesting will vary. The ordering depends on the relative relationship of the view position to the volume.

A back-to-front order allows us to composite our data using the method illustrated in Figure **7–3**. But a front-to-back order provides advantages in some cases. If we are compositing opaque samples, we can stop the compositing process for a pixel once a voxel has been mapped there. This is because any voxel mapped to the same pixel at a later time is occluded by the first pixel. This procedure can be extended to non-opaque voxels by stopping the composite process once the alpha value at a pixel becomes equal to a value of one. Also, with a front-to-back method, we can obtain useful intermediate results by compositing just a portion of the voxels. With a back-to-front procedure the value of a pixel may change dramatically during the rendering process. The front-to-back order generates images that smoothly converge to the final image.

Now that we know in which order to composite voxels, the question is *what* are we compositing? Westover [Westover90] offers one approach. We composite a density function. Typically we use a spherical Gaussian kernel projected onto a plane perpendicular to the view direction (Figure **7–11**). The projected kernel is

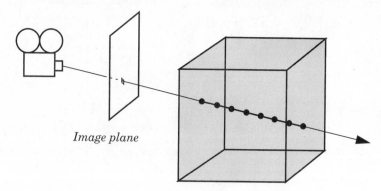

Figure 7–12 Casting a ray through a volume.

known as a *footprint*. The footprint is evaluated on a grid as shown in the figure. The extent of the footprint and its resolution is specified by the user. The footprint must be chosen carefully. If it is too small, then pixels on the image plane may not receive sufficient contribution. If it is too large, details in the image will be lost as the data is composited.

Westover extends his method to non-cubical voxels as well. The splats are then elliptical. One important aspect of this technique is that the footprint for each voxel remains constant if the view projection is orthographic. Thus, the footprint needs only be calculated once. For perspective viewing the footprint varies across the volume. Because of the expense of computing the footprint, perspective viewing is much slower relative to orthographic viewing.

Other researchers have described an alternative technique for compositing that takes advantage of conventional surface rendering hardware [Shirley90], [Wilhelms91]. Voxels are decomposed into partially transparent polygons and then sent through the graphics hardware. These techniques require careful selection of alpha and color values to avoid artifacts in the image. Similar to Westover's splatting technique, the polygonal decomposition is constant if the view is orthographic. Perspective views require position dependent decomposition of the voxels.

Image-Order Techniques

In image-order techniques, we determine how data samples affect each pixel in the image plane. This is done using a variation of the ray-casting technique we described in Chapter 3. The difference is that for surface ray casting, the rays interact only with the surface and surface properties of the object. In volume ray casting, the rays interact with interior of the object.

The basic process is as follows. A ray is cast from the camera through a selected pixel in the image plane and into the volume (Figure **7–12**). The ray is sampled at discrete points separated by a distance d. At each point within the volume, color and opacity is accumulated. (This is a numerical integration process.) Once the opacity reaches a value of one, or the ray exits the volume, the process terminates. This is repeated for each pixel in the image plane.

To compute the data value at d we can use either constant or linear interpolation. With constant or zero-order interpolation, the voxel value is used for the data value at d. For linear interpolation we use the tri-linear interpolation functions of Figure **8–10**. Linear interpolation gives superior results as compared to constant order interpolation, but requires extra computation.

There are several techniques we can use to speed up this process. The first is to limit the sampling to the region of the ray within the volume. This idea can be extended further to limit the sampling to points within the data of interest. Often, volumes consist of "empty" space, or regions where the data values are not of interest or contribute negligibly to the final image. By avoiding sampling in these regions, a significant speedup can be achieved. An algorithm known as *polygon assisted ray casting,* or PARC, limits ray sampling by bounding the data of interest with a polyhedron. Only points within the bounding polyhedron are sampled.

Another approach to improving performance is to organize volume data into encoded structures. Octree and run-length encoded representations are both commonly used. When properly constructed, these data structures can quickly distinguish between empty and non-empty regions in the volume. This allows the algorithm to process only those regions contributing to the final image. A benefit to this approach is that the volume data is often compressed to a size smaller than its original.

Shading

Volume rendered images benefit from shading just as surface rendered images do. The major difference is that light is affected as it passes into and out of the volume. During its traversal, the light also can be scattered or reflected repeatedly. Although we can simulate these effects using more elaborate ray-tracing techniques, there are simpler methods that achieve reasonable results. We will discuss two such methods: z-buffer *gradient-shading* and *gray-level shading*.

If we want to shade opaque volume rendered images we can use z-buffer gradient shading. This method requires knowledge of the z-depth of each sample. So for example, if we use an object-order technique we keep track of depth while compositing. For image-order techniques we keep track of the point at which the ray strikes the object and compute the view depth.

Once we have a z-buffer we can compute an approximate normal. We use a finite difference approximation to the gradient at the point x_0, y_0 in the image plane.

$$\frac{\partial Z}{\partial x} = \frac{Z(x_0 + \Delta x, y_0) - Z(x_0 - \Delta x, y_0)}{2\Delta x}$$

$$\frac{\partial Z}{\partial y} = \frac{Z(x_0, y_0 + \Delta y) - Z(x_0, y_0 - \Delta y)}{2\Delta y} \qquad \textbf{(7-3)}$$

$$\frac{\partial Z}{\partial z} = 1$$

This vector is then normalized to yield a normal vector. We can then use standard lighting equations with this normal to shade the pixel.

For both opaque and non-opaque volume data we can use gray-level shading. We simply approximate the normal using the data gradient given by Equation **7-3**. This information, in combination with the light direction and standard lighting equations we described earlier, can be used to modulate the intensity of the image value.

The Future of Volume Rendering

Some researchers believe that volume rendering will eventually replace surface rendering as the basis for computer graphics rendering techniques. Kaufman [Kaufman93] is a staunch advocate of this point of view. His claim is that volume rendering is to surface rendering, as raster graphics was to vector graphics. This analogy draws on the early years of computer graphics, when vector graphics (i.e., stroked lines) were the only graphics available. Although these techniques were useful, the arrival of raster graphics supplanted vector graphics, mainly because of superior image quality (i.e., surface shading, texture mapping, etc.). Volume rendering offers improvements in image quality over surface rendering in some areas as well. So the question remains: will volume rendering surpass surface rendering as the rendering technique of choice?

There are major obstacles to adopting volume rendering in wide application. These are

1. data size is large,

2. performance is poor, and

3. volume modelling techniques are limited in accuracy.

The size of volume data is large (as compared to equivalent surface representation). This is intimately connected with item number 3 above, and is a function of the structure of volume data. The basic problem is that the data is represented on a regular grid. To capture detail on such a structure requires refining the entire volume. This is a $O(n^3)$ process, where n is the number of samples in the x-y-z directions. Current computer systems are incapable of treating large volumes (e.g., 1024^3 or 1,073,741,824 voxels, or larger). This includes processing the data, as well as storing and accessing the data on disc and across the network (or bus).

The performance of volume rendering is currently too slow for many types of interactive work. This is a direct consequence of item 1 above, as well as the fact that conventional computer systems do not support volume rendering in hardware. Some researchers including Lacroute and Levoy [Lacroute94] and Sobierajski and Avila [Sobierajski95] have reported impressive speedups based on algorithmic improvements (e.g., preprocessing the data). However, it is only when computers directly support volume rendering, or parallel computation methods are widely used, that volume-rendered frame rates may approach the current rates for surface rendering.

Finally, volume modelling is not precise enough for many types of geometric representation. It is not atypical for an industrial application to require 0.05mm accuracy across a distance of one meter. To translate this into volume rendering terms, this would require a volume of dimensions $20,000^3$. As a result, volume modelling will be used in a limited form for the foreseeable future. Most likely a volume system would be capable of voxelizing surface primitives on the fly, similar to the way line primitives are rasterized currently.

Despite these obstacles there is promise for the future. Items numbered 1 and 2 are related to computer system issues. Advances in parallel systems, computer speed, memory, and networks are certain to continue at a tremendous rate. Hardware support for volume rendering will eventually appear. Thus, items 1 and 2, as obstacles to volume rendering are likely to disappear in time. Item number 3 is a matter of how we choose to model data. Choosing a mixed representation of surface primitives plus volumes will go a long way to resolving this issue. This will allow users to model their data in the form most appropriate to the data. Thus, volume rendering is likely to become more widespread in the future.

7.8 Putting It All Together

This chapter has covered a wide variety of topics. In this section we demonstrate applications of each topic to some simple problems.

Red-Blue Stereo

In our first example, we will be looking at using red-blue stereo rendering. We start off with the example shown in Figure **7–13**, which renders something akin to a mace. Then, in Figure **7–13** we add in red-blue stereo rendering by adding two lines near the bottom which invoke the `StereoRenderOn()` and `SetStereoType()` methods. Once these two methods have been invoked, further rendering will be done in stereo. The picture in the upper right corner displays a grayscale version of the resulting image.

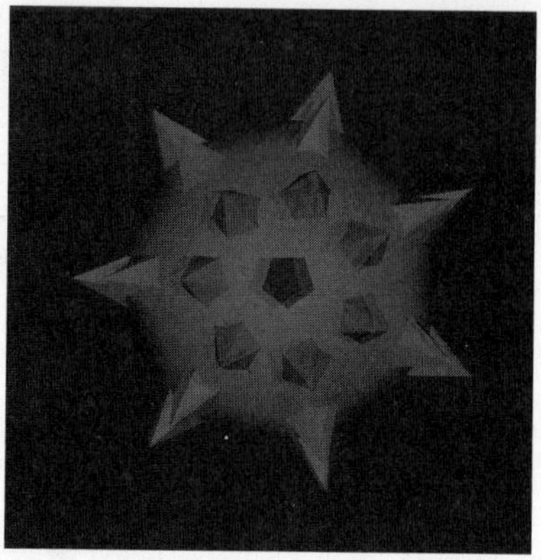

```
main ()
{
  vtkRenderMaster rm;
  vtkRenderer *ren1;
  vtkRenderWindow *renWin;
  vtkSphereSource *sphere;
  vtkConeSource *cone;
  vtkGlyph3D *glyph;
  vtkActor *sphereActor, *spikeActor;
  vtkPolyMapper *sphereMapper;
  vtkPolyMapper *spikeMapper;
  vtkRenderWindowInteractor *iren;

  // create the rendering objects
  renWin = rm.MakeRenderWindow();
  iren = renWin->MakeRenderWindowInteractor();
  ren1 = renWin->MakeRenderer();

  // create the pipeline, ball and spikes
  sphere = new vtkSphereSource(7);
  sphereMapper = new vtkPolyMapper;
  sphereMapper->SetInput(sphere->GetOutput());
  sphereActor = new vtkActor;
  sphereActor->SetMapper(sphereMapper);

  // sphereActor->GetProperty()->SetColor(0.8,0.8,0.8);
  cone = new vtkConeSource(5);
  glyph = new vtkGlyph3D;
  glyph->SetInput(sphere->GetOutput());
  glyph->SetSource(cone->GetOutput());
  glyph->UseNormal();
  glyph->ScaleByVector();
  glyph->SetScaleFactor(0.25);
  spikeMapper = new vtkPolyMapper;
  spikeMapper->SetInput(glyph->GetOutput());
  spikeActor = new vtkActor;
  spikeActor->SetMapper(spikeMapper);
  ren1->AddActors(sphereActor);
  ren1->AddActors(spikeActor);
  ren1->SetBackground(0.1,0.2,0.4);

  // zoom in a little
  ren1->GetActiveCamera()->Zoom(1.4);
  renWin->StereoRenderOn();
  renWin->SetStereoType(VTK_STEREO_RED_BLUE);
  renWin->Render();
```

Figure 7–13 An example of red-blue stereo rendering (Mace3.cc).

```
// changes and additions to the
// preceding example's source

// variables for the new actors
spikeActor2 = new vtkActor;
spikeActor2->SetMapper(spikeMapper);
spikeActor2->SetPosition(0,-0.7,0);
sphereActor2->SetPosition(0,-0.7,0);

ren1->AddActors(sphereActor2);
ren1->AddActors(spikeActor2);

// zoom in a little
ren1->GetActiveCamera()->Zoom(1.5);

renWin->SetSubFrames(21);
for (i = 0; i <= 1.0; i = i + 0.05)
  {
  spikeActor2->RotateY(2);
  sphereActor2->RotateY(2);
  renWin->Render();
  }
iren->Start();
```

Figure 7–14 Example of motion blur (MotBlur.cc).

Motion Blur

In our second example, we show how to simulate motion blur using the *Visualization Toolkit*. As shown in Figure **7–14**, we begin with our previous example. We then remove the two lines controlling stereo rendering and add a few lines to create another mace. We position the first mace in the top of the rendering window and the second mace at the bottom. We then use the SetSubFrames() method to start performing subframe accumulation. Here, we will perform twenty-one renders to produce the final image. For motion blur to be noticeable, something must be moving, so we set up a loop to rotate the bottom mace by two degrees between each subframe. Over the twenty-one subframes it will rotate forty degrees from its initial position. It is important to remember that the resulting image is not displayed until the required number of subframes have been rendered.

Focal Depth

Now we will change the previous example to illustrate focal depth. First, we change the position of the bottom mace, moving it farther away from us. Since it

```
// changes and additions to the
// preceding example's source

// set the actors position and scale
spikeActor->SetPosition(0,0.7,0);
sphereActor->SetPosition(0,0.7,0);
spikeActor2->SetPosition(0,-0.7,-10);
sphereActor2->SetPosition(0,-0.7,-10);
spikeActor2->SetScale(2,2,2);
sphereActor2->SetScale(2,2,2);
```

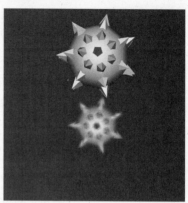

```
// zoom in a little
ren1->GetActiveCamera()->SetFocalPoint(0,0,0);
ren1->GetActiveCamera()->Zoom(4);
ren1->GetActiveCamera()->SetFocalDisk(0.05);

renWin->SetFDFrames(11);
renWin->Render();

iren->Start();
```

Figure 7–15 Example of a scene rendered with focal depth (`CamBlur.cc`).

is farther away it will appear smaller, so we scale it by a factor of two to maintain reasonable image size. We then remove the code for rendering the subframes and instead set the number of frames for focal depth rendering. We also set the camera's focal point and focal disk to appropriate values. The resulting image and the required changes to the source code are shown in Figure **7–15**.

Texture Mapping

Figure **7–16** shows the complete source code for a simple texture mapping example. You will notice that most of the code is similar to what we used in the preceding examples. The key step here is the creation of a `vtkTexture` object. This object interfaces between its data input and the texture mapping functions of the graphics library. The `vtkTexture` instance is associated with an actor. More than one texture instance may be shared between multiple actors. For texture mapping to function properly, texture coordinates must be defined by the actor's modeller.

One interesting note regarding the `vtkTexture` object. Instances of this class are mappers that have an `Input` instance variable that is updated during each render. The input type is a `vtkStructuredPoints` dataset type. Thus, a

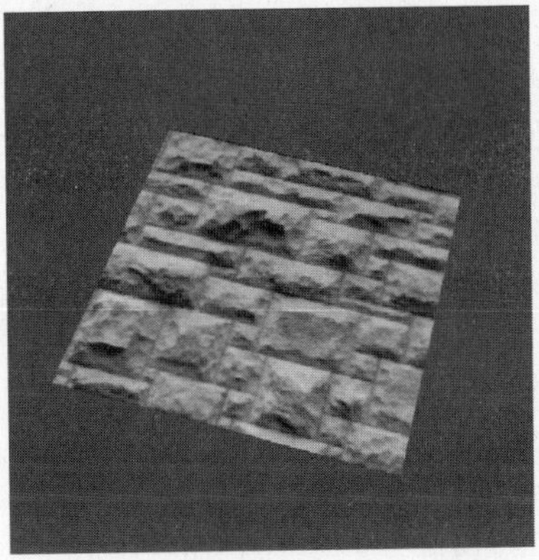

```
#include "vtk.hh"

main ()
{
  vtkRenderMaster rm;
  vtkRenderWindow *renWin;
  vtkRenderer *ren1;
  vtkActor planeActor;
  vtkPlaneSource plane;
  vtkPolyMapper planeMapper;
  vtkRenderWindowInteractor *iren;
  vtkTexture *atext;
  vtkPNMReader pnm;

  renWin = rm.MakeRenderWindow();
  iren = renWin->MakeRenderWindowInteractor();
  ren1 = renWin->MakeRenderer();

  // load the texture map
  atext = new vtkTexture;
  pnm.SetFilename("../../data/masonry.ppm");
  atext->SetInput(pnm.GetOutput());
  atext->InterpolateOn();

  planeMapper.SetInput(plane.GetOutput());
  planeActor.SetMapper(planeMapper);
  planeActor.SetTexture(atext);

  ren1->AddActors(&planeActor);
  ren1->SetBackground(0.2,0.3,0.4);
  renWin->SetSize(500,500);

  // zoom and then interact with data
  ren1->GetActiveCamera()->Zoom(1.4);
  iren->Initialize();

  iren->Start();
}
```

Figure 7–16 Example of texture mapping (`TPlane.cc`).

visualization pipeline can be constructed to read, process, and/or generate the texture map. This includes using the object `vtkRendererSource`, which converts the renderer's image into a structured point dataset. The input texture map can be either 2D (a pixmap) or 3D (a volume).

A few words of warning when using textures. Some renderers only support 2D texture, or may not support alpha textures. Also, some rendering systems require that each dimension of the structured point dataset is an exact power of two. (At the time of printing this was true of OpenGL.)

Volume Rendering

Our final example focuses on volume rendering. The source code shown in Figure **7–17** begins by creating the usual objects. Then we use a `vtkStructuredPointsReader` to read in a volume dataset for a high potential iron protein. We pass the data on to a `vtkOutlineFilter`, `vtkPolyMapper` and finally the actor, which will draw the boundaries of the volume dataset. We do a quick rendering of the outline and then zoom in a little for a better view. Now we set up the volume rendering side of things. We assign a volume renderer (`volRen` in this example) to our renderer `ren1`. When we send a render to `renWin`, that is forwarded to `ren1`. `ren1` will render the outline and then forward the render message on to `volRen`. `volRen` then renders each of its volumes and composites its results with the image that `ren1` created. The result is then displayed.

The volume renderer implemented in **vtk** uses an image-order ray casting technique. When applying this technique, it is important to make sure that the step size, specified in world coordinates, is consistent with respect to the data. If your data occupies a $10 \times 10 \times 10$ unit cube in world coordinates, then you would certainly want your step size to be less than ten units. A reasonable value of 0.1 units would result in about one hundred steps as the ray passes through the volume. Another important factor is the transfer functions that map the scalar values into RGBA values. If you specified the alpha value range as $(1,1)$ (the default value), the rays would stop as soon as they hit the volume. Most volume rendered images require translucent transfer functions for best results.

7.9 Chapter Summary

In this chapter we focused on a number of advanced topics in computer graphics. Stereo rendering techniques create two separate views for the right and left eyes. This simulates binocular parallax and allows us to see depth in the image. Time multiplexed techniques alternate left and right eye views in rapid succession. Time parallel techniques display both images at the same time.

Alpha opacity is a graphics method to simulate transparent objects. Compositing is the process of blending translucent samples in order. Alpha compositing requires the data to be ordered properly.

Texture mapping is a powerful technique to introduce additional detail into an image without extensive geometric modelling. Applying 2D texture maps to the surface of an object is analogous to pasting a picture. The location of the texture map is specified via texture coordinates.

Raster devices often suffer from aliasing effects. Antialiasing techniques are used to minimize the effects of aliasing. These techniques create blended images that soften the boundary of hard edges.

By using an accumulation buffer we can create interesting effects, including motion blur and camera focus. In motion blurring we accumulate multiple renders as the actors move. To simulate camera depth, we jitter the camera position and hold its focal point constant.

```
main ()
{
  vtkRenderMaster rm;
  vtkRenderWindow *renWin;
  vtkRenderer *ren1;
  vtkRenderWindowInteractor *iren;
  vtkVolumeRenderer volRen;
  vtkVolume vol;
  vtkStructuredPointsReader reader;
  vtkActor *outline1Actor;
  vtkPolyMapper outlineMapper;
  vtkOutlineFilter outline;
  float range[2];
  char c;
  renWin = rm.MakeRenderWindow();
  iren = renWin->MakeRenderWindowInteractor();
  ren1 = renWin->MakeRenderer();
  renWin->DoubleBufferOff();

  // Read data
  reader.SetFilename("../../data/ironProtein.vtk");
  reader.Update();
  reader.GetOutput()->GetPointData()->GetScalars()-
>GetRange(range);

  // Create outline
  outline.SetInput(reader.GetOutput());
  outlineMapper.SetInput(outline.GetOutput());
  outline1Actor = new vtkActor;
  outline1Actor->SetMapper(&outlineMapper);
  ren1->SetBackground(0.1,0.2,0.4);
  ren1->AddActors(outline1Actor);
  renWin->SetSize(150,150);
  renWin->Render();
  ren1->GetActiveCamera()->Zoom(1.5);
  ren1->SetVolumeRenderer(&volRen);
  volRen.AddVolume(&vol);
  volRen.SetStepSize(0.3);
  vol.SetInput(reader.GetOutput());
  vol.GetLookupTable()->SetAlphaRange(0,0.3);
  vol.SetScalarRange(range);
  // interact with data
  renWin->Render();
  cin >> c;
}
```

Figure 7–17 Volume rendering of a high potential iron protein (vol.cc).

Volume rendering is a powerful technique for directly viewing 3D datasets. Volume techniques may be classified as image-order, object-order, or a combination of the two. Object-order techniques composite voxels in front-to-back or back-to-front order. Image-order techniques use ray casting through pixels in the image plane to sample the volume.

7.10 Bibliographic Notes

Turn to the references in our earlier chapter on computer graphics (Chapter 3) for more in-depth coverage of the topics. Since these topics tend to be more obscure you will probably find that relevant papers may be more valuable [Kelly94] [Hodges92].

Volume rendering and volume visualization are active areas of research. A good introductory source can be found in [Kaufman91]. You may also wish to read about methods to improve the performance of volume rendering. Lacroute and Levoy [Lacroute94] describe one method to render images in a few seconds, as compared to the more typical many minutes of earlier systems. Their software implementation (VolPack) is available on the web at `http://www-graphics.stanford.edu/software/volpack/`.

Another important center of volume visualization research is at SUNY Stony Brook. They offer a volume rendering package called VolVis. VolVis is a comprehensive volume visualization system available free of charge. Both source and executable versions are available. See the web site `http://www.cs.sunysb.edu/~volvis` for more information.

7.11 References

[Kelly94]

> M. Kelly, K. Gould, S. Winner, A. Yen. "Hardware Accelerated Rendering of CSG and Transparency." *Computer Graphics (SIGGRAPH '94)*, pp. 177-184.

[Hodges92]

> L. F. Hodges. "Tutorial: Time-Multiplexed Stereoscopic Computer Graphics." *IEEE Computer Graphics & Applications,* March 1992.

[Kaufman91]

> A. Kaufman (editor). *Volume Visualization.* IEEE Computer Society Press, Los Alamitos, CA, 1991.

[Kaufman93]

> A. Kaufman, R. Yagel, D. Cohen. "Volume Graphics." *IEEE Computer*, 26(7):51-64, July 1993.

[Lacroute94]

> P. Lacroute and M. Levoy. "Fast Volume Rendering Using a Shear-Warp Factorization of the Viewing Transformation." In *Proceedings of SIGGRAPH '94*, pp. 451-458, Addison-Welsey, Reading, MA, 1994.

[Shirley90]

P. Shirley and A. Tuchman. "A Polygonal Approximation to Direct Volume Rendering." *Computer Graphics*, 24(5):63-70, 1990.

[Sobierajski95]

L. Sobierajski and R. Avila. "A Hardware Acceleration Method for Volumetric Ray Tracing." In *Proceedings of Visualization '95*, pp. 27-34, IEEE Computer Society Press, Los Alamitos, CA, October 1995.

[Wilhelms91]

J. Wilhelms and A. Van Gelder. "A Coherent Projection Approach for Direct Volume Rendering." *Computer Graphics (SIGGRAPH '91)*, 25(4):275-284, 1991.

[Westover90]

L. Westover. "Footprint Evaluation for Volume Rendering." *Computer Graphics (SIGGRAPH '90)*, 24(4):367-376, 1990.

7.12 Exercises

7.1   In astronomy, photographs can be taken that show the movements of the stars over a period of time by keeping the camera's shutter open. Without accounting for the rotation of the earth, these photographs display a swirl of circular arcs all centered about a common point. Such time lapse photography is essentially capturing motion blur. If we tried to simulate these images using the motion blur technique described in this chapter, they would look very different from the photographs. Why is this? How could you change the simple motion blur algorithm to correct this?

7.2   In Figure **7–1** we show the difference between stereo rendering with two or one view planes. If you were viewing a rectangle head on (its surface normal parallel to your direction), what artifacts would be introduced by rendering onto one view plane while using the equations for two planes?

7.3   On some graphics systems transparent objects are rendered using a technique called screen door transparency. Basically, every pixel is either completely opaque or completely transparent. Any value in between is approximated using dithering. So a polygon that was 50% opaque would be rendered by drawing only half of the pixels. What visual artifacts does this introduce? What blending problems can arise in using such a technique?

7.4   In this chapter we describe a few different techniques for antialiased rendering. One technique involved rendering a large image and then scaling it down to the desired size using bilinear interpolation. Another technique involved rendering multiple images at the desired size using small camera movements, and then accumulating them into a final image. When rendering a model with a surface representation, these two techniques will produce roughly the same result. When rendering a model with a wireframe representation there will be significant differences. Why is this?

Data Representation II

This chapter examines advanced topics in data representation. This includes topological and geometric relationships, and computational methods for cells and datasets.

8.1 Coordinate Systems

We will examine three different coordinate systems: the global, dataset, and structured coordinate systems. Figure **8–1** shows the relationship between the global and dataset coordinate systems, and depicts the structured coordinate system.

Global Coordinate System

The global coordinate system is a Cartesian, three-dimensional space. Each point is expressed as a triplet of values (x,y,z) along the x, y, and z axes. This is the same system that was described in Chapter 3 (see "Coordinate Systems" on page 47).

The global coordinate system is always used to specify dataset geometry (i.e., the point coordinates), and data attributes such as normals and vectors. We will use the word "position" to indicate that we are using global coordinates.

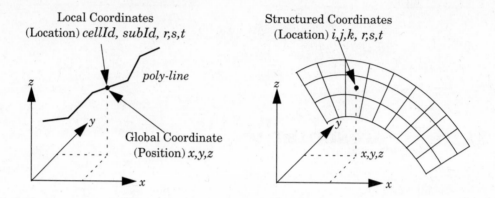

Figure 8–1 Local and global coordinate systems.

Dataset Coordinate System

The dataset, or local, coordinate system is based on combined topological and geometric coordinates. The topological coordinate is used to identify a particular cell, and the geometric coordinate is used to identify a particular location within the cell. Together they uniquely specify a location in the dataset. Here we will use the word "location" to refer to local or dataset coordinates.

The topological coordinate is an "id": a unique, non-negative integer number referring to either a dataset point or cell. For a composite cell, we use an additional "sub-id" to refer to a particular primary cell that composes the composite cell. The sub-id is also unique and non-negative. The id and sub-id together select a particular primary cell.

To specify a location within the primary cell, we use geometric coordinates. These geometric coordinates, or *parametric coordinates*, are coordinates "natural" or canonical to the particular topology and dimension of a cell.

We can best explain local coordinates by referring to an example. If we consider the poly-line cell type shown in Figure **8–1**, we can specify the position of a point by indicating 1) the poly-line cell id, 2) the primary cell (i.e., line) sub-id and 3) the parametric coordinate of the line. Because the line is one-dimensional, the natural or parametric coordinate is based on the one-dimensional parameter r. Then any point *along* the line is given by a linear combination of the two end points of the line x_i and x_{i+1}

$$x(r) = (1-r)x_i + rx_{i+1} \qquad \textbf{(8-1)}$$

where the parametric coordinate r is constrained between $(0,1)$. In this equation we are assuming that the sub-id is equal to i.

The number of parametric coordinates corresponds to the topological dimension of the cell. Three-dimensional cells will be characterized by the three parametric coordinates (r, s, t). For cells of topological order less than three, we will ignore the last *(3 - n)* parametric coordinates, where n is the topological order of the cell. For convenience and consistency, we also will constrain each parametric coordinate to range between *(0,1)*.

Every cell type will have its own parametric coordinate system. Later in this chapter we will describe the parametric coordinate systems in detail. But first we will examine another coordinate system, the *structured coordinate system*.

Structured Coordinate System

Many dataset types are structured. This includes structured points and structured grids. Because of their inherent structure, they have their own natural coordinate system. This coordinate system is based on the *i-j-k* indexing scheme that we touched on in Chapter 5 (see "Structured Points" on page 118).

The structured grid coordinate system is a natural way to describe components of a structured dataset. By fixing some indices, and allowing the others to vary within a limited range, we can specify points, lines, surfaces, and volumes. For example, by fixing the *i* index $i = i_0$, and allowing the *j* and *k* indices to range between their minimum and maximum values, we specify a surface. If we fix three indices, we specify a point, if we fix two indices, we specify a line, and if we allow three indices to vary, we specify a volume (or sub-volume). The structured coordinate system is generally used to specify a *region of interest* (or ROI). The region of interest is an area that we want to visualize, or to operate on.

There is a simple relationship between the point and cell id of the dataset coordinate system and the structured coordinate system. To obtain a point id p_{id} given the indices (i_p, j_p, k_p) and dimensions (n_x, n_y, n_z) we use

$$p_{id} = i_p + j_p n_x + k_p n_x n_y \qquad \text{(8-2)}$$

with $0 \le i_p < n_x$, $0 \le j_p < n_y$, $0 \le k_p < n_z$. (We can use this id to index into an array of points or point attribute data.) This equation implicitly assumes an ordering of the points in topological space. Points along the *i* axis vary fastest, followed by the *j* and then the *k* axes. A similar relationship exists for cell id's

$$cell_{id} = i_p + j_p (n_x - 1) + k_p (n_x - 1)(n_y - 1) \qquad \text{(8-3)}$$

Here we've taken into account that there are one fewer cells along each topological axes than there are points.

8.2 Interpolation Functions

Computer visualization deals with discrete data. The data is either supplied at a finite number of points, or created by sampling continuous data at a finite number of points. But we often need information at positions other than these supplied points. This may be for rendering, or for sub-sampling the data during algorithm execution. We need to interpolate data from known points to some intermediate point using *interpolation functions*.

Interpolation functions relate the values at cell points to the interior of the cell. Thus, we assume that information is defined at cell points, and that we must interpolate from these points. We can express the result as a weighted average of the data values at each cell point.

General Form

To interpolate data from the cell points p_i to a point p that is inside the cell, we need three pieces of information:

1. the data values at each cell point,

2. the parametric coordinates of the point p within the cell, and

3. the cell type including interpolation functions.

Given this information, the interpolation is a linear combination of the data values at the cell points

$$d = \sum_{i=0}^{n-1} W_i \cdot d_i \qquad \text{(8-4)}$$

where d is the data value at the interior cell location (r,s,t); d_i is the data value at the ith cell point; and W_i is a weight at the ith cell point. The weights, or *interpolation functions*, are functions of the parametric coordinates $W_i = W(r,s,t)$. In addition, because we want $d = d_i$ when the interior point coincides with a cell point, we can place additional constraints on the weights

$$W_i = 1, W_j = 0 \quad \text{when } p = p_i \text{ and } i \neq j \qquad \text{(8-5)}$$

We also desire the interpolated data value d to be no smaller than the minimum d_i and no larger than the maximum d_i. Thus the weights should also satisfy

$$\sum_i W_i = 1, \quad 0 \leq W_i \leq 1 \qquad \text{(8-6)}$$

The interpolation functions are of a characteristic shape. They reach their maximum value $W_i = 1$ at cell point p_i, and are zero at all other points. Examining Equation **8-1**, we draw Figure **8–2** and see that each interpolation function has the shape of a peaked "hat", and that interpolation is a linear combination of these hat functions, scaled by the data value at each point.

Equation **8-4** is the general form for cell interpolation. It is used to interpolate any data value defined at the cell points to any other point within the cell. We have only to define the specific interpolation functions W_i for each cell type.

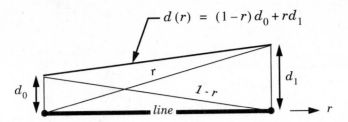

Figure 8–2 Interpolation is a linear combination of local interpolation functions. Interpolation functions are scaled by data values at cell points.

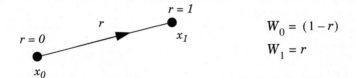

Figure 8–3 Parametric coordinate system and interpolation functions for a line.

Specific Forms

Each cell type has its own interpolation functions. The weights W_i are functions of the parametric coordinates r-s-t. In this section we will define the parametric coordinate system and interpolation function for each primary cell type. Composite cells use the interpolation functions and parametric coordinates of their composing primary cells. The only difference in coordinate system specification between primary and composite cells is that composite cells use the additional sub-id to specify a particular primary cell.

Vertex

Vertex cells do not require parametric coordinates or interpolation functions since they are zero-dimensional. The single weighting function is $W_0 = 1$.

Line

Figure **8–3** shows the parametric coordinate system and interpolation functions for a line. The line is described using the single parametric coordinate r.

Pixel

Figure **8–4** shows the parametric coordinate system and interpolation functions for a pixel cell type. The pixel is described using the two parametric coordinates (r,s). Note that the pixel edges are constrained to lie parallel to the global coordinate axes.

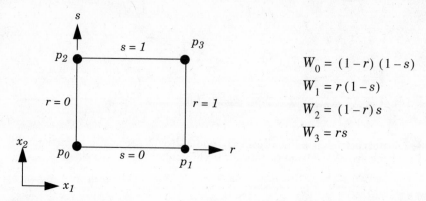

Figure 8–4 Parametric coordinate system and interpolation functions for a pixel.

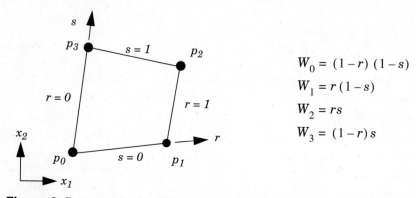

Figure 8–5 Parametric coordinate system and interpolation functions for a quadrilateral.

Quadrilateral

Figure **8–5** shows the parametric coordinate system and interpolation functions for a quadrilateral cell type. The quadrilateral is described using the two parametric coordinates (r,s).

Triangle

Figure **8–6** shows the parametric coordinate system and interpolation functions for a triangle cell type. The triangle is characterized using the two parametric coordinates (r,s).

Polygon

Figure **8–7** shows the parametric coordinate system and interpolation functions for a polygon cell type. The polygon is characterized using the two parametric coordinates (r,s). The parametric coordinate system is defined by creating a rect-

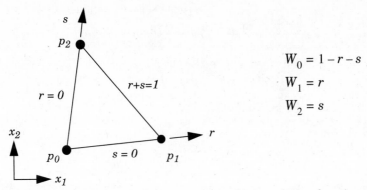

$$W_0 = 1 - r - s$$
$$W_1 = r$$
$$W_2 = s$$

Figure 8–6 Parametric coordinate system and interpolation functions for a triangle.

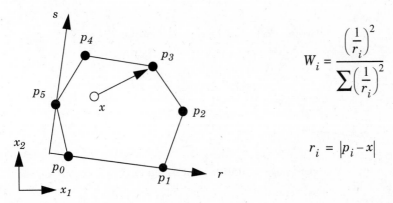

$$W_i = \frac{\left(\dfrac{1}{r_i}\right)^2}{\sum \left(\dfrac{1}{r_i}\right)^2}$$

$$r_i = |p_i - x|$$

Figure 8–7 Parametric coordinate system and interpolation functions for a polygon.

angle oriented along the first edge of the polygon. The rectangle also must bound the polygon.

The polygon poses a special problem since we do not know how many vertices define the polygon. As a result, it is not possible to create general interpolation functions in the fashion of the previous functions we have seen. Instead, we use a function based on weighted distance squared from each polygon vertex.

The weighted distance squared interpolation functions work well in practice. However, there are certain rare cases where points topologically distant from the interior of a polygon have an undue effect on the polygon interior (Figure 8–8). These situations occur only if the polygon is concave and wraps around on itself.

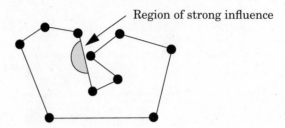

Figure 8–8 Potential problem with distance-based interpolation function.

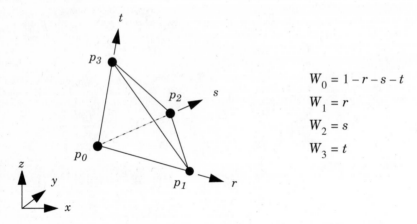

$$W_0 = 1 - r - s - t$$
$$W_1 = r$$
$$W_2 = s$$
$$W_3 = t$$

Figure 8–9 Parametric coordinate system and interpolation functions for a tetrahedron.

Tetrahedron

Figure **8–9** shows the parametric coordinate system and interpolation functions for a tetrahedron cell type. The tetrahedron is described using the three parametric coordinates *(r,s,t)*.

Voxel

Figure **8–10** shows the parametric coordinate system and interpolation functions for a voxel cell type. The voxel is described using the three parametric coordinates *(r,s,t)*. Note that the voxel edges are constrained to lie parallel to the global coordinate axes.

Hexahedron

Figure **8–11** shows the parametric coordinate system and interpolation functions for a hexahedron cell type. The hexahedron is described using the three parametric coordinates *(r,s,t)*.

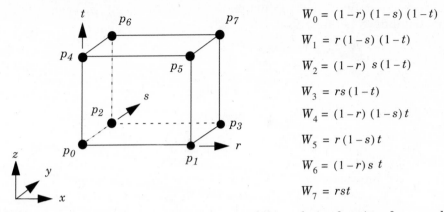

$$W_0 = (1-r)(1-s)(1-t)$$
$$W_1 = r(1-s)(1-t)$$
$$W_2 = (1-r)s(1-t)$$
$$W_3 = rs(1-t)$$
$$W_4 = (1-r)(1-s)t$$
$$W_5 = r(1-s)t$$
$$W_6 = (1-r)st$$
$$W_7 = rst$$

Figure 8–10 Parametric coordinate system and interpolation functions for a voxel.

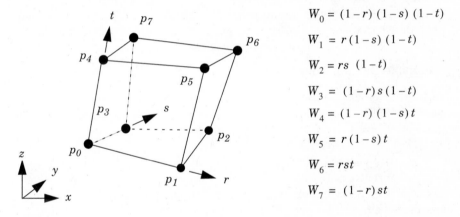

$$W_0 = (1-r)(1-s)(1-t)$$
$$W_1 = r(1-s)(1-t)$$
$$W_2 = rs(1-t)$$
$$W_3 = (1-r)s(1-t)$$
$$W_4 = (1-r)(1-s)t$$
$$W_5 = r(1-s)t$$
$$W_6 = rst$$
$$W_7 = (1-r)st$$

Figure 8–11 Parametric coordinate system and interpolation functions for a hexahedron.

8.3 Coordinate Transformation

Coordinate transformation is a common visualization operation. This may be either transformation from dataset coordinates to global coordinates, or global coordinates to dataset coordinates.

Dataset to Global Coordinates

Transforming between dataset coordinates and global coordinates is straightforward. We start by identifying a primary cell using the cell id and sub-id. Then the global coordinates are generated from the parametric coordinates by using the interpolation functions of Equation **8-4**. Given cell points $p_i = p_i(x_i, y_i, z_i)$ the global coordinate p is simply

$$p = \sum_{i=0}^{n-1} W_i\left(r_0, s_0, t_0\right) p_i \tag{8-7}$$

where the interpolation weights W_i are evaluated at the parametric coordinate (r_0, s_0, t_0).

In the formulation presented here, we have used the same order interpolation functions for both data and cell geometry. (By order we mean the polynomial degree of the interpolating polynomials.) This is termed *iso-parametric* interpolation. It is possible to use different interpolation functions for geometry and data. *Super-parametric* interpolation is used when the order of the interpolation functions for geometry is greater than those used for data. *Sub-parametric* interpolation is used when the order of the interpolation functions for geometry is less than those used for data. Using different interpolation functions is commonly used in numerical analysis techniques such as the finite element method. We will always use the iso-parametric interpolation for visualization applications.

Global to Dataset Coordinates

Global to dataset coordinate transformations are expensive compared to dataset to global transformations. There are two reasons for this. First, we must identify the particular cell C_i that contains the global point p. Second, we must solve Equation **8-4** for the parametric coordinates of p.

To identify the cell C_i means doing some form of searching. A simple but inefficient approach is to visit every cell in a dataset and determine whether p lies inside any cell. If so, then we have found the correct cell and stop the search. Otherwise, we check the next cell in the list.

This simple technique is not fast enough for large data. Instead, we use accelerated search techniques. These are based on spatially organizing structures such as an octree or three-dimensional hash table. The idea is as follows: we create a number of "buckets", or data place holders, that are accessed by their location in global space. Inside each bucket we tag all the points or cells that are partially or completely inside the bucket. Then, to find a particular cell that contains point p, we find the bucket that contains p, and obtain all the cells associated with the bucket. We then evaluate inside/outside for this abbreviated cell list to find the single cell containing p. (See "Searching" on page 241 for a more detailed description.)

The second reason that global to dataset coordinate transformation is expensive is because we must solve the interpolation function for the parametric coordinates of p. Sometimes we can do this analytically, but in other cases we must solve for the parametric coordinates using numerical techniques.

Consider the interpolation functions for a line (Figure **8–1**). We can solve this equation exactly and find that

$$r = \frac{(x - x_0)}{(x_1 - x_0)} = \frac{(y - y_0)}{(y_1 - y_0)} = \frac{(z - z_0)}{(z_1 - z_0)} \qquad \textbf{(8-8)}$$

Similar relations exist for any cell whose interpolation functions are linear combinations of parametric coordinates. This includes vertices, lines, triangles, and tetrahedra. The quadrilateral and hexahedron interpolation functions are nonlinear because they are products of linear expressions for the parametric coordinates. As a result, we must resort to numerical techniques to compute global to dataset coordinate transformations. The interpolation functions for pixels and voxels are non-linear as well, but because of their special orientation with respect to the x-y-z coordinate axes, we can solve them exactly. (We will treat pixel and voxel types in greater depth in "Special Techniques for Structured Points" on page 245.)

To solve the interpolation functions for parametric coordinates we must use non-linear techniques for the solution of a system of equations. A simple and effective technique is Newton's method [Conte72].

To use Newton's method we begin by defining three functions for the known global coordinate $p = p(x,y,z)$ in terms of the interpolation functions $W_i = W_i(r,s,t)$

$$
\begin{aligned}
f(r, s, t) &= 0 = x - \sum W_i x_i \\
g(r, s, t) &= 0 = y - \sum W_i y_i \\
h(r, s, t) &= 0 = z - \sum W_i z_i
\end{aligned}
\qquad \textbf{(8-9)}
$$

and then, expanding the functions using a Taylor's series approximation,

$$
\begin{aligned}
f = 0 &= f_0 + \frac{\partial f}{\partial r}(r - r_0) + \frac{\partial f}{\partial s}(s - s_0) + \frac{\partial f}{\partial t}(t - t_0) + \dots \\
g = 0 &= g_0 + \frac{\partial g}{\partial r}(r - r_0) + \frac{\partial g}{\partial s}(s - s_0) + \frac{\partial g}{\partial t}(t - t_0) + \dots \\
h = 0 &= h_0 + \frac{\partial h}{\partial r}(r - r_0) + \frac{\partial h}{\partial s}(s - s_0) + \frac{\partial h}{\partial t}(t - t_0) + \dots
\end{aligned}
\qquad \textbf{(8-10)}
$$

we can develop an iterative procedure to solve for the parametric coordinates. This yields the general form

$$
\begin{bmatrix} r_{i+1} \\ s_{i+1} \\ t_{i+1} \end{bmatrix} = \begin{bmatrix} r_i \\ s_i \\ t_i \end{bmatrix} - \begin{bmatrix} \frac{\partial f}{\partial r} & \frac{\partial f}{\partial s} & \frac{\partial f}{\partial t} \\ \frac{\partial g}{\partial r} & \frac{\partial g}{\partial s} & \frac{\partial g}{\partial t} \\ \frac{\partial h}{\partial r} & \frac{\partial h}{\partial s} & \frac{\partial h}{\partial t} \end{bmatrix}^{-1} \begin{bmatrix} f_i \\ g_i \\ h_i \end{bmatrix}
\qquad \textbf{(8-11)}
$$

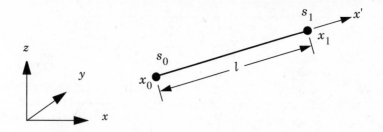

Figure 8–12 Computing derivatives in a 1D line cell.

Fortunately, Newton's method converges quadratically when it converges, and the interpolation functions that we have presented here are well-behaved. In practice, Equation **8-11** converges in just a few iterations.

8.4 Computing Derivatives

Interpolation functions enable us to compute data values at arbitrary locations within a cell. They also allow us to compute the rate of change, or derivatives, of data values. For example, given displacements at cell points we can compute cell strains and stresses. Or, given pressure values we can compute the pressure gradient at a specified location.

To introduce this process, we will begin by examining the simplest case: computing derivatives in a 1D line (Figure **8–12**). Using geometric arguments, we can compute the derivatives in the r parametric space according to

$$\frac{ds}{dr} = \frac{(s_1 - s_0)}{1} = (s_1 - s_0) \tag{8-12}$$

where s_i is the data value at point i. In the local coordinate system x', which is parallel to the r coordinate system (that is, it lies along the vector $\vec{x}_1 - \vec{x}_0$), the derivative is

$$\frac{ds}{dx'} = \frac{(s_1 - s_0)}{l} \tag{8-13}$$

where l is the length of the line.

Another way to derive Equation **8-13** is to use the interpolation functions of Figure **8–3** and the chain rule for derivatives. The chain rule

$$\frac{d}{dr} = \frac{d}{dx'} \cdot \frac{d}{dr} x' \tag{8-14}$$

allows us to compute the derivative d/dx' using

$$\frac{d}{dx'} = \left(\frac{d}{dr}\right) / \frac{d}{dr}x' \tag{8-15}$$

With the interpolation functions we can compute the x' derivatives with respect to r as

$$\frac{d}{dr}x' = \frac{d}{dr}\left(\sum_{i=0}^{1} W_i \cdot x'_i\right) = -x_0' + x_1' = l \tag{8-16}$$

which, when combined with Equation **8-15** and Equation **8-12** for the s derivatives, yields Equation **8-13**.

One final step remains. The derivatives in the $\vec{x}$ coordinate system must be converted to the global x-y-z system. We can do this by creating a unit vector $\vec{v}$ as

$$\vec{v} = \frac{(\vec{x}_1 - \vec{x}_0)}{|x_1 - x_0|} \tag{8-17}$$

where $\vec{x}_0$ and $\vec{x}_1$ are the locations of the two end points of the line. Then the derivatives in the x, y, and z directions can be computed by taking the dot products along the axes.

$$\frac{ds}{dx} = \left(\frac{s_1 - s_0}{l}\right)\vec{v} \cdot (1, 0, 0)$$

$$\frac{ds}{dy} = \left(\frac{s_1 - s_0}{l}\right)\vec{v} \cdot (0, 1, 0) \tag{8-18}$$

$$\frac{ds}{dz} = \left(\frac{s_1 - s_0}{l}\right)\vec{v} \cdot (0, 0, 1)$$

To summarize this process, derivatives are computed in the local r-s-t parametric space using cell interpolation. These are then transformed into a local $x' - y' - z'$ Cartesian system. Then, if the $x' - y' - z'$ system is not aligned with the global $x - y - z$ coordinate system, another transformation is required to generate the result.

We can generalize this process to three dimensions. From the chain rule for partial derivatives

$$\frac{\partial}{\partial x} = \frac{\partial}{\partial r}\frac{\partial r}{\partial x} + \frac{\partial}{\partial s}\frac{\partial s}{\partial x} + \frac{\partial}{\partial t}\frac{\partial t}{\partial x}$$

$$\frac{\partial}{\partial y} = \frac{\partial}{\partial r}\frac{\partial r}{\partial y} + \frac{\partial}{\partial s}\frac{\partial s}{\partial y} + \frac{\partial}{\partial t}\frac{\partial t}{\partial y} \tag{8-19}$$

$$\frac{\partial}{\partial z} = \frac{\partial}{\partial r}\frac{\partial r}{\partial z} + \frac{\partial}{\partial s}\frac{\partial s}{\partial z} + \frac{\partial}{\partial t}\frac{\partial t}{\partial z}$$

or after rearranging

$$
\begin{bmatrix} \dfrac{\partial}{\partial r} \\[2mm] \dfrac{\partial}{\partial s} \\[2mm] \dfrac{\partial}{\partial t} \end{bmatrix} = \begin{bmatrix} \dfrac{\partial x}{\partial r} & \dfrac{\partial y}{\partial r} & \dfrac{\partial z}{\partial r} \\[2mm] \dfrac{\partial y}{\partial s} & \dfrac{\partial y}{\partial s} & \dfrac{\partial z}{\partial s} \\[2mm] \dfrac{\partial z}{\partial t} & \dfrac{\partial y}{\partial t} & \dfrac{\partial z}{\partial t} \end{bmatrix} \begin{bmatrix} \dfrac{\partial}{\partial x} \\[2mm] \dfrac{\partial}{\partial y} \\[2mm] \dfrac{\partial}{\partial z} \end{bmatrix} = J \begin{bmatrix} \dfrac{\partial}{\partial x} \\[2mm] \dfrac{\partial}{\partial y} \\[2mm] \dfrac{\partial}{\partial z} \end{bmatrix} \qquad \textbf{(8-20)}
$$

The 3×3 matrix J is called the Jacobian matrix, and it relates the parametric coordinate derivatives to the global coordinate derivatives. We can rewrite Equation **8-20** into more compact form

$$
\frac{\partial}{\partial r_i} = J \frac{\partial}{\partial x_i} \qquad \textbf{(8-21)}
$$

and solve for the global derivatives by taking the inverse of the Jacobian matrix

$$
\frac{\partial}{\partial x_i} = J^{-1} \frac{\partial}{\partial r_i} \qquad \textbf{(8-22)}
$$

The inverse of the Jacobian always exists as long as there is a one-to-one correspondence between the parametric and global coordinate systems. This means that for any (r, s, t) coordinate there corresponds only one (x, y, z) coordinate. This holds true for any of the parametric coordinate systems presented here, as long as pathological conditions such as cell self-intersection or a cell folding in on itself are avoided. (An example of cell folding is when a quadrilateral becomes non-convex.)

In our one-dimensional example, the derivatives along the line were constant. However, other interpolation functions (e.g., Figure **8–5**) may yield non-constant derivatives. Here, the Jacobian is a function of position in the cell, and must be evaluated at a particular (r, s, t) coordinate value.

8.5 Topological Operations

Many visualization algorithms require information about the topology of a cell or dataset. Operations that provide such information are called *topological operations*. Examples of these operations include obtaining the topological dimension of a cell, or accessing neighboring cells that share common edges or faces. We might use these operations to decide whether to render a cell (e.g., render only one-dimensional lines) or to propagate particles through a flow field (e.g., traversing cells across common boundaries).

Before proceeding we need to define some terms from topology. *Manifold topology* describes a region surrounding a point that is topologically connected. That is, a region around the point is topologically equivalent to a small "disk" (in

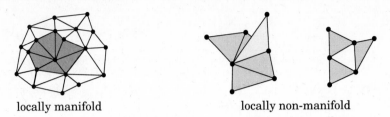

locally manifold   locally non-manifold

Figure 8–13   Manifold and non-manifold surface topology. If the local neighborhood around a vertex is topologically a 2D disk (i.e., a small disk can be placed on the surface without tearing or overlapping), then the surface is manifold at that vertex.

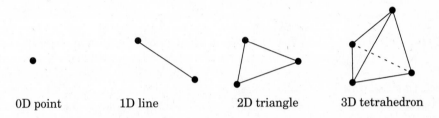

0D point   1D line   2D triangle   3D tetrahedron

Figure 8–14   Simplices of dimension three and lower.

two-dimensions) or "ball" (in three-dimensions). Topology that is not manifold is termed *non-manifold*. Examples of manifold and non-manifold geometry are shown in Figure **8–13**.

There are some simple rules we can use to decide whether a surface or region approximated with cells is manifold or non-manifold. In two dimensions, if every edge of a two-dimensional cell is used by exactly one other cell, than the surface is locally manifold. In three dimensions, if every face of a three-dimensional cell is used by exactly one other cell, than the region is locally manifold.

We also will use the term *simplex* on some occasions. A simplex of dimension n is the convex region defined by a set of $n+1$ independent points. A vertex, line, triangle, and tetrahedron are simplices of dimension 0, 1, 2, and 3, respectively. These are shown in Figure **8–14**.

Cell Operations

Cell operations return information about the topology of a cell. Typically we want to know the topological order of the cell or the topology of the cell boundary.

Given a cell C_i of topological dimension d, the cell is (implicitly) composed of boundary cells of topological order $d-1$ and lower. For example, a tetrahedron is composed of four two-dimensional triangles, six one-dimensional edges, and four zero-dimensional vertices. Cell operations return information about the number of boundary cells of a particular topological dimension, as well as the ordered list of points that define each bounding cell.

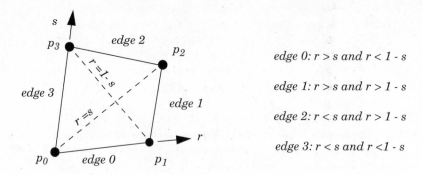

Figure 8–15 Closest boundary cell operation for quadrilateral cell.

Another useful cell operation returns the closest boundary cell of dimension *d-1* given the parametric coordinates of the cell. This operation ties the geometry to the topology of the cell, as compared to the parametric coordinate system, which ties the topology to the geometry. The closest boundary cell operation is implemented by partitioning each cell into various regions, as illustrated in Figure **8–15**. To determine the closest boundary cell we need only to identify the parametric region that the point lies in, and then return the appropriate boundary cell.

Another useful cell operation is cell decomposition into simplices. Every cell can be decomposed into a collection of simplices. By doing so, and by operating on the simplex decomposition rather than the cell itself, we can create algorithms that are independent of cell type. For example, if we want to intersect two datasets of varied cell type, without simplex decomposition we would have to create methods to intersect every possible combination of cells. With simplex decomposition, we can create a single intersection operation that operates on only the limited set of simplices. The significant advantage of this approach is that as new cells are added to the visualization system, only the cell object (including its method for simplex decomposition) must be implemented, and no other objects need be modified.

Dataset Operations

Dataset operations return information about the topology of a dataset, or topological information about the adjacency of cells. Typical operations include determining the neighbors to a cell, or returning a list of all cells that use a particular point.

We can formalize the adjacency operations by continuing the discussion of "Cell Types" on page 109. Adjacency methods are used to obtain information about the neighbors of a cell. A neighbor of a particular cell C_i is simply a cell that shares one or more points in common with C_i. A vertex neighbor is a neighbor that shares one or more vertices. An edge neighbor is a neighbor that shares one or more edges. A face neighbor is a cell that shares vertices that define one of the faces of the cell. Note that a face neighbor is also an edge neighbor, and an edge neighbor is also a vertex neighbor.

The adjacency operators are simple set operations. For a particular cell C_i defined by points

$$C_i = \{p_1, p_2, ..., p_n\} = P \tag{8-23}$$

and a point list $\bar{P} = (\bar{p}_1, \bar{p}_2, ..., \bar{p}_n)$ with $\bar{P} \subset P$, where $\bar{P}$ typically corresponds to the points defining a boundary cell of C_i, the neighbors of C_i is the adjacency set $A(\bar{C}, \bar{P})$. The adjacency set is simply the intersection of the use sets for each point, excluding the cell C_i.

$$A\left(C_i, \bar{P}\right) = \left(\bigcap_{i=1}^{n} U(\bar{p}_i)\right) - C_i \tag{8-24}$$

The adjacency set represents a variety of useful information. In a manifold object represented by a polyhedra, for example, each polygon must have exactly one edge neighbor for each of its edges. Edges that have no neighbors are boundary edges; edges that have more than one edge neighbor represent non-manifold topology. Datasets that consist of three-dimensional cells (e.g., unstructured grids) are topologically consistent only if, for each cell, there is exactly one face neighbor for each face. Faces that have no neighbors are on the boundary of the dataset. More than one face neighbor implies that the neighbors are self-intersecting.

8.6 Searching

Searching is an operation to find the cell containing a specified point p, or to locate cells or points in a region surrounding p. Algorithms requiring this operation include streamline generation, where we need to find the starting location within a cell, probing, where the data values at a point are interpolated from the containing cell, or collision detection, where cells in a certain region must be evaluated for intersection. Sometimes (e.g., structured point datasets), searching is a simple operation because of the regularity of data. However, in less structured data the searching operation is more complex.

To find the cell containing p, we can use the following naive search procedure. Traverse all cells in the dataset, finding the one (if any) that contains p. To determine whether a cell contains a point, the cell interpolation functions are evaluated for the parametric coordinates (r,s,t). If these coordinates lie within the cell, then p lies in the cell. The basic assumption here is that cells do not overlap, so that at most a single cell contains the given point p. To determine cells or points lying in the region surrounding p, we can traverse cells or points to see whether they lie within the region around p. For example, we can choose to define the region as a sphere centered at p. Then, if a point or the points composing a cell lie in the sphere, the point or cell is considered to be in the region surrounding p.

These naive procedures are unacceptable for all but the smallest datasets, since they are of order $O(n)$, where n is the number of cells or points. To improve the performance of searching, we need to introduce supplemental data structures to support spatial searching. Such structures are well-known and include MIP maps, octrees, kd-trees, and binary sphere trees (see "Bibliographic Notes" on page 265 at the end of this chapter).

The basic idea behind these spatial search structures is that the search space is subdivided into smaller parts, or buckets. Each bucket contains a list of the points or cells that lie within it. Buckets are organized in structured fashion so that constant time or logarithmic time access to any bucket is possible. For example, if we assign a portion of 2D Euclidean space into a grid of n by m buckets, the location of p in a particular bucket can be determined with two subtractions and two divisions: a constant time access. Similarly, the location of p in a non-uniformly subdivided octree is determined in logarithmic time, since recursive insertion into octant children is required. Once the bucket is found, the search is then limited to the points or cells contained within it. In a properly designed spatial search structure, the number of points or cells in a bucket is a small portion of the total and less then a fixed value. Thus, the time to search within a bucket can be bounded by a fixed constant. The result is that introducing spatial search structures reduces search times to a maximum $O(log\ n)$.

We have two options when applying spatial search structures. We may insert points into the search structure, or we may insert cells, depending on the application. There are advantages and disadvantages to both approaches. Inserting cells into buckets is not a trivial operation. In general, cells are arbitrarily oriented and shaped, and will not fit completely into a single bucket. As a result, cells often span multiple buckets. To reliably determine whether a cell is in a bucket requires geometric intersection tests, a costly operation. Another approach is to use the *bounding box* of a cell to decide which bucket(s) a cell belongs in. We only need to intersect the bounding box with a bucket to determine whether the cell may belong in the bucket. Unfortunately, even though this operation is generally fast, often cells are associated with buckets even though they may not actually lie inside them, wasting (in large models) memory resources and extra processing time.

Inserting points into a search structure is easier because points can be uniquely placed into a bucket. Inserting points also allows us to search for both points *and* cells. Cells can be found by using p to index into the appropriate bucket. The closest point(s) p_i to p are then located. Using the topological adjacency operator to retrieve the cells using points p_i, we can then search these cells for the cell containing p. This procedure must be used with caution, however, since the closest points may not be used by the cells containing p (Figure **8–16**).

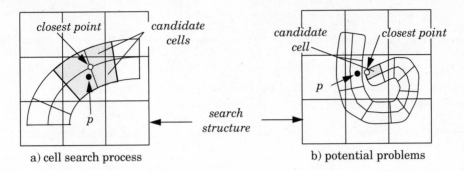

Figure 8–16 Using search structure (containing points) to find cells. a) Points are associated with appropriate bucket. Point p is used to index into bucket, and closest point(s) p_i is found. Cells using p_i are evaluated for containing cell. b) Sometimes closest points p_i are not used by cells containing p.

8.7 Cell / Line Intersection

An important geometric operation is intersection of a line with a cell. This operation can be used to interactively select a cell from the rendering window, to perform ray-casting for rendering, or to geometrically query data.

In the *Visualization Toolkit* each cell must be capable of intersecting itself against a line. Figure **8–17** summarizes these operations for the nine primitive cell types supported by **vtk**. (Intersections on composite cells are implemented by intersecting each primitive cell in turn.)

Line/cell intersection for 0D, 1D, and 2D cells follows standard approaches. Intersection against 3D cells is difficult. This is because the surfaces of these cells are described parametrically, and are not necessarily planar. For example, to intersect a line with a tetrahedron, we can intersect the line against the four triangular faces of the tetrahedron. Hexahedron, however, may have non-planar faces. Thus, we cannot intersect the line against six quadrilateral, planar faces. Instead, we use line/face intersection as an initial guess, and project the intersection point onto the surface of the cell. This produces an approximate result, but is accurate enough for most applications.

8.8 Scalars and Colors

There is a close correspondence between scalar data and colors. We saw this in "Color Mapping" on page 143, where we saw how to use a color table to map scalar values into a color specification (i.e., red, green, and blue or *RGB*). There are cases, however, when we want to circumvent this mapping process. Such cases occur when color data is supplied instead of scalar data.

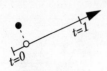

Vertex	Line	Triangle
- project point onto ray	- 3D line intersection	- line/plane intersection
- distance to line must be within tolerance	- distance between lines must be within tolerance	- intersection point must lie in triangle
- t must lie between [0,1]	- s,t must lie between [0,1]	- t must lie between [0,1]

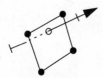

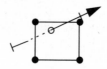

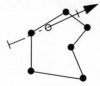

Quadrilateral	Pixel	Polygon
- line/plane intersection	- line/plane intersection	- line/plane intersection
- intersection point must lie in quadrilateral	- intersection point must lie in pixel (uses efficient in/out test)	- intersection point must lie in polygon (uses ray casting for polygon in/out)
- t must lie between [0,1]	- t must lie between [0,1]	- t must lie between [0,1]

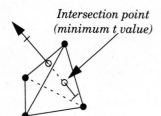

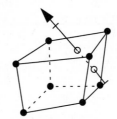

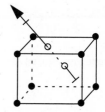

Tetrahedron	Hexahedron	Voxel
- intersect each (triangle) face	- intersect each (quadrilateral) face	- intersect each (pixel) face
- t must lie between [0,1]	- since face may be non-planar, project previous result onto hexahedron surface	- t must lie between [0,1]
	- t must lie between [0,1]	

Figure 8–17 Summary of line/cell intersection operations for nine primitive cell types. Line is assumed normalized in parametric coordinate t with $0 \leq t \leq 1$.

A common example occurs in imaging. Recall that an image is a regular, two-dimensional array of points. The points define pixels, which in turn form a two-dimensional structured points dataset. Images are frequently stored as a pair of dimensions along with data values. The data values may be one of black and white (e.g., a bitmap), grayscale, or color (e.g., a pixmap). Bitmaps and gray-scale images can be directly cast into the form of single-values scalar data, and we can use our earlier approach. Pixmaps, however, consist of (at a minimum) three values per pixel of red, green, and blue. (Sometimes, a fourth alpha opacity value may also be included.) Thus, pixmaps cannot be directly cast into scalar form.

To accommodate color data, special types of scalar objects needs to be created. Each class must act as if it were a scalar: that is, a request for data at a particular point must return a *single* scalar value. This allows us to use standard scalar visualization techniques such as contouring or warping. Thus a mapping from *RGB* or *RGBA* color coordinates to a single scalar value is required.

One simple mapping returns the *luminance Y* of a color. Given three components, *RGB*, the luminance is

$$Y = 0.30R + 0.59G + 0.11B \qquad \textbf{(8-25)}$$

If the color includes transparency, *RGBA*, the luminance is

$$Y = A \cdot (0.30R + 0.59G + 0.11B) \qquad \textbf{(8-26)}$$

Using this abstraction allows us to treat single-valued scalars and scalars consisting of multi-valued colors the same. The end result is that we can mix both types of scalar data into our visualization networks.

8.9 Special Techniques for Structured Points

A significant attraction of the structured points dataset is the speed and simplicity of computation. In this section, we will explore specific techniques that exploit the special regular topology and geometry of structured point datasets.

Coordinate Transformation

Given a point p we can find the structured coordinates by performing three division operations (Figure **8–18**). Taking the integer `floor` function yields the structured coordinates. Taking the fractional part of the result yields the parametric coordinates of the cell. We can then use Equation **8-3** to convert to dataset coordinates.

Derivative Computation

Because the structured point dataset is oriented parallel to the coordinate x, y, and z axes, and because the spacing of points in each of these directions is regu-

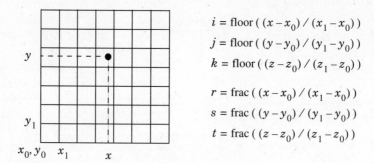

$$i = \text{floor}\,(\,(x - x_0)\,/\,(x_1 - x_0)\,)$$
$$j = \text{floor}\,(\,(y - y_0)\,/\,(y_1 - y_0)\,)$$
$$k = \text{floor}\,(\,(z - z_0)\,/\,(z_1 - z_0)\,)$$

$$r = \text{frac}\,(\,(x - x_0)\,/\,(x_1 - x_0)\,)$$
$$s = \text{frac}\,(\,(y - y_0)\,/\,(y_1 - y_0)\,)$$
$$t = \text{frac}\,(\,(z - z_0)\,/\,(z_1 - z_0)\,)$$

Figure 8–18 Structured point coordinate transformation.

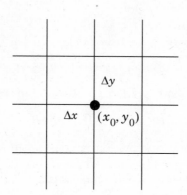

Figure 8–19 Using finite differences to compute derivatives on structured points dataset.

lar, finite difference schemes can be used to compute partial derivatives at the cell points. Referring to Figure **8–19**, we see that central differences can be used in each of the three directions according to

$$g_x = \frac{d\,(x_0 + \Delta x,\, y_0,\, z_0) - d\,(x_0 - \Delta x,\, y_0,\, z_0)}{2\Delta x}$$

$$g_y = \frac{d\,(x_0,\, y_0 + \Delta y,\, z_0) - d\,(x_0,\, y_0 - \Delta y,\, z_0)}{2\Delta y}$$

$$g_z = \frac{d\,(x_0,\, y_0,\, z_0 + \Delta z) - d\,(x_0,\, y_0,\, z_0 - \Delta z)}{2\Delta z}$$

(8-27)

(Note that at the boundary of the dataset, one-sided differences may be used.) We can use these equations to compute derivatives within the cell as well. We simply compute the derivatives at each cell point from Equation **8-27**, and then use the cell interpolation functions to compute the derivative at the point inside the cell.

Topology

Structured datasets lend themselves to efficient topological operations (i.e., both structured points and structured grids). Given a cell id, it is possible to determine vertex, edge, or face neighbors using simple constant time operations. First, given the cell id in a three-dimensional structured dataset, we use a combination of division and modulo arithmetic to compute the structured coordinates

$$i = id \ \text{modulo} \ (n_x - 1)$$
$$j = (id / (n_x - 1)) \ \text{modulo} \ (n_y - 1) \tag{8-28}$$
$$k = id / ((n_x - 1)(n_y - 1))$$

Face neighbors are determined by incrementing one of the $i, j,$ or k indices. Edge neighbors are determined by incrementing any two indices, while vertex neighbors are found by incrementing all three indices. Care must be taken while incrementing to insure that the indices fall in the range

$$0 \le i < (n_x - 1)$$
$$0 \le j < (n_y - 1) \tag{8-29}$$
$$0 \le k < (n_z - 1)$$

An attempt to index outside these ranges indicates that the neighbor in question does not exist.

Searching

Given a point $p = (x, y, z)$ we can determine the cell containing p by using the equations given in Figure **8–18**. These equations generate the structured coordinates (i, j, k), which can then be converted to cell id (i.e., dataset coordinates) using Equation **8-3**.

To find the closest point to p, we compute the structured coordinates by rounding to the nearest integer value (instead of using the floor function). Thus,

$$i = \text{int} \ ((x - x_0) / (x_1 - x_0))$$
$$j = \text{int} \ ((y - y_0) / (y_1 - y_0)) \tag{8-30}$$
$$k = \text{int} \ ((z - z_0) / (z_1 - z_0))$$

8.10 Putting It All Together

In this section we will finish our earlier description of an implementation for unstructured data. We also define a high-level, abstract interface for cells and datasets. This interface allows us to implement the general (i.e., dataset specific) algorithms in the *Visualization Toolkit*. We also describe implementations for color scalars, searching and picking, and conclude with a series of examples to demonstrate some of these concepts.

Unstructured Topology

In Chapter 5 we described data representations for the unstructured dataset types `vtkPolyData` and `vtkUnstructuredGrid`. Close examination of this data structure reveals that operations to retrieve topological adjacency are inefficient. In fact, to implement any operation to retrieve vertex, edge, or face neighbors requires a search of the cell list, resulting in $O(n)$ time complexity. This is unacceptable for all but the smallest applications, since any algorithm traversing the cell list and retrieving adjacency information is at a minimum $O(n^2)$.

The reason for this inefficiency is that the data representation is a "downward" hierarchy (Figure **8–21**(b)). That is, given a cell we can quickly determine the topological features lower in the topological hierarchy such as faces, edges, and points. However, given a face, edge, or point we must search the cell list to determine the owning cells. To improve the efficiency of this data representation, we must introduce additional information into the hierarchy that allows "upward" hierarchy traversal (similar to that shown in Figure **8–21**(a)).

The solution to this problem is to extend the unstructured data structure with a *link list*. The link list is a list of lists of cells that use each point and corresponds to the upward links of Figure **8–21**(c). The link list transforms the hierarchical structure of Figure **5–10** into a ring structure. Cells reference their composing points, and points in turn reference the cells that use them. The full unstructured data structure is shown in Figure **8–20**.

The link is in fact an implementation of the use sets of Equation **5-1**. We can use this equation to compute adjacency operation in constant time, if the maximum number of cells using a point is much smaller than the number of points in a dataset. To see this, we refer to Equation **8-24** and see that the adjacency operations consist of a finite number of set intersections. Each operation is an intersection of the link lists for each point. If the number of cells in each link list is "small", then the intersection operation can be bounded by a fixed constant in time, and the total operation can be considered a constant time operation.

There are several important characteristics of this data representation.

- The link list is an extension of the basic unstructured data representation. As a result, we can defer the construction of the link lists until they are required. Often the link lists are never needed and require no computer resources to compute or store.

- Building the link list is a linear $O(n)$ operation. Each cell is traversed and for every point that the cell uses, the list of using cells for that point is

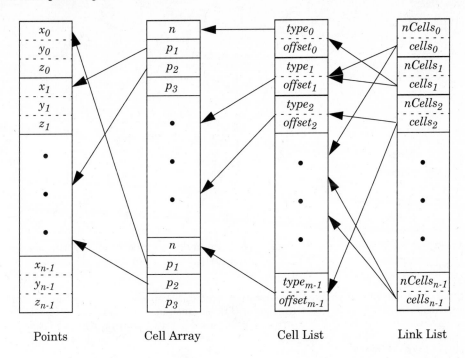

Figure 8–20 Complete unstructured data representation including link lists. There are m cells and n points. The n structures in the link list are lists of cells that use each vertex. Each link list is variable in length.

extended to include the current cell. Building the link list is only needed once as an initialization step.

- The data representation is compact relative to other topology representation schemes (e.g., the winged-edge structure and the radial-edge structures [Baumgart74] [Weiler88]). These other data structures contain explicit representation of intermediate topology such as edges, loops, faces, or special adjacency information such as adjacent edges (winged-edge structure), or extensive "use" descriptions (radial-edge structure). The compactness of representation is particularly important for visualization, since the data size is typically large.

The unstructured data structure in the *Visualization Toolkit* is implemented using the four classes vtkPoints (and subclasses), vtkCellArray, vtkCellList, and vtkLinkList. The building of this data structure is incremental. At a minimum, the points and cells are represented using vtkPoints and vtkCellArray. If random access or extra type information is required, then the object vtkCellList is used. If adjacency information is required, an instance of the class vtkLinkList is created. These operations are carried out behind the scenes, and generally do not require extra knowledge by the application programmer.

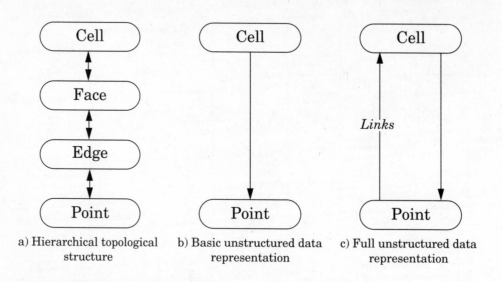

a) Hierarchical topological   b) Basic unstructured data   c) Full unstructured data
        structure   representation   representation

Figure 8–21 Enhancing hierarchical unstructured data representation. a) Conventional topological hierarchy for geometric model. b) Basic unstructured data hierarchy. c) Full unstructured data hierarchy. By introducing upward references from points to cells, the unstructured data hierarchy may be efficiently traversed in both directions, and is more compact than conventional topological hierarchies.

Abstract Interfaces

With the completion of Chapters 5 and 8, we can summarize the abstract interface for cells, datasets, and the point data attributes. These pseudo-code descriptions encapsulate the core functionality of the classes vtkDataSet, vtkCell, and vtkPointData and their subclasses. All algorithms presented in this text can be implemented using combinations of these methods.

Dataset Abstraction

The dataset is the central data representation in the *Visualization Toolkit*. Datasets are composed of one or more cells and points. Associated with the points are attribute data consisting of scalars, vectors, normals, texture coordinates, and user defined data.

```
type = GetDataType()
```
   Return the type of dataset (e.g., vtkPolyData, vtkStructured-Points, vtkStructuredGrid, vtkUnstructuredGrid).

```
numPoints = GetNumberOfPoints()
```
   Return the number of points in the dataset.

```
numCells = GetNumberOfCells()
```
   Return the number of cells in the dataset.

`x = GetPointCoordinate(ptId)`
> Given a point id, return the *x-y-z* coordinates of the point.

`cell = GetCell(cellId)`
> Given a cell id, return a pointer to a cell object.

`cells = GetPointCells(ptId)`
> Given a point id, return the cells that use this point.

`neighbors = GetCellNeighbors(cellId, ptIds)`
> Given a cell id and a list of points composing a boundary face of the cell, return the neighbors of that cell sharing the points.

`cellId = FindCell(x, cell, tol2, subId, pcoords, weights)`
> Given a coordinate value x, an initial search cell, and a tolerance measure, return the id and sub-id of the cell containing the point and its interpolation function weights. The initial search cell is used to speed up the search process when the position x is known to be near the cell. If no cell is found, `cellId` < 0 is returned.

`pointData = GetPointData()`
> Return a pointer to the object maintaining point attribute data. This includes scalars, vectors, normals, tensors, texture coordinates, and user defined data.

`bounds = GetBounds()`
> Get the bounding box of the dataset.

`dataSet = MakeObject()`
> Make a copy of the current dataset. A "virtual" constructor. (Typically reference counting methods are used to copy data.)

`CopyStructure(dataSet)`
> Update the current structure definition (i.e., geometry and topology) with the supplied dataset.

Cell Abstraction

Cells are the atomic structures of the *Visualization Toolkit*. Cells consist of a topology, which is defined by a sequence of ordered point ids, and a geometry, which are the point coordinates. The cell coordinate consists of a cell id, a sub-cell id, and a parametric coordinate. The sub-id specifies a primary cell that lies within a composite cell such as a triangle strip. Edges and faces of cells are defined implicitly from the topological definition of the cell.

`type = GetType()`
> Return the type of the cell. Must be one of the twelve **vtk** cell types.

`dim = GetDimension()`
> Return the topological definition of the cell.

`numberPoints = GetNumberOfPoints()`
    Return the number of points that define the cell.

`points = GetPoints()`
    Return a list of point ids defining the cell.

`numberEdges = GetNumberOfEdges()`
    Return the number of edges in the cell.

`edge = GetEdge(i)`
    Given an edge id ($0 \leq i <$ numberEdges) return a pointer to a cell that represents an edge of the cell.

`numberFaces = GetNumberOfFaces()`
    Return the number of faces in a cell.

`face = GetFace(i)`
    Given an face id ($0 \leq i <$ numberFaces) return a pointer to a cell that represents an face of the cell.

`inOutStatus = GetBoundary(subId, pcoords, poindIds)`
    Given a cell subId and parametric coordinates, return a list of point ids that define the closest boundary face of the cell. Also return whether the point is actually in the cell.

`inOutStatus = EvaluatePosition(x, closestPoint, subId, pcoords, weights, dist2)`
    Given a point coordinate x, return the sub-id, parametric coordinates, and interpolation weights of the cell if x lies inside the cell. The position `closestPoint` is the closest point on the cell to x (may be the same) and `dist2` is the squared distance between them. The method returns an `inOutStatus` indicating whether x is *topologically* inside or outside the cell. That is, the point may satisfy parametric coordinate conditions but may lie off the surface of the cell (e.g., point lies above polygon). Use both `inOutStatus` and `dist2` to determine whether point is both topologically and geometrically in the cell.

`EvaluateLocation(subId, pcoords, x, weights)`
    Given a point location (i.e., sub-id and parametric coordinates), return the position x of the point and the interpolation weights.

`Contour(value, cellScalars, points, verts, lines, polys, scalars)`
    Given a contour value and scalar values at the cell ponts, generate contour primitives (vertices, lines, or polygons with associated points and scalar values).

`Derivatives(subId, pcoords, values, dim, derivs)`
    Given a cell location (i.e., subId and parametric coordinates) and data values at the cell points, return dim*3 derivatives (i.e., corresponds to the x, y, and z directions times dimension of data).

IntersectWithLine(p1, p2, tol, t, x, pcoords, subId)
> Given a finite line defined by the two points p1 and p2 and an intersection tolerance, return the point of intersection x. The parametric coordinate t along the line and cell location at the point of intersection are also returned.

Triangulate(index, points)
> Decompose cell into simplices of dimension equal to the topological cell dimension. The index is an integer value that controls the triangulation if more than one triangulation is possible (e.g., voxel or hexahedron).

bounds = GetBounds()
> Return the bounding box of the cell.

Point Attribute Abstraction

Point attribute data is information associated with the points of a cell/dataset. This information consists of scalars, vectors, normals, tensors, texture coordinates, and/or user defined data. There is a one-to-one relationship between the points in a dataset and the attribute data. For example, scalar value at location 100 is associated with point id 100.

Many of the methods described below deal with moving data from the input to the output of a filter. Since the possibility exists that new types of attribute data could be added in the future, the details of moving data is hidden as much as possible (i.e., minimize the knowledge that the filter has about specific attribute types). Thus, generic functions like CopyData() allow for copying data from the input to the output without knowing what this data is.

CopyScalarsOn() / CopyScalarsOff()
> Turn on/off boolean flag controlling copying of scalar data from input to output of filter.

CopyVectorsOn() / CopyVectorsOff()
> Turn on/off boolean flag controlling copying of vector data from input to output of filter.

CopyNormalsOn() / CopyNormalsOff()
> Turn on/off boolean flag controlling copying of normal data from input to output of filter.

CopyTensorsOn() / CopyTensorsOff()
> Turn on/off boolean flag controlling copying of tensor data from input to output of filter.

CopyTextureCoordsOn() / CopyTextureCoordsOff()
> Turn on/off boolean flag controlling copying of texture coordinates data from input to output of filter.

CopyUserDefinedOn() / CopyUserDefinedOff()
> Turn on/off boolean flag controlling copying of user defined data from input to output of filter.

CopyAllOn() / CopyAllOff()
> Turn on/off all boolean flags controlling copying of data from input to output of filter.

PassData(pointData)
> Transfer all input point attribute data to the output according to the copy flags listed previously.

CopyAllocate(pointData)
> Initialize and allocate storage for point-by-point copy process.

CopyData(pointData, fromId, toId)
> Given input point data and a specific point id, copy the input point's attribute data to the output point.

InterpolateAllocate(pointData)
> Initialize and allocate storage for point-by-point interpolation process.

InterpolatePoint(pointData, toId, ptIds, weights)
> Given input point data and a list of points and their interpolation weights, interpolate data to the specified output point.

NullPoint(int ptId)
> Set the data value(s) of the specified output point id to a null value.

SetScalars() / GetScalars()
> Set / return scalar data.

SetVectors() / GetVectors()
> Set / return vector data.

SetNormals() / GetNormals()
> Set / return normal data.

SetTensors() / GetTensors()
> Set / return tensor data.

SetTextureCoords() / GetTextureCoords()
> Set / return texture coordinate data.

SetUserDefined() / GetUserDefined()
> Set / return user defined data.

Traversing Intermediate Topology

The dataset abstraction implemented by **vtk** provides simple techniques to traverse points and cells. Sometimes we want to traverse intermediate topology such as edges or faces. For example, to identify boundary edges in a triangular

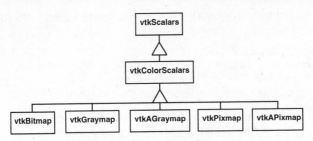

Figure 8–22 Color scalars object model.

mesh we must traverse each edge, counting the number of triangles that use each edge. (Recall that boundary edges are used by just one triangle.) Unfortunately, there is no obvious way to traverse edges. The same problem holds true if we want to traverse the faces of a dataset containing 3D cells.

A simple solution is to traverse each cell, and then obtain the edges (or faces) that compose the cell. The problem with this approach is that edges and faces are generally used by more than one cell, resulting in multiple visits to the same face or edge. This may be acceptable in some algorithms, but usually we count on visiting each edge or face only once.

A better solution to this problem is to traverse each cell as before, but only process intermediate topology if the current cell has the smallest cell id. (The current cell is the cell being visited in the traversal process.) To determine whether the current cell has the smallest cell id, we obtain all cells using the intermediate topology. This information can be obtained using the topological adjacency operators described earlier (e.g., Equation **8-24**).

To illustrate this process consider visiting the edges of a polygonal mesh. We begin by visiting the first polygon, p, and then its edges. For each edge we determine the adjacent polygon(s) (if any) that use the edge. If the id of the adjacent polygon(s) is greater than polygon p's id, or there are no adjacent polygons, then we know to process the current edge. (Of course the first polygon will always have the smallest id – but this will change as the traversal proceeds.) We then continue traversing the polygon list for new p's. In this way all the edges of the mesh will be visited.

Color Scalar Data

Multi-valued scalar data, or scalars represented by various color representations, are a special type in the *Visualization Toolkit*. These classes are of generic type vtkColorScalars, which is in turn a subclass of vtkScalars (Figure **8–22**).

vtkColorScalars is an abstract class that specifies a uniform interface to its concrete subclasses, as well as implementing the methods required by vtkScalars. Special features of this class are as follows.

- Subclasses of vtkColorScalars operate on color specification in the

RGBA (i.e., red-green-blue-alpha transparency) format. The internal representation of data may be different, but must be converted to this form to satisfy the abstract interface. For example, vtkGraymap, which represents data as a single unsigned char value, converts its value to RGBA by setting its alpha value $\alpha = 1$ and each color component to the gray value $R = G = B = \text{gray}$.

- To satisfy the abstract interface specified by vtkScalars, subclasses of vtkColorScalars must also be capable of converting their multi-valued color values into a single value. Equation **8-25** and Equation **8-26** are used.

- Special methods provide information about the type of scalar, either SingleValued or ColorScalar, and the number of data values per scalar (i.e., GetScalarType() and GetNumberOfValuesPerScalar()). This information allows us to differentiate between general types of scalar, and to perform special operations like texture mapping and writing data to disk.

- Every subclass of vtkColorScalars must be capable of returning an array of unsigned char values. The array consists of 1-4 values per scalar (depending on the number of values per scalar). This operation is used for high-performance texture and imaging operations.

Searching

The *Visualization Toolkit* provides two classes to perform searches for dataset points and cells. These are vtkLocator and vtkCellLocator. vtkLocator is used to search for points and, if used with the topological dataset operator GetPointCells(), to search for cells as well. vtkCellLocator is used to search for cells.

vtkLocator is implemented as a regular grid of buckets (i.e., same topology and geometry as a structured point set). The number of buckets can be user specified, or more conveniently, automatically computed based on the number of dataset points. On average, vtkLocator provides constant time access to points. However, in cases where the point distribution is not uniform, the number of points in a bucket may vary widely, giving $O(n)$ worst case behavior. In practice this is rarely a problem, but adaptive spatial search structures (e.g., an octree) may be a better choice sometimes.

Determining closest point to a point p using vtkLocator (as well as other spatial search structures) is a three step process. In the first step, the bucket containing p is found using the appropriate insertion scheme. (For vtkLocator this is three divisions to determine bucket indices *(i, j, k)*.) Next, the list of points in this bucket is searched to determine the closest point. However, as Figure **8-23** shows, this may not be the true closest point, since points in neighboring buckets may be closer. Consequently, a final search of neighboring buckets is necessary. The search distance is a function of the distance to the current closest point. Once all neighbors within this distance are searched, the closest point is returned.

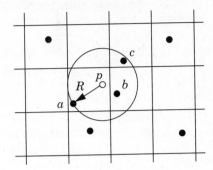

Figure 8–23 Determining closest point to p in vtkLocator. Initial search in bucket results in point a. Search must extend beyond local bucket as a function of search radius R, resulting in point b.

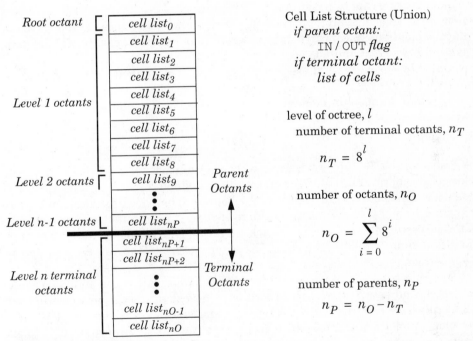

Figure 8–24 Structure of spatial search structure vtkCellLocator. The data structure represents a uniformly subdivided octree.

vtkCellLocator is implemented as a uniformly subdivided octree with some peculiar characteristics (Figure **8–24**). Conventional octree representations use upward parent and downward children pointers to track parent and children octants. Besides the required list of entities (i.e., points or cells) in each octant, additional information about octant level, center, and size may also be maintained. This results in a flexible structure with significant overhead. The overhead is the memory resources to maintain pointers, plus the cost to allocate and delete memory.

In contrast, `vtkCellLocator` uses a single array to represent the octree. The array is divided into two parts. The first part contains a list of parent octants, ordered according to level and octant child number. In the second part are the terminal, or leaf octants. The terminal octants are ordered on a regular array of buckets, just the same as `vtkLocator`. The terminal octants contain a list of the entities inside the octant. The parent octants maintain a value indicating whether the octant is empty, or whether something is inside it. (Both types of information are represented in the same portion of the octant structure.) Because the octree is uniformly subdivided, parent-child relationships, as well as octant locations, can be computed quickly using simple division operations.

The advantage of this structure is that memory can be allocated and deleted quickly. In addition, insertion into the octree is exactly the same as with `vtkLocator`, and is simpler than conventional octrees. The parent octants provide quick culling capability, since their status (empty or non-empty) allows us to stop certain types of search operations. On the down side, because the octree is uniformly subdivided, this structure is wasteful of memory resources if the data is non-uniformly distributed.

Our experience with these search structures described here is that they work well for many types of visualization data. However, if your data is non-uniform, you may want to implement your own special search classes.

Picking

The *Visualization Toolkit* provides three classes to perform actor, point, and cell picking. The object `vtkPicker` intersects a ray defined from camera position to a screen (i.e., pixel coordinate) against the bounding box of all pickable and non-transparent actors. (An actor is pickable if its `Pickable` instance variable is true.) The result of the `vtkPicker` pick operation is to return a list of the actors whose bounding box is intersected. The actor closest to the camera position is also returned.

The object `vtkPointPicker` intersects the ray against the points defining each actor, and returns the point coordinate closest to the camera position, as well as the actor that the point belongs to. Since screen resolution prevents precise selection of a point, a tolerance around the ray must be specified. The tolerance is expressed as a fraction of the rendering window size. (Rendering window size is measured across the window diagonal.) Points must lie within this tolerance to be picked.

The object `vtkCellPicker` intersects the ray with the cells defining each actor, and returns the point of intersection, as well as the actor that the cell belongs to. If you are trying to select a unique actor, `vtkCellPicker` is the object to use because it performs surface (or cell) intersection. Picking actors using `vtkPicker` can yield undesirable results because of the overlap of bounding boxes. The same is true of `vtkPointPicker` because of tolerance problems.

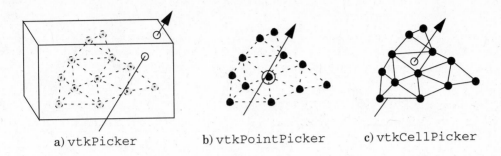

a) vtkPicker   b) vtkPointPicker   c) vtkCellPicker

Figure 8–25 Summary of picking operations.

Unfortunately, vtkCellPicker is the slowest object of the three because of greater computational requirements.

Figure **8–25** summarizes these three picking classes. Picking is built into the vtkRenderWindowInteractor class using the "p" key (see "Introducing vtkRenderWindowInteractor" on page 66). By default a vtkCellPicker is created, but you are free to specify your own picker type.

Examples

To conclude this section, we will examine how some of the dataset, cell, and point attribute operations are used. These operations tend to be used by class developers. You will not need to use them if you build applications by constructing visualization pipelines with existing filters.

Find Free Edges

In our first example we will take a peek inside the filter vtkLinearExtrusion-Filter. This filter implements the following modelling operation. Given a polygonal mesh, extrude the mesh in a given direction, constructing a "skirt" or "walls" from the free edges. If the polygonal example is a single square, the result of this operation is a cube. Or, if the polygonal data consists of a single line, the result of the operation is a quadrilateral. A point will generate a line as shown in Figure **8–26**(a).

Recall that free edges are edges used by only one polygon. We can determine this information using the dataset topology operation GetCellEdgeNeighbors(). We use the two points defining the edge of the polygon and Equation **8-24** to determine the adjacency set (i.e., the polygons sharing this edge). If no other polygon uses this edge, then the edge is extruded to generate a triangle strip. The C++ pseudo code is as follows.

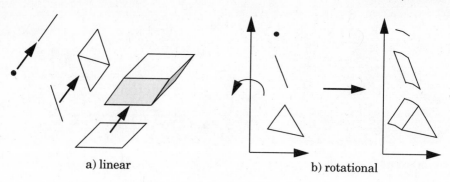

a) linear   b) rotational

Figure 8–26 Depiction of linear and rotational extrusion.

```
for (cellId=0; cellId < numCells; cellId++)
  {
  cell = mesh.GetCell(cellId);
  if ((dim=cell->GetCellDimension()) == 0)
  //create lines from points
  else if ( dim == 1 )
  // create strips from lines

  else if ( dim == 2 ) // create strips from boundary edges
    {
    numEdges = cell->GetNumberOfEdges();
    for (i=0; i<numEdges; i++)
      {
      edge = cell->GetEdge(i);
      for (j=0; j<(edge->GetNumberOfPoints()-1); j++)
        {
        p1 = edge->PointIds.GetId(j);
        p2 = edge->PointIds.GetId(j+1);
        mesh.GetCellEdgeNeighbors(cellId, p1, p2, cellIds);
        if ( cellIds.GetNumberOfIds() < 1 )
          {
          //generate triangle strip
          }
        } //for each sub-edge
      } //for each edge
    } //for each polygon or triangle strip
  } //for each cell
```

This same approach is used in the `vtkRotationalExtrusionFilter` (Figure **8–26**(b)). The difference between these two functions is that the type of motion is rotational as compared to linear (`vtkLinearExtrusionFilter`). These two filters can be used to perform some nifty modelling operations. Linear extrusion can be used to create bar charts with arbitrary cross sections, or to

a) Linearly extruded fonts to show letter frequency in text (`alphaFreq.cc`).

b) Rotationally symmetric objects
(`bottle.tcl`).

c) Rotation in combination with linear
displacement and radius variation
(`spring.tcl`).

Figure 8–27 Models created using linear and rotational extrusion.

sweep out three-dimensional fonts. The rotational extrusion filter can be used to create rotationally symmetric objects such as bottles or wine glasses. Examples of these techniques are shown in Figure **8–27**.

Find Cells

In this example we combine picking and a topological operation to select cells sharing a common point. Specifically, we use `vtkPointPicker` and the topological dataset operation `GetPointCells()`. This operation is depicted in Figure **8–28**. We have also included a fragment of C++ code implementing this procedure. Note that this procedure will work for any dataset type, even if the geometry is implicitly defined (e.g. `vtkStructuredPoints`).

The most difficult part of this procedure is the picking process. The selection point must be specified in pixel coordinates. The `vtkPointPicker` converts

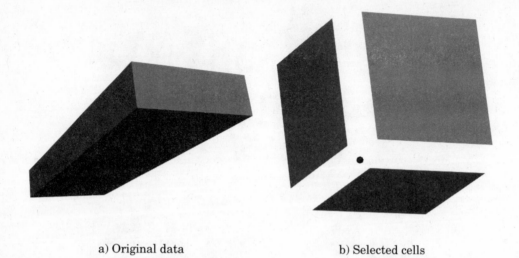

a) Original data   b) Selected cells

```
sphereActor->SetPosition(picker->GetPickPosition());
if ( picker->GetPointId() >= 0 )  // picked a point
  {
  cout << "Point id: " << picker->GetPointId() << "\n";
  cellsActor->VisibilityOn();
  plateActor->VisibilityOff();
  cells->Initialize();
  cells->Allocate(100);
  cells->SetPoints(plateOutput->GetPoints());
  plateOutput->GetPointCells(picker->GetPointId(), cellIds);
  for (i=0; i < cellIds.GetNumberOfIds(); i++)
    {
    cellId = cellIds.GetId(i);
    plateOutput->GetCellPoints(cellId, ptIds);
    cells->InsertNextCell(plateOutput->GetCellType(cellId), pt
    }
  }
else  //didn't pick anything
  {
  cellsActor->VisibilityOff();
  plateActor->VisibilityOn();
  }
renWin->Render();
```

c) C++ code (pickCells.cc)

Figure 8–28 Selecting group of cells sharing a common point. a) Original data. b) Selected cells sharing point on corner. Cells shrunk for clarity. The small sphere indicates the selected point. c) C++ code fragment in pick routine.

these coordinates into world and then dataset coordinates using the renderer in which the pick occurred. (The renderer uses the transformation matrix of its active camera to perform coordinate transformation.)

The picking process is conveniently managed in `vtkRenderWindowInter-actor`. This object allows the specification of functions to execute just before picking and just after picking (i.e., `StartPickMethod()` and `EndPick-Method()`). Using this facility we can define a post-picking function to retrieve the point id and then execute the `GetPointCells()` operation. This process is shown in Figure **8–28**.

Interpolate Point

In this example we will show how to build a point probe using the dataset and cell operations described in this chapter. A point probe is defined as follows. Given a *x-y-z* point coordinate, find the cell coordinates (i.e., cell id, sub-cell id, and parametric coordinates) and the interpolation weights. Once the interpolation weights are found, we can then compute local data values at *x-y-z*.

The point probe is implemented using the dataset operation `FindCell()`. This method requires a point specified in global coordinates (our *x-y-z* value), and a tolerance. The tolerance is often necessary because of numerical precision or when picking near the surface of 3D cells, or on 0D, 1D, and 2D cells. The `Find-Cell()` operation returns the information we require, plus the interpolation weights of the cell containing our point probe. To determine the data value at our probe point, we need to retrieve the data values on the cell points. We can then use the interpolation functions of Equation **8-4** to determine the probe scalar value.

Figure **8–29** depicts this process and includes C++ code. In the example we use the combustor dataset with the objects `vtkCursor3D`, `vtkProbeFilter` and `vtkGlyph3D`. The purpose of the cursor is to control the position of the probe point. The class `vtkProbeFilter` performs the probing operation just described. (This filter has been generalized so that it can handle more than one input point.) `vtkGlyph3D` is used to place an oriented, scaled cone at the cursor focal point. This gives us visual feedback about the scalar and vector quantities at the probe. Of course, we can extract numeric values and display them to the user if this is important.

8.11 Chapter Summary

Three important visualization coordinate systems are the world, dataset, and structured coordinate systems. The world coordinate system is an *x-y-z* Cartesian three-dimensional space. The dataset coordinate system consists of a cell id, sub-cell id, and parametric coordinates. The structured coordinate system consists of *i-j-k* integer indices into a rectangular topological domain.

Visualization data is generally in discrete form. Interpolation functions are used to obtain data at points between the known data values. Interpolation func-

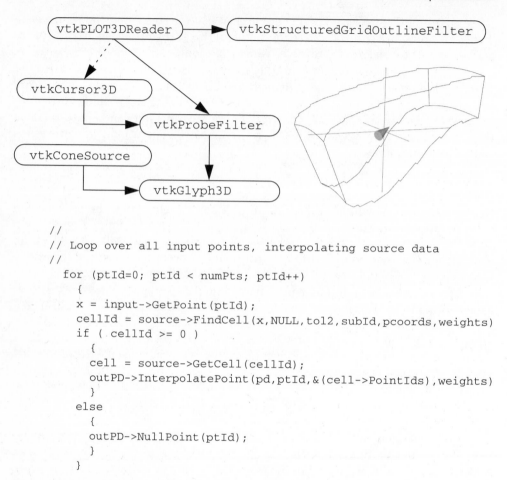

```
//
// Loop over all input points, interpolating source data
//
   for (ptId=0; ptId < numPts; ptId++)
     {
     x = input->GetPoint(ptId);
     cellId = source->FindCell(x,NULL,tol2,subId,pcoords,weights)
     if ( cellId >= 0 )
       {
       cell = source->GetCell(cellId);
       outPD->InterpolatePoint(pd,ptId,&(cell->PointIds),weights)
       }
     else
       {
       outPD->NullPoint(ptId);
       }
     }
```

Figure 8–29 Creating a point probe. Visualization network, C++ code for probe filter and resulting image shown (probe.cc).

tions vary depending on the particular cell type. The form of the interpolation functions are weighting values located at each of the cells points. The interpolations functions form the basis for conversion from dataset to global coordinates and vice-versa. The interpolation functions also are used to compute data derivatives.

Topological operators provide information about the topology of a cell or dataset. Obtaining neighboring cells to a particular cell is an important visualization operation. This operation can be used to determine whether cell boundaries are on the boundary of a dataset or to traverse datasets on a cell-by-cell basis.

Because of the inherent regularity of structured point datasets, operations can be efficiently implemented compared to other dataset types. These operations include coordinate transformation, derivative computation, topological query, and searching.

8.12 Bibliographic Notes

Interpolation functions are employed in a number of numerical techniques. The finite element method in particular depends on interpolation functions. If you want more information about interpolation functions refer to the finite element references suggested below [Cook89] [Gallagher75] [Zienkiewicz87]. These texts also discuss derivative computation in the context of interpolation functions.

Basic topology references are available from a number of sources. Two good descriptions of topological data structures are available from Weiler [Weiler86] [Weiler88] and Baumgart [Baumgart74]. Weiler describes the radial-edge structure. This data structure can represent manifold and non-manifold geometry. The winged-edge structure described by Baumgart is widely known. It is used to represent manifold geometry. Shephard [Shephard88] describes general finite element data structures. These are similar to visualization structures but with extra information related to analysis and geometric modelling.

There are extensive references regarding spatial search structures. Samet [Samet90] provides a general overview of some. Octrees were originally developed by Meagher [Meagher82] for 3D imaging. See [Williams83], [Bentley75], and [Quinlan94] for information about MIP maps, kd-trees, and binary sphere trees, respectively.

8.13 References

[Baumgart74]

B. G. Baumgart. "Geometric Modeling for Computer Vision." Ph.D. thesis, Stanford University, Palo Alto, CA, 1974.

[Bentley75]

J. L. Bentley. "Multidimensional Binary Search Trees Used for Associative Search." *Communications of the ACM*, 18(9):509-516, 1975.

[Conte72]

S. D. Conte and C. de Boor. *Elementary Numerical Analysis*. McGraw-Hill Book Company, 1972.

[Cook89]

R. D. Cook, D. S. Malkus, and M. E. Plesha. *Concepts and Applications of Finite Element Analysis*. John Wiley and Sons, New York, 1989.

[Gallagher75]

R. H. Gallagher. *Finite Element Analysis: Fundamentals*. Prentice Hall, Upper Saddle River, NJ, 1975.

[Meagher82]

D. J. Meagher. "Efficient Synthetic Image Generation of Arbitrary 3D Objects." In *Proceedings of the IEEE Conference on Pattern Recognition and Image Processing*, pp. 473-478, 1982.

[Quinlan94]

S. Quinlan. "Efficient Distance Computation Between Non-Convex Objects." In *Proceedings of IEEE International Conference on Robotics and Automation*, 1994.

[Samet90]

H. Samet. *Design and Analysis of Spatial Data Structures*. Addison-Wesley, Reading, MA, 1990.

[Shephard88]

M. S. Shephard and P. M. Finnigan. "Toward Automatic Model Generation." *State-of-the-Art Surveys on Computational Mechanics*, A. K. Noor and J. T. Oden, editors, ASME, pp. 335-366, 1989.

[Weiler86]

K. J. Weiler. *Topological Structures for Geometric Modeling*. Ph.D. thesis, Rensselaer Polytechnic Institute, Troy, NY, May 1986.

[Weiler88]

K. J. Weiler. "The Radial-Edge Structure: A Topological Representation for Non-Manifold Geometric Boundary Representations." In M. J. Wozny, H. W. McLaughlin, and J. L. Encarnacao, editors, *Geometric Modeling for CAD Applications*, pp. 3-36, North Holland, 1988.

[Williams83]

L. Williams. "Pyramidal Parametrics." *Computer Graphics (SIGGRAPH '83)*, 17(3):1-11, 1983.

[Zienkiewicz87]

O. C. Zienkiewicz and R. L. Taylor. *The Finite Element Method - Volume 1*. McGraw Hill Book Co., NY, 4th edition, 1987.

8.14 Exercises

8.1 Given a volume of dimensions $5 \times 10 \times 15$ with origin (1.0, 2.0, 3.0) and voxel aspect ratio (0.5, 0.5, 1.0).

a) Compute minimum point position.

b) Compute maximum point position.

c) For cell id 342, compute cell minimum point position and maximum point position.

d) What points (list ids) define cell id 342?

e) Given point specified in structured coordinates as $i, j, k = (3, 6, 4)$; $r, s, t = (0.1, 0.2, 0.5)$, compute global coordinates.

f) Given point id 342; compute global coordinates.

8.2 Compute global coordinates and interpolation weights for the points specified in dataset coordinates (refer to Figure **8–30**(a-d)).

a) Line with $r = 0.5$.

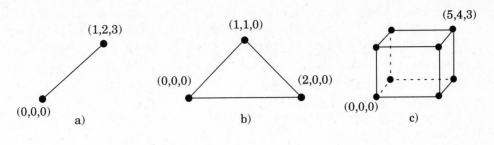

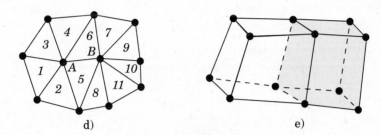

Figure 8–30 Exercise figures.

b) Triangle with $r, s = (0.25, 0.33)$
c) Voxel with $r, s, t = (0.25, 0.33, 0.5)$.

8.3 Compute parametric coordinates for cells shown in Figure **8–30**(a-d).
a) Line with $x, y, z = (0.3, 0.6, 0.9)$
b) Triangle with $x, y, z = (0.5, 0.25, 0.0)$
c) Voxel with $x, y, z = (0.5, 0.4, 2.0)$

8.4 Given the line shown in Figure **8–30**(a), if scalar data values are $(s_0, s_1) = (0.0, 0.25)$, what are the derivatives in the x, y, z directions?

8.5 Refer to Figure **8–30**(d) and let the numbers indicate cell ids and the letters indicate point ids.
a) List the cells using point A.
b) List the cells using point B.
c) List cells using edge (A, B) . How does this list correspond to your answers in parts a) and b) above?

8.6 Refer to Figure **8–30**(e).
a) How many boundary faces are there?
b) How many "internal" faces?

8.7 Describe a procedure to intersect two finite lines. How does tolerance value come into play?

8.8 Describe a procedure to intersect a line and triangle. Are there special characteristics of a triangle that can be used to speed this operation?

8.9 Compare memory requirements for the three unstructured grid data structures shown in Figure **8–21**. Assume that two cells use each face, four faces use each cell, and six edges use each vertex (i.e., a structured dataset).

8.10 Using the abstract cell and dataset interface, write a program to compute
a) number of points in a dataset,
b) number of cells in a dataset,
c) number of edges in a dataset,
d) number of faces in a dataset.

8.11 Given a volume of dimensions $5 \times 10 \times 15$.
a) How many internal faces are there (i.e. used by two voxels)?
b) How many boundary faces are there (i.e., used by one voxel)?

8.12 Write a general extrusion filter that sweeps an object along a path to construct a new surface. Assume that the path is defined by a sequence of transformation matrices. Can you think of a way to prevent self-intersection?

Algorithms II

We return again to visualization algorithms. This chapter describes algorithms that are either more complex to implement, or less widely used for 3D visualization applications. Recall that we classify algorithms as either scalar, vector, tensor, or modelling algorithms.

9.1 Scalar Algorithms

As we have seen, scalar algorithms often involve mapping scalar values through a lookup table, or creating contour lines or surfaces. In this section, we examine another contouring algorithm, *dividing cubes*, which generates contour surfaces using dense point clouds. We also describe carpet plots. Carpet plots are not true 3D visualization techniques, but are widely used to visualize many types of scalar data.

Dividing Cubes

Dividing cubes is a contouring algorithm similar to marching cubes [Cline88]. Unlike marching cubes, dividing cubes generates point primitives as compared to triangles (3D) or lines (2D). If the number of points on the contour surface is large, the rendered appearance of the contour surface appears "solid". To achieve this solid appearance, the density of the points must be at or greater than screen

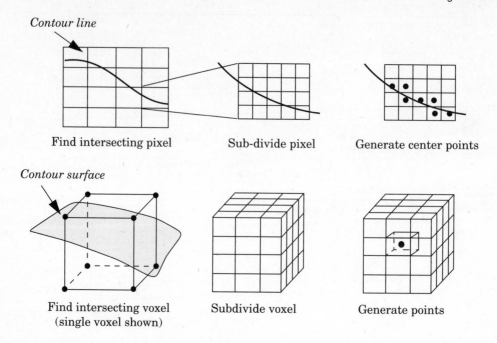

Contour line

Find intersecting pixel   Sub-divide pixel   Generate center points

Contour surface

Find intersecting voxel   Subdivide voxel   Generate points
(single voxel shown)

Figure 9–1 Overview of dividing cubes algorithm. Each voxel through which contour passes is subdivided into subvoxels at less than screen resolution. If the contour passes through a subvoxel, a center point is generated.

resolution. (Also, the points must be rendered using the standard lighting and shading equations used in surface rendering.)

The motivation for dividing cubes is that rendering points is much faster than rendering polygons. This varies depending upon rendering hardware/software. Special purpose hardware has been developed to render shaded points at high speed. In other systems, greater attention has been placed on polygon rendering, and the rendering speed differences are not so great. Also, certain geometric operations such as cutting and merging data are simple operations with points. Comparable operations with polygons are much more difficult to implement.

One disadvantage of creating contours with dense point clouds is that magnification of the surface (via camera zooming, for example) reveals the disconnected nature of the surface. Thus, the point set must be constructed for maximum zoom, or constructed dynamically based on the relative relationship between the camera and contour.

Although dividing cubes was originally developed for volume datasets, it is possible to adapt the algorithm to other dataset types by subdividing in parametric coordinates. Our presentation assumes that we are working with volumes.

Figure **9–1** provides an overview of the dividing cubes algorithm. Like other contouring algorithms, we first choose a contour value. We begin by visiting each

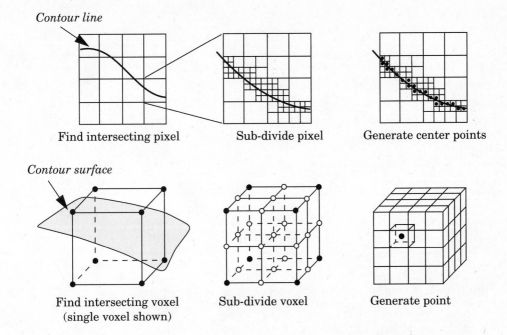

Contour line

Find intersecting pixel   Sub-divide pixel   Generate center points

Contour surface

Find intersecting voxel   Sub-divide voxel   Generate point
(single voxel shown)

Figure 9–2 Recursive dividing cubes algorithm. Top half of figure shows algorithm depicted in two dimensions. Lower half depicts algorithm in three dimensions.

voxel and select those through which the isosurface passes. (The isosurface passes through a voxel when there are scalar values both above and below the contour value.) We also compute the gradient at each voxel point for use in computing point normals.

After selecting a voxel that the isosurface passes through, the voxel is subdivided into a regular grid of $n_1 \times n_2 \times n_3$ subvoxels. The number of divisions is controlled by the width of a voxel w_i in combination with screen resolution R. The screen resolution is defined as the distance between adjacent pixels in world coordinates. We can express the number of divisions n_i along the coordinate axes x_i as

$$n_i = \frac{w_i}{R} \qquad \qquad \textbf{(9-1)}$$

where the quotient is rounded-up to the nearest integer. The scalar values at the sub-points are generated using the interpolation functions for a voxel (see Figure **8–10**). Then we determine whether the contour passes through each subvoxel. If it does, we simply generate a point at the center of the subvoxel and compute its normal using the standard interpolation functions.

An interesting variation on this algorithm is a recursive implementation as shown in Figure **9–2**. Instead of subdividing the voxel directly (i.e., procedurally) into a regular grid we recursively divide the voxel (similar to octree decomposi-

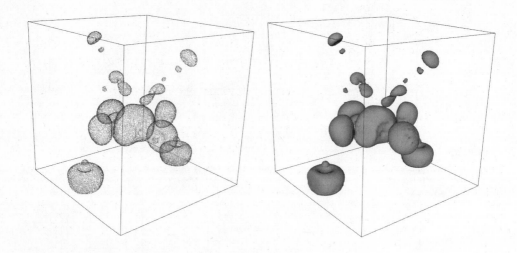

Figure 9–3 Examples of dividing cubes isosurface. The left image consists of 50,078 points, and the right image consists of 2,506,989 points (`dcubes.tcl`).

tion). The voxel is subdivided regularly creating eight sub-voxels and 19 new points (12 mid-edge points, 6 mid-face points, and 1 mid-voxel point). The scalar values at the new points are interpolated from the original voxel using the tri-linear interpolation functions. The process repeats for each sub-voxel if the isosurface passes through it. This process continues until the size of the sub-voxel is less than or equal to screen resolution. In this case, a point is generated at the center of the sub-voxel. The collection of all such points composes the dividing cubes isosurface.

The advantage of the recursive implementation is that the subdivision process terminates prematurely in those regions of the voxel where the contour cannot pass. On the other hand, the recursive subdivision requires that the voxel subdivision occurs in powers of two. This can generate far more points than the procedural implementation.

Figure **9–3** shows two examples of dividing cubes isosurfaces. The contour surface on the left consists of 50,078 points. Because the points are not generated at display resolution, it is possible to see through the contour surface. The second contour surface on the right is composed of 2,506,989 points. The points are generated at display resolution, and as a result the contour surface appears solid.

As Figure **9–1** and Figure **9–2** show, the points generated by dividing cubes do not lie exactly on the contour surface. We can determine the maximum error by examining the size of the terminal sub-voxels. Assume that a terminal sub-voxel is a cube, and that the length of the side of the cube is given by l. Then the maximum error is half the length of the cube diagonal, or $l\sqrt{3}/2$.

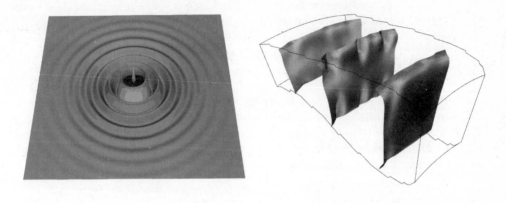

a) Exponential cosine function   b) Flow energy

Figure 9–4 Carpet plots. a) Visualization of an exponential cosine function. Function values are indicated by surface displacement. Colors indicate derivative values (exp-Cos.cc). b) Carpet plot of combustor flow energy in a structured grid. Colors and plane height indicate energy values (warpComb.tcl).

Carpet Plots

A common data form is a 2D structured point set with associated scalar data. *Carpet plots* can visualize data in this form. A carpet plot is created by warping a 2D surface in the direction of the surface normal (or possibly some user defined direction). The amount of warping is controlled by the scalar value, possibly in combination with a scale factor. Carpet plots are similar to the vector displacement plots (see "Displacement Plots" on page 157).

Although carpet plots are typically applied to structured point data, they can be used to visualize datasets composed of 2D structured grids or 2D unstructured grids. In their basic form carpet plots can be used to visualize only three variables: two surface position coordinates and a scalar value. However, it is common to introduce another variable by using color mapping on the surface.

Figure **9–4** illustrates application of carpet plots. Figure **9–4**(a) shows the exponential cosine function centered at the origin with points located at radius r

$$F(r) = e^{-r} \cos(10r)$$ **(9-2)**

The function values are used to warp the surface while the function derivatives are used to color it.

Figure **9–4**(b) shows a carpet plot that visualizes flow energy in a structured grid. Both displacement and color are used to show the energy values. Although this figure is similar to Figure **6–14**(b) there are some important differences. Figure **6–14**(b) displays vector data whereas Figure **9–4**(b) displays scalar data. Figure **9–4**(b) deforms the surface in the direction of surface normal (or possibly a user defined direction). The vector data (i.e., vector orientation) controls the direction of deformation in Figure **6–14**(b).

9.2 Vector Algorithms

In *Algorithms I* we showed how to create simple vector glyphs and how to integrate particles through a vector field to create streamlines. In this section we extend these concepts to create streamribbons and streampolygons. In addition, we introduce the concept of vector field topology, and show how to characterize a vector field using topological constructs.

Streamribbons and Streamsurfaces

Streamlines depict particle paths in a vector field. By coloring these lines, or creating local glyphs (such as dashed lines or oriented cones), we can represent additional scalar and temporal information. However, these techniques can convey only elementary information about the vector field. Local information (e.g., flow rotation or derivatives) and global information (e.g., structure of a field such as vortex tubes) is not represented. Streamribbons and streamsurfaces are two techniques used to represent local and global information.

A natural extension of the streamline technique widens the line to create a ribbon. The ribbon can be constructed by generating two adjacent streamlines and then bridging the lines with a polygonal mesh. This technique works well as long as the streamlines remain relatively close to one another. If separation occurs, so that the streamlines diverge, the resulting ribbon will not accurately represent the flow, because we expect the surface of the ribbon to be everywhere tangent to the vector field (i.e., definition of streamline). The ruled surface connecting two widely separated streamlines does not generally satisfy this requirement.

The streamribbon provides information about important flow parameters: the vector vorticity and flow divergence. *Vorticity* $\vec{\omega}$ is the measure of rotation of the vector field, expressed as a vector quantity: a direction (axis of rotation) and magnitude (amount of rotation). *Streamwise vorticity* Ω is the projection of $\vec{\omega}$ along the instantaneous velocity vector, $\vec{v}$. Said another way, streamwise vorticity is the rotation of the vector field around the streamline defined as follows.

$$\Omega = \frac{\vec{v} \cdot \vec{\omega}}{|\vec{v}||\vec{\omega}|} \qquad \textbf{(9-3)}$$

The amount of twisting of the streamribbon approximates the streamwise vorticity. Flow *divergence* is a measure of the "spread" of the flow. The changing width of the streamribbon is proportional to the cross-flow divergence of the flow.

A streamsurface is a collection of an infinite number of streamlines passing through a *base curve*. The base curve, or *rake*, defines the starting points for the streamlines. If the base curve is closed (e.g., a circle) the surface is closed and a streamtube results. Thus, streamribbons are specialized types of streamsurfaces with a narrow width compared to length.

Compared to vector icons or streamlines, streamsurfaces provide additional information about the structure of the vector field. Any point on the streamsurface is tangent to the velocity vector. Consequently, taking an example from fluid flow, no fluid can pass through the surface. Streamtubes are then representations of constant mass flux. Streamsurfaces show vector field structure better than streamlines or vector glyphs because they do not require visual interpolation across icons.

Streamsurfaces can be computed by generating a set of streamlines from a user specified rake. A polygonal mesh is then constructed by connecting adjacent streamlines. One difficulty with this approach is that local vector field divergence can cause streamlines to separate. Separation can introduce large errors into the surface, or possibly cause self intersection, which is not physically possible.

Another approach to computing streamsurfaces has been taken by Hultquist [Hultquist92]. The streamsurface is a collection of streamribbons connected along their edges. In this approach, the computation of the streamlines and tiling of the streamsurface is carried out concurrently. This allows streamlines to be added or removed as the flow separates or converges. The tiling can also be controlled to prevent the generation of long, skinny triangles. The surface may also be "torn", i.e., ribbons separated, if the divergence of the flow becomes too high.

Stream Polygon

The techniques described so far provide approximate measures of vector field quantities such as streamwise vorticity and divergence. However, vector fields contain more information than these techniques can convey. As a result, other techniques have been devised to visualize this information. One such technique is the *stream polygon* [Schroeder91], which serves as the basis for a number of advanced vector and tensor visualization methods. The stream polygon is used to visualize local properties of strain, displacement, and rotation. We begin by describing the effects of a vector field on the local state of strain.

Non-uniform vector fields give rise to local deformation in the region where they occur. If the vector field is displacement in a physical medium such as a fluid or a solid, the deformation consists of local strain (i.e., local distortion) and rigid body motion. To mathematically describe the deformation we examine a 3D vector $\vec{v} = (u, v, w)$ at a specified point $\vec{x} = (x, y, z)$. Using a first order Taylor's series expansion about $\vec{x}$, we can express the local deformation e_{ij} as

$$e_{ij} = \varepsilon_{ij} + \omega_{ij} \tag{9-4}$$

where ε_{ij} is the local strain and ω_{ij} is the local rotation. Note that these variables are expressed as 3×3 tensors. (Compare this equation to that given in

Figure **6–20**. Note that this equation and the following Equation **9-5** differ in their off-diagonal terms by a factor of 1/2. This is because Figure **6–20** expresses *engineering shear strain* which is used in the study of elasticity. Equation **9-5** expresses a tensor quantity and is mathematically consistent.)

The local strain is expressed as a combination of the partial derivatives at $\dot{x}$ as follows.

$$
\varepsilon_{ij} = \begin{bmatrix}
\dfrac{\partial u}{\partial x} & \dfrac{1}{2}\left(\dfrac{\partial u}{\partial y}+\dfrac{\partial v}{\partial x}\right) & \dfrac{1}{2}\left(\dfrac{\partial u}{\partial z}+\dfrac{\partial w}{\partial x}\right) \\[2ex]
\dfrac{1}{2}\left(\dfrac{\partial u}{\partial y}+\dfrac{\partial v}{\partial x}\right) & \dfrac{\partial v}{\partial y} & \dfrac{1}{2}\left(\dfrac{\partial v}{\partial z}+\dfrac{\partial w}{\partial y}\right) \\[2ex]
\dfrac{1}{2}\left(\dfrac{\partial u}{\partial z}+\dfrac{\partial w}{\partial x}\right) & \dfrac{1}{2}\left(\dfrac{\partial v}{\partial z}+\dfrac{\partial w}{\partial y}\right) & \dfrac{\partial w}{\partial z}
\end{bmatrix}
\tag{9-5}
$$

The terms on the diagonal of ε_{ij} are the normal components of strain. The off-diagonal terms are the shear strain. The local rigid-body rotation is given by

$$
\omega_{ij} = \begin{bmatrix}
0 & \dfrac{1}{2}\left(\dfrac{\partial u}{\partial y}-\dfrac{\partial v}{\partial x}\right) & \dfrac{1}{2}\left(\dfrac{\partial u}{\partial z}-\dfrac{\partial w}{\partial x}\right) \\[2ex]
\dfrac{1}{2}\left(\dfrac{\partial v}{\partial x}-\dfrac{\partial u}{\partial y}\right) & 0 & \dfrac{1}{2}\left(\dfrac{\partial v}{\partial z}-\dfrac{\partial w}{\partial y}\right) \\[2ex]
\dfrac{1}{2}\left(\dfrac{\partial w}{\partial x}-\dfrac{\partial u}{\partial z}\right) & \dfrac{1}{2}\left(\dfrac{\partial w}{\partial y}-\dfrac{\partial v}{\partial z}\right) & 0
\end{bmatrix}
\tag{9-6}
$$

Equation **9-6** can also be represented using tensor notation as

$$
\omega_{ij} = -\frac{1}{2}\varepsilon_{ijk}\vec{\omega}
\tag{9-7}
$$

where $\vec{\omega}$ is the vorticity vector referred to in the previous section. The vorticity, or local rigid body rotation is then

$$
\vec{\omega} = \begin{bmatrix}
\dfrac{\partial w}{\partial y}-\dfrac{\partial v}{\partial z} \\[2ex]
\dfrac{\partial u}{\partial z}-\dfrac{\partial w}{\partial x} \\[2ex]
\dfrac{\partial v}{\partial x}-\dfrac{\partial u}{\partial y}
\end{bmatrix}
\tag{9-8}
$$

For the reader unfamiliar with tensor notation, this presentation is certainly less than complete. However, the matrices in Equation **9-5** and Equation **9-6** directly translate into visual form, which will help clarify the concepts presented here. Referring to Figure **9–5**, the normal strain, shear strain, and rigid body motion create distinct deformation modes. These modes combine

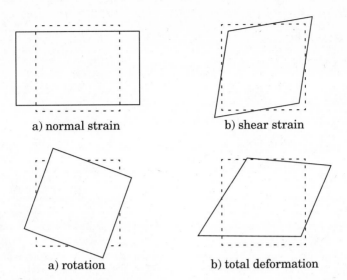

a) normal strain   b) shear strain

a) rotation   b) total deformation

Figure 9–5 Components of local deformation due to vector field. Dotted line shows initially undeformed object.

to produce the total deformation. Modes of normal strain cause compression or extension in the direction perpendicular to a surface, while shear strains cause angular distortions. These strains combined with rigid body rotation around an axis yield the total strain at a point.

The essence of the stream polygon technique is to show these modes of deformation. A regular n-sided polygon (Figure **9–6**) is placed into a vector field at a specified point and then deformed according to the local strain. The components of strain may be shown separately or in combination. The orientation of the normal of the polygon is arbitrary. However, it is convenient to align the normal with the local vector. Then the rigid body rotation about the vector is the streamwise vorticity, and the effects of normal and shear strain are in the plane perpendicular to a streamline passing through the point.

The stream polygon offers other interesting possibilities. The stream polygon may be swept along a trajectory, typically a streamline, to generate tubes. The radius of the tube r can be modified according to some scalar function. One application is to visualize fluid flow. In incompressible flow with no shear, the radius of the tube can vary according to the scalar function vector magnitude. Then the equation

$$r(\vec{v}) = r_{max}\sqrt{\frac{|\vec{v}_{min}|}{|\vec{v}|}} \qquad\qquad \textbf{(9-9)}$$

represents an area of constant mass flow. Thus, the tube will thicken as the flow slows, and narrow as the velocity increases. Each of the n sides of the tube can be

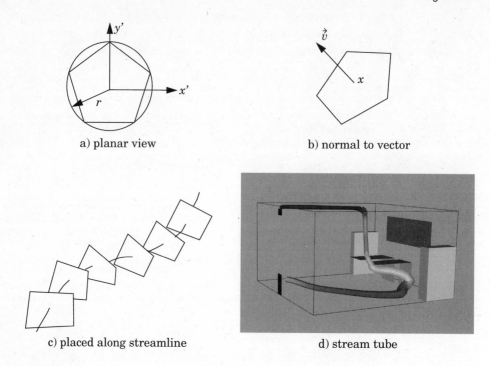

a) planar view

b) normal to vector

c) placed along streamline

d) stream tube

Figure 9–6 The stream polygon. a) Planar view. b) Aligned with vector. c) Aligned along streamline. d) Sweeping polygon to form tube (`officeTube.tcl`).

colored with a different scalar function, although for visual clarity at most one or two functions should be used.

The streamtubes generated by the streampolygon and the streamtubes we described in the previous section are not the same. The streampolygon does not necessarily lie along a streamline. If it does, the streampolygon represents information at a point, while the streamtube is an approximation constructed from multiple streamlines. Also, the radial variation in the tubes constructed from streampolygon sweeps do not necessarily relate to mass flow since the radius in a streampolygon can be tied to an arbitrary scalar variable.

Vector Field Topology

Vector fields have a complex structure characterized by special features called *critical points* [Globus91] [Helman91]. Critical points are locations in the vector field where the local vector magnitude goes to zero and the vector direction becomes undefined. At these points the vector field either converges or diverges, and/or local circulation around the point occurs.

Critical points lie in dataset cells where the u, v, and w components of the vector field each pass through zero. These points are located using an iterative search procedure such as the bi-section technique. Each iteration evaluates the cell interpolation function until the zero vector is found. Once a critical point is found, its local behavior is determined from the matrix of partial derivatives. This is because at the critical point the velocity is zero, and the vector field can be approximated by a first-order expansion of partial derivatives [Helman91]

$$u \approx \frac{\partial u}{\partial x}dx + \frac{\partial u}{\partial y}dy + \frac{\partial u}{\partial z}dz$$

$$v \approx \frac{\partial v}{\partial x}dx + \frac{\partial v}{\partial y}dy + \frac{\partial v}{\partial z}dz \qquad\qquad \textbf{(9-10)}$$

$$w \approx \frac{\partial w}{\partial x}dx + \frac{\partial w}{\partial y}dy + \frac{\partial w}{\partial z}dz$$

The matrix of partial derivatives J can be written in vector notation as

$$\vec{u} = J d\vec{x} \text{ with } J = \begin{bmatrix} \frac{\partial u}{\partial x} & \frac{\partial u}{\partial y} & \frac{\partial u}{\partial z} \\[2mm] \frac{\partial v}{\partial x} & \frac{\partial v}{\partial y} & \frac{\partial v}{\partial z} \\[2mm] \frac{\partial w}{\partial x} & \frac{\partial w}{\partial y} & \frac{\partial w}{\partial z} \end{bmatrix} \qquad\qquad \textbf{(9-11)}$$

which is referred to as the Jacobian. The behavior of the vector field in the vicinity of a critical point is characterized by the eigenvalues of J. The eigenvalues consist of an imaginary and real component. The imaginary component describes the rotation of the vector field around the critical point, while the real part describes the relative attraction or repulsion of the vector field to the critical point. In two dimensions the critical points are as shown in Figure 9–7.

A number of visualization techniques have been developed to construct vector field topology from an analysis of critical points. These techniques provide a global understanding of the field, including points of *attachment* and *detachment* and field *vortices*. Using a fluid flow analogy, points of attachment and detachment occur on the surface of an object where the tangential component of the vector field goes to zero, and the flow is perpendicular to the surface. Thus, streamlines will begin or end at these points. There is no common definition for a vortex, but generally speaking vortices are regions of relatively concentrated vorticity (e.g., flow rotation). The study of vortices is important because they represent areas of energy loss, or can have significant impact on downstream flow conditions (e.g., trailing vortices behind large aircraft).

One useful visualization technique creates vector field skeletons that divide the vector field into separate regions. Within each region the vector field is topologically equivalent to uniform flow. These skeletons are created by locating critical points, and then connecting the critical points with streamlines. In 3D vector field analysis this technique can be applied to the surface of objects to locate

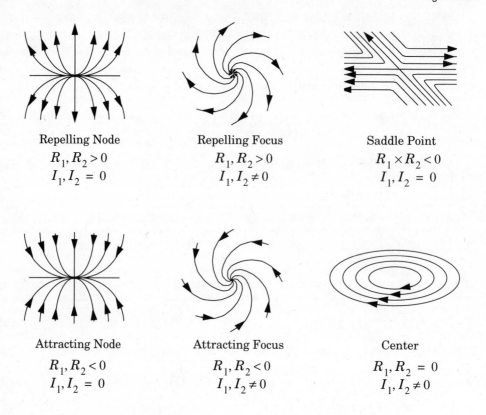

Figure 9–7 Critical points in two dimensions. The real part of the eigenvalues (R_1, R_2) of the matrix of first derivatives control the attraction or repulsion of the vector field. The imaginary part of the eigenvalues (I_1, I_2) controls the rotation.

lines of flow separation and attachment and other important flow features. Also, in general 3D flow, the regions of uniform flow are separated by surfaces, and creation of 3D flow skeletons is a current research topic.

Vortex visualization is another area of current research. One simple technique computes the *helicity-density*

$$H_d = \vec{v} \cdot \vec{w} = |\vec{v}||\vec{w}|\cos\varphi \tag{9-12}$$

This is a scalar function of the vector dot product between the vorticity and the local vector. Large positive values of H_d result in right-handed vortices, while large negative values indicate left-handed vortices. Helicity-density can be conveniently shown using isosurfaces, which gives an indication for the location and structure of a vortex.

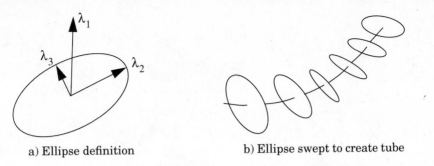

a) Ellipse definition   b) Ellipse swept to create tube

Figure 9–8 Creation of hyperstreamlines. Ellipse is swept along streamline of eigen-field. Major/minor axes of ellipse controlled by other two eigenvectors.

9.3 Tensor Algorithms

In Chapter 6 we saw that 3×3 real symmetric tensors can be characterized by the eigenvalues and eigenvectors of the tensor. Recall that we can express the eigenvectors of the system as

$$\vec{v}_i = \lambda_i e_i, \text{ with } i = 1, 2, 3 \qquad\qquad \textbf{(9-13)}$$

where e_i is a unit vector in the direction of the eigenvalue, and λ_i are the eigenvalues. Thus, we can decompose a 3×3 real symmetric tensor field into three vector fields, each field defined by one of the three eigenvectors from Equation **9-13**. We call these vector fields *eigenfields*, since they are derived from the eigenvectors of the tensor field.

Decomposition of the tensor field in this fashion provides additional insight into visualizing 3×3 real symmetric tensors. We can directly use the vector field visualization techniques presented previously, or use variations of them. One such technique is a novel extension of the streampolygon technique, the method of *hyperstreamlines*.

Hyperstreamlines

Hyperstreamlines are constructed by creating a streamline through one of the three eigenfields, and then sweeping a geometric primitive along the streamline [Delmarcelle93]. Typically an ellipse is used as the geometric primitive, where the remaining two eigenvectors define the major and minor axes of the ellipse (Figure **9–8**). Sweeping the ellipse along the eigenfield streamline results in a tubular shape. Another useful generating geometric primitive is a cross. The length and orientation of the arms of the cross are controlled by two of the eigenvectors. Sweeping the cross results in a helical shape since the eigenvectors (and therefore cross arms) will rotate in some tensor fields.

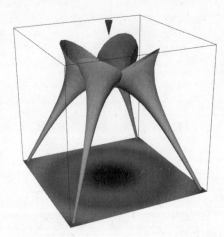

Figure 9–9 Example of hyperstreamlines (`Hyper.tcl`). The four hyperstreamlines shown are integrated along the minor principle stress axis. A plane (colored with a different lookup table) is also shown.

Figure **9–9** shows an example of hyperstreamlines. The data is from a point load applied to a semi-infinite domain. Compare this figure to Figure **6–22** that used tensor ellipsoids to visualize the same data. Notice that there is less clutter and more information available from the hyperstreamline visualization.

9.4 Modelling Algorithms

Visualizing Geometry

One of the most common applications of visualization is to view geometry. We may have a geometric representation of a part or complex assembly (perhaps designed on a CAD system) and want to view the part or assembly before it is manufactured. While viewing geometry is better addressed in a text on computer graphics, often there is dataset structure we wish to view in the same way. For example, we may want to see data mapped on a particular portion of the dataset, or view the structure of the dataset itself (e.g., view a finite element mesh).

Three-dimensional datasets have a surface and interior. Typically we want to visualize the surface of the dataset, or perhaps a portion of the interior. (Note: volume rendering is a different matter – see "Volume Rendering" on page 209.) To visualize the dataset we must extract a portion of the dataset topology/geometry (and associated data) as some form of surface primitives such as polygons. If the surface of the dataset is opaque, we may also wish to eliminate occluded interior detail.

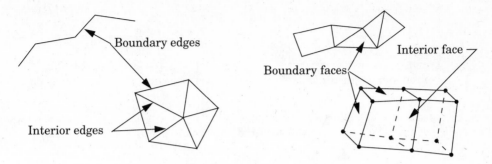

Figure 9–10 Boundary edges and faces.

We have already seen how structured datasets, such as structured points or structured grids, have a natural *i-j-k* coordinate system that allows extraction of points, lines, and planes from the interior of the dataset (see "Structured Coordinate System" on page 227). For example, to extract the fifth *i*-plane from a structured grid of dimensions (i_m, j_m, k_m) , we specify the data extents using $(4, 4, 0, (j_m - 1), 0, (k_m - 1))$ (assuming zero-offset addressing).

More generally, we can extract boundary edges and faces from a dataset. A boundary edge is a 1D cell type (e.g., line or polyline), or the edge of a 2D cell used by only that single cell. Similarly, a boundary face is a 2D cell type (e.g., polygon, triangle strip), or the face of a 3D cell used by only that single cell (Figure **9–10**). We can obtain this information using the topological operators of the previous chapter. Cells of dimension 2 or less are extracted as is, while boundary edges and faces are determined by counting the number of cell neighbors for a particular topological boundary (i.e., edge or face neighbors). If there are no neighbors, the edge or face is a boundary edge or boundary face, and is extracted.

Using these techniques we can view the structure of our dataset. However, there are also situations where we want more control in the selection of the data. We call this *data extraction*.

Data Extraction

Often we want to extract portions of data from a dataset. This may be because we want to reduce the size of the data, or because we are interested in visualizing only a portion of it.

Reducing dataset size is an important practical capability, because visualization data size can be huge. By reducing data size, reductions in computation and memory requirements can be realized. This results in better interactive response.

We also may need to reduce data size in order to visualize the important features of a large dataset. This can be used to reduce image clutter and improve the effectiveness of the visualization. Smaller data size also enables the visual-

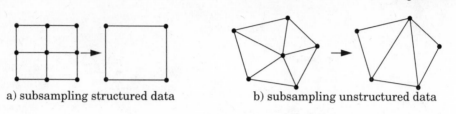

a) subsampling structured data   b) subsampling unstructured data

Figure 9–11 Subsampling data. a) Structured data can be subsampled by choosing every n^{th} point. b) Subsampling unstructured data requires local re-triangulation.

ization user to navigate through and inspect data more quickly relative to larger datasets. Next we describe two techniques to extract data. One is based on *geometry extraction*, and the other is based on *data thresholding*, or *thresholding*.

Geometry Extraction

Geometry extraction selects data based on geometric or topological characteristics. A common extraction technique selects a set of points and cells that lie within a specified range of id's. A typical example is selecting all cells having id's between 0-100, or all cells using point id's 250-500. Finite element analysts use this method frequently to isolate the visualization to just a few key regions.

Another useful technique called *spatial extraction*, selects dataset structure and associated data attributes lying within a specified region in space. For example, a point and radius can be used to select (or deselect) data within an enclosing sphere. Implicit functions are particularly useful tools for describing these regions. Points that evaluate negative are inside the region, while points outside the region evaluate positive. Thus, cells whose points are all positive are outside the region, and cells whose points are all negative are inside the region.

Subsampling (Figure **9–11**) is a method that reduces data size by selecting a subset of the original data. The subset is specified by choosing a parameter n, specifying that every n^{th} data point is to be extracted. For example, in structured datasets such as structured points and grids, selecting every n^{th} point produces the results shown in Figure **9–11**(a).

Subsampling modifies the topology of a dataset. When points or cells are not selected, this leaves a topological "hole". Dataset topology must be modified to fill the hole. In structured data, this is simply a uniform selection across the *i*-*j*-*k* coordinates. In unstructured data (Figure **9–11**(b)), the hole must be filled in by using triangulation or other complex tessellation schemes. Subsampling is not typically performed on unstructured data because of its inherent complexity.

A related technique is *data masking*. In data masking we select every n^{th} cell. At a minimum this leaves one or more topological "holes" in the dataset. Masking also may change the topology of the dataset, since partial selections of cells from structured datasets can only be represented using unstructured grids. Masking is typically used to improve interactive performance, or to quickly process portions of data.

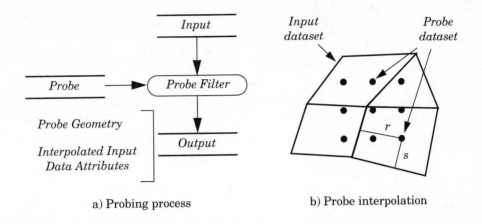

a) Probing process   b) Probe interpolation

Figure 9–12   Probing data. The geometry of one dataset *(Probe)* is used to extract dataset attributes from another dataset *(Input)*.

Thresholding

Data thresholding selects data based on the values of dataset attributes. For example, we may select all cells having a point with scalar value between (0,1), or all points having a velocity magnitude greater than 1.0.

   Scalar thresholding is easily implemented. The threshold is either a single value that scalar values are greater than or less than, or a range of values. Cells or points whose associated scalar values satisfy the threshold criteria can be extracted. Other dataset attribute types such as vectors, normals, or tensors can be extracted in similar fashion by converting the type to a single scalar value. For example, vectors can be extracted using vector magnitude, and tensors using matrix determinate.

   A problem with both geometry extraction and thresholding is that the approaches presented thus far extract "atomic" pieces of data, i.e., a complete cell. Sometimes the cell may lie across the boundary of the threshold. In this case the cell must be "cut", similar to a contour operation, and only a portion of the cell is extracted.

Probing

Probing is a method that obtains dataset attributes by sampling one dataset (the input) with a set of points (the probe) as shown in Figure **9–12**(a). Probing is also called "resampling". Examples include probing an input dataset with a sequence of points along a line, on a plane, or in a volume. The result of the probing is a new dataset (the output) with the topological and geometric structure of the probe dataset, and point attributes interpolated from the input dataset. Once the probing operation is completed, the output dataset can be visualized with any of the appropriate techniques described in this text.

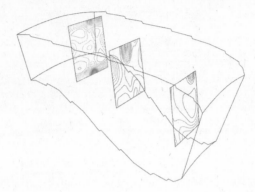

Figure 9–13 Probing data in a combustor. Probes are regular array of 50^2 points which are then passed through a contouring filter (probeComb.tcl).

Figure **9–12**(b) illustrates the details of the probing process. For every point in the probe dataset, the location in the input dataset (i.e., cell, sub-cell, and parametric coordinates) and interpolation weights are determined. Then the data values from the cell are interpolated to the probe point. Probe points that are outside the input dataset are assigned a nil (or appropriate) value. This process repeats for all points in the probe dataset.

Probing can be used to reduce data or to view data in a particular fashion.

• Data is reduced when the probe operation is limited to a sub-region of the input dataset, or the number of probe points is less than the number of input points.

• Data can be viewed in particular fashion by sampling on specially selected datasets. Using a probe dataset consisting of a line enables x-y plotting along a line, or using a plane allows surface color mapping or line contouring.

Probing must be used carefully or errors may be introduced. Under-sampling data in a region can miss important high frequency information, or localized data variations. Over-sampling data, while not creating error, can give false confidence in the accuracy of the data. Thus the sampling frequency should have a similar density as the input dataset, or if higher density, the visualization should be carefully annotated as to the original data frequency.

One important application of probing converts irregular or unstructured data to structured form using a volume of appropriate resolution as a probe to sample the unstructured data. This is useful if we use volume rendering or other volume visualization techniques to view our data.

Figure **9–13** shows an example of three probes. The probes sample flow density in a structured grid. The output of the probes is passed through a contour filter to generate contour lines. As this figure illustrates, we can be selective with the location and extent of the probe, allowing us to focus on important regions in the data.

Triangle Strip Generation

Triangle strips are compact representations of triangle polygons as described in "Triangle Strip" on page 111. Many rendering libraries include triangle strips as graphics primitives because they are a high-performance alternative to general polygon rendering.

Visualization and graphics data is often represented with triangles. Marching cubes, for example, generates thousands and potentially millions of triangles to represent an isosurface. To achieve greater performance in our visualizations, we can convert triangle polygons into triangle strips. Or, if data is represented using polygons, we can first triangulate the polygons and then create triangle strips.

A simple method to generate triangle strips uses greedy gathering of triangles into a strip (Figure **9–14**). The method proceeds as follows. An "unmarked" triangle is found to initialize the strip. Unmarked triangles are triangles that have not yet been gathered into a triangle strip. Starting with the initial triangle, the strip may grow in one of three directions, corresponding to the three edges of the triangle. We choose to grow the strip in the direction of the first unmarked neighbor triangle we encounter. If there are no unmarked neighbors the triangle strip is complete. Otherwise the strip is extended by adding triangles to the list that satisfy triangle strip topology. The strip is grown until no unmarked neighbor can be found. Additional strips are then created using the same procedure until every triangle is marked.

The length of the triangle strips varies greatly depending on the structure of the triangle mesh. Figure **9–15**(a) shows triangle strips each of length 390 triangles from a dataset that was originally structured. Such a case is an exception: unstructured triangle meshes typically average about 5-6 triangles per strip (Figure **9–15**(b)). Even so, the memory savings are impressive. A triangle strip of length 6 requires 8 points to represent, while 8 triangles require 24 points, for a memory savings of 66.7%. Rendering speed may be greatly affected too, depending upon the capabilities of the rendering system.

Connectivity

Inter-cell connectivity is a topological property of datasets. Cells are topologically connected when they share boundary features such as points, edges, or faces (Figure **9–16**). Connectivity is useful in a number of modelling applications, particularly when we want to separate out "parts" of a dataset.

One application of connectivity extracts a meaningful portion of an isosurface. If the isosurface is generated from measured data such as an MRI or CT scan, it likely contains "noise" or unimportant anatomical structure. Using connectivity algorithms we can separate out the part of the isosurface that we desire, either by eliminating noise or undesirable anatomical structure.

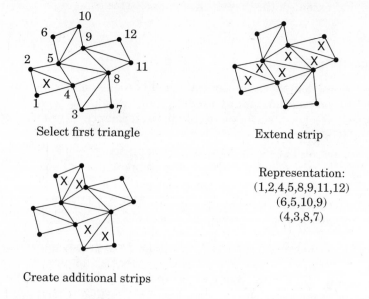

Select first triangle

Extend strip

Representation:
(1,2,4,5,8,9,11,12)
(6,5,10,9)
(4,3,8,7)

Create additional strips

Figure 9–14 Creating triangle strips.

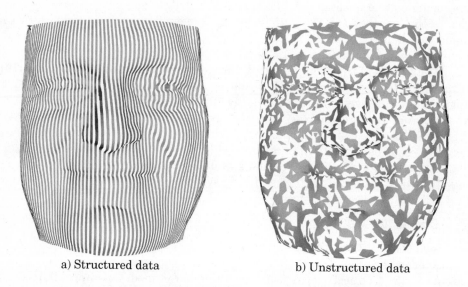

a) Structured data

b) Unstructured data

Figure 9–15 Triangle strip examples. a) Structured triangle mesh consisting of 134 strips each of 390 triangles (stripF.tcl). b) Unstructured triangle mesh consisting of 2227 strips of average length 3.94, longest strip 101 triangles. Images are generated by displaying every other triangle strip (uStripeF.tcl).

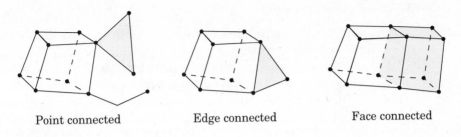

Point connected   Edge connected   Face connected

Figure 9–16 Connected cells.

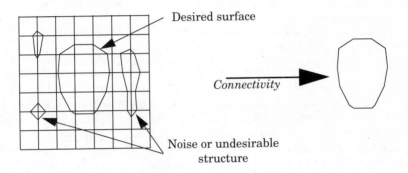

Figure 9–17 Extracting portion of isosurface of interest using connectivity.

Figure **9–17** is an example where a 2D surface of interest (e.g., an isocontour) is extracted from a noisy signal.

Connectivity algorithms can be implemented using a recursive visit method. We begin by choosing an arbitrary cell and mark it "visited". Then, depending upon the type of connectivity desired (i.e., point, edge, face), we gather the appropriate neighbors and mark them visited. This process repeats recursively until all connected cells are visited. We generally refer to such a set of connected cells as a connected "surface" even though the cells may be of a topological dimension other than 2.

To identify additional connected surfaces we locate another unvisited cell and repeat the process described previously. We continue to identify connected surfaces until every cell in the dataset is visited. As each connected surface is identified, it is assigned a surface number. We can use this number to specify the surfaces to extract or we can specify "seed" points or cells and extract the surfaces connected to them.

In some cases the recursion depth of the connectivity algorithm becomes larger than the computer system can manage. In this case we can specify a maximum recursion depth. When this depth is exceeded, recursion is terminated and the current cells in the recursion are used as seeds to restart the recursion.

Polygon Normal Generation

Gouraud and Phong shading (see Chapter 3) can improve the appearance of rendered polygons. Both techniques require point normals. Unfortunately polygonal meshes do not always contain point normals, or data file formats may not support point normals. Examples include the marching cubes algorithm for general datasets (typically will not generate surface normals) and the stereo lithography file format (does not support point normals). Figure **9–18**(a) shows a model defined from stereo-lithography format. The facetting of the model is clearly evident.

To address this situation we can compute surface normals from the polygonal mesh. A simple approach follows. First, polygon normals are computed around a common point. These normals are then averaged at the point, and the normal is re-normalized (i.e., $|n| = 1$) and associated with the point. This approach works well under two conditions.

1. The orientation of all polygons surrounding the point are consistent as shown in Figure **9–18**(b). A polygon is oriented consistently if the order of defining polygon points is consistent with its edge neighbors. That is, if polygon p is defined by points *(1,2,3)*, then the polygon edge neighbor p_{23} must use the edge *(2,3)* in the direction *(3,2)*. If not consistent, then the average point normal may be zero or not accurately represent the orientation of the surface. This is because the polygon normal is computed from a cross product of the edges formed by its defining points.

2. The angular difference in surface normals between adjacent polygons is small. Otherwise, sharp corners or edges will have a washed out appearance when rendered, resulting in an unsatisfactory image (Figure **9–18**(c)).

To avoid these problems we adopt a more complex polygon normal generation algorithm. This approach includes steps to insure that polygons are oriented consistently, and an edge splitting scheme that duplicates points across sharp edges.

To orient edges consistently we use a recursive neighbor traversal. An initial polygon is selected and marked "consistent". For each edge neighbor of the initial polygon, the ordering of the neighbor polygon points is checked. If not consistent, the ordering is reversed. The neighbor polygon is then marked "consistent". This process repeats recursively for each edge neighbor until all neighbors are marked "consistent". In some cases there may be more than one connected surface, so that the process may have to be repeated until all polygons are visited.

A similar traversal method splits sharp edges. A sharp edge is an edge shared by two polygons whose normals vary by a user specified *feature angle*. The feature angle between two polygons is the angle between their normals (Figure **9–19**(a)). When sharp edges are encountered during the recursive traversal, the points along the edge are duplicated, effectively disconnecting the mesh along that edge (Figure **9–19**(b)). Then, when shared polygon normals are

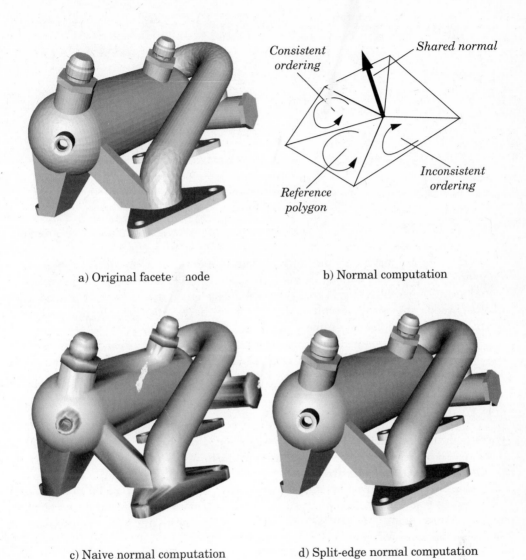

a) Original facetted model

b) Normal computation

c) Naive normal computation

d) Split-edge normal computation

Figure 9–18 Surface normal generation. a) Facetted model without normals. b) Polygons must be consistently oriented to accurately compute normals. c) Sharp edges are poorly represented using shared normals as shown on the corners of this cube. d) Normal generation with sharp edges split (Normals.cc).

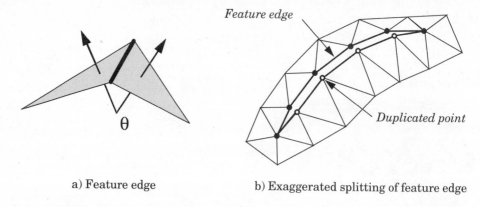

a) Feature edge   b) Exaggerated splitting of feature edge

Figure 9–19 Computing feature angles (a) and splitting edges (b).

computed later in the process, contributions to the average normal across sharp edges is prevented.

On some computers limitations on recursion depth may become a problem. Polygonal surfaces can consist of millions of polygons, resulting in large recursion depth. Hence the depth of recursion can be specified by the user. If recursion depth exceeds the specified value, the recursion halts and the polygons on the boundary of the recursion become seeds to begin the process again.

Figure **9–18**(d) shows the result of the advanced normal generation technique with a feature angle of 60 degrees. Sharp edges are well-defined and curved areas lack the facetting evident in the original model.

Decimation

Various data compression techniques have been developed in response to large data size. The UNIX utilities `compress/uncompress` and the PC utility `zip` compress data files. The MPEG compression algorithm compresses video sequences. These techniques may be loss-less, meaning that no data is lost between the compression/decompression steps, or lossy, meaning that data is lost during compression. The utilities `compress/uncompress` and `zip` are loss-less, while MPEG is lossy.

In graphics, data compression techniques have been developed as well. The sub-sampling methods we saw earlier in this chapter are an example of simple data compression techniques for visualization data. Another emerging area of graphics data compression is polygon reduction techniques.

Polygon reduction techniques reduce the number of polygons required to model an object. The size of models, in terms of polygon count, has grown tremendously over the last few years. This is because many models are created using digital measuring devices such as laser scanners or satellites. These devices can generate data at tremendous rates. For example, a laser digitizer can generate on the order of 500,000 triangles in a 15-second scan. Visualization algorithms such as marching cubes also generate large numbers of polygons: one to three million triangles from a 512^3 volume is typical.

One polygon reduction technique is the decimation algorithm [Schroeder92a]. The goal of the decimation algorithm is to reduce the total number of triangles in a triangle mesh, preserving the original topology and forming a good approximation to the original geometry. A triangle mesh is a special form of a polygonal mesh, where each polygon is a triangle. If need be, a polygon mesh can be converted to a triangle mesh using standard polygon triangulation methods.

Decimation is related to the subsampling technique for unstructured meshes described in Figure **9–11**(b). The differences are that

- decimation treats only triangle meshes, not arbitrary unstructured grids;

- the choice of which points to delete is a function of a *decimation criterion*, a measure of the local error introduced by deleting a point; and

- the triangulation of the hole created by deleting the point is carried out in a way as to preserve edges or other important features.

Decimation proceeds by iteratively visiting each point in a triangle mesh. For each point, three basic steps are carried out (Figure **9–20**). The first step classifies the local geometry and topology in the neighborhood of the point. The classification yields one of the five categories shown in the figure: simple, boundary, complex, edge, and corner point. Based on this classification, the second step uses a local error measure (i.e., the decimation criterion) to determine whether the point can be deleted. If the criterion is satisfied, the third step deletes the point (along with associated triangles), and triangulates the resulting hole. A more detailed description of each of these steps and example applications follow.

Point Classification

The first step of the decimation algorithm characterizes the local geometry and topology for a given point. The outcome of classification determines whether the vertex is a potential candidate for deletion, and if it is, which criteria to use.

Each point may be assigned one of five possible classifications: simple, complex, boundary, interior edge, or corner vertex. Examples of each type are shown in Figure **9–20**.

A *simple point* is surrounded by a complete cycle of triangles, and each edge that uses the point is used by exactly two triangles. If the edge is not used by two triangles, or if the point is used by a triangle not in the cycle of triangles, then the point is *complex*. These are non-manifold cases.

A point that is on the boundary of a mesh, i.e., within a semi-cycle of triangles, is a *boundary point*.

A simple point can be further classified as an *interior edge* or *corner point*. These classifications are based on the local mesh geometry. If the surface normal angle between two adjacent triangles is greater than a specified *feature angle*, then a *feature edge* exists (see Figure **9–19**(a)). When a point is used by two fea-

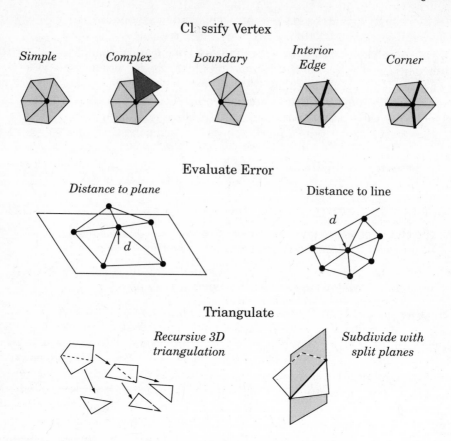

Figure 9–20 Overview of decimation algorithm.

ture edges, the point is an interior edge point. If one or three or more feature edges use the point, the point is a *corner point*.

Complex vertices and corner vertices are not deleted from the triangle mesh. All other vertices become candidates for deletion.

Decimation Criterion

Once we have a candidate point for deletion, we estimate the error that would result by deleting the point and then replacing it (and its associated triangles) with another triangulation. There are a number of possible error measures; but the simplest are based on distance measures of local planarity or local co-linearity (Figure **9–20**).

In the local region surrounding a simple point, the mesh is considered nearly "flat", since there are by definition no feature edges. Hence, simple points use an error measure based on distance to plane. The plane passing through the local region can be computed either using a least-squares plane, or by computing an area averaged plane.

Points classified as boundary or interior edge are considered to lay on an edge, and use a distance to edge error measure. That is, we compute the distance that the candidate point is from the new edge formed during the triangulation process.

A point satisfies the decimation criterion d if its distance measure is less than d. The point can then be deleted. All triangles using the point are deleted as well, leaving a "hole" in the mesh. This hole is patched using a local triangulation process.

Triangulation

After deleting a point, the resulting hole must be re-triangulated. Although the hole, defined by a loop of edges, is topologically two dimensional, it is generally non-planar, and therefore general purpose 2D triangulation techniques cannot be used. Instead, we use a special recursive 3D divide-and-conquer technique to triangulate the loop.

Triangulation proceeds as follows. An initial split plane is chosen to divide the loop in half and create two sub-loops. If all the points in each sub-loop lie on opposite sides of the plane, then the split is a valid one. In addition, an *aspect ratio* check insures that the loop is not too long and skinny, thereby resulting in needle-like triangles. The aspect ratio is the ratio between the length of the split line to the minimum distance of a point in the sub-loop to the split plane. If the candidate split plane is not valid, or does not satisfy the aspect ratio criterion, then another candidate split plane is evaluated. Once a split plane is found, then the subdivision of each sub-loop continues recursively until a sub-loop consists of three edges. In this case, the sub-loop generates a triangle and halts the recursion.

Occasionally triangulation fails because no split plane can be found. In this case, the candidate point is not deleted and the mesh is left in its original state. This poses no problem to the algorithm and decimation continues by visiting the next point in the dataset.

Results and Advanced Techniques

Typical compression rates for the decimation algorithm range from 2:1 to 100:1, with 10:1 a nominal figure for "large" (i.e., 10^5 triangles) datasets. The results vary greatly depending upon the type of data. CAD models typically reduce the least because these models have many sharp edges and other features, and the CAD modellers usually produce minimal triangulations. Terrain data, especially if relatively flat regions are present, may reduce at rates of 100:1.

Figure **9–21** shows two applications of decimation to laser digitized data and to a terrain model of Honolulu, Hawaii, USA. In both cases the reduction was on the order of 90% for a 10:1 compression ratio. Wireframe images are shown to accentuate the density of the polygonal meshes. The left hand image in each pair is the original data. The right hand image is the decimated mesh. Notice the gradations in the decimated mesh around feature of high curvature.

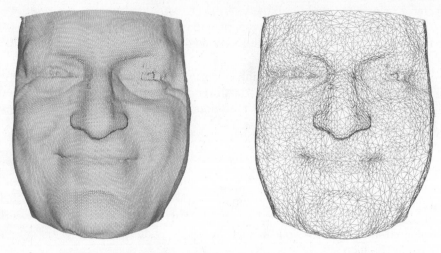

a) Decimation of laser digitizer data (deciFran.tcl).

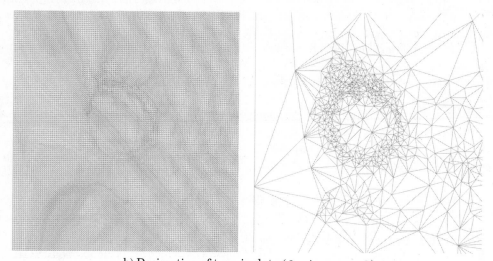

b) Decimation of terrain data (deciHawa.tcl).

Figure 9–21 Examples of decimation algorithm. Triangle meshes are shown in wireframe.

The advantage of decimation, as compared to subsampling techniques, is that the mesh is adaptively modified to retain more details in areas of high curvature.

Swept Volumes and Surfaces

Consider moving an object (e.g., your hand) over some path (e.g., raise your hand). How can we visualize this motion? The obvious answer is to form a time-animation sequence as the hand is moved. But what if we wish to statically represent the motion as well as the space that is traversed by the hand? Then we can use *swept surfaces* and *swept volumes*.

A swept volume is the volume of space occupied by an object as it moves through space along an arbitrary trajectory. A swept surface is the surface of the swept volume. Together, swept volumes and swept surfaces can statically represent the motion of objects.

Past efforts at creating swept surfaces and volumes have focused on analytical techniques. The mathematical representation of various 3D geometric primitives (e.g., lines, polygons, splines) was extended to include a fourth dimension of time (the path). Unfortunately, these approaches have never been practically successful, partly due to mathematical complexity, and partly due to problem degeneracies.

Degeneracies occur when an n-dimensional object moves in such a way that its representation becomes $(n\text{-}1)$-dimensional. For example, moving a plane in the direction of its normal, sweeps out a 3D "cubical" volume. Sweeping the plane in a direction perpendicular to its normal, however, results in a degenerate condition, since the plane sweeps out a 2D "rectangle".

Instead of creating swept surfaces analytically, numerical approximation techniques can be used [Schroeder94]. Implicit modelling provides the basis for an effective technique to visualize object motion via swept surfaces and volumes. The technique is immune to degeneracies and can treat any geometric representation for which a distance function can be computed, including the 12 cell types in **vtk**.

The technique to generate swept surfaces and volumes using an implicit modelling approach proceeds as follows. The geometric model, or part, and a path describing the parts motion, or sweep trajectory ST, must be defined. Then we use the following four steps as depicted in Figure **9–22**.

1. Generate an implicit model from the part. This results in an implicit representation in the form of a volume. We call this the implicit model V_I.

2. Construct another volume, the workspace volume V_W, that strictly bounds V_I as it moves along the path ST. Then sweep V_I through V_W by moving in small steps, Δx, along ST. At each step, s, sample V_I with the workspace volume V_W. We use a boolean union operation to perform the sampling.

3. Extract isosurface, or offset surface(s) from V_W using a contouring algorithm such as marching cubes.

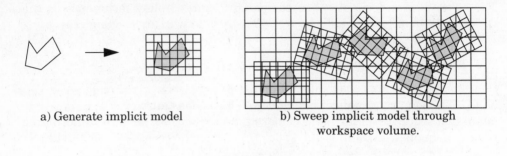

a) Generate implicit model   b) Sweep implicit model through
                                        workspace volume.

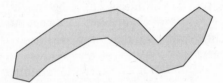

c) Generate swept surface via isosurface extraction.
Use connectivity to extract single surface.

Figure 9–22 Overview of swept surface technique.

4. Step 3 may create multiple connected surfaces. If a single surface is
    desired, use connectivity to extract the single "largest" surface (in terms of
    number of triangles). This surface is an approximation to the swept surface,
    and the volume it encloses is an approximation to the swept volume.

   There are a few points that require additional explanation. This algorithm
uses two volumes, the implicit model and the workspace volume. Both are
implicit models, but the workspace volume is used to accumulate the part as it
moves along the sweep trajectory. In theory, the part could be sampled directly
into the workspace volume to create the implicit model of the swept surface. Performance issues dictate that the implicit model is sampled into the workspace
volume. This is because it is much faster to sample the implicit model of the part
rather than the part itself, since computing the distance function from a part
that may consist of tens of thousands of cells is relatively time consuming, compared to sampling the implicit model V_I.

   Sampling V_I is depicted in Figure **9–23**. The sweep trajectory is defined by
a series of transformation matrices $ST = \{t_1, t_2, ..., t_m\}$. As the part moves
along ST, interpolation is used to compute an in-between transformation matrix
t. Sampling is achieved by inverse transforming V_W into the local space of V_I
using t. Then, similar to the probe operation described in section y, the points of
V_W are transformed by the inverse of the transformation matrix t^{-1} , and used
to interpolate the distance values from the implicit model V_I.

   Because we are dealing with an implicit modelling technique, parts with
concave features can generate multiple surfaces. As discussed in "Connectivity"

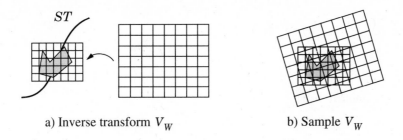

a) Inverse transform V_W b) Sample V_W

Figure 9–23 Generating workspace volume by sampling implicit volume.

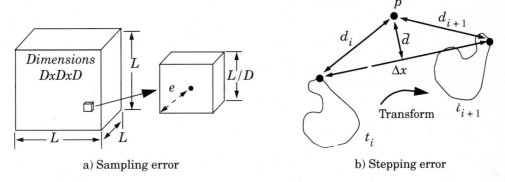

a) Sampling error   b) Stepping error

Figure 9–24 Computing sampling and stepping error.

on page 287, the connectivity algorithm is used to separate out the swept surface. This final surface is an approximation to the actual swept surface, since we are sampling the actual geometric representation on an array of points (i.e., the implicit model), and then sampling the implicit model on another volume (i.e., the workspace volume). Also, stepping along the sweep trajectory generates errors proportional to the step size Δx.

These errors can be characterized as follows (Figure **9–24**). Given a voxel size L/D, where L is the edge length of the volume, and D is the dimension of the volume (assumed uniform for convenience), the maximum sampling error is

$$e \le \frac{\sqrt{3}}{2}\left(\frac{L}{D}\right) \tag{9-14}$$

The error due to stepping, which includes both translation and rotational components, is bounded by $\Delta x/2$, where Δx is the maximum displacement of any point on the implicit model at any given translational step. Combining these terms for sampling both volumes and the error due to stepping, the total error is

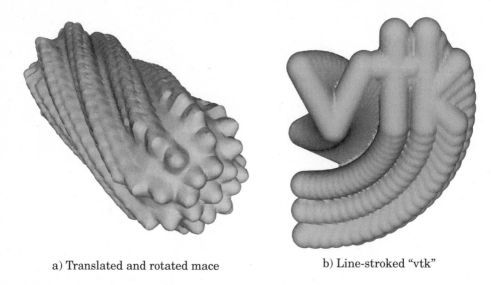

a) Translated and rotated mace   b) Line-stroked "vtk"

Figure 9–25 Swept surfaces. a) Swept mace sampled at 25 locations (`sweptMac.cc`).
b) Swept vtk sampled at 21 locations (`sweptVtk.tcl`).

$$e_{\text{tot}} \leq \frac{\sqrt{3}}{2}\left(\frac{L_I}{D_I} + \frac{L_W}{D_W}\right) + \frac{\Delta x}{2} \qquad \textbf{(9-15)}$$

where the subscripts I and W refer to the implicit model and workspace volume, respectively.

To show the application of this algorithm, we have generated swept surfaces for the letters "**vtk**" and the "mace" model as shown in Figure **9–25**. We have purposely chosen a step size to exaggerate the stepping error. Using more steps would smooth out the surface "bumps" due to stepping. Also, the appearance of the surface varies greatly with the selected isosurface value. Larger values give rounder, smoother surfaces. If you use small values near zero (assuming positive distance function) the surface may break up. To correct this you need to use a higher resolution workspace or compute negative distances. Negative distances are computed during the implicit modelling step by negating all points *inside* the original geometry. Negative distances allow us to use a zero isosurface value or to generate internal offset surfaces. Negative distances can only be computed for closed (i.e., manifold) objects.

Visualizing Unstructured Points

Unstructured point datasets consist of points at irregular positions in 3D space. The relationship between points is arbitrary. Examples of unstructured point

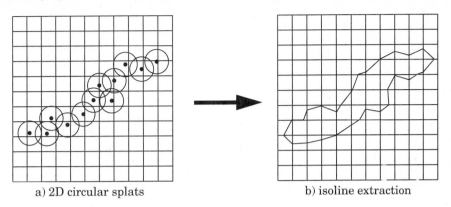

a) 2D circular splats   b) isoline extraction

Figure 9–26 Splatting techniques depicted in 2D. a) Injecting points into structured point dataset (circular splats). b) Visualizing structured point dataset via contouring.

datasets are visualizing temperature distribution from an array of (arbitrarily) placed thermocouples, or rainfall level measured at scattered positions over a geographic region.

Unlike structured points and grids, or even unstructured grids, unstructured point dataset have no topological component relating one point to another. For these reasons unstructured points are simple to represent but difficult to visualize. They are difficult to visualize because there is no inherent "structure" to which we can apply our library of visualization techniques. Beyond just displaying points (possibly colored with scalar value, or using oriented vector glyphs) none of the techniques discussed thus far can be used. Thus, to visualize unstructured points we have to build structure to which we can apply our visualization techniques.

There are several approaches available to build topological structure given a random set of points. One common approach samples unstructured points with a structured point set, and then visualizes the data using standard volume rendering or surface-based rendering techniques. Another approach creates *n*-dimensional triangulations from the unstructured points, thereby creating topological structure. Some common techniques are described in the following sections.

Splatting Techniques

Splatting techniques build topological structure by sampling unstructured points with a structured point set (Figure **9–26**). The sampling is performed by creating special influence, or splatting, functions $SF(x,y,z)$ that distribute the data value of each unstructured point over the surrounding region. To sample the unstructured points, each point is inserted into a structured point dataset SP, and the data values are distributed through SP using the splatting functions $SF(x,y,z)$. Once the topological structure is built, any structured point visualization technique can be used (including volume rendering).

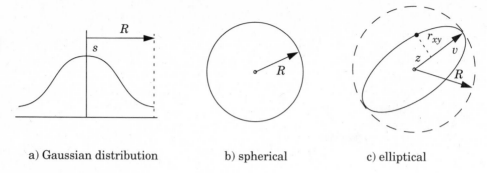

a) Gaussian distribution   b) spherical   c) elliptical

Figure 9–27 Gaussian splatting functions. a) one-dimensional, b) 2D spherical, and c) 2D elliptical.

A common splatting function is a uniform Gaussian distribution centered at a point p_i. The function is conveniently cast into the form

$$SF(x, y, z) = se^{-f(r/R)^2} \tag{9-16}$$

where s is a scale factor that multiplies the exponential, f is the exponent scale factor $f \geq 0$, r is the distance between the point and the Gaussian center point $r = \|p - p_i\|$, and R is the radius of influence of the Gaussian, where $r \leq R$.

The Gaussian function (Figure **9–27**(a)) becomes a circle in cross-section in two dimensions (Figure **9–27**(b)) and a sphere in three-dimensions. Since the value of the function is maximum when $r = 0$, the maximum value is given by the scale factor s. The parameter f controls the rate of decay of the splat. Scalar values can be used to set the value of s, so that relatively large scalar values create bigger splats than smaller values.

Splats may be accumulated using the standard implicit modelling boolean operations (Equation **6-13**, Equation **6-14**, and Equation **6-15**). That is, we may choose to form a union, intersection, or difference of the splats. The union and intersection operators are used most frequently.

Another interesting variation modifies the shape of the splat according to a vector quantity such as surface normal or vector data. Figure **9–27**(c) shows an example where the splat shape is elongated in the direction parallel to a vector. Thus, if we have a set of points and normals, we can create a polygonal surface by combining splatting with isosurface extraction.

To generate oriented splats we modify Equation **9-16** by introducing an eccentricity factor E and the vector $\vec{v}$.

$$SF(x, y, z) = se^{-f\left(\frac{\left(\frac{r_{xy}}{E}\right)^2 + z^2}{R^2}\right)} \tag{9-17}$$

where z and r_{xy} are computed from

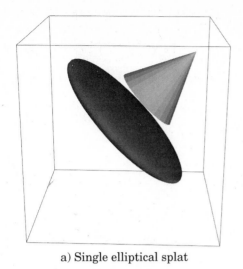

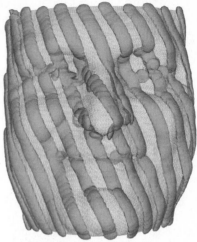

a) Single elliptical splat   b) Surface reconstruction

Figure 9–28 Elliptical splatting. a) Single elliptical splat with eccentricity $E=10$. Cone shows orientation of vector (singleSplat.cc). b) Surface reconstructed using elliptical splats into 100^3 volume followed by isosurface extraction. Points regularly subsampled and overlayed on original mesh (splatF.tcl).

$$z = \vec{v} \cdot (p - p_i), \text{ with } |\vec{v}| = 1$$
$$r_{xy} = r^2 - z^2$$
(9-18)

The parameter z is the distance along the vector $\vec{v}$, and the parameter r_{xy} is the distance perpendicular to v to the point p. The eccentricity factor controls the shape of the splat. A value $E = 1$ results in spherical splats, whereas $E > 1$ yields flattened splats and $E < 1$ yields elongated splats in the direction of the vector v.

Figure **9–28**(a) shows an elliptical splat with $E = 10$. (The splat surface is created by using isosurface extraction.) As expected the splat is an ellipsoid. Figure **9–28**(b) is an application of elliptical splatting used to reconstruct a surface from an unstructured set of points. The advantage of using an elliptical splat is that we can flatten the splat in the plane perpendicular to the point normal. This tends to bridge the space between the point samples. The surface itself is extracted using a standard isosurface extraction algorithm.

Interpolation Techniques

Interpolation techniques construct a function to smoothly interpolate a set of unstructured points. That is, given a set of n points $p_i = (x_i, y_i, z_i)$ and function values $F_i(p_i)$, a new function $F(p)$ is created that interpolates the points p_i.

Once the interpolation function is constructed, we can build topological structure from the unstructured points by sampling $F(p)$ over a structured point dataset. We can then visualize the structured point dataset using the various techniques presented throughout the text.

Shepard's method is an inverse distance weighted interpolation technique [Wixom78]. The interpolation functions can be written

$$F(p) = \frac{\displaystyle\sum_{i=1}^{n} \frac{F_i}{|p - p_i|^2}}{\displaystyle\sum_{i=1}^{n} \frac{1}{|p - p_i|^2}} \qquad (9\text{-}19)$$

where $F(p_i) = F_i$. Shepard's method is easy to implement, but has the undesirable property that limits its usefulness for most practical application. The interpolation functions generate a local "flat spot" at each point p_i since the derivatives are zero

$$\frac{\partial F}{\partial x} = \frac{\partial F}{\partial y} = \frac{\partial F}{\partial z} = 0 \qquad (9\text{-}20)$$

As a result Shepard's method is overly constrained in the region around each point.

Shepard's method is an example of a basis function method. That is, the interpolation function $F(p)$ consists of a sum of functions centered at each data point p_i. Other basis function methods have been developed as described by Nielson [Nielson91]. They vary in localization of the basis functions and the sophistication of the interpolation function. Localization of basis functions means that their effect is isolated to a small region. Examples of more sophisticated basis functions include quadratic polynomials and cubic splines. Please see the references for more information.

Triangulation Techniques

Triangulation techniques build topology directly from the unstructured points. The points are *triangulated* to create a topological structure consisting of n-dimensional simplices that completely bound the points and linear combinations of the points (the so-called *convex hull*). The result of triangulation is a set of triangles (2D) or tetrahedra (3D), depending upon the dimension of the input data [Lawson86].

An n-dimensional triangulation of a point set $P = (p_1, p_2, p_3, ..., p_n)$ is a collection of n-dimensional simplices whose defining points lie in P. The simplices do not intersect one another and share only boundary features such as edges or faces. The Delaunay triangulation is a particularly important form [Bowyer81] [Watson81]. It has the property that the circumsphere of any n-dimensional sim-

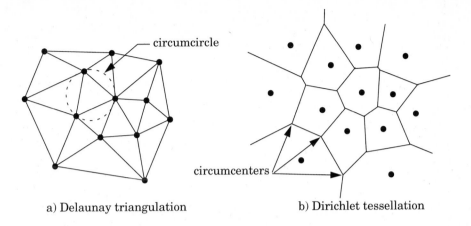

a) Delaunay triangulation   b) Dirichlet tessellation

Figure 9–29 The Delaunay triangulation (a) and Dirichlet tessellation (b). The circumcircle of each triangle in a Delaunay triangulation contains no other points but the three vertices of the triangle. The region surrounding each point p_i in a Dirichlet tessellation is the set of points closest to p_i.

plex contains no other points of P except the $n+1$ defining points of the simplex (Figure **9–29**(a)).

The Delaunay triangulation has many interesting properties. In two dimensions, the Delaunay triangulation has been shown to be the optimal triangulation. That is, the minimum interior angle of a triangle in a Delaunay triangulation is greater than or equal to the minimum interior angle of any other possible triangulation. The Delaunay triangulation is the dual of the Dirichlet tessellation (Figure **9–29**(b)), another important construction in computational geometry. The Dirichlet tessellation, also known as the Voronoi tessellation, is a tiling of space where each tile represents the space closest to a point p_i. (The tiles are called Voronoi cells.) An n-dimensional Delaunay triangulation can be constructed from the Dirichlet tessellation by creating edges between Voronoi cells that share common $n-1$ boundaries (e.g., faces in 3D and edges in 2D). Conversely, the vertices of the Dirichlet tessellation are located at the circumcenters of the Delaunay circumcircles.

The Delaunay triangulation can be computed using a variety of techniques. We describe a particularly elegant technique introduced independently by Watson [Watson81] and Bowyer [Bowyer81] (Figure **9–30**). The algorithm begins by constructing an initial Delaunay triangulation that strictly bounds the point set P, the so-called bounding triangulation. This bounding triangulation can be as simple as a single triangle (2D) or tetrahedron (3D). Then, each point of P is injected one by one into the current triangulation. If the injected point lies within the circumcircle of any simplex, then the simplex is deleted, leaving a "hole" in the triangulation. After deleting all simplices, the $n-1$ dimensional faces on the boundary of the hole, along with the injected point, are used to construct a modified triangulation. This is a Delaunay triangulation, and the process contin-

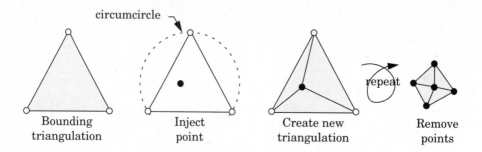

circumcircle

| Bounding triangulation | Inject point | Create new triangulation | Remove points |

Figure 9–30 Computing the Delaunay triangulation using technique of Watson and Boyer. Points are injected into triangulation forming new Delaunay triangulations. In the final step, the initial bounding points are removed to reveal final triangulation.

ues until all points are injected into the triangulation. The last step removes the simplices connecting the points forming the initial bounding triangulation to reveal the completed Delaunay triangulation.

This simplistic presentation of triangulation techniques has shown how to create topological structure from a set of unstructured points. We have ignored some difficult issues such as degeneracies and numerical problems. Degeneracies occur when points in a Delaunay triangulation lie in such a way that the triangulation is not unique. For example, the points lying at the vertices of a square, rectangle, or hexagon are degenerate because they can be triangulated in more than one way, where each triangulation is equivalent (in terms of Delaunay criterion) to the other. Numerical problems occur when we attempt to compute circumcenters, especially in higher-dimensional triangulations, or when simplices of poor aspect ratio are present.

Despite these problems, triangulation methods are a powerful tool for visualizing unstructured points. Once we convert the data into a triangulation (or in our terminology, an unstructured grid), we can directly visualize our data using standard unstructured grid techniques.

Hybrid Techniques

Recent work has focused on combining triangulation and basis function techniques for interpolating 2D bivariate data. The basic idea is as follows. A triangulation of P is constructed. Then an interpolating network of curves is defined over the edges of the triangulation. These curves are constructed with certain minimization properties of interpolating splines. Finally, the curve network is used to construct a series of triangular basis functions, or surface patches, that exhibit continuity in function value, and possibly higher order derivatives. (See [Nielson91] for more information.)

Multi-Dimensional Visualization

The treatment of multi-dimensional data sets is an important data visualization issue. Each point in a dataset is described by an n-dimensional coordinate, where $n \geq 3$. Here we assume that each coordinate is an independent variable, and that we wish to visualize a single dependent variable. (Multi-dimensional visualization of vectors and tensors is an open research area.) An application of multi-dimensional data is financial visualization, where we might want to visualize return on investment as a function of interest rate, initial investment, investment period, and income, to name just a few possibilities.

There are two fundamental problems that we must address when applying multi-dimensional visualization. These are the problems of *projection* and *understanding*.

The problem of projection is that using computer graphics we have two dimensions in which to present our data, or possibly three or four if we use specialized methods. Using 3D graphics we can give the illusion of three dimensions, or we can use stereo viewing techniques to achieve three dimensions. We can also use time as a fourth dimension by animating images. However, except for these limited situations, general n-dimensional data cannot be represented on a 2D computer screen.

The problem of understanding, is that humans do not easily comprehend more than three dimensions, or possibly three dimensions plus time. Thus, even if we could create a technique to display data of many dimensions, the difficulty in understanding the data would impair the usefulness of the technique.

Most multi-dimensional visualization techniques work with some form of dimension mapping, where n dimensions are mapped to three dimensions and then displayed with 3D computer graphics techniques. The mapping is achieved by fixing all variables except three, and then applying the visualization techniques described throughout the text to the resulting data. For maximum benefit, the process of fixing independent variables, mapping to three dimensions, and then generating visualization must be interactive. This improves the effectiveness of the visualization process, allowing the user to build an internal model of the data by manipulating different parts of the data.

One novel approach to multi-dimensional visualization has been proposed by Inselberg and Dimsdale [Inselberg87]. This approach uses *parallel coordinate systems*. Instead of plotting points on orthogonal axes, the ith dimensional coordinate of each point is plotted along separate, parallel axes. This is shown in Figure **9–31** for a five-dimensional point. In parallel coordinate plots, points appear as lines. As a result, plots of n-dimensional points appear as sequences of line segments that may intersect or group to form complex fan patterns or groups. In so doing, the human pattern recognition capability is engaged. Unfortunately, if the number of points becomes large, and the data is not strongly correlated, the resulting plots can become a solid mass of black, and any data trends are drowned in the visual display.

Another useful multi-variable technique uses glyphs. Although glyphs cannot generally be designed for arbitrary n-dimensional data, in many applications

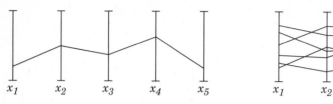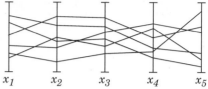

a) Plot of five-dimensional point   b) Plot of six points

Figure 9–31   Plotting a five-dimensional point using parallel coordinates. a) plot of single point, b) plot of many points.

we can create glyphs to convey the information we are interested in. Refer to "Glyphs" on page 173 for more information about glyphs.

Texture Algorithms

Texturing is a common tool in computer graphics used to introduce detail without the high cost of graphics primitives. As we suggested in Chapter 7, texture mapping can also be used to visualize data. We explore a few techniques in the following sections.

Texture Thresholding

We saw earlier how to threshold data based on scalar values (see "Thresholding" on page 285). We refer to this approach as *geometric thresholding* because structural components of a dataset (e.g., points and cells) are extracted based on data value. In contrast, we can use texture mapping techniques to achieve similar results. We call this technique *texture thresholding*.

Texture thresholding conceals features we do not want to see, and accentuates features that we want to see. There are many variations on this theme. A feature can be concealed by making it transparent or translucent, by reducing its intensity, or using muted colors. A feature can be accentuated by making it opaque, increasing its intensity, or adding bright color. In the following paragraphs we describe a technique that combines intensity and transparency.

Texture thresholding requires two pieces of information: a texture map and an index into the map, or texture coordinate. In the simplest case we can devise a texture map that consists of two distinct regions as shown in Figure **9–32**(a). The first region is alternatively referred to as "conceal", "off", or "outside". The second region is referred to as "accentuate", "on", or "inside". (These different labels are used depending upon the particular application.) With this texture map in hand we can texture threshold by computing an appropriate texture coordinate. Areas that we wish to accentuate are assigned a coordinate to map into the "accentuate" portion of the texture map. Areas that we want to conceal are assigned a coordinate to map into the "conceal" portion of the texture map.

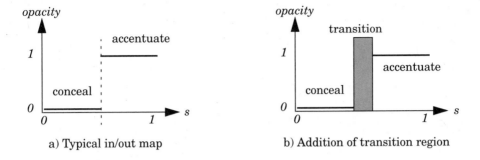

a) Typical in/out map

b) Addition of transition region

Figure 9–32 1D texture map. a) In/out map. b) Addition of transition region to in/out map.

One texture threshold technique uses transparency. We can conceal a region by setting its alpha opacity value to zero (transparent), and accentuate it by setting the alpha value to one (opaque). Thus, the texture map consists of two regions: a concealed region with $\alpha = 0$, and an accentuated region with $\alpha = 1$. Of course, the effect can be softened by using intermediate alpha values to create translucent images.

An extension of this technique introduces a third region into the texture map: a transition region (Figure **9–32**(b)). The transition region is the region between the concealed and accentuated regions. We can use the transition region to draw a border around the accentuated region, further highlighting the region.

To construct the texture map we use *intensity-alpha,* or $I\alpha$ values. The intensity modulates the underlying color, while the alpha value controls transparency (as described previously). In the accentuated region, the intensity and opacity values are set high. In the concealed region, the intensity value can be set to any value (if $\alpha = 0$) or to a lower value (if $\alpha \neq 0$). The transition region can use various combinations of α and intensity. A nice combination produces a black, opaque transition region (i.e., $I = 0$ and $\alpha = 1$).

To visualize information with the thresholding technique, we must map data to texture coordinates. As we saw previously, we can use scalar values in combination with a threshold specification to map data into the concealed, transition, and accentuated regions of the texture map. Figure **9–33**(a) shows an example of texture thresholding applied to scalar data from a simulation of fluid flow. A scalar threshold s_T is set to show only data with scalar value greater than or equal to s_T.

Another useful texture thresholding application uses implicit functions to map point position to texture coordinate. This is a form of *geometric clipping.* As we saw in "Implicit Functions" on page 167, implicit functions naturally map a (x, y, z) coordinate value into three regions: $F(x, y, z) < 0$, $F(x, y, z) = 0$, and $F(x, y, z) > 0$; or equivalently, the concealed, transition, and accentuated regions of the texture map. Using boolean combinations of implicit functions, we can create complex cuts of our data as illustrated in Figure **9–33**(b). This figure

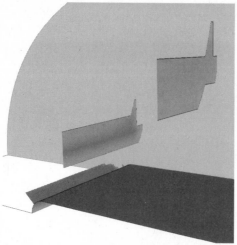 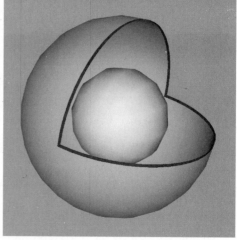

a) Thresholding data with texture   b) Sphere cut with transparent texture

Figure 9–33 Examples of texture thresholding. a) Using scalar threshold to show values of flow density on plane above value of 1.5 (`texThresh.tcl`). b) Boolean combination of two planes to cut nested spheres (`tcutSph.cc`).

shows two nested spheres. The outer sphere is cut by a boolean combination of two planes to show the inner sphere.

Boolean Textures

Texture thresholding can be extended into two or higher dimensions. That is, 2D or 3D texture coordinates can be used to map two or three data variables into a texture map. One such technique is *boolean textures*, a method to clip geometry using a 2D texture map and two implicit functions [Lorensen93].

Boolean textures extend texture thresholding for geometric clipping from 1D to 2D. Instead of using a single implicit function to label regions "in" or "out", two implicit functions are used. This results in four different regions corresponding to all possible combinations of "in" and "out". The boolean texture map is modified to reflect this as shown in Figure **9–34**. As with 1D texture thresholding, transition regions can be created to separate the four regions.

The boolean texture map can be created with combinations of intensity and transparency values to achieve a variety of effects. By combining the four combinations of in/out (i.e., four regions of Figure **9–34**), with the two combinations of "conceal" and "accentuate", sixteen different boolean textures are possible. Figure **9–35**(a) illustrates these combinations expressed as boolean combinations of two implicit functions A and B. The "inside" of the implicit functions is indicated with subscript i, while the outside is indicated with subscript o. The boolean expressions indicate the regions that we wish to conceal, as shown by open circles. The darkened circles are the regions that are accentuated. We can see in

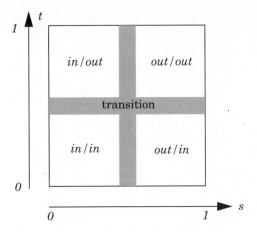

Figure 9–34 2D Boolean texture.

Figure **9–35**(b) the effects of applying these different boolean textures to a sphere. The implicit functions in this figure are two elliptical cylinders sharing a common axis, and rotated 90 degrees from one another. In addition, transition regions have been defined with $I = 0$ to generate the dark cut edges shown. All sixteen spheres share the same texture coordinates; only the texture map changes.

Texture Animation

Time-based animation techniques can illustrate motion or temporal data variation. This process often requires relatively large amounts of computer resource to read, process, and display the data. As a result, techniques to reduce computer resource are desirable when animating data.

Texture mapping can be used to animate certain types of data. In these techniques, the data is not regenerated frame by frame, instead a time-varying texture map is used to change the visual appearance of the data. An example of this approach is texture animation of vector fields [Yamrom95].

As we saw in "Hedgehogs and Oriented Glyphs" on page 155, vector fields can be represented as oriented and scaled lines. Texture animation can transform this static representational scheme into a dynamic representation. The key is to construct a series of 1D texture maps that when applied rapidly in sequence create the illusion of motion. Figure **9–36**(a) shows a series of sixteen such texture maps. The maps consist of intensity-alpha ($I\alpha$) values, A portion of the texture map is set fully opaque with full intensity ($I = 1, \quad \alpha = 1$). This is shown as the "dark" pattern in Figure **9–36**(a). The remainder of the map is set fully transparent with arbitrary intensity ($I = 1, \quad \alpha = 0$) shown as the "white" portion. As is evidenced by the figure, the sequence of sixteen texture maps scanned top to bottom generate the appearance of motion from left to right. Notice also how the texture maps are designed to wrap around to from a continuous pattern.

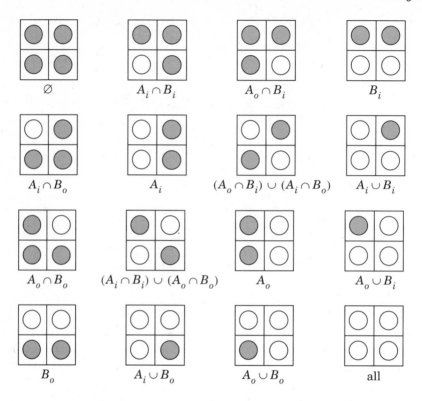

a) Combinations of 2D in/out textures

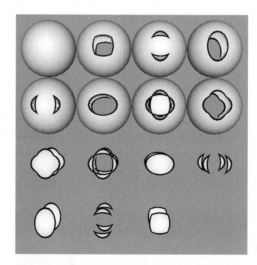

b) Sixteen boolean textures (from above) applied to sphere (`quadricCut.cc`)

Figure 9–35 Sixteen boolean textures.a) Sixteen combinations of in/out. b) Textures applied to sphere using two elliptical cylinder implicit functions.

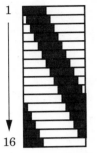

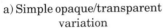

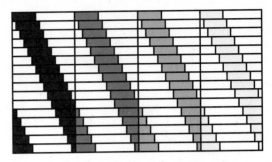

a) Simple opaque/transparent variation

b) Feathered opaque/transparent variation

Figure 9–36 Texture maps for vector animation. Sixteen textures applied in succession create effect of motion along a vector. a) Simple map. b) Varying intensity "feathers" effect of motion.

Along with the 1D texture map the texture coordinate *s* must also be generated. On a line this is straightforward. The beginning of the line receives texture coordinate *s = 0*, while the line terminus receives texture coordinate value *s = 1*. Any intermediate points (if the vector is a polyline) are parameterized in monotonic fashion in the interval (0,1). Texture coordinates need only be generated once. Only the texture map is varied to generate the vector animation.

Other effects are possible by modifying the texture map. Figure **9–36**(b) shows a texture map with a repeating sequence of opaque/transparent regions. In each opaque region the intensity is gradually reduced from left to right. The result is that this tends to "feather" the appearance of the vector motion. The resulting image is more pleasing to the eye.

9.5 Putting It All Together

With the conclusion of this chapter we have covered the basics of data visualization. In this section we show you how to use some of the advanced algorithms as implemented in the *Visualization Toolkit*.

Dividing Cubes / Point Generation

Dividing cubes is implemented in **vtk** with the class vtkDividingCubes. It has been specialized to operate with structured point datasets. Besides specifying the contour value, you must specify a separation distance between points (using the method SetDistance()). If you desire a solid appearance, pick a distance that is less than or equal to display resolution.

The separation distance controls the accuracy of point generation. It is possible to generate points that appear to form a solid surface when rendered, but are not accurately located on the contour surface. Although this usually is not an

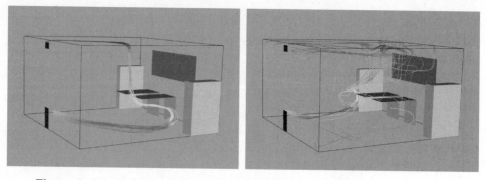

Figure 9–37 Using random point seeds to create streamlines (office.tcl).

issue when viewing contour surfaces, if the accuracy of the point positions is important, the distance value must be set smaller. However, this can result in huge numbers of points. To reduce the number of points you can use the Set-Increment() method, which specifies that every n^{th} point is to be generated. Using this approach, you can obtain good accuracy and control the total number of points. An example where point positions are important is when the points are used to locate glyphs or as seed points for streamline generation.

The *Visualization Toolkit* provides other point generation techniques. The source object vtkPointSource generates a user-specified number of points within a spherical region. The point positions are random within the sphere. (Note that there is a natural tendency for higher point density near the center of the sphere because the points are randomly generated along the radius and spherical angles ϕ and θ.)

Figure **9–37** is an example use of vtkPointSource to generate streamlines. The dataset is a structured grid of dimensions $21 \times 20 \times 20$ with flow velocity and a scalar pressure field. The dataset is a CFD simulation of flow in a small office. As this picture shows, there are a couple of bookcases, desks, a window, and an inlet and outlet for the ventilation system. On one of the desks is a small, intense heat source (e.g., a cigarette). In the left image twenty-five streamlines are started near the inlet using a vtkPointSource point generator. The second image shows what happens when we move the point source slightly to the left. By adjusting a single parameter (e.g., the center of the point source) it is possible to quickly explore our simulation data.

Another convenient object for point generation is the class vtkEdge-Points. vtkEdgePoints generates points on an isosurface. The points are generated by locating cell edges whose points are both above and below the isosurface value. Linear interpolation is used to generate the point. Since vtkEdgePoints operates on any cell type, this filter's input type is any dataset type (e.g., vtkDataSet). Unlike vtkDividingCubes this filter will not typically generate dense point clouds that appear solid.

Swept Volumes and Surfaces

Swept surfaces can be applied in two interesting ways. First, they can be used as a modelling tool to create unusual shapes and forms. In this sense swept surfaces are an advanced implicit modelling technique. Second, swept surfaces can be used to statically to model object motion. This is an important visualization technique in itself and has many important applications. One of these applications is design for maintainability.

When a complex mechanical system like a car engine is designed, it is important to design proper access to critical engine components. These components, like spark plugs, require higher levels of service and maintenance. It is important that these components can be easily reached by a mechanic. We've read horror stories of how it is necessary to remove an engine to change a spark plug. Insuring ready access to critical engine parts prevents situations like this from occurring.

Swept surface can assist in the design of part access. We simply define a path to remove the part (early in the design process), and then generate a swept surface. This surface (sometimes referred to as a maintenance access solid or MAS) is then placed back into the CAD system. From this point on, the design of surrounding components such as fuel lines or wiring harnesses must avoid the MAS. As long as the MAS is not violated, the part can be removed. If the MAS is violated, a reevaluation of the removal path or redesign of the part or surrounding components is necessary.

Figure **9–38** shows how to create a swept surface from a simple geometric representation. The geometry is simply a line-stroked **vtk**. The next step is to define a motion path. This path is defined by creating a list of transformation matrices. Linear interpolation is used to generate intermediate points along the path if necessary.

In Figure **9–38** we also see the basic procedure to construct the swept surface. First, we must construct an implicit representation of the part by using vtkImplictModeller. This is then provided as input to vtkSweptSurface. It is important that the resolution of the implicit model is greater than that of vtkSweptSurface. This will minimize errors when we construct the surface. A bounding box surrounding the part and its motion can be defined, or it will be computed automatically. For proper results, this box must strictly contain the part as its moves. We also can set the number of interpolation steps, or allow this to be computed automatically as well. In the figure, we have chosen a small number to better illustrate the stepping of the algorithm.

Once vtkSweptSurface executes, we extract the swept surface using an isosurfacing algorithm. The isosurface value is an offset distance; thus we can create surfaces that take into account geometry tolerance. (This is particularly important if we are designing mechanical systems.) The implementation of the implicit modeller in **vtk** uses a positive distance function; so the isosurface value should always be positive. To create swept surfaces of zero and negative value requires a modification to the implicit modeller.

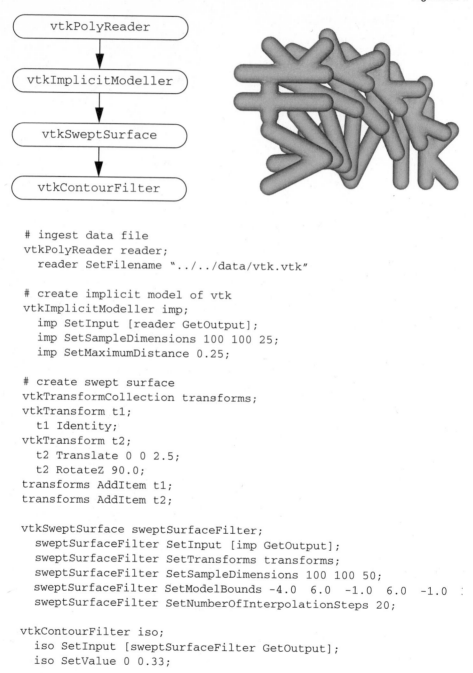

```
# ingest data file
vtkPolyReader reader;
   reader SetFilename "../../data/vtk.vtk"

# create implicit model of vtk
vtkImplicitModeller imp;
   imp SetInput [reader GetOutput];
   imp SetSampleDimensions 100 100 25;
   imp SetMaximumDistance 0.25;

# create swept surface
vtkTransformCollection transforms;
vtkTransform t1;
   t1 Identity;
vtkTransform t2;
   t2 Translate 0 0 2.5;
   t2 RotateZ 90.0;
transforms AddItem t1;
transforms AddItem t2;

vtkSweptSurface sweptSurfaceFilter;
   sweptSurfaceFilter SetInput [imp GetOutput];
   sweptSurfaceFilter SetTransforms transforms;
   sweptSurfaceFilter SetSampleDimensions 100 100 50;
   sweptSurfaceFilter SetModelBounds -4.0  6.0  -1.0  6.0  -1.0  :
   sweptSurfaceFilter SetNumberOfInterpolationSteps 20;

vtkContourFilter iso;
   iso SetInput [sweptSurfaceFilter GetOutput];
   iso SetValue 0 0.33;
```

Figure 9–38 Generating swept surface from line-stroked "vtk" (sweptVtk.tcl).

Multi-Dimensional Visualization

An important characteristic of multi-dimensional datasets is that they cannot be categorized according to any of the types defined in the *Visualization Toolkit*. This has an important implication for source objects interfacing with multi-dimensional data. That is, the source objects are responsible for converting the data they interface with into one of the types defined in **vtk**.

Other visualization systems treat this problem differently. In these systems a dataset type is defined that can represent multi-dimensional data. This dataset type is essentially an *n*-dimensional matrix. Additional filters are defined that allow the user to extract pieces of the dataset and assemble them into a more conventional dataset type, such as a volume or structured grid. After mapping the data from multi-dimensional form to conventional form standard visualization techniques can be applied. (Future implementations of **vtk** may include this functionality. At the current time you must map multi-dimensional data into a known **vtk** form.)

To demonstrate these ideas we will refer to Figure **9–39**. This is an example of multi-dimensional financial data. The data reflects parameters associated with monetary loans. In the file `financial.txt` there are six different variables: `TIME_LATE`, `MONTHLY_PAYMENT`, `UNPAID_PRINCIPLE`, `LOAN_AMOUNT`, `INTEREST_RATE`, and `MONTHLY_INCOME`. (Note: this is simulated data, don't make financial decisions based upon this!)

We will use Gaussian splatting to visualize this data (see "Splatting Techniques" on page 301). Our first step is to choose dependent and independent variables. This choice is essentially a mapping from multi-dimensional data into an unstructured point dataset. In this example we will choose `MONTHLY_PAYMENT`, `INTEREST_RATE`, and `LOAN_AMOUNT` as our *x-y-z* point coordinates, and `TIME_LATE` as a scalar value. This maps four of six variables. For now we will ignore the other two variables.

We use `vtkGaussianSplatter` to perform the splatting operation (i.e., conversion from unstructured points to volume dataset). This is followed by an isosurface extraction. We splat the data two times. The first time we splat the entire population. This is to show context and appears as gray/wireframe in the figure. The second time we splat the data and scale it by the value of `TIME_LATE`. As a result, only payments that are late contribute to the second isosurface.

The results of this visualization are interesting. First, we see that there is a strong correlation between the two independent variables `MONTHLY_PAYMENT` and `LOAN_AMOUNT`. (This is more evident when viewing the data interactively.) We see that the data falls roughly on a plane at a 45 degree angle between these two axes. With a little reflection this is evident: the monthly payment is strongly a function of loan amount (as well as interest rate and payment period). Second, we see that there is a clustering of delinquent accounts within the total population. The cluster tends to grow with larger interest rates and shrink with smaller monthly payment and loan amount. Although the relationship with interest rate is expected, the clustering towards smaller monthly payment is not. Thus our visualization has provided a clue into the data. Further exploration into the data

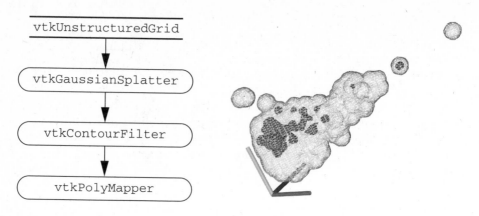

```
// construct pipeline for delinquent population
lateSplatter = new vtkGaussianSplatter;
  lateSplatter->SetInput(dataSet);
  lateSplatter->SetSampleDimensions(50,50,50);
  lateSplatter->SetRadius(0.05);
  lateSplatter->SetScaleFactor(0.005);
  lateSplatter->DebugOn();

lateSurface = new vtkContourFilter;
  lateSurface->SetInput(lateSplatter->GetOutput());
  lateSurface->SetValue(0,0.01);
  lateSurface->DebugOn();

lateMapper = new vtkPolyMapper;
  lateMapper->SetInput(lateSurface->GetOutput());
  lateMapper->ScalarsVisibleOff();

lateActor = new vtkActor;
  lateActor->SetMapper(lateMapper);
  lateActor->GetProperty()->SetColor(1.0,0.0,0.0);
```

Figure 9–39 Visualization of multi-dimensional financial data. Visualization network, output image, and sample C++ code are shown (`finance.cc`). The gray/wireframe surface represents the total data population. The dark surface represents data points delinquent on loan payment.

may reveal the reason(s), or we may perform additional data analysis and acquisition to understand the phenomena.

One important note about multi-dimensional visualization. Because we tend to combine variables in odd ways (e.g., the use of MONTHLY_PAYMENT, INTEREST_RATE, and LOAN_AMOUNT as *x-y-z* coordinates), normalization of the data is usually required. To normalize data we simply adjust data values to lie between (0,1). Otherwise our data can be badly skewed and result in poor visualizations.

Connectivity

Many useful visualization algorithms often borrow from other fields. Topological connectivity analysis is one such technique. This technique is best categorized as a method in computational geometry, but serves many useful purposes in computer graphics and visualization.

To illustrate the application of connectivity analysis, we will use an MRI dataset generated by Janet MacFall at the Center for In Vivo Microscopy at Duke University. The dataset is a volume of dimensions 256^3 and is included on the CD-ROM. The data is of the root system of a small pine tree. Using the class vtkSliceCubes, an implementation of marching cubes for large volumes, we generate an initial isosurface represented by 351,118 triangles. (We have placed the file pine_root.tri on CD-ROM. This is a faster way of manipulating this data. If you have a large enough computer you can process the volume directly with vtkVolume16Reader and vtkMarchingCubes.)

Figure **9–40**(a) shows the initial dataset. Notice that there are many small, disconnected isosurfaces due to noise and isolated moisture in the data. We use vtkConnectivityFilter to remove these small, disconnected surfaces. Figure **9–40**(b) shows the result of applying the filter. Over 50,000 triangles were removed, leaving 299,480 triangles.

The vtkConnectivityFilter is a general filter taking datasets as input, and generating an unstructured grid as output. It functions by extracting cells that are connected at points (i.e., share common points). In this example the single largest surface is extracted. It is also possible to specify cell ids and point ids and extract surfaces connected to these.

Decimation

Decimation is a 3D data compression technique for surfaces represented as triangle meshes. We use it most often to improve rendering interactive response for large models.

Figure **9–41** shows the application of decimation to the data from the pine root example. The original model of 351,118 triangles is reduced to 81,111 triangles using a combination of decimation and connectivity. The decimation parameters are fairly conservative. Here we see a reduction of approximately 55%.

The most common parameters to adjust in the vtkDecimate filter are the TargetReduction, InitialError, ErrorIncrement, MaximumIterations,

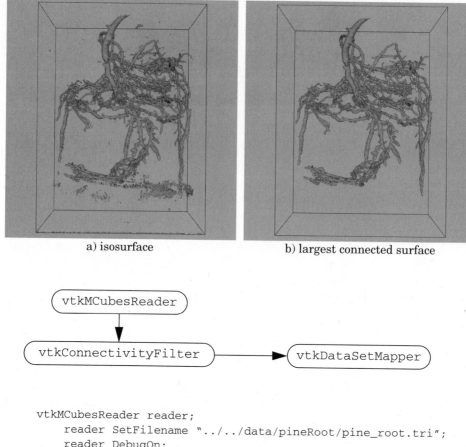

a) isosurface   b) largest connected surface

```
vtkMCubesReader reader;
    reader SetFilename "../../data/pineRoot/pine_root.tri";
    reader DebugOn;
vtkPolyMapper isoMapper;
    isoMapper SetInput [reader GetOutput];
    isoMapper ScalarsVisibleOff;
vtkActor isoActor;
    isoActor SetMapper isoMapper;
    eval [isoActor GetProperty] SetColor $raw_sienna;

vtkOutlineFilter outline;
    outline SetInput [reader GetOutput];
vtkPolyMapper outlineMapper;
    outlineMapper SetInput [outline GetOutput];
vtkActor outlineActor;
    outlineActor SetMapper outlineMapper;
    [outlineActor GetProperty] SetColor 0 0 0;
```

Figure 9–40 Applying connectivity filter to remove noisy isosurfaces (connPineRoot.tcl). Data is from 256^3 volume data of the root system of a pine tree.

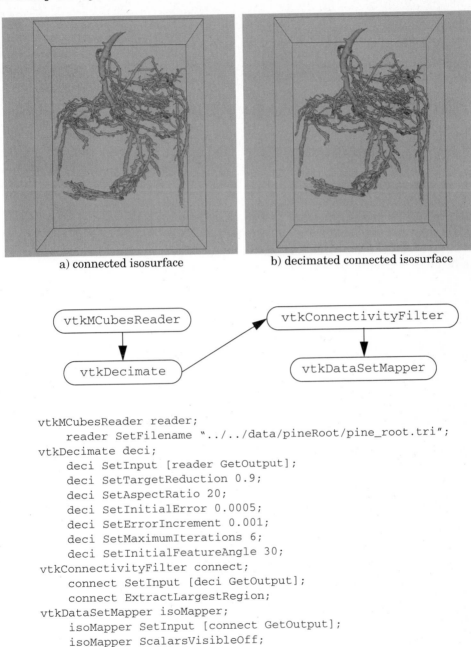

a) connected isosurface   b) decimated connected isosurface

```
vtkMCubesReader reader;
    reader SetFilename "../../data/pineRoot/pine_root.tri";
vtkDecimate deci;
    deci SetInput [reader GetOutput];
    deci SetTargetReduction 0.9;
    deci SetAspectRatio 20;
    deci SetInitialError 0.0005;
    deci SetErrorIncrement 0.001;
    deci SetMaximumIterations 6;
    deci SetInitialFeatureAngle 30;
vtkConnectivityFilter connect;
    connect SetInput [deci GetOutput];
    connect ExtractLargestRegion;
vtkDataSetMapper isoMapper;
    isoMapper SetInput [connect GetOutput];
    isoMapper ScalarsVisibleOff;
```

Figure 9–41 Applying connectivity and decimation filters to remove noisy isosurfaces and reduce data size (deciPineRoot.tcl). Data is from 256^3 volume data of the root system of a pine tree.

and `InitialFeatureAngle`. `TargetReduction` specifies the compression factor (numbers closer to one represent higher compression). Because of topological, decimation criterion, aspect ratio, and feature angle constraints this reduction may not be realized (i.e., `TargetReduction` is a desired goal, not a guaranteed output). The `InitialError` and `ErrorIncrement` control the decimation criterion. As the filter starts, the decimation criterion is set to `InitialError`. Then, for each iteration the decimation criterion is incremented by `ErrorIncrement`. The algorithm terminates when either the target reduction is achieved, or the number of iterations reaches `MaximumIterations`. The `InitialFeatureAngle` is used to compute feature edges. Smaller angles force the algorithm to retain more surface detail.

Other important parameters are the `AspectRatio` and `MaximumSubIterations`. `AspectRatio` controls the triangulation process. All triangles must satisfy this criterion or the vertex will not be deleted during decimation. A sub-iteration is an iteration where the decimation criterion is not incremented. This can be used to coalesce triangles during rapid rates of decimation. `MaximumSubIterations` controls the number of sub-iterations. This parameter is typically set to 2.

Texture Cutting

Texture mapping is a powerful visualization technique. Besides adding detail to images with minimal effort, we can perform important viewing and modelling operations. One of these operations is cutting data to view the internal structure.

Figure **9–42** is an example of texture cutting using a transparent texture map. The motor show consists of five complex parts, some of which are hidden by the outer casing. To see the inside of the motor we define an implicit cutting function. This function is simply the intersection of two planes to form a cutting "corner". The object `vtkImplicitTextureCoords` is used in combination with this implicit function to generate texture coordinates. These objects are then rendered with the appropriate texture map and the internal parts of the motor can be seen.

The texture map consists of three regions (as described previously in the chapter). The concealed region is transparent. The transition region is opaque but with a black (zero intensity) color. The highlighted region is full intensity and opaque. As can be seen from Figure **9–42**, the cuts appear as black borders giving a nice visual effect.

The importance of texture techniques is that we can change the appearance of objects and even perform modelling operations like cutting with little effort. We need only change the texture map. This process is much faster relative to the alternative approach of geometric modelling. Also, hardware support of texture is becoming common. Thus the rendering rate remains high despite the apparent increase in visual complexity.

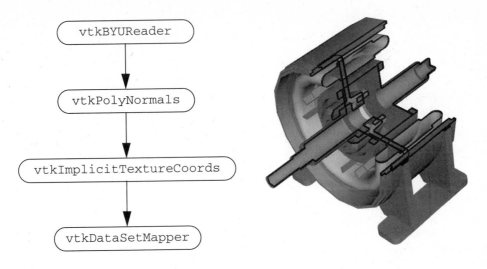

```
# texture
vtkStructuredPointsReader texReader;
    texReader SetFilename "../../data/texThres.vtk"
vtkTexture texture;
    texture SetInput [texReader GetOutput];
    texture InterpolateOff;
    texture RepeatOff;

# read motor parts...each part colored separately
vtkBYUReader byu;
    byu SetGeometryFilename "../../data/motor.g"
    byu SetPartNumber 1;
    byu DebugOn;
vtkPolyNormals normals;
    normals SetInput [byu GetOutput];
    normals DebugOn;
vtkImplicitTextureCoords tex1;
    tex1 SetInput [normals GetOutput];
    tex1 SetRFunction planes;
vtkDataSetMapper byuMapper;
    byuMapper SetInput [tex1 GetOutput];
vtkActor byuActor;
    byuActor SetMapper byuMapper;
    byuActor SetTexture texture;
    eval [byuActor GetProperty] SetColor $cold_grey;
```

Figure 9–42 Texture cut used to reveal internal structure. Two cut planes are used in combination with transparent texture (`motor.tcl`).

9.6 Chapter Summary

Dividing cubes is a scalar contouring operation that generates points rather than surface primitives such as lines or polygons. Dense point clouds appear solid because of the limited resolution of computer images.

Vector fields have complex structure. This structure can be visualized using streamribbons, streamsurfaces, and streampolygons. The topology of a vector field can be characterized by connecting critical points with streamlines.

Tensor fields consist of three orthogonal vector fields. The vector fields are the major, medium, and minor eigenvectors of the tensor field. Hyperstreamlines can be used to visualize tensor fields.

Dataset topology operations generate triangle strips, extract connected surfaces, and compute surface normals. Decimation is a polygon reduction algorithm that reduces the number of triangles in a triangle mesh. Implicit modelling techniques can be used to construct swept surfaces and volumes. Unstructured points are easy to represent but difficult to visualize. Splatting, interpolation, and triangulation techniques are available to construct structure for unstructured points. Multi-variate visualization is required for data of dimension four and higher. Data must be mapped to three dimensions before standard visualization techniques can be used. Parallel coordinates techniques are also available to visualize multi-variate data.

Modelling algorithms extract geometric structure from data, reduce the complexity of the data or create geometry. Spatial extraction selects dataset structure and associated data attributes lying within a specified region in space. Subsampling reduces data by selecting every n^{th} data point. A related technique, data masking, selects every n^{th} cell. Subsets of a dataset can also be selected using thresholding, which selects cells or points that lie within a range of scalar values. Probing resamples data at a set of points. The probe produces a dataset that has the topology of the probe with data values from the probed dataset. Generating triangle strips can reduce storage requirements and improve rendering speeds on some systems. If a dataset has multiple disjoint structures, a connectivity algorithm can uniquely identify the separate structures. For polygonal data that does not have vertex normals defined, normal generation algorithms can compute these values that are suitable for interpolation by Gouraud of Phong shading. Decimation, another data reduction technique, removes triangles in "flat" regions and fills the resulting gaps with new triangles. Unstructured points present a challenge because these data do not have topology. Splatting represents each point in the data with a structured point set and accumulates these splats using implicit modelling techniques. Triangulation techniques build topology directly from the unstructured points.

Multi-dimensional visualization techniques focus on data that has many scalar data values for each point. Parallel coordinates is an interesting approach that plots the scalar values for a data point along a parallel axis. The observer looks for trends and relationships between the lines that represent each point's data.

Texture algorithms use texture coordinates and texture maps to select or highlight portions of a dataset. Texture thresholding assigns texture coordinates based on a scalar value. The scalar value and texture map determines how a cell or portion of a cell is rendered. Boolean textures extend this concept to 2D and 3D. Careful design of a boolean texture map permits the "cutting" of geometry with combinations of implicit surfaces. Texture can also be used to animate vector fields.

9.7 Bibliographic Notes

Dividing cubes is an interesting algorithm because of the possibilities it suggests [Cline88]. Point primitives are extremely simple to render and manipulate. This simplicity can be used to advantage to build accelerated graphics boards, perform 3D editing, or build parallel visualization algorithms.

Many plotting and visualization systems use carpet plots extensively. Carpet plots are relatively easy to represent and render. Often 2D plotting techniques are used (i.e., lighting and perspective effects ignored). Check [Wang90] for additional information on rendering carpet plots.

In recent years a number of powerful vector visualization techniques have emerged. These techniques include streamsurfaces [Hultquist92], streampolygons [Schroeder91], vector field topology [Helman91] [Globus91], streamballs [Brill94], and vorticity visualization [Banks94]. The streamballs technique is a recent technique that combines techniques from implicit modelling. You may also wish to see references [Crawfis92] [vanWijk93] and [Max94]. These describe volume rendering and other advanced techniques for vector visualization, topics not well covered in this text.

Some abstract yet beautiful visualization images are due to Delmarcelle and Hesselink [Delmarcelle93]. Their rendering of hyperstreamlines reflect the underlying beauty and complexity of tensor fields.

Polygon reduction is a relatively new field of study. SIGGRAPH '92 marked a flurry of interest with the publication of two papers on this topic [Schroeder92a] [Turk92]. Since then a number of valuable techniques have been published. One of the best techniques, in terms of quality of results, is given by [Hoppe93], although it is limited in time and space because it is based on formal optimization techniques. Other interesting methods include [Hinker93] and [Rossignac93]. A promising area of research is multi-resolution analysis, where wavelet decomposition is used to build multiple levels of detail in a model [Eck95].

The use of texture for visualization is relatively unexploited. In part this has been due to lack of texture support in most graphics software and hardware. This is now changing, as more vendors support texture and software systems (such as OpenGL) that provide an API for texture. Important references here include the boolean textures [Lorensen93] and surface convolution techniques [Cabral93] [Stalling95].

Unstructured or unorganized point visualization is likely to play a prominent role in visualization as the field matures and more complex data is encountered. Nielson *et al.* have presented important work in this field [Nielson91].

Multidimensional visualization is another important focus of visualization research [Bergeron89] [Mihalisin90]. Much real-world data is both unstructured and multidimensional. This includes financial databases, marketing statistics, and multidimensional optimization. Addressing these types of data is important to achieve future advances in understanding and application. Feiner [Feiner90] has presented a simple projection method combined with virtual reality techniques. [Inselberg87] has introduced parallel coordinates. These techniques have been shown to be powerful for many types of visual analysis.

9.8 References

[Banks94]

D. C. Banks and B. A. Singer. "Vortex Tubes in Turbulent Flows: Identification, Representation, Reconstruction." In *Proceedings of Visualization '94*, pp. 132-139, IEEE Computer Society Press, Los Alamitos, CA, 1994.

[Bergeron89]

R. D. Bergeron and G. Grinstein. "A Reference Model for the Visualization of Multidimensional Data." In *Proceedings Eurographics '89*, pp. 393-399, North Holland, Amsterdam, 1989.

[Bowyer81]

A. Bowyer. "Computing Dirichlet Tessellations." *The Computer Journal*, 24(2):162-166, 1981.

[Brill94]

M. Brill, H. Hagen, H-C. Rodrian, W. Djatschin, S. V. Klimenko. "Streamball Techniques for Flow Visualization." In *Proceedings of Visualization '94*, pp. 225-231, IEEE Computer Society Press, Los Alamitos, CA, 1994.

[Cabral93]

B. Cabral and L. Leedom. "Imaging Vector Fields Using Line Integral Convolution." In *Proceedings of SIGGRAPH '93*, pp. 263-270, Addison-Wesley, Reading, MA, 1993.

[Cline88]

H. E. Cline, W. E. Lorensen, S. Ludke, C. R. Crawford, and B. C. Teeter, "Two Algorithms for the Three-Dimensional Construction of Tomograms." *Medical Physics*, 15(3):320-327, June 1988.

[Crawfis92]

R, Crawfis and N. Max. "Direct Volume Visualization of Three Dimensional Vector Fields." In *Proceedings 1992 Workshop on Volume Visualization*, pp. 55-60, ACM Siggraph, New York, 1992.

[Delmarcelle93]

T. Delmarcelle and L. Hesselink. "Visualizing Second-Order Tensor Fields with Hyperstreamlines." *IEEE Computer Graphics and Applications*, 13(4):25-33, 1993.

[Eck95]

M. Eck, T. DeRose, T. Duchamp, H. Hoppe, M. Lounsbery, W. Stuetzle. "Multi-resolution Analysis of Arbitrary Meshes." In *Proceedings SIGGRAPH '95*, pp. 173-182, Addison-Wesley, Reading, MA, August 1995.

[Feiner90]

S. Feiner and C. Beshers. "Worlds within Worlds: Metaphors for Exploring *n*-Dimensional Virtual Worlds." In *Proceedings UIST '90 (ACM Symp. on User Interface Software)*, pp. 76-83, October, 1990.

[Globus91]

A. Globus, C. Levit, and T. Lasinski. "A Tool for Visualizing the Topology of Three-Dimensional Vector Fields." In *Proceedings of Visualization '91*, pp. 33-40, IEEE Computer Society Press, Los Alamitos, CA, 1991.

[Helman91]

J. L. Helman and L. Hesselink. "Visualization of Vector Field Topology in Fluid Flows." *IEEE Computer Graphics and Applications*, 11(3):36-46, 1991.

[Hinker93]

P. Hinker and C. Hansen. "Geometric Optimization." In *Proceedings of Visualization '93*, pp. 189-195, IEEE Computer Society Press, Los Alamitos, CA, October 1993.

[Hoppe93]

H. Hoppe, T. DeRose, T. Duchamp, J. McDonald, W. Stuetzle. "Mesh Optimization." In *Proceedings of SIGGRAPH '93*, pp. 19-26, August 1993.

[Hultquist92]

J. P. M. Hultquist. "Constructing Stream Surfaces in Steady 3-D Vector Fields." In *Proceedings of Visualization '92*, pp. 171-178, IEEE Computer Society Press, Los Alamitos, CA, 1992.

[Inselberg87]

A. Inselberg and B. Dimsdale. "Parallel Coordinates for Visualizing Multi-Dimensional Geometry." In *Computer Graphics 1987 (Proceedings of CG International '87)*, pp. 25-44, Springer-Verlag, 1987.

[Lawson86]

C. L. Lawson. "Properties of *n*-Dimensional Triangulations." *Computer-Aided Geometric Design*, 3:231-246, 1986.

[Lorensen93]

W. Lorensen. "Geometric Clipping with Boolean Textures." in *Proceedings of Visualization '93*, pp. 268-274, IEEE Computer Society Press, Los Alamitos, CA, Press, October 1993.

[Max94]

N. Max, R. Crawfis, C. Grant. "Visualizing 3D Vector Fields Near Contour Surfaces." In *Proceedings of Visualization '94*, pp. 248-255, IEEE Computer Society Press, Los Alamitos, CA, 1994.

[Mihalisin90]

T. Mihalisin, E. Gawlinski, J. Timlin, and J. Schwegler. "Visualizing a Scalar Field on an *n*-Dimensional Lattice." In *Proceedings of Visualization '90, pp. 255-262,* IEEE Computer Society Press, Los Alamitos, CA, October 1990.

[Nielson91]
G. M. Nielson, T. A. Foley, B. Hamann, D. Lane. "Visualizing and Modeling Scattered Multivariate Data." *IEEE Computer Graphics and Applications*, 11(3):47-55, 1991.

[Rossignac93]
J. Rossignac and P. Borrel. "Multi-Resolution 3D Approximations for Rendering Complex Scenes." In *Modeling in Computer Graphics: Methods and Applications*, B. Falcidieno and T. Kunii, editors, pp. 455-465, Springer-Verlag Berlin, 1993.

[Schroeder91]
W. Schroeder, C. Volpe, and W. Lorensen. "The Stream Polygon: A Technique for 3D Vector Field Visualization." In *Proceedings of Visualization '91*, pp. 126-132, IEEE Computer Society Press, Los Alamitos, CA, October 1991.

[Schroeder92a]
W. Schroeder, J. Zarge, and W. Lorensen. "Decimation of Triangle Meshes." *Computer Graphics (SIGGRAPH '92)*, 26(2):65-70, August 1992.

[Schroeder92b]
W. Schroeder, W. Lorensen, G. Montanaro, and C. Volpe. "Visage: An Object-Oriented Scientific Visualization System." In *Proceedings of Visualization '92*, pp. 219-226, IEEE Computer Society Press, Los Alamitos, CA, October 1992.

[Schroeder94]
W. Schroeder, W. Lorensen, and S. Linthicum, "Implicit Modeling of Swept Surfaces and Volumes." In *Proceedings of Visualization '94*, pp. 40-45, IEEE Computer Society Press, Los Alamitos, CA, October 1994.

[Stalling95]
D. Stalling and H-C. Hege. "Fast and Independent Line Integral Convolution." In *Proceedings of SIGGRAPH '95*, pp. 249-256, Addison-Wesley, Reading, MA, 1995.

[Turk92]
G. Turk. "Re-Tiling of Polygonal Surfaces." *Computer Graphics (SIGGRAPH '92)*, 26(2):55-64, July 1992.

[vanWijk93]
J. J. van Wijk. "Flow Visualization with Surface Particles." *IEEE Computer Graphics and Applications*, 13(4):18-24, 1993.

[Wang90]
S-L C. Wang and J. Staudhammer. "Visibility Determination on Projected Grid Surfaces." *IEEE Computer Graphics and Applications*, 10(4):36-43, 1990.

[Watson81]
D. F. Watson. "Computing the n-Dimensional Delaunay Tessellation with Application to Voronoi Polytopes." *The Computer Journal*, 24(2):167-172, 1981.

[Wixom78]
J. Wixom and W. J. Gordon. "On Shepard's Method of Metric Interpolation to Scattered Bivariate and Multivariate Data." *Math. Comp.*, 32:253-264, 1978.

[Yamrom95]
B. Yamrom and K. M. Martin. "Vector Field Animation with Texture Maps." *IEEE Computer Graphics and Applications*, 15(2):22-24, 1995.

9.9 Exercises

9.1 Describe an approach to adapt dividing cubes to other 3D cell types. Can your method be adapted to 1D and 2D cells?

9.2 Discuss the advantages and disadvantages of representing surfaces with points versus polygons.

9.3 Streamribbons can be constructed by either i) connecting two adjacent streamlines with a surface, or ii) placing a ribbon on the streamline and orienting the surface according to streamwise vorticity vector. Discuss the differences in the resulting visualization.

9.4 Write the following programs to visualize velocity flow in the combustor.
a) Use `vtkProbeFilter` and `vtkHedgeHog`.
b) Use `vtkProbeFilter` and `vtkStreamLine`.
c) Use `vtkProbeFilter` and `vtkWarpVector`.
d) Use `vtkProbeFilter` and `vtkVectorNorm`.
e) Use `vtkProbeFilter` and `vtkVectorDot`.

9.5 Describe a method to extract geometry using an arbitrary dataset. (That is, extract geometry that lies within the culling dataset.) (*Hint:* how would you evaluate in/out of points?)

9.6 The filter `vtkPolyNormals` is often used in combination with the filters `vtkCleanPolyData` and `vtkContourFilter` to generate smooth isosurfaces.
a) Write a class to combine these three filters into one filter. Can you eliminate intermediate storage?
b) Rewrite this class by constructing a subclass of `vtkContourFilter` and using `vtkMergePoints` directly. How does this improve efficiency?
c) What is the difference between the surface normals created by `vtkMarchingCubes` and `vtkPolyNormals`?

9.7 Assume that we have a database consisting of interest rate R, monthly payment P, monthly income I, and days payment is late L.
a) If R, P, I are all sampled regularly, how would you visualize this data?
b) If all data is irregularly sampled, list three methods to visualize it.

9.8 Why do you think triangle strips are often faster to render than general polygons?

9.9 The normal generation technique described in this chapter creates consistently oriented surface normals.
a) Do the normals point inside or outside of a closed surface?
b) Describe a technique to orient normals so that they point out of a closed surface.
c) Can surface normals be used to eliminate visible triangles prior to rendering? (*Hint:* what is the relationship between camera view and surface normal?)

9.10 Describe a technique to partially threshold a cell (i.e., to cut a cell as necessary to satisfy threshold criterion). Can an approach similar to marching cubes be used?

9.11 The class `vtkRendererSource` allows us to use the rendered image as a texture map (or structured points dataset). Write a program to construct iterated textures, that is textures that consist of repeated images. Can the same image be generated using texture coordinates?

9.12 Describe how you would modify the decimation algorithm to treat general polygons.

Interpreters

*I*n this chapter we investigate interpreted languages for data visualization. We compare their strengths and weaknesses against traditional compiled languages. Then, we provide a quick introduction to the syntax of the interpreted language Tcl, how we integrated the *Visualization Toolkit* into Tcl, and some example programs.

10.1 Interpreted versus Compiled Languages

Programming languages can be categorized as either compiled or interpreted. These categories correspond to the way in which we interact with the language. In a compiled language, the source code is first compiled (i.e., translated into machine instructions), linked (modules gathered together and symbols resolved), and then executed. When an error is detected, the source code must be edited, recompiled and relinked before it can be tested. Programmers can spend significant amounts of time waiting on the compiler. An interpreted language requires no compilation or linking. Instead, instructions are typed directly to the computer, or a file is edited and re-parsed, and the language instructions are carried out immediately. Using an interpreted language can drastically reduce development time, especially in situations where many small tweaks are required to achieve the desired result (e.g., developing user interfaces).

While development times may be reduced for interpreted languages, compilation results in the fastest execution times. Compilers produce executables that are more difficult to reverse engineer, and they often have efficient methods to manipulate and represent complex data structures. While there are a few languages that support both interpretation and compilation, the most commonly used languages today are one or the other.

For the software that accompanies this book, we decided to write our objects in the compiled language C++ because of its object-oriented capabilities, efficient execution speed, and large following. We also wanted to be able to rapidly develop applications (including graphical user interfaces) with the **vtk** toolkit, so we "wrapped" the Tcl interpreted language around the C++ objects. Tcl offers a simple interpreted language that can be imbedded into programs, plus the graphical user interface Tk. Tcl/Tk is widely used and is available free of charge.

The end result is a toolkit that offers you the choice of building interpreted or compiled applications. Moreover, because each object is implemented in a compiled language, even the interpreted applications execute relatively quickly. The interpreter is generally only used for high-level object manipulation, and is rarely involved in tight execution loops. Now let's take a look at some of the issues involved with our implementation of the Tcl interpreted language.

10.2 Introduction to Tcl

Tcl is an interpretive language developed by John Ousterhout during the late 1980's [Ousterhout94]. It was designed to provide a flexible command language that could be easily integrated with a variety of applications. Tcl itself is written in the C programming language, and has a well-defined API for integrating in new functions. Its syntax is very similar to C shell programming. The example script below illustrates some of its basic features. Any line that starts with a pound sign is a comment and is ignored, command lines consist of a command name possibly followed by arguments. A semicolon or new line indicates the end of a command.

```
# Tcl script to compute the circumference of a circle
set pi 3.1416;
set radius 2;
set area [expr $pi*$radius*2.0];
puts $area
```

The set command takes two arguments: the name of a variable to create and its initial value. The second line in the example uses this command to create a variable named pi with a value of 3.1416. All variables in Tcl are stored as strings. Integer and floating point values are converted to strings as necessary. The third line creates a variable named radius. In the fourth line a variable named area is created using the set command, but its initialization is more complex. Enclosing brackets allow you to use a Tcl statement as an argument to a command. The format of a nested statement is the same as any other, except that a pair of brackets enclose it. Inside the brackets we want to calculate the area of the circle so we use the `expr` command, which evaluates its arguments as a mathematical expression and returns the result. Notice that there are dollar signs in front of the two variables we created earlier. This causes Tcl to perform variable substitution and use the value of the variable, not just its name. The fifth line uses the `puts` command to print out the result which is stored in the variable `area`.

Now let's look at another example. The script below prints the numbers one through ten and their squares. The first two lines are comments. The remaining lines are all part of a `for` command which takes four arguments. Each of these arguments is enclosed in braces (not brackets), which tells Tcl to take whatever is between them as the argument. Unlike brackets, no variable substitution or evaluation is done.

The first argument of a `for` loop is the initialization script. Before the loop starts iterating, it will evaluate its first argument, which in this case is a `set` command that creates and initializes a variable named `num`. The second argument is the test condition. This argument will be evaluated before each iteration through the loop. Looping continues until this expression becomes false. The third argument is evaluated at the end of each iteration. This argument is typically used to increment the loop variable. In the script below we use the `incr` command to increment the variable `num`. The fourth argument is the body of the loop which is evaluated with each iteration.

The braces are important because they prevent the arguments from being evaluated before they are passed to the `for` loop. Otherwise, the result of $num <= 10 would have been passed as the second argument, instead of the actual script $num <= 10. Double quotations perform a similar function, except that variable substitution does occur before the argument is passed to the command. In our example, the values for `num` and `numsqr` will be substituted before the enclosed string is passed to the `puts` command.

```
# Tcl script to print the numbers 1-10 and their squares
#
for {set num 1} {$num <= 10} {incr num} {
  set numsqr [expr $num*$num];
  puts "$num => $numsqr";
  }
```

That covers most of Tcl's syntax and the example scripts later in this chapter will help to clarify some of these points. There are hundreds of Tcl commands beyond what we introduced, and fortunately John Ousterhout's book, titled *Tcl and the Tk Toolkit*, covers them clearly and effectively.

10.3 How vtk is Integrated with Tcl

To use the Tcl interpreter with the *Visualization Toolkit* classes you need to understand a little about how the two are integrated. Between the C++ code of **vtk** and the Tcl interpreter there is a layer of wrapper code. This code, written in the C programming language, controls the exchange of information between Tcl and **vtk**'s C++ methods.

For every class in **vtk** a command is added to Tcl with the same name as the class. These commands create instances of their respective classes. In the first line of the following example, the vtkRenderMaster command creates an instance of that class. The one argument to an instantiation command is the name to assign to the resulting instance.

Once an instance has been created, the instance name also becomes a command. This may seem a little odd at first, but it is well suited to the object-oriented nature of **vtk**. After creating an instance of vtkRenderMaster named renMas, we can invoke methods on this instance by using its name as a command. In the second line of this example we use this technique to invoke the Print() method for the instance of vtkRenderMaster we just created. To invoke a method that takes arguments, you just add them onto the command as shown in the third line of this example.

```
vtkRenderMaster renMas;
renMas Print;
renMas SetDebug 1;
puts [renMas GetDebug];
set renWin [renMas MakeRenderWindow];
$renWin Print;
set ren1 [$renWin MakeRenderer];
```

Methods with return values can be used just like Tcl commands that return values. Since every return value in Tcl must be a string, the wrapper code will automatically convert integers and floating point values into strings before returning them. For methods that return pointers, it's a bit more difficult. Since we cannot return the pointer, we must convert the pointer into a unique string name. To accomplish this we keep hash tables that convert between instance pointers and string names. Whenever you create a **vtk** object in a Tcl script, that object's name and instance pointer are stored in hash tables. If you use that name as an argument to a method, the string name will automatically be converted to an instance pointer using these hash tables. When a method needs to return a pointer to an instance that wasn't created in the Tcl script, we create a unique string name such as vtkTemp0, vtkTemp1, etc. The pointer and generated name are also entered into the hash tables for future use. For example, in the fifth line of the above example, we use the set command to create a new variable called renWin. Its initial value is the result of invoking the MakeRenderWindow() method on our instance renMas. Normally this method returns a C++ pointer, but the wrapper code converts the pointer value into a generic string name and returns that. The sixth line shows how this result can then be used through the variable `renWin`.

Most of the arguments going to and from methods, consist of simple types such as integers and floats. Where a method takes a fixed size array, such as `float fargs[3]`, we break up the array into individual arguments. A C++ method such as `anInstance->amethod(int iarg, float fargs[3])` can be called from Tcl as `anInstance amethod iarg fargs1 fargs2 fargs3`. For methods that return a pointer to an array we perform the opposite. We are limited to returning one string by Tcl. For methods that return arrays we create a space delimited list of values.

Pointers to objects are passed back and forth using either the name specified upon creation or their generated name as described above. The argument to a user defined functions (e.g. `SetStartRender(void (*f)(void *), void *arg)`) in C++ is a pointer to a function. In our Tcl implementation, you specify a string argument that will be interpreted when the user defined function is called. The following example prints out the message "Executing the mapper" at the start of `polyMapper1`'s `Render()` method.

```
# excerpt from a Tcl script
polyMapper1 SetStartRender {puts "Executing the mapper"};
```

Because of the differences between C++ and Tcl, not all of the methods that are available from C++ are accessible in Tcl. We developed a program in Lex and Yacc to read in the C++ header files and automatically generate the wrapper code. After augmenting the information from the C++ header files with a `hints` file, it still does not provide enough flexibility for us to safely wrap some methods. The few methods that could not be wrapped are unavailable from the Tcl interpreter.

On the other hand, there are some methods that are available only from the Tcl interpreter. The `ListMethods` method prints a listing of all the methods that are available for an object from Tcl. It also lists the number of arguments that the method takes. For example:

```
vtk>vtkLight light1;
light1
vtk>light1 ListMethods;
Methods from vtkObject:
  Delete
  GetClassName
  DebugOn
  DebugOff
  GetDebug
  GetMTime
  Modified
Methods from vtkLight:
  GetClassName
  Render          with 2 args
```

```
SetColor        with 3 args
GetColor
SetPosition     with 3 args
GetPosition
SetFocalPoint   with 3 args
GetFocalPoint
SetIntensity    with 1 arg
GetIntensity
...
```

10.4 Examples

Figure **10–1** compares the C++ and Tcl code to render a cube. Note how the pointers in C++ are dealt with from the Tcl script. Most of the code in this example can be used as a starting point for other scripts. The next example is a Tcl version of Mace.cc that was presented in Figure **4–13**. In it we create the same visualization pipeline and then execute a `for` loop which modifies the actor's properties.

Near the end of the script, we set the UserMethod() of the vtkRenderWindowInteractor to {wm deiconify .vtkInteract}. This command lets

```
// C++ code to draw a cube          # Tcl code to draw a cube
#include "RenderM.hh"
#include "CubeSrc.hh"
#include "PolyMap.hh"

main ()                             vtkRenderMaster renMas;
{                                   vtkCubeSource cubeSrc;
  vtkRenderMaster renMas;           vtkPolyMapper cubeMpr;
  vtkCubeSource cubeSrc;            vtkActor cube1;
  vtkPolyMapper cubeMpr;
  vtkRenderWindow *renWin;
  vtkRenderer *ren1;
  vtkActor *cube1;
  renWin =                          set renWin \
    renMas.MakeRenderWindow();        [renMas MakeRenderWindow];
  ren1 = renWin->MakeRenderer();    set ren1 \
                                      [$renWin MakeRenderer];

  cubeMpr.SetInput(                 cubeMpr SetInput \
    cubeSrc->GetOutput());            [cubeSrc GetOutput];
  cube1 = new vtkActor;
  cube1->SetMapper(cubeMpr);        cube1 SetMapper cubeMpr;
  ren1->AddActor(cube1);            $ren1 AddActor cube1;
  renWin->Render();                 $renWin Render;
}
```

Figure 10–1 A comparison between the C++ and Tcl code to render a cube.

us access an interpreter widget (the "interactor ui") into which we can type Tcl commands. This widget is created at the beginning of the example by sourcing the file vtkInt.tcl. We can then access this widget by typing "u" in the rendering window. This can be very useful for making small changes and immediately seeing the effects of them.

```tcl
# this is a tcl version of the Mace example
# include get the vtk interactor ui
source vtkInt.tcl

# Create the render master
#
vtkRenderMaster rm;

# Now create the RenderWindow, Renderer and both Actors
#
set renWin [rm MakeRenderWindow];
set ren1   [$renWin MakeRenderer];
set iren [$renWin MakeRenderWindowInteractor];

# create a sphere source and actor
#
vtkSphereSource sphere;
vtkPolyMapper    sphereMapper;
    sphereMapper SetInput [sphere GetOutput];
vtkActor sphereActor;
    sphereActor SetMapper sphereMapper;

# create the spikes using a cone source and the sphere source
#
vtkConeSource cone;
vtkGlyph3D glyph;
    glyph SetInput [sphere GetOutput];
    glyph SetSource [cone GetOutput];
    glyph UseNormal;
    glyph ScaleByVector;
    glyph SetScaleFactor 0.25;
vtkPolyMapper spikeMapper;
    spikeMapper SetInput [glyph GetOutput];
vtkActor spikeActor;
    spikeActor SetMapper spikeMapper;

# Add the actors to the renderer, set the background and size
#
$ren1 AddActors sphereActor;
$ren1 AddActors spikeActor;
$ren1 SetBackground 0.1 0.2 0.4;
$renWin SetSize 450 450;
```

```
# Get handles to some useful objects
#
$iren SetUserMethod {wm deiconify .vtkInteract};
$iren Initialize;
$renWin Render;
set cam1 [$ren1 GetActiveCamera];
set sphereProp [sphereActor GetProperty];
set spikeProp [spikeActor GetProperty];

# Create a loop to draw some pretty pictures
#
for {set i 0} {$i < 360} {incr i; incr i} {
   $cam1 Azimuth 5;
   $ren1 SetBackground 0.6 0.0 [expr (360.0 - $i) / 400.0];
   $sphereProp SetColor \
      0.5 [expr $i / 440.0] [expr (360.0 - $i) / 440.0];
   $spikeProp SetColor \
      [expr (360.0 - $i) / 440.0] 0.5 [expr $i / 440.0];
   $renWin Render;
}

# prevent the default tk window from showing up
wm withdraw .
```

10.5 User Interfaces with Tk

If you have been experimenting with the example Tcl scripts, you may have noticed an empty window appearing along with the rendering window. This window is intended to hold the user interface for your application. This user interface is written in Tk, an extension to Tcl. Tk provides support for common user interface components such as push buttons, text widgets and scroll bars. Figure **10–2** shows an example of a simple user interface for a Tcl program. Developing applications using the Tk user interface is covered in John Ousterhout's book [Ousterhout94]. If you want to use Tcl, and prevent the empty window from popping up, you can add the following lines to your scripts. They indicate that the top level window of the user interface should not be mapped (i.e., displayed) but otherwise nothing else changes.

```
# prevent the default tk window from showing up
wm withdraw .
```

A nice feature of Tk is that it is window system independent. You can create user interfaces that will work in both the X Window system and the Microsoft Windows windowing system. Thus, applications you build in Tcl/Tk are computer platform independent. You also may be interested in one of the Tcl/Tk user inter-

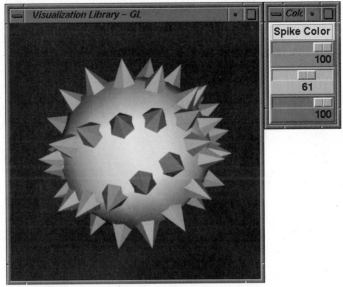

Figure 10–2 Mace with Tk user interface.

face design tools. These tools allow you to layout graphical user interfaces interactively by directly placing buttons, sliders, and other widgets in their correct position.

10.6 Chapter Summary

In this chapter we discussed the differences between compiled and interpreted languages. We find ourselves most frequently working with interpreted languages, since our work tends to be rapid prototyping or small visualization programs. The *Visualization Toolkit* allows you to use either C++ or Tcl as your primary development language. This allows you to pick the environment that best suits you, or to mix them together, doing your prototyping in Tcl and then writing the final program in C++. We then described the basic syntax of Tcl and provided a few example scripts to explain how Tcl handles variables and recursive interpretation. We then looked at how **vtk** is wrapped with Tcl and what limitations that creates. The chapter concluded with a few example scripts and a brief discussion of combining Tk's user interfaces with **vtk**.

10.7 Bibliographic Notes

For more information on interpreted languages or interpreted graphics systems, you can turn to Ousterhout's book on Tcl and Tk [Ousterhout94]. You also might want to look into other popular languages such as Python, Perl or Scheme. AVS and Iris Explorer are two packages that might not be thought of as interpreted systems. They both use a visual programming interface that provides the same sort of functionality that one typically associates with a command line interpreter. If you are familiar with electronic news groups, then you might be interested in the following groups: `comp.lang.tcl`; `comp.lang.python`; `comp.lang.scheme`; `comp.graphics.avs`; `comp.graphics.explorer`. For information on Lex and Yacc [Levine92] provides a good starting point. For some background on the authors' experiences in the interpreted language LYMB you can look into [Schroeder92].

10.8 References

[Ousterhout94]
J. K. Ousterhout. *Tcl and the Tk Toolkit*. Addison-Wesley Publishing Company, Reading, MA, 1984.

[Levine92]
J. R. Levine, T. Mason, and D. Brown. *Lex & Yacc*. O'Reilly & Associates, Sebastopol, CA, 1992.

[Schroeder92]
W. J. Schroeder, W.E. Lorensen, G.D. Montanaro, and C. R. Volpe. "VISAGE: An Object-Oriented Scientific Visualization System." In *Proceedings IEEE Visualization '92*, IEEE Computer Society Press, Los Alamitos, CA, 1992.

10.9 Exercises

10.1 Create a Tcl script to perform the same visualization as presented in Figure **4–12**. Be careful of the `vtkSphereSource` constructor, since it creates an instance of the class as well as setting the sphere resolution.

10.2 Extend Exercise 10.1 by adding a `for` loop that will azimuth the active camera through 360 degrees, creating a short animation.

10.3 Describe the advantages and pitfalls of using the Tcl interface (as compared to C++) in **vtk**. Be sure to discuss the possible performance issues, taking into account the compiled/interpreted hybrid nature of **vtk**. Also consider issues of scale associated with building large or complex applications in such an environment.

Applications

We described the design and implementation of an extensive toolkit of visualization techniques. In this chapter we show how to use these tools to gain insight into several application areas. These areas are medical imaging, financial visualization, modelling, computational fluid dynamics, finite element analysis, and algorithm visualization. For each case, we briefly describe the problem domain and what information we expect to obtain through visualization. Then, we design an application to show the results. Each application will supplement the tools in the *Visualization Toolkit* with application-specific tools. Finally, we present a sample program with resulting images.

The visualization design process we go through is similar in each case. First, we read or generate application-specific data and transform it into one of the data representation types in the *Visualization Toolkit*. Often this first step is the most difficult one because we have to write custom computer code. In the next step, we choose visualizations for the relevant data within the application. Sometimes this means choosing or creating models corresponding to physical structure. Examples include spheres for atoms, polygonal surfaces to model physical objects, or computational surfaces to model flow boundaries. Other times we generate more abstract models, such as isosurfaces or glyphs, corresponding to important application data. In the last step we combine the physical components with the abstract components to create a visualization that aids the user in understanding the data.

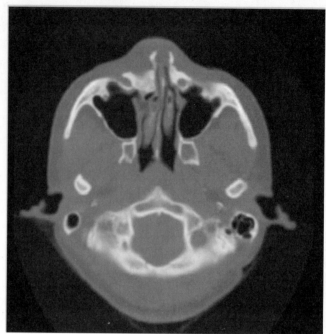

Figure 11–1 A CT slice through a human head.

11.1 3D Medical Imaging

Radiology is a medical discipline that deals with images of human anatomy. These images come from a variety of medical imaging devices, including X-ray, X-ray Computed Tomography (CT), Magnetic Resonance Imaging (MRI), and ultrasound. Each imaging technique, called an imaging modality, has particular diagnostic strengths; and the choice of modality is the job of the radiologist and the referring physician. For the most part, radiologists deal with two dimensional images, but there are situations when three-dimensional models can assist the radiologist's diagnosis. Radiologists have special training to interpret the two dimensional images, and understand the complex anatomical relationships in these two-dimensional representations. However, in dealing with referring physicians and surgeons, the radiologist sometimes has difficulty communicating these relationships. After all, a surgeon works in three-dimensions during the planning and execution of an operation. Surgeons are much more comfortable looking at and working with three-dimensional models.

This case study deals with CT data. Computed tomography measures the attenuation of X-rays as they pass through the body. A CT image consists of levels of gray that vary from black (for air), to gray (for soft tissue), to white (for bone). Figure **11–1** shows a CT cross-section through a head. This slice is taken perpendicular to the spine approximately through the middle of the ears. The gray boundary around the head clearly shows the ears and bridge of the nose.

The dark regions on the interior of the slice are the nasal passages and ear canals. The bright areas are bone. This study contains 93 such slices, spaced 1.5 mm apart. Each slice has 256^2, 0.8 mm pixels with 12 bits of gray level.

Our challenge is to take this massive amount of gray scale data (over 12 megabytes) and convert it into information that will aid the surgeon. Fortunately, our visualization toolkit has just the right technique. We will use isocontouring techniques to extract the skin and bone surfaces. From experience we know that a density value of 600 will define the air/skin boundary, and a value of 11500 will define the soft tissue / bone boundary.

Medical imaging slice data is structured point data. Recall from Chapter 5 that for structured point data, the topology and geometry of the data is implicitly known, requiring only dimensions, an origin, and an aspect ratio.

The steps we follow in this case study is common to many three-dimensional medical studies.

1. Read the input.

2. For each anatomical feature of interest, create an isosurface.

3. Transform the models from patient space to world space.

4. Render the models.

In this case study we will go into detail to show you how to read input data and extract anatomical features using isocontouring. Along the way we will also show you how to render the data. We finish with a brief discussion of medical data transformation.

Read the input

Medical images come in many flavors of file formats. This study is stored as flat files without header information. Each 16-bit pixel is stored with the bytes swapped. Also, as is often the case, each slice is stored in a separate file, with the file suffix being the slice number.

Assume for the moment that **vtk** does not have a reader that can read the data in our format, and that we have to create an object to do that. This is an instructive example, because it demonstrates the process you may have to go through to read your own data.

Because of the object-oriented design of **vtk**, our task is not too difficult. In **vtk** terminology, our reader is a source and our data is structured points. So, we look for any existing objects that are of type vtkStructuredPointsSource. The object vtkPNMReader that reads Pozkanzer Portable Pixmap (PPM) files can serve as a guide.

As for any source object in **vtk**, we must provide at a minimum three methods: a constructor, Execute() and PrintSelf(). We also need to decide what instance variables our object will require to perform it's duties. From our experience with medical imaging data, we know that each slice is usually kept in a separate file with a suffix that is a number. The format of the number varies. Some files will be of the form `prefix.1`, `prefix.2`, ... while others will be of the form `prefix.001`, `prefix.002`, ... We could just choose the first style since that's the style our case study data uses, but we'll try to generalize the file naming so that others can use our object later. To make the file naming general, we introduce a `FilePattern` instance variable that holds a string that we can use to build a file name from a prefix and a number. Medical imaging files often have a header of a certain size before the image data starts. The size of the header varies from file format to file format. We handle this variance by introducing a `HeaderSize` instance variable. This will contain the number of bytes to seek over before getting to the image data. Since each pixel in our image data is two bytes long, the bytes may have to be swapped to be the proper format for our visualization application. We add a `SwapBytes` instance variable to indicate whether or not swapping is required. We also need a `DataOrigin` and `DataAspectRatio` to define where the first slice starts and the x, y, z aspect ratios for the `vtkStructured-Points`. Finally, another complication is that sometimes one or more bits in each 16-bit pixel is used to mark connectivity between voxels, or for other purposes unrelated to the current case study. So we add a `DataMask` instance variable to allow us to mask out extraneous information.

We will call our object `vtkVolume16Reader`. It is a source object that reads files and creates a structured points dataset. We will subclass from the convenience class `vtkStructuredPointsSource`. The header file, which reflects our design choices described above, is shown in the following.

```
#ifndef __vtkVolume16Reader_h
#define __vtkVolume16Reader_h

#include "vtkShortScalars.hh"
#include "vtkStructuredPointsSource.hh"

class vtkVolume16Reader : public vtkStructuredPointsSource
{
public:
  vtkVolume16Reader();
  char *GetClassName() {return "vtkVolume16Reader";};
  void PrintSelf(ostream& os, vtkIndent indent);

  // Description:
  // Specify file prefix for the image file(s).
  vtkSetStringMacro(FilePrefix);
  vtkGetStringMacro(FilePrefix);

  // Description:
  // The sprintf format to use to build filename from FilePrefix
  // and number.
  vtkSetStringMacro(FilePattern);
  vtkGetStringMacro(FilePattern);
```

```
// Description:
// Set the range of files to read.
vtkSetVector2Macro(ImageRange,int);
vtkGetVectorMacro(ImageRange,int,2);

// Description:
// Specify an aspect ratio for the data.
vtkSetVector3Macro(DataAspectRatio,float);
vtkGetVectorMacro(DataAspectRatio,float,3);


// Description:
// Specify the origin for the data.
vtkSetVector3Macro(DataOrigin,float);
vtkGetVectorMacro(DataOrigin,float,3);

// Description:
// Specify the dimensions for the data.
vtkSetVector2Macro(DataDimensions,int);
vtkGetVectorMacro(DataDimensions,int,2);

// Description:
// Specify a mask used to eliminate data in the data file (e.g.,
// connectivity bits).
vtkSetMacro(DataMask,short);
vtkGetMacro(DataMask,short);

// Description:
// Specify the number of bytes to seek over at start of image
vtkSetMacro(HeaderSize,int);
vtkGetMacro(HeaderSize,int);

// Description:
// Turn on/off byte swapping
vtkSetMacro(SwapBytes,int);
vtkGetMacro(SwapBytes,int);
vtkBooleanMacro(SwapBytes,int);

// Other objects make use of these methods
vtkShortScalars *ReadImage(int sliceNumber, int dim[2]);
vtkShortScalars *ReadVolume(int first, int last, int dim[2]);

protected:
  void Execute();
  char *FilePrefix;
  char *FilePattern;
  int ImageRange[2];
  float DataAspectRatio[3];
  int   DataDimensions[2];
  float DataOrigin[3];
```

```
short DataMask;
int   SwapBytes;
int   HeaderSize;

int Read16BitImage(FILE *fp, short *pixels, int xsize,
                   int ysize, int skip, int swapBytes);
};
#endif
```

As you can see, the header file follows our idea of what this reader object should look like. We have introduced a few methods to perform various read operations. The key method, which is `protected`, is `Read16BitImage()`. This method has the task of actually reading the slice files. Two other methods, `ReadImage()` and `ReadVolume()`, utilize `Read16BitImage()` to read images and volumes, respectively. These methods are made public because we suspect that other objects in the system may be able to use them. (For example, the object `vtkSliceCubes` uses the method `ReadImage()`.)

Now let's walk briefly through the C++ code to see how we put things together. The constructor for `vtkVolume16Reader` sets the defaults for each of our instance variables:

```
vtkVolume16Reader::vtkVolume16Reader()
{
  this->FilePrefix = NULL;
  this->FilePattern = "%s.%d";
  this->ImageRange[0] = this->ImageRange[1] = 1;

  this->DataOrigin[0] = this->DataOrigin[1] =
                        this->DataOrigin[2] = 0.0;
  this->DataAspectRatio[0] = this->DataAspectRatio[1] =
                            this->DataAspectRatio[2] = 1.0;

  this->DataMask = 0x0000;
  this->HeaderSize = 0;
  this->SwapBytes = 0;
}
```

The `Execute()` method is the critical method for any source or filter. We initialize the filter, validate instance variables, read in the data as a scalar field, and store it as a structured points dataset.

```
void vtkVolume16Reader::Execute()
{
  vtkShortScalars *newScalars;
  int first, last;
  int numberSlices;
  int *dim;
  vtkStructuredPoints *output= this->GetOutput();
```

```
      // Validate instance variables
      if (this->FilePrefix == NULL)
        {
        vtkErrorMacro(<< "FilePrefix is NULL");
        return;
        }

      if (this->HeaderSize < 0)
        {
        vtkErrorMacro(<< "HeaderSize " << this->HeaderSize
                       << " must be >= 0");
        return;
        }

    dim = this->DataDimensions;
     if (dim[0] <= 0 || dim[1] <= 0)
        {
        vtkErrorMacro(<< "x, y dimensions " << dim[0] << ", " << dim[1]
                       << "must be greater than 0.");
        return;
        }

      if ( (this->ImageRange[1]-this->ImageRange[0]) <= 0 )
        {
        numberSlices = 1;
        newScalars = this->ReadImage(this->ImageRange[0], dim);
        }
      else
        {
        first = this->ImageRange[0];
        last = this->ImageRange[1];
        numberSlices = last - first + 1;
        newScalars = this->ReadVolume(first, last, dim);
        }

     output->SetDimensions(dim[0], dim[1], numberSlices);
     output->SetAspectRatio(this->DataAspectRatio);
     output->SetOrigin(this->DataOrigin);
      if ( newScalars )
        {
        output->GetPointData()->SetScalars(newScalars);
        newScalars->Delete();
        }
    }
```

The Execute() method is relatively straightforward. The structured point dataset is defined by setting the origin, aspect ratio, and dimensions. The scalar data is obtained by reading the slice data, and then associating it with the dataset. The only tricky part is the use of reference counting: we have to create the scalar object (newScalars above), assign it to the dataset (with the SetScalars() method), and then unregister our use of the object (with the Delete() method). (If reference counting is a mystery to you, see Appendix A for more information.)

The method Read16BitImage() is the heart of this object. The methods ReadImage() and ReadVolume() both make use of it. Here we will show the C++ code for Read16BitImage(); you can view the code for ReadImage() and ReadVolume() on the CD-ROM included with this book.

```
int vtkVolume16Reader:: Read16BitImage (FILE *fp, short *pixels,
                                        int xsize, int ysize,
                                        int skip, int swapBytes)
{
    int numShorts = xsize * ysize;
    int status;

    if (skip) fseek (fp, skip, 0);
    status = fread (pixels, sizeof (short), numShorts, fp);

    if (status && swapBytes)
      {
      unsigned char *bytes = (unsigned char *) pixels;
      unsigned char tmp;
      int i;
      for (i = 0; i < numShorts; i++, bytes += 2)
        {
        tmp = *bytes;
        *bytes = *(bytes + 1);
        *(bytes + 1) = tmp;
        }
      }

    if (status && this->DataMask != 0x0000 )
      {
      short *dataPtr = pixels;
      int i;
      for (i = 0; i < numShorts; i++, dataPtr++)
        {
        *dataPtr &= this->DataMask;
        }
      }

    return status;
}
```

Observe that the instance variables HeaderSize (via the variable skip), Swap-Bytes (via the variable swapBytes), and DataMask all come into play in this method. Also, the data dimensions are used to compute the number of data items to read.

We can easily check our new object with a simple test program:

```
#include "vtkVolume16Reader.hh"
main () {
    vtkVolume16Reader *aVolume = new vtkVolume16Reader;
    aVolume->SetDataDimensions(256, 256);
    aVolume->SwapBytesOn();
    aVolume->SetFilePrefix ("../../../data/fullHead/headsq");
    aVolume->SetImageRange(1, 93);
    aVolume->SetDataAspectRatio (.8, .8, 1.5);
    aVolume->Update();
    cout << "Our Volume: " << *aVolume;
}
```

The Update() method forces our object to Execute().

The first step, and for this case study the most complicated, is complete! We can read our input data and we tried to generalize our object so that others that use it later for data in a slightly different format. Notice that we did not go overboard trying to make the object too general. Now we can begin to explore this interesting medical data.

Create an isosurface

We can choose from three techniques for isosurface visualization: volume rendering, marching cubes, and dividing cubes. We assume that we want to interact with our data at the highest possible speed, so we will not use volume rendering. We prefer marching cubes if we have polygonal rendering hardware available, or if we need to move up close to or inside the extracted surfaces. Even with hardware assisted rendering, we may have to reduce the polygon count to get reasonable rendering speeds. Dividing cubes is appropriate for software rendering. For this application we'll use marching cubes.

For medical volumes, marching cubes generates a large number of triangles. To be practical, we'll do this case study with a reduced resolution dataset. We took the original 256^2 data and reduced it to 64^2 slices by averaging neighboring pixels twice in the slice plane. We call the resulting dataset quarter since it has 1/4 the resolution of the original data. We adjust the DataAspectRatio for the reduced resolution dataset to 3.2 mm per pixel. Our first program will generate an isosurface for the skin.

The flow in the program is similar to most **vtk** applications.

1. Generate some data.

2. Process it with filters.

3. Create a mapper to make rendering primitives.

4. Create actors for all mappers.

5. Render the results.

The filter we have chosen to use is `vtkMarchingCubes`. We could also use `vtkContourFilter`, but we know that `vtkMarchingCubes` is faster for this type of data (see Figure **6–36**). To complete this example, we take the output from the isosurface generator `vtkMarchingCubes` and connect it to a mapper and actor via `vtkPolyMapper` and `vtkActor`. The C++ code is as follows.

```cpp
#include "vtk.hh"
main ()
{
  // create the renderer stuff
  vtkRenderMaster aRendermaster;
  vtkRenderWindow *ourRenderingWindow =
              aRendermaster.MakeRenderWindow();
  vtkRenderWindowInteractor *ourInteractor =
              ourRenderingWindow->MakeRenderWindowInteractor();


  // read the volume
  vtkVolume16Reader *v16 = new vtkVolume16Reader;
    v16->SetDataDimensions(64,64);
    v16->SwapBytesOn();
    v16->SetFilePrefix ("../../../data/headsq/quarter");
    v16->SetImageRange(1, 93);
    v16->SetDataAspectRatio (3.2, 3.2, 1.5);


  // extract the skin
  vtkMarchingCubes *skinExtractor = new vtkMarchingCubes;
    skinExtractor->SetInput(v16->GetOutput());
    skinExtractor->SetValue(0, 500);
  vtkPolyMapper *skinMapper = new vtkPolyMapper;
    skinMapper->SetInput(skinExtractor->GetOutput());
    skinMapper->ScalarsVisibleOff();
  vtkActor *skin = new vtkActor;
    skin->SetMapper(skinMapper);


  // get an outline
  vtkOutlineFilter *outlineData = new vtkOutlineFilter;
    outlineData->SetInput(v16->GetOutput());
  vtkPolyMapper *mapOutline = new vtkPolyMapper;
    mapOutline->SetInput(outlineData->GetOutput());
  vtkActor *outline = new vtkActor;
    outline->SetMapper(mapOutline);
    outline->GetProperty()->SetColor(0,0,0);
```

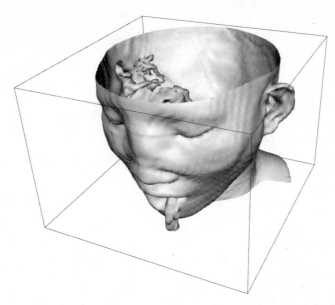

Figure 11-2 The skin extracted from a CT dataset of the head.

```
// create a camera with the correct view up
vtkCamera *aCamera = new vtkCamera;
  aCamera->SetViewUp (0, 0, -1);
  aCamera->SetPosition (0, -1, 0);
  aCamera->SetFocalPoint (0, 0, 0);
  aCamera->CalcViewPlaneNormal();

// now, make a renderer and tell it our lights and actors
vtkRenderer *aRenderer = ourRenderingWindow->MakeRenderer();
  aRenderer->AddActors(outline);
  aRenderer->AddActors(skin);
  aRenderer->SetActiveCamera(aCamera);
  aRenderer->ResetCamera ();
  aRenderer->SetBackground(1, 1, 1);

// interact with data
ourRenderingWindow->Render();
ourInteractor->Start();
}
```

Figure **11-2** shows the resulting image of the patient's skin.

We can improve this visualization in a number of ways. First, we can choose a more appropriate color (and other surface properties) for the skin. We use the vtkProperty method SetColor() to set the skin color to a fleshy tone. Next, we can add additional isosurfaces corresponding to various anatomical features.

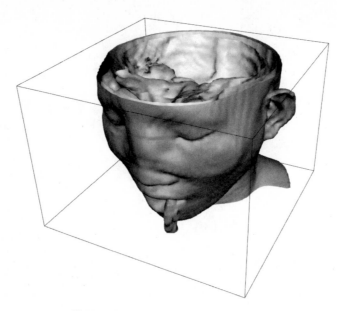

Figure 11–3 Skin and bone isosurfaces.

Here we choose to extract the bone surface by adding an additional pipeline segment. The segment consists of a vtkContourFilter, vtkPolyMapper, and vtkActor, just as we did with the skin. Finally, to improve rendering performance on our system, we create triangle strips from the output of the contouring process. This requires adding two filters: vtkCleanPolyData and vtkStripper. The purpose of the first filter is to remove degenerate triangles, and to merge coincident points. This way the triangle strip filter will produce better results. Figure **11–3** shows the resulting image, and the following is the C++ code for the pipeline.

```
// extract the skin
vtkMarchingCubes *skinExtractor = new vtkMarchingCubes;
  skinExtractor->SetInput(v16->GetOutput());
  skinExtractor->SetValue(0, 500);
vtkCleanPolyData *skinCleaner = new vtkCleanPolyData;
  skinCleaner->SetInput(skinExtractor->GetOutput());
vtkStripper *skinStripper = new vtkStripper;
  skinStripper->SetInput(skinCleaner->GetOutput());
vtkPolyMapper *skinMapper = new vtkPolyMapper;
  skinMapper->SetInput(skinStripper->GetOutput());
  skinMapper->ScalarsVisibleOff();
vtkActor *skin = new vtkActor;
  skin->SetMapper(skinMapper);
  skin->GetProperty()->SetDiffuseColor(1, .49, .25);
```

```
   skin->GetProperty()->SetSpecular(.3);
   skin->GetProperty()->SetSpecularPower(20);


// extract the bone
vtkMarchingCubes *boneExtractor = new vtkMarchingCubes;
   boneExtractor->SetInput(v16->GetOutput());
   boneExtractor->SetValue(0, 1150);
vtkCleanPolyData *boneCleaner = new vtkCleanPolyData;
   boneCleaner->SetInput(boneExtractor->GetOutput());
vtkStripper *boneStripper = new vtkStripper;
   boneStripper->SetInput(boneCleaner->GetOutput());
vtkPolyMapper *boneMapper = new vtkPolyMapper;
   boneMapper->SetInput(boneStripper->GetOutput());
   boneMapper->ScalarsVisibleOff();
vtkActor *bone = new vtkActor;
   bone->SetMapper(boneMapper);
   bone->GetProperty()->SetDiffuseColor(1, 1, .9412);
```

The *Visualization Toolkit* provides other useful techniques besides isocontouring for exploring volume data. The `vtkStructuredPointsGeometry-Filter` extracts geometry (e.g., lines, planes, or sub-volumes) from objects of type `vtkStructuredPoints`. Each point in the extracted geometry will have a scalar value from the original data. (Recall that in this case study the scalar value is the X-ray density.)

We can use this filter to extract three orthogonal planes corresponding to the axial, sagittal and coronal cross-sections that are familiar to radiologists. The axial plane is perpendicular to the patient's neck, sagittal passes from left to right, and coronal passes from front to back. For illustrative purposes, we render each of these planes with a different color lookup table. For the axial plane, we use a grey scale. The sagittal and coronal planes vary the saturation and hue table, respectively. We combine this with a translucent rendering of the skin. The following **vtk** code creates the three lookup tables.

```
// create a b/w lookup table
vtkLookupTable *bwLut = new vtkLookupTable;
  bwLut->SetTableRange (0, 2000);
  bwLut->SetSaturationRange (0, 0);
  bwLut->SetHueRange (0, 0);
  bwLut->SetValueRange (0, 1);


// create a hue lookup table
vtkLookupTable *hueLut = new vtkLookupTable;
  hueLut->SetTableRange (0, 2000);
  hueLut->SetHueRange (0, 1);
  hueLut->SetSaturationRange (1, 1);
  hueLut->SetValueRange (1, 1);
```

```
// create a saturation lookup table
vtkLookupTable *satLut = new vtkLookupTable;
  satLut->SetTableRange (0, 2000);
  satLut->SetHueRange (.6, .6);
  satLut->SetSaturationRange (0, 1);
  satLut->SetValueRange (1, 1);
```

For each plane, we need a vtkStructuredPointsGeometryFilter, a vtk-
PolyMapper and a vtkActor. The C++ code is as follows.

```
// sagittal
vtkStructuredPointsGeometryFilter *saggitalSection =
    new vtkStructuredPointsGeometryFilter;
  saggitalSection->SetExtent (32,32, 0,63, 0, 93);
  saggitalSection->SetInput (v16->GetOutput());
vtkPolyMapper *saggitalMapper = new vtkPolyMapper;
  saggitalMapper->SetInput(saggitalSection->GetOutput());
  saggitalMapper->ScalarsVisibleOn();
  saggitalMapper->SetScalarRange (0, 2000);
  saggitalMapper->SetLookupTable (bwLut);
vtkActor *sagittal = new vtkActor;
  sagittal->SetMapper(saggitalMapper);

// axial
vtkStructuredPointsGeometryFilter *axialSection =
    new vtkStructuredPointsGeometryFilter;
  axialSection->SetExtent (0,63, 0,63, 46, 46);
  axialSection->SetInput (v16->GetOutput());
vtkPolyMapper *axialMapper = new vtkPolyMapper;
  axialMapper->SetInput(axialSection->GetOutput());
  axialMapper->ScalarsVisibleOn();
  axialMapper->SetScalarRange (0, 2000);
  axialMapper->SetLookupTable (hueLut);
vtkActor *axial = new vtkActor;
  axial->SetMapper(axialMapper);

// coronal
vtkStructuredPointsGeometryFilter *coronalSection =
    new vtkStructuredPointsGeometryFilter;
  coronalSection->SetExtent (0,63, 32, 32, 0, 92);
  coronalSection->SetInput (v16->GetOutput());
vtkPolyMapper *coronalMapper = new vtkPolyMapper;
  coronalMapper->SetInput(coronalSection->GetOutput());
  coronalMapper->ScalarsVisibleOn();
  coronalMapper->SetScalarRange (0, 2000);
  coronalMapper->SetLookupTable (satLut);
vtkActor *coronal = new vtkActor;
  coronal->SetMapper(coronalMapper);
```

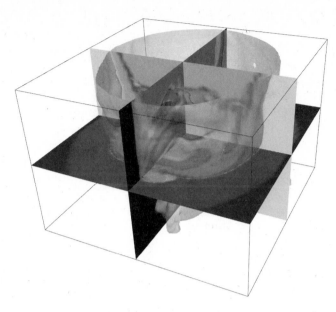

Figure 11–4 Composite image of three planes and translucent skin.

Figure **11–4** shows the resulting composite image.

In this example, the actor named skin is rendered last because we are using a translucent surface. Recall from "Transparency and Alpha Values" on page 199 that we must order the polygons composing transparent surfaces for proper results. We render the skin last by adding it to aRenderer's actor list last.

We need to make one last point about processing medical imaging data, Medical images can be acquired in a variety of orders that refer to the relationship of consecutive slices to the patient. Radiologists view an image as though they were looking at the patient's feet. This means that on the display, the patient's left appears on the right. For CT there are two standard orders: top to bottom or bottom to top. In a top to bottom acquisition, slice i is farther towards the patient's feet than slice i - 1. Why do we worry about this order? It is imperative in medical applications that we retain the left / right relationship. Ignoring the slice acquisition order can result in a flipping of left and right. In fact, the images we have produced so far have their left / right sense reversed. To correct this, we need to transform either the original dataset or the geometry we have extracted. (See "Exercises" on page 383.)

11.2 Financial Visualization

The application of 3D visualization techniques to financial data is relatively new. Historically, financial data has been represented using 2D plotting techniques such as line, scatter plots, bar charts, and pie charts. These techniques are especially well suited for the display of price and volume information for stocks, bonds, and mutual funds. Three-dimensional techniques are becoming more important because the volume of information has increased in recent years, and 3D graphics and visualization techniques are becoming interactive. Interactive rates means that visualization can be applied to the day-to-day processing of data. Our belief is that this will allow deeper understanding of today's complex financial data, and more timely decisions.

In this example we go through the process of obtaining data, converting it to a form that we can use, and then using visualization techniques to view it. Some of the external software tools used in this example may be unfamiliar to you. This should not be a large concern. We have simply chosen the tools with which we are familiar. Where we have used an Awk script, you might choose to write a small C program to do the same thing. The value of the example lies in illustrating the high level process of solving a visualization problem.

The first step is to obtain the data. We obtained our data from a public site on the World Wide Web (WWW) that archives stock prices and volumes for many publicly traded stocks. If you have no experience with the World Wide Web, there are many books and software products listed in the bibliographic notes that can provide an introduction. Using a web browser such as Netscape or Mosaic, and a computer that can reach the Internet, we can visit the web site `http://www.ai.mit.edu/stocks.html`. This site provides a wealth of stock information, including a directory of historical data files for many stocks. From this directory we downloaded four files: GE, GM, DEC and IBM. These files also can be obtained using anonymous ftp from the machine `ftp.ai.mit.edu` in the directory `/pub/stocks/results`.

Once we have obtained the data, we convert it to a format that can be read into **vtk**. While **vtk** can read in a variety of data formats, frequently your data will not be in one of those. The data files we obtained are stored in the following format:

```
930830   49.375   48.812   49.250   1139.2   56.1056
930831   49.375   48.938   49.125   1360.4   66.8297
930902   49.188   48.688   48.750   1247.2   60.801
. . .
```

Each line stores the data for one day of trading. The first number is the date, stored as the last two digits of the year followed by a two digit month and finally the day of the month. The next three values represent the high, low, and closing price of the stock for that day. The next value is the volume of trading in thousands of shares. The final value is the volume of trading in millions of dollars.

We used an Awk script to convert the original data format into a **vtk** data file. (See "vtk File Formats" on page 416.) This conversion could be done using many other approaches, such as writing a C program or a Tcl script.

```
BEGIN {print "# vtk DataSet Version 1.0\n
Data values for stock\nASCII\n\nDATASET POLYDATA"}
{count += 1}
{ d = $1%100}
{ m = int(($1%10000)/100)}
{ if (m == 2) d += 31}
{ if (m == 3) d += 59}
{ if (m == 4) d += 90}
{ if (m == 5) d += 120}
{ if (m == 6) d += 151}
{ if (m == 7) d += 181}
{ if (m == 8) d += 212}
{ if (m == 9) d += 243}
{ if (m == 10) d += 273}
{ if (m == 11) d += 304}
{ if (m == 12) d += 334}
{ d = d + (int($1/10000) - 93)*365}
{dates[count] = d; prices[count] = $4; volumes[count] = $5}
END {
    print "POINTS " count " float";
    for (i = 1; i <= count; i++) print dates[i] " " prices[i] " 0 ";
    print "\nLINES 1 " (count + 1) " " count;
    for (i = 0; i < count; i++) print i;
    print "\nPOINT_DATA " count "\nSCALARS volume float";
    print "LOOKUP_TABLE default";
    for (i = 1; i <= count; i++) print volumes[i];
    }
```

The above Awk script performs the conversion. Its first line outputs the required header information indicating that the file is a **vtk** data file containing polygonal data. It also includes a comment indicating that the data represents stock values. There are a few different **vtk** data formats that we could have selected. It is up to you to decide which format best suits the data you are visualizing. We have judged the polygonal format (vtkPolyData) as best suited for this particular stock visualization.

The next line of the Awk script creates a variable named count that keeps track of how many days worth of information is in the file. This is equivalent to the number of lines in the original data file.

The next fourteen lines convert the six digit date into a more useful format, since the original format has a number of problems. If we were to blindly use the original format and plot the data using the date as the independent variable, there would be large gaps in our plot. For example, 931231 is the last day of 1993 and 940101 is the first day of 1994. Chronologically these two dates are sequential, but mathematically there are (940101 - 931231) 8870 values between them. A simple solution would be to use the line number as our independent variable.

This would work as long as we knew that every trading day was recorded in the data file. It would not properly handle the situation where the market was open, but for some reason data was not recorded. A better solution is to convert the dates into numerically ordered days. The preceding Awk script sets January 1, 1993, as day number one, and then numbers all the following days from there. At the end of these fourteen lines the variable, d, will contain the resulting value.

The next line in our Awk script stores the converted date, closing price, and dollar volume into arrays indexed by the line number stored in the variable count. Once all the lines have been read in and stored into the arrays, we write out the rest of the **vtk** data file. We have selected the date as our independent variable and x coordinate. The closing price we store as the y coordinate, and the z coordinate we set to zero. After indicating the number and type of points to be stored, the Awk script loops through all the points and writes them out to the **vtk** data file. It then writes out the line connectivity list. In this case we just connect one point to the next to form a polyline for each stock. Finally, we write out the volume information as scalar data associated with the points. Portions of the resulting **vtk** data file are shown below.

```
# vtk DataFile Version 1.0
Data values for stock
ASCII

DATASET POLYDATA
POINTS 348 float
242 49.250 0
243 49.125 0
245 48.750 0
246 48.625 0
...


LINES 1 349 348
0
1
2
3
...


POINT_DATA 348
SCALARS volume float
LOOKUP_TABLE default
1139.2
1360.4
1247.2
1745.4
...
```

Now that we have generated the **vtk** data file, we can start the process of creating a visualization for the stock data. To do this, we wrote a Tcl script to be used with the Tcl-based **vtk** executable. At a high level the script reads in the stock data, sends it through a tube filter, creates a label for it, and then creates an outline around the resulting dataset. Ideally, we would like to display multiple stocks in the same window. To facilitate this, we designed the Tcl script to use a procedure to perform operations on a per stock basis. The resulting script is listed below.

```tcl
# this is a tcl script for the stock case study
# First create the render master
vtkRenderMaster rm;

# Now create the RenderWindow, Renderer and both Actors
set renWin [rm MakeRenderWindow];
set ren1   [$renWin MakeRenderer];
set iren   [$renWin MakeRenderWindowInteractor];

#create the outline
vtkAppendPolyData apf;
vtkOutlineFilter olf;
olf SetInput [apf GetOutput];
vtkPolyMapper outlineMapper;
outlineMapper SetInput [olf GetOutput];
vtkActor outlineActor;
outlineActor SetMapper outlineMapper;
outlineActor SetScale 0.15 1 1;

# create the stocks
proc AddStock {prefix name x y z} {
    global ren1 zpos;

    # create labels
    vtkTextSource $prefix.TextSrc;
    $prefix.TextSrc SetText "$name";
    vtkPolyMapper $prefix.LabelMapper;
    $prefix.LabelMapper SetInput \
      [$prefix.TextSrc GetOutput];
    vtkFollower $prefix.LabelActor;
    $prefix.LabelActor SetMapper $prefix.LabelMapper;
    $prefix.LabelActor SetPosition $x $y $z;
    $prefix.LabelActor SetScale 0.25 0.25 0.25;
    eval $prefix.LabelActor SetOrigin \
      [$prefix.LabelMapper GetCenter];
    # read in the data and create the tube filter etc.
    vtkPolyReader $prefix.PolyRead;
    $prefix.PolyRead SetFilename "$prefix.vtk";
    vtkTubeFilter $prefix.TubeFilter;
    $prefix.TubeFilter SetInput \
      [$prefix.PolyRead GetOutput];
    $prefix.TubeFilter SetNumberOfSides 8;
```

```
    $prefix.TubeFilter SetRadius 0.5;
    $prefix.TubeFilter SetRadiusFactor 10000;
    # transform the tube to the correct scale & position
    vtkTransform $prefix.Transform;
    $prefix.Transform Translate 0 0 $zpos;
    $prefix.Transform Scale 0.15 1 1;
    vtkTransformPolyFilter $prefix.TransformFilter;
    $prefix.TransformFilter SetInput \
      [$prefix.TubeFilter GetOutput];
    $prefix.TransformFilter SetTransform $prefix.Transform;

    # increment zpos
    set zpos [expr $zpos + 10];

    vtkPolyMapper $prefix.StockMapper;
    $prefix.StockMapper SetInput \
      [$prefix.TransformFilter GetOutput];
    vtkActor $prefix.StockActor;
    $prefix.StockActor SetMapper $prefix.StockMapper;
    $prefix.StockMapper SetScalarRange 0 8000;
    [$prefix.StockActor GetProperty] SetAmbient 0.5;
    [$prefix.StockActor GetProperty] SetDiffuse 0.5;

    apf AddInput [$prefix.TransformFilter GetOutput];
    $ren1 AddActors $prefix.StockActor;
    $ren1 AddActors $prefix.LabelActor;
    $prefix.LabelActor SetCamera [$ren1 GetActiveCamera];
}

# set up the stocks
AddStock GE "GE" 67 50 3;
AddStock GM "GM" 60 36 13;
AddStock IBM "IBM" 62 74 17;
AddStock DEC "DEC" 40 19 27;

# Add the actors to the renderer, set the background and size
$ren1 AddActors outlineActor;
$ren1 SetBackground 0.1 0.2 0.4;
$renWin SetSize 500 500;

# render the image
$iren Initialize;
[$ren1 GetActiveCamera] SetViewAngle 10;
$ren1 ResetCamera;
[$ren1 GetActiveCamera] Zoom 1.5;

# prevent the tk window from showing up
wm withdraw .
```

The first part of this script consists of the standard procedure for renderer and interactor creation that can be found in almost all of the **vtk** Tcl scripts. The next section creates the objects necessary for drawing an outline around all of the stock data. An `vtkAppendPolyData` filter is used to append all of the stock data together. This is then sent through a `vtkOutlineFilter` to create a bounding box around the data. A mapper and actor are created to display the result.

In the next part of this script we define the procedure to add stock data to this visualization. The procedure takes five arguments: the name of the stock, the label we want displayed, and the x, y, z coordinates defining where to position the label. The first line of the procedure indicates that the variable `ren1` should be visible to this procedure. By default the procedure can only access its own local variables. Next we, create the label using a `vtkTextSource`, `vtkPoly-Mapper`, and `vtkFollower`. The names of these objects are all prepended with the variable `$prefix` – thus the names will be unique. An instance of `vtkFollower` is used instead of the usual `vtkActor`, because we always want the text to be right side up and facing the camera. The `vtkFollower` class provides this functionality. The remaining lines position and scale the label appropriately. We set the origin of the label to the center of its data. This insures that the follower will rotate about its center point.

The next group of lines creates the required objects to read in the data, pass it through a tube filter and a transform filter, and finally display the result. The tube filter uses the scalar data (stock volume in this example) to determine the radius of the tube. The mapper also uses the scalar data to determine the coloring of the tube. The transform filter uses a transform object to set the stock's position based on the value of the variable `zpos`. For each stock, we will increment `zpos` by ten, effectively shifting the next stock over ten units from the current stock. This prevents the stocks from being stacked on top of each other. We also use the transform to compress the x-axis to make the data easier to view. Next, we add this stock as an input to the append filter and add the actors and followers to the renderer. The last line of the procedure sets the follower's camera to be the active camera of the renderer.

Back in the main body of the Tcl script, we invoke the `AddStock` procedure four times with four different stocks. Finally, we add the outline actor and customize the renderer and camera to produce a nice initial view. Two different views of the result are displayed in Figure **11–5**. The top view shows a history of stock closing prices for our four stocks. The color and width of these lines corresponds to the volume of the stock on that day. The lower view more clearly illustrates the changes in stock volume by looking at the data from the top down.

A legitimate complaint with Figure **11–5** is that the changing width of the tube makes it more difficult to see the true shape of the price verses time curve. We can solve this problem by using a ribbon filter followed by a linear extrusion filter, instead of the tube filter. The ribbon filter will create a ribbon whose width will vary in proportion to the scalar value of the data. We then use the linear extrusion filter to extrude this ribbon along the y-axis so that it has a constant thickness. The resulting views are shown in Figure **11–6**.

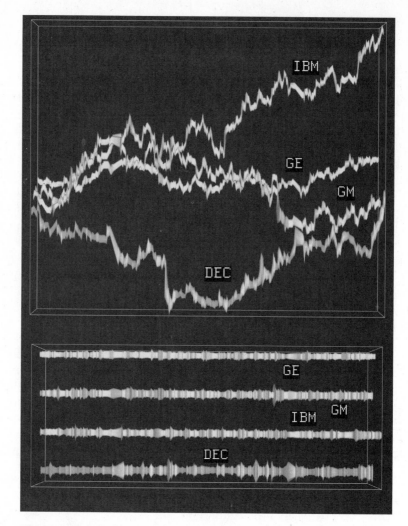

Figure 11–5 Two views from the stock visualization script. The top shows closing price over time. The bottom shows volume over time.

11.3 Implicit Modelling

The *Visualization Toolkit* has some useful geometric modelling capabilities. One of the most powerful features is implicit modelling. In this example we show how to use polygonal descriptions of objects and create "blobby" models of them using the implicit modelling objects in **vtk**. This example generates a logo for the *Visualization Toolkit* from polygonal representations of the letters *v*, *t*, and *k*.

We create three separate visualization pipelines, one for each letter. Figure **11–7** shows the visualization pipeline. As is common in **vtk** applications,

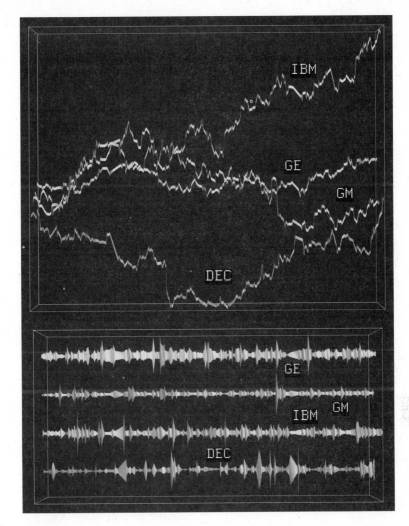

Figure 11–6 Two more views of the stock case study. Here the tube filter has been replaced by a ribbon filter followed with a linear extrusion filter.

we design a pipeline and fill in the details of the instance variables just before we render. We pass the letters through a `vtkTransformPolyFilter` to position them relative to each other. Then we combine all of the polygons from the transformed letters into one polygon dataset using the `vtkAppendPolyData` filter. The `vtkImplicitModeller` creates a volume dataset of dimension 64^3 with each voxel containing a scalar value that is the distance to the nearest polygon. Recall from "Implicit Modelling" on page 171, that the implicit modelling algorithm lets us specify the region of influence of each polygon. Here we set that using the `SetMaximumDistance()` method of the `vtkImplicitModeller`. By restricting the region of influence, we can significantly improve performance of

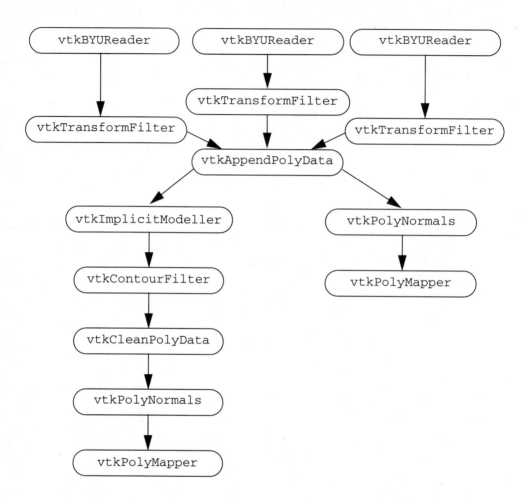

Figure 11–7 The visualization pipeline for the **vtk** blobby logo.

the implicit modelling algorithm. Then we use vtkContourFilter to extract an isosurface that approximates a distance of 1.0 from each polygon. Since we want our blobby logo to appear smooth, we apply vtkCleanPolyData to remove duplicate vertices and vtkPolyNormals to create normals. We create two actors: one for the blobby logo and one for the original polygon letters. Notice that both actors share the polygon data created by vtkAppendPolyData. Because of the nature of the **vtk** visualization pipeline (see "Implicit Control of Execution" on page 92), the appended data will only be created once by the portion of the pipeline that is executed first. As a final touch, we move the polygonal logo in front of the blobby logo. Now we will go through the example in detail.

First, we read the geometry files that contain polygonal models of each letter in the logo. The data is in MOVIE.BYU format, so we use vtkBYUReader.

```
vtkBYUReader *letterVBYU = new vtkBYUReader;
   letterVBYU->SetGeometryFilename ("v.geo");
vtkBYUReader *letterTBYU = new vtkBYUReader;
   letterTBYU->SetGeometryFilename ("t.geo");
vtkBYUReader *letterKBYU = new vtkBYUReader;
   letterKBYU->SetGeometryFilename ("k.geo");
```

We want to transform each letter into its appropriate location and orientation
within the logo. We create the transform filters here, but defer specifying the
location and orientation until later in the program.

```
// create a transform and transform filter for each letter
vtkTransform *VTransform = new vtkTransform;
vtkTransformPolyFilter *VTransformFilter = new
    vtkTransformPolyFilter;
  VTransformFilter->SetInput (letterVBYU->GetOutput());
  VTransformFilter->SetTransform (VTransform);

vtkTransform *TTransform = new vtkTransform;
vtkTransformPolyFilter *TTransformFilter = new
    vtkTransformPolyFilter;
  TTransformFilter->SetInput (letterTBYU->GetOutput());
  TTransformFilter->SetTransform (TTransform);

vtkTransform *KTransform = new vtkTransform;
vtkTransformPolyFilter *KTransformFilter = new
    vtkTransformPolyFilter;
  KTransformFilter->SetInput (letterKBYU->GetOutput());
  KTransformFilter->SetTransform (KTransform);
```

We collect all of the transformed letters into one set of polygons by using an
instance of the class vtkAppendPolyData.

```
// now append them all
vtkAppendPolyData *appendAll = new vtkAppendPolyData;
  appendAll->AddInput (VTransformFilter->GetOutput());
  appendAll->AddInput (TTransformFilter->GetOutput());
  appendAll->AddInput (KTransformFilter->GetOutput());
```

Since the geometry for each letter did not have surface normals, we add them
here. We use vtkPolyNormals. We complete this portion of the pipeline by creating a mapper and an actor.

```
// create normals
vtkPolyNormals *logoNormals = new vtkPolyNormals;
  logoNormals->SetInput (appendAll->GetOutput());
  logoNormals->SetFeatureAngle (60);
```

```
   // map to rendering primitives
   vtkPolyMapper *logoMapper = new vtkPolyMapper;
     logoMapper->SetInput (logoNormals->GetOutput());

   vtkActor *logo = new vtkActor;
     logo->SetMapper (logoMapper);
```

We create the blobby logo with the implicit modeller.

```
   vtkImplicitModeller *blobbyLogoImp = new vtkImplicitModeller;
     blobbyLogoImp->SetInput (appendAll->GetOutput());
     blobbyLogoImp->SetMaximumDistance (.05);
     blobbyLogoImp->SetSampleDimensions (64,64,64);

   vtkContourFilter *blobbyLogoIso = new vtkContourFilter;
     blobbyLogoIso->SetInput (blobbyLogoImp->GetOutput());
     blobbyLogoIso->SetValue (1, 1.0);
```

To get a smooth appearance, we merge coincident vertices generated from the implicit modeller and generate surface normals. We complete the network by creating a mapper and actor.

```
   vtkCleanPolyData *blobbyLogoClean = new vtkCleanPolyData;
     blobbyLogoClean->SetInput (blobbyLogoIso->GetOutput());

   vtkPolyNormals *blobbyLogoNormals = new vtkPolyNormals;
     blobbyLogoNormals->SetInput (blobbyLogoClean->GetOutput());
     blobbyLogoNormals->SetFeatureAngle (60.0);

   vtkPolyMapper *blobbyLogoMapper = new vtkPolyMapper;
     blobbyLogoMapper->SetInput (blobbyLogoNormals->GetOutput());
     blobbyLogoMapper->ScalarsVisibleOff ();

   vtkActor *blobbyLogo = new vtkActor;
     blobbyLogo->SetMapper (blobbyLogoMapper);
```

To improve the look of our resulting visualization, we define a couple of organic colors. Softer colors show up better on some electronic media (e.g., VHS videotape) and are pleasing to the eye.

```
   vtkProperty *tomato = new vtkProperty;
     tomato->SetDiffuseColor(1, .3882, .2784);
     tomato->SetSpecular(.3);
     tomato->SetSpecularPower(20);

   vtkProperty *banana = new vtkProperty;
     banana->SetDiffuseColor(.89, .81, .34);
     banana->SetDiffuse (.7);
```

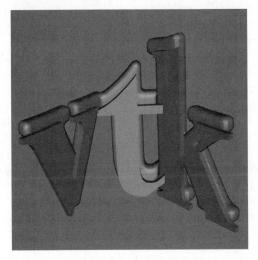

Figure 11–8 A logo created with `vtkImplicitModeller`.

```
banana->SetSpecular(.4);
banana->SetSpecularPower(20);
```

These colors are then assigned to the appropriate actors.

```
blobbyLogo->SetProperty (tomato);
logo->SetProperty (banana);
```

And finally, we position the letters in the logo, and move the polygonal logo out in front of the blobby logo by modifying the actor's position. The resulting image is shown in Figure **11–8**.

```
VTransform->Translate (-13.1,0,15.4);
VTransform->RotateY (50);
KTransform->Translate (12.1, 0, 0);
KTransform->RotateY (-50);
logo->SetPosition (0, 0, 6);
```

11.4 Computational Fluid Dynamics

Computational Fluid Dynamics (CFD) visualization poses a challenge to any visualization toolkit. CFD studies the flow of fluids in and around complex structures. Often, large amounts of supercomputer time is used to derive scalar and vector data in the flow field. Since CFD computations produce multiple scalar and vector data types, we will apply many of the tools described in this book. The challenge is to combine multiple representations into meaningful visualizations that extract information without overwhelming the user.

CFD analysts usually employ finite difference grids. A finite difference grid represents the discretization of the problem domain into small computational cells. The grid allows the analyst to create a large system of equations that can then be solved on a computer. The grid is topologically uniform in *i-j-k* space, but the corresponding physical coordinates need not be uniformly distributed. This is what we call a structured grid in **vtk**.

There are a number of techniques we can use when we first look at the complex data presented by CFD applications. Since we need to apply several algorithms to the data, and since there will be many parameter changes for these algorithms, we suggest using the Tcl interpreter rather than C++ code. Our strategy for visualizing this CFD data include will be as follows.

1. Display the computational grid. The analyst carefully constructed the finite difference grid to have a higher density in regions where rapid changes occur in the flow variables. We will display the gird in wireframe so we can see the computational cells.

2. Display the scalar fields on the computational grid. This will give us an overview of where the scalar data is changing. We will experiment with the extents of the grid extraction to focus on interesting areas.

3. Explore the vector field by seeding streamlines with a spherical cloud of points. Move the sphere through areas of rapidly changing velocity.

4. Try using the computational grid itself as seeds for the streamlines. Of course we will have to restrict the extent of the grid you use for this purpose. Using the grid, we will be able to place more seeds in regions where the analyst expected more action.

For this case study, we use a dataset from NASA called the LOx Post. It simulates the flow of liquid oxygen across a flat plate with a cylindrical post perpendicular to the flow [Rogers86]. This analysis models the flow in a rocket engine. The post promotes mixing of the liquid oxygen.

We start by exploring the scalar and vector fields in the data. We derive a scalar field by calculating the magnitude of the velocity vectors. This study has a particularly interesting vector field around the post. We seed the field with multiple streamlines lines and experiment with parameters for the streamlines. Streampolygons are particularly appropriate here and do a nice job of showing the flow downstream from the post. We animate the streamline creation by moving the seeding line or rake back and forth behind the post.

Following our own advice, we first display the computational grid. The following Tcl code produced Figure **11–9**.

```
# read data
vtkPLOT3DReader pl3d;
pl3d SetXYZFilename "../../data/lox/postxyz.bin"
pl3d SetQFilename "../../data/lox/postq.bin"
pl3d SetScalarFunctionNumber 153;
pl3d SetVectorFunctionNumber 200;
```

```
# create the computational grids: the floor
vtkStructuredGridGeometryFilter floorComp;
   floorComp SetExtent 0 37 0 75 0 0;
   floorComp SetInput [pl3d GetOutput];
vtkPolyMapper floorMapper;
   floorMapper SetInput [floorComp GetOutput];
   floorMapper ScalarsVisibleOff;
vtkActor floorActor;
   floorActor SetMapper floorMapper;
   [floorActor GetProperty] SetWireframe;
   [floorActor GetProperty] SetColor 0 0 0;

# the post
vtkStructuredGridGeometryFilter postComp;
   postComp SetExtent 0 0 0 75 0 37;
   postComp SetInput [pl3d GetOutput];
vtkPolyMapper postMapper;
   postMapper SetInput [postComp GetOutput];
   postMapper ScalarsVisibleOff;
vtkActor postActor;
   postActor SetMapper postMapper;
   [postActor GetProperty] SetWireframe;
   [postActor GetProperty] SetColor 0 0 0;

# a plane upstream of the flow
vtkStructuredGridGeometryFilter fanComp;
   fanComp SetExtent 0 37 38 38 0 37;
   fanComp SetInput [pl3d GetOutput];
vtkPolyMapper fanMapper;
   fanMapper SetInput [fanComp GetOutput];
   fanMapper ScalarsVisibleOff;
vtkActor fanActor;
   fanActor SetMapper fanMapper;
   [fanActor GetProperty] SetWireframe;
   [fanActor GetProperty] SetColor 0 0 0;

# outline
vtkStructuredGridOutlineFilter outline;
   outline SetInput [pl3d GetOutput];
vtkPolyMapper outlineMapper;
   outlineMapper SetInput [outline GetOutput];
vtkActor outlineActor;
   outlineActor SetMapper outlineMapper;
   set outlineProp [outlineActor GetProperty];
   eval $outlineProp SetColor 0 0 0;

# Add the actors to the renderer, set the background and size
$ren1 AddActors outlineActor;
$ren1 AddActors floorActor;
$ren1 AddActors postActor;
```

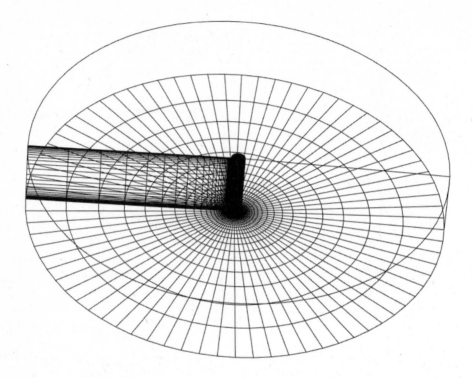

Figure 11–9 Portion of computational grid for the LoX post.

```
$ren1 AddActors fanActor;
$ren1 SetBackground 1 1 1;
$renWin SetSize 750 750;
```

To display the scalar field using color mapping, we just turn on scalar visibility for each vtkPolyMapper and render again, producing Figure **11–10**.

```
postMapper ScalarsVisibleOn;
fanMapper ScalarsVisibleOn;
floorMapper ScalarsVisibleOn;
```

Now, we explore the vector field using vtkPointSource. Recall that this object generates a random cloud of points around a spherical center point. We will use this cloud of points to generate streamlines. We place the center of the cloud near the post since this is where the velocity seems to be changing most rapidly. During this exploration, we use streamlines rather than streamtubes for reasons of efficiency. The Tcl code is as follows.

Figure 11–10 Scalar field displayed on three computational grids.

```
# seeds for streamlines
vtkPointSource rake;
   rake SetCenter -.74 0 .3
   rake SetNumberOfPoints 10

# the streamlines
vtkStreamLine streamers;
   streamers SetInput [pl3d GetOutput];
   streamers SetSource [rake GetOutput];
   streamers SetMaximumPropagationTime 100;
   streamers SpeedScalarsOn;
   streamers SetIntegrationStepLength .2;
   streamers SetStepLength .2;
   streamers Update;
```

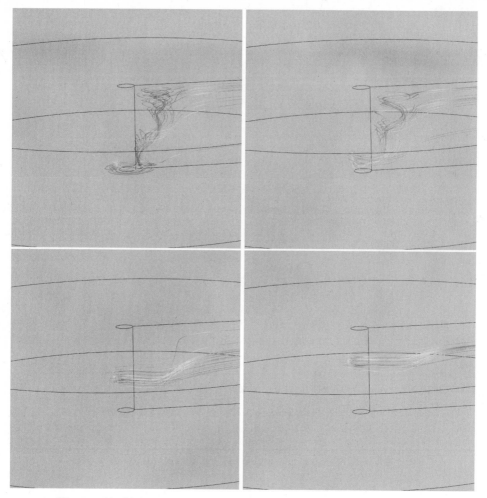

Figure 11-11 Streamlines seeded with spherical cloud of points.
Four separate cloud positions are shown.

```
vtkPolyMapper mapTubes;
  mapTubes SetInput [streamers GetOutput];
  eval mapTubes SetScalarRange \
    [[pl3d GetOutput] GetScalarRange];
vtkActor tubesActor;
  tubesActor SetMapper mapTubes;
```

Figure **11-11** shows streamlines seeded from four locations along the post.
Notice how the structure of the flow begins to emerge as the starting positions
for the streamlines are moved up and down in front of the post. This is particularly true if we do this interactively; the mind assembles the behavior of the
streamlines into a global understanding of the flow field.

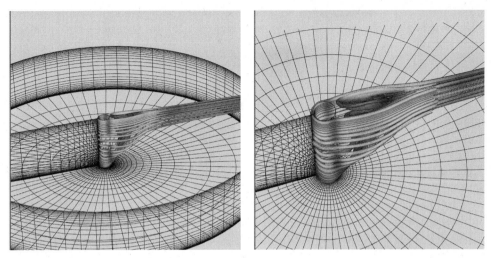

Figure 11–12 Streamtubes created by using the computational grid just in front of the post as a source for seeds.

As a final example, we use the computational grid to seed the streamlines and display the streamlines as streamtubes as is shown in Figure **11–12**. A nice feature of this approach is that we generate more streamlines in regions where the analyst constructed a denser grid.

```
vtkStructuredGridGeometryFilter seedsComp;
   seedsComp SetExtent 10 10 37 39 1 35;
   seedsComp SetInput [pl3d GetOutput];

   streamers SetSource [seedsComp GetOutput];
   streamers SetMaximumPropagationTime 100;
   streamers SpeedScalarsOn;
   streamers SetIntegrationStepLength .2;
   streamers SetStepLength .2;

vtkTubeFilter tubes
   tubes SetInput [cleaner GetOutput];
   tubes SetNumberOfSides 8
   tubes SetRadius .08
   tubes VaryRadiusOff

# change input to stream tubes
mapTubes SetInput [tubes GetOutput];
```

There are a number of other methods we could use to visualize this data. As we saw in "Vector Field Topology" on page 278, there are regions where the velocity vanishes. We can use the object vtkVectorTopology to identify these region(s) and generate streamlines. Another useful visualization would be to identify regions of vorticity. We could use Equation **9-12** in conjunction with an isocontouring algorithm (e.g., `vtkContourFilter`) to creates isosurfaces of large helical-density.

11.5 Finite Element Analysis

Finite element analysis is a widely used numerical technique for finding solutions of partial differential equations. Applications of finite element analysis include linear and non-linear structural, thermal, dynamic, electromagnetic, and flow analysis. In this application we will visualize the results of a blow molding process.

In the extrusion blow molding process, a material is extruded through an annular die to form a hollow cylinder. This cylinder is called a *parison*. Two mold halves are then closed on the parison, while at the same time the parison is inflated with air. Some of the parison material remains within the mold while some becomes waste material. The material is typically a polymer plastic softened with heat, but blow molding has been used to form metal parts. Plastic bottles are often manufactured using a blow molding process.

Designing the parison die and molds is not easy. Improper design results in large variations in the wall thickness. In some cases the part may fail in thin-walled regions. As a result, analysis tools have been developed to assist in the design of molds and dies. These tools are based on finite element techniques.

The results of one such analysis are shown in Figure **11–13**. The polymer was molded using an isothermal, nonlinear-elastic, incompressible (rubber-like) material. Triangular membrane finite elements were used to model the parison, while a combination of triangular and quadrilateral finite elements were used to model the mold. The mold surface is assumed to be rigid, and the parison is assumed to attach to the mold upon contact. Thus, the thinning of the parison is controlled by its stretching during inflation and the sequence in which it contacts the mold.

Figure **11–13** illustrates ten steps of one analysis. The color of the parison indicates its thickness. Using a rainbow scale, red areas are thinnest while blue regions are thickest (see Color Plates). Our visualization shows clearly one problem with the analysis technique we are using. Note that while the nodes (i.e., points) of the finite element mesh are prevented from passing through the mold, the interior of the triangular elements are not. This is apparent from the occlusion of the mold wireframe by the parison mesh.

To generate these images, we used a Tcl script shown in Figure **11–14** and Figure **11–15**. The input data is in **vtk** format, so a `vtkUnstructuredGridReader` was used as a source object. The mesh displacement is accomplished using an instance of `vtkWarpVector`. At this point the pipeline splits. We wish to treat the mold and parison differently (different properties such as wireframe versus surface), but the data for both mold and parison is combined. Fortunately we can easily separate the data using two instances of class `vtkConnectivityFilter`. One filter extracts the parison, while the other extracts both parts of the

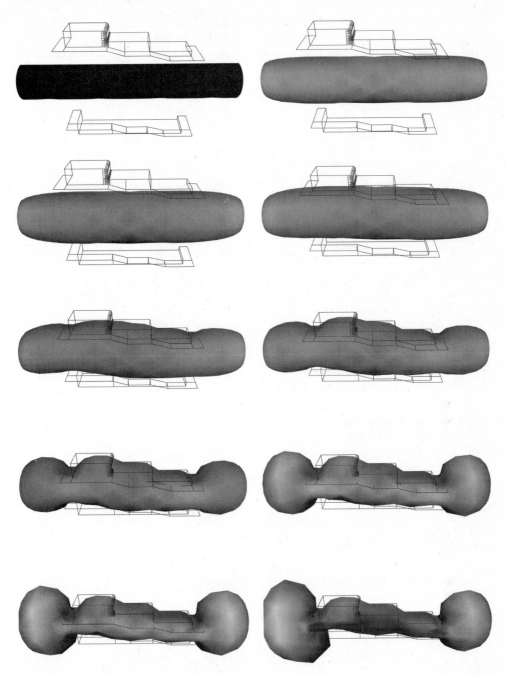

Figure 11–13 Ten frames from a blow molding finite element analysis. Mold halves (shown in wireframe) are closed around a parison as the parison is inflated. Coloring indicates thickness - red areas are thinner than blue. (See Color Plate 52.)

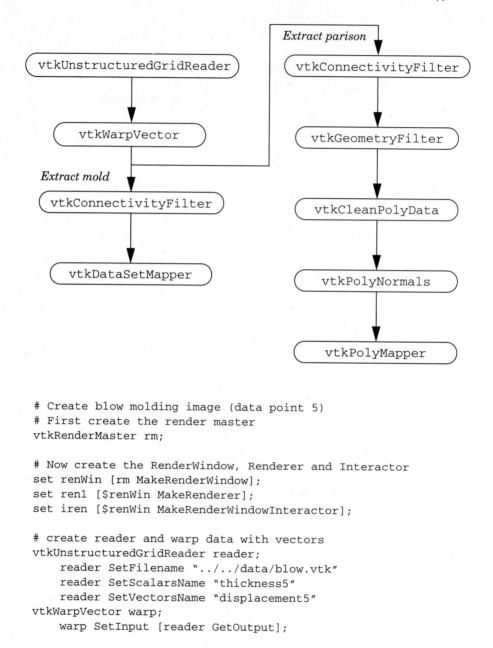

```
# Create blow molding image (data point 5)
# First create the render master
vtkRenderMaster rm;

# Now create the RenderWindow, Renderer and Interactor
set renWin [rm MakeRenderWindow];
set ren1 [$renWin MakeRenderer];
set iren [$renWin MakeRenderWindowInteractor];

# create reader and warp data with vectors
vtkUnstructuredGridReader reader;
    reader SetFilename "../../data/blow.vtk"
    reader SetScalarsName "thickness5"
    reader SetVectorsName "displacement5"
vtkWarpVector warp;
    warp SetInput [reader GetOutput];
```

Figure 11–14 Tcl script to generate blow molding image. Network topology and initial portion of script are shown (part 1 of 2).

```
# extract mold from mesh using connectivity
vtkConnectivityFilter connect;
    connect SetInput [warp GetOutput];
    connect ExtractSpecifiedRegions;
    connect AddSpecifiedRegion 0;
    connect AddSpecifiedRegion 1;
vtkDataSetMapper moldMapper;
    moldMapper SetInput [connect GetOutput];
    moldMapper ScalarsVisibleOff;
vtkActor moldActor;
    moldActor SetMapper moldMapper;
set moldProp [moldActor GetProperty];
    $moldProp SetColor .2 .2 .2;
    $moldProp SetWireframe;

# extract parison from mesh using connectivity
vtkConnectivityFilter connect2;
    connect2 SetInput [warp GetOutput];
    connect2 ExtractSpecifiedRegions;
    connect2 AddSpecifiedRegion 2;
vtkGeometryFilter parison;
    parison SetInput [connect2 GetOutput];
vtkCleanPolyData clean2
    clean2 SetInput [parison GetOutput];
vtkPolyNormals normals2;
    normals2 SetInput [clean2 GetOutput];
    normals2 SetFeatureAngle 60;
vtkLookupTable lut;
    lut SetHueRange 0.0 0.66667;
vtkPolyMapper parisonMapper;
    parisonMapper SetInput [normals2 GetOutput];
    parisonMapper SetLookupTable lut;
    parisonMapper SetScalarRange 0.12 1.0
vtkActor parisonActor;
    parisonActor SetMapper parisonMapper;

# Add the actors to the renderer, set the background and size
$ren1 AddActors moldActor;
$ren1 AddActors parisonActor;
$ren1 SetBackground 1 1 1;
$iren Initialize;
```

Figure 11–15 Tcl script to generate blow molding image (part 2 of 2).

mold. Finally, to achieve a smooth surface appearance on the parison, we use a
vtkPolyNormals filter. In order to use this filter, we have to convert the data
type from vtkUnstructuredGrid (output of vtkConnectivityFilter) to
type vtkPolyData. The filter vtkGeometryFilter does this nicely, and we
merge duplicate points using vtkCleanPolyData.

11.6 Algorithm Visualization

Visualization can be used to display algorithms and data structures. Representing this information often requires creative work on the part of the application
programmer. For example, Robertson *et al.* [Robertson91] have shown 3D techniques for visualizing directory structures and navigating through them. Their
approach involves building three dimensional models (the so-called "cone trees")
to represent files, directories, and associations between files and directories.
Similar approaches can be used to visualize stacks, queues, linked lists, trees,
and other data structures.

In this example we will visualize the operation of the recursive *Towers of
Hanoi* puzzle. In this puzzle there are three pegs (Figure **11–16**). In the initial
position there are one or more disks (or pucks) of varying diameter on the pegs.
The disks are sorted according to disk diameter, so that the largest disk is on the
bottom, followed by the next largest (and so on). The goal of the puzzle is to move
the disks from one peg to another, moving the disks one at a time, and never
placing a larger disk on top of a smaller disk.

The classical solution to this puzzle is based on a divide-and-conquer
approach [AhoHopUll83]. The problem of moving *n* disks from the initial peg to
the second peg can be thought of as solving two sub-problems of size *n-1*. First
move *n-1* disks from the initial peg to the third peg. Then move the nth disk to
the second peg. Finally, move the *n-1* disks on the third peg back to the second
peg.

The solution to this problem can be elegantly implemented using recursion.
We have shown portions of the C++ code in Figure **11–17** and Figure **11–18**. In
the first part of the solution (which is not shown in Figure **11–17**) the table top,
pegs and disks are created using the classes vtkPlaneSource and vtkCylinderSource. The function Hanoi() is then called to begin the recursion. The
routine MovePuck() is responsible for moving a disk from one peg to another. It
has been jazzed up to move the disk in small, user specified increments, and to
flip the disc over as it moves from one peg to the next. This gives a pleasing
visual effect and adds the element of fun to the visualization.

Because of the clear relationship between algorithm and physical reality,
the Towers of Hanoi puzzle is relatively easy to visualize. A major challenge facing visualization researchers is to visualize more abstract information, such as
information on the Internet, the structure of documents, or the effectiveness of
advertising/entertainment in large market segments. This type of visualization,
known as information visualization, is likely to emerge in the future as an
important research challenge.

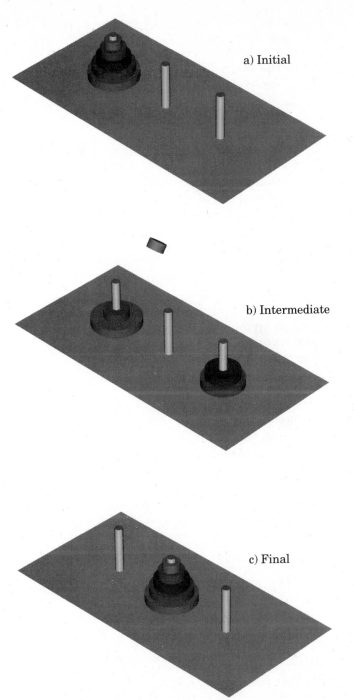

Figure 11–16 Towers of Hanoi. a) Initial configuration. 2) Intermediate configuration. c) Final configuration.

```
// Recursive solution of Towers of Hanoi. Parameters are number of
// and orinating peg, final peg, and intermediate peg.
static void Hanoi (int n, int peg1, int peg2, int peg3)
{
  if ( n != 1 )
    {
    Hanoi (n-1, peg1, peg3, peg2);
    Hanoi (1, peg1, peg2, peg3);
    Hanoi (n-1, peg3, peg2, peg1);
    }
  else
    {
    MovePuck (peg1, peg2);
    }
}
```

Figure 11–17 C++ code for recursive solution of Towers of Hanoi.

11.7 Chapter Summary

This chapter presented several case studies covering a variety of visualization techniques. The examples used different data representations including polygonal data, volumes, structured grids, and unstructured grids. Both C++ and Tcl code was used to implement the case studies.

Medical imaging is a demanding application area due to the size of the input data. Three-dimensional visualization of anatomy is generally regarded by radiologists as a communication tool for referring physicians and surgeons. Medical datasets are typically structured point data (or volumes) or 2D images that form volumes. Common visualization tools for medical imaging include isosurfaces, cut planes, and image display on volume slices.

Next, we presented an example that applied 3D visualization techniques to financial data. In this case study, we began by showing how to import data from an external source. We applied tube filters to the data and varied the width of the tube to show the volume of stock trading. We saw how different views can be used to present different pieces of information. In this case, we saw that by viewing the visualization from the front, we saw a conventional price display. Then, by viewing the visualization from above, we saw trade volume.

In the modelling case study we showed how to use polygonal models and the implicit modelling facilities in **vtk** to create a stylistic logo. The final model was created by extracting an isosurface at a user-selected offset.

Computational fluid dynamics frequently employs structured grid data. We examined some strategies for exploring the scalar and vector fields. The computational grid created by the analyst serves as a staring point for analyzing the data. We displayed geometry extracted from the finite difference grid, scalar color mapping, and streamlines and streamtubes to investigate the data.

```
// Routine is responsible for moving disks from one peg to the next.
void MovePuck (int peg1, int peg2)
{
  float distance, flipAngle;
  vtkActor *movingActor;
  int i;

  NumberOfMoves++;
  // get the actor to move
  movingActor = (vtkActor *)pegStack[peg1].Pop();
  // get the distance to move up
  distance = (H - (L * (pegStack[peg1].GetNumberOfItems() -
1)) + rMax) / NumberOfSteps;
  for (i=0; i<NumberOfSteps; i++)
    {
    movingActor->AddPosition(0,distance,0);
    Renwin->Render();
    }
  // get the distance to move across
  distance = (peg2 - peg1) * D / NumberOfSteps;
  flipAngle = 180.0 / NumberOfSteps;
  for (i=0; i<NumberOfSteps; i++)
    {
    movingActor->AddPosition(distance,0,0);
    movingActor->RotateX(flipAngle);
    Renwin->Render();
    }
  // get the distance to move down
  distance = ((L * (pegStack[peg2].GetNumberOfItems() - 1)) - H -
rMax) / NumberOfSteps;
  for (i=0; i<NumberOfSteps; i++)
    {
    movingActor->AddPosition(0,distance,0);
    Renwin->Render();
    }
  pegStack[peg2].Push(movingActor);
}
```

Figure 11–18 Function to move disks from one peg to another in the Towers of Hanoi example. Motion is in small steps with additional flip of disk.

In the finite element case study, we looked at unstructured grids used in a simulation of a blow molding process. We displayed the deformation of the geometry using displacement plots, and represented the material thickness using color mapping. We saw how we can create simple animations by generating a sequence of images.

We concluded the case studies by visualizing the *Towers of Hanoi* algorithm. Here we showed how to combine the procedural power of C++ with the visualization capabilities in **vtk**. We saw how visualization often requires our creative resources to cast data structures and information into visual form.

11.8 Bibliographic Notes

The case studies presented in the chapter rely on having interesting data to visualize. Sometimes the hardest part of practicing visualizing is finding these sort of data. The Internet is a tremendous resource for this task. Paul Gilster [Gilster94] has written a good introduction to many of the tools for accessing information on the Internet. There are many more books available on this subject in the local bookstore.

In the stock case study we used a programming tool called AWK to convert our data into a form suitable for **vtk**. More information on AWK can be found in *The AWK Programming Language* [Aho88]. Another popular text processing languages is Perl [Perl95].

If you would like to know more about information visualization you can start with the references listed here [Becker95] [Ding90] [Eick93] [Feiner88] [Johnson91] [Robertson91]. This is a relatively new field but will certainly grow in the near future.

11.9 References

[Aho88]

A. V. Aho, B. W. Kernighan, and P. J. Weinberger. *The AWK Programming Language*. Addison-Wesley, Reading MA, 1988.

[AhoHopUll83]

A. V. Aho, J. E. Hopcroft, and J. D. Ullman. *Data Structures and Algorithm*s. Addison-Wesley, Reading, MA, 1983.

[Becker95]

R. A. Becker, S. G. Eick, and A. R. Wilks. "Visualizing Network Data." *IEEE Transactions on Visualization and Graphics*, 1(1):16-28,1995.

[deLorenzi93]

H. G. deLorenzi and C. A. Taylor. "The Role of Process Parameters in Blow Molding and Correlation of 3-D Finite Element Analysis with Experiment." *International Polymer Processing,* 3(4):365-374, 1993.

[Ding90]
C. Ding and P. Mateti. "A Framework for the Automated Drawing of Data Structure Diagrams." *IEEE Transactions on Software Engineering*, 16(5):543-557, May 1990.

[Eick93]
S. G. Eick and G. J. Wills. "Navigating Large Networks with Hierarchies." In *Proceedings of Visualization '93*, pp. 204-210, IEEE Computer Society Press, Los Alamitos, CA, October 1993.

[Feiner88]
S. Feiner. "Seeing the Forest for the Trees: Hierarchical Displays of Hypertext Structures." In *Conference on Office Information Systems*, Palo Alto, CA, 1988.

[Gilster94]
P. Gilster. *Finding It on the Internet: The Essential Guide to Archie, Veronica, Gopher, WAIS, WWW (including Mosaic), and Other Search and Browsing Tools.* John Wiley & Sons, Inc., 1994.

[Johnson91]
B. Johnson and B. Shneiderman. "Tree-Maps: A Space-Filling Approach to the Visualization of Hierarchical Information Structures." In *Proceedings of Visualization '91*, pp. 284-291, IEEE Computer Society Press, Los Alamitos, CA, October, 1991.

[Perl95]
D. Till. *Teach Yourself Perl in 21 Days*. Sams Publishing, Indianapolis, Indiana, 1995.

[Robertson91]
G. G. Robertson, J. D. Mackinlay, and S. K. Card. "Cone Trees: Animated 3D Visualizations of Hierarchical Information." In *Proceedings of ACM CHI '91 Conference on Human Factors in Computing Systems*, pp. 189-194, 1991.

[Rogers86]
S. E. Rogers, D. Kwak, and U. K. Kaul, "A Numerical Study of Three-Dimensional Incompressible Flow Around Multiple Post." in *Proceedings of AIAA Aerospace Sciences Conference*, vol. AIAA Paper 86-0353, Reno, Nevada, 1986.

11.10 Exercises

11.1 Modify medical dataset so that resulting images have proper relationship of left to right.
a) Use actor's transformation methods.
b) Use a `vtkTransformFilter`.
c) What are the advantages/disadvantages of the above approaches?

11.2 Change the medical case study to use dividing cubes for the skin surface.

11.3 Modify the medical case study to use `vtkContourFilter`, `vtkClean-PolyData`, and `vtkPolyNormals`.
a) Compare the visual results. What are the differences?
b) Compare execution time. Which objects are fastest? Why?

11.4 Create polygonal / line stroked models of your initials and build your own logo. Experiment with different transformations.

11.5 Enhance the appearance of Towers of Hanoi visualization.
a) Texture map disks, base plane, and pegs.
b) Create disks with central holes.

11.6 Use the blow molding example as a starting point for the following.
a) Create an animation of the blow molding sequence. Is it possible to interpolate between time steps? How would you do this?
b) Create the second half of the parison using symmetry. What transformation matrix do you need to use?

11.7 Start with the stock visualization example presented in this chapter.
a) Modify the example code to use a ribbon filter and linear extrusion filter as described in the text. Be careful of the width of the generated ribbons.
b) Can you think of a way to present high/low trade values for each day?

Software Guide

Our focus in this text has been visualization architecture, algorithms, and applications. We have avoided discussing lower-level software design and implementation details for the most part. Instead, we have included a C++ software library that we feel demonstrates important concepts in a simple, easily understood manner. If you are interested in using this software, we recommend that you read the first section *Software Conventions* in this appendix. If you plan on extending the software, or are especially interested in understanding its internal organization, please read the *Development Guide* as well.

A.1 Software Conventions

We adopted a number of conventions during the design and implementation of the *Visualization Toolkit*. We have done this to make the software easy to understand and work with. Hopefully you will spend more time learning about visualization than the idiosyncracies of our software. Understanding the following conventions is a good starting point towards this goal.

Naming Conventions

There are a number of simple naming conventions in **vtk**. Becoming familiar with these conventions will help you better understand and use the software library. In general, we use long, descriptive names for classes, instance variables, and methods. Each name begins with a capital letter, and separations between words are indicated by case change (e.g., NumberOfPoints). Specific conventions are as follows.

Classnames. Each class name begins with the prefix vtk. (The prefix prevents name clashes when mixing C++ libraries).

Filenames. Filenames are the same as the name of the class they contain. We use the suffix .hh for include files, and .cc for source files.

Data Member Names. We use long, descriptive names beginning with a capital letter and case change to indicate word separation. When referring to data members we use an explicit this-> pointer. We find that the resulting code is easier to understand and less confusing.

Automatic Variables. Automatic variables generally begin with a lowercase letter. Our major convention is to make the variable names descriptive.

#define. We use all uppercase with the underscore character separating words. All constants should start with "VTK_" . If a constant will only be used and defined within one .cc file, then you can name it whatever you want, although we still encourage you to use the "VTK_" prefix.

On-Line Documentation

We have provided a minimal, but complete, set of documentation for **vtk**. The documentation exists in at least three forms. First, all documentation is embedded directly in the source code. The include files (.hh) contain the object synopsis and description, as well as virtual and inline method descriptions. The source files (.cc) contain additional method descriptions. Second, we have extracted this embedded information and reformatted it into UNIX man pages (and the electronic form included in this text). You can view the source code directly to obtain information, or you can use your system help facilities (such as man). The latter part of this text (see "Object Descriptions" on page 465) contains this information formatted for your convenience. To use this information effectively, you will need to follow a few guidelines.

Documentation is inherited. Often, methods (especially virtual methods) are documented in a base class and not in its derived classes. Or some functionality may be present and documented in a base class, so the derived class inherits this as well.

Methods are documented once. Typically, there are two or more forms for a method. For example, SetColor(float,float,float) and SetColor(float *). Documentation is provided for only one of the methods, since the action performed is identical for both, even though the arguments are in different forms.

Standard or obvious methods are not documented. Constructors, destructors, standard methods (see following section), or obvious methods are not documented. Obvious methods are methods that are obvious from context, and need no additional description.

Standard Methods

Objects in **vtk** use the same names for common methods. Becoming familiar with these methods will help you understand the source code. We assume that you are familiar with the usual C++ constructor forms and omit them from the following list.

`<class pointer> *MakeObject()`. This method is effectively a virtual constructor. That is, invoking this method causes an object to make a copy of itself and then return a pointer to the new object.

`void Delete()`. Use this to delete a **vtk** object created with the new or `MakeObject()` method. Depending upon the nature of the object being deleted, this may or may not actually delete the object. For example, reference counted objects will only be deleted if their reference count goes to zero (see "Special Objects" on page 391).

`void DebugOn()/DebugOff()`. Turn debugging information on or off.

`void PrintSelf()`. Print out the object including superclass information.

`char *GetClassName()`. Return the name of the class.

`void Modified()`. This updates the internal modification time stamp for the object. This method should be called whenever the object has been modified.

`unsigned long GetMTime()`. Return the last modification time of an object. The value is guaranteed to be unique and monotonically increasing.

Additional standard methods exist for objects that manage memory. These methods are not common for all objects, but are common to objects that allocate and delete memory.

`int Allocate()`. Obtain memory via the new operator. If the object has allocated memory previously, the memory is deleted and then new memory is acquired. If memory allocation fails, a 0 is returned.

`void Initialize()`. Cause an object to release any memory acquired with the new operator. The object is not deleted.

`void Reset()`. Memory acquired with the new operator is retained and reused. The object's old data is written over top of.

Visualization Toolkit **Macros**

The *Visualization Toolkit* uses a number of #define macros (found in the file vtkSetGet.hh). These macros greatly simplify programming tasks and enforce uniform object behavior. Their uses include setting and getting instance variables including proper treatment of modified time and reference counting, and provide simple output for debugging, warnings, and error conditions.

Many macros are used to create standard object methods. To properly understand the .hh files you will need to know how these macros expand. A summary of these macros, with examples, follows.

> vtkSetMacro(Name,Type) is used to set the value of instance variables. The macro expands into the method: void SetName(Type). For example vtkSetMacro(Scale,float) expands to void SetScale(float).

> vtkGetMacro(Name,Type) is used to get the value of an instance variable. The macro expands into the method: Type GetName(). For example vtkGetMacro(Scale,float) expands to float GetScale().

> vtkBooleanMacro(Name,Type) is used to create convenience methods for boolean (i.e., true/false or 1/0) instance variables. The macro expands into the two methods: void NameOn() and void NameOff(). For example vtkBooleanMacro(Visibility, float) expands into void VisibilityOn() and void VisibilityOff().

> vtkSetStringMacro(Name) is used to set the value of a character string instance variable. The macro expands into the method void SetName(char *). For example vtkSetStringMacro(Filename) expands into void SetFilename(char *).

> vtkGetStringMacro(Name) is used to get the value of a character string instance variable. The macro expands into the method char *GetName(). For example vtkGetStringMacro(Filename) expands into char *GetFilename().

> vtkSetObjectMacro(Name,Type) is used to set instance variables that are pointers to other objects (i.e., an association). The macro expands into the two methods void SetName(Type *) and void SetName(Type &). For example vtkSetObjectMacro(Transform,vtkTransform) expands into void SetTransform(vtkTransform *) and void SetTransform(vtkTransform &).

> vtkGetObjectMacro(Name,Type) is used to get instance variables that are pointers to other objects. The macro expands into the method Type *GetName(). For example vtkGetObjectMacro(Transform,vtkTransform) expands into vtkTransform *GetTransform().

`vtkSetRefCountedObject(Name,Type)` is used to set instance variables that are pointers to reference counted objects. (The use of a reference counted object may need to be `Registered()` or `UnRegistered()`, as appropriate.) The macro expands into the two methods `void SetName(Type *)` and `void SetName(Type &)`. For example `vtkSetRefCountedObjectMacro(Points,vtkPoints)` expands into `void SetPoints(vtkPoints *)` and `void SetPoints(vtkPoints &)`.

`vtkSetVector2Macro(Name,Type)` is used to set instance variables that are arrays of length `[2]`. The macro expands into the two methods `void SetName(Type,Type)` and `void SetName(Type array[2])`. For example `vtkSetVector2Macro(HueRange, float)` expands into `void SetHueRange(float,float)` and `void SetHueRange(float array[2])`.

`vtkSetVector3Macro(Name,Type)` is used to set instance variables that are arrays of length `[3]`. The macro expands into the two methods `void SetName(Type, Type, Type)` and `void SetName(Type array[3])`. For example `vtkSetVector3Macro(Color,float)` expands into `void SetColor(float,float,float)` and `void SetColor(float array[3])`.

`vtkSetVector4Macro(Name,Type)` is used to set instance variables that are arrays of length `[4]`. The macro expands into the two methods `void SetName(Type, Type, Type, Type)` and `void SetName(Type array[4])`. For example `vtkSetVector4Macro (WorldPoint,float)` expands into `void SetWorldPoint (float,float,float,float)` and `void SetWorldPoint (float array[4])`.

`vtkSetVectorMacro(Name,Type,Count)` is used to set instance variables that are arrays. The macro expands into the method `void SetName(Type data[Count])`. For example `vtkSetVector (Bounds,float,6)` expands into `void SetBounds(float data[6])`.

`vtkGetVectorMacro(Name,Type,Count)` is used to get an array of data. The macro expands into the two methods `Type *GetName()` and `void GetName(Type data[Count])`. (The first macro returns a pointer to the data, the second copies the data into user provided array.) For example `vtkGetVector(Color,float,3)` expands into `float *GetColor()` and `void GetColor(float data[3])`.

`vtkDebugMacro(msg)` is used to print out debugging messages. (Debugging messages are printed when the `Debug` instance variable is true, otherwise no messages appear.) The `msg` parameter is a text string that includes the `iostream` operator `<<`. For example

`vtkDebugMacro(<<"S="<<s)` expands into (in a nutshell) `cerr`
`<< "Debug: (some info)" << "S=" << s << "\n"`.

`vtkWarningMacro(msg)` is used to print out warning messages. (Warning
messages are informational in nature – the system behaves normally but an unusual situation has been encountered.) The `msg`
parameter is a text string that includes the `iostream` operator `<<`.
For example `vtkWarningMacro(<<"S="<<s)` expands into (in a
nutshell) `cerr << Warning: (some info)" << "S=" << s <<`
`"\n"`.

`vtkErrorMacro(msg)` is used to print out error messages. (Error messages indicate that a significant problem has been encountered.) The
`msg` parameter is a text string that includes the `iostream` operator `<<`. For example `vtkWarningMacro(<<"S="<<s)` expands into
(in a nutshell) `cerr << ERROR: (some info)" << "S=" << s`
`<< "\n"`.

Pointers, References, and Copying

The object-oriented paradigm encapsulates data and procedures into objects.
One implication of this is that access into the internal data representation of an
object is not allowed. Thus, the proper way to obtain information from an object
is to copy information from the object into an accessible memory location.

From a software development point of view, this results in robust, safe systems. Unfortunately, copying data can be unacceptably inefficient. For example,
if an object contains 1,000,000 `float` values, copying this data results in both
computational and memory overhead.

In **vtk** we address this dilemma by offering a choice. Most every data access
method comes in a pair. The first returns either a pointer or reference to an
object or memory location. The second copies data into user provided memory, or
offers a copy constructor or equivalent method to copy an object. Typical examples are shown in Figure **A–1**.

As a user you may choose to copy or reference data. Bear in mind this cau-
tionary note: *pointers and references often refer to dynamic data, that is, data
that may be deleted or may change during program execution.* We guarantee that
data referred to by a pointer or reference will not change as long as another **vtk**
method is not executed. Use pointers and references quickly, and for reasons of
efficiency. Otherwise, use the safer object-oriented approach and copy the data.

If you do decide to copy data, make sure that you free all memory. Automatic variables will be freed when scope is exited, but objects created with the
`MakeObject()` or `new` methods must be deleted by you (using the `Delete()`
method).

Return Reference or Pointer

```
float *GetColor();
float *x= this->GetPoint(id);
vtkIdList *l= cell->GetPointIds();
vtkCell *c = this->GetCell(id);
```

Copy Data

```
float c[3]; void GetColor(c[3]);
float x[3]; this->GetPoint(id,x[3]);
vtkIdList l = *(cell->GetPointIds());
vtkCell *c = this->GetCell(id)->MakeObject();
```

Figure A–1 Example methods to access data by pointer or reference; or to copy data.

Special Objects

There are objects in **vtk** that require special treatment during construction and deletion. These are device dependent graphics objects and reference counted objects.

Device dependent graphics objects include `vtkRenderWindow` and `vtkRenderer`. Although these objects can be created manually, using either the new operator or via ordinary type declaration, we highly recommend that you use the standard construction procedure. In this case you would use `vtkRenderMaster` and `vtkRenderWindow` to construct these objects as follows.

```
vtkRenderMaster rm;
vtkRenderWindow *renWin = rm.MakeRenderWindow();
vtkRenderer *renderer = renWin->MakeRenderer();
```

The standard construction procedure insures proper device initialization and promotes device independent applications. The specific type of renderer is determined at run time or by setting the environment variable `VTK_RENDERER`.

Reference counted objects are another type of special object. These objects exist as long as they are referred to by other objects. Once their reference count goes to zero, they will self-destruct. This behavior has important implications if you are planning to do heavy-duty development programming using **vtk**.

Reference counting is implemented as follows. Every reference counted object (call it *O* for convenience) when constructed has a reference count of 1. When *O* is used by another object (call it *U*), the using object registers its use of *O* by executing *O*'s `Register()` method. This bumps *O*'s reference count to 2.

When U no longer uses (or references) O it executes O's UnRegister() method. Thus the reference count is decremented to a value of 1. At this point a call to O's Delete() method will reduce the reference count to 0 and O will destruct.

From the previous discussion we can create two simple rules for creating reference counted objects. First, for every new method there must be a matching Delete() method. And second, for every Register() method there must be a matching UnRegister() method. If these rules are observed you will avoid memory leaks and memory corruption problems.

In filter implementations these rules result in code that can appear misleading at first glance. A snippet of code is shown in the following.

```
points = new vtkFloatPoints
...//filter does its thing
output->SetPoints(points);
points->Delete();
```

In this example points (a reference counted object) is created with the new method and then assigned to its output with the SetPoints() method. Then the points are deleted with the Delete() method. Although it might appear that points has been deleted, in actuality the SetOutput() registers the use of points by the output object. Hence the Delete() method does not destroy points, instead it simply decrements the reference count.

This scheme works well except for one situation: creating automatic variables that are reference counted objects. In this case the object is created with a reference count of one. Then, when scope is exited, the object is automatically deleted by the compiler. This results in warnings from **vtk**, since a reference counted object with a non-zero reference count is being deleted. To remedy this situation you can use the method ReferenceCountingOff() as follows.

```
{
  vtkFloatPoints pts;
  pts.ReferenceCountingOff();
  ...//other stuff
} //scope is exited and pts deleted automatically
```

If you do encounter the warning message for automatic variables mentioned previously, it is most likely innocuous. But for better performance and cleaner running code, we recommend that you eliminate these warning messages.

A.2 Object Synopsis

The following is an alphabetical list of the classes in the *Visualization Toolkit*. Each list item consists of the class name and a brief synopsis of its functionality. We have organized the synopsis according to functionality. These functional categories are as follows.

- *Foundation.* Foundation objects supply basic functionality for other objects throughout the *Visualization Toolkit.* These objects often serve as base classes (e.g., vtkObject), as computational classes (e.g., vtkMath), or provide fundamental data representation capability (e.g., vtkFloatArray).

- *Datasets.* Dataset objects are the fundamental visualization data types. These objects are input to and output from sources, filters, and mappers. The abstract object vtkDataSet specifies an interface that all derived classes must provide.

- *Cells.* Cells are the fundamental abstraction of visualization data. Datasets are composed of collections of various types of cells. The object vtkCell specifies an abstract interface for all cells.

- *Pipeline.* Pipeline objects include reference counted objects and abstract classes for the visualization network architecture. Reference counted objects do the dirty work of representing cells and datasets. They are used in the visualization pipeline and are frequently passed from one object to the next during network execution. The abstract classes enforce network topology via type checking, and provide various methods to manipulate visualization classes.

- *Sources.* Source objects initialize visualization networks. Source objects have no other objects as input, and frequently read from external data files i.e., readers) or create data from instance variables (i.e., procedural objects). Source objects create one or more datasets on output.

- *Filters.* Filter objects have at least one input dataset and generate one or more datasets on output. The compiler enforces the way filters can be connected together. That is, the SetInput() method controls which types of objects can be input. The output of a filter is determined by the type returned from its GetOutput() (or equivalent) method.

- *Mappers.* Mappers terminate the visualization network. Mapper objects take one or more input objects. Writers are mapper objects that write data to a file. Device mappers are objects that map visualization data to a particular display device or graphics library.

- *Graphics.* Graphics objects provide the core rendering functionality. These allow manipulation of lights, cameras, and actors, as well as various actor properties and rendering attributes (e.g., renderer background color).

- *OpenGL Renderer.* There are a variety of renderers supported by the *Visualization Toolkit.* A representative renderer is OpenGL. The description of objects in other rendering libraries is the same as for the objects in openGL.

- *Window-System Specific.* Certain objects are specific to a particular window system (i.e., X Window System or Windows). These objects capture user events such as key press and mouse motion.

Foundation

vtkBitArray - dynamic, self-adjusting array of bits

vtkByteSwap - perform machine dependent byte swapping

vtkCollection - create and manipulate unsorted lists of objects

vtkDoubleArray - dynamic, self-adjusting double precision array

vtkFloatArray - dynamic, self-adjusting floating point array

vtkIndent - a simple class to control print indentation

vtkIntArray - dynamic, self-adjusting integer array

vtkLWObject - abstract base class for visualization library

vtkMath - performs common math operations

vtkObject - abstract base class for most of vtk

vtkRefCount - subclasses of this object are reference counted

vtkShortArray - dynamic, self-adjusting short integer array

SetGet - standard macros for setting/getting instance variables

vtkStack - create and manipulate lists of objects

vtkTimeStamp - record modification and/or execution time

vtkUnsignedCharArray - dynamic, self-adjusting unsigned character array

vtkVoidArray - dynamic, self-adjusting array of void* pointers

Datasets

vtkDataSet - abstract class to specify dataset behavior

vtkImage - a regular array of 2D scalar floating point data

vtkPointSet - abstract class for specifying dataset behavior

vtkPolyData - concrete dataset represents vertices, lines, polygons, and triangle strips

vtkPointData - represent and manipulate point attribute data

vtkStructuredGrid - topologically regular array of data

vtkStructuredData - abstract class for topologically regular data

vtkStructuredPoints - topologically and geometrically regular array of data

vtkUnstructuredGrid - dataset represents arbitrary combinations of all possible cell types

Cells

vtkCell - abstract class to specify cell behavior

vtkCellType - define types of cells

vtkHexahedron - a cell that represents a 3D parallelpiped

vtkLine - a cell that represents a 1D line

vtkPixel - a cell that represents a orthogonal quadrilateral vtkPolyLine - a cell that represents a set of 1D lines

vtkPolyVertex - a cell that represents a set of 0D vertices

vtkPolygon - a cell that represents an n-sided polygon

vtkQuad - a cell that represents a convex quadrilateral

vtkTetra - a cell that represents a tetrahedron

vtkTriangle - a cell that represents a triangle

vtkTriangleStrip - a cell that represents a triangle strip

vtkVertex - a cell that represents a 3D point

vtkVoxel - a cell that represents a 3D orthogonal parallelepiped

Pipeline

vtkAGraymap - scalar data in intensity + alpha (grayscale + opacity) form

vtkAPixmap - scalar data in rgba (color + opacity) form

vtkBitScalars - packed bit (0/1) representation of scalar data

vtkBitmap - scalar data in bitmap form

vtkCellArray - object represents cell connectivity

vtkCellList - object provides direct access to cells in vtkCellArray

vtkCellLocator - octree-based spatial search object to quickly locate cells

vtkColorScalars - abstract class represents scalar data in color specification

vtkCone - implicit function for a cone

vtkCylinder - implicit function for a cylinder

vtkDataSetCollection - maintain an unordered list of dataset objects

vtkDataSetFilter - filter that takes vtkDataSet as input

vtkFloatNormals - floating point representation of 3D normals

vtkFloatPoints - floating point representation of 3D points

vtkFloatScalars - floating point representation of scalar data

vtkFloatTCoords - floating point representation of texture coordinates

vtkFloatTensors - floating point representation of tensor data

vtkFloatVectors - floating point representation of 3D vectors

vtkFilter - abstract class for specifying filter behaviour

vtkGraymap - scalar data in grayscale form

vtkIntPoints - integer representation of 3D points

vtkIntScalars - integer representation of scalar data

vtkIdList - list of point or cell ids

vtkImplicitBoolean - implicit function consisting of boolean combinations of implicit functions

vtkImplicitFunction - abstract interface for implicit functions

vtkImplicitFunctionCollection - maintain a list of implicit functions

vtkLinkList - object represents upward pointers from points to list of cells using each point

vtkLocator - spatial search object to quickly locate points

vtkMatrix4x4 - represent and manipulate 4x4 transformation matrices

vtkMergePoints - merge exactly coincident points

vtkNormals - abstract interface to 3D normals

vtkPixmap - scalar data in RGB (color) form

vtkPlane - perform various plane computations

vtkPlanes - implicit function for convex set of planes

vtkPoints - abstract interface to 3D points

vtkPolyDataCollection - maintain a list of polygonal data objects

vtkPolyFilter - filter that takes vtkPolyData as input

vtkPointSetFilter - filter that takes vtkPointSet as input

vtkQuadric - evaluate implicit quadric function

vtkStructuredGridFilter - filter that takes vtkStructuredGrid as input

vtkShortScalars - short integer representation of scalar data

vtkScalars - abstract interface to array of scalar data

vtkSphere - implicit function for a sphere

vtkStructuredPointsCollection - maintain a list of structured points data objects

vtkStructuredPointsFilter - filter that takes vtkStructuredPoints as input

vtkTCoords - abstract interface to texture coordinates

vtkTensor - supporting class to enable assignment and referencing of tensors

vtkTensors - abstract interface to tensors

vtkUnsignedCharScalars - unsigned char representation of scalar data

vtkUnstructuredGridFilter - filter that takes unstructured grid as input

vtkUserDefined - interface to user defined data

vtkVectors - abstract interface to 3D vectors

Sources

vtkAxes - create an x-y-z axes

vtkBYUReader - read MOVIE.BYU polygon files

vtkBooleanTexture - generate 2D texture map based on combinations of inside, outside, and on region boundary

vtkConeSource - generate polygonal cone

vtkCubeSource - create a polygonal representation of a cube

vtkCursor3D - generate a 3D cursor representation

vtkCyberReader - read Cyberware laser digitizer files

vtkCylinderSource - generate a cylinder centered at origin

vtkDataReader - helper class for objects that read **vtk** data files

vtkDataSetReader - class to read any type of **vtk** dataset vtkDiskSource - create a disk with hole in center

vtkLineSource - create a line defined by two end points

vtkMCubesReader - read binary marching cubes file

vtkOutlineSource - create wireframe outline around bounding box

vtkPlaneSource - create an array of quadrilaterals located in the plane

vtkPLOT3DReader - read PLOT3D data files

vtkPNMReader - read pnm (i.e., portable anymap) files

vtkPointLoad - compute stress tensors given point load on semi-inifinite domain

vtkPolyReader - read **vtk** polygonal data file

vtkPointSource - create a random cloud of points

vtkPolySource - abstract class whose subclasses generate polygonal data

vtkRendererSource - take a renderer into the pipeline

vtkStructuredGridReader - read **vtk** structured grid data file

vtkStructuredGridSource - abstract class whose subclasses generate structured grid data

vtkStructuredPointsReader - read **vtk** structured points data file

vtkStructuredPointsSource - abstract class whose subclasses generate structured points data

vtkSTLReader - read ASCII or binary stereo lithography files

vtkSampleFunction - sample an implicit function over a structured point set

vtkSource - abstract class specifies interface of data sources

vtkSphereSource - create a sphere centered at the origin

vtkTextSource - create polygonal text

vtkUnstructuredGridReader - read **vtk** unstructured grid data file

vtkUnstructuredGridSource - abstract class whose subclasses generate unstructured grid data

vtkVolume16Reader -read 16 bit image files

vtkVoxelReader -read a binary 0/1 bit voxel file

Filters

vtkAppendFilter - appends one or more datasets together into a single unstructured grid

vtkAppendPolyData - appends one or more polygonal datasets together

vtkBooleanStructuredPoints - combine two or more structured point sets

vtkBrownianPoints - assign random vector to points

vtkCleanPolyData - merge duplicate points and remove degenerate primitives

vtkConnectivityFilter - extract geometry based on geometric connectivity

vtkContourFilter - generate isosurfaces/isolines from scalar values

vtkCutter - Cut vtkDataSets with user-specified implicit function vtkDataSetToDataSetFilter - abstract filter class

vtkDataSetToPolyFilter - abstract filter class

vtkDataSetToStructuredGridFilter - abstract filter class

vtkDataSetToStructuredPointsFilter - abstract filter class

vtkDataSetToUnstructuredGridFilter - abstract filter class

vtkDashedStreamLine - generate constant-time dashed streamline in arbitrary dataset

vtkDecimate - reduce the number of triangles in a mesh

vtkDividingCubes - create points lying on isosurface

vtkEdgePoints - generate points on isosurface

vtkElevationFilter - generate scalars along a specified direction

vtkExtractGeometry - extract cells that lie either entirely inside or outside of a specified implicit function

vtkExtractVectorComponents - extract components of vector as separate scalars

vtkFeatureEdges - extract boundary, non-manifold, and/or sharp edges from polygonal data

vtkFeatureVertices - extract boundary, non-manifold, and/or sharp vertices from polygonal data (operates on line primitives)

vtkGaussianSplatter - splat points with Gaussian distribution

vtkGeometryFilter - extract geometry from data (or convert data to polygonal type)

vtkGlyph3D - copy oriented and scaled geometry to every input point

vtkHedgeHog - create oriented lines from vector data

vtkHyperStreamLine - generate streamline in arbitrary dataset

vtkStructuredPointsGeometryFilter - extract geometry for structured points

vtkImageFilter - a filter that takes a `vtkImage` as input

vtkImageToImageFilter - filter with `vtkImage` as input and output

vtkImageToPolyDataFilter - abstract filter class

vtkImplicitModeller - compute distance from input geometry on structured point set

vtkImplicitTextureCoords - generate 1D, 2D, or 3D texture coordinates based on implicit function(s)

vtkLinearExtrusionFilter - sweep polygonal data creating "skirt" from free edges and lines, and lines from vertices

vtkMarchingCubes - generate isosurface(s) from volume

vtkMaskPolyData - sample subset of input polygonal data

vtkMaskPoints - selectively filter points

vtkMergeFilter - extract separate components of data from different datasets

vtkOutlineFilter - create wireframe outline for arbitrary dataset

vtkPolyToPolyFilter - abstract filter class

vtkPolyNormals - compute normals for polygonal mesh

vtkProbeFilter - compute data values at specified point locations

vtkPointSetToPointSetFilter - abstract filter class

vtkRecursiveDividingCubes - create points lying on isosurface (using recursive approach)

vtkRibbonFilter - create oriented ribbons from lines defined in polygonal dataset

vtkRotationalExtrusionFilter - sweep polygonal data creating "skirt" from free edges and lines, and lines from vertices

vtkShepardMethod - sample unstructured points onto structured points using Shepard's method

vtkShrinkFilter - shrink cells composing an arbitrary dataset

vtkShrinkPolyData - shrink cells composing PolyData

vtkSliceCubes - generate isosurface(s) from volume four slices at a time

vtkStreamLine - generate streamline in arbitrary dataset

vtkStreamPoints - generate points along streamer separated by constant time increment

vtkStreamer - abstract object implements integration of massless particle through vector field

vtkStripper - create triangle strips

vtkStructuredGridToPolyFilter - abstract filter class

vtkStructuredGridGeometryFilter - extract geometry for structured grid

vtkStructuredGridOutlineFilter - create wireframe outline for structured grid

vtkStructuredPointsToImageFilter - convert structured points to an image

vtkStructuredPointsToPolyDataFilter - abstract filter class

vtkStructuredPointsToStructuredPointsFilter - abstract filter class

vtkStructuredPointsGeometryFilter - extract geometry for structured points

vtkSweptSurface - given a path and input geometry generate an (implicit) representation of a swept surface

vtkTensorGlyph - scale and orient glyph according to tensor eigenvalues and eigenvectors

vtkTextureMapToBox - generate 3D texture coordinates by mapping points into bounding box

vtkTextureMapToPlane - generate texture coordinates by mapping points to plane

vtkThreshold - extracts cells where scalar value of every point in cell satisfies threshold criterion

vtkThresholdPoints - extracts points whose scalar value satisfies threshold criterion

vtkThresholdTextureCoords - compute 1D, 2D, or 3D texture coordinates based on scalar threshold

vtkTransformFilter - transform points and associated normals and vectors vtkTransformPolyFilter - transform points and associated normals and vectors for polygonal dataset

vtkTransformStructuredPoints - transform (and resample) vtkStructuredPoints

vtkTriangleFilter - create triangle polygons from input polygons and triangle strips

vtkTubeFilter - filter that generates tubes around lines

vtkVectorDot - generate scalars from dot product of vectors and normals (e.g., show displacement plot)

vtkVectorNorm - generate scalars from euclidean norm of vectors

vtkVectorTopology - mark points where the vector field vanishes (singularities exist)

vtkVoxelModeller - convert an arbitrary dataset to a voxel representation

vtkWarpScalar - deform geometry with scalar data

vtkWarpTo - deform geometry by warping towards a point

vtkWarpVector - deform geometry with vector data

Mappers

vtkBYUWriter - write MOVIE.BYU files

vtkDataSetMapper - map `vtkDataSet` and subclasses to graphics primitives

vtkDataSetWriter - write any type of **vtk** dataset to file

vtkDataWriter - helper class for objects that write **vtk** data files

vtkMapper - abstract class specifies interface to map data to graphics primitives

vtkPolyMapper - map `vtkPolyData` to graphics primitives

vtkSTLWriter - write stereo lithography files

vtkVoxelWriter - write out 0/1 voxel data from `vtkVoxelModeller`

vtkPolyWriter - write **vtk** polygonal data

vtkStructuredGridWriter - write **vtk** structured grid data file

vtkStructuredPointsWriter - write **vtk** structured points data file

vtkUnstructuredGridWriter - write **vtk** unstructured grid data file

vtkWriter - abstract class to write data to file(s)

Graphics

vtkActor - an entity in a rendered image

vtkActorCollection - a list of actors

vtkCamera - a virtual camera for 3D rendering

vtkCameraDevice - abstract definition of a hardware dependent camera

vtkCellPicker - select a cell by shooting a ray into graphics window

vtkFollower - a subclass of actor that always faces the camera

vtkGeometryPrimitive - abstract interface for geometric data vtkLODActor - a subclass of actor that supports Levels Of Detail

vtkLogLookupTable - map scalar values into colors using logarithmic (base 10) color table

vtkLookupTable - map scalar values into colors or colors to scalars; generate color table

vtkLight - a virtual light for 3D rendering

vtkLightCollection - a list of lights

vtkLightDevice - abstract definition of a hardware dependent light

vtkPicker - select an actor by shooting a ray into graphics window

vtkPointPicker - select a point by shooting a ray into graphics window

vtkProperty - represent surface properties of a geometric object

vtkPropertyDevice - abstract definition of a hardware dependent property

vtkRenderMaster - create a device specific rendering window

vtkRenderWindow - create a window for renderers to draw into

vtkRenderWindowInteractor - an event-driven interface to rendering window

vtkRenderer - abstract specification for renderers

vtkRendererCollection - a list of renderers

vtkTexture - handles properties associated with a texture map

vtkTextureDevice - abstract definition of a hardware dependent texture

vtkTransform - a general matrix transformation class

vtkTransformCollection - maintain a list of transforms

vtkVolume - a volumetric entity in a rendered image

vtkVolumeCollection - a list of volumes

vtkVolumeRenderer - renders volumetric data

OpenGL Renderer

vtkOglrCamera - OpenGL camera

vtkOglrLight - OpenGL light

vtkOglrLines - OpenGL line primitive

vtkOglrPoints - OpenGL point primitive

vtkOglrPolygons - OpenGL polygon primitive

vtkOglrPrimitive - a geometry primitive for the OpenGL library

vtkOglrProperty - OpenGL property

vtkOglrRenderWindow - OpenGL rendering window

vtkOglrRenderer - OpenGL renderer

vtkOglrTexture - OpenGL texture map

vtkOglrTriangleMesh - OpenGL triangle strip primitive

Device Specific

vtkWin32OglrRenderWindow - OpenGL rendering window for Windows

vtkWin32RenderWindowInteractor - an MS Windows based event handler for a
`vtkWin32OglrRenderWindow`

vtkXRenderWindow - a rendering window for the X Window system

vtkXRenderWindowInteractor - an X event handler for a `vtkXRenderWindow`

For additional information, such as object inheritance, see the object diagrams. More extensive documentation (including descriptions of methods and instance variables) is available from on-line documentation included on the CD-ROM. Note that this synopsis is not complete: some objects are omitted for compactness. Most of the omitted objects are from graphics libraries (SGI gl and HP starbase, for example).

A.3 Object Diagrams

The following section contains abbreviated object diagrams using the OMT graphical language. The purpose of this section is to convey the essence of the software structure, particularly inheritance and object associations. Due to space limitation, not all objects are shown, particularly "leaf" (i.e., bottom of the inheritance tree) objects. Instead we choose a single leaf object to represent other sibling objects. The organization of the objects follows that of the synopsis.

Foundation

The foundation object diagram is shown in Figure **A–2**. These represent the core data objects, as well as other object manipulation classes.

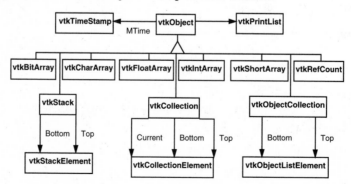

Figure A–2 Foundation object diagram.

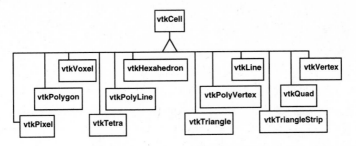

Figure A–4 Cell object diagram.

Datasets

The dataset object diagram is shown in Figure **A–3**. Currently four concrete dataset types are supported. Unstructured point data can be represented by any of the subclasses of `vtkPointSet`. Rectilinear grids are represented using `vtkStructuredGrid`.

Cells

The cell object diagram is shown in Figure **A–4**. Currently twelve types are supported in **vtk**.

Pipeline

The pipeline object diagram is shown in Figure **A–5**. These are the core objects to represent data.

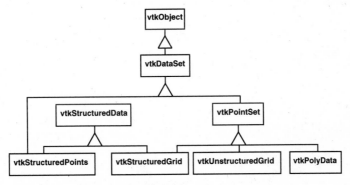

Figure A–3 Dataset object diagram.

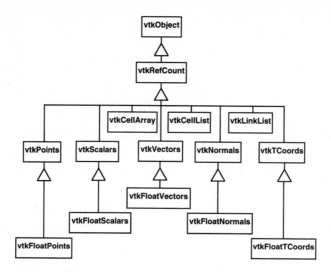

Figure A–5 Pipeline object diagram.

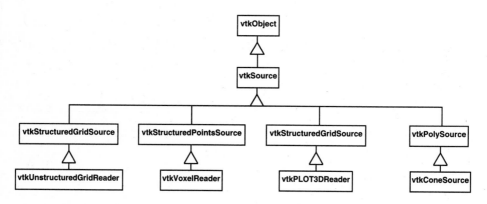

Figure A–6 Source object diagram.

Sources

The source object diagram is shown in Figure **A–6**.

Filters

The filter object diagram is shown in Figure **A–7**.

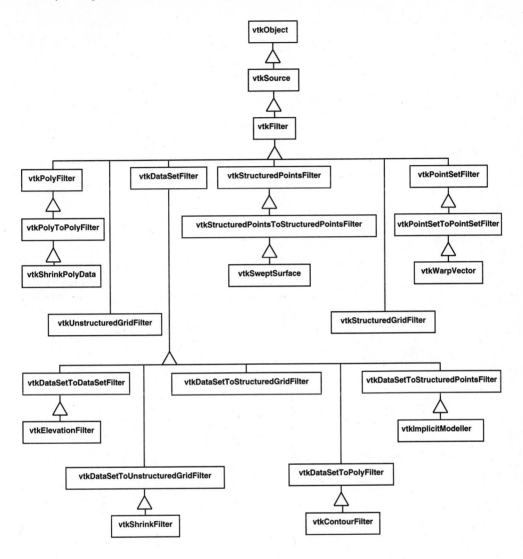

Figure A–7 Filter object diagram.

Mappers

The mapper object diagram is shown in Figure **A–8**. There are basically two types: graphics mappers that map visualization data to the graphics system, and writers that write data to output file (or other I/O device).

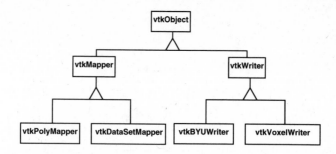

Figure A–8 Mapper object diagram.

Graphics

The graphics object diagram is shown in Figure **A–9**. The diagram has been extended to include some associations with objects in the system. If you are unfamiliar with the object-oriented graphics notation see Rumbaugh *et al.*, *Object-Oriented Modeling and Design*. (Full reference in Chapter 2 reference section.)

OpenGL Renderer

The OpenGL renderer object diagram is shown in Figure **A–10**. Note that there are other rendering libraries in **vtk**. The OpenGL object diagram is representative of these other libraries.

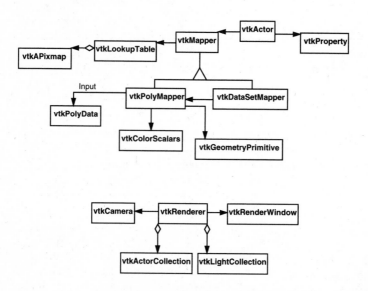

Figure A–9 Graphics object diagram.

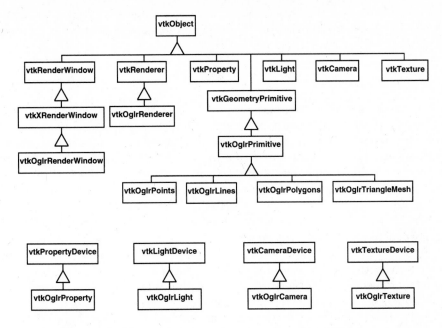

Figure A–10 OpenGL / graphics interface object diagram.

A.4 Development Guide

In this section we've included general tips for extending the *Visualization Toolkit* C++ class library.

Reference Counting

We saw in Chapter 4 how reference counting is used to conserve memory resources. To implement reference counting we derive a class from `vtkRefCount`. This object defines two methods: `Register()` and `UnRegister()`, and an instance variable `RefCount`. The `Register()` method increments the reference count while the `UnRegister()` method decrements the count. When the reference count returns to zero, the object invokes its own destructor.

In order for the reference counting mechanism to work correctly, we have to create and assign a reference counted object properly. When a reference counted object is first created, *its count is initially one*. When the object is assigned to another object, its count is incremented by one. Of course, each additional object association bumps the reference count by one. The reference count is reduced as using objects are deleted or no longer use the reference counted object. Therefore, the correct procedure when dealing with reference counted objects is to create it with the new method, assign it to another object or use it as necessary, and then free it with the `Delete()` method. Please refer to "Special Objects" on page 391 for more information on reference counting and example use of reference counted objects.

Modified Time

Correct execution of the visualization network requires tracking object modification times. In **vtk** an objects modification time is a unique, monotonically increasing unsigned integer. During network execution, modified times are compared between objects. If the input to a process object has been changed, or the object itself has been changed, then the process object must re-execute. In most cases tracking modified time is handled automatically via methods inherited from the objects superclass(es), or by using the standard **vtk** Set/Get macros. In some special cases you may have to understand the modified time mechanism to properly design and implement an object.

Every subclass of `vtkObject` inherits the standard `GetMTime()` method. This virtual method generally provides the proper default behavior. However, if an object A depends upon object B (i.e., B is either an instance variable or association), and B can be modified independently of A, then A must implement its own `GetMTime()` method. In this method both the modified times of A and B must be compared, and the larger value must be returned. Of course, if A depends upon more than one object, then a comparison is required between the modified time of each object.

A good example to look at is the filter `vtkTransformFilter`. This filter has a pointer to a `vtkTransform` object. Because the transform object can be modified independent of `vtkTransformFilter`, the filter must check both its own modified time as well as the transform object's modified time.

One special note. In the example above, B must not be a data flow input to A. The `GetMTime()` method must return the modified time of the local object, not of the network. Comparison between the local process object and its inputs is handled by the network update procedure (i.e., when invoking `Update()`).

Network Updates

The implicit execution technique implemented in **vtk** requires repeated network updates as process objects are modified or input datasets change. This process is implemented using two methods: `Execute()` and `Update()`. The `Update()` method compares object modification time with its input modified time, and if necessary, executes (via `Execute()`) the process object. In most cases this procedure is handled automatically via methods inherited from the objects superclasses. However, there are cases where you will have to understand the network update mechanism to properly implement a process object.

The `Update()` method must be overloaded if the object has more than one input, more than one output, or does not use the standard `Input/Output` instance variables. The basic procedure is to issue an `Update()` method to each input, and then compare modified times between the input objects and the filters execute time. If the modified time of any input object is greater than the local object's execute time, or the local object's modified time is greater than its execution time, then the local object must re-execute. In addition, the local process object may have released data to conserve memory. If this is so then it must re-execute. See vtkFilter for an example of the network update procedure. You may also want to refer to "Multiple Input / Output" on page 92.

Deriving a New Source Object

Source objects initiate a visualization network. They read data from a file or communications device, or procedurally generate it. To create a new source object you must decide what kind of **vtk** specific data type to generate: vtkPolyData, vtkStructuredPoints, vtkUnstructuredGrid, or vtkStructuredGrid. (Or, if none of these is suitable, you will have to define your own dataset type.)

Your new source object should be a subclass of vtkSource. For the data types currently in **vtk** there are convenience base classes available for subclassing: vtkPolySource, vtkStructuredPointsSource, vtkStructuredGridSource, and vtkUnstructuredGridSource. If you use these objects as base classes, you need only to create standard constructors, destructors, instance variable methods, and the single most important method: Execute(). Execute() is the method that is invoked during pipeline execution to generate output data. Good examples of source objects to study are vtkConeSource or vtkPlaneSource.

The body of the source object Execute() method generally consists of five major parts (refer to Figure **A–11**).

1. *Declaration.* Variables are declared, including the appropriate **vtk** types, pointers, and references. A pointer to the output of the source is declared and initialized using the GetOutput() method to perform any typecasting.

2. *Initialization.* In this step we insure the validity and consistency of the input. We may also include debugging information since it provides feedback to users about entry into the filter and other important statistics.

3. *Allocation.* Visualization data is allocated using the C++ new operator. (Operator new should always be used with reference counted objects.)

4. *Body.* The body of the algorithm follows. Data values are created as appropriate.

5. *Output.* The visualization objects allocated in step 3 are set as output. This includes any geometry, topology, and point attributes objects. You may wish to provide debugging output such as summarizing results to the user. Also any objects you've create with the new operator should be deleted with the Delete() operator as necessary.

The details of each step will vary depending upon the particular data type.

```
void vtkLineSource::Execute()
{
    int numLines=this->Resolution;
    int numPts=this->Resolution+1;
    float x[3], tc[2], v[3];
    int i, j;
    int pts[2];
    vtkFloatPoints *newPoints;
    vtkFloatTCoords *newTCoords;
    vtkCellArray *newLines;
    vtkPolyData *output = this->GetOutput();
```
Declaration

```
    vtkDebugMacro(<<"Creating line");
```
Initialization
```
    newPoints = new vtkFloatPoints(numPts);
    newTCoords = new vtkFloatTCoords(numPts,2);
    newLines = new vtkCellArray;
    newLines->Allocate(newLines->EstimateSize(numLines,2));
```
Allocation
```
    //
    // Generate points and texture coordinates
    //
    for (i=0; i<3; i++) v[i] = this->Pt2[i] - this->Pt1[i];
    tc[1] = 0.0;
    for (i=0; i<numPts; i++)
      {
      tc[0] = ((float)i/this->Resolution);
      for (j=0; j<3; j++) x[j] = this->Pt1[j] + tc[0]*v[j];
      newPoints->InsertPoint(i,x);
      newTCoords->InsertTCoord(i,tc);
      }
    //
    //  Generate lines
    //
    for (i=0; i < numLines; i++)
      {
      pts[0] = i;
      pts[1] = i+1;
      newLines->InsertNextCell(2,pts);
      }
```
Body
```
    //
    // Update ourselves and release memory
    //
    output->SetPoints(newPoints);
    newPoints->Delete();
    output->GetPointData()->SetTCoords(newTCoords);
    newTCoords->Delete();
    output->SetLines(newLines);
    newLines->Delete();
}
```
Output

Figure A–11 Example source object implementation. This is the Execute() method from vtkLineSource.

Deriving a New Filter Object

Filter objects transform input data into output data. The key to deriving a new filter object is to identify the type of input and output data. The data types you choose depend upon the desired level of generality and performance.

The more general a filter is, the larger the number of dataset types it can process. The advantage of general filters is that if a new type of data is created, a general filter can immediately accommodate it. For example, filters that input vtkDataSet can process any new or existing type of data, since every data type is a subclass of vtkDataSet. General filters are typically not as efficient as filters written with a particular data form in mind. We saw an example of this in Figure **6–36**. You will have to decide what the cost of generality means to your application.

You also may wish to create filters based on the inherent type of the data. The filter vtkStructuredGridGeometryFilter is used to extract geometry from topologically regular grids expressed via a local *i-j-k* coordinate system. Such a filter makes sense only in the context of structured data. Since it is impossible to extract unstructured geometry or polygonal geometry using a *i-j-k* indexing scheme, the filter is not applicable to those data types.

Care must also be used when selecting the output form of a filter. Usually the filtering algorithm dictates the output data type, but if you have a choice we encourage you to choose the most general form. A more general output form means that your filter can be connected a greater number of other filters.

Once you have decided upon your input and output data types, you can implement your filter. A number of special classes exist for you to derive your filter from. These classes combine the instance variable Input and Output and the methods GetOutput() and SetInput() into a single class. Examples include the following.

vtkDataSetToDataSetFilter. Given an input dataset, generate an output dataset. The most general of all filters.

vtkDataSetToPolyFilter. Given an input dataset, generate polygonal data on output.

vtkDataSetToStructuredPointsFilter. Given an input dataset, generate structured points on output.

vtkDataSetToStructuredGridFilter. Given an input dataset, generate a structured grid on output.

vtkDataSetToUnstructuredGridFilter. Given an input dataset, generate unstructured grid data on output.

vtkPolyToPolyFilter. Input and output polygonal data.

vtkPointSetToPointSetFilter. General filter to create a point set from an input point set. Point sets are data that explicitly represent points with a point array (i.e., subclasses of vtkPoints).

vtkStructuredGridToPolyFilter. Create polygonal data from any type of structured data.

vtkStructuredPointsToPolyDataFilter. Given input structured points, create polygonal data on output.

vtkStructuredPointsToStructuredPointsFilter. Input and output structured points.

You should derive your objects from these abstract classes, if possible. To actually create your filter, implement the usual standard constructor, destructor, and instance variable methods. Finally, the algorithm itself is implemented in the Execute() method. Good examples of filter objects to study are vtkWarpVector or vtkContourFilter.

The body of the filter object Execute() method follows the same five steps that the source object does. There are a few important differences. A filter object has an Input instance variable of general type vtkDataSet. Input may have to be cast to the appropriate input type, as enforced by its superclass. The value of Input is guaranteed to be non-NULL upon entry into the Execute() method. Also, in the body of the method, use the convenience methods of vtkPointData to copy and interpolate data whenever possible. Example code illustrating this process is shown in Figure **A–12**.

Deriving a Reference Counted Object

Reference counted objects are objects that are used by datasets to represent data arrays. These objects are passed between filters as network execution proceeds. They are subclasses of vtkRefCount. Examples of reference counted objects include vtkPoints, vtkScalars, vtkVectors, vtkNormals, vtkTCoords, and their subclasses.

The subclasses of these objects depend upon type-specific arrays for implementation. For example, vtkFloatPoints is used to represent arrays of floats, and is a concrete class of vtkPoints. In turn, the class vtkFloatArray is used to represent the data within vtkFloatPoints. Hence, to derive a reference counted object, you must identify the appropriate abstract superclass (e.g., vtkPoints) as well as the particular type you are interested in representing (e.g., float, int, short, or your own type). Then you must create or identify a previously defined type-specific array to support the object you wish to derive. For examples of similar classes, see vtkFloatPoints or vtkIntScalars.

Deriving a New Dataset

Deriving a new dataset means creating a subclass of vtkDataSet. You must design your new dataset to satisfy the abstract interface specified by vtkDataSet. In addition, you may need to construct additional source, filter, and mapper objects, as appropriate. Try to take advantage of the abstract classes vtkPointSet and vtkStructuredData if you can, since they implement many of the virtual functions found in vtkDataSet.

```
void vtkWarpVector::Execute()
{
  vtkPoints *inPts;
  vtkFloatPoints *newPts;
  vtkPointData *pd;
  vtkVectors *inVectors;                                          Declaration
  int i, ptId;
  float *x, *v, newX[3];
  vtkPointSet *input=(vtkPointSet *)this->Input;
  vtkPointSet *output=(vtkPointSet *)this->Output;
  vtkDebugMacro(<<"Warping data with vectors");
  inPts = input->GetPoints();
  pd = input->GetPointData();
  inVectors = pd->GetVectors();
  if ( !inVectors || !inPts )                                     Initialization
    {
    vtkErrorMacro(<<"No input data");
    return;
    }
  newPts = new vtkFloatPoints(inPts->GetNumberOfPoints());        Allocation
//
// Loop over all points, adjusting locations
//
  for (ptId=0; ptId < inPts->GetNumberOfPoints(); ptId++)
    {
    x = inPts->GetPoint(ptId);
    v = inVectors->GetVector(ptId);
    for (i=0; i<3; i++)                                           Body
      {
      newX[i] = x[i] + this->ScaleFactor * v[i];
      }
    newPts->SetPoint(ptId, newX);
    }
//
// Update ourselves and release memory
//
  output->GetPointData()->CopyNormalsOff(); //geom modified
  output->GetPointData()->PassData(input->GetPointData());       Output
  output->SetPoints(newPts);
  newPts->Delete();
}
```

Figure A–12 Example filter object implementation. This is the `Execute()` method from `vtkWarpVector`.

Deriving a New Cell Type

Deriving a new cell type means creating a subclass of vtkCell. To derive a new cell you must design your new cell type to satisfy the abstract interface specified by vtkCell, you must modify CellType.hh, and you must modify the dataset vtkUnstructuredGrid.

To modify CellType.hh you must add a #define to associate a numeric tag with the cell name. This tag is used internally by the class vtkUnstruc-turedGrid and vtkCell::GetCellType() to map cells into appropriate data structures.

The class vtkUnstructuredGrid is modified since it must represent every cell type. Hence the method vtkUnstructuredGrid::GetCell() must be modified accordingly.

One special note: if you create a new cell type you must implement methods to return the "boundary" faces and edges of the cell. These boundary faces and edges are expressed as a type of cell, so they must be valid cell types. This may require implementing new cell types to represent the boundaries of the cell as well.

Interfacing to a Rendering Library

The *Visualization Toolkit* has been designed to accommodate different types of rendering libraries. This includes both *retained* as well as *immediate-mode* rendering libraries.

Retained libraries typically implement a two-step rendering process. In the first step, a library-specific data structure or display list is built. In the second step, the structure is traversed and displayed. The build process is often slow, while the traversal is relatively fast. An example of a retained library is PHIGS.

Immediate-mode libraries display immediately upon loading graphics data. Only a single step is required to render data.

In **vtk** all graphics primitives reflect the two-step process of a retained library, but can accommodate the immediate libraries as well. The two steps are manifested in each graphics primitive as the methods Build() and Draw(). The Build() step provides the opportunity to construct a structure or build a display list. The Draw() step provides the opportunity to traverse the display list, or in the case of immediate-mode renderers, load data directly into the graphics library.

To construct a new renderer for **vtk**, you must construct two general types of objects: the renderer and graphics primitives. The renderer is responsible for coordinating lights, cameras, actors, and actor properties. This entails proper initialization and control of the graphics library. Graphics primitives are lower-level objects that define the lights, cameras, geometry, and properties to the graphics library. They are responsible for converting internal **vtk** data to the appropriate form, and loading the data into the library. (Start by studying the OpenGL object diagram in Figure **A–10**.)

We encourage you to try and use our object design to implement your library interface. The advantages are device independence and system consistency. You may need to extend the graphics classes, particularly the lights or property classes, in order to provide access to special graphics functionality.

Deriving a New Mapper Object

Mappers interface the visualization pipeline to the graphics system, or are used to write data to file. If you need to add a graphics mapper, you may also have to modify the graphics system, so please read that section as well.

Mappers are similar to graphics primitives in that they also implement the Build() and Draw() methods. Mappers must create the appropriate device primitives (e.g., points, polygons, lines, etc.). by interfacing to the renderer. Mappers may also need to map data through a lookup table. Follow the example set by vtkPolyMapper as a starting point.

Writers are easy to implement. The single method WriteData() must be implemented (besides the usual constructor/destructor and instance variable methods).

Introducing User Defined Data

The *Visualization Toolkit* supports user defined data in the visualization network. This is an array of pointers to void* data. Thus user defined data can be arbitrarily complex.

The nature of this support is that user defined data will be passed through the network if it is present and if the filters are such that they copy data from input to output. No mechanism to read, write, or display user defined data is available in **vtk**. To introduce user defined data into the network you will have to add some or all of this functionality.

Improving Performance

The *Visualization Toolkit* has been written to demonstrate visualization algorithms and architecture. We have not made a serious attempt to optimize performance. If you wish to improve performance we suggest you begin by eliminating virtual function access to data, and replace them with inline functions.

The reference counted objects such as vtkPoints, vtkScalars, vtkVectors, vtkNormals, and vtkTCoords are particularly important. These abstract objects specify a interface to concrete classes such as vtkFloatPoints or vtkIntScalars. This design provides the benefit that new concrete types can be introduced without modifying any other objects. The downside is that data is accessed via virtual function pointers.

If you wish to eliminate virtual access, you will have to select a single representation type such as float or double. (For example, if the representation type float is chosen, all point coordinates would be represented with floating point numbers.) Once a type is chosen modify the abstract classes so that they become concrete. Make sure that you use `inline` data access functions.

A variation of this idea is to allow some data types to be abstract, while others are concrete. As an example, you might allow scalars to be of various types (`char`, `short`, `int`, `float`), while all other data is represented with `float`'s.

Another area to improve performance is to tune the interface to the graphics libraries. The *Visualization Toolkit* has been designed to be portable across a variety of graphics libraries. Thus, we have sacrificed performance for flexibility and portability. If your application is to run with a particular library, or your data is of a particular form, you can often take advantage of characteristics of the graphics library. For example, some graphics libraries allow you to load large amounts of data (i.e., a display list) with a single function call. By converting the **vtk** data structures into a display list, rendering can be greatly accelerated.

A.5 vtk File Formats

The *Visualization Toolkit* provides a number of source and writer objects to read and write various data file formats. The *Visualization Toolkit* also provides some of its own file formats. The main reason for creating yet another data file format is to offer a consistent data representation scheme for a variety of dataset types, and to provide a simple method to communicate data between software. Whenever possible, we recommend that you use formats that are more widely used. But if this is not possible, the *Visualization Toolkit* formats described here can be used instead. Note, however, that these formats are not yet supported by other tools.

The visualization file formats consist of five basic parts.

1. The first part is the file version and identifier. This part contains the single line: `# vtk DataFile Version x.x`. This line must be exactly as shown with the exception of the version number `x.x`, which will vary with different releases of **vtk**.

2. The second part is the header. The header consists a character string terminated by end-of-line character `\n`. The header is 256 characters maximum. The header can be used to describe the data and include any other pertinent information.

3. The next part is the file format. The file format describes the type of file, either ASCII or binary. On this line the single word `ASCII` or `BINARY` must appear.

4. The fourth part is the dataset structure. The geometry part describes the geometry and topology of the dataset. This part begins with a line containing the keyword `DATASET` followed by a keyword describing the type of dataset. Then, depending upon the type of dataset, other keyword/data combinations define the actual data.

```
# vtk DataFile Version 1.0  ⌉(1)
Really cool data  ⌉(2)
ASCII | BINARY  ⌉(3)
DATASET type      ⌉
...                (4)
POINT_DATA n     ⌉
...                (5)
```

Part 1: Header

Part 2: Title (256 characters maximum, terminated with newline \n character)

Part 3: Data type, either ASCII or BINARY

Part 4: Geometry/topology. *Type* is one of: STRUCTURED_POINTS
STRUCTURED_GRID
UNSTRUCTURED_GRID
POLYDATA

Part 5: Dataset attributes. The number of data items *n* of each type must match the number of points in the dataset.

Figure A–13 Overview of five parts of **vtk** data file format.

5. The final part describes the dataset attributes. This part begins with the keyword POINT_DATA, followed by an integer number specifying the number of points. Other keyword/data combinations then define the actual data values.

An overview of the file format is shown in Figure **A–13**. The first three parts are mandatory, but the other two are optional. Thus you have the flexibility of mixing and matching dataset attributes and geometry, either by operating system file manipulation, or using **vtk** filters to merge data. Keywords are case insensitive, and may be separated by whitespace.

Before describing the data file formats please note the following.

- *dataType* is one of the types bit, unsigned_char, short, int, float, or double. These keywords are used to describe the form of the data, both for reading from file, as well as constructing the appropriate internal objects. Not all data types are supported for all classes.

- All keyword phrases are written in ASCII form whether the file is binary or ASCII. The binary section of the file (if in binary form) is the data proper; i.e., the numbers that define points coordinates, scalars, cell indices, etc.

- Indices are 0-offset. Thus the first point is point id 0.

- If both the data attribute and geometry/topology part are present in the file, then the number of data values defined in the data attribute part must exactly match the number of points defined in the geometry/topology part.

- Cell types and indices are of type `int`.

- Binary data must be placed into the file immediately after the "newline" (`\n`) character from the previous ASCII keyword and parameter sequence.

- The geometry/topology description must occur prior to the data attribute description. .

Dataset Format

The *Visualization Toolkit* supports four different dataset formats: structured points, structured grid, unstructured grid, and polygonal data. These formats are as follows.

- Structured Points
  The file format supports 1D, 2D, and 3D structured point datasets. The dimensions n_x, n_y, n_z must be greater than or equal to 1. The aspect ratios a_x, a_y, a_z must be greater than 0.

  ```
  DATASET STRUCTURED_POINTS
  DIMENSIONS n_x n_y n_z
  ORIGIN x y z
  ASPECT_RATIO a_x a_y a_z
  ```

- Structured Grid
  The file format supports 1D, 2D, and 3D structured grid datasets. The dimensions n_x, n_y, n_z must be greater than or equal to 1. The point coordinates are defined by the data in the `POINTS` section. This consists of *x-y-z* data values for each point.

  ```
  DATASET STRUCTURED_GRID
  DIMENSIONS n_x n_y n_z
  POINTS n dataType
  p_0x p_0y p_0z
  p_1x p_1y p_1z
  ...
  p_(n-1)x p_(n-1)y p_(n-1)z
  ```

- Polygonal Data
  The polygonal dataset consists of arbitrary combinations of surface graphics primitives points (and poly-points), lines (and poly-lines), polygons (of various types), and triangle strips. Polygonal data is defined by the `POINTS` `VERTICES`, `LINES`, `POLYGONS`, or `TRIANGLE_STRIPS` sections. The `POINTS` definition is the same as we saw for structured grid datasets. The `VERTICES`, `LINES`, `POLYGONS`, or `TRIANGLE_STRIPS` keywords define the polygo-

nal dataset topology. Each of these keywords requires two parameters: the number of cells n and the size of the cell list *size*. The cell list size is the total number of integer values required to represent the list (i.e., sum of *numPoints* and connectivity indices over each cell). None of the keywords VERTICES, LINES, POLYGONS, or TRIANGLE_STRIPS is required.

```
DATASET POLYDATA
POINTS n dataType
```
$p_{0x}\ p_{0y}\ p_{0z}$
$p_{1x}\ p_{1y}\ p_{1z}$

...

$p_{(n-1)x}\ p_{(n-1)y}\ p_{(n-1)z}$

```
VERTICES n size
```
$numPoints_0,\ i_0,\ j_0,\ k_0,\ ...$
$numPoints_1,\ i_1,\ j_1,\ k_1,\ ...$

...

$numPoints_{n-1},\ i_{n-1},\ j_{n-1},\ k_{n-1},\ ...$

```
LINES n size
```
$numPoints_0,\ i_0,\ j_0,\ k_0,\ ...$
$numPoints_1,\ i_1,\ j_1,\ k_1,\ ...$

...

$numPoints_{n-1},\ i_{n-1},\ j_{n-1},\ k_{n-1},\ ...$

```
POLYGONS n size
```
$numPoints_0,\ i_0,\ j_0,\ k_0,\ ...$
$numPoints_1,\ i_1,\ j_1,\ k_1,\ ...$

...

$numPoints_{n-1},\ i_{n-1},\ j_{n-1},\ k_{n-1},\ ...$

```
TRIANGLE_STRIPS n size
```
$numPoints_0,\ i_0,\ j_0,\ k_0,\ ...$
$numPoints_1,\ i_1,\ j_1,\ k_1,\ ...$

...

$numPoints_{n-1},\ i_{n-1},\ j_{n-1},\ k_{n-1},\ ...$

- Unstructured Grid

  The unstructured grid dataset consists of arbitrary combinations of any possible cell type. Unstructured grids are defined by points, cells, and cell types. The CELLS keyword requires two parameters: the number of cells n and the size of the cell list *size*. The cell list size is the total number of integer values required to represent the list (i.e., sum of *numPoints* and connectivity indices over each cell). The CELL_TYPES keyword requires a single parameter: the number of cells n. This value should match the value specified by the CELLS keyword. The cell types data is a single integer value per cell that specified cell type (see Cell.hh or Figure **A–14**).

```
DATASET UNSTRUCTURED_GRID
POINTS n dataType
```
$p_{0x}\, p_{0y}\, p_{0z}$
$p_{1x}\, p_{1y}\, p_{1z}$
...
$p_{(n-1)x}\, p_{(n-1)y}\, p_{(n-1)z}$

```
CELLS n size
```
$numPoints_0,\ i, j, k, l, ...$
$numPoints_1,\ i, j, k, l, ...$
$numPoints_2,\ i, j, k, l, ...$
...
$numPoints_{n-1},\ i, j, k, l, ...$

```
CELL_TYPES n
```
$type_0$
$type_1$
$type_2$
...
$type_{n-1}$

Attribute Format

The *Visualization Toolkit* supports the following point attributes: scalars (single-valued as well as color scalars of 1, 2, 3, and 4 bytes), vectors, normals, texture coordinates (1D, 2D, and 3D), and 3×3 tensors. In addition, a lookup table using the RGBA color specification can be defined as well.

Each type of point attribute data has a *dataName* associated with it. This is a character string (without embedded whitespace) used to identify a particular data. The *dataName* is used by the **vtk** readers to extract data. As a result, more than one point attribute of the same type can be included in a file. For example, two different scalar fields, pressure and temperature, can be contained in the same file. (If the appropriate *dataName* is not specified in the **vtk** reader, then the first data of that type is extracted from the file.)

- Scalars
  Scalar definition includes specification of a lookup table. The definition of a lookup table is optional. If not specified, the default **vtk** table will be used (and *tableName* should be "default").

```
SCALARS dataName dataType
LOOKUP_TABLE tableName
```

s_0

s_1

...

s_{n-1}

The definition of color scalars varies depending upon the number of values (*nValues*) per scalar. If the file format is ASCII, the color scalars are defined using *nValues* float values between (0,1). If the file format is BINARY, the stream of data consists of *nValues* unsigned char values per scalar value.

COLOR_SCALARS *dataName nValues*

$c_{00}\ c_{01}\ \cdots\ c_{0(nValues-1)}$

$c_{10}\ c_{11}\ \cdots\ c_{1(nValues-1)}$

...

$c_{(n-1)0}\ c_{(n-1)1}\ \cdots\ c_{(n-1)(nValues-1)}$

- Lookup Table

  The *tableName* field is a character string (without imbedded white space) used to identify the lookup table. This label is used by the **vtk** reader to extract a specific table.

  Each entry in the lookup table is a rgba[4] (*red-green-blue-alpha*) array (*alpha* is opacity where *alpha=0* is transparent). If the file format is ASCII, the lookup table values must be float values between (0,1). If the file format is BINARY, the stream of data must be four unsigned char values per table entry.

  LOOKUP_TABLE *tableName size*

  $r_0\ g_0\ b_0\ a_0$

  $r_1\ g_1\ b_1\ a_1$

  ...

  $r_{size-1}\ g_{size-1}\ b_{size-1}\ a_{size-1}$

- Vectors

  VECTORS *dataName dataType*

  $v_{0x}\ v_{0y}\ v_{0z}$

  $v_{1x}\ v_{1y}\ v_{1z}$

  ...

  $v_{(n-1)x}\ v_{(n-1)y}\ v_{(n-1)z}$

- Normals

  Normals are assumed normalized $|n| = 1$.

NORMALS *dataName dataType*

$n_{0x}\, n_{0y}\, n_{0z}$

$n_{1x}\, n_{1y}\, n_{1z}$

...

$n_{(n-1)x}\, n_{(n-1)y}\, n_{(n-1)z}$

- Texture Coordinates
  Texture coordinates of 1, 2, and 3 dimensions are supported.

  TEXTURE_COORDINATES *dataName dim dataType*

  $t_{00}\, t_{01} \cdots t_{0(dim-1)}$

  $t_{10}\, t_{11} \cdots t_{1(dim-1)}$

  ...

  $t_{(n-1)0}\, t_{(n-1)1} \cdots t_{(n-1)(dim-1)}$

- Tensors
  Currently only 3×3 real-valued, symmetric tensors are supported.

  TENSORS *dataName dataType*

  $t^0{}_{00}\, t^0{}_{01}\, t^0{}_{02}$

  $t^0{}_{10}\, t^0{}_{11}\, t^0{}_{12}$

  $t^0{}_{20}\, t^0{}_{21}\, t^0{}_{22}$

  $t^1{}_{00}\, t^1{}_{01}\, t^1{}_{02}$

  $t^1{}_{10}\, t^1{}_{11}\, t^1{}_{12}$

  $t^1{}_{20}\, t^1{}_{21}\, t^1{}_{22}$

  ...

  $t^{n-1}{}_{00}\, t^{n-1}{}_{01}\, t^{n-1}{}_{02}$

  $t^{n-1}{}_{10}\, t^{n-1}{}_{11}\, t^{n-1}{}_{12}$

  $t^{n-1}{}_{20}\, t^{n-1}{}_{21}\, t^{n-1}{}_{22}$

Examples

The first example is a cube represented by six polygonal faces. There are scalar data associated with the eight vertices. A lookup table of eight colors is also defined.

```
# vtk DataFile Version 1.0
Cube example
ASCII
DATASET POLYDATA
POINTS 8 float
```

```
0.0 0.0 0.0
1.0 0.0 0.0
1.0 1.0 0.0
0.0 1.0 0.0
0.0 0.0 1.0
1.0 0.0 1.0
1.0 1.0 1.0
0.0 1.0 1.0
POLYGONS 6 30
4 0 1 2 3
4 4 5 6 7
4 0 1 5 4
4 2 3 7 6
4 0 4 7 3
4 1 2 6 5
POINT_DATA 8
SCALARS sample_scalars float
LOOKUP_TABLE my_table
0.0
1.0
2.0
3.0
4.0
5.0
6.0
7.0
LOOKUP_TABLE my_table 8
0.0 0.0 0.0 1.0
1.0 0.0 0.0 1.0
0.0 1.0 0.0 1.0
1.0 1.0 0.0 1.0
0.0 0.0 1.0 1.0
1.0 0.0 1.0 1.0
0.0 1.0 1.0 1.0
1.0 1.0 1.0 1.0
```

The next example is a volume of dimension $3 \times 4 \times 5$. Since no lookup table is defined, either the user must create one in **vtk**, or the default lookup table will be used.

```
# vtk DataFile Version 1.0
Volume example
ASCII
DATASET STRUCTURED_POINTS
DIMENSIONS 3 4 6
ASPECT_RATIO 1 1 1
ORIGIN 0 0 0
POINT_DATA 72
SCALARS volume_scalars char
LOOKUP_TABLE default
0 0 0 0 0 0 0 0 0 0 0 0
0 5 10 15 20 25 25 20 15 10 5 0
0 10 20 30 40 50 50 40 30 20 10 0
```

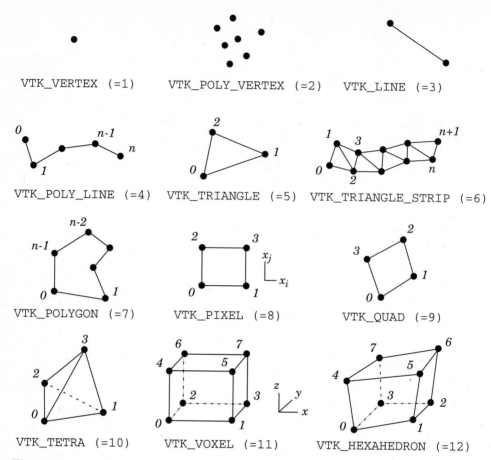

Figure A–14 Cell type specification. Use the include file `CellType.hh` to manipulate cell types.

```
0 10 20 30 40 50 50 40 30 20 10 0
0 5 10 15 20 25 25 20 15 10 5 0
0 0 0 0 0 0 0 0 0 0 0 0
```

The third example is an unstructured grid containing all twelve cell types. The file contains scalar and vector data.

```
# vtk DataFile Version 1.0
Unstructured Grid Example
ASCII

DATASET UNSTRUCTURED_GRID
POINTS 27 float
0 0 0    1 0 0    2 0 0    0 1 0    1 1 0    2 1 0
0 0 1    1 0 1    2 0 1    0 1 1    1 1 1    2 1 1
```

```
0 1 2     1 1 2     2 1 2     0 1 3     1 1 3     2 1 3
0 1 4     1 1 4     2 1 4     0 1 5     1 1 5     2 1 5
0 1 6     1 1 6     2 1 6

CELLS 11 60
8 0 1 4 3 6 7 10 9
8 1 2 5 4 7 8 11 10
4 6 10 9 12
4 5 11 10 14
6 15 16 17 14 13 12
6 18 15 19 16 20 17
4 22 23 20 19
3 21 22 18
3 22 19 18
2 26 25
1 24

CELL_TYPES 11
12
12
10
10
7
6
9
5
5
3
1


POINT_DATA 27
SCALARS scalars float
LOOKUP_TABLE default
0.0     1.0     2.0     3.0     4.0     5.0
6.0     7.0     8.0     9.0     10.0     11.0
12.0     13.0     14.0     15.0     16.0     17.0
18.0     19.0     20.0     21.0     22.0     23.0
24.0     25.0     26.0
VECTORS vectors float
1 0 0     1 1 0     0 2 0     1 0 0     1 1 0     0 2 0
1 0 0     1 1 0     0 2 0     1 0 0     1 1 0     0 2 0
0 0 1     0 0 1     0 0 1     0 0 1     0 0 1     0 0 1
0 0 1     0 0 1     0 0 1     0 0 1     0 0 1     0 0 1
0 0 1     0 0 1     0 0 1
```

Additional examples are available in the data examples directory.

CD-ROM Organization

Now that we have dealt with the complexities of data visualization, we face the greatest challenge of all: reading and extracting information from the CD-ROM. This appendix quickly discusses what is on the CD-ROM, how to access it, and potential problems you may encounter. Since the contents of the CD-ROM may change at some point in the future, the final word on these topics will be found in the README files on the CD-ROM itself.

B.1 Introduction

The CD-ROM that comes with this book has been designed to work with both Unix and Microsoft Windows systems. Since these two systems store their information differently, there will be some parts of the CD-ROM that only apply to Unix systems and vice-versa.

The first example of this is in the top level README files: README.vtk and README.TXT. The README files contain important information that may be more recent than the information in this appendix. Many of the directories on the CD-ROM have README files. At the top level, README.UNIX is formatted so that it can be read on Unix systems, while README.TXT has been formatted for Microsoft Windows. Please read these README files, and assume that the information contained there is the final word on installing and accessing the data on the CD-ROM.

At the top level directory of the CD-ROM you will find the following main directories:

- `binaries` - pre-compiled libraries and executables for some Unix systems,

- `dist` - source code and data for **vtk** on Unix and Windows,

- `images` - a collection of pictures stored in GIF format,

- `pcdist` - files used by the Windows setup program, and

- `vtkData` - HTML (Hyper-Text Markup Language) files for **vtk**.

If you use pre-compiled binaries and/or libraries make sure that the compiler, operating system, and shared libraries are all consistent. Otherwise, you will likely encounter unexpected behavior.

B.2 Microsoft Windows Systems

This CD-ROM is designed to work with Microsoft Windows95 or Microsoft WindowsNT. It will not work properly under Microsoft Windows 3.0, 3.1 or 3.11.

Installing Pre-Compiled Binaries

Installing the pre-compiled executables on Windows systems requires running the program SETUP.EXE on the CD-ROM. This will guide you through an installation process, create a program group, and set up a number of examples. You can run the examples by double clicking on their icons. This process should be quick and easy.

Extracting Source Code

Source code for **vtk** under Windows is kept in the directory dist\win32. There is a README file in that directory describing what is there. Currently we have placed a tar file that contains all the source and include files for the PC. Run the tar.exe (found on the CD-ROM) on the tar file to extract the source code on your hard drive. (We did this because the CD-ROM readers typically mangle the filenames. Using the tar process extracts the filenames intact.) This is likely to change in the future – refer to the README file as necessary.

Note that not all the examples found in the text have been placed into the PC distribution. This goes for both Tcl and C++ files. However, the source code is available on the CD-ROM, so you can retrieve it as required. These files are found in the dist directory. The dist\examples\cc directory contains C++ code; while the dist\examples\tcl directory contains Tcl/Tk examples. Note that there are differences in carriage returns between Windows and Unix systems; you will have to accommodate this.

B.3 Unix Systems

This CD-ROM has been created using the Rock Ridge extensions. These extensions enable us to store Unix filenames and directories. Unfortunately some Unix systems cannot handle these extensions. If you install the CD-ROM and the filenames are all upper case and truncated to eight characters followed by a three character extension, then your system cannot handle Rock Ridge extensions.

For these systems we have created a Unix tar file called CD.TAR;1. This file contains the important, core information on the CD-ROM. The location of the file CD.TAR;1 is at the top level directory on the CD-ROM. (Note: on some systems the name of the file will appear as CD.TAR without the version number.) You can untar the file using a command like the following:

```
cd /to/where_you/want_vtk/to_go
tar -xvf /cdrom_location/CD.TAR\;1
```

This will give you all of the images, binaries, vtkData and dist directories excluding the dist/data directory. This will take up about 80 megabytes of disk space. To access the data files you should probably create symbolic links to the ones you want to use since they are quite large. The Unix ln command can be used to create symbolic links.

B.4 HTML Files

Much of the documentation for the *Visualization Toolkit* is stored in HTML (Hyper-Text Markup Language) files. These files can be viewed using any web browser such as Mosaic or Netscape. You should start with the file vtk.html which provides an overview and links to the rest of the HTML files.

B.5 Problems

If you encounter problems the first step is to make sure you have read all of the README files on the CD-ROM. If you have access to the World Wide Web you should try looking at the Frequently Asked Questions (FAQ) list that can be found at http://www.cs.rpi.edu/~martink. We will be placing bug fixes, new classes and data, and other interesting information at this site. Good luck!

Color Plates

*I*n the following pages we have collected many of the black and white images in this text and reproduced them in color. Our goals are to provide you with an overview of the most common visualization algorithms, and to demonstrate their practical application.

The color plates have been organized according to the categories listed below. For each category we have included a series of color plates demonstrating important visualization concepts or techniques. These categories are as follows:

- *Computer Graphics*. In this section we demonstrate various concepts in computer graphics including surface properties, shading methods, and rendering techniques.

- *Scalar Visualization*. We show how to visualize single-valued scalar data using color mapping, a variety of contouring techniques, carpet plots, and scalar generation.

- *Vector Visualization*. Vectors are data consisting of a magnitude and direction. In this section we show how to visualize vectors using hedgehogs, warping, displacement plots, time animation, and streamlines.

- *Tensor Visualization*. Tensors can be described as n-dimensional tables. We show how to visualize 3×3 real-valued, symmetric tensors. Methods described include tensor ellipsoids and hyperstreamlines.

- *Modelling*. Modelling is a catchall category for many visualization, dataset transformation, and geometric construction algorithms. In this section we describe techniques for modelling geometry; specialized visualization methods like resampling, probing, and glyphing; operations on datasets; texture-based algorithms; and multi-dimensional visualization.

- *Applications*. Here we've collected images from the applications chapter (Chapter 11), and a few other spots throughout the text.

If any of these concepts are unfamiliar to you, or you would like additional information, please refer to the text proper. The computer graphics images are from Chapters 3 and 7. The algorithms are described in the two chapters on visualization algorithms, Chapters 6 and 9.

Part of the fun of practicing visualization is the sheer aesthetic pleasure of the image. Unlike computer graphics, the purpose of visualization is to convey information – visualizations are not necessarily physically realistic or artful. But despite this quality, visualizations are beautiful anyway, mostly due to the fact that they are eminently useful. To better appreciate these images, you may wish to reflect on the size and complexity of the underlying data. The true value of these images is based on their ability to communicate information in a clear and simple manner.

We hope you enjoy these images.

Computer Graphics. Computer graphics is the foundation of data visualization. From a practical point of view, visualization techniques transform data into graphics primitives. The methods of computer graphics are then used to create the final images.

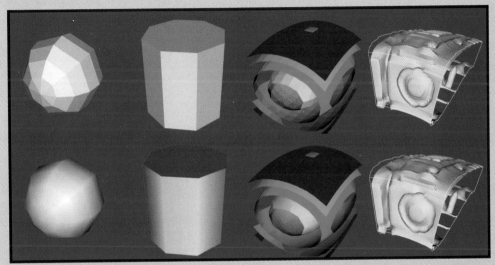

Plate 1   Flat and Gouraud shading. Different shading methods can dramatically improve the look of an object represented with polygons. On the top, flat shading uses a constant surface normal across each polygon. On the bottom, Gouraud shading interpolates colors from polygon vertices to give a smoother look.

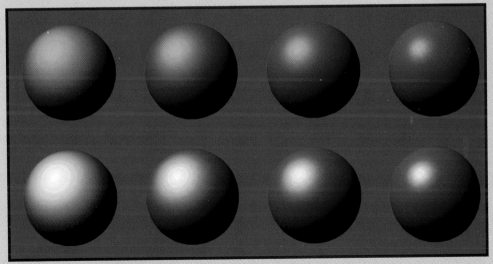

Plate 2   Effects of specular coefficients. Specular coefficients control the apparent "shininess" of objects. The top row has a specular intensity value of 0.5; the bottom row 1.0. Along the horizontal direction the specular power changes. The values (from left to right) are 5, 10, 20, 40.

Plate 3   Camera movement centered at the focal point.The plate to the right shows some common camera movements. Azimuth is rotation around the view up vector. Elevation is rotation around the vector defined as the cross product between the projection and view up vectors. Roll is a rotation around the view plane normal, which is typically parallel to the projection vector.

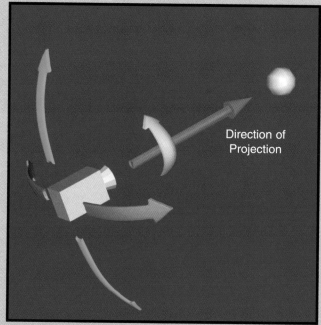

Plate 4   Camera movement centered at the camera position. Yaw is a rotation of the camera around the view up vector. Roll is a rotation around the view plane normal. Pitch is a rotation around the vector defined by the cross product between the view up vector and view plane normal.

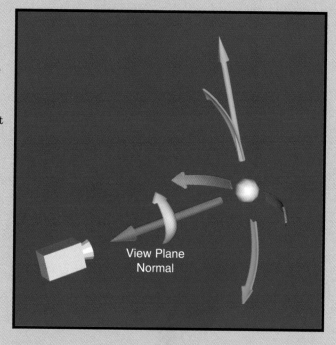

Scalar Visualization. Scalars are single valued data items. Examples of scalar data include pressure, temperature, or X-ray intensity. Scalar data are the simplest and most common form of visualization data.

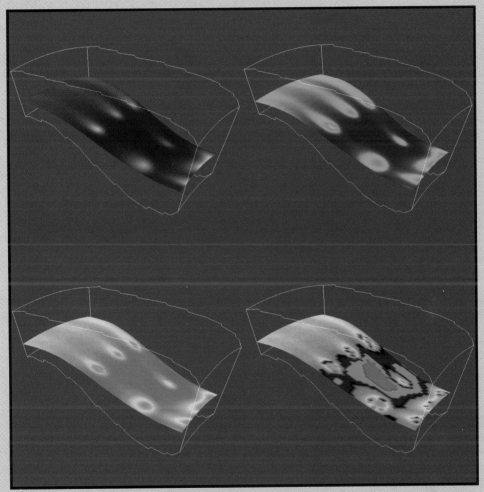

Plate 13 Comparison of four color maps in a combustion chamber. Effective color mapping requires careful selection of a color lookup table, or transfer function. This selection requires sensitivity to the qualities of human perception, plus any special features in the data itself. The image in the upper left uses a gray-scale lookup table. The image in the upper right uses a blue to red rainbow table. The lower left image uses a red to blue table. The final image uses a special table designed to accentuate transitions in the data. The data shown is flow density.

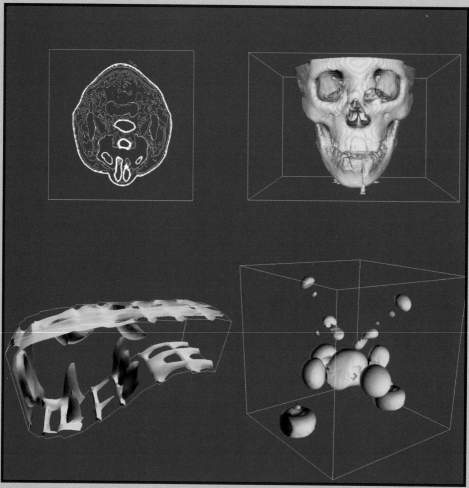

Plate 14   Applications of contouring. Contouring is one of the most important and widely used visualization techniques. Contouring is used to generate lines of constant scalar value in 2D (isolines), and isosurfaces in 3D. The contour lines in the upper left were generated from medical slice data. The isosurface in the upper right was generated from a series of slices (i.e., a volume) using the marching cubes isosurface algorithm. The lower left image shows an isosurface of flow density. The lower right image is an isosurface from a high potential iron protein molecule.

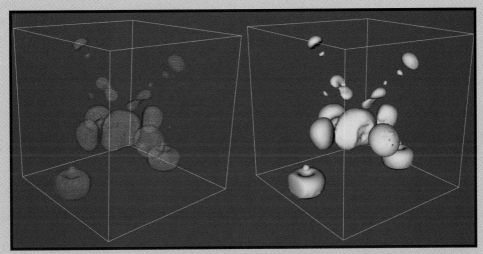

Plate 15   Dividing cubes. Dividing cubes is a contouring algorithm that represents isocontours with dense point clouds. As long as the points are generated at display resolution, the point clouds appear solid. The left image consists of 154,857 points. The right image consists of 1,917,900 points.

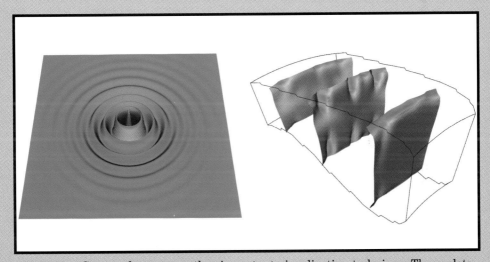

Plate 16   Carpet plots are another important visualization technique. These plots are typically used to visualize functions of the form . $F(x,y) = z$. A plane (in the x-y plane) is distorted according to z function value. Color mapping is often used to introduce another variable into the visualization. The left image above shows the function $F(x,y) = e^{-r} \cos (10r)$. The colors indicate derivative values. The right image shows displacement of planes with flow energy. The colors also correspond to flow energy.

Vector Visualization. Vectors are data items with both a magnitude and direction. Typical examples of 3D vectors are velocity, displacement, and momentum. Vector data is especially important in computational fluid dynamics (CFD). CFD is the study of fluid flow using computers.

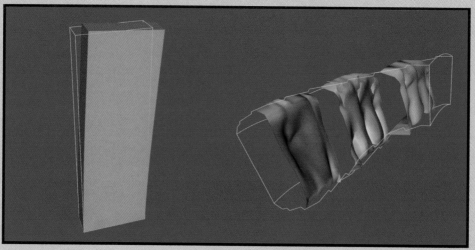

Plate 17   Warping geometry with vector data. The left image shows a simple beam deformed with displacement vectors. The wireframe outline represents the undeformed configuration. On the right, planes are deformed with flow velocity. The color map depicts flow density.

Plate 18   Displacement plot in combination with vector warping to visualize vibration. A displacement plot is created by computing the dot product between the vector and surface normal at each vertex. The resulting scalar value is color mapped to indicate relative surface motion. Red areas are moving in the direction of the surface normal; blue areas in the opposite direction. Black areas indicate little or no motion in the direction of the surface normal. These black regions are similar to nodal lines used to visualize modes of vibration. The vibration mode shown here is the second torsional.

Plate 19 Hedgehogs of blood flow in the human carotid arteries. Hedgehogs are created by placing a line in the direction of the vector at a particular point. The line is also scaled proportional to the vector magnitude. Scalar data is often used to color the line. In 2D and for small numbers of 3D vectors, hedgehogs are quite effective. For greater numbers of vectors, such as the image shown here, it is difficult to see which direction the line is pointing, and to distinguish information in the resulting visual clutter. This MRI data has been specially acquired to determine tissue density as well as blood velocity.

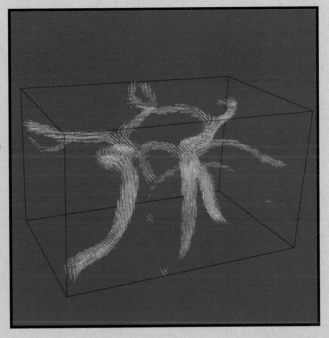

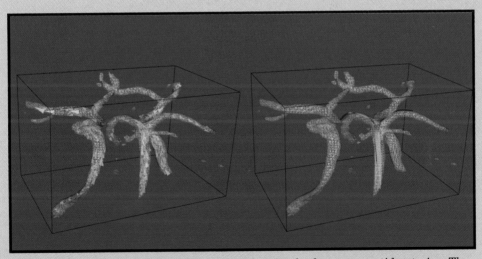

Plate 20 3D vector glyphs and streamtubes in the human carotid arteries. The cone glyphs in the left image clearly indicate vector direction, but small numbers must be used for visual clarity. A natural extension of hedgehogs is to connect the line segments (via a numerical integration technique) into extended lines, or as shown on the right, thick lines or tubes.

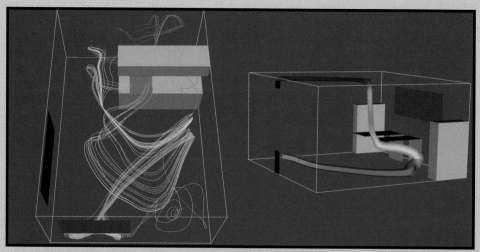

Plate 21   Examples of streamlines and streamtubes. On the left, streamlines are computed from a CFD analysis of ventilation in a small kitchen. The streamlines are color mapped with air pressure data. Thirty streamlines are initiated under a window and allowed to travel through the kitchen. On the right, a single streamtube is initiated in an office near a ventilation duct. The streamtube travels through the office and exits through an exhaust duct at top. The radius of the tube varies according to flow velocity. Slower speeds result in fatter tubes; larger speeds result in thinner tubes. (Data Courtesy Dr. L. Besse, ETH, Zurich.)

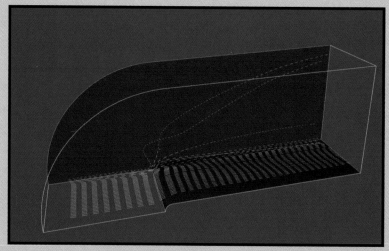

Plate 22   Dashed streamlines. More than two dozen streamlines are initiated upstream of a blunt fin projecting into a moving air stream. Each dash is of equal length measured in units of time. As a result, longer dashes are in regions of higher velocity.

Tensor Visualization. General tensors can be described as n-dimensional tables. Recent research has focused on visualizing 3 x 3 real-valued, symmetric matrices. These types of tensors are found in the study of materials (both solid and liquid). Examples include strain

Plate 23   Tensor ellipsoids. The eigenvectors of a 3 **x** 3 real symmetric matrix define the axes of an ellipsoid. The length of the axes is determined by the eigenvalues. In stress analysis, these axes are the principle axes of stress. In this example a single point load is applied to an elastic material, resulting in singular stress and strain values. At the surface of the material the ellipsoids flatten because there is no stress perpendicular to the surface. Near the singularity the ellipsoids elongate and point in the direction of the load point.

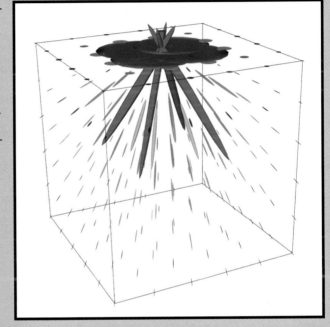

Plate 24
Hyperstreamlines. The tensor eigenvectors define three perpendicular vector fields corresponding to the major, medium, and minor eigenvalues. One of these fields is used to generate a streamline. The other two fields control the cross-section of an ellipse that is swept along the streamline. In this example, the hyperstreamlines flare as they approach the stress singularity. A plane is also shown to show the symmetric nature of the stress field. The plane is colored by effective stress, and uses a different lookup table then the hyperstreamlines.

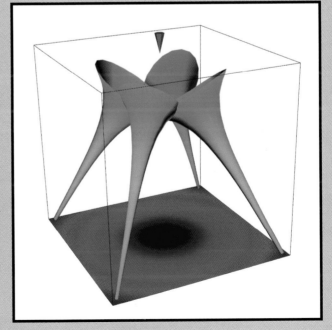

Modelling. Many visualization techniques cannot be easily classified as scalar, vector, or tensor techniques. We categorize these as modelling techniques. Examples include glyphing, resampling, and texture methods. Other algorithms are used to generate geometry or operate on data. Implicit modelling, calculating surface normals, polygon reduction, and data extraction are typical examples. We also classify these as modelling techniques

Plate 25   Examples of source objects that procedurally generate polygonal models. These nine images represent some of the capability of the Visualization Toolkit. From upper left in reading order: sphere, cone, cylinder, cube, plane, text, random point cloud, disk (with or without holes), and line source. More complex geometry can be read from CAD or other modelling systems via reader objects.

Plate 26 Implicit modelling used to construct geometric objects. Implicit modelling employs functions of the form , where c is a constant. These so-called implicit functions can be sampled on a regular grid (i.e., a volume) and then rendered with surface or volume rendering techniques. Moreover, it is easy to combine these functions using boolean operations such as union, intersection, and difference. This ice cream cone was generated using a cone clipped with two planes, and a sphere intersected with another sphere. An isosurface was then extracted with marching cubes by choosing a value for the constant c.

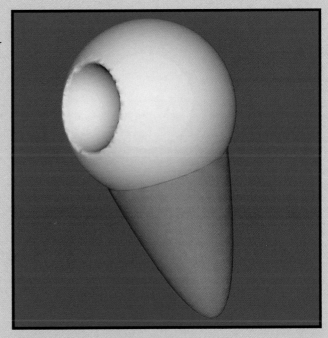

Plate 27 Implicit functions can also be used to select data. In this example, two ellipsoidal quadric functions are joined in a boolean operation and then used to select a subsample of the original volume data. The extracted voxel data (shown colored and slightly shrunk), is much smaller in size than the original dataset. Thus, data in important regions can be selected and processed much faster than if the whole dataset was processed.

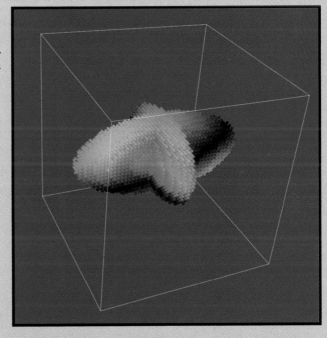

Plate 28   Implicit modelling based on distance function. Implicit models can be created by methods other than implicit functions. In this example, the lines (shown in purple) spell the word "HELLO". Then, for each point in a volume, a distance function to the line segments are computed. An offset surface at a specified distance from the lines is then extracted using marching cubes. The offset surface is shown in translucent red.

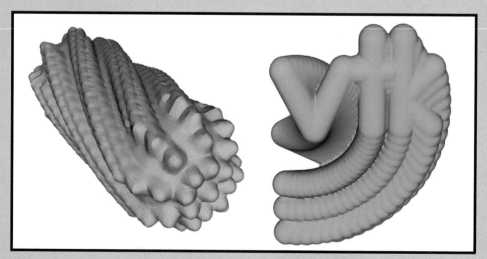

Plate 29   Implicit modelling used to create swept surfaces. The method described in the previous plate is combined with the boolean union operation as a part moves through a volume. In the left image, a mace is translated and rotated to create the swept surface shown. In the right, the letters "vtk" are rotated and translated to create the swept vtk. The bumps in the surface can be eliminated by choosing a smaller step size.

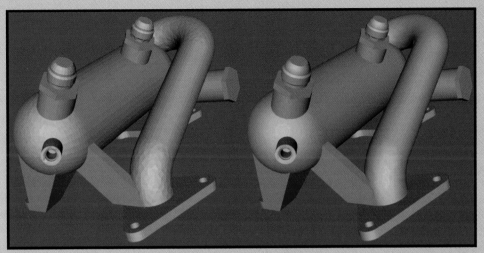

Plate 30 Generating surface normals. Geometry in graphics systems is often represented with polygons. To achieve smooth shading (compared to a faceted look), surface normals at the vertices of polygons are required. These images show how computed surface normals improve the rendered appearance.

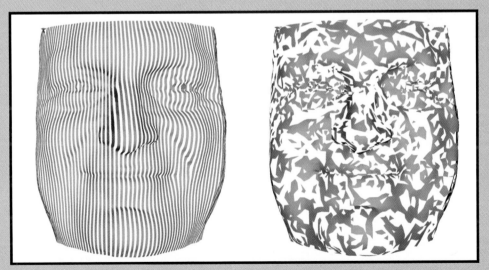

Plate 31 Creating triangle strips. Triangle strips are a type of graphics primitive that can be compactly stored in memory, and are often faster to render. The image on the left shows a selected set of triangle strips (every other strip turned off) generated from a structured dataset. The image on the right shows a selected subset of triangle strips generated from an unstructured dataset.

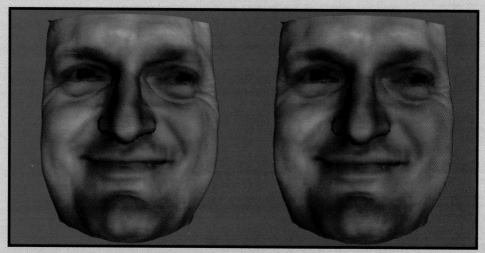

Plate 32   Decimation of a triangle mesh. Decimation is one of a family of polygon reduction techniques. These techniques aim at reducing the size of a polygonal mesh while preserving a good approximation to the original data. This example compares two triangle meshes. The one on the right has been reduced 90%.

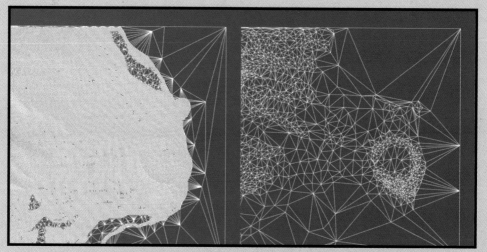

Plate 33   Decimation of digital elevation data from Honolulu, Hawaii. The mesh on the left has been reduced 31.1% by removing co-planar triangles (from 403,680 to 277,952 triangles). A portion of the shoreline is shown. On the right, the same area with total reduction 92.6% (29,525 triangles remaining). Data source Lee Moore, Webster Research Center, Xerox Corporation.

Plate 34   Glyphs used to indicate surface normals. Glyphing is one of the most versatile visualization techniques. Glyphs are often designed to show many variables simultaneously. The secret to good glyph design is a simple, and intuitive, relationship between data variable(s) and glyph features.

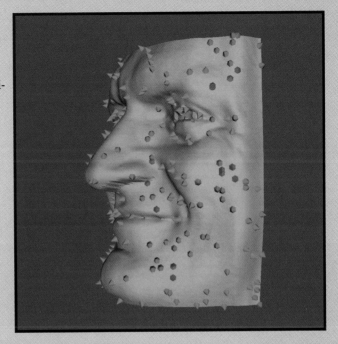

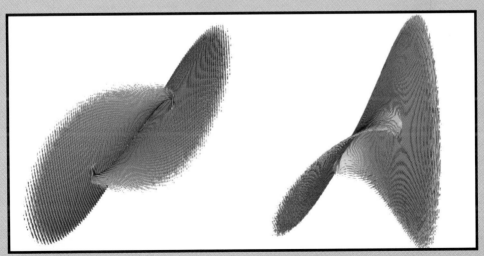

Plate 35   The Lorenz strange attractor. The Lorenz equations are expressed as a system of differential equations. These equations are numerically integrated to form a trajectory. To generate the isosurface shown, we count the number of times the trajectory passes through the voxels of a volume dataset. The isosurface value is a user-specified count value.

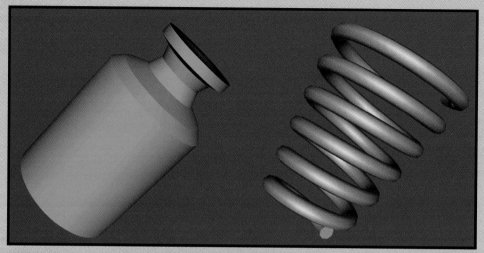

Plate 36 Rotational extrusion. Extrusion, or sweeping, is a simple, but powerful, modelling technique. On the left an axisymmetric bottle is created by sweeping a profile curve. On the right, a spring is created by sweeping a circle while varying its sweep radius and translating it at the same time.

Plate 37 Linear extrusion tied to data values. The letters of the alphabet are used as extrusion primitives. The amount of extrusion is controlled by the frequency of occurrence of the letters in a text document.

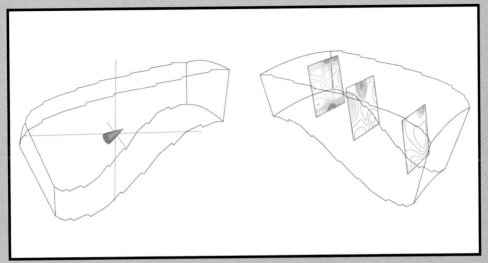

Plate 38 Probing datasets. Probing is a method of interpolating data values at one or more points. The left image shows a cone glyph oriented and sized according to vector and scalar data. The position of the cone is at the focus of the 3D cursor (shown in red). The scalar and vector values at the focus point are computed through a probe operation. Probing is also used to resample data on a set of points. In the right image, three planes are used as probes in the original data. Contour lines (of flow density) are then generated on the sampled planes.

Plate 39 Cut plane through dataset. Cutting allows us to view data on surfaces that "pass through", or cut, a dataset. In this image, a computational surface of the structured grid dataset is shown in wireframe. A cut plane (shown as colored surface) is then used to cut through the dataset at an arbitrary position and orientation. The colors correspond to flow density. Cutting surfaces are not necessarily planes: implicit functions such as spheres, cylinders, and quadrics can also be used.

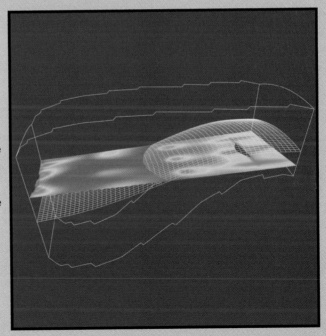

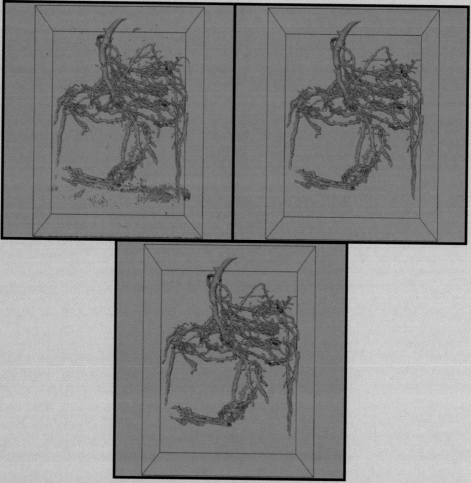

Plate 40   Connectivity and decimation used to select and reduce data. The original isosurface is generated from a 256^3 volume and consists of 351,118 triangles (shown upper left). The next image (shown upper right) has been modified by extracting the largest, topologically connected surface, resulting in 299,480 triangles. In the bottom image, decimation has been applied to reduce the mesh size to a final count of 81,111 triangles. (Data origin J. McFall at the Center for In Vivo Microscopy at Duke University.)

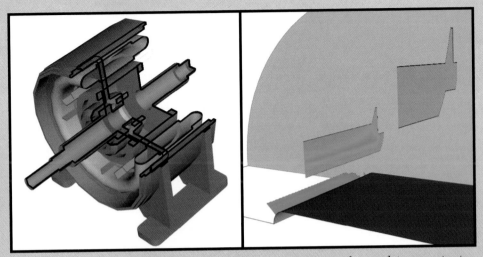

Plate 41 Texture mapping techniques. Texture maps can be used to accentuate important data characteristics, or to reveal features. In the left image, the outer portions of a motor are cut away using transparent texture. In the right image, scalar data controls the application of a texture map. Portions of three planes are set transparent when their scalar values are less than a specified threshold.

Plate 42 Boolean textures. Texture maps can be subdivided into separate regions, each region corresponding to a particular data range. In this example, a 2D texture map is created consisting of opaque, transition (shown in black), and transparent regions along both the *s* and *t* texture axes. Implicit functions are used to associate a part of the sphere surface with the texture map. Different results are obtained depending on the combination of opacity and transparency for each texture map. This shows the 16 possible combinations applied to a sphere.

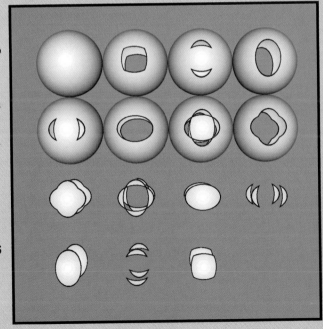

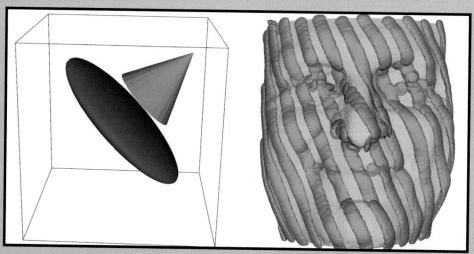

Plate 43 Splatting data to build topological structure. Each splat is a fuzzy ellipse that influences nearby regions with an exponential function. The shape of the ellipse can be controlled by vector or normal data. The size of the splat can be controlled by scalar magnitude. The left image shows a single elliptical splat (in blue) modified by a vector (shown as a cone). The right image shows a regular subsampling of points used to reconstruct a surface. The original surface is shown as a teal, wireframe mesh.

Plate 44 Visualization of multi-dimensional data. The splatting technique shown in the previous plate is used to visualize financial data. This data is from over 3,000 loan accounts. For each account there are six different variables. The axes in this example are monthly payment, interest rate, and loan amount. The grayish surface shows the total population. The red surfaces indicate accounts that are delinquent on loan payment. This information could be used to characterize bad credit risks.

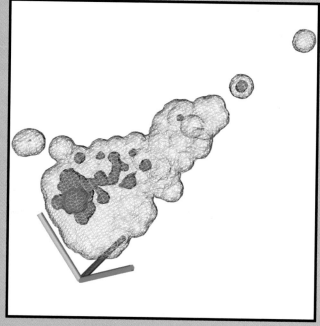

Applications. These examples represent but a few of the many possible application areas of visualization. These applications draw on many of the concepts and visualization techniques presented earlier.

Plate 45 Medical imaging. Two isosurfaces are shown corresponding to the human skin and bone. Data is from CT scan with 94 slice planes at 1282^2 resolution.

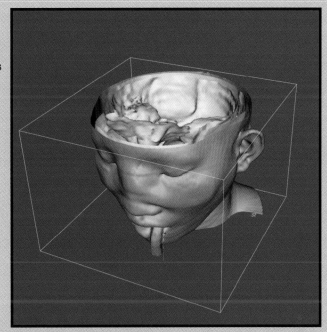

Plate 46 Medical imaging. This image shows an isosurface of the human skin plus additional image planes. Each plane is colored with a different color lookup table. The skin is rendered translucent.

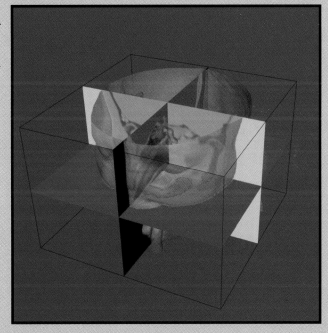

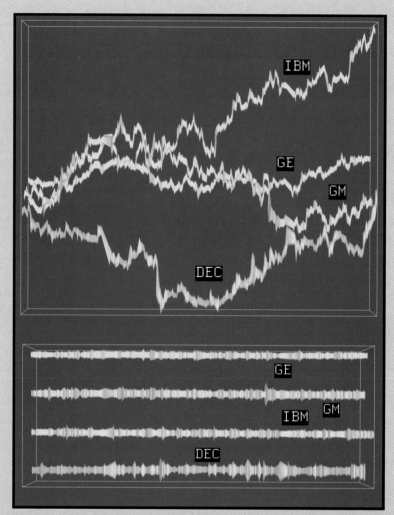

Plate 47 Financial visualization of stock market data. Typical stock value plot extended using the third dimension. Lines have been wrapped with variable-radius tubes. Radius of tube and color correspond to trade volume. Images show front and top views.

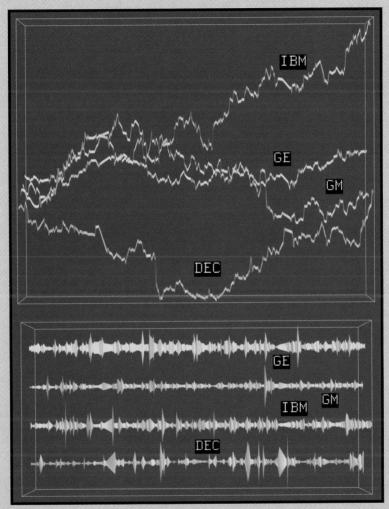

Plate 48 Financial visualization. The previous example was modified to use a constant-width ribbon (width of each plot is constant in front view). Ribbon is extruded in third direction to represent stock trade volume (shown top view).

Plate 49 Computational fluid dynamics (CFD) visualization. Portions of grid (corresponding to physical boundaries) are colored with velocity magnitude. This analysis simulates the flow of liquid oxygen over a post projecting from a flat surface. The post promotes mixing of liquid oxygen.

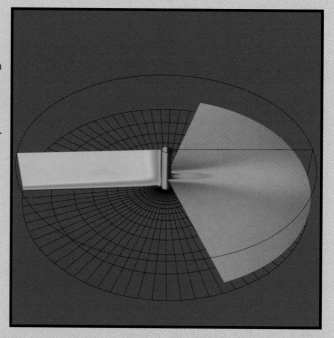

Plate 50 CFD visualization. Portions of grid are used to seed streamtubes. Notice flow vortices around post.

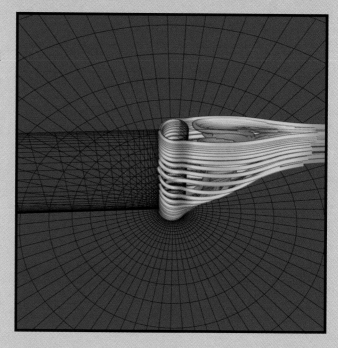

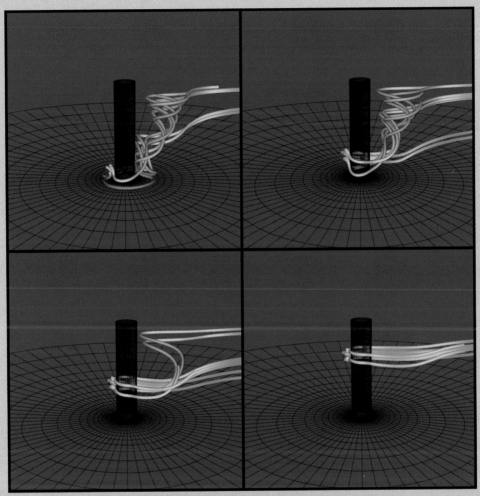

Plate 51   CFD Visualization of a vertical post in fluid flow. Four images from a sequence of streamline generation. A spherical cloud of points is used to generate the streamlines. The seed cloud is moved up along the front of the post.

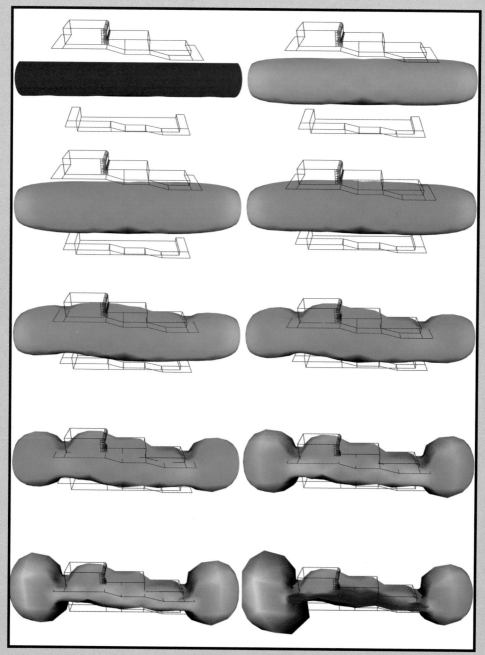

Plate 52   Finite element visualization. Ten frames from a simulated blow molding process are shown. A balloon-like plastic parison is simultaneously inflated and pressed with a die (shown in wireframe). The red color indicates thin walls. Blue indicates thicker walls.

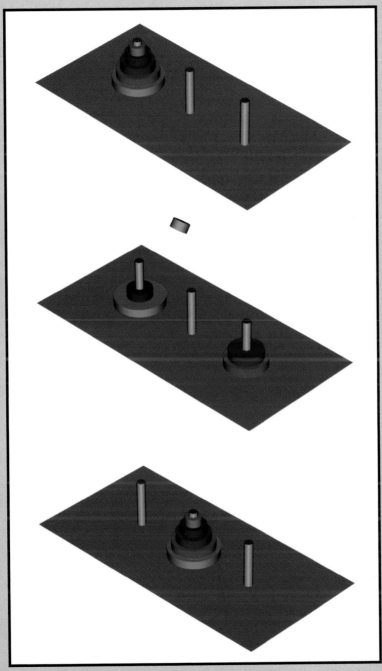

Plate 53   Algorithm visualization. Three images from *Towers of Hanoi* simulation are shown. The top image shows the starting configuration; the middle image shows an intermediate configuration; and the bottom image shows the final configuration.

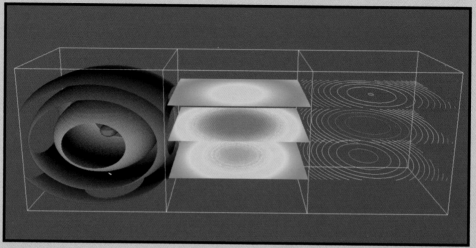

Plate 54 Visualizing the quadric $F(x,y,z) = x^2 + 2y^2 + 3z^2 + yz$ in three parts. The left part of the image shows isosurfaces $F(x,y,z) = c$. In the middle part, color mapped planes indicate function value. In the right part, contour lines illustrate regions of constant function value.

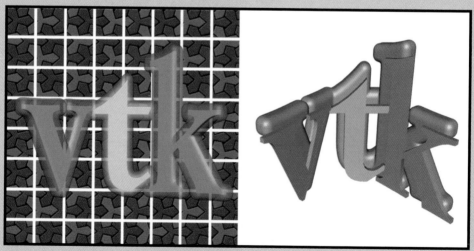

Plate 55 Implicit modelling to create stylistic logo. The original letters "v", "t", and "k" (shown in reddish hue in right image) are represented with a polygonal mesh. A structured point dataset is used to sample the distance from these letters, and an isosurface technique extracts the blobby "vtk" at a specified distance value. The left image shows a different version of the logo with a texture mapped plane whose cells have been passed through a shrink filter.

Object Descriptions

*I*n the following pages we provide a synopsis of the objects in the *Visualization Toolkit*. Each object description consists of at least four parts. The *Name* is a one-line description of the object. The *Class Hierarchy* lists the superclass(es). This information is important because you may need to refer to the superclass for further documentation. The *Description* includes a more detailed summary of the object's implementation and/or functionality. The final part is a *Summary* of the object methods. For some objects you may also find the *Caveats*, *See Also*, and *Defines*. These describe any special features of the object, refer to related objects, and list the #define parameters defined by the object include file.

This documentation is also available in the source code. Most of the documentation will be found in the include file, but some method descriptions will be found associated with the method definitions in the source file. (Please observe that we use a standard naming convention for the C++ source and include files. If the class name is vtkFoo, then the include file will be named vtkFoo.hh and the source code will be named vtkFoo.cc.)

You also may want to refer to Appendix A, specifically the description of classes by category (see "Object Synopsis" on page 392). Using the synopsis you can search for objects based on functionality, and then visit these object descriptions for more information. You also may want to see the various examples included on CD-ROM. These illustrate the use of objects in a typical application.

vtkAGraymap

NAME

vtkAGraymap - scalar data in intensity + alpha (grayscale + opacity) form

CLASS HIERARCHY

class vtkAGraymap : public vtkColorScalars

DESCRIPTION

vtkAGraymap is a concrete implementation of vtkColorScalars. vtkAGraymap represents scalars using one value for intensity (grayscale) and one value for alpha (opacity). The intensity and alpha values range between (0,255) (i.e., an unsigned char value).

If you use the method SetColor() (inherited from superclass vtkColorScalars) the RGBA components are converted to intensity-alpha using the standard luminance equation Luminance = 0.30*red + 0.59*green + 0.11*blue.

SEE ALSO

vtkGraymap vtkPixmap vtkAPixmap vtkBitmap

SUMMARY

void SetColor(int i, unsigned char rgba[4])
Set a RGBA color value at a particular array location. Does not do range checking.

void InsertColor(int i, unsigned char rgba[4])
Insert a RGBA color value at a particular array location. Does range checking and will allocate additional memory if necessary.

int InsertNextColor(unsigned char rgba[4])
Insert a RGBA color value at the next available slot in the array. Will allocate memory if necessary.

unsigned char *GetPtr(const int id)
Get pointer to array of data starting at data position "id". Form of data is a list of repeated intensity/alpha pairs.

unsigned char *WritePtr(const int id, const int number)
Get pointer to data array. Useful for direct writes of data. MaxId is bumped by number (and memory allocated if necessary). Id is the location you wish to write into; number is the number of scalars to write. Use the method WrotePtr() to mark completion of write.

void WrotePtr()
Terminate direct write of data. Although dummy routine now, reserved for future use.

unsigned char *GetColor(int id)
Return an unsigned char RGBA color value for a particular point id.

vtkAGraymap

void   GetColor(int id, unsigned char rgba[4])
Copy RGBA color value components into user provided array for specified point id.

vtkAGraymap& operator=(const vtkAGraymap& fs)
Deep copy of scalars.

unsigned char *GetAGrayValue(int id)
Return an unsigned char gray-alpha value for a particular point id.

void   GetAGrayValue(int id, unsigned char ga[2])
Copy gray-alpha components into user provided array for specified point id.

void   SetAGrayValue(int i, unsigned char ga[2])
Set a gray-alpha value at a particular array location. Does not do range checking.

void   InsertAGrayValue(int i, unsigned char ga[2])
Insert a gray-alpha value at a particular array location. Does range checking and will allocate additional memory if necessary.

int   InsertNextAGrayValue(unsigned char ga[2])
Insert a gray-alpha value at the next available slot in the array. Will allocate memory if necessary.

vtkAPixmap

NAME

vtkAPixmap - scalar data in RGBA (color + opacity) form

CLASS HIERARCHY

class vtkAPixmap : public vtkColorScalars

DESCRIPTION

vtkAPixmap is a concrete implementation of vtkColorScalars. Scalars are represented using three values for color (red, green, blue) plus alpha opacity value. Each of r,g,b,a components ranges from (0,255) (i.e., an unsigned char value).

SEE ALSO

vtkGraymap vtkAGraymap vtkPixmap vtkBitmap

SUMMARY

unsigned char *GetColor(int i)
Return a RGBA color at array location i.

unsigned char *GetPtr(const int id)
Get pointer to array of data starting at data position "id".

unsigned char *WritePtr(const int id, const int number)
Get pointer to data array. Useful for direct writes of data. MaxId is bumped by number (and memory allocated if necessary). Id is the location you wish to write into; number is the number of scalars to write. Use the method WrotePtr() to mark completion of write.

void WrotePtr()
Terminate direct write of data. Although dummy routine now, reserved for future use.

vtkAPixmap& operator=(const vtkAPixmap& fs)
Deep copy of scalars.

void GetColor(int id, unsigned char rgba[4])
Copy RGBA components into user provided array rgba[4] for specified point id.

void SetColor(int id, unsigned char rgba[4])
Insert color into object. No range checking performed (fast!).

void InsertColor(int id, unsigned char rgba[4])
Insert color into object. Range checking performed and memory allocated as necessary.

int InsertNextColor(unsigned char rgba[4])
Insert color into next available slot. Returns point id of slot.

vtkActor

NAME

vtkActor - represents an object (geometry & properties) in a rendered scene

CLASS HIERARCHY

class vtkActor : public vtkObject

DESCRIPTION

vtkActor is used to represent an entity in a rendering scene. It handles functions related to the actors position, orientation and scaling. It combines these instance variables into one four-by-four transformation matrix as follows: [x y z 1] = [x y z 1] Translate(-origin) Scale(scale) Rot(y) Rot(x) Rot (z) Trans(origin) Trans(position). The actor also maintains a reference to the defining geometry (i.e., the mapper), rendering properties and possibly a texture map.

SEE ALSO

vtkProperty vtkTexture vtkMapper vtkFollower vtkLODActor

SUMMARY

void SetProperty(vtkProperty *lut);
void SetProperty(vtkProperty& lut)
vtkProperty *GetProperty();
Set/Get the property object that controls this actors surface properties. This should be an instance of a vtkProperty object. Every actor must have a property associated with it. If one isn't specified, then one will be generated automatically. Multiple actors can share one property object.

void SetTexture(vtkTexture*)
void SetTexture(vtkTexture&)
vtkTexture *GetTexture()
Set/Get the texture object to control rendering texture maps. This will be a vtkTexture object. An actor does not need to have an associated texture map and multiple actors can share one texture.

void SetMapper(vtkMapper*)
void SetMapper(vtkMapper&)
This is the method that is used to connect an actor to the end of a visualization pipeline, i.e. the mapper. This should be a subclass of vtkMapper. Typically vtkPolyMapper and vtkDataSetMapper will be used.

vtkMapper *GetMapper()
Returns the Mapper that this actor is getting it's data from.

void SetUserMatrix(vtkMatrix4x4*)
void SetUserMatrix(vtkMatrix4x4&)
vtkMatrix4x4 *GetUserMatrix()
In addition to the instance variables, such as position and orientation, you can specify your own four-by-four transformation matrix that will get concatenated with the actor's four-by-four matrix as determined by the other instance variables. If the other instance variables such as position and orientation are left with their

vtkActor

default values then they will result in the identity matrix. And the resulting matrix will be the user defined matrix.

void SetPosition(float, float, float)
void SetPosition(float *)
float *GetPosition()
void GetPosition(float data[3])
void AddPosition(float deltaPosition[3]);
void AddPosition(float deltaX,float deltaY,float deltaZ);
Set/Get/Add the position of the actor in world coordinates.

void SetOrigin(float, float, float)
void SetOrigin(float *)
float *GetOrigin()
void GetOrigin(float data[3])
Set/Get the origin of the actor. This is the point about which all rotations take place.

void SetScale(float, float, float)
void SetScale(float *)
float *GetScale()
void GetScale(float data[3])
Set/Get the scale of the actor. Scaling in performed independently on the X, Y and Z axis. A scale of zero is illegal and will be replaced with one.

void SetVisibility(int)
int GetVisibility()
void VisibilityOn()
void VisibilityOff()
Set/Get the visibility of the actor. Visibility is like a light switch for actors. Use it to turn them on or off.

void SetPickable(int)
int GetPickable()
void PickableOn()
void PickableOff()
Set/Get the pickable instance variable. This determines if the actor can be picked (typically using the mouse). Also see dragable.

void SetDragable(int)
int GetDragable()
void DragableOn()
void DragableOff()
Set/Get the value of the dragable instance variable. This determines if an actor, once picked, can be dragged (translated) through space. This is typically done through an interactive mouse interface. This does not affect methods such as SetPosition, which will continue to work. It is just intended to prevent some actors from being dragged from within a user interface.

vtkActor()
Creates an actor with the following defaults: origin(0,0,0) position=(0,0,0) scale=(1,1,1) visibility=1 pickable=1 dragable=1 orientation=(0,0,0). No user defined matrix and no texture map.

vtkActor

void Render(vtkRenderer *ren)

This causes the actor to be rendered. It in turn will render the actor's property, texture map, and then mapper. If a property hasn't been assigned, then the actor will create one automatically.

void SetOrientation (float x,float y,float z)

Sets the orientation of the actor. Orientation is specified as X,Y and Z rotations in that order, but they are performed as RotateZ, RotateX and finally RotateY.

float *GetOrientation ()

Returns the orientation of the actor as s vector of X,Y, and Z rotation. The ordering in which these rotations must be done to generate the same matrix is RotateZ, RotateX, and finally RotateY. See also SetOrientation.

void AddOrientation (float a1,float a2,float a3)

Add to the current orientation. See SetOrientation and GetOrientation for more details. This basically does a GetOrientation, adds the passed in arguments, and then calls SetOrientation.

void RotateX (float angle)

Rotate the actor in degrees about the X axis using the right hand rule.

void RotateY (float angle)

Rotate the actor in degrees about the Y axis using the right hand rule.

void RotateZ (float angle)

Rotate the actor in degrees about the Z axis using the right hand rule.

void RotateWXYZ (float degree, float x, float y, float z)

Rotate the actor in degrees about an arbitrary axis specified by the last three arguments.

void GetMatrix(vtkMatrix4x4& result)

Copy the actor's composite 4x4 matrix into the matrix provided.

vtkMatrix4x4& GetMatrix()

Return a reference to the actor's 4x4 composite matrix.

float *GetBounds()

Get the bounds for this Actor as (Xmin,Xmax,Ymin,Ymax,Zmin,Zmax).

float *GetCenter()

Get the center of the bounding box in world coordinates.

float *GetXRange()

Get the actor's x range in world coordinates.

float *GetYRange()

Get the actor's y range in world coordinates.

float *GetZRange()

Get the actor's z range in world coordinates.

vtkActorCollection

NAME

vtkActorCollection - a list of actors

CLASS HIERARCHY

class vtkActorCollection : public vtkCollection

DESCRIPTION

vtkActorCollection represents and provides methods to manipulate a list of actors (i.e., vtkActor and subclasses). The list is unsorted and duplicate entries are not prevented.

SEE ALSO

vtkActor vtkCollection

SUMMARY

void AddItem(vtkActor *a)
Add an actor to the list.

void RemoveItem(vtkActor *a)
Remove an actor from the list.

int IsItemPresent(vtkActor *a)
Determine whether a particular actor is present. Returns its position in the list.

vtkActor *GetNextItem()
Get the next actor in the list.

vtkAppendFilter

NAME

vtkAppendFilter - appends one or more datasets together into a single unstructured grid

CLASS HIERARCHY

class vtkAppendFilter : public vtkDataSetToUnstructuredGridFilter

DESCRIPTION

vtkAppendFilter is a filter that appends one of more datasets into a single unstructured grid. All geometry is extracted and appended, but point attributes (i.e., scalars, vectors, normals) are extracted and appended only if all datasets have the point attributes available. (For example, if one dataset has scalars but another does not, scalars will not be appended.)

SEE ALSO

vtkAppendPolyData

SUMMARY

void AddInput(vtkDataSet *ds)
Add a dataset to the list of data to append.

void RemoveInput(vtkDataSet *ds)
Remove a dataset from the list of data to append.

vtkAppendPolyData

NAME

vtkAppendPolyData - appends one or more polygonal datasets together

CLASS HIERARCHY

class vtkAppendPolyData : public vtkFilter

DESCRIPTION

vtkAppendPolyData is a filter that appends one of more polygonal datasets into a single polygonal dataset. All geometry is extracted and appended, but point attributes (i.e., scalars, vectors, normals) are extracted and appended only if all datasets have the point attributes available. (For example, if one dataset has scalars but another does not, scalars will not be appended.)

SEE ALSO

vtkAppendFilter

SUMMARY

vtkPolyData *GetOutput()
Get the output of this filter.

void AddInput(vtkPolyData *ds)
Add a dataset to the list of data to append.

void RemoveInput(vtkPolyData *ds)
Remove a dataset from the list of data to append.

vtkAxes

NAME

vtkAxes - create an x-y-z axes

CLASS HIERARCHY

class vtkAxes : public vtkPolySource

DESCRIPTION

vtkAxes creates three lines that form an x-y-z axes. The origin of the axes is user specified (0,0,0 is default), and the size is specified with a scale factor. Three scalar values are generated for the three lines and can be used (via color map) to indicate a particular coordinate axis.

SUMMARY

void SetOrigin(float, float, float)
void SetOrigin(float *)
float *GetOrigin()
void GetOrigin(float data[3])
    Set the origin of the axes.

void SetScaleFactor(float)
float GetScaleFactor()
    Set the scale factor of the axes. Used to control size.

vtkAxes()
    Construct with origin=(0,0,0) and scale factor=1.

vtkBYUReader

NAME

vtkBYUReader - read MOVIE.BYU polygon files

CLASS HIERARCHY

class vtkBYUReader : public vtkPolySource

DESCRIPTION

vtkBYUReader is a source object that reads MOVIE.BYU polygon files. These files consist of a geometry file (.g), a scalar file (.s), a displacement or vector file (.d), and a 2D texture coordinate file (.t).

SUMMARY

> void **SetGeometryFilename(char *)**
> char ***GetGeometryFilename()**
>> Specify name of geometry filename.

> void **SetDisplacementFilename(char *)**
> char ***GetDisplacementFilename()**
>> Specify name of displacement filename.

> void **SetScalarFilename(char *)**
> char ***GetScalarFilename()**
>> Specify name of scalar filename.

> void **SetTextureFilename(char *)**
> char ***GetTextureFilename()**
>> Specify name of texture coordinates filename.

> void **SetReadDisplacement(int)**
> int   **GetReadDisplacement()**
> void **ReadDisplacementOn()**
> void **ReadDisplacementOff()**
>> Turn on/off the reading of the displacement file.

> void **SetReadScalar(int)**
> int   **GetReadScalar()**
> void **ReadScalarOn()**
> void **ReadScalarOff()**
>> Turn on/off the reading of the scalar file.

> void **SetReadTexture(int)**
> int   **GetReadTexture()**
> void **ReadTextureOn()**
> void **ReadTextureOff()**
>> Turn on/off the reading of the texture coordinate file. Specify name of geometry filename.

vtkBYUWriter

NAME

vtkBYUWriter - write MOVIE.BYU files

CLASS HIERARCHY

class vtkBYUWriter : public vtkWriter

DESCRIPTION

vtkBYUWriter writes MOVIE.BYU polygonal files. These files consist of a geometry file (.g), a scalar file (.s), a displacement or vector file (.d), and a 2D texture coordinate file (.t). These files must be specified to the object, the appropriate boolean variables must be true, and data must be available from the input for the files to be written.

SUMMARY

void SetGeometryFilename(char *)
char *GetGeometryFilename()
Specify the name of the geometry file to write.

void SetDisplacementFilename(char *)
char *GetDisplacementFilename()
Specify the name of the displacement file to write.

void SetScalarFilename(char *)
char *GetScalarFilename()
Specify the name of the scalar file to write.

void SetTextureFilename(char *)
char *GetTextureFilename()
Specify the name of the texture file to write.

void SetWriteDisplacement(int)
int   GetWriteDisplacement()
void WriteDisplacementOn()
void WriteDisplacementOff()
Turn on/off writing the displacement file.

void SetWriteScalar(int)
int   GetWriteScalar()
void WriteScalarOn()
void WriteScalarOff()
Turn on/off writing the scalar file.

void SetWriteTexture(int)
int   GetWriteTexture()
void WriteTextureOn()
void WriteTextureOff()
Turn on/off writing the texture file.

vtkBYUWriter()
Create object so that it writes displacement, scalar, and texture files (if data is available).

vtkBYUWriter

void **SetInput(vtkPolyData *input)**
Specify the input data or filter.

void **WriteData()**
Write out data in MOVIE.BYU format.

vtkBitArray

NAME

vtkBitArray - dynamic, self-adjusting array of bits

CLASS HIERARCHY

class vtkBitArray : public vtkObject

DESCRIPTION

vtkBitArray is an array of bits (0/1 data value). The array is packed so that each byte stores eight bits. vtkBitArray provides methods for insertion and retrieval of bits, and will automatically resize itself to hold new data.

SUMMARY

unsigned char *GetPtr(const int id)
Get the address of a particular data index.

unsigned char *WritePtr(const int id, const int number)
Get the address of a particular data index. Make sure data is allocated for the number of items requested. Set MaxId according to the number of data values requested.

vtkBitArray& SetValue(const int id, const int i)
Insert data at a specified position in the array. Does not perform range checking.

vtkBitArray& InsertValue(const int id, const int i)
Insert data at a specified position in the array.

int   InsertNextValue(const int i)
Insert data at the end of the array. Return its location in the array.

void Squeeze()
Resize object to just fit data requirement. Reclaims extra memory.

int   GetSize()
Get the allocated size of the object in terms of number of data items.

int   GetMaxId()
Returning the maximum index of data inserted so far.

void Reset()
Reuse the memory allocated by this object. Objects appear as if no data has been previously inserted.

int   GetValue(const int id)
Get the data at a particular index.

int   Allocate(const int sz, const int ext)
Allocate memory for this array. Delete old storage if present.

void Initialize()
Release storage and reset array to initial state.

vtkBitArray(const int sz, const int ext)
Construct with specified storage and extend value.

vtkBitArray

vtkBitArray(const vtkBitArray& ia)
Construct array from another array. Copy each element of other array.

vtkBitArray& operator=(const vtkBitArray& ia)
Deep copy of another array.

vtkBitArray& operator+=(const vtkBitArray& ia)
Append one array onto the end of this array.

vtkBitScalars

NAME

vtkBitScalars - packed bit (0/1) representation of scalar data

CLASS HIERARCHY

class vtkBitScalars : public vtkScalars

DESCRIPTION

vtkBitScalars is a concrete implementation of vtkScalars. Scalars are represented using a packed bit array. Only possible scalar values are (0/1).

SUMMARY

unsigned char *GetPtr(const int id)
Get pointer to array of data starting at data position "id".

unsigned char *WritePtr(const int id, const int number)
Get pointer to data array. Useful for direct writes of data. MaxId is bumped by number (and memory allocated if necessary). Id is the location you wish to write into; number is the number of scalars to write. Use the method WrotePtr() to mark completion of write.

void WrotePtr()
Terminate direct write of data. Although dummy routine now, reserved for future use.

vtkBitScalars& operator=(const vtkBitScalars& cs)
Deep copy of scalars.

vtkBitmap

NAME

vtkBitmap - scalar data in bitmap form

CLASS HIERARCHY

class vtkBitmap : public vtkColorScalars

DESCRIPTION

vtkBitmap is a concrete implementation of vtkColorScalars. Scalars are represented using a packed character array of (0,1) values.

If you use the method SetColor() (inherited method) the conversion to bit value is as follows. Any non-black color is set "on" and black is set "off".

SEE ALSO

vtkGraymap vtkAGraymap vtkPixmap vtkAPixmap

SUMMARY

unsigned char *GetPtr(const int id)
Get pointer to byte containing bit in question. You will have to decompose byte to obtain appropriate bit value.

unsigned char *WritePtr(const int id, const int number)
Get pointer to data. Useful for direct writes into object. MaxId is bumped by number (and memory allocated if necessary). Id is the location you wish to write into; number is the number of RGBA colors to write.

vtkBitmap& operator=(const vtkBitmap& fs)
Deep copy of scalars.

unsigned char *GetColor(int id)
Return a RGBA color for a particular point id.

void GetColor(int id, unsigned char rgba[4])
Get RGBA color value for id indicated.

void SetColor(int id, unsigned char rgba[4])
Insert RGBA color value into object. No range checking performed (fast!).

void InsertColor(int id, unsigned char rgba[4])
Insert RGBA color value into object. Range checking performed and memory allocated as necessary.

int InsertNextColor(unsigned char rgba[4])
Insert RGBA color value into next available slot. Returns point id of slot.

vtkBooleanStructuredPoints

NAME

vtkBooleanStructuredPoints - combine two or more structured point sets

CLASS HIERARCHY

class vtkBooleanStructuredPoints : public vtkFilter

DESCRIPTION

vtkBooleanStructuredPoints is a filter that performs boolean combinations on two or more input structured point sets. Operations supported include union, intersection, and difference. A special method is provided that allows incremental appending of data to the filter output.

CAVEATS

To boolean two structured point datasets together requires that the dimensions of each dataset is identical. The origin and aspect ratio are ignored.

DEFINES

VTK_UNION_OPERATOR 0
VTK_INTERSECTION_OPERATOR 1
VTK_DIFFERENCE_OPERATOR 2

SUMMARY

void SetOperationType(int)
int   GetOperationType()
Specify the type of boolean operation.

vtkStructuredPoints *GetOutput()
Get the output of this filter.

vtkBooleanStructuredPoints()
Construct with sample resolution of (50,50,50) and automatic computation of sample bounds. Initial boolean operation is union.

void AddInput(vtkStructuredPoints *sp)
Add another structured point set to the list of objects to boolean.

void RemoveInput(vtkStructuredPoints *sp)
Remove an object from the list of objects to boolean.

void Append(vtkStructuredPoints *sp)
Perform boolean operations by appending to current output data.

void SetSampleDimensions(int i, int j, int k)
Set the i-j-k dimensions on which to perform boolean operation.

void SetModelBounds(float *bounds)
Set the size of the volume on which to perform the sampling.

vtkBooleanTexture

NAME

vtkBooleanTexture - generate 2D texture map based on combinations of inside, outside, and on region boundary

CLASS HIERARCHY

class vtkBooleanTexture : public vtkStructuredPointsSource

DESCRIPTION

vtkBooleanTexture is a filter to generate a 2D texture map based on combinations of inside, outside, and on region boundary. The "region" is implicitly represented via 2D texture coordinates. These texture coordinates are normally generated using a filter like vtkImplicitTextureCoords, which generates the texture coordinates for any implicit function.

vtkBooleanTexture generates the map according to the s-t texture coordinates plus the notion of being in, on, or outside of a region. An in region is when the texture coordinate is between (0,0.5-thickness/2). An out region is where the texture coordinate is (0.5+thickness/2). An on region is between (0.5-thickness/2,0.5+thickness/2). The combination in, on, and out for each of the s-t texture coordinates results in 16 possible combinations (see text). For each combination, a different value of intensity and transparency can be assigned. To assign maximum intensity and/or opacity use the value 255. A minimum value of 0 results in a black region (for intensity) and a fully transparent region (for transparency).

SEE ALSO

vtkImplicitTextureCoords vtkThresholdTextureCoords

SUMMARY

void SetXSize(int)
int GetXSize()
Set the X texture map dimension.

void SetYSize(int)
int GetYSize()
Set the Y texture map dimension.

void SetThickness(int)
int GetThickness()
Set the thickness of the "on" region.

void SetInIn(unsigned char, unsigned char)
void SetInIn(unsigned char *)
unsigned char *GetInIn()
void GetInIn(unsigned char data[2])
Specify intensity/transparency for "in/in" region.

void SetInOut(unsigned char, unsigned char)
void SetInOut(unsigned char *)

vtkBooleanTexture

unsigned char *GetInOut()
void GetInOut(unsigned char data[2])

> Specify intensity/transparency for "in/out" region.

void SetOutIn(unsigned char, unsigned char)
void SetOutIn(unsigned char *)
unsigned char *GetOutIn()
void GetOutIn(unsigned char data[2])

> Specify intensity/transparency for "out/in" region.

void SetOutOut(unsigned char, unsigned char)
void SetOutOut(unsigned char *)
unsigned char *GetOutOut()
void GetOutOut(unsigned char data[2])

> Specify intensity/transparency for "out/out" region.

void SetOnOn(unsigned char, unsigned char)
void SetOnOn(unsigned char *)
unsigned char *GetOnOn()
void GetOnOn(unsigned char data[2])

> Specify intensity/transparency for "on/on" region.

void SetOnIn(unsigned char, unsigned char)
void SetOnIn(unsigned char *)
unsigned char *GetOnIn()
void GetOnIn(unsigned char data[2])

> Specify intensity/transparency for "on/in" region.

void SetOnOut(unsigned char, unsigned char)
void SetOnOut(unsigned char *)
unsigned char *GetOnOut()
void GetOnOut(unsigned char data[2])

> Specify intensity/transparency for "on/out" region.

void SetInOn(unsigned char, unsigned char)
void SetInOn(unsigned char *)
unsigned char *GetInOn()
void GetInOn(unsigned char data[2])

> Specify intensity/transparency for "in/on" region.

void SetOutOn(unsigned char, unsigned char)
void SetOutOn(unsigned char *)
unsigned char *GetOutOn()
void GetOutOn(unsigned char data[2])

> Specify intensity/transparency for "out/on" region.

vtkBrownianPoints

NAME

vtkBrownianPoints - assign random vector to points

CLASS HIERARCHY

class vtkBrownianPoints : public vtkDataSetToDataSetFilter

DESCRIPTION

vtkBrownianPoints is a filter object that assigns a random vector (i.e., magnitude and direction) to each point. The minimum and maximum speed values can be controlled by the user.

SUMMARY

void SetMinimumSpeed(float)
float GetMinimumSpeed()
    Set the minimum speed value.

void SetMaximumSpeed(float)
float GetMaximumSpeed()
    Set the maximum speed value.

vtkByteSwap

NAME

vtkByteSwap - perform machine dependent byte swapping

CLASS HIERARCHY

class vtkByteSwap

DESCRIPTION

vtkByteSwap is used by other classes to perform machine dependent byte swapping. Byte swapping is often used when reading or writing binary files.

EXAMPLES

STLRead.cc

SUMMARY

void Swap4BE(char *mem_ptr1)
Swap four byte word.

void Swap4BERange(char *mem_ptr1,int num)
Swap bunch of bytes. Num is the number of four byte words to swap.

void Swap4LE(char *mem_ptr1)
Swap four byte word.

void Swap4LERange(char *mem_ptr1,int num)
Swap bunch of bytes. Num is the number of four byte words to swap.

vtkCamera

NAME

vtkCamera - a virtual camera for 3D rendering

CLASS HIERARCHY

class vtkCamera : public vtkObject

DESCRIPTION

vtkCamera is a virtual camera for 3D rendering. It provides methods to position and orient the view point and focal point. Convenience methods for moving about the focal point also are provided. More complex methods allow the manipulation of the computer graphics model including view up vector, clipping planes, and camera perspective.

SEE ALSO

vtkCameraDevice

SUMMARY

void SetPosition(float x, float y, float z);
void SetPosition(float a[3]);
float *GetPosition()
void GetPosition(float data[3])
Set/Get the position of the camera in world coordinates.

void SetFocalPoint(float x, float y, float z);
void SetFocalPoint(float a[3]);
float *GetFocalPoint()
void GetFocalPoint(float data[3])
Set/Get the focal point of the camera in world coordinates

void SetViewUp(float vx, float vy, float vz);
void SetViewUp(float a[3]);
float *GetViewUp()
void GetViewUp(float data[3])
Set/Get the view up direction for the camera.

void SetClippingRange(float front, float back);
void SetClippingRange(float a[2]);
float *GetClippingRange()
void GetClippingRange(float data[2])
Set/Get the location of the front and back clipping planes along the direction of projection. These are positive distances along the direction of projection. How these values are set can have a large impact on how well z-buffering works. In particular the front clipping plane can make a very big difference. Setting it to 0.01 when it really could be 1.0 can have a big impact on your z-buffer resolution farther away.

virtual void Render(vtkRenderer *ren);
This method causes the camera to set up whatever is required for viewing the scene. This is actually handled by an instance of vtkCameraDevice, which is created automatically.

vtkCamera

void SetViewAngle(float)
float GetViewAngle()
> Set/Get the camera view angle (i.e., the width of view in degrees). Larger values yield greater perspective distortion.

void SetEyeAngle(float)
float GetEyeAngle()
> Set/Get the separation between eyes (in degrees). This is used when generating stereo images.

int   GetStereo()
> Is this camera rendering in stereo?

void SetWindowCenter(float, float)
void SetWindowCenter(float *)
float *GetWindowCenter()
void GetWindowCenter(float data[2])
> Set/Get the center of the window.

void SetFocalDisk(float)
float GetFocalDisk()
> Set the size of the cameras lens in world coordinates. This is only used when the renderer is doing focal depth rendering. When that is being done the size of the focal disk will effect how significant the depth effects will be.

void SetSwitch(int)
int   GetSwitch()
void SwitchOn()
void SwitchOff()
> Set/Get the value of the Switch instance variable. This indicates if the camera is on or off.

vtkCamera()
> Construct camera instance with its focal point at the origin, and position=(0,0,1). The view up is along the y-axis, view angle is 30 degrees, and the clipping range is (.1,1000).

void SetThickness(float X)
> Set the distance between clipping planes. A side effect of this method is to adjust the back clipping plane to be equal to the front clipping plane plus the thickness.

void SetDistance(float X)
> Set the distance of the focal point from the camera. The focal point is modified accordingly. This should be positive.

void CalcViewPlaneNormal()
> Compute the view plane normal from the position and focal point.

void SetRoll(float roll)
> Set the roll angle of the camera about the view plane normal.

float GetRoll()
> Returns the roll of the camera.

void CalcDistance ()
> Compute the camera distance, which is the distance between the focal point and position.

vtkCamera

float *GetOrientation ()
Returns the orientation of the camera. This is a vector of X, Y, and Z rotations that when performed in the order RotateZ, RotateX, and finally RotateY will yield the same 3x3 rotation matrix for the camera.

void CalcViewTransform()
Compute the view transform matrix. This is used in converting between view and world coordinates. It does not include any perspective effects but it does include shearing and scaling.

void CalcPerspectiveTransform(float aspect, float nearz, float farz)
Compute the perspective transform matrix. This is used in converting between view and world coordinates.

vtkMatrix4x4 &GetPerspectiveTransform(float aspect, float nearz, float farz)
Return the perspective transform matrix. See CalcPerspectiveTransform.

vtkMatrix4x4 &GetViewTransform()
Return the perspective transform matrix. See CalcPerspectiveTransform.

vtkMatrix4x4 &GetCompositePerspectiveTransform(float aspect, float nearz, float farz)
Return the perspective transform matrix. See CalcPerspectiveTransform.

void OrthogonalizeViewUp()
Recompute the view up vector so that it is perpendicular to the view plane normal.

void Dolly(float amount)
Move the position of the camera along the view plane normal. Moving towards the focal point (e.g., > 1) is a dolly-in, moving away from the focal point (e.g., < 1) is a dolly-out.

void Zoom(float amount)
Change the ViewAngle of the camera so that more or less of a scene occupies the viewport. A value > 1 is a zoom-in. A value < 1 is a zoom-out.

void Azimuth (float angle)
Rotate the camera about the view up vector centered at the focal point.

void Elevation (float angle)
Rotate the camera about the cross product of the view plane normal and the view up vector centered on the focal point.

void Yaw (float angle)
Rotate the focal point about the view up vector centered at the camera's position.

void Pitch (float angle)
Rotate the focal point about the cross product of the view up vector and the view plane normal, centered at the camera's position.

void Roll (float angle)
Rotate the camera around the view plane normal.

vtkCamera

void SetViewPlaneNormal(float X,float Y,float Z)
Set the direction that the camera points. Adjusts position to be consistent with the view plane normal.

vtkCameraDevice

NAME

vtkCameraDevice - abstract definition of a hardware dependent camera

CLASS HIERARCHY

class vtkCameraDevice : public vtkObject

DESCRIPTION

vtkCameraDevice is the superclass of the hardware dependent cameras such as vtkOglrCamera and vtkSbrCamera. This object is typically created automatically by a vtkCamera object when it renders. The user should never see this class.

SEE ALSO

vtkCamera

SUMMARY

virtual void Render(vtkCamera *cam, vtkRenderer *ren) = 0;
This is the only method that the subclasses must supply.

vtkCell

NAME

vtkCell - abstract class to specify cell behavior

CLASS HIERARCHY

class vtkCell : public vtkObject

DESCRIPTION

vtkCell is an abstract class that specifies the interfaces for data cells. Data cells are simple topological elements like points, lines, polygons, and tetrahedra of which visualization datasets are composed. In some cases visualization datasets may explicitly represent cells (e.g., vtkPolyData, vtkUnstructuredGrid), and in some cases, the datasets are implicitly composed of cells (e.g., vtkStructuredPoints).

CAVEATS

The #define VTK_CELL_SIZE is a parameter used to construct cells and provide a general guideline for controlling object execution. This parameter is not a hard boundary: you can create cells with more points.

DEFINES

VTK_CELL_SIZE 512
VTK_TOL 1.e-05 // Tolerance for geometric calculation

SUMMARY

virtual vtkCell *MakeObject() = 0;
Create concrete copy of this cell.

virtual int GetCellType() = 0;
Return the type of cell.

virtual int GetCellDimension() = 0;
Return the topological dimensional of the cell (0,1,2, or 3).

vtkFloatPoints *GetPoints()
Get the point coordinates for the cell.

int   GetNumberOfPoints()
Return the number of points in the cell.

virtual int GetNumberOfEdges() = 0;
Return the number of edges in the cell.

virtual int GetNumberOfFaces() = 0;
Return the number of faces in the cell.

vtkIdList *GetPointIds()
Return the list of point ids defining the cell.

int   GetPointId(int ptId)
For cell point i, return the actual point id.

vtkCell

virtual vtkCell *GetEdge(int edgeId) = 0;

> Return the edge cell from the edgeId of the cell.

virtual vtkCell *GetFace(int faceId) = 0;

> Return the face cell from the faceId of the cell.

virtual int CellBoundary(int subId, float pcoords[3], vtkIdList& pts) = 0;

> Given parametric coordinates of a point, return the closest cell boundary, and whether the point is inside or outside of the cell. The cell boundary is defined by a list of points (pts) that specify a face (3D cell), edge (2D cell), or vertex (1D cell). If the return value of the method is != 0, then the point is inside the cell.

virtual int EvaluatePosition(float x[3], float closestPoint[3],
int& subId, float pcoords[3],
float& dist2, float *weights) = 0;

> Given a point x[3] return inside(=1) or outside(=0) cell; evaluate parametric coordinates, sub-cell id (!=0 only if cell is composite), distance squared of point x[3] to cell (in particular, the sub-cell indicated), closest point on cell to x[3], and interpolation weights in cell. (The number of weights is equal to the number of points defining the cell). Note: on rare occasions a -1 is returned from the method. This means that numerical error has occurred and all data returned from this method should be ignored. Also, inside/outside is determine parametrically. That is, a point is inside if it satisfies parametric limits. This can cause problems for cells of topological dimension 2 or less, since a point in 3D can project onto the cell within parametric limits but be "far" from the cell. Thus, the value dist2 may be checked to determine true in/out.

virtual void EvaluateLocation(int& subId, float pcoords[3],
float x[3], float *weights) = 0;

> Determine global coordinate (x[3]) from subId and parametric coordinates. Also returns interpolation weights. (The number of weights is equal to the number of points in the cell.)

virtual void Contour(float value, vtkFloatScalars *cellScalars,
vtkFloatPoints *points, vtkCellArray *verts,
vtkCellArray *lines, vtkCellArray *polys,
vtkFloatScalars *scalars) = 0;

> Generate contouring primitives.

virtual int IntersectWithLine(float p1[3], float p2[3], float tol, float& t,
float x[3], float pcoords[3], int& subId) = 0;

> Intersect with a ray. Return parametric coordinates (both line and cell) and global intersection coordinates, given ray definition and tolerance. The method returns non-zero value if intersection occurs.

virtual int Triangulate(int index, vtkFloatPoints &pts) = 0;

> Generate simplices of proper dimension. If cell is 3D, tetrahedron are generated; if 2D triangles; if 1D lines; if 0D points. The form of the output is a sequence of points, each n+1 points (where n is topological cell dimension) defining a simplex. The index is a parameter that controls which triangulation to use (if more than one is possible). If numerical degeneracy encountered, 0 is returned, otherwise 1 is returned.

vtkCell

virtual void Derivatives(int subId, float pcoords[3], float *values,
int   dim, float *derivs) = 0;
Compute derivatives given cell subId and parametric coordinates. The values array is a series of data value(s) at the cell points. There is a one-to-one correspondence between cell point and data value(s). Dim is the number of data values per cell point. Derivs are derivatives in the x-y-z coordinate directions for each data value. Thus, if computing derivatives for a scalar function in a hexahedron, dim=1, 8 values are supplied, and 3 deriv values are returned (i.e., derivatives in x-y-z directions). On the other hand, if computing derivatives of velocity (vx,vy,vz) dim=3, 24 values are supplied ((vx,vy,vz)1, (vx,vy,vz)2, ...()8), and 9 deriv values are returned ((d(vx)/dx),(d(vx)/dy),(d(vx)/dz), (d(vy)/dx),(d(vy)/dy), (d(vy)/dz), (d(vz)/dx),(d(vz)/dy),(d(vz)/dz)).

vtkCell():
Points(VTK_CELL_SIZE), PointIds(VTK_CELL_SIZE)
Construct cell.

char HitBBox (float bounds[6], float origin[3], float dir[3],
float coord[3], float& t)
Bounding box intersection modified from Graphics Gems Vol I. Note: the intersection ray is assumed normalized such that valid intersections can only occur between [0,1]. Method returns non-zero value if bounding box is hit. Origin[3] starts the ray, dir[3] is the components of the ray in the x-y-z directions, coord[3] is the location of hit, and t is the parametric coordinate along line.

float *GetBounds ()
Compute cell bounding box (xmin,xmax,ymin,ymax,zmin,zmax). Return pointer to array of six float values.

void GetBounds(float bounds[6])
Compute cell bounding box (xmin,xmax,ymin,ymax,zmin,zmax). Copy result into user provided array.

float GetLength2 ()
Compute Length squared of cell (i.e., bounding box diagonal squared).

vtkCellArray

NAME

vtkCellArray - object represents cell connectivity

CLASS HIERARCHY

class vtkCellArray : public vtkRefCount

DESCRIPTION

vtkCellArray is a supporting object that explicitly represents cell connectivity. The cell array structure is a raw integer list of the form: (n,id1,id2,...,idn, n,id1,id2,...,idn, ...) where n is the number of points in the cell, and id is a zero-offset index into an associated point list.

Advantages of this data structure are its compactness, simplicity, and easy interface to external data. However, it is totally inadequate for random access. This functionality (when necessary) is accomplished by using the vtkCellList and vtkLinkList objects to extend the definition of the data structure.

SEE ALSO

vtkCellList vtkLinkList

SUMMARY

int   GetNumberOfCells()
Get the number of cells in the array.

int   InsertNextCell(int npts, int* pts)
Create a cell by specifying the number of points and an array of point id's.

int   InsertNextCell(vtkIdList &pts)
Create a cell by specifying a list of point ids.

int   InsertNextCell(int npts)
Create cells by specifying count, and then adding points one at a time using method InsertCellPoint(). If you don't know the count initially, use the method UpdateCellCount() to complete the cell.

void InsertCellPoint(int id)
Used in conjunction with InsertNextCell(int npts) to add another point to the list of cells.

void UpdateCellCount(int npts)
Used in conjunction with InsertNextCell(int npts) and InsertCellPoint() to update the number of points defining the cell.

int   InsertNextCell(vtkCell *cell)
Insert a cell object.

int   EstimateSize(int numCells, int maxPtsPerCell)
Utility routine helps manage memory of cell array. EstimateSize() returns a value used to initialize and allocate memory for array based on number of cells and maximum number of points making up cell. If every cell is the same size (in

vtkCellArray

terms of number of points), then the memory estimate is guaranteed exact. (If not exact, use Squeeze() to reclaim any extra memory.)

void Reset()
Reuse list. Reset to initial condition.

void Squeeze()
Reclaim any extra memory.

void InitTraversal()
A cell traversal methods that is more efficient than vtkDataSet traversal methods. InitTraversal() initializes the traversal of the list of cells.

int GetNextCell(int& npts, int* &pts)
A cell traversal methods that is more efficient than vtkDataSet traversal methods. GetNextCell() gets the next cell in the list. If end of list is encountered, 0 is returned.

int GetSize()
Get the size of the allocated connectivity array.

int GetNumberOfConnectivityEntries()
Get the total number of entries (i.e., data values) in the connectivity array. This may be much less than the allocated size (i.e., return value from GetSize().)

void GetCell(int loc, int &npts, int* &pts)
Internal method used to retrieve a cell given an offset into the internal array.

int GetLocation(int npts)
Computes the current location within the internal array. Used in conjunction with GetCell(int loc,...).

void ReverseCell(int loc)
Special method inverts ordering of current cell. Must be called carefully or the cell topology may be corrupted.

void ReplaceCell(int loc, int npts, int *pts)
Replace the point ids of the cell with a different list of point ids.

int *GetPtr()
Get pointer to array of cell data.

int *WritePtr(const int ncells, const int size)
Get pointer to data array for purpose of direct writes of data. Size is the total storage consumed by the cell array. ncells is the number of cells represented in the array. Use the method WrotePtr() to mark completion of write.

void WrotePtr()
Terminate direct write of data. Although dummy routine now, reserved for future use.

int GetMaxCellSize()
Returns the size of the largest cell. The size is the number of points defining the cell.

vtkCellList

NAME

vtkCellList - object provides direct access to cells in vtkCellArray

CLASS HIERARCHY

class vtkCellList : public vtkRefCount

DESCRIPTION

Supplemental object to vtkCellArray to allow random access into cells. The "location" field is the location in the vtkCellArray list in terms of an integer offset. An integer offset was used instead of a pointer for easy storage and inter-process communication.

SEE ALSO

vtkCellArray vtkLinkList

SUMMARY

_vtkCell_s &GetCell(const int id)
Return a reference to a cell list structure.

unsigned char GetCellType(const int cellId)
Return the type of cell.

int   GetCellLocation(const int cellId)
Return the location of the cell in the associated vtkCellArray.

void DeleteCell(int cellId)
Delete cell by setting to NULL cell type.

void InsertCell(const int cellId, const unsigned char type, const int loc)
Add a cell to structure.

int   InsertNextCell(const unsigned char type, const int loc)
Add a cell to the object in the next available slot.

void Squeeze()
Reclaim any extra memory.

void Reset()
Initialize object without releasing memory.

vtkCellLocator

NAME

vtkCellLocator - octree-based spatial search object to quickly locate cells

CLASS HIERARCHY

class vtkCellLocator : public vtkObject

DESCRIPTION

vtkCellLocator is a spatial search object to quickly locate cells in 3D. vtkCellLocator uses a uniform-level octree subdivision, where each octant carries an indication of whether it is empty or not, and each leaf octant carries a list of the cells inside of it. (An octant is not empty if it has one or more cells inside of it.) Typical operations are intersection with a line to return candidate cells, or intersection with another vtkCellLocator to return candidate cells.

CAVEATS

Many other types of spatial locators have been developed, such as variable depth octrees and kd-trees. These are often more efficient for the operations described here.

SUMMARY

void SetDataSet(vtkDataSet*)
void SetDataSet(vtkDataSet&)
vtkDataSet *GetDataSet()
    Set list of cells to insert into locator.

void SetLevel(int)
int   GetLevel()
    Set the level of the octree (set automatically if Automatic is true).

void SetMaxLevel(int)
int   GetMaxLevel()
    Set the maximum allowable level for the octree.

void SetAutomatic(int)
int   GetAutomatic()
void AutomaticOn()
void AutomaticOff()
    Boolean controls whether automatic subdivision size is computed from average number of cells in octant.

void SetNumberOfCellsInOctant(int)
int   GetNumberOfCellsInOctant()
    Specify the average number of cells in each octant.

void SetTolerance(float)
float GetTolerance()
    Specify absolute tolerance (in world coordinates) for performing intersection computations.

vtkCellLocator()
    Construct with automatic computation of divisions, averaging 25 cells per octant.

vtkCellLocator

**int   IntersectWithLine(float a0[3], float a1[3], float tol,
        float& t, float x[3], float pcoords[3],
        int &subId)**

Return list of octants that are intersected by line. The octants are ordered along the line and are represented by octant number. To obtain the cells in the octant, use the method GetOctantCells().

vtkIdList* GetOctantCells(int octantId)

Get the cells in an octant.

int   IntersectWithCellLocator(vtkCellLocator& locator, vtkIdList cells)

Intersect against another vtkCellLocator returning cells that lie in intersecting octants.

vtkCellPicker

NAME

vtkCellPicker - select a cell by shooting a ray into graphics window

CLASS HIERARCHY

class vtkCellPicker : public vtkPicker

DESCRIPTION

vtkCellPicker is used to select a cell by shooting a ray into graphics window and intersecting with actor's defining geometry - specifically its cells. Beside returning coordinates, actor and mapper, vtkCellPicker returns the id of the closest cell within the tolerance along the pick ray, and the dataset that was picked.

SEE ALSO

vtkPicker vtkPointPicker

SUMMARY

int   GetCellId()
Get the id of the picked cell. If CellId = -1, nothing was picked.

int   GetSubId()
Get the subId of the picked cell. If SubId = -1, nothing was picked.

float *GetPCoords()
void   GetPCoords(float data[3])
Get the parametric coordinates of the picked cell. Only valid if pick was made.

vtkCleanPolyData

NAME

vtkCleanPolyData - merge duplicate points and remove degenerate primitives

CLASS HIERARCHY

class vtkCleanPolyData : public vtkPolyToPolyFilter

DESCRIPTION

vtkCleanPolyData is a filter that takes polygonal data as input and generates polygonal as output. vtkCleanPolyData merges duplicate points (within specified tolerance), and transforms degenerate topology into appropriate form (for example, triangle is converted into line if two points of triangle are merged).

If tolerance is specified precisely=0.0, then this object will use the vtkMergePoints object to merge points (very fast). Otherwise the slower vtkLocator is used.

CAVEATS

Merging points can alter topology, including introducing non-manifold forms. Tolerance should be chosen carefully to avoid these problems.

SUMMARY

void SetTolerance(float)
float GetTolerance()
Specify tolerance in terms of percentage of bounding box.

void CreateDefaultLocator();
Create default locator. Used to create one when none is specified.

vtkCleanPolyData()
Construct object with initial tolerance of 0.0.

void SetLocator(vtkLocator *locator)
Specify a spatial locator for speeding the search process. By default an instance of vtkLocator is used.

vtkCollection

NAME

vtkCollection - create and manipulate unsorted lists of objects

CLASS HIERARCHY

class vtkCollection : public vtkObject

DESCRIPTION

vtkCollection is a general object for creating and manipulating lists of objects. The lists are unsorted and allow duplicate entries. vtkCollection also serves as a base class for lists of specific types of objects.

SUMMARY

void InitTraversal()

Initialize the traversal of the collection. This means the data pointer is set at the beginning of the list.

vtkObject *GetNextItem()

Get the next item in the collection. NULL is returned if the collection is exhausted.

vtkCollection()

Construct with empty list.

void AddItem(vtkObject *a)

Add an object to the list. Does not prevent duplicate entries.

void RemoveItem(vtkObject *a)

Remove an object from the list. Removes the first object found, not all occurrences. If no object found, list is unaffected.

void RemoveAllItems()

Remove all objects from the list.

int   IsItemPresent(vtkObject *a)

Search for an object and return location in list. If location == 0, object was not found.

int   GetNumberOfItems()

Return the number of objects in the list.

vtkColorScalars

NAME

vtkColorScalars - abstract class represents scalar data in color specification

CLASS HIERARCHY

class vtkColorScalars : public vtkScalars

DESCRIPTION

vtkColorScalars is an abstract class whose subclasses represent scalar data using a color specification such as rgb, grayscale, RGBA, hsv, etc.

In order to be a vtkScalar subclass, vtkColorScalars must be able to return a single value given a point id. By default, this operation is performed by computing luminance (or equivalent) as the single value. Concrete subclasses of vtkColorScalars may have additional methods to convert multi-dimensional color information into a single scalar value.

CAVEATS

Derived classes of vtkColorScalars treat colors differently. All derived classes will return a RGBA (red-green-blue-alpha transparency) array in response to "GetColor()" methods. However, when setting colors, the RGBA data is converted to internal form. For example, a vtkGrayMap converts RGBA into a luminance value and stores that.

SUMMARY

virtual unsigned char *GetPtr(const int id) = 0;
Get pointer to array of data starting at data position "id".

int   GetNumberOfColors()
Return number of colors (same as number of scalars).

virtual unsigned char *GetColor(int id) = 0;
Return an unsigned char RGBA for a particular point id. No matter what internal representation of color, derived class must convert it to RGBA.

virtual void GetColor(int id, unsigned char rgba[4]) = 0;
Copy color components into user provided array rgba[4] for specified point id. No matter what internal representation of color, derived class must convert it to RGBA form.

virtual void SetColor(int id, unsigned char rgba[4]) = 0;
Insert color into object. No range checking performed (fast!).

virtual void InsertColor(int id, unsigned char rgba[4]) = 0;
Insert color into object. Range checking performed and memory allocated as necessary.

virtual int InsertNextColor(unsigned char rgba[4]) = 0;
Insert color into next available slot. Returns point id of slot.

virtual int Allocate(const int sz, const int ext=1000) = 0;
Allocate space for color data.

vtkColorScalars

float GetScalar(int i)
Convert internal color representation into scalar value.

void SetScalar(int i, float s)
Map through lookup table to set the color.

void InsertScalar(int i, float s)
Map through lookup table to set the color.

int InsertNextScalar(float s)
Map through lookup table to set the color.

void GetColors(vtkIdList& ptId, vtkAPixmap& p)
Given list of point id's, return colors for each point.

unsigned char *GetComponentRange ()
Compute range of color RGBA data (rmin,rmax, gmin,gmax, bmin,bmax, amin,amax). Return pointer to array of length 8.

void GetComponentRange(unsigned char range[8])
Compute range of color RGBA data (rmin,rmax, gmin,gmax, bmin,bmax, amin,amax). Copy result into user provided array.

vtkCone

NAME

vtkCone - implicit function for a cone

CLASS HIERARCHY

class vtkCone : public vtkImplicitFunction

DESCRIPTION

vtkCone computes the implicit function and function gradient for a cone. vtkCone is a concrete implementation of vtkImplicitFunction. The cone vertex is located at the origin with axis of rotation coincident with z-axis. (Use the superclass' vtkImplicitFunction transformation matrix if necessary to reposition.) The angle specifies the angle between the axis of rotation and the side of the cone.

CAVEATS

The cone is infinite in extent. To truncate the cone use the vtkImplicitBoolean in combination with clipping planes.

SUMMARY

void SetAngle(float)
float GetAngle()
Set/Get the cone angle (expressed in degrees).

vtkConeSource

NAME

vtkConeSource - generate polygonal cone

CLASS HIERARCHY

class vtkConeSource : public vtkPolySource

DESCRIPTION

vtkConeSource creates a cone centered at origin and pointing down the x-axis. Depending upon the resolution of this object, different representations are created. If resolution=0 a line is created; if resolution=1, a single triangle is created; if resolution=2, two crossed triangles are created. For resolution > 2, a 3D cone (with resolution number of sides) is created. It also is possible to control whether the bottom of the cone is capped with a (resolution-sided) polygon, and to specify the height and radius of the cone.

SUMMARY

```
void  SetHeight(float)
float GetHeight()
```
Set the height of the cone.

```
void  SetRadius(float)
float GetRadius()
```
Set the radius of the cone.

```
void  SetResolution(int)
int   GetResolution()
```
Set the number of facets used to represent the cone.

```
void  SetCapping(int)
int   GetCapping()
void  CappingOn()
void  CappingOff()
```
Turn on/off whether to cap the cone with a polygon.

vtkConeSource(int res)
Construct with default resolution 6, height 1.0, radius 0.5, and capping on.

vtkConnectivityFilter

NAME

vtkConnectivityFilter - extract data based on geometric connectivity

CLASS HIERARCHY

class vtkConnectivityFilter : public vtkDataSetToUnstructuredGridFilter

DESCRIPTION

vtkConnectivityFilter is a filter that extracts cells that share common points. The filter works in one of four ways: 1) extract the largest connected region in the dataset; 2) extract specified region numbers; 3) extract all regions sharing specified point ids; or 4) extract all regions sharing specified cell ids.

DEFINES

VTK_EXTRACT_POINT_SEEDED_REGIONS 1
VTK_EXTRACT_CELL_SEEDED_REGIONS 2
VTK_EXTRACT_SPECIFIED_REGIONS 3
VTK_EXTRACT_LARGEST_REGION 4

SUMMARY

void SetMaxRecursionDepth(int)
int   GetMaxRecursionDepth()
The connectivity extraction algorithm works recursively. In some systems the stack depth is limited. This methods specifies the maximum recursion depth.

void SetColorRegions(int)
int   GetColorRegions()
void ColorRegionsOn()
void ColorRegionsOff()
Turn on/off the coloring of connected regions.

vtkConnectivityFilter()
Construct with default extraction mode to extract largest regions.

int   GetNumberOfExtractedRegions()
Obtain the number of connected regions.

void ExtractPointSeededRegions()
Set the extraction mode to extract regions sharing specified point ids.

void ExtractCellSeededRegions()
Set the extraction mode to extract regions sharing specified cell ids.

void ExtractSpecifiedRegions()
Set the extraction mode to extract regions of specified id. You may have to execute filter first (with debug turned on) to determine region ids.

void ExtractLargestRegion()
Set the extraction mode to extract the largest region found.

void InitializeSeedList()
Initialize list of point ids/cell ids used to seed regions.

vtkConnectivityFilter

void AddSeed(int id)
Add a seed id (point or cell id). Note: ids are 0-offset.

void DeleteSeed(int id)
Delete a seed id (point or cell id). Note: ids are 0-offset.

void InitializeSpecifiedRegionList()
Initialize list of region ids to extract.

void AddSpecifiedRegion(int id)
Add a region id to extract. Note: ids are 0-offset.

void DeleteSpecifiedRegion(int id)
Delete a region id to extract. Note: ids are 0-offset.

vtkContourFilter

NAME

vtkContourFilter - generate isosurfaces/isolines from scalar values

CLASS HIERARCHY

class vtkContourFilter : public vtkDataSetToPolyFilter

DESCRIPTION

vtkContourFilter is a filter that takes as input any dataset and generates on output isosurfaces and/or isolines. The exact form of the output depends upon the dimensionality of the input data. Data consisting of 3D cells will generate isosurfaces, data consisting of 2D cells will generate isolines, and data with 1D or 0D cells will generate isopoints. Combinations of output type are possible if the input dimension is mixed.

If the input type is volume (e.g., 3D structured point dataset), you may wish to use vtkMarchingCubes. This class is specifically tailored for volumes and is therefore much faster.

CAVEATS

vtkContourFilter uses variations of marching cubes to generate output primitives. The output primitives are disjoint - that is, points may be generated that are coincident but distinct. You may want to use vtkCleanPolyData to remove the coincident points. Also, the isosurface is not generated with surface normals. Use vtkPolyNormals to create them, if desired.

SEE ALSO

vtkMarchingCubes vtkSliceCubes vtkDividingCubes

DEFINES

VTK_MAX_CONTOURS 256

SUMMARY

float *GetValues()
void GetValues(float data[VTK_MAX_CONTOURS])
Return array of contour values (size of numContours).

vtkContourFilter()
Construct object with initial range (0,1) and single contour value of 0.0.

void SetValue(int i, float value)
Set a particular contour value at contour number i. The index i ranges between 0<=i<NumberOfContours.

void GenerateValues(int numContours, float range[2])
Generate numContours equally spaced contour values between specified range. Contour values will include min/max range values.

vtkCubeSource

NAME

vtkCubeSource - create a polygonal representation of a cube

CLASS HIERARCHY

class vtkCubeSource : public vtkPolySource

DESCRIPTION

vtkCubeSource creates a cube centered at origin. The cube is represented with four-sided polygons. It is possible to specify the length, width, and height of the cube independently.

SUMMARY

void SetXLength(float)
float GetXLength()
> Set the length of the cube in the x-direction.

void SetYLength(float)
float GetYLength()
> Set the length of the cube in the y-direction.

void SetZLength(float)
float GetZLength()
> Set the length of the cube in the z-direction.

void SetCenter(float, float, float)
void SetCenter(float *)
float *GetCenter()
void GetCenter(float data[3])
> Set the center of the cube.

void SetBounds(float bounds[6])
> Convenience method allows creation of cube by specifying bounding box.

vtkCursor3D

NAME

vtkCursor3D - generate a 3D cursor representation

CLASS HIERARCHY

class vtkCursor3D : public vtkPolySource

DESCRIPTION

vtkCursor3D is an object that generates a 3D representation of a cursor. The cursor consists of a wireframe bounding box, three intersecting axes lines that meet at the cursor focus, and "shadows" or projections of the axes against the sides of the bounding box. Each of these components can be turned on/off.

This filter generates two output datasets. The first (Output) is just the geometric representation of the cursor. The second (Focus) is a single point at the focal point.

SUMMARY

void SetFocalPoint(float, float, float)
void SetFocalPoint(float *)
float *GetFocalPoint()
void GetFocalPoint(float data[3])
 Specify the position of cursor focus.

void SetOutline(int)
int   GetOutline()
void OutlineOn()
void OutlineOff()
 Turn on/off the wireframe bounding box.

void SetAxes(int)
int   GetAxes()
void AxesOn()
void AxesOff()
 Turn on/off the wireframe axes.

void SetXShadows(int)
int   GetXShadows()
void XShadowsOn()
void XShadowsOff()
 Turn on/off the wireframe x-shadows.

void SetYShadows(int)
int   GetYShadows()
void YShadowsOn()
void YShadowsOff()
 Turn on/off the wireframe y-shadows.

void SetZShadows(int)
int   GetZShadows()

vtkCursor3D

void ZShadowsOn()
void ZShadowsOff()
> Turn on/off the wireframe z-shadows.

void SetWrap(int)
int GetWrap()
void WrapOn()
void WrapOff()
> Turn on/off cursor wrapping. If the cursor focus moves outside the specified bounds, the cursor will either be restrained against the nearest "wall" (Wrap=off), or it will wrap around (Wrap=on).

vtkPolyData *GetFocus()
> Get the focus for this filter.

vtkCursor3D()
> Construct with model bounds = (-1,1,-1,1,-1,1), focal point = (0,0,0), all parts of cursor visible, and wrapping off.

void SetModelBounds(float xmin, float xmax, float ymin, float ymax,
> **float zmin, float zmax)**
> Set the boundary of the 3D cursor.

vtkCutter

NAME

vtkCutter - Cut vtkDataSets with user-specified implicit function

CLASS HIERARCHY

class vtkCutter : public vtkDataSetToPolyFilter

DESCRIPTION

vtkCutter is a filter to cut through data using any subclass of vtkImplicitFunction. That is, a polygonal surface is created corresponding to the implicit function $F(x,y,z) = 0$.

SEE ALSO

vtkImplicitFunction

SUMMARY

vtkCutter(vtkImplicitFunction *cf)
Construct with user-specified implicit function.

unsigned long GetMTime()
Overload standard modified time function. If cut functions is modified, then this object is modified as well.

vtkCyberReader

NAME

vtkCyberReader - read Cyberware laser digitizer files

CLASS HIERARCHY

class vtkCyberReader : public vtkPolySource

DESCRIPTION

vtkCyberReader is a source object that reads a Cyberware laser digitizer file. (Original source code provided courtesy of Cyberware, Inc.)

SUMMARY

void SetFilename(char *)
char *GetFilename()
    Specify Cyberware file name.

vtkCylinder

NAME

vtkCylinder - implicit function for a cylinder

CLASS HIERARCHY

class vtkCylinder : public vtkImplicitFunction

DESCRIPTION

vtkCylinder computes the implicit function and function gradient for a cylinder. vtkCylinder is a concrete implementation of vtkImplicitFunction. Cylinder is centered at origin and axes of rotation is along z-axis. (Use the superclass' vtkImplicitFunction transformation matrix if necessary to reposition.)

CAVEATS

The cylinder is infinite in extent. To truncate the cylinder use the vtkImplicitBoolean in combination with clipping planes.

SUMMARY

void SetRadius(float)
float GetRadius()
      Set/Get cylinder radius.

vtkCylinderSource

NAME

vtkCylinderSource - generate a cylinder centered at origin

CLASS HIERARCHY

class vtkCylinderSource : public vtkPolySource

DESCRIPTION

vtkCylinderSource creates a polygonal cylinder centered at the origin. The axis of the cylinder is aligned along the global y-axis. The height and radius of the cylinder can be specified, as well as the number of sides. It is also possible to control whether the cylinder is open-ended or capped.

SUMMARY

void SetHeight(float)
float GetHeight()
Set the height of the cylinder.

void SetRadius(float)
float GetRadius()
Set the radius of the cylinder.

void SetResolution(int)
int   GetResolution()
Set the number of facets used to define cylinder.

void SetCapping(int)
int   GetCapping()
void CappingOn()
void CappingOff()
Turn on/off whether to cap cylinder with polygons.

vtkDashedStreamLine

NAME

vtkDashedStreamLine - generate constant-time dashed streamline in arbitrary dataset

CLASS HIERARCHY

class vtkDashedStreamLine : public vtkStreamLine

DESCRIPTION

vtkDashedStreamLine is a filter that generates a "dashed" streamline for an arbitrary dataset. The streamline consists of a series of dashes, each of which represents (approximately) a constant time increment. Thus, in the resulting visual representation, relatively long dashes represent areas of high velocity, and small dashes represent areas of low velocity.

vtkDashedStreamLine introduces the instance variable DashFactor. DashFactor interacts with its superclass' instance variable StepLength to create the dashes. DashFactor is the percentage of the StepLength line segment that is visible. Thus, if DashFactor=0.75, the dashes will be "three-quarters on" and "one-quarter off".

SEE ALSO

vtkStreamer vtkStreamLine vtkStreamPoints

SUMMARY

void SetDashFactor(float)
float GetDashFactor()
For each dash, specify the fraction of the dash that is "on". A factor of 1.0 will result in a continuous line, a factor of 0.5 will result in dashed that are half on and half off.

vtkDataReader

NAME

vtkDataReader - helper class for objects that read vtk data files

CLASS HIERARCHY

class vtkDataReader : public vtkObject

DESCRIPTION

vtkDataReader is a helper class that reads the **vtk** data file header and point data (e.g., scalars, vectors, normals, etc.) from a **vtk** data file. See text for format.

DEFINES

VTK_ASCII 1
VTK_BINARY 2

SUMMARY

void SetFilename(char *)
char *GetFilename()
Specify file name of **vtk** data file to read.

int GetFileType()
Get the type of file (VTK_ASCII or VTK_BINARY)

void SetScalarsName(char *)
char *GetScalarsName()
Set the name of the scalar data to extract. If not specified, first scalar data encountered is extracted.

void SetVectorsName(char *)
char *GetVectorsName()
Set the name of the vector data to extract. If not specified, first vector data encountered is extracted.

void SetTensorsName(char *)
char *GetTensorsName()
Set the name of the tensor data to extract. If not specified, first tensor data encountered is extracted.

void SetNormalsName(char *)
char *GetNormalsName()
Set the name of the normal data to extract. If not specified, first normal data encountered is extracted.

void SetTCoordsName(char *)
char *GetTCoordsName()
Set the name of the texture coordinate data to extract. If not specified, first texture coordinate data encountered is extracted.

vtkDataReader

void SetLookupTableName(char *)
char *GetLookupTableName()

> Set the name of the lookup table data to extract. If not specified, uses lookup table named by scalar. Otherwise, this specification supersedes.

vtkDataReader()

> Construct object.

FILE *OpenVTKFile()

> Open a **vtk** data file. Returns NULL if error.

int ReadHeader(FILE *fp)

> Read the header of a **vtk** data file. Returns 0 if error.

int ReadPointData(FILE *fp, vtkDataSet *ds, int numPts)

> Read the point data of a **vtk** data file. The number of points (from the dataset) must match the number of points defined in point attributes (unless no geometry was defined).

int ReadPoints(FILE *fp, vtkPointSet *ps, int numPts)

> Read point coordinates. Return 0 if error.

int ReadScalarData(FILE *fp, vtkDataSet *ds, int numPts)

> Read scalar point attributes. Return 0 if error.

int ReadVectorData(FILE *fp, vtkDataSet *ds, int numPts)

> Read vector point attributes. Return 0 if error.

int ReadNormalData(FILE *fp, vtkDataSet *ds, int numPts)

> Read normal point attributes. Return 0 if error.

int ReadTensorData(FILE *fp, vtkDataSet *ds, int numPts)

> Read tensor point attributes. Return 0 if error.

int ReadCoScalarData(FILE *fp, vtkDataSet *ds, int numPts)

> Read color scalar point attributes. Return 0 if error.

int ReadTCoordsData(FILE *fp, vtkDataSet *ds, int numPts)

> Read texture coordinates point attributes. Return 0 if error.

int ReadLutData(FILE *fp, vtkDataSet *ds)

> Read lookup table. Return 0 if error.

int ReadCells(FILE *fp, int size, int *data)

> Read lookup table. Return 0 if error.

void CloseVTKFile(FILE *fp)

> Close a **vtk** file.

vtkDataSet

NAME

vtkDataSet - abstract class to specify dataset behavior

CLASS HIERARCHY

class vtkDataSet : public vtkObject

DESCRIPTION

vtkDataSet is an abstract class that specifies an interface for data objects. (Data objects are synonymous with datasets.) vtkDataSet also provides methods to provide informations about the data, such as center, bounding box, and representative length.

SUMMARY

virtual void Update();
Provides opportunity for data to insure internal consistency before access.

virtual vtkDataSet *MakeObject() = 0;
Create concrete instance of this dataset.

virtual void CopyStructure(vtkDataSet *ds) = 0;
Copy the geometric and topological structure of an object. Note that the invoking object and the object pointed to by the parameter ds must be of the same type.

virtual char *GetDataType() = 0;
Return class name of data type. This is one of vtkStructuredGrid, vtkStructuredPoints, vtkUnstructuredGrid, vtkPolyData.

virtual int GetNumberOfPoints() = 0;
Determine number of points composing dataset.

virtual int GetNumberOfCells() = 0;
Determine number of cells composing dataset.

virtual float *GetPoint(int ptId) = 0;
Get point coordinates with ptId such that: 0 <= ptId < NumberOfPoints.

virtual void GetPoint(int id, float x[3]);
Copy point coordinates into user provided array x[3] for specified point id.

virtual vtkCell *GetCell(int cellId) = 0;
Get cell with cellId such that: 0 <= cellId < NumberOfCells.

virtual int GetCellType(int cellId) = 0;
Get type of cell with cellId such that: 0 <= cellId < NumberOfCells.

virtual void GetCellPoints(int cellId, vtkIdList& ptIds) = 0;
Topological inquiry to get points defining cell.

virtual void GetPointCells(int ptId, vtkIdList& cellIds) = 0;
Topological inquiry to get cells using point.

virtual void GetCellNeighbors(int cellId, vtkIdList& ptIds, vtkIdList& cellIds);
Topological inquiry to get all cells using list of points exclusive of cell specified (e.g., cellId).

vtkDataSet

virtual int FindCell(float x[3], vtkCell *cell, float tol2, int& subId,
float pcoords[3], float *weights) = 0;
> Locate cell based on global coordinate x and tolerance squared. If cell is non-NULL, then search starts from this cell and looks at immediate neighbors. Returns cellId >= 0 if inside, < 0 otherwise. The parametric coordinates are provided in pcoords[3]. The interpolation weights are returned in weights[]. (The number of weights is equal to the number of points in the found cell). Tolerance is used to control how close the point is to be considered "in" the cell.

void ReleaseData();
> Release data back to system to conserve memory resource. Used during visualization network execution.

int ShouldIReleaseData();
> Return flag indicating whether data should be released after use by a filter.

void SetDataReleased(int)
int GetDataReleased()
> Set/Get the DataReleased ivar.

void SetReleaseDataFlag(int)
int GetReleaseDataFlag()
void ReleaseDataFlagOn()
void ReleaseDataFlagOff()
> Turn on/off flag to control whether this object's data is released after being used by a filter.

void SetGlobalReleaseDataFlag(int)
int GetGlobalReleaseDataFlag()
void GlobalReleaseDataFlagOn()
void GlobalReleaseDataFlagOff()
> Turn on/off flag to control whether every object releases its data after being used by a filter.

virtual void Squeeze();
> Reclaim any extra memory used to store data.

void SetSource(vtkSource*)
void SetSource(vtkSource&)
> Set the owner of this data object for Sources.

float *GetScalarRange();
> Convenience method to get the range of the scalar data if there is any. Otherwise it will return (0,1).

virtual int GetMaxCellSize() = 0;
> Convenience method returns largest cell size in dataset. This is generally used to allocate memory for supporting data structures.

vtkDataSet ()
> Constructor with default bounds (0,1, 0,1, 0,1).

vtkDataSet (const vtkDataSet& ds) :
PointData(ds.PointData)
> Copy constructor.

vtkDataSet

void ComputeBounds()
Compute the data bounding box from data points.

float *GetBounds()
Return a pointer to the geometry bounding box in the form (xmin,xmax, ymin,ymax, zmin,zmax).

float *GetCenter()
Get the center of the bounding box.

float GetLength()
Return the length of the diagonal of the bounding box.

vtkDataSetCollection

NAME

vtkDataSetCollection - maintain an unordered list of dataset objects

CLASS HIERARCHY

class vtkDataSetCollection : public vtkCollection

DESCRIPTION

vtkDataSetCollection is an object that creates and manipulates lists of datasets.

SEE ALSO

vtkCollection

SUMMARY

void   AddItem(vtkDataSet *ds)
Add a dataset to the list.

void   RemoveItem(vtkDataSet *ds)
Remove a dataset from the list.

int   IsItemPresent(vtkDataSet *ds)
Determine whether a particular dataset is present. Returns its position in the list.

vtkDataSet *GetNextItem()
Get the next dataset in the list.

vtkDataSetFilter

NAME

vtkDataSetFilter - filter that takes vtkDataSet as input

CLASS HIERARCHY

class vtkDataSetFilter : public vtkFilter

DESCRIPTION

vtkDataSetFilter is a filter that takes a single vtkDataSet data object as input.

SUMMARY

void   SetInput(vtkDataSet *input)
Specify the input data or filter.

vtkDataSetMapper

NAME

vtkDataSetMapper - map vtkDataSet and derived classes to graphics primitives

CLASS HIERARCHY

class vtkDataSetMapper : public vtkMapper

DESCRIPTION

vtkDataSetMapper is a mapper to map data sets (i.e., vtkDataSet and all derived classes) to graphics primitives. The mapping procedure is as follows: all 0D, 1D, and 2D cells are converted into points, lines, and polygons/triangle strips, and then mapped to the graphics system. The 2D faces of 3D cells are mapped only if they are used by only one cell, i.e., on the boundary of the data set.

SUMMARY

void SetInput(vtkDataSet *in);
void SetInput(vtkDataSet& in)
    Specify the input data to map.

kDataSetToStructuredGridFilter

NAME

vtkDataSetToStructuredGridFilter - abstract filter class

CLASS HIERARCHY

class vtkDataSetToStructuredGridFilter : public vtkDataSetFilter

DESCRIPTION

vtkDataSetToStructuredGridFilter is an abstract filter class whose subclasses take as input any dataset and generate a structured grid on output.

SUMMARY

vtkStructuredGrid *GetOutput()
Get the output of this filter.

---

vtkDataSetReader

NAME

vtkDataSetReader - class to read any type of **vtk** dataset

CLASS HIERARCHY

class vtkDataSetReader : public vtkSource

DESCRIPTION

vtkDataSetReader is a class that provides instance variables and methods to read any type of dataset in visualization library format. The output type of this class will vary depending upon the type of data file.

CAVEATS

These **vtk** formats are not standard. Use other more standard formats when you can.

SUMMARY

vtkDataSet *GetOutput()
Get the output of this source.

void SetFilename(char *name)
Specify file name of **vtk** data file to read.

int GetFileType()
Get the type of file (VTK_ASCII or VTK_BINARY).

void SetScalarsName(char *name)
Set the name of the scalar data to extract. If not specified, first scalar data encountered is extracted.

void SetVectorsName(char *name)
Set the name of the vector data to extract. If not specified, first vector data encountered is extracted.

void SetTensorsName(char *name)
Set the name of the tensor data to extract. If not specified, first tensor data encountered is extracted.

void SetNormalsName(char *name)
Set the name of the normal data to extract. If not specified, first normal data encountered is extracted.

void SetTCoordsName(char *name)
Set the name of the texture coordinate data to extract. If not specified, first texture coordinate data encountered is extracted.

void SetLookupTableName(char *name)
Set the name of the lookup table data to extract. If not specified, uses lookup table named by scalar. Otherwise, this specification supersedes.

vtkDataSetToDataSetFilter

NAME

vtkDataSetToDataSetFilter - abstract filter class

CLASS HIERARCHY

class vtkDataSetToDataSetFilter : public vtkDataSetFilter

DESCRIPTION

vtkDataSetToDataSetFilter is an abstract filter class. Subclasses of
vtkDataSetToDataSetFilter take a dataset as input and create a dataset as output. The
form of the input geometry is not changed in these filters, only the point attributes (e.g.
scalars, vectors, etc.).

SUMMARY

void SetInput(vtkDataSet *input)
Specify the input data or filter.

void Update()
Update input to this filter and the filter itself. Note that we are overloading this
method because the output is an abstract dataset type. This requires special
treatment.

vtkDataSet *GetOutput()
Get the output of this filter. If output is NULL then input hasn't been set which is
necessary for abstract objects.

vtkData

NAME

vtkDataSetToPolyFilter - abstract filter class

CLASS HIERARCHY

class vtkDataSetToPolyFilter : public vtkDataSetFilter

DESCRIPTION

vtkDataSetToPolyFilter is an abstract filter class whose subclasses take as
dataset and generate polygonal data on output.

SUMMARY

vtkPolyData *GetOutput()
Get the output of this filter.

vtkDataSetToStructuredPointsFilter

NAME

vtkDataSetToStructuredPointsFilter - abstract filter class

CLASS HIERARCHY

class vtkDataSetToStructuredPointsFilter : public vtkDataSetFilter

DESCRIPTION

vtkDataSetToStructuredPointsFilter is an abstract filter class whose subclasses take as input any dataset and generate structured points data on output.

SUMMARY

vtkStructuredPoints *GetOutput()

Get the output of this filter.

vtkDataSetToUnstructuredGridFilter

NAME

vtkDataSetToUnstructuredGridFilter - abstract filter class

CLASS HIERARCHY

class vtkDataSetToUnstructuredGridFilter : public vtkDataSetFilter

DESCRIPTION

vtkDataSetToUnstructuredGridFilter is an abstract filter class whose subclasses take as input any dataset and generate an unstructured grid on output.

SUMMARY

vtkUnstructuredGrid *GetOutput()
    Get the output of this filter.

vtkDataSetWriter

NAME

vtkDataSetWriter - write any type of **vtk** dataset to file

CLASS HIERARCHY

class vtkDataSetWriter : public vtkDataWriter

DESCRIPTION

vtkDataSetWriter is an abstract class for mapper objects that write their data to disk (or into a communications port). The input to this object is a dataset of any type.

SUMMARY

void SetInput(vtkDataSet *input)
Specify the input data or filter.

vtkDataWriter

NAME

vtkDataWriter - helper class for objects that write **vtk** data files

CLASS HIERARCHY

class vtkDataWriter : public vtkWriter

DESCRIPTION

vtkDataWriter is a helper class that opens and writes the **vtk** header and point data (e.g., scalars, vectors, normals, etc.) from a **vtk** data file. See text for various formats.

SUMMARY

    void SetFilename(char *)
    char *GetFilename()
       Specify file name of **vtk** polygon data file to write.

    void SetHeader(char *)
    char *GetHeader()
       Specify the header for the **vtk** data file.

    void SetFileType(int)
    int   GetFileType()
       Specify file type (VTK_ASCII or VTK_BINARY) for **vtk** data file.

    void SetScalarsName(char *)
    char *GetScalarsName()
       Give a name to the scalar data. If not specified, uses default name "scalars".

    void SetVectorsName(char *)
    char *GetVectorsName()
       Give a name to the vector data. If not specified, uses default name "vectors".

    void SetTensorsName(char *)
    char *GetTensorsName()
       Give a name to the tensors data. If not specified, uses default name "tensors".

    void SetNormalsName(char *)
    char *GetNormalsName()
       Give a name to the normals data. If not specified, uses default name "normals".

    void SetTCoordsName(char *)
    char *GetTCoordsName()
       Give a name to the texture coordinates data. If not specified, uses default name "textureCoords".

    void SetLookupTableName(char *)
    char *GetLookupTableName()
       Give a name to the lookup table. If not specified, uses default name "lookupTable".

vtkDataWriter

vtkDataWriter()
Created object with default header, ASCII format, and default names for scalars, vectors, tensors, normals, and texture coordinates.

FILE *OpenVTKFile()
Open a **vtk** data file. Returns NULL if error.

int   WriteHeader(FILE *fp)
Write the header of a **vtk** data file. Returns 0 if error.

int   WritePointData(FILE *fp, vtkDataSet *ds)
Write the point data (e.g., scalars, vectors, ...) of a **vtk** data file. Returns 0 if error.

void CloseVTKFile(FILE *fp)
Close a **vtk** file.

vtkDecimate

NAME

vtkDecimate - reduce the number of triangles in a mesh

CLASS HIERARCHY

class vtkDecimate : public vtkPolyToPolyFilter

DESCRIPTION

vtkDecimate is a filter to reduce the number of triangles in a triangle mesh, while preserving the original topology and a forming good approximation to the original geometry. The input to vtkDecimate is a vtkPolyData object, and only triangles are treated. If you desire to decimate polygonal meshes, first triangulate the polygons with the vtkTriangleFilter object.

The algorithm proceeds as follows. Each vertex in the triangle list is evaluated for local planarity (i.e., the triangles using the vertex are gathered and compared to an "average" plane). If the region is locally planar, that is if the target vertex is within a certain distance of the average plane (i.e., the error), and there are no edges radiating from the vertex that have a dihedral angle greater than a user-specified edge angle (i.e., feature angle), and topology is not altered, then that vertex is deleted. The resulting hole is then patched by re-triangulation. The process creates over the entire vertex list (this constitutes an iteration). Iterations proceed until a target reduction is reached or a maximum iteration count is exceeded.

There are a number of additional parameters you can set to control the decimation algorithm. The error may be increased over each iteration with the error increment. Edge preservation may be disabled or enabled. You can turn on/off edge vertex deletion. (Edge vertices are vertices that lie along boundaries of meshes.) Sub iterations are iterations that are performed without changing the decimation criterion. The aspect ratio controls the shape of the triangles that are created, and is the ratio of maximum edge length to minimum edge length. The degree is the number of triangles using a single vertex. Vertices of high degree are considered "complex" and are never deleted.

This implementation has been adapted for a global error bound decimation criterion. That is, the error is a global bound on distance to original surface.

DEFINES

VTK_NUMBER_STATISTICS 12

SUMMARY

void SetInitialError(float)
float GetInitialError()
Set the decimation error bounds. Expressed as a fraction of the longest side of the input data's bounding box.

void SetErrorIncrement(float)
float GetErrorIncrement()
Set the value of the increment by which to increase the decimation error after each iteration.

vtkDecimate

void SetMaximumError(float)
float GetMaximumError()

Set the largest decimation error that can be achieved by incrementing error.

void SetTargetReduction(float)
float GetTargetReduction()

Specify the desired reduction in the total number of polygons. Because of various constraints, this level of reduction may not be realizable.

void SetMaximumIterations(int)
int   GetMaximumIterations()

Specify the maximum number of iterations to attempt. If decimation target is reached first, this value will not be reached.

void SetMaximumSubIterations(int)
int   GetMaximumSubIterations()

Specify the maximum sub-iterations to perform. If no triangles are deleted in a sub-iteration, the sub-iteration process is stopped.

void SetInitialFeatureAngle(float)
float GetInitialFeatureAngle()

Specify the mesh feature angles.

void SetFeatureAngleIncrement(float)
float GetFeatureAngleIncrement()

Set increment by which to increase feature angle over each iteration.

void SetMaximumFeatureAngle(float)
float GetMaximumFeatureAngle()

Set the largest permissible feature angle.

void SetPreserveEdges(int)
int   GetPreserveEdges()
void PreserveEdgesOn()
void PreserveEdgesOff()

Turn on/off the preservation of feature edges.

void SetBoundaryVertexDeletion(int)
int   GetBoundaryVertexDeletion()
void BoundaryVertexDeletionOn()
void BoundaryVertexDeletionOff()

Turn on/off the deletion of vertices on the boundary of a mesh.

void SetAspectRatio(float)
float GetAspectRatio()

Specify the maximum allowable feature angle during triangulation.

void SetDegree(int)
int   GetDegree()

If the number of triangles connected to a vertex exceeds "Degree", then the vertex is considered complex and is never deleted. (NOTE: the complexity of the triangulation algorithm is proportional to Degree^2.)

vtkDecimate

vtkDecimate()

Create object with target reduction of 90%, feature angle of 30 degrees, initial error of 0.0, error increment of 0.005, maximum error of 0.1, and maximum iterations of 6.

vtkDiskSource

NAME

vtkDiskSource - create a disk with hole in center

CLASS HIERARCHY

class vtkDiskSource : public vtkPolySource

DESCRIPTION

vtkDiskSource creates a polygonal disk with a hole in the center. The disk has zero height. The user can specify the inner and outer radius of the disk, and the radial and circumferential resolution of the polygonal representation.

SEE ALSO

vtkLinearExtrusionFilter

SUMMARY

void SetInnerRadius(float)
float GetInnerRadius()
Specify inner radius of hole in disc.

void SetOuterRadius(float)
float GetOuterRadius()
Specify outer radius of disc.

void SetRadialResolution(int)
int GetRadialResolution()
Set the number of points in radius direction.

void SetCircumferentialResolution(int)
int GetCircumferentialResolution()
Set the number of points in circumferential direction.

vtkDividingCubes

NAME

vtkDividingCubes - create points lying on isosurface

CLASS HIERARCHY

class vtkDividingCubes : public vtkStructuredPointsToPolyDataFilter

DESCRIPTION

vtkDividingCubes is a filter that generates points lying on a surface of constant scalar value (i.e., an isosurface). Dense point clouds (i.e., at screen resolution) will appear as a surface. Less dense clouds can be used as a source to generate streamlines or to generate "transparent" surfaces. This filter is based on the generate program written by H. Cline, S. Ludke and W. Lorensen.

The density of the point cloud is controlled by the Distance instance variable. This is a distance value in global coordinates specifying the approximate distance between points.

SUMMARY

void SetValue(float)
float GetValue()
Set isosurface value.

void SetDistance(float)
float GetDistance()
Specify sub-voxel size at which to generate point.

void SetIncrement(int)
int GetIncrement()
Every "Increment" point is added to the list of points. This parameter, if set to a large value, can be used to limit the number of points while retaining good accuracy.

vtkDividingCubes()
Construct object with Value=0.0, Distance=0.1, and Increment=1.

vtkDoubleArray

NAME

vtkDoubleArray - dynamic, self-adjusting double precision array

CLASS HIERARCHY

class vtkDoubleArray : public vtkObject

DESCRIPTION

vtkDoubleArray is an array of double precision numbers. It provides methods for insertion and retrieval of double precision values, and will automatically resize itself to hold new data.

SUMMARY

double GetValue(const int id)
Get the data at a particular index.

double *GetPtr(const int id)
Get the address of a particular data index.

double *WritePtr(const int id, const int number)
Get the address of a particular data index. Make sure data is allocated for the number of items requested. Set MaxId according to the number of data values requested.

vtkDoubleArray& InsertValue(const int id, const double f)
Insert data at a specified position in the array.

int   InsertNextValue(const double f)
Insert data at the end of the array. Return its location in the array.

double& operator[](const int i)
Does insert or get (depending on location on lhs or rhs of statement). Does not do automatic resizing - user's responsibility to range check.

void   Squeeze()
Resize object to just fit data requirement. Reclaims extra memory.

int   GetSize()
Get the allocated size of the object in terms of number of data items.

int   GetMaxId()
Returning the maximum index of data inserted so far.

void   Reset()
Reuse the memory allocated by this object. Object appears as if no data has been previously inserted.

int   Allocate(const int sz, const int ext)
Allocate memory for this array. Delete old storage if present.

void   Initialize()
Release storage and reset array to initial state.

vtkDoubleArray

vtkDoubleArray(const int sz, const int ext)
Construct with specified storage and extend value.

vtkDoubleArray(const vtkDoubleArray& fa)
Construct array from another array. Copy each element of other array.

vtkDoubleArray& operator=(const vtkDoubleArray& fa)
Deep copy of another array.

void operator+=(const vtkDoubleArray& fa)
Append one array onto the end of this array.

vtkEdgePoints

NAME

vtkEdgePoints - generate points on isosurface

CLASS HIERARCHY

class vtkEdgePoints : public vtkDataSetToPolyFilter

DESCRIPTION

vtkEdgePoints is a filter that takes as input any dataset and generates for output a set of points that lie on an isosurface. The points are created by interpolation along cells edges whose end-points are below and above the contour value.

CAVEATS

vtkEdgePoints can be considered a "poor man's" dividing cubes algorithm (see vtkDividingCubes). Points are generated only on the edges of cells, not in the interior, and at lower density than dividing cubes. However, it is more general than dividing cubes since it treats any type of dataset.

SUMMARY

void SetValue(float)
float GetValue()
    Set/get the contour value.

vtkEdgePoints()
    Construct object with contour value of 0.0.

vtkElevationFilter

NAME

vtkElevationFilter - generate scalars along a specified direction

CLASS HIERARCHY

class vtkElevationFilter : public vtkDataSetToDataSetFilter

DESCRIPTION

vtkElevationFilter is a filter to generate scalar values from a dataset. The scalar values lie within a user specified range, and are generated by computing a projection of each dataset point onto a line. The line can be oriented arbitrarily. A typical example is to generate scalars based on elevation or height above a plane.

SUMMARY

void SetLowPoint(float, float, float)
void SetLowPoint(float *)
float *GetLowPoint()
void GetLowPoint(float data[3])
 Define one end of the line (small scalar values).

void SetHighPoint(float, float, float)
void SetHighPoint(float *)
float *GetHighPoint()
void GetHighPoint(float data[3])
 Define other end of the line (large scalar values).

void SetScalarRange(float, float)
void SetScalarRange(float *)
float *GetScalarRange()
void GetScalarRange(float data[2])
 Specify range to map scalars into.

vtkElevationFilter()
 Construct object with LowPoint=(0,0,0) and HighPoint=(0,0,1). Scalar range is (0,1).

vtkExtractGeometry

NAME

vtkExtractGeometry - extract cells that lie either entirely inside or outside of a specified implicit function

CLASS HIERARCHY

class vtkExtractGeometry : public vtkDataSetToUnstructuredGridFilter

DESCRIPTION

vtkExtractGeometry extracts from its input dataset all cells that are either completely inside or outside of a specified implicit function. Any type of dataset can be input to this filter. On output the filter generates an unstructured grid.

SUMMARY

void SetImplicitFunction(vtkImplicitFunction*)
void SetImplicitFunction(vtkImplicitFunction&)
vtkImplicitFunction *GetImplicitFunction()
Specify the implicit function for inside/outside checks.

void SetExtractInside(int)
int   GetExtractInside()
void ExtractInsideOn()
void ExtractInsideOff()
Boolean controls whether to extract cells that are inside of implicit function (ExtractInside == 1) or outside of implicit function (ExtractInside == 0).

vtkExtractGeometry(vtkImplicitFunction *f)
Construct object with ExtractInside turned on.

unsigned long GetMTime()
Overload standard modified time function. If implicit function is modified, then this object is modified as well.

vtkExtractVectorComponents

NAME

vtkExtractVectorComponents - extract components of vector as separate scalars

CLASS HIERARCHY

class vtkExtractVectorComponents : public vtkFilter

DESCRIPTION

vtkExtractVectorComponents is a filter that extracts vector components as separate scalars. This is accomplished by creating three different outputs. Each output is the same as the input, except that the scalar values will be one of the three components of the vector. These can be found in the VxComponent, VyComponent, and VzComponent.

CAVEATS

This filter is unusual in that it creates multiple outputs. Hence, it cannot take advantage of the convenience classes (e.g., vtkPolyToPolyFilter) for deriving concrete filters. Instead, it overloads the Update() method of its superclasses and provides methods for retrieving the output.

SUMMARY

vtkDataSet *GetVxComponent()

Get the output dataset representing velocity x-component. If output is NULL then input hasn't been set, which is necessary for abstract objects.

vtkDataSet *GetVyComponent()

Get the output dataset representing velocity y-component. If output is NULL then input hasn't been set, which is necessary for abstract objects.

vtkDataSet *GetVzComponent()

Get the output dataset representing velocity z-component. If output is NULL then input hasn't been set, which is necessary for abstract objects.

void SetInput(vtkDataSet *input)

Specify the input data or filter.

void Update()

Update input to this filter and the filter itself. Note that we are overloading this method because the output is an abstract dataset type. This requires special treatment.

vtkFeatureEdges

NAME

vtkFeatureEdges - extract boundary, non-manifold, and/or sharp edges from polygonal data

CLASS HIERARCHY

class vtkFeatureEdges : public vtkPolyToPolyFilter

DESCRIPTION

vtkFeatureEdges is a filter to extract special types of edges from input polygonal data. These edges are either 1) boundary (used by one polygon) or a line cell; 2) non-manifold (used by three or more polygons); or 3) feature edges (edges used by two triangles and whose dihedral angle > FeatureAngle). These edges may be extracted in any combination. Edges may also be "colored" (i.e., scalar values assigned) based on edge type.

SEE ALSO

vtkFeatureVertices

SUMMARY

void   SetBoundaryEdges(int)
int   GetBoundaryEdges()
void   BoundaryEdgesOn()
void   BoundaryEdgesOff()
Turn on/off the extraction of boundary edges.

void   SetFeatureEdges(int)
int   GetFeatureEdges()
void   FeatureEdgesOn()
void   FeatureEdgesOff()
Turn on/off the extraction of feature edges.

void   SetFeatureAngle(float)
float GetFeatureAngle()
Specify the feature angle for extracting feature edges.

void   SetNonManifoldEdges(int)
int   GetNonManifoldEdges()
void   NonManifoldEdgesOn()
void   NonManifoldEdgesOff()
Turn on/off the extraction of non-manifold edges.

void   SetColoring(int)
int   GetColoring()
void   ColoringOn()
void   ColoringOff()
Turn on/off the coloring of edges by type.

vtkFeatureEdges()
Construct object with feature angle = 30; all types of edges extracted and colored.

vtkFeatureVertices

NAME

vtkFeatureVertices - extract boundary, non-manifold, and/or sharp vertices from polygonal data (operates on line primitives)

CLASS HIERARCHY

class vtkFeatureVertices : public vtkPolyToPolyFilter

DESCRIPTION

vtkFeatureVertices is a filter to extract special types of vertices from input polygonal data. In particular, the filter operates on the line primitives in the polygonal data. The vertex types are: 1) boundary (used by one line) or a vertex cell type; 2) non-manifold (used by three or more lines); or 3) feature edges (vertices used by two lines and whose orientation angle > FeatureAngle). The orientation angle is computed from the dot product between the two lines. These vertices may be extracted in any combination. Vertices may also be "colored" (i.e., scalar values assigned) based on vertex type.

CAVEATS

This filter operates only on line primitives in polygonal data. Some data may require pre-processing with vtkCleanPolyData to merge coincident points. Otherwise points may be flagged as boundary. (This is true when running vtkFeatureEdges and then vtkFeatureVertices.)

SEE ALSO

vtkFeatureEdges

SUMMARY

    void SetBoundaryVertices(int)
    int   GetBoundaryVertices()
    void BoundaryVerticesOn()
    void BoundaryVerticesOff()
        Turn on/off the extraction of boundary vertices.

    void SetFeatureVertices(int)
    int   GetFeatureVertices()
    void FeatureVerticesOn()
    void FeatureVerticesOff()
        Turn on/off the extraction of feature vertices.

    void SetFeatureAngle(float)
    float GetFeatureAngle()
        Specify the feature angle for extracting feature vertices.

    void SetNonManifoldVertices(int)
    int   GetNonManifoldVertices()
    void NonManifoldVerticesOn()
    void NonManifoldVerticesOff()
        Turn on/off the extraction of non-manifold vertices.

vtkFeatureVertices

void SetColoring(int)
int GetColoring()
void ColoringOn()
void ColoringOff()
Turn on/off the coloring of vertices by type.

vtkFeatureVertices()
Construct object with feature angle = 30; all types of vertices extracted and colored.

vtkFilter

NAME

vtkFilter - abstract class for specifying filter behavior

CLASS HIERARCHY

class vtkFilter : public vtkSource

DESCRIPTION

vtkFilter is an abstract class that specifies the interface for data filters. Each filter must have an Update() and Execute() method that will cause the filter to execute if its input or the filter itself has been modified since the last execution time.

SEE ALSO

vtkSource

SUMMARY

void Update();
All filters must provide a method to update the visualization pipeline. (Method interface inherited from vtkSource.)

vtkFilter()
Construct new filter without start or end methods.

void Update()
Update input to this filter and the filter itself.

vtkFloatArray

NAME

vtkFloatArray - dynamic, self-adjusting floating point array

CLASS HIERARCHY

class vtkFloatArray : public vtkObject

DESCRIPTION

vtkFloatArray is an array of floating point numbers. It provides methods for insertion and retrieval of floating point values, and will automatically resize itself to hold new data.

SUMMARY

float   GetValue(const int id)
Get the data at a particular index.

float   *GetPtr(const int id)
Get the address of a particular data index.

float   *WritePtr(const int id, const int number)
Get the address of a particular data index. Make sure data is allocated for the number of items requested. Set MaxId according to the number of data values requested.

vtkFloatArray& InsertValue(const int id, const float f)
Insert data at a specified position in the array.

int   InsertNextValue(const float f)
Insert data at the end of the array. Return its location in the array.

float& operator[](const int i)
Does insert or get (depending on location on lhs or rhs of statement). Does not do automatic resizing - user's responsibility to range check.

void   Squeeze()
Resize object to just fit data requirement. Reclaims extra memory.

int   GetSize()
Get the allocated size of the object in terms of number of data items.

int   GetMaxId()
Returning the maximum index of data inserted so far.

void   Reset()
Reuse the memory allocated by this object. Object appears as if no data has been previously inserted.

int   Allocate(const int sz, const int ext)
Allocate memory for this array. Delete old storage if present.

void   Initialize()
Release storage and reset array to initial state.

vtkFloatArray

vtkFloatArray(const int sz, const int ext)
Construct with specified storage and extend value.

vtkFloatArray(const vtkFloatArray& fa)
Construct array from another array. Copy each element of other array.

vtkFloatArray& operator=(const vtkFloatArray& fa)
Deep copy of another array.

void operator+=(const vtkFloatArray& fa)
Append one array onto the end of this array.

vtkFloatNormals

NAME

vtkFloatNormals - floating point representation of 3D normals

CLASS HIERARCHY

class vtkFloatNormals : public vtkNormals

DESCRIPTION

vtkFloatNormals is a concrete implementation of vtkNormals. Normals are represented using float values.

SUMMARY

float *GetPtr(const int id)
Get pointer to array of data starting at data position "id".

float *WritePtr(const int id, const int number)
Get pointer to data array. Useful for direct writes of data. MaxId is bumped by number (and memory allocated if necessary). Id is the location you wish to write into; number is the number of normals to write. Use the method WrotePtr() to mark completion of write.

void WrotePtr()
Terminate direct write of data. Although dummy routine now, reserved for future use.

vtkFloatNormals& operator=(const vtkFloatNormals& fn)
Deep copy of normals.

vtkFloatPoints

NAME

vtkFloatPoints - floating point representation of 3D points

CLASS HIERARCHY

class vtkFloatPoints : public vtkPoints

DESCRIPTION

vtkFloatPoints is a concrete implementation of vtkPoints. Points are represented using float values.

SUMMARY

float *GetPtr(const int id)
Get pointer to array of data starting at data position "id".

float *WritePtr(const int id, const int number)
Get pointer to data array. Useful for direct writes of data. MaxId is bumped by number (and memory allocated if necessary). Id is the location you wish to write into; number is the number of scalars to write. Use the method WrotePtr() to mark completion of write.

void WrotePtr()
Terminate direct write of data. Although dummy routine now, reserved for future use.

vtkFloatPoints& operator=(const vtkFloatPoints& fp)
Deep copy of points.

vtkFloatScalars

NAME

vtkFloatScalars - floating point representation of scalar data

CLASS HIERARCHY

class vtkFloatScalars : public vtkScalars

DESCRIPTION

vtkFloatScalars is a concrete implementation of vtkScalars. Scalars are represented using float values.

SUMMARY

float *GetPtr(const int id)
Get pointer to array of data starting at data position "id".

float *WritePtr(const int id, const int number)
Get pointer to data array. Useful for direct writes of data. MaxId is bumped by number (and memory allocated if necessary). Id is the location you wish to write into; number is the number of scalars to write. Use the method WrotePtr() to mark completion of write.

void WrotePtr()
Terminate direct write of data. Although dummy routine now, reserved for future use.

vtkFloatScalars& operator=(const vtkFloatScalars& fs)
Deep copy of scalars.

vtkFloatTCoords

NAME

vtkFloatTCoords - floating point representation of texture coordinates

CLASS HIERARCHY

class vtkFloatTCoords : public vtkTCoords

DESCRIPTION

vtkFloatTCoords is a concrete implementation of vtkTCoords. Texture coordinates are represented using float values.

SUMMARY

float *GetPtr(const int id)
Get pointer to array of data starting at data position "id".

float *WritePtr(const int id, const int number)
Get pointer to data array. Useful for direct writes of data. MaxId is bumped by number (and memory allocated if necessary). Id is the location you wish to write into; number is the number of texture coordinates to write. Use the method WrotePtr() to mark completion of write. Make sure the dimension of the texture coordinate is set prior to issuing this call.

void WrotePtr()
Terminate direct write of data. Although dummy routine now, reserved for future use.

vtkFloatTCoords& operator=(const vtkFloatTCoords& ftc)
Deep copy of texture coordinates.

vtkFloatTensors

NAME

vtkFloatTensors - floating point representation of tensor data

CLASS HIERARCHY

class vtkFloatTensors : public vtkTensors

DESCRIPTION

vtkFloatTensors is a concrete implementation of vtkTensors. Tensor values are represented using float values.

SUMMARY

float *GetPtr(const int id)

Get pointer to array of data starting at data position "id".

float *WritePtr(const int id, const int number)

Get pointer to data array. Useful for direct writes of data. MaxId is bumped by number (and memory allocated if necessary). Id is the location you wish to write into; number is the number of tensors to write. Use the method WrotePtr() to mark completion of write. Make sure the dimension of the tensor is set prior to issuing this call.

void WrotePtr()

Terminate direct write of data. Although dummy routine now, reserved for future use.

vtkFloatTensors& operator=(const vtkFloatTensors& ft)

Deep copy of tensors.

vtkFloatVectors

NAME

vtkFloatVectors - floating point representation of 3D vectors

CLASS HIERARCHY

class vtkFloatVectors : public vtkVectors

DESCRIPTION

vtkFloatVectors is a concrete implementation of vtkVectors. Vectors are represented using float values.

SUMMARY

float *GetPtr(const int id)

Get pointer to array of data starting at data position "id".

float *WritePtr(const int id, const int number)

Get pointer to data array. Useful for direct writes of data. MaxId is bumped by number (and memory allocated if necessary). Id is the location you wish to write into; number is the number of vectors to write. Use the method WrotePtr() to mark completion of write.

void WrotePtr()

Terminate direct write of data. Although dummy routine now, reserved for future use.

vtkFloatVectors& operator=(const vtkFloatVectors& fv)

Deep copy of vectors.

vtkFollower

NAME

vtkFollower - a subclass of actor that always faces the camera

CLASS HIERARCHY

class vtkFollower : public vtkActor

DESCRIPTION

vtkFollower is a subclass of vtkActor that always follows its specified camera. More specifically it will not change its position or scale, but it will continually update its orientation so that it is right side up and facing the camera. This is typically used for text labels in a scene. All of the adjustments that can be made to an actor also will take effect with a follower. So, if you change the orientation of the follower by 90 degrees, then it will follow the camera, but be off by 90 degrees.

SEE ALSO

vtkActor vtkCamera

SUMMARY

void SetCamera(vtkCamera*)
void SetCamera(vtkCamera&)
vtkCamera *GetCamera()
Set/Get the Camera to follow. If this is not set, then the follower won't know who to follow.

vtkFollower()
Creates a follower with no camera set

void GetMatrix(vtkMatrix4x4& result)
Copy the follower's composite 4x4 matrix into the matrix provided.

vtkGaussianSplatter

NAME

vtkGaussianSplatter - splat points with Gaussian distribution

CLASS HIERARCHY

class vtkGaussianSplatter : public vtkDataSetToStructuredPointsFilter

DESCRIPTION

vtkGaussianSplatter is a filter that injects input points into a structured points dataset. As each point is injected, it "splats" or distributes values to neighboring voxels in the structured points dataset. Data is distributed using a Gaussian distribution function. The distribution function is modified using scalar values (expands distribution) or normals/vectors (creates ellipsoidal distribution rather than spherical).

SUMMARY

void SetRadius(float)
float GetRadius()
Specify the radius of propagation of the splat. This value is expressed as a percentage of the sampling structured point set. Smaller numbers greatly reduce execution time.

void SetScaleFactor(float)
float GetScaleFactor()
Multiply Gaussian splat distribution by this value.

void SetExponentFactor(float)
float GetExponentFactor()
Specify sharpness of decay of splat

void SetEccentricity(float)
float GetEccentricity()
Control the shape of elliptical splatting. Eccentricity is the ratio of the major axis (aligned along normal) to the minor (axes) aligned along other two axes.

void SetModelBounds(float data[6])
void SetModelBounds(float *)
float *GetModelBounds()
void GetModelBounds(float data[6])
void SetModelBounds(float xmin, float xmax, float ymin, float ymax,
float zmin, float zmax);
Set the (xmin,xmax, ymin,ymax, zmin,zmax) bounding box in which the sampling is performed.

void SetNormalWarping(int)
int   GetNormalWarping()
void NormalWarpingOn()
void NormalWarpingOff()
Turn on/off the generation of elliptical splats.

void SetScalarWarping(int)
int   GetScalarWarping()

vtkGaussianSplatter

void ScalarWarpingOn()
void ScalarWarpingOff()
Turn on/off the scaling of splats by scalar value.

void SetCapping(int)
int   GetCapping()
void CappingOn()
void CappingOff()
Turn on/off the capping of the outside parts of the structured point set by setting to a specified cap value.

void SetCapValue(float)
float GetCapValue()
Specify the cap value to use.

vtkGaussianSplatter()
Construct object with dimensions=(50,50,50); automatic computation of bounds; a splat radius of 0.1; an exponent factor of -5; and normal and scalar warping turned on.

void ComputeModelBounds()
Compute the size of the sample bounding box automatically from the input data.

void SetSampleDimensions(int i, int j, int k)
Set the dimensions of the sampling structured point set.

vtkGeometryFilter

NAME

vtkGeometryFilter - extract geometry from data (or convert data to polygonal type)

CLASS HIERARCHY

class vtkGeometryFilter : public vtkDataSetToPolyFilter

DESCRIPTION

vtkGeometryFilter is a general-purpose filter to extract geometry (and associated data) from any type of dataset. Geometry is obtained as follows: all 0D, 1D, and 2D cells are extracted. All 2D faces that are used by only one 3D cell (i.e., boundary faces) are extracted. It also is possible to specify conditions on point ids, cell ids, and on bounding box (referred to as "Extent") to control the extraction process.

This filter also may be used to convert any type of data to polygonal type. The conversion process may be less than satisfactory for some 3D datasets. For example, this filter will extract the outer surface of a volume or structured grid dataset. (For structured data you may want to use vtkStructuredPointsGeometryFilter or vtkStructuredGridGeometryFilter.)

CAVEATS

When vtkGeometryFilter extracts cells (or boundaries of cells) it may create duplicate points. Use vtkCleanPolyData to merge duplicate points.

SEE ALSO

vtkStructuredPointsGeometryFilter vtkStructuredGridGeometryFilter

SUMMARY

    void SetPointClipping(int)
    int   GetPointClipping()
    void PointClippingOn()
    void PointClippingOff()
        Turn on/off selection of geometry by point id.

    void SetCellClipping(int)
    int   GetCellClipping()
    void CellClippingOn()
    void CellClippingOff()
        Turn on/off selection of geometry by cell id.

    void SetExtentClipping(int)
    int   GetExtentClipping()
    void ExtentClippingOn()
    void ExtentClippingOff()
        Turn on/off selection of geometry via bounding box.

    void SetPointMinimum(int)
    int   GetPointMinimum()
        Specify the minimum point id for point id selection.

vtkGeometryFilter

void SetPointMaximum(int)
int   GetPointMaximum()
　　　Specify the maximum point id for point id selection.

void SetCellMinimum(int)
int   GetCellMinimum()
　　　Specify the minimum cell id for point id selection.

void SetCellMaximum(int)
int   GetCellMaximum()
　　　Specify the maximum cell id for point id selection.

vtkGeometryFilter()
　　　Construct with all types of clipping turned off.

void SetExtent(float xMin, float xMax, float yMin,
**　　　　　　　　　float yMax, float zMin, float zMax)**
　　　Specify a (xmin,xmax, ymin,ymax, zmin,zmax) bounding box to clip data.

void SetExtent(float *extent)
　　　Specify a (xmin,xmax, ymin,ymax, zmin,zmax) bounding box to clip data.

vtkGeometryPrimitive

NAME

vtkGeometryPrimitive - abstract interface for geometric data

CLASS HIERARCHY

class vtkGeometryPrimitive : public vtkObject

DESCRIPTION

vtkGeometryPrimitive is an abstract specification for objects that interface to the polygonal based rendering libraries. Subclasses of vtkGeometryPrimitive interface indirectly to a renderer during its two pass rendering process. In the first pass (Build()), the vtkGeometryPrimitive object is asked to build its data from its input polygonal data. In the next pass (Draw()), the object is asked to load its data into the graphics pipeline. Typically the user will never encounter this object or its subclasses. It is used to interface the Mappers to the underlying graphics library.

SEE ALSO

vtkMapper

SUMMARY

virtual void Initialize(vtkRenderer *ren) = 0;
Initialize the loading of geometric data during the rendering process.

virtual void Build(vtkPolyData *data, vtkColorScalars *c) = 0;
Build appropriate graphical data representation for the particular library.

virtual void Draw(vtkRenderer *ren) = 0;
Load data into specific graphics library.

vtkProperty *GetProperty()
Return the current property.

void SetProperty(vtkProperty *p)
Set the current property.

vtkGeometryPrimitive ()
Construct empty geometry primitive.

vtkGlyph3D

NAME

vtkGlyph3D - copy oriented and scaled geometry to every input point

CLASS HIERARCHY

class vtkGlyph3D : public vtkDataSetToPolyFilter

DESCRIPTION

vtkGlyph3D is a filter that copies a geometric representation (specified as polygonal data) to every input point. The geometry may be oriented along the input vectors or normals, and it may be scaled according to scalar data or vector magnitude. The geometry is supplied via the Source instance variable; the points come from the Input.

SEE ALSO

vtkTensorEllipsoid

DEFINES

VTK_SCALE_BY_SCALAR 0
VTK_SCALE_BY_VECTOR 1
VTK_USE_VECTOR 0
VTK_USE_NORMAL 1

SUMMARY

void   SetSource(vtkPolyData*)
void   SetSource(vtkPolyData&)
vtkPolyData *GetSource()
        Specify the geometry to copy to each point.

void   SetScaling(int)
void   ScalingOn()
void   ScalingOff()
int   GetScaling()
        Turn on/off scaling of input geometry.

void   SetScaleMode(int)
int   GetScaleMode()
void   ScaleByScalar()
void   ScaleByVector()
        Either scale by scalar or by vector/normal magnitude.

void   SetScaleFactor(float)
float GetScaleFactor()
        Specify scale factor to scale object by.

void   SetRange(float, float)
void   SetRange(float *)
float *GetRange()
void   GetRange(float data[2])
        Specify range to map scalar values into.

vtkGlyph3D

void	**SetOrient(int)**
void	**OrientOn()**
void	**OrientOff()**
int	**GetOrient()**

Turn on/off orienting of input geometry along vector/normal.

void	**SetClamping(int)**
void	**ClampingOn()**
void	**ClampingOff()**
int	**GetClamping()**

Turn on/off clamping of scalar values to range.

void	**SetVectorMode(int)**
int	**GetVectorMode()**
void	**UseVector()**
void	**UseNormal()**

Specify whether to use vector or normal to perform vector operations.

void	**Update()**

Override update method because execution can branch two ways (Input and Source).

vtkGraymap

NAME

vtkGraymap - scalar data in grayscale form

CLASS HIERARCHY

class vtkGraymap : public vtkColorScalars

DESCRIPTION

vtkGraymap is a concrete implementation of vtkScalars. Scalars are represented using a single unsigned char for components of gray. Gray values range from (0,255) with 0 being black.

SUMMARY

unsigned char *GetPtr(const int id)
Get pointer to array of data starting at data position "id".

unsigned char *WritePtr(const int id, const int number)
Get pointer to data array. Useful for direct writes of data. MaxId is bumped by number (and memory allocated if necessary). Id is the location you wish to write into; number is the number of scalars to write. Use the method WrotePtr() to mark completion of write.

void   WrotePtr()
Terminate direct write of data. Although dummy routine now, reserved for future use.

vtkGraymap& operator=(const vtkGraymap& fs)
Deep copy of scalars.

unsigned char *GetColor(int id)
Return a RGBA color for a particular point id. (Note: gray value converted into full RGBA.)

void   GetColor(int id, unsigned char rgba[4])
Copy gray components into user provided array for specified point id. (Note: gray value converted into full RGBA color value.)

void   SetColor(int id, unsigned char rgba[4])
Insert gray value into object. No range checking performed (fast!). (Note: RGBA color value converted to grayscale.)

void   InsertColor(int id, unsigned char rgba[4])
Insert RGBA color value into object. Range checking performed and memory allocated as necessary. (Note: RGBA converted to gray value.)

int   InsertNextColor(unsigned char rgba[4])
Insert RGBA color value into next available slot. Returns point id of slot. (Note: RGBA converted to gray value.)

unsigned char GetGrayValue(int id)
Return a gray value for a particular point id.

vtkGraymap

void SetGrayValue(int id, unsigned char g)
Insert gray value into object. No range checking performed (fast!).

void InsertGrayValue(int id, unsigned char g)
Insert gray value into object. Range checking performed and memory allocated as necessary.

int   InsertNextGrayValue(unsigned char g)
Insert gray value into next available slot. Returns point id of slot.

vtkHedgeHog

NAME

vtkHedgeHog - create oriented lines from vector data

CLASS HIERARCHY

class vtkHedgeHog : public vtkDataSetToPolyFilter

DESCRIPTION

vtkHedgeHog creates oriented lines from the input data set. Line length is controlled by vector magnitude times scale factor. Vectors are colored by scalar data, if available.

SUMMARY

void SetScaleFactor(float)
float GetScaleFactor()
Set scale factor to control size of oriented lines.

vtkHexahedron

NAME

vtkHexahedron - a cell that represents a 3D rectangular hexahedron

CLASS HIERARCHY

class vtkHexahedron : public vtkCell

DESCRIPTION

vtkHexahedron is a concrete implementation of vtkCell to represent a 3D rectangular hexahedron (e.g., "brick" topology).

SUMMARY

vtkHexahedron(const vtkHexahedron& h)
Deep copy of cell.

**void   JacobianInverse(float pcoords[3], float inverse[9],
                                      float derivs[24])**
Given parametric coordinates compute inverse Jacobian transformation matrix. Returns 9 elements of 3x3 inverse Jacobian plus interpolation function derivatives.

vtkHyperStreamline

NAME

vtkHyperStreamline - generate hyperstreamline in arbitrary dataset

CLASS HIERARCHY

class vtkHyperStreamline : public vtkDataSetToPolyFilter

DESCRIPTION

vtkHyperStreamline is a filter that integrates through tensor field to generate a hyperstreamline. The integration is along the maximum eigenvector and the cross section of the hyperstreamline is defined by the two other eigenvectors. Thus the shape of the hyperstreamline is "tube-like", with the cross section being elliptical. Hyperstreamlines are used to visualize tensor fields.

The starting point of a hyperstreamline can be defined in one of two ways. First, you may specify an initial position. This is a x-y-z global coordinate. The second option is to specify a starting location. This is cellId, subId, and cell parametric coordinates.

The integration of the hyperstreamline occurs through the major eigenvector field. IntegrationStepLength controls the step length within each cell (i.e., this is the fraction of the cell length). The length of the hyperstreamline is controlled by MaximumPropagationDistance. This parameter is the length of the hyperstreamline in units of distance. The tube itself is composed of many small sub-tubes - NumberOfSides controls the number of sides in the tube, and StepLength controls the length of the sub-tubes.

Because hyperstreamlines are often created near regions of singularities, it it possible to control the scaling of the tube cross section by using a logarithmic scale. Use LogScalingOn to turn this capability on. The Radius value controls the initial radius of the tube.

SEE ALSO

vtkTensorEllipsoids vtkStreamer

DEFINES

```
VTK_INTEGRATE_FORWARD 0
VTK_INTEGRATE_BACKWARD 1
VTK_INTEGRATE_BOTH_DIRECTIONS 2
VTK_START_FROM_POSITION 0
VTK_START_FROM_LOCATION 1
```

SUMMARY

void SetMaximumPropagationDistance(float)
float GetMaximumPropagationDistance()
Specify the maximum length of the hyperstreamline expressed as absolute distance (i.e., arc length) value.

vtkHyperStreamline

void SetIntegrationStepLength(float)
float GetIntegrationStepLength()
Specify a nominal integration step size (expressed as a fraction of the size of each cell).

void SetStepLength(float)
float GetStepLength()
Specify the length of a tube segment composing the hyperstreamline. The length is specified as a fraction of the diagonal length of the input bounding box.

void SetIntegrationDirection(int)
VTK_INTEGRATE_FORWARD,VTK_INTEGRATE_BOTH_DIRECTIONS);
int GetIntegrationDirection()
Specify the direction in which to integrate the hyperstreamline.

void SetTerminalEigenvalue(float)
float GetTerminalEigenvalue()
Set/get terminal eigenvalue. If major eigenvalue falls below this value, hyperstreamline terminates propagation.

void SetNumberOfSides(int)
int GetNumberOfSides()
Set the number of sides for the hyperstreamlines. At a minimum, number of sides is 3.

void SetRadius(float)
float GetRadius()
Set the initial tube radius. This is the maximum "elliptical" radius at the beginning of the tube. Radius varies based on ratio of eigenvalues. Note that tube section is actually elliptical and may become a point or line in cross section in some cases.

void SetLogScaling(int)
int GetLogScaling()
void LogScalingOn()
void LogScalingOff()
Turn on/off logarithmic scaling. If scaling is on, the log base 10 of the computed eigenvalues are used to scale the cross section radii.

vtkHyperStreamline()
Construct object with initial starting position (0,0,0); integration step length 0.2; step length 0.01; forward integration; terminal eigenvalue 0.0; number of sides 6; radius 0.5; and logarithmic scaling off.

void SetStartLocation(int cellId, int subId, float pcoords[3])
Specify the start of the hyperstreamline in the cell coordinate system. That is, cellId and subId (if composite cell), and parametric coordinates.

void SetStartLocation(int cellId, int subId, float r, float s, float t)
Specify the start of the hyperstreamline in the cell coordinate system. That is, cellId and subId (if composite cell), and parametric coordinates.

int GetStartLocation(int& subId, float pcoords[3])
Get the starting location of the hyperstreamline in the cell coordinate system. Returns the cell that the starting point is in.

vtkHyperStreamline

void SetStartPosition(float x[3])
Specify the start of the hyperstreamline in the global coordinate system. Starting from position implies that a search must be performed to find initial cell to start integration from.

void SetStartPosition(float x, float y, float z)
Specify the start of the hyperstreamline in the global coordinate system. Starting from position implies that a search must be performed to find initial cell to start integration from.

float *GetStartPosition()
Get the start position of the hyperstreamline in global x-y-z coordinates.

void IntegrateMajorEigenvector()
Use the major eigenvector field as the vector field through which to integrate. The major eigenvector is the eigenvector whose corresponding eigenvalue is closest to positive infinity.

void IntegrateMediumEigenvector()
Use the major eigenvector field as the vector field through which to integrate. The major eigenvector is the eigenvector whose corresponding eigenvalue is between the major and minro eigenvalues.

void IntegrateMinorEigenvector()
Use the major eigenvector field as the vector field through which to integrate. The major eigenvector is the eigenvector whose corresponding eigenvalue is closest to negative infinity.

vtkIdList

NAME

vtkIdList - list of point or cell ids

CLASS HIERARCHY

class vtkIdList : public vtkObject

DESCRIPTION

vtkIdList is used to represent and pass data id's between objects. vtkIdList may represent any type of integer id, but usually represent point and cell ids.

SUMMARY

int   GetNumberOfIds()

Return the number of id's in the list.

int   GetId(const int i)

Return the id at location i.

void   SetId(const int i, const int id)

Set the id at location i. Doesn't do range checking.

void   InsertId(const int i, const int id)

Set the id at location i. Does range checking and allocates memory as necessary.

int   InsertNextId(const int id)

Add the id specified to the end of the list. Range checking is performed.

int   getChunk(const int sz)

Get a piece of memory to write into. Allocates memory as necessary.

int   IsId(int id)

Return 1 if id specified is contained in list; 0 otherwise.

void   DeleteId(int Id)

Delete specified id from list.

void   IntersectWith(vtkIdList& otherIds)

Intersect this list with another vtkIdList. Updates current list according to result of intersection operation.

NAME

vtkImage - a regular array of 2D scalar floating point data

CLASS HIERARCHY

class vtkImage : public vtkStructuredPoints

DESCRIPTION

vtkImage is a data object that is a concrete implementation of vtkDataSet. vtkImage represents a geometric structure that is a topological and geometrical regular array of points. Examples include volumes (voxel data) and pixmaps. It is more restrictive than its parent vtkStructuredPoints in that it only uses vtkFloatScalars for scalar value storage. This object should probably be named vtkFloatImage.

vtkImageFilter

NAME

vtkImageFilter - a filter that takes a vtkImage as input

CLASS HIERARCHY

class vtkImageFilter : public vtkFilter

DESCRIPTION

vtkImageFilter is an abstract class which defines filters that input vtkImage data types.
This is done for performance reasons so that an image processing algorithm can know
that it is working with a floating point data array instead of being required to use the
more generic, but slower methods.

SEE ALSO

vtkImage vtkFilter

SUMMARY

void SetInput(vtkImage *input);
void SetInput(vtkImage &input)
vtkImage *GetInput()
Set/Get the input to this filter. This must be of type vtkImage or a subclass of it.

void SetInput(vtkImage *input)
Specify the input data or filter.

vtkImageToImageFilter

NAME

vtkImageToImageFilter -a filter with vtkImage as input and output

CLASS HIERARCHY

class vtkImageToImageFilter : public vtkImageFilter

DESCRIPTION

vtkImageToImageFilter is an abstract class which defines filters that input and output vtkImage data types. This is done for performance reasons so that an image processing algorithm can know that it is working with a floating point data array instead of being required to use the more generic, but slower methods.

SEE ALSO

vtkImage vtkImageFilter vtkImageToPolyDataFilter vtkStructuredPointsToImageFilter

SUMMARY

vtkImage *GetOutput()

Get the output of this filter.

vtkImageToPolyDataFilter

NAME

vtkImageToPolyDataFilter - abstract filter class

CLASS HIERARCHY

class vtkImageToPolyDataFilter : public vtkImageFilter

DESCRIPTION

vtkImageToPolyDataFilter is an abstract filter class whose subclasses take on input a vtkImage and generate polygonal data on output.

SEE ALSO

vtkImage vtkPolyData

SUMMARY

vtkPolyData *GetOutput()
Get the output of this filter.

vtkImplicitBoolean

NAME

vtkImplicitBoolean - implicit function consisting of boolean combinations of implicit functions

CLASS HIERARCHY

class vtkImplicitBoolean : public vtkImplicitFunction

DESCRIPTION

vtkImplicitBoolean is an implicit function consisting of boolean combinations of implicit functions. The class has a list of functions (FunctionList) that are combined according to a specified operator (VTK_UNION or VTK_INTERSECTION or VTK_DIFFERENCE). You can use nested combinations of vtkImplicitFunctions (and/ or vtkImplicitBoolean) to create elaborate implicit functions. vtkImplicitBoolean is a concrete implementation of vtkImplicitFunction.

The operators work as follows. The VTK_UNION operator takes the minimum value of all implicit functions. The VTK_INTERSECTION operator takes the maximum value of all implicit functions. The VTK_DIFFERENCE operator subtracts the 2nd through last implicit functions from the first.

DEFINES

VTK_UNION 0
VTK_INTERSECTION 1
VTK_DIFFERENCE 2
VTK_UNION_OF_MAGNITUDES 3

SUMMARY

void   SetOperationType(int)
int   GetOperationType()

Specify the type of boolean operation.

vtkImplicitBoolean()

void   AddFunction(vtkImplicitFunction *f)

Add another implicit function to the list of functions.

void   RemoveFunction(vtkImplicitFunction *f)

Remove a function from the list of implicit functions to boolean.

vtkImplicitFunction

NAME

vtkImplicitFunction - abstract interface for implicit functions

CLASS HIERARCHY

class vtkImplicitFunction : public vtkObject

DESCRIPTION

vtkImplicitFunction specifies an abstract interface for implicit functions. Implicit functions are of the form $F(x,y,z) = 0$. Two primitive operations are required: the ability to evaluate the function and the function gradient at a given point.

vtkImplicitFunction provides a mechanism to transform the implicit function(s) via a transformation matrix. This capability can be used to translate, orient, or scale implicit functions. For example, a sphere implicit function can be transformed into an oriented ellipse. This is accomplished by using an instance of vtkTransform.

CAVEATS

The transformation matrix transforms a point into the space of the implicit function (i.e., the model space). Typically we want to transpose the implicit model into world coordinates. In this case the inverse of the transform is required.

SEE ALSO

vtkTransform

SUMMARY

virtual float EvaluateFunction(float x[3]) = 0;

Evaluate function at position x-y-z and return value. Must be implemented by derived class.

virtual void EvaluateGradient(float x[3], float g[3]) = 0;

Evaluate function gradient at position x-y-z and pass back vector. Must be implemented by derived class.

void SetTransform(vtkTransform*)
void SetTransform(vtkTransform&)
vtkTransform *GetTransform()

Set/Get transformation matrix to transform implicit function.

float FunctionValue(float x[3])

Evaluate function at position x-y-z and return value. Point x[3] is transformed through transform (if provided).

void FunctionGradient(float x[3], float g[3])

Evaluate function gradient at position x-y-z and pass back vector. Point x[3] is transformed through transform (if provided).

vtkImplicitFunctionCollection

NAME

vtkImplicitFunctionCollection - maintain a list of implicit functions

CLASS HIERARCHY

class vtkImplicitFunctionCollection : public vtkCollection

DESCRIPTION

vtkImplicitFunctionCollection is an object that creates and manipulates lists of objects of type vtkImplicitFunction.

SEE ALSO

vtkCollection

SUMMARY

void AddItem(vtkImplicitFunction *f)
Add a implicit function to the list.

void RemoveItem(vtkImplicitFunction *f)
Remove a implicit function from the list.

int IsItemPresent(vtkImplicitFunction *f)
Determine whether a particular implicit function is present. Returns its position in the list.

vtkImplicitFunction *GetNextItem()
Get the next implicit function in the list.

vtkImplicitModeller

NAME

vtkImplicitModeller - compute distance from input geometry on structured point set

CLASS HIERARCHY

class vtkImplicitModeller : public vtkDataSetToStructuredPointsFilter

DESCRIPTION

vtkImplicitModeller is a filter that computes the distance from the input geometry on a structured point set. This distance function can then be "contoured" to generate new, offset surfaces from the original geometry.

SEE ALSO

vtkSampleFunction

SUMMARY

int   *GetSampleDimensions()
void GetSampleDimensions(int data[3])
void SetSampleDimensions(int i, int j, int k);
void SetSampleDimensions(int dim[3]);
Set/Get the i-j-k dimensions on which to sample distance function.

void SetMaximumDistance(float)
float GetMaximumDistance()
Specify distance away from surface of input geometry to sample. Smaller values make large increases in performance.

void SetModelBounds(float data[6])
void SetModelBounds(float *)
float *GetModelBounds()
void GetModelBounds(float data[6])
void SetModelBounds(float xmin, float xmax, float ymin, float ymax, float zmin, float zmax);
Specify the region in space in which to perform the sampling.

void SetCapping(int)
int   GetCapping()
void CappingOn()
void CappingOff()
The outer boundary of the structured point set can be assigned a particular value. This can be used to close or "cap" all surfaces.

void SetCapValue(float)
float GetCapValue()
Specify the capping value to use.

vtkImplicitModeller()
Construct with sample dimensions=(50,50,50), so that model bounds are automatically computed from input. Capping is turned on with CapValue equal to a large positive number.

vtkImplicitModeller

float ComputeModelBounds()
Compute ModelBounds from input geometry.

void SetSampleDimensions(int i, int j, int k)
Set the i-j-k dimensions on which to sample the distance function.

vtkImplicitTextureCoords

NAME

vtkImplicitTextureCoords - generate 1D, 2D, or 3D texture coordinates based on implicit function(s)

CLASS HIERARCHY

class vtkImplicitTextureCoords : public vtkDataSetToDataSetFilter

DESCRIPTION

vtkImplicitTextureCoords is a filter to generate 1D, 2D, or 3D texture coordinates from one, two, or three implicit functions, respectively. In combinations with a vtkBooleanTexture map, the texture coordinates can be used to highlight (via color or intensity) or cut (via transparency) dataset geometry without any complex geometric processing. (Note: the texture coordinates are referred to as r-s-t coordinates.)

The texture coordinates are automatically normalized to lie between (0,1). Thus, no matter what the implicit functions evaluate to, the resulting texture coordinates lie between (0,1), with the zero implicit function value mapped to the 0.5 texture coordinates value. Depending upon the maximum negative/positive implicit function values, the full (0,1) range may not be occupied (i.e., the positive/negative ranges are mapped using the same scale factor).

A boolean variable InvertTexture is available to flip the texture coordinates around 0.5 (value 1.0 becomes 0.0, 0.25->0.75). This is equivalent to flipping the texture map (but a whole lot easier).

CAVEATS

You can use the transformation capabilities of vtkImplicitFunction to orient, translate, and scale the implicit functions. Also, the dimension of the texture coordinates is implicitly defined by the number of implicit functions defined.

SEE ALSO

vtkImplicitFunction vtkTexture vtkBooleanTexture

SUMMARY

void SetRFunction(vtkImplicitFunction*)
void SetRFunction(vtkImplicitFunction&)
vtkImplicitFunction *GetRFunction()
　　Specify an implicit function to compute the r texture coordinate.

void SetSFunction(vtkImplicitFunction*)
void SetSFunction(vtkImplicitFunction&)
vtkImplicitFunction *GetSFunction()
　　Specify an implicit function to compute the s texture coordinate.

void SetTFunction(vtkImplicitFunction*)
void SetTFunction(vtkImplicitFunction&)
vtkImplicitFunction *GetTFunction()
　　Specify an implicit function to compute the t texture coordinate.

vtkImplicitTextureCoords

void SetFlipTexture(int)
int   GetFlipTexture()
void FlipTextureOn()
void FlipTextureOff()
　　　Specify a implicit function to compute the t texture coordinate.

vtkImplicitTextureCoords()
　　　Create object with texture dimension=2 and no r-s-t implicit functions defined
　　　and FlipTexture turned off.

vtkIndent

NAME

vtkIndent - a simple class to control print indentation

CLASS HIERARCHY

class vtkIndent

DESCRIPTION

vtkIndent is used to control indentation during the chaining print process. This way nested objects can correctly indent themselves.

SUMMARY

vtkIndent GetNextIndent()
Determine the next indentation level. Keep indenting by two until the max of forty.

ostream& operator<<(ostream& os, vtkIndent& ind)
Print out the indentation. Basically output a bunch of spaces.

vtkIntArray

NAME

vtkIntArray - dynamic, self-adjusting integer array

CLASS HIERARCHY

class vtkIntArray : public vtkObject

DESCRIPTION

vtkIntArray is an array of integer numbers. It provides methods for insertion and retrieval of integer values, and will automatically resize itself to hold new data.

SUMMARY

int   **GetValue(const int id)**
Get the data at a particular index.

int   ***GetPtr(const int id)**
Get the address of a particular data index.

int   ***WritePtr(const int id, const int number)**
Get the address of a particular data index. Make sure data is allocated for the number of items requested. Set MaxId according to the number of data values requested.

vtkIntArray& InsertValue(const int id, const int i)
Insert data at a specified position in the array.

int   **InsertNextValue(const int i)**
Insert data at the end of the array. Return its location in the array.

int& operator[](const int i)
Does insert or get (depending on location on lhs or rhs of statement). Does not do automatic resizing - user's responsibility to range check.

void **Squeeze()**
Resize object to just fit data requirement. Reclaims extra memory.

int   **GetSize()**
Get the allocated size of the object in terms of number of data items.

int   **GetMaxId()**
Return the maximum index of data inserted so far.

void **Reset()**
Reuse the memory allocated by this object. Object appears as if no data has been previously inserted.

int   **Allocate(const int sz, const int ext)**
Allocate memory for this array. Delete old storage if present.

void **Initialize()**
Release storage and reset array to initial state.

vtkIntArray(const int sz, const int ext)
Construct with specified storage and extend value.

vtkIntArray

vtkIntArray(const vtkIntArray& ia)
Construct array from another array. Copy each element of other array.

vtkIntArray& operator=(const vtkIntArray& ia)
Deep copy of another array.

void operator+=(const vtkIntArray& ia)
Append one array onto the end of this array.

vtkIntPoints

NAME

vtkIntPoints - integer representation of 3D points

CLASS HIERARCHY

class vtkIntPoints : public vtkPoints

DESCRIPTION

vtkIntPoints is a concrete implementation of vtkPoints. Points are represented using integer values.

SUMMARY

int   *GetPtr(const int id)

Get pointer to array of data starting at data position "id".

int   *WritePtr(const int id, const int number)

Get pointer to data array. Useful for direct writes of data. MaxId is bumped by number (and memory allocated if necessary). Id is the location you wish to write into; number is the number of points to write. Use the method WrotePtr() to mark completion of write.

void   WrotePtr()

Terminate direct write of data. Although dummy routine now, reserved for future use.

vtkIntPoints& operator=(const vtkIntPoints& fp)

Deep copy of points.

vtkIntScalars

NAME

vtkIntScalars - integer representation of scalar data

CLASS HIERARCHY

class vtkIntScalars : public vtkScalars

DESCRIPTION

vtkIntScalars is a concrete implementation of vtkScalars. Scalars are represented using integer values.

SUMMARY

int   *GetPtr(const int id)
Get pointer to array of data starting at data position "id".

int   *WritePtr(const int id, const int number)
Get pointer to data array. Useful for direct writes of data. MaxId is bumped by number (and memory allocated if necessary). Id is the location you wish to write into; number is the number of scalars to write. Use the method WrotePtr() to mark completion of write.

void WrotePtr()
Terminate direct write of data. Although dummy routine now, reserved for future use.

vtkIntScalars& operator=(const vtkIntScalars& is)
Deep copy of scalars.

vtkLODActor

NAME

vtkLODActor - an actor that supports multiple levels of detail

CLASS HIERARCHY

class vtkLODActor : public vtkActor

DESCRIPTION

vtkLODActor is an actor that stores multiple Levels of Detail and can automatically switch between them. It selects which level of detail to use based on how much time it has been allocated to render. Currently a very simple method of TotalTime/ NumberOfActors is used. In the future this should be modified to dynamically allocate the rendering time between different actors based on their needs. There are currently three levels of detail. The top level is just the normal data. The lowest level of detail is a simple bounding box outline of the actor. The middle level of detail is a point cloud of a fixed number of points that have been randomly sampled from the Mappers input data. Point attributes are copied over to the point cloud. These two lower levels of detail are accomplished by creating instances of a vtkOutlineFilter, vtkGlyph3D, and vtkPointSource.

SEE ALSO

vtkActor vtkRenderer

SUMMARY

int   GetNumberOfCloudPoints()
void SetNumberOfCloudPoints(int)
Set/Get the number of random points for the point cloud.

vtkLODActor()
Creates a vtkLODActor with the following defaults: origin(0,0,0) position=(0,0,0) scale=(1,1,1) visibility=1 pickable=1 dragable=1 orientation=(0,0,0). NumberOfCloudPoints is set to 150.

void Render(vtkRenderer *ren)
This causes the actor to be rendered. It, in turn, will render the actor's property and then mapper.

vtkLWObject

NAME

vtkLWObject - abstract base class for visualization library

CLASS HIERARCHY

class vtkLWObject

DESCRIPTION

vtkLWObject is the base class for many objects that use multiple inheritance. vtkLWObject is a "light weight" version of vtkObject, whose sole function is to resolve issues of multiple inheritance. (NOTE: This was done because the alternative, virtual base classes, causes many problems with current C++ compilers. Also, the ability to "cast down" is not possible with virtual base classes.)

This class reimplements some of the methods and instance variables found in vtkObject. It uses the same naming scheme, but prepends each with a "_" character.

DEFINES

vtk_DebugMacro(x)
vtk_WarningMacro(x)
vtk_ErrorMacro(x)

SUMMARY

vtkLWObject()
Construct object.

void _Modified()
Update the modification time for this object.

unsigned long int _GetMTime()
Return the modification for this object.

void _DebugOn()
Turn debug printout on.

void _DebugOff()
Turn debug printout off.

vtkLight

NAME

vtkLight - a virtual light for 3D rendering

CLASS HIERARCHY

class vtkLight : public vtkObject

DESCRIPTION

vtkLight is a virtual light for 3D rendering. It provides methods to locate and point the light, turn it on and off, and set its brightness and color. In addition to the basic infinite distance point light source attributes, you also can specify the light attenuation values and cone angle. These attributes are only used if the light is a positional light. The default is a directional light (e.g. infinite point light source).

SEE ALSO

vtkLightDevice

SUMMARY

virtual void Render(vtkRenderer *ren,int light_index);
Abstract interface to renderer. Each concrete subclass of vtkLight will load its data into the graphics system in response to this method invocation. The actual loading is performed by a vtkLightDevice subclass, which will be created automatically.

void SetColor(float, float, float)
void SetColor(float *)
float *GetColor()
void GetColor(float data[3])
Set/Get the color of the light.

void SetPosition(float, float, float)
void SetPosition(float *)
float *GetPosition()
void GetPosition(float data[3])
Set/Get the position of the light.

void SetFocalPoint(float, float, float)
void SetFocalPoint(float *)
float *GetFocalPoint()
void GetFocalPoint(float data[3])
Set/Get the point at which the light is shining.

void SetIntensity(float)
float GetIntensity()
Set/Get the brightness of the light (from one to zero).

void SetSwitch(int)
int   GetSwitch()

vtkLight

void SwitchOn()
void SwitchOff()
Turn the light on or off.

void SetPositional(int)
int GetPositional()
void PositionalOn()
void PositionalOff()
Turn positional lighting on or off.

void SetExponent(float)
float GetExponent()
Set/Get the exponent of the cosine used in positional lighting.

void SetConeAngle(float)
float GetConeAngle()
Set/Get the lighting cone angle of a positional light in degrees.

void SetAttenuationValues(float, float, float)
void SetAttenuationValues(float *)
float *GetAttenuationValues()
void GetAttenuationValues(float data[3])
Set/Get the quadratic attenuation constants. They are specified as constant, linear, and quadratic, in that order.

vtkLight()
Create a light with the focal point at the origin and its position set to (0,0,1). The lights color is white, intensity=1, and the light is turned on.

vtkLightCollection

NAME

vtkLightCollection - a list of lights

CLASS HIERARCHY

class vtkLightCollection : public vtkCollection

DESCRIPTION

vtkLightCollection represents and provides methods to manipulate a list of lights (i.e., vtkLight and subclasses). The list is unsorted and duplicate entries are not prevented.

SEE ALSO

vtkCollection vtkLight

SUMMARY

void AddItem(vtkLight *a)
Add a light to the list.

void RemoveItem(vtkLight *a)
Remove a light from the list.

int IsItemPresent(vtkLight *a)
Determine whether a particular light is present. Returns its position in the list.

vtkLight *GetNextItem()
Get the next light in the list. NULL is returned when the collection is exhausted.

vtkLightDevice

NAME

vtkLightDevice - abstract definition of a hardware dependent light

CLASS HIERARCHY

class vtkLightDevice : public vtkObject

DESCRIPTION

vtkLightDevice is the superclass of the hardware dependent lights such as vtkOglrLight and vtkSbrLight. This object is typically created automatically by a vtkLight object when it renders. The user should never see this class.

SEE ALSO

vtkLight

SUMMARY

virtual void Render(vtkLight *lgt, vtkRenderer *ren,int light_index) = 0;
This is the only method that the subclasses must supply.

vtkLine

NAME

vtkLine - cell represents a 1D line

CLASS HIERARCHY

class vtkLine : public vtkCell

DESCRIPTION

vtkLine is a concrete implementation of vtkCell to represent a 1D line.

SUMMARY

vtkLine(const vtkLine& l)
Deep copy of cell.

float DistanceToLine(float x[3], float p1[3], float p2[3],
float &t, float closestPoint[3])
Compute distance to finite line.

float DistanceToLine (float x[3], float p1[3], float p2[3])
Determine the distance of the current vertex to the edge defined by the vertices
provided. Returns distance squared. Note: line is assumed infinite in extent.

vtkLineSource

NAME

vtkLineSource - create a line defined by two end points

CLASS HIERARCHY

class vtkLineSource : public vtkPolySource

DESCRIPTION

vtkLineSource is a source object that creates a polyline defined by two endpoints. The number of segments composing the polyline is controlled by setting the object resolution.

SUMMARY

> **void SetPoint1(float, float, float)**
> **void SetPoint1(float *)**
> **float *GetPoint1()**
> **void GetPoint1(float data[3])**
> Set position of first end point.

> **void SetPoint2(float, float, float)**
> **void SetPoint2(float *)**
> **float *GetPoint2()**
> **void GetPoint2(float data[3])**
> Set position of other end point.

> **void SetResolution(int)**
> **int   GetResolution()**
> Divide line into resolution number of pieces.

vtkLinearExtrusionFilter

NAME

vtkLinearExtrusionFilter - sweep polygonal data creating a "skirt" from free edges and lines, and lines from vertices

CLASS HIERARCHY

class vtkLinearExtrusionFilter : public vtkPolyToPolyFilter

DESCRIPTION

vtkLinearExtrusionFilter is a modelling filter. It takes polygonal data as input and generates polygonal data on output. The input dataset is swept according to some extrusion function and creates new polygonal primitives. These primitives form a "skirt" or swept surface. For example, sweeping a line results in a quadrilateral, and sweeping a triangle creates a "wedge".

There are a number of control parameters for this filter. You can control whether the sweep of a 2D object (i.e., polygon or triangle strip) is capped with the generating geometry via the "Capping" ivar. Also, you can extrude in the direction of a user specified vector, towards a point, or in the direction of vertex normals (normals must be provided - use vtkPolyNormals if necessary). The amount of extrusion is controlled by the "ScaleFactor" instance variable.

The skirt is generated by locating certain topological features. Free edges (edges of polygons or triangle strips only used by one polygon or triangle strips) generate surfaces. This is true also of lines or polylines. Vertices generate lines.

This filter can be used to create 3D fonts, 3D irregular bar charts, or to model 2 1/2D objects like punched plates. It also can be used to create solid objects from 2D polygonal meshes.

CAVEATS

Some polygonal objects have no free edges (e.g., sphere). When swept, this will result in two separate surfaces if capping is on, or no surface if capping is off.

SEE ALSO

vtkRotationalExtrusionFilter

DEFINES

VTK_VECTOR_EXTRUSION 1
VTK_NORMAL_EXTRUSION 2
VTK_POINT_EXTRUSION 3

SUMMARY

void SetExtrusionType(int)
int GetExtrusionType()
Set/Get the type of extrusion.

vtkLinearExtrusionFilter

void **SetCapping(int)**
int **GetCapping()**
void **CappingOn()**
void **CappingOff()**
Turn on/off the capping of the skirt.

void **SetScaleFactor(float)**
float **GetScaleFactor()**
Set/Get extrusion scale factor,

void **SetVector(float, float, float)**
void **SetVector(float *)**
float ***GetVector()**
void **GetVector(float data[3])**
Set/Get extrusion vector. Only needs to be set if VectorExtrusion is turned on.

void **SetExtrusionPoint(float, float, float)**
void **SetExtrusionPoint(float *)**
float ***GetExtrusionPoint()**
void **GetExtrusionPoint(float data[3])**
Set/Get extrusion point. Only needs to be set if PointExtrusion is turned on. This
is the point towards which extrusion occurs.

vtkLinearExtrusionFilter()
Create object with normal extrusion type, capping on, scale factor=1.0, vector
(0,0,1), and extrusion point (0,0,0).

vtkLinkList

NAME

vtkLinkList - object represents upward pointers from points to list of cells using each point

CLASS HIERARCHY

class vtkLinkList : public vtkRefCount

DESCRIPTION

vtkLinkList is a supplemental object to CellArray and CellList to allow access from points to cells using the points. LinkList is a collection of Links, each link represents a dynamic list of cell id's using the point. The information provided by this object can be used to determine neighbors and construct other local topological information.

SEE ALSO

vtkCellArray vtkCellList

SUMMARY

_vtkLink_s &GetLink(int ptId)
Get a link structure given a point id.

unsigned short GetNcells(int ptId)
Get the number of cells using the point.

int   *GetCells(int ptId)
Return a list of cell ids using the point.

void IncrementLinkCount(int ptId)
Increment the count of the number of cells using the point.

void InsertCellReference(int ptId, unsigned short pos, int cellId)
Insert a cell id into the list of cells using the point.

void DeletePoint(int ptId)
Delete point (and storage) by destroying links to using cells.

void InsertNextCellReference(int ptId, int cellId)
Insert a cell id into the list of cells (at the end) using the cell id provided. (Make sure to extend the link list (if necessary) using the method ResizeCellList().)

void RemoveCellReference(int cellId, int ptId)
Delete the reference to the cell (cellId) from the point (ptId). This removes the reference to the cellId from the cell list, but does not resize the list (recover memory with ResizeCellList(), if necessary).

void ResizeCellList(int ptId, int size)
Increase the length of the list of cells using a point by the size specified.

void AllocateLinks(int n)
Allocate memory for the list of lists of cell ids.

vtkLinkList

void Squeeze()
Reclaim any unused memory.

void BuildLinks(vtkDataSet *data)
Build the link list array.

vtkLocator

NAME

vtkLocator - spatial search object to quickly locate points

CLASS HIERARCHY

class vtkLocator : public vtkObject

DESCRIPTION

vtkLocator is a spatial search object to quickly locate points in 3D. vtkLocator works by dividing a specified region of space into a regular array of "rectangular" buckets, and then keeping a list of points that lie in each bucket. Typical operation involves giving a position in 3D and finding the closest point.

CAVEATS

Many other types of spatial locators have been developed such as octrees and kd-trees. These are often more efficient for the operations described here.

SUMMARY

void SetPoints(vtkPoints*)
void SetPoints(vtkPoints&)
vtkPoints *GetPoints()
      Set list of points to insert into locator.

void SetDivisions(int, int, int)
void SetDivisions(int *)
int   *GetDivisions()
void GetDivisions(int data[3])
      Set the number of divisions in x-y-z directions.

void SetAutomatic(int)
int   GetAutomatic()
void AutomaticOn()
void AutomaticOff()
      Boolean controls whether automatic subdivision size is computed from average number of points in bucket.

void SetNumberOfPointsInBucket(int)
int   GetNumberOfPointsInBucket()
      Specify the average number of points in each bucket.

void SetTolerance(float)
float GetTolerance()
      Specify absolute tolerance (in world coordinates) for performing merge operations.

vtkLocator()
      Construct with automatic computation of divisions, averaging 25 points per bucket.

int   FindClosestPoint(float x[3])
      Given a position x, return the id of the point closest to it.

vtkLocator

int ***MergePoints()**
Merge points together based on tolerance specified. Return a list that maps unmerged point ids into new point ids.

int **InitPointInsertion(vtkPoints *newPts, float bounds[6])**
Initialize the point insertion process. The newPts is an object representing point coordinates into which incremental insertion methods place their data. Bounds are the box that the points lie in.

int **InsertPoint(float x[3])**
Incrementally insert a point into search structure, merging the point with pre-inserted point (if within tolerance). If point is merged with pre-inserted point, pre-inserted point id is returned. Otherwise, new point id is returned. Before using this method you must make sure that newPts have been supplied, the bounds has been set properly, and that divs are properly set. (See InitPointInsertion().)

vtkLogLookupTable

NAME

vtkLogLookupTable - map scalar values into colors using logarithmic (base 10) color table

CLASS HIERARCHY

class vtkLogLookupTable : public vtkLookupTable

DESCRIPTION

vtkLogLookupTable is an object that is used by mapper objects to map scalar values into RGBA (red-green-blue-alpha transparency) color specification, or RGBA into scalar values. The difference between this class and its superclass vtkLookupTable is that this class performs scalar mapping based on a logarithmic lookup process. (Uses log base 10.)

If non-positive ranges are encountered, then they are converted to positive values using absolute value.

SEE ALSO

vtkLookupTable

SUMMARY

vtkLogLookupTable(int sze, int ext):
vtkLookupTable(sze,ext)
Construct with effective range 1->10 (based on logarithmic values).

void   SetTableRange(float min, float max)
Set the minimum/maximum scalar values for scalar mapping. Scalar values less than minimum range value are clamped to minimum range value. Scalar values greater than maximum range value are clamped to maximum range value. (The log base 10 of these values is taken and mapping is performed in logarithmic space.)

unsigned char *MapValue(float v)
Given a scalar value v, return an RGBA color value from lookup table. Mapping performed log base 10 (negative ranges are converted into positive values).

vtkLookupTable

NAME

vtkLookupTable - map scalar values into colors or colors to scalars; generate color table

CLASS HIERARCHY

class vtkLookupTable : public vtkRefCount

DESCRIPTION

vtkLookupTable is an object that is used by mapper objects to map scalar values into RGBA (red-green-blue-alpha transparency) color specification, or RGBA into scalar values. The color table can be created by direct insertion of color values, or by specifying hue, saturation, value, and alpha range and generating a table.

This class is designed as a base class for derivation by other classes. The Build(), MapValue(), and SetTableRange() methods are virtual and may require overloading in subclasses.

CAVEATS

vtkLookupTable is a reference counted object. Therefore, you should always use operator "new" to construct new objects. This procedure will avoid memory problems (see text).

SEE ALSO

vtkLogLookupTable

SUMMARY

void SetNumberOfColors(int)
int GetNumberOfColors()
Set the number of colors in the lookup table.

void SetHueRange(float, float)
void SetHueRange(float *)
float *GetHueRange()
void GetHueRange(float data[2])
Set the range in hue (using automatic generation). Hue ranges from (0,1).

void SetSaturationRange(float, float)
void SetSaturationRange(float *)
float *GetSaturationRange()
void GetSaturationRange(float data[2])
Set the range in saturation (using automatic generation). Hue ranges from (0,1).

void SetValueRange(float, float)
void SetValueRange(float *)
float *GetValueRange()
void GetValueRange(float data[2])
Set the range in value (using automatic generation). Value ranges from (0,1).

void SetAlphaRange(float, float)
void SetAlphaRange(float *)

vtkLookupTable

float *GetAlphaRange()
void GetAlphaRange(float data[2])
> Set the range in alpha (using automatic generation). Alpha ranges from (0,1).

unsigned char *GetPtr(const int id)
> Get pointer to color table data. Format is array of unsigned char r-g-b-a-r-g-b-a...

unsigned char *WritePtr(const int id, const int number)
> Get pointer to data. Useful for direct writes into object. MaxId is bumped by number (and memory allocated if necessary). Id is the location you wish to write into; number is the number of RGBA values to write. Use the method WrotePtr() to mark completion of write.

void WrotePtr()
> Terminate direct write of data. Although dummy routine now, reserved for future use.

vtkLookupTable(int sze, int ext)
> Construct with range=(0,1); and hsv ranges set up for rainbow color table (from red to blue).

int Allocate(int sz, int ext)
> Allocate a color table of specified size.

void SetTableRange(float r[2])
> Set the minimum/maximum scalar values for scalar mapping. Scalar values less than minimum range value are clamped to minimum range value. Scalar values greater than maximum range value are clamped to maximum range value.

void SetTableRange(float min, float max)
> Set the minimum/maximum scalar values for scalar mapping. Scalar values less than minimum range value are clamped to minimum range value. Scalar values greater than maximum range value are clamped to maximum range value.

void Build()
> Generate lookup table from hue, saturation, value, alpha min/max values. Table is built from linear ramp of each value.

unsigned char *MapValue(float v)
> Given a scalar value v, return an RGBA color value from lookup table.

void SetTableValue (int indx, float rgba[4])
> Directly load color into lookup table. Use [0,1] float values for color component specification.

void SetTableValue(int indx, float r, float g, float b, float a)
> Directly load color into lookup table. Use [0,1] float values for color component specification.

float *GetTableValue (int indx)
> Return a RGBA color value for the given index into the lookup table. Color components are expressed as [0,1] float values.

void GetTableValue (int indx, float rgba[4])
> Return a RGBA color value for the given index into the lookup table. Color components are expressed as [0,1] float values.

vtkMCubesReader

NAME

vtkMCubesReader - read binary marching cubes file

CLASS HIERARCHY

class vtkMCubesReader : public vtkPolySource

DESCRIPTION

vtkMCubesReader is a source object that reads binary marching cubes files. (Marching cubes is an isosurfacing technique that generates many triangles.) The binary format is supported by B. Lorensen's marching cubes program (and the vtkSliceCubes object). The format repeats point coordinates, so this object will merge the points with a vtkLocator object. You can choose to supply the vtkLocator or use the default.

CAVEATS

Binary files assumed written in sun/hp/sgi form.

Because points are merged when read, degenerate triangles may be removed. Thus the number of triangles read may be fewer than the number of triangles written.

SEE ALSO

vtkMarchingCubes vtkSliceCubes

SUMMARY

    void SetFilename(char *)
    char *GetFilename()
        Specify file name of marching cubes file.

    void SetLimitsFilename(char *)
    char *GetLimitsFilename()
        Specify file name of marching cubes limits file.

    void SetFlipNormals(int)
    int GetFlipNormals()
    void FlipNormalsOn()
    void FlipNormalsOff()
        Specify whether to flip normals in opposite direction.

    void SetNormals(int)
    int GetNormals()
    void NormalsOn()
    void NormalsOff()
        Specify whether to read normals.

    void CreateDefaultLocator();
        Create default locator. Used to create one when none is specified.

    vtkMCubesReader()
        Construct object with FlipNormals and Normals set to true.

vtkMCubesReader

void SetLocator(vtkLocator *locator)
Specify a spatial locator for merging points. By default, an instance of
vtkMergePoints is used.

vtkMapper

NAME

vtkMapper - abstract class specifies interface to map data to graphics primitives

CLASS HIERARCHY

class vtkMapper : public vtkObject

DESCRIPTION

vtkMapper is an abstract class to specify interface between data and graphics primitives. Subclasses of vtkMapper map data through a lookuptable and control the creation of rendering primitives that interface to the graphics library. The mapping can be controlled by supplying a lookup table and specifying a scalar range to map data through.

SUMMARY

virtual void Render(vtkRenderer *) = 0;

Method initiates the mapping process. Generally sent by the actor as each frame is rendered.

virtual void CreateDefaultLookupTable();

Create default lookup table. Generally used to create one when none is available.

void   SetScalarsVisible(int)
int   GetScalarsVisible()
void   ScalarsVisibleOn()
void   ScalarsVisibleOff()

Turn on/off flag to control whether scalar data is used to color objects.

void   SetScalarRange(float, float)
void   SetScalarRange(float *)
float *GetScalarRange()
void   GetScalarRange(float data[2])

Specify range in terms of (smin,smax), through which to map scalars into lookup table.

virtual float *GetBounds() = 0;

Return bounding box of data in terms of (xmin,xmax, ymin,ymax, zmin,zmax). Used in the rendering process to automatically create a camera in the proper initial configuration.

vtkMapper()

Construct with initial range (0,1).

unsigned long GetMTime()

Overload standard modified time function. If lookup table is modified, then we are modified as well.

void   SetStartRender(void (*f)(void *), void *arg)

Specify a function to be called before rendering process begins. Function will be called with argument provided.

vtkMapper

void SetStartRenderArgDelete(void (*f)(void *))
Set the arg delete method. This is used to free user memory.

void SetEndRenderArgDelete(void (*f)(void *))
Set the arg delete method. This is used to free user memory.

void SetEndRender(void (*f)(void *), void *arg)
Specify a function to be called when rendering process completes. Function will be called with argument provided.

void SetLookupTable(vtkLookupTable *lut)
Specify a lookup table for the mapper to use.

vtkMarchingCubes

NAME

vtkMarchingCubes - generate isosurface(s) from volume

CLASS HIERARCHY

class vtkMarchingCubes : public vtkStructuredPointsToPolyDataFilter

DESCRIPTION

vtkMarchingCubes is a filter that takes as input a volume (e.g., 3D structured point set) and generates on output one or more isosurfaces. One or more contour values must be specified to generate the isosurfaces. Alternatively, you can specify a min/max scalar range and the number of contours to generate a series of evenly spaced contour values. The current implementation requires that the scalar data is defined with "short int" data values.

CAVEATS

The output primitives are disjoint - that is, points may be generated that are coincident but distinct. You may want to use vtkCleanPolyData to remove the coincident points.

This filter is specialized to volumes. If you are interested in contouring other types of data, use the general vtkContourFilter.

SEE ALSO

vtkContourFilter vtkSliceCubes vtkDividingCubes

DEFINES

VTK_MAX_CONTOURS 256

SUMMARY

float *GetValues()
void GetValues(float data[VTK_MAX_CONTOURS])
    Return array of contour values (size of numContours).

vtkMarchingCubes()
    Construct object with initial range (0,1) and single contour value of 0.0.

void SetValue(int i, float value)
    Set a particular contour value at contour number i.

void GenerateValues(int numContours, float range[2])
    Generate numContours equally spaced contour values between specified range.

void GenerateValues(int numContours, float r1, float r2)
    Generate numContours equally spaced contour values between specified range.

vtkMaskPoints

NAME

vtkMaskPoints - selectively filter points

CLASS HIERARCHY

class vtkMaskPoints : public vtkDataSetToPolyFilter

DESCRIPTION

vtkMaskPoints is a filter that passes through points and point attributes from input dataset. (Other geometry is not passed through.) It is possible to mask every nth point, and to specify an initial offset to begin masking from. A special random mode feature enables random selection of points.

SUMMARY

void SetOnRatio(int)
int   GetOnRatio()
Turn on every nth point.

void SetMaximumNumberOfPoints(int)
int   GetMaximumNumberOfPoints()
Limit the number of points that can be passed through.

void SetOffset(int)
int   GetOffset()
Start with this point.

void SetRandomMode(int)
int   GetRandomMode()
void RandomModeOn()
void RandomModeOff()
Special flag causes randomization of point selection. If this mode is on, statically every nth point (i.e., OnRatio) will be displayed.

vtkMaskPolyData

NAME

vtkMaskPolyData - sample subset of input polygonal data

CLASS HIERARCHY

class vtkMaskPolyData : public vtkPolyToPolyFilter

DESCRIPTION

vtkMaskPolyData is a filter that sub-samples input polygonal data. The user specifies every nth item, with an initial offset to begin sampling.

SUMMARY

void SetOnRatio(int)
int   GetOnRatio()
    Turn on every nth entity,

void SetOffset(int)
int   GetOffset()
    Start with this point.

vtkMath

NAME

vtkMath - performs common math operations

CLASS HIERARCHY

class vtkMath

DESCRIPTION

vtkMath is provides methods to perform common math operations. These include providing constants such as Pi; conversion from degrees to radians; vector operations such as dot and cross products and vector norm; matrix determinant for 2x2, 3x3, and 4x4 matrices; and random number generation.

SUMMARY

float Dot(float x[3], float y[3])
Dot product of two 3-vectors.

float Norm(float x[3])
Compute the norm of 3-vector.

float Normalize(float x[3])
Normalize (in place) a 3-vector. Returns norm of vector.

float Determinant2x2(float c1[2], float c2[2])
Compute determinant of 2x2 matrix. Two columns of matrix are input.

double Determinant2x2(double a, double b, double c, double d)
Calculate the determinant of a 2x2 matrix: | a b | | c d |

float Determinant3x3(float c1[3], float c2[3], float c3[3])
Compute determinant of 3x3 matrix. Three columns of matrix are input.

double Determinant3x3(double a1, double a2, double a3,
| a1, b1, c1 | | a2, b2, c2 | | a3, b3, c3 |

float Distance2BetweenPoints(float x[3], float y[3])
Compute distance squared between two points.

float Random(float min, float max)
Generate random number between (min,max)

float Random()
Generate random numbers between 0.0 and 1.0 This is used to provide portability across different systems. Based on code in "Random Number Generators: Good Ones are Hard to Find," by Stephen K. Park and Keith W. Miller in *Communications of the ACM*, 31, 10 (Oct. 1988) pp. 1192-1201. Borrowed from: Fuat C. Baran, Columbia University, 1988.

void RandomSeed(long s)
Initialize seed value. NOTE: Random() has the bad property that the first random number returned after RandomSeed() is called is proportional to the seed value! To help solve this, I call RandomSeed() a few times inside seed. This doesn't ruin the repeatability of Random().

vtkMath

void Cross(float x[3], float y[3], float z[3])
Cross product of two 3-vectors. Result vector in z[3].

int Jacobi(float **a, float *w, float **v)
Jacobi iteration for the solution of eigenvectors/eigenvalues of a 3x3 real symmetric matrix. Square 3x3 matrix a; output eigenvalues in w; and output eigenvectors in v. Resulting eigenvalues/vectors are sorted in decreasing order; eigenvectors are normalized.

vtkMatrix4x4

NAME

vtkMatrix4x4 - represent and manipulate 4x4 transformation matrices

CLASS HIERARCHY

class vtkMatrix4x4 : public vtkObject

DESCRIPTION

vtkMatrix4x4 is a class to represent and manipulate 4x4 matrices. Specifically, it is designed to work on 4x4 transformation matrices found in 3D rendering using homogeneous coordinates [x y z w].

SEE ALSO

vtkTransform

SUMMARY

vtkMatrix4x4 ()

Construct a 4x4 identity matrix.

void operator= (float element)

Set all the elements of the matrix to the given value.

void MultiplyPoint(float in[4],float result[4])

Multiply this matrix by a point (in homogeneous coordinates). and return the result in result. The in[4] and result[4] arrays must both be allocated but they can be the same array.

void PointMultiply(float in[4],float result[4])

Multiply a point (in homogeneous coordinates) by this matrix, and return the result in result. The in[4] and result[4] arrays must both be allocated, but they can be the same array.

void Invert (vtkMatrix4x4 in,vtkMatrix4x4 & out)

Matrix Inversion (by Richard Carling from "Graphics Gems," Academic Press, 1990).

float Determinant (vtkMatrix4x4 & in)

Compute the determinant of the matrix and return it.

void Adjoint (vtkMatrix4x4 & in,vtkMatrix4x4 & out)

Compute adjoint of the matrix and put it into out.

void Transpose (vtkMatrix4x4 in,vtkMatrix4x4 & out)

Transpose the matrix and put it into out.

vtkMergeFilter

NAME

vtkMergeFilter - extract separate components of data from different datasets

CLASS HIERARCHY

class vtkMergeFilter : public vtkFilter

DESCRIPTION

vtkMergeFilter is a filter that extracts separate components of data from different datasets and merges them into a single dataset. The output from this filter is of the same type as the input (i.e., vtkDataSet.)

SUMMARY

void SetGeometry(vtkDataSet *input);
void SetGeometry(vtkDataSet &input)
vtkDataSet *GetGeometry()
> Specify object from which to extract geometry information.

vtkDataSet *GetOutput()
> Get the output of this source.

void SetScalars(vtkDataSet*)
void SetScalars(vtkDataSet&)
vtkDataSet *GetScalars()
> Specify object from which to extract scalar information.

void SetVectors(vtkDataSet*)
void SetVectors(vtkDataSet&)
vtkDataSet *GetVectors()
> Specify object from which to extract vector information.

void SetNormals(vtkDataSet*)
void SetNormals(vtkDataSet&)
vtkDataSet *GetNormals()
> Specify object from which to extract normal information.

void SetTCoords(vtkDataSet*)
void SetTCoords(vtkDataSet&)
vtkDataSet *GetTCoords()
> Specify object from which to extract texture coordinates information.

void SetTensors(vtkDataSet*)
void SetTensors(vtkDataSet&)
vtkDataSet *GetTensors()
> Specify object from which to extract tensor data.

void SetUserDefined(vtkDataSet*)
void SetUserDefined(vtkDataSet&)
vtkDataSet *GetUserDefined()
> Specify object from which to extract user defined data.

vtkMergePoints

NAME

vtkMergePoints - merge exactly coincident points

CLASS HIERARCHY

class vtkMergePoints : public vtkLocator

DESCRIPTION

vtkMergePoints is a locator object to quickly locate points in 3D. The primary difference between vtkMergePoints and its superclass vtkLocator is that vtkMergePoints merges precisely coincident points and is therefore much faster.

SEE ALSO

vtkCleanPolyData

SUMMARY

int   *MergePoints()
Merge points together if they are exactly coincident. Return a list that maps unmerged point ids into new point ids. User is responsible for freeing list (use delete []).

int   InsertPoint(float x[3])
Incrementally insert a point into search structure, merging the point with pre-inserted point (if precisely coincident). If point is merged with pre-inserted point, pre-inserted point id is returned. Otherwise, new point id is returned. Before using this method you must make sure that newPts have been supplied, the bounds has been set properly, and that divs are properly set (see InitPointInsertion() from superclass.)

vtkNormals

NAME

vtkNormals - abstract interface to 3D normals

CLASS HIERARCHY

class vtkNormals : public vtkRefCount

DESCRIPTION

vtkNormals provides an abstract interface to 3D normals. The data model for vtkNormals is an array of nx-ny-nz triplets accessible by point id. (Each normal is assumed normalized $|n| = 1$.) The subclasses of vtkNormals are concrete data types (float, int, etc.) that implement the interface of vtkNormals.

SUMMARY

virtual vtkNormals *MakeObject(int sze, int ext=1000) = 0;
Create a copy of this object.

virtual char *GetDataType() = 0;
Return data type. One of "bit", "unsigned char", "short", "int", "float", or "double".

virtual int GetNumberOfNormals() = 0;
Return number of normals in array.

virtual float *GetNormal(int id) = 0;
Return a float normal n[3] for a particular point id.

virtual void GetNormal(int id, float n[3]);
Copy normal components into user provided array n[3] for specified point id.

virtual void SetNormal(int id, float n[3]) = 0;
Insert normal into object. No range checking performed (fast!).

virtual void InsertNormal(int id, float n[3]) = 0;
void InsertNormal(int id, float nx, float ny, float nz);
Insert normal into object. Range checking performed and memory allocated as necessary.

virtual int InsertNextNormal(float n[3]) = 0;
int   InsertNextNormal(float nx, float ny, float nz);
Insert normal into next available slot. Returns point id of slot.

virtual void Squeeze() = 0;
Reclaim any extra memory.

void InsertNormal(int id, float nx, float ny, float nz)
Insert normal into position indicated.

int   InsertNextNormal(float nx, float ny, float nz)
Insert normal into position indicated.

void GetNormals(vtkIdList& ptId, vtkFloatNormals& fp)
Given a list of pt ids, return an array of corresponding normals.

vtkObject

NAME

vtkObject - abstract base class for most of the vtk objects

CLASS HIERARCHY

class vtkObject

DESCRIPTION

vtkObject is the base class for many objects in the visualization toolkit. vtkObject provides methods for tracking modification times, debugging, and printing. Most objects created within the vtk framework should be a subclass of vtkObject or one of its children. The few exceptions tend to be very small helper classes that usually never get instantiated or situations where multiple inheritance gets in the way. Then, LWObject might be required.

SEE ALSO

vtkLWObject

SUMMARY

void Modified()
Update the modification time for this object. Many filters rely on the modification time to determine if they need to recompute their data.

ostream& operator<<(ostream& os, vtkObject& o)
This operator allows all subclasses of vtkObject to be printed via <<. It in turn invokes the Print method, which in turn will invoke the PrintSelf method that all objects should define (if they have anything interesting to print out).

vtkObject()
Create an object with Debug turned off and modified time initialized to zero.

void Delete()
Delete a vtk object. This method should always be used to delete an object when the new operator was used to create it. Using the C++ delete method will not work with reference counting.

unsigned long int GetMTime()
Return the modification for this object.

void PrintSelf(ostream& os, vtkIndent indent)
Chaining method to print an object's instance variables, as well as its superclasses.

void DebugOn()
Turn debugging output on.

void DebugOff()
Turn debugging output off.

int GetDebug()
Get the value of the debug flag.

vtkOutlineFilter

NAME

vtkOutlineFilter - create wireframe outline for arbitrary data set

CLASS HIERARCHY

class vtkOutlineFilter : public vtkDataSetToPolyFilter

DESCRIPTION

vtkOutlineFilter is a filter that generates a wireframe outline of any data set. The outline consists of the twelve edges of the dataset bounding box.

vtkOutlineSource

NAME

vtkOutlineSource - create wireframe outline around bounding box

CLASS HIERARCHY

class vtkOutlineSource : public vtkPolySource

DESCRIPTION

vtkOutlineSource creates a wireframe outline around a user specified bounding box.

SUMMARY

  void SetBounds(float data[6])
  void SetBounds(float *)
  float *GetBounds()
  void GetBounds(float data[6])
    Specify the bounding box for this object.

vtkPLOT3DReader

NAME

vtkPLOT3DReader - read PLOT3D data files

CLASS HIERARCHY

class vtkPLOT3DReader : public vtkStructuredGridSource

DESCRIPTION

vtkPLOT3D is a reader object that reads PLOT3D formatted files and generates a structured grid on output. PLOT3D is a computer graphics program designed to visualize the grids and solutions of computational fluid dynamics. Please see the "PLOT3D User's Manual" available from NASA Ames Research Center, Moffett Field CA.

PLOT3D files consist of a grid file (also known as XYZ file), an optional solution file (also known as a Q file), and an optional function file that contains user created data. The Q file contains solution information as follows: the four parameters free stream mach number (Fsmach), angle of attack (Alpha), Reynolds number (Re), and total integration time (Time). In addition, the solution file contains the flow density (scalar), flow momentum (vector), and flow energy (scalar).

The reader can generate additional scalars and vectors (or "functions") from this information. To use vtkPLOT3DReader, you must specify the particular function number for the scalar and vector you want to visualize. This implementation of the reader provides the following functions. The scalar functions are: -1 - don't read or compute any scalars   100 - density   110 - pressure   120 - temperature   130 - enthalpy   140 - internal energy   144 - kinetic energy   153 - velocity magnitude   163 - stagnation energy   170 - entropy   184 - swirl.

The vector functions are: -1 - don't read or compute any vectors   200 - velocity   201 - vorticity   202 - momentum   210 - pressure gradient (other functions are described in the PLOT3D spec, but only those listed are implemented here). Note that by default, this reader creates the density scalar (100) and momentum vector (202) as output. (These are just read in from the solution file.) Please note that the validity of computation is a function of this class's gas constants (R, Gamma) and the equations used. They may not be suitable for your computational domain.

The format of the function file is as follows. An integer indicating number of grids, then an integer specifying number of functions per each grid. This is followed by the (integer) dimensions of each grid in the file. Finally, for each grid, and for each function, a float value per each point in the current grid. Note: if both a function from the function file is specified, as well as a scalar from the solution file (or derived from the solution file), the function file takes precedence.

DEFINES

VTK_WHOLE_SINGLE_GRID_NO_IBLANKING 0
VTK_WHOLE_MULTI_GRID_NO_IBLANKING 2

vtkPLOT3DReader

SUMMARY

void SetFileFormat(int)
int GetFileFormat()
Specify the PLOT3D file format to use

void SetXYZFilename(char *)
char *GetXYZFilename()
Set/Get the PLOT3D geometry filename.

void SetQFilename(char *)
char *GetQFilename()
Set/Get the PLOT3D solution filename.

void SetFunctionFilename(char *)
char *GetFunctionFilename()
Set/Get the PLOT3D function filename.

void SetGridNumber(int)
int GetGridNumber()
Specify the grid to read.

void SetScalarFunctionNumber(int)
int GetScalarFunctionNumber()
Specify the scalar function to extract. If =-1, then no scalar function is extracted.

void SetVectorFunctionNumber(int)
int GetVectorFunctionNumber()
Specify the vector function to extract. If =-1, then no vector function is extracted.

void SetFunctionFileFunctionNumber(int)
int GetFunctionFileFunctionNumber()
Specify which function to extract from the function file. If =-1, then no function is extracted.

float GetFsmach()
Get the free-stream mach number.

float GetAlpha()
Get the angle of attack.

float GetRe()
Get the Reynold's number.

float GetTime()
Get the total integration time.

void SetR(float)
float GetR()
Set/Get the gas constant.

void SetGamma(float)
float GetGamma()
Set/Get the ratio of specific heats.

void SetUvinf(float)
float GetUvinf()
Set/Get the x-component of the free-stream velocity.

vtkPLOT3DReader

void SetVvinf(float)
float GetVvinf()
Set/Get the y-component of the free-stream velocity.

void SetWvinf(float)
float GetWvinf()
Set/Get the z-component of the free-stream velocity.

vtkPNMReader

NAME

vtkPNMReader - read pnm (i.e., portable anymap) files

CLASS HIERARCHY

class vtkPNMReader : public vtkStructuredPointsSource

DESCRIPTION

vtkPNMReader is a source object that reads pnm (portable anymap) files. This includes .pbm (bitmap), .pgm (grayscale), and .ppm (pixmap) files. (Currently this object only reads binary versions of these files.)

PNMReader creates structured point datasets. The dimension of the dataset depends upon the number of files read. Reading a single file results in a 2D image, while reading more than one file results in a 3D volume.

To read a volume, files must be of the form "filename.<number>" (e.g., foo.ppm.0, foo.ppm.1, ...). You must also specify the image range. This range specifies the beginning and ending files to read (range can be any pair of non-negative numbers).

The default behavior is to read a single file. In this case, the form of the file is simply "filename" (e.g., foo.bar, foo.ppm, foo.pnm). To differentiate between reading images and volumes, the image range is set to (-1,-1) to read a single image file.

SUMMARY

void SetFilename(char *)
char *GetFilename()
Specify file name of pnm file(s).

void SetImageRange(int, int)
void SetImageRange(int *)
int   *GetImageRange()
void GetImageRange(int data[2])
Set the range of files to read.

void SetDataAspectRatio(float, float, float)
void SetDataAspectRatio(float *)
float *GetDataAspectRatio()
void GetDataAspectRatio(float data[3])
Specify an aspect ratio for the data.

void SetDataOrigin(float, float, float)
void SetDataOrigin(float *)
float *GetDataOrigin()
void GetDataOrigin(float data[3])
Specify the origin for the data.

vtkPicker

NAME

vtkPicker - select an actor by shooting a ray into a graphics window

CLASS HIERARCHY

class vtkPicker : public vtkObject

DESCRIPTION

vtkPicker is used to select actors by shooting a ray into a graphics window and intersecting with the actor's bounding box. The ray is defined from a point defined in window (or pixel) coordinates, and a point located from the camera's position.

vtkPicker may return more than one actor, since more than one bounding box may be intersected. vtkPicker returns the list of actors that were hit, the pick coordinates in world and untransformed mapper space, and the actor and mapper that are "closest" to the camera. The closest actor is the one whose center point (i.e., center of bounding box) projected on the ray is closest to the camera.

CAVEATS

vtkPicker and its subclasses will not pick actors that are "unpickable" (see vtkActor) or are fully transparent.

SEE ALSO

vtkPicker is used for quick picking. If you desire to pick points or cells, use the subclass vtkPointPicker or vtkCellPicker, respectively.

SUMMARY

vtkRenderer *GetRenderer()
Get the renderer in which pick event occurred.

float *GetSelectionPoint()
void GetSelectionPoint(float data[3])
Get the selection point in screen (pixel) coordinates. The third value is related to z-buffer depth. (Normally should be =0.)

void SetTolerance(float)
float GetTolerance()
Specify tolerance for performing pick operation. Tolerance is specified as fraction of rendering window size. (Rendering window size is measured across diagonal.)

float *GetPickPosition()
void GetPickPosition(float data[3])
Return position in global coordinates of pick point.

float *GetMapperPosition()
void GetMapperPosition(float data[3])
Return position in mapper (i.e., non-transformed) coordinates of pick point.

vtkPicker

vtkActor *GetActor()
Return actor that was picked.

vtkMapper *GetMapper()
Return mapper that was picked.

vtkDataSet *GetDataSet()
Get a pointer to the dataset that was picked. If nothing was picked then NULL is returned.

vtkPicker()
Construct object with initial tolerance of 1/40th of window.

int   Pick(float selectionX, float selectionY, float selectionZ, vtkRenderer *renderer)
Perform pick operation with selection point provided. Normally the first two values for the selection point are x-y pixel coordinate, and the third value is =0. Return non-zero if something was successfully picked.

vtkPixel

NAME

vtkPixel - a cell that represents an orthogonal quadrilateral

CLASS HIERARCHY

class vtkPixel : public vtkCell

DESCRIPTION

vtkPixel is a concrete implementation of vtkCell to represent a 2D orthogonal quadrilateral. Unlike vtkQuad, the corners are at right angles, and aligned along x-y-z coordinate axes leading to large increases in computational efficiency.

SUMMARY

vtkPixel(const vtkPixel& p)
Deep copy of cell.

vtkPixmap

NAME

vtkPixmap - scalar data in RGB (color) form

CLASS HIERARCHY

class vtkPixmap : public vtkColorScalars

DESCRIPTION

vtkPixmap is a concrete implementation of vtkScalars. Scalars are represented using three values for color (red, green, blue). Each of r,g,b ranges from (0,255) (i.e., an unsigned char value).

SUMMARY

void SetColor(int i, unsigned char rgba[4])

Set a RGBA color value at a particular array location. Does not do range checking.

void InsertColor(int i, unsigned char rgba[4])

Insert a RGBA color value at a particular array location. Does range checking and will allocate additional memory if necessary.

int InsertNextColor(unsigned char *rgba)

Insert a RGBA value at the next available slot in the array. Will allocate memory if necessary.

unsigned char *GetPtr(const int id)

Get pointer to array of data starting at data position "id".

unsigned char *WritePtr(const int id, const int number)

Get pointer to data array. Useful for direct writes of data. MaxId is bumped by number (and memory allocated if necessary). Id is the location you wish to write into; number is the number of scalars to write. Use the method WrotePtr() to mark completion of write.

void WrotePtr()

Terminate direct write of data. Although dummy routine now, reserved for future use.

vtkPixmap& operator=(const vtkPixmap& fs)

Deep copy of scalars.

unsigned char *GetColor(int i)

Return a RGBA color at array location i.

void GetColor(int id, unsigned char rgba[4])

Copy RGBA components into user provided array rgb[4] for specified point id.

vtkPlane

NAME

vtkPlane - perform various plane computations

CLASS HIERARCHY

class vtkPlane : public vtkImplicitFunction

DESCRIPTION

vtkPlane provides methods for various plane computations. These include projecting points onto a plane, evaluating the plane equation, and returning plane normal. vtkPlane is a concrete implementation of the abstract class vtkImplicitFunction.

SUMMARY

void SetNormal(float, float, float)
void SetNormal(float *)
float *GetNormal()
void GetNormal(float data[3])
Set/get plane normal. Plane is defined by point and normal.

void SetOrigin(float, float, float)
void SetOrigin(float *)
float *GetOrigin()
void GetOrigin(float data[3])
Set/get point through which plane passes. Plane is defined by point and normal.

float Evaluate(float normal[3], float origin[3], float x[3])
Quick evaluation of plane equation n(x-origin)=0.

float DistanceToPlane(float x[3], float n[3], float p0[3])
Return the distance of a point x to a plane defined by $n(x-p0) = 0$. The normal n[3] must be magnitude=1.

int IntersectWithLine(float p1[3], float p2[3], float n[3],
**   float p0[3], float& t, float x[3])**
Given a line defined by the two points p1,p2; and a plane defined by the normal n and point p0, compute an intersection. The parametric coordinate along the line is returned in t, and the coordinates of intersection are returned in x. A 0 is returned if the plane and line are parallel.

vtkPlaneSource

NAME

vtkPlaneSource - create an array of quadrilaterals located in the plane

CLASS HIERARCHY

class vtkPlaneSource : public vtkPolySource

DESCRIPTION

vtkPlaneSource creates an m x n array of quadrilaterals arranged as a regular tiling in the plane. The plane is centered at the origin, and orthogonal to the global z-axis. The resolution of the plane can be specified in both the x and y directions (i.e., specify m and n, respectively).

SUMMARY

void SetResolution(const int xR, const int yR)
Set the number of x-y subdivisions in the plane.

vtkPlanes

NAME

vtkPlanes - implicit function for convex set of planes

CLASS HIERARCHY

class vtkPlanes : public vtkImplicitFunction

DESCRIPTION

vtkPlanes computes the implicit function and function gradient for a set of planes. The planes must define a convex space.

The function value is the closest distance of a point to any of the planes. The function gradient is the plane normal at the function value. Note that the normals must point outside of the convex region. Thus, a negative function value means that a point is inside the convex region.

To define the planes you must create two objects: a subclass of vtkPoints (e.g., vtkFloatPoints) and a subclass of vtkNormals (e.g., vtkFloatNormals). The points define a point on the plane, and the normals specify plane normals.

SUMMARY

void SetPoints(vtkPoints*)
void SetPoints(vtkPoints&)
vtkPoints *GetPoints()
Specify a list of points defining points through which the planes pass.

void SetNormals(vtkNormals*)
void SetNormals(vtkNormals&)
vtkNormals *GetNormals()
Specify a list of normal vectors for the planes. There is a one-to-one correspondence between plane points and plane normals.

vtkPointData

NAME

vtkPointData - represent and manipulate point attribute data

CLASS HIERARCHY

class vtkPointData : public vtkObject

DESCRIPTION

vtkPointData is a class that is used to represent and manipulate point attribute data (e.g., scalars, vectors, normals, texture coordinates, etc.) Special methods are provided to work with filter objects, such as passing data through filter, copying data from one point to another, and interpolating data given cell interpolation weights.

SUMMARY

void SetScalars(vtkScalars*)
void SetScalars(vtkScalars&)
vtkScalars *GetScalars()
    Set scalar data.

void SetVectors(vtkVectors*)
void SetVectors(vtkVectors&)
vtkVectors *GetVectors()
    Set vector data.

void SetNormals(vtkNormals*)
void SetNormals(vtkNormals&)
vtkNormals *GetNormals()
    Set normal data.

void SetTCoords(vtkTCoords*)
void SetTCoords(vtkTCoords&)
vtkTCoords *GetTCoords()
    Set texture coordinates data.

void SetTensors(vtkTensors*)
void SetTensors(vtkTensors&)
vtkTensors *GetTensors()
    Set tensor data.

void SetUserDefined(vtkUserDefined*)
void SetUserDefined(vtkUserDefined&)
vtkUserDefined *GetUserDefined()
    Set user defined data.

void SetCopyScalars(int)
int GetCopyScalars()
void CopyScalarsOn()
void CopyScalarsOff()
    Turn on/off the copying of scalar data.

void SetCopyVectors(int)
int GetCopyVectors()

vtkPointData

void CopyVectorsOn()
void CopyVectorsOff()
Turn on/off the copying of vector data.

void SetCopyNormals(int)
int   GetCopyNormals()
void CopyNormalsOn()
void CopyNormalsOff()
Turn on/off the copying of normals data.

void SetCopyTCoords(int)
int   GetCopyTCoords()
void CopyTCoordsOn()
void CopyTCoordsOff()
Turn on/off the copying of texture coordinates data.

void SetCopyTensors(int)
int   GetCopyTensors()
void CopyTensorsOn()
void CopyTensorsOff()
Turn on/off the copying of tensor data.

void SetCopyUserDefined(int)
int   GetCopyUserDefined()
void CopyUserDefinedOn()
void CopyUserDefinedOff()
Turn on/off the copying of user defined data.

vtkPointData()
Construct object with copying turned on for all data.

vtkPointData& operator=(vtkPointData& pd)
Shallow copy of data.

void CopyData(vtkPointData* fromPd, int fromId, int toId)
Copy the point data from one point to another.

void PassData(vtkPointData* pd)
Pass entire arrays of input data through to output. Obey the "copy" flags.

void CopyAllocate(vtkPointData* pd, int sze, int ext)
Allocates point data for point-by-point copy operation. If sze=0, then use the input PointData to create (i.e., find initial size of) new objects; otherwise use the sze variable.

void InterpolateAllocate(vtkPointData* pd, int sze, int ext)
Initialize point interpolation.

void InterpolatePoint(vtkPointData *fromPd, int toId, vtkIdList *ptIds, float *weights)
Interpolate data from points and interpolation weights.

void CopyAllOn()
Turn on copying of all data.

void CopyAllOff()
Turn off copying of all data.

vtkPointLoad

NAME

vtkPointLoad - compute stress tensors given point load on semi-infinite domain

CLASS HIERARCHY

class vtkPointLoad : public vtkStructuredPointsSource

DESCRIPTION

vtkPointLoad is a source object that computes stress tensors on a volume. The tensors are computed from the application of a point load on a semi-infinite domain. (The analytical results are adapted from Saada - see text.) It also is possible to compute effective stress scalars if desired. This object serves as a specialized data generator for some of the examples in the text.

SEE ALSO

vtkTensorGlyph vtkHyperStreamline

SUMMARY

> **void SetLoadValue(float)**
> **float GetLoadValue()**
> > Set/Get value of applied load.

> **void SetModelBounds(float data[6])**
> **void SetModelBounds(float *)**
> **float *GetModelBounds()**
> **void GetModelBounds(float data[6])**
> **void SetModelBounds(float xmin, float xmax, float ymin, float ymax,**
> **float zmin, float zmax);**
> > Specify the region in space over which the tensors are computed. The point load is assumed to be applied at top center of the volume.

> **void SetPoissonsRatio(float)**
> **float GetPoissonsRatio()**
> > Set/Get Poisson's ratio.

> **void SetComputeEffectiveStress(int)**
> **int GetComputeEffectiveStress()**
> **void ComputeEffectiveStressOn()**
> **void ComputeEffectiveStressOff()**
> > Turn on/off computation of effective stress scalar.

> **vtkPointLoad()**
> > Construct with ModelBounds=(-1,1,-1,1,-1,1), SampleDimensions=(50,50,50), and LoadValue = 1.

> **void SetSampleDimensions(int i, int j, int k)**
> > Specify the dimensions of the volume. A stress tensor will be computed for each point in the volume.

vtkPointLoad

void SetSampleDimensions(int dim[3])
Specify the dimensions of the volume. A stress tensor will be computed for each point in the volume.

vtkPointPicker

NAME

vtkPointPicker - select a point by shooting a ray into a graphics window

CLASS HIERARCHY

class vtkPointPicker : public vtkPicker

DESCRIPTION

vtkPointPicker is used to select a point by shooting a ray into a graphics window and intersecting with actor's defining geometry - specifically its points. Beside returning coordinates, actor, and mapper, vtkPointPicker returns the id of the closest point within the tolerance along the pick ray.

SEE ALSO

vtkPicker vtkCellPicker

SUMMARY

int   GetPointId()
Get the id of the picked point. If PointId = -1, nothing was picked.

vtkPointSet

NAME

vtkPointSet - abstract class for specifying dataset behavior

CLASS HIERARCHY

class vtkPointSet : public vtkDataSet

DESCRIPTION

vtkPointSet is an abstract class that specifies the interface for datasets that explicitly use "point" arrays to represent geometry. For example, vtkPolyData and vtkUnstructuredGrid require point arrays to specify point position, while vtkStructuredPoints generates point positions implicitly.

SUMMARY

void SetPoints(vtkPoints*)
void SetPoints(vtkPoints&)
vtkPoints *GetPoints()
  Specify point array to define point coordinates.

void CopyStructure(vtkDataSet *ds)
  Copy the geometric structure of an input point set object.

vtkPointSetFilter

NAME

vtkPointSetFilter - filter that takes vtkPointSet as input

CLASS HIERARCHY

class vtkPointSetFilter : public vtkFilter

DESCRIPTION

vtkPointSetFilter is a filter that takes a single vtkPointSet data object as input.

SUMMARY

void SetInput(vtkPointSet *input)
Specify the input data or filter.

vtkPointSetToPointSetFilter

NAME

vtkPointSetToPointSetFilter - abstract filter class

CLASS HIERARCHY

class vtkPointSetToPointSetFilter : public vtkPointSetFilter

DESCRIPTION

vtkPointSetToPointSetFilter is an abstract filter class whose subclasses take as input a point set and generates a point set on output. At a minimum, the concrete subclasses of vtkPointSetToPointSetFilter modify their point coordinates. They never modify their topological form, however.

SUMMARY

void SetInput(vtkPointSet *input)
Specify the input data or filter.

void Update()
Update input to this filter and the filter itself. Note that we are overloading this method because the output is an abstract dataset type. This requires special treatment.

vtkPointSet *GetOutput()
Get the output of this filter. If output is NULL then input hasn't been set which is necessary for abstract objects.

vtkPointSource

NAME

vtkPointSource - create a random cloud of points

CLASS HIERARCHY

class vtkPointSource : public vtkPolySource

DESCRIPTION

vtkPointSource is a source object that creates a user-specified number of points within a specified radius about a specified center point. The location of the points is random within the sphere.

SUMMARY

void SetNumberOfPoints(int)
int GetNumberOfPoints()
Set the number of points to generate.

void SetCenter(float, float, float)
void SetCenter(float *)
float *GetCenter()
void GetCenter(float data[3])
Set the center of the point cloud.

void SetRadius(float)
float GetRadius()
Set the radius of the point cloud.

vtkPoints

NAME

vtkPoints - abstract interface to 3D points

CLASS HIERARCHY

class vtkPoints : public vtkRefCount

DESCRIPTION

vtkPoints provides an abstract interface to 3D points. The data model for vtkPoints is an array of x-y-z triplets accessible by point id. The subclasses of vtkPoints are concrete data types (float, int, etc.) that implement the interface of vtkPoints.

SUMMARY

virtual vtkPoints *MakeObject(int sze, int ext=1000) = 0;
Create a copy of this object.

virtual char *GetDataType() = 0;
Return data type. One of "bit", "char", "short", "int", "float", or "double".

virtual int GetNumberOfPoints() = 0;
Return number of points in list.

virtual float *GetPoint(int id) = 0;
Return a pointer to a float array x[3] for a specified point id.

virtual void GetPoint(int id, float x[3]);
Copy point coordinates into user provided array x[3] for specified point id.

virtual void SetPoint(int id, float x[3]) = 0;
Insert point into object. No range checking performed (fast!).

virtual void InsertPoint(int id, float x[3]) = 0;
void InsertPoint(int id, float x, float y, float z);
Insert point into object. Range checking performed and memory allocated as necessary.

virtual int InsertNextPoint(float x[3]) = 0;
int   InsertNextPoint(float x, float y, float z);
Insert point into next available slot. Returns point id of slot.

virtual void Squeeze() = 0; // reclaim memory
Reclaim any extra memory.

virtual void GetPoints(vtkIdList& ptId, vtkFloatPoints& fp);
Get the point coordinates for the point ids specified.

void InsertPoint(int id, float x, float y, float z)
Insert point into position indicated.

int   InsertNextPoint(float x, float y, float z)
Insert point into position indicated.

void GetPoints(vtkIdList& ptId, vtkFloatPoints& fp)
Given a list of pt ids, return an array of point coordinates.

vtkPoints

void ComputeBounds()
    Determine (xmin,xmax, ymin,ymax, zmin,zmax) bounds of points.

float *GetBounds()
    Return the bounds of the points.

void GetBounds(float bounds[6])
    Return the bounds of the points.

vtkPolyData

NAME

vtkPolyData - concrete dataset represents vertices, lines, polygons, and triangle strips

CLASS HIERARCHY

class vtkPolyData : public vtkPointSet

DESCRIPTION

vtkPolyData is a data object that is a concrete implementation of vtkDataSet. vtkPolyData represents a geometric structure consisting of vertices, lines, polygons, and triangle strips. Point attribute values (e.g., scalars, vectors, etc.) also are represented.

The actual cell types (CellType.hh) supported by vtkPolyData are: VTK_VERTEX, VTK_POLY_VERTEX, VTK_LINE, VTK_POLY_LINE, VTK_TRIANGLE, VTK_TRIANGLE_STRIP, VTK_POLYGON, VTK_PIXEL, and VTK_QUAD.

One important feature of vtkPolyData objects is that special traversal and data manipulation methods are available to process data. These methods are generally more efficient than vtkDataSet methods and should be used whenever possible. For example, traversing the cells in a dataset we would use GetCell(). To traverse cells with vtkPolyData we would retrieve the cell array object representing polygons (for example) and then use vtkCellArray's InitTraversal() and GetNextCell() methods.

SUMMARY

void GetPointCells(int ptId, unsigned short& ncells,
Efficient method to obtain cells using a particular point. Make sure that routine BuildLinks() has been called.

int IsTriangle(int v1, int v2, int v3)
Given three vertices, determine whether it's a triangle. Make sure BuildLinks() has been called first.

int IsPointUsedByCell(int ptId, int cellId)
Determine whether a point is used by a particular cell. If it is, return non-zero. Make sure BuildCells() has been called first.

int IsEdge(int p1, int p2)
Determine whether two points form an edge. If they do, return non-zero. Make sure BuildLinks() has been called first.

vtkPolyData(const vtkPolyData& pd) :
vtkPointSet(pd)
Perform shallow construction of vtkPolyData.

void CopyStructure(vtkDataSet *ds)
Copy the geometric and topological structure of an input poly data object.

void SetVerts (vtkCellArray* v)
Set the cell array defining vertices.

vtkPolyData

vtkCellArray* GetVerts()
Get the cell array defining vertices. If there are no vertices, an empty array will be returned (convenience to simplify traversal).

void SetLines (vtkCellArray* l)
Set the cell array defining lines.

vtkCellArray* GetLines()
Get the cell array defining lines. If there are no lines, an empty array will be returned (convenience to simplify traversal).

void SetPolys (vtkCellArray* p)
Set the cell array defining polygons.

vtkCellArray* GetPolys()
Get the cell array defining polygons. If there are no polygons, an empty array will be returned (convenience to simplify traversal).

void SetStrips (vtkCellArray* s)
Set the cell array defining triangle strips.

vtkCellArray* GetStrips()
Get the cell array defining triangle strips. If there are no triangle strips, an empty array will be returned (convenience to simplify traversal).

void Initialize()
Restore object to initial state. Release memory back to system.

void BuildCells()
Create data structure that allows random access of cells.

void BuildLinks()
Create upward links from points to cells that use each point. Enables topologically complex queries.

void GetCellPoints(int cellId, vtkIdList& ptIds)
Copy a cells point ids into list provided. (Less efficient.)

void GetCellPoints(int cellId, int& npts, int* &pts)
Return a pointer to a list of point ids defining cell. (More efficient.) Assumes that cells have been built (with BuildCells()).

void Allocate(int numCells, int extSize)
Method allocates initial storage for vertex, line, polygon, and triangle strip arrays. Use this method before the method PolyData::InsertNextCell(). (Or, provide vertex, line, polygon, and triangle strip cell arrays.)

int InsertNextCell(int type, int npts, int *pts)
Insert a cell of type vtkVERTEX, vtkPOLY_VERTEX, vtkLINE, vtkPOLY_LINE, vtkTRIANGLE, vtkQUAD, vtkPOLYGON, or vtkTRIANGLE_STRIP. Make sure that the PolyData::Allocate() function has been called first or that vertex, line, polygon, and triangle strip arrays have been supplied. Note: will also insert vtkPIXEL, but converts it to vtkQUAD.

int InsertNextCell(int type, vtkIdList &pts)
Insert a cell of type VTK_VERTEX, VTK_POLY_VERTEX, VTK_LINE, VTK_POLY_LINE, VTK_TRIANGLE, VTK_QUAD, VTK_POLYGON, or

vtkPolyData

VTK_TRIANGLE_STRIP. Make sure that the PolyData::Allocate() function has been called first or that vertex, line, polygon, and triangle strip arrays have been supplied. Note: will also insert VTK_PIXEL, but converts it to VTK_QUAD.

void Squeeze()
Recover extra allocated memory when creating data whose initial size is unknown. Examples include using the InsertNextCell() method, or when using the CellArray::EstimateSize() method to create vertices, lines, polygons, or triangle strips.

void Reset()
Begin inserting data all over again. Memory is not freed but otherwise objects are returned to their initial state.

void ReverseCell(int cellId)
Reverse the order of point ids defining the cell.

void ReplaceCell(int cellId, int npts, int *pts)
Replace the points defining cell "cellId" with a new set of points.

void GetCellEdgeNeighbors(int cellId, int p1, int p2, vtkIdList& cellIds)
Get the neighbors at an edge. More efficient than the general GetCellNeighbors(). Assumes links have been built (with BuildLinks()), and looks specifically for edge neighbors.

vtkPolyDataCollection

NAME

vtkPolyDataCollection - maintain a list of polygonal data objects

CLASS HIERARCHY

class vtkPolyDataCollection : public vtkCollection

DESCRIPTION

vtkPolyDataCollection is an object that creates and manipulates lists of datasets of type vtkPolyData.

SEE ALSO

vtkDataSetCollection vtkCollection

SUMMARY

void AddItem(vtkPolyData *pd)
Add a poly data to the list.

void RemoveItem(vtkPolyData *pd)
Remove an poly data from the list.

int IsItemPresent(vtkPolyData *pd)
Determine whether a particular poly data is present. Returns its position in the list.

vtkPolyData *GetNextItem()
Get the next poly data in the list.

vtkPolyFilter

NAME

vtkPolyFilter - filter that takes vtkPolyData as input

CLASS HIERARCHY

class vtkPolyFilter : public vtkFilter

DESCRIPTION

vtkPolyFilter is a filter that takes a single vtkPolyData data object as input.

SUMMARY

void   SetInput(vtkPolyData *input)
Specify the input data or filter.

vtkPolyLine

NAME

vtkPolyLine - cell represents a set of 1D lines

CLASS HIERARCHY

class vtkPolyLine : public vtkCell

DESCRIPTION

vtkPolyLine is a concrete implementation of vtkCell to represent a set of 1D lines.

SUMMARY

vtkPolyLine(const vtkPolyLine& pl)
Deep copy of cell.

int GenerateNormals(vtkPoints *pts, vtkCellArray *lines, vtkFloatNormals *normals)
Given points and lines, compute normals to lines.

int GenerateSlidingNormals(vtkPoints *pts, vtkCellArray *lines, vtkFloatNormals *normals)
Given points and lines, compute normals to lines. These are not true normals, they are "orientation" normals used by classes like vtkTubeFilter that control the rotation around the line. The normals try to stay pointing in the same direction as much as possible (i.e., minimal rotation).

vtkPolyMapper

NAME

vtkPolyMapper - map vtkPolyData to graphics primitives

CLASS HIERARCHY

class vtkPolyMapper : public vtkMapper

DESCRIPTION

vtkPolyMapper is a mapper to map polygonal data (i.e., vtkPolyData) to graphics primitives. It is possible to control which geometric primitives are displayed using the boolean variables provided.

SUMMARY

    void SetInput(vtkPolyData *in);
    void SetInput(vtkPolyData& in)

        Specify the input data to map.

    void SetVertsVisibility(int)
    int   GetVertsVisibility()
    void VertsVisibilityOn()
    void VertsVisibilityOff()

        Control the visibility of vertices.

    void SetLinesVisibility(int)
    int   GetLinesVisibility()
    void LinesVisibilityOn()
    void LinesVisibilityOff()

        Control the visibility of lines.

    void SetPolysVisibility(int)
    int   GetPolysVisibility()
    void PolysVisibilityOn()
    void PolysVisibilityOff()

        Control the visibility of polygons.

    void SetStripsVisibility(int)
    int   GetStripsVisibility()
    void StripsVisibilityOn()
    void StripsVisibilityOff()

        Control the visibility of triangle strips.

    vtkPolyMapper()

        Construct mapper with vertices, lines, polygons, and triangle strips turned on.

vtkPolyNormals

NAME

vtkPolyNormals - compute normals for polygonal mesh

CLASS HIERARCHY

class vtkPolyNormals : public vtkPolyToPolyFilter

DESCRIPTION

vtkPolyNormals is a filter that computes point normals for a polygonal mesh. The filter can reorder polygons to insure consistent orientation across polygon neighbors. Sharp edges can be split and points duplicated with separate normals to give crisp (rendered) surface definition. It is also possible to globally flip the normal orientation.

The algorithm works by determining normals for each polygon and then averaging them at shared points. When sharp edges are present, the edges are split and new points generated to prevent blurry edges (due to Gouraud shading).

SUMMARY

void SetFeatureAngle(float)
float GetFeatureAngle()
Specify the angle that defines a sharp edge. If the difference in angle across neighboring polygons is greater than this value, the shared edge is considered "sharp".

void SetSplitting(int)
int   GetSplitting()
void SplittingOn()
void SplittingOff()
Turn on/off the splitting of sharp edges.

void SetConsistency(int)
int   GetConsistency()
void ConsistencyOn()
void ConsistencyOff()
Turn on/off the enforcement of consistent polygon ordering.

void SetFlipNormals(int)
int   GetFlipNormals()
void FlipNormalsOn()
void FlipNormalsOff()
Turn on/off the global flipping of normal orientation.

void SetMaxRecursionDepth(int)
int   GetMaxRecursionDepth()
Control the depth of recursion used in this algorithm. (Some systems have limited stack depth.)

vtkPolyNormals()
Construct with feature angle=30, splitting and consistency turned on, and flipNormals turned off.

vtkPolyReader

NAME

vtkPolyReader - read vtk polygonal data file

CLASS HIERARCHY

class vtkPolyReader : public vtkPolySource

DESCRIPTION

vtkPolyReader is a source object that reads ASCII or binary polygonal data files in vtk format. See text for format details.

CAVEATS

Binary files written on one system may not be readable on other systems.

SUMMARY

void   SetFilename(char *name)
Specify file name of vtk polygonal data file to read.

int   GetFileType()
Get the type of file (VTK_ASCII or VTK_BINARY)

void   SetScalarsName(char *name)
Set the name of the scalar data to extract. If not specified, first scalar data encountered is extracted.

void   SetVectorsName(char *name)
Set the name of the vector data to extract. If not specified, first vector data encountered is extracted.

void   SetTensorsName(char *name)
Set the name of the tensor data to extract. If not specified, first tensor data encountered is extracted.

void   SetNormalsName(char *name)
Set the name of the normal data to extract. If not specified, first normal data encountered is extracted.

void   SetTCoordsName(char *name)
Set the name of the texture coordinates data to extract. If not specified, first texture coordinates data encountered is extracted.

void   SetLookupTableName(char *name)
Set the name of the lookup table data to extract. If not specified, uses lookup table named by scalar. Otherwise, this specification supersedes.

vtkPolySource

NAME

vtkPolySource - abstract class whose subclasses generate polygonal data

CLASS HIERARCHY

class vtkPolySource : public vtkSource

DESCRIPTION

vtkPolySource is an abstract class whose subclasses generate polygonal data.

SUMMARY

vtkPolyData *GetOutput()
Get the output of this source.

vtkPolyToPolyFilter

NAME

vtkPolyToPolyFilter - abstract filter class

CLASS HIERARCHY

class vtkPolyToPolyFilter : public vtkPolyFilter

DESCRIPTION

vtkPolyToPolyFilter is an abstract filter class whose subclasses take as input polygonal data and generate polygonal data on output.

SUMMARY

vtkPolyData *GetOutput()
Get the output of this filter.

vtkPolyVertex

NAME

vtkPolyVertex - cell represents a set of 0D vertices

CLASS HIERARCHY

class vtkPolyVertex : public vtkCell

DESCRIPTION

vtkPolyVertex is a concrete implementation of vtkCell to represent a set of 3D vertices.

SUMMARY

vtkPolyVertex(const vtkPolyVertex& pp)
Deep copy of cell.

vtkPolyWriter

NAME

vtkPolyWriter - write **vtk** polygonal data

CLASS HIERARCHY

class vtkPolyWriter : public vtkDataWriter

DESCRIPTION

vtkPolyWriter is a source object that writes ASCII or binary polygonal data files in **vtk** format. See text for format details.

CAVEATS

Binary files written on one system may not be readable on other systems.

SUMMARY

void SetInput(vtkPolyData *input)
Specify the input data or filter.

vtkPolygon

NAME

vtkPolygon - a cell that represents an n-sided polygon

CLASS HIERARCHY

class vtkPolygon : public vtkCell

DESCRIPTION

vtkPolygon is a concrete implementation of vtkCell to represent a 2D n-sided polygon. The polygons cannot have any internal holes, and cannot self-intersect.

SUMMARY

vtkPolygon(const vtkPolygon& p)
Deep copy of cell.

void ComputeNormal(vtkPoints *p, int numPts, int *pts, float *n)
Compute the polygon normal from a points list, and a list of point ids that index into the points list.

void ComputeNormal(float *v1, float *v2, float *v3, float *n)
Compute the polygon normal from three points.

void ComputeNormal(vtkFloatPoints *p, float *n)
Compute the polygon normal from a list of floating points.

int ParameterizePolygon(float *p0, float *p10, float& l10, float *p20,float &l20, float *n)
Create a local s-t coordinate system for a polygon.

int PointInPolygon (float bounds[6], float *x, float *n)
Determine whether point is inside polygon. Function uses ray-casting to determine if point is inside polygon. Works for arbitrary polygon shape (e.g., non-convex).

int Triangulate(vtkIdList &outTris)
Triangulate polygon. Tries to use the fast triangulation technique first, and if that doesn't work, uses more complex routine that is guaranteed to work.

int CanSplitLoop (int fedges[2], int numVerts, int *verts, int& n1, int *l1, int& n2, int *l2, float& ar)
Determine whether the loop can be split / build loops.

void SplitLoop (int fedges[2], int numVerts, int *verts, int& n1, int *l1, int& n2, int* l2)
Creates two loops from splitting plane provided.

void ComputeWeights(float x[3], float *weights)
Compute interpolation weights using $1/r^{**}2$ normalized sum.

vtkProbeFilter

NAME

vtkProbeFilter - sample data values at specified point locations

CLASS HIERARCHY

class vtkProbeFilter : public vtkDataSetToDataSetFilter

DESCRIPTION

vtkProbeFilter is a filter that computes point attributes (e.g., scalars, vectors, etc.) at specified point positions. The filter has two inputs: the Input and Source. The Input geometric structure is passed through the filter. The point attributes are computed at the Input point positions by interpolating into the source data. For example, we can compute data values on a plane (plane specified as Input) from a volume (Source).

SUMMARY

void SetSource(vtkDataSet*)
void SetSource(vtkDataSet&)
vtkDataSet *GetSource()
Specify the point locations used to probe input. Any geometry can be used.

void Update()
Overload update method because execution can branch two ways (Input and Source). Also input and output are abstract.

vtkProperty

NAME

vtkProperty - represent surface properties of a geometric object

CLASS HIERARCHY

class vtkProperty : public vtkObject

DESCRIPTION

vtkProperty is an object that represents lighting and other surface properties of a geometric object. The primary properties that can be set are colors (overall, ambient, diffuse, specular, and edge color); specular power; opacity of the object; the representation of the object (points, wireframe, or surface); and the shading method to be used (flat, Gouraud, and Phong).

SEE ALSO

vtkActor vtkPropertyDevice

SUMMARY

virtual void Render(vtkRenderer *ren);

This method causes the property to set up whatever is required for its instance variables. This is actually handled by an instance of vtkPropertyDevice, which is created automatically.

void SetFlat(void);
void SetGouraud(void);
void SetPhong(void);

Set the interpolation of this actor. These three are mutually exclusive.

int GetRepresentation()

Get the method of representation for the object.

int GetInterpolation()

Get the shading method for the object.

void SetColor(float r,float g,float b);
void SetColor(float a[3])
float *GetColor()
void GetColor(float data[3])

Set the color of the object. Has the side effect of setting the ambient diffuse and specular colors as well. This is basically a quick overall color setting method.

void SetAmbient(float)
float GetAmbient()

Set/Get the ambient lighting coefficient.

void SetDiffuse(float)
float GetDiffuse()

Set/Get the diffuse lighting coefficient.

vtkProperty

void SetSpecular(float)
float GetSpecular()
> Set/Get the specular lighting coefficient.

void SetSpecularPower(float)
float GetSpecularPower()
> Set/Get the specular power.

void SetOpacity(float)
float GetOpacity()
> Set/Get the object's opacity. 1.0 is totally opaque and 0.0 is completely
> transparent.

int   GetEdgeVisibility()
void SetEdgeVisibility(int)
void EdgeVisibilityOn()
void EdgeVisibilityOff()
> Turn on/off the visibility of edges. On some renderers it is possible to render the
> edges of geometric primitives separately from the interior.

int   GetBackface()
void SetBackface(int)
void BackfaceOn()
void BackfaceOff()
> Turn backface properties on and off (not implemented yet).

void SetAmbientColor(float, float, float)
void SetAmbientColor(float *)
float *GetAmbientColor()
void GetAmbientColor(float data[3])
> Set/Get the ambient surface color. Not all renderers support separate ambient and
> diffuse colors. From a physical standpoint it really doesn't make too much sense
> to have both. For the rendering libraries that don't support both, the diffuse color
> is used.

void SetDiffuseColor(float, float, float)
void SetDiffuseColor(float *)
float *GetDiffuseColor()
void GetDiffuseColor(float data[3])
> Set/Get the diffuse surface color.

void SetSpecularColor(float, float, float)
void SetSpecularColor(float *)
float *GetSpecularColor()
void GetSpecularColor(float data[3])
> Set/Get the specular surface color.

void SetEdgeColor(float, float, float)
void SetEdgeColor(float *)
float *GetEdgeColor()
void GetEdgeColor(float data[3])
> Set/Get the color of primitive edges (if edge visibility enabled).

vtkProperty

vtkProperty()
Construct object with object color, ambient color, diffuse color, specular color, and edge color white; ambient coefficient=0; diffuse coefficient=0; specular coefficient=0; specular power=1; Gouraud shading; and surface representation.

vtkPropertyDevice

NAME

    vtkPropertyDevice - abstract definition of a hardware dependent property

CLASS HIERARCHY

    class vtkPropertyDevice : public vtkObject

DESCRIPTION

    vtkPropertyDevice is the superclass of a hardware dependent vtkProperty (e.g., vtkOglrProperty and vtkSbrProperty). This object is typically created automatically by a vtkProperty object when it renders. The user should never see this class.

SEE ALSO

    vtkProperty

SUMMARY

    virtual void Render(vtkProperty *prp, vtkRenderer *ren) = 0;
      This is the only method that the subclasses must supply.

vtkQuad

NAME

vtkQuad - a cell that represents a 2D quadrilateral

CLASS HIERARCHY

class vtkQuad : public vtkCell

DESCRIPTION

vtkQuad is a concrete implementation of vtkCell to represent a 2D quadrilateral.

SUMMARY

vtkQuad(const vtkQuad& q)
Deep copy of cell.

vtkQuadric

NAME

vtkQuadric - evaluate implicit quadric function

CLASS HIERARCHY

class vtkQuadric : public vtkImplicitFunction

DESCRIPTION

vtkQuadric evaluates the quadric function $F(x,y,z) = a0*x^2 + a1*y^2 + a2*z^2 + a3*x*y + a4*y*z + a5*x*z + a6*x + a7*y + a8*z + a9$. vtkQuadric is a concrete implementation of vtkImplicitFunction.

vtkRecursiveDividingCubes

NAME

vtkRecursiveDividingCubes - create points lying on isosurface (using recursive approach)

CLASS HIERARCHY

class vtkRecursiveDividingCubes : public vtkStructuredPointsToPolyDataFilter

DESCRIPTION

vtkRecursiveDividingCubes is a filter that generates points lying on a surface of constant scalar value (i.e., an isosurface). Dense point clouds (i.e., at screen resolution) will appear as a surface. Less dense clouds can be used as a source to generate streamlines or to generate "transparent" surfaces.

This implementation differs from vtkDividingCubes in that it uses a recursive procedure. In many cases this can result in generating more points than the procedural implementation of vtkDividingCubes. This is because the recursive procedure divides voxels by multiples of powers of two. This can over-constrain subdivision. One of the advantages of the recursive technique is that the recursion is terminated earlier, which in some cases can be more efficient.

SEE ALSO

vtkDividingCubes vtkContourFilter vtkMarchingCubes

SUMMARY

void SetValue(float)
float GetValue()
Set isosurface value.

void SetDistance(float)
float GetDistance()
Specify sub-voxel size at which to generate point.

void SetIncrement(int)
int   GetIncrement()
Every "Increment" point is added to the list of points. This parameter, if set to a large value, can be used to limit the number of points while retaining good accuracy.

vtkRefCount

NAME

vtkRefCount - subclasses of this object are reference counted

CLASS HIERARCHY

class vtkRefCount : public vtkObject

DESCRIPTION

vtkRefCount is the base class for objects that are reference counted. Objects that are reference counted exist as long as another object uses them. Once the last reference to a reference counted object is removed, the object will spontaneously destruct. Typically only data objects that are passed between objects are reference counted.

CAVEATS

Note: in **vtk** objects are generally created with combinations of new/Delete() methods. This works great until you want to allocate objects off the stack (i.e., automatic objects). Automatic objects, when automatically deleted (by exiting scope), will cause warnings to occur. You can avoid this by turing reference counting off (i.e., use the method ReferenceCountingOff()).

SUMMARY

void ReferenceCountingOff()

Turn off reference counting for this object. This allows you to create automatic reference counted objects and avoid warning messages when scope is exited. (Note: It is preferable to use the combination new/Delete() to create and delete **vtk** objects.)

vtkRefCount()

Construct with initial reference count = 1 and reference counting on.

void Delete()

Overload vtkObject's Delete() method. For reference counted objects the Delete() method simply unregisters the use of the object. This may or may not result in the destruction of the object, depending upon whether another object is referencing it.

~vtkRefCount()

Destructor for reference counted objects. Reference counted objects should almost always use the combination of new/Delete() to create and delete objects. Automatic reference counted objects (i.e., creating them on the stack) are not encouraged. However, if you desire to do this, you will have to use the ReferenceCountingOff() method to avoid warning messages when the objects are automatically deleted upon scope termination.

void Register(vtkObject* o)

Increase the reference count (mark as used by another object).

void UnRegister(vtkObject* o)

Decrease the reference count (release by another object).

vtkRenderMaster

NAME

vtkRenderMaster - create a device specific rendering window

CLASS HIERARCHY

class vtkRenderMaster : public vtkObject

DESCRIPTION

vtkRenderMaster is used to create a device specific rendering window. vtkRenderMaster interfaces with the operating system to determine which type of rendering library to use. If the environment variable VTK_RENDERER is set, then that rendering library is used. If VTK_RENDERER is not set then it will try to pick the best renderer it can based on what was compiled into **vtk**.

SEE ALSO

vtkRenderWindow vtkRenderer

SUMMARY

vtkRenderWindow *MakeRenderWindow(char *type)

Create a vtkRenderWindow to match the type given. Current values for type include sbr for starbase; glr for SGI's gl; oglr for OpenGL and Mesa; xglr for Sun's XGL.

vtkRenderWindow *MakeRenderWindow(void)

Create renderer based on environment variable VTK_RENDERER. If VTK_RENDERER is not set then it will try to pick the best renderer it can.

vtkRenderWindow

NAME

vtkRenderWindow - create a window for renderers to draw into

CLASS HIERARCHY

class vtkRenderWindow : public vtkObject

DESCRIPTION

vtkRenderWindow is an abstract object to specify the behavior of a rendering window. A rendering window is a window in a graphical user interface where renderers draw their images. Methods are provided to synchronize the rendering process, set window size, and control double buffering.

SEE ALSO

vtkRenderer vtkRenderMaster vtkRenderWindowInteractor

DEFINES

VTK_STEREO_CRYSTAL_EYES 1
VTK_STEREO_RED_BLUE   2

SUMMARY

virtual void Start() = 0;
Initialize the rendering process.

virtual void Frame() = 0;
Performed at the end of the rendering process to swap buffers (if necessary).

virtual void CopyResultFrame();
Performed at the end of the rendering process to generate image. This is typically done right before swapping buffers.

virtual vtkRenderer *MakeRenderer() = 0;
Create a device specific renderer. This is the only way to create a renderer that will work. This method is implemented in the subclasses of vtkRenderWindow so that each subclass will return the correct renderer for its graphics library.

virtual vtkLightDevice *MakeLight() = 0;
Create a device specific light. This is used by vtkLight to create the correct type of vtkLightDevice.

virtual vtkCameraDevice   *MakeCamera() = 0;
Create a device specific camera. This is used by vtkCamera to create the correct type of vtkCameraDevice.

virtual vtkPropertyDevice   *MakeProperty() = 0;
Create a device specific property. This is used by vtkProperty to create the correct type of vtkPropertyDevice.

virtual vtkTextureDevice   *MakeTexture() = 0;
Create a device specific texture. This is used by vtkTexture to create the correct type of vtkTextureDevice.

vtkRenderWindow

virtual vtkRenderWindowInteractor *MakeRenderWindowInteractor() = 0;

Create an interactor to control renderers in this window. We need to know what type of interactor to create, because we might be in X Windows or MS Windows.

virtual int *GetPosition() = 0;
virtual void SetPosition(int,int);
virtual void SetPosition(int a[2]);

Set/Get the position in screen coordinates of the rendering window.

virtual int *GetSize() = 0;
virtual void SetSize(int,int) = 0;
virtual void SetSize(int a[2]);

Set/Get the size of the window in screen coordinates.

virtual void SetFullScreen(int) = 0;
int   GetFullScreen()
void   FullScreenOn()
void   FullScreenOff()

Turn on/off rendering full screen window size.

void   SetBorders(int)
int   GetBorders()
void   BordersOn()
void   BordersOff()

Turn on/off window manager borders. Typically, you shouldn't turn the borders off, because that bypasses the window manager and can cause undesirable behavior.

void   SetMapped(int)
int   GetMapped()
void   MappedOn()
void   MappedOff()

Keep track of whether the rendering window has been mapped to screen.

void   SetDoubleBuffer(int)
int   GetDoubleBuffer()
void   DoubleBufferOn()
void   DoubleBufferOff()

Turn on/off double buffering.

int   GetStereoRender()
void   SetStereoRender(int)
void   StereoRenderOn()
void   StereoRenderOff()

Turn on/off stereo rendering.

int   GetStereoType()
void   SetStereoType(int)

Set/Get what type of stereo rendering to use.

void   SetErase(int)
int   GetErase()

vtkRenderWindow

void EraseOn()
void EraseOff()

Turn on/off erasing the screen between images. This allows multiple exposure sequences if turned on. You will need to turn double buffering off or make use of the SwapBuffers methods to prevent you from swapping buffers between exposures.

void SetSwapBuffers(int)
int GetSwapBuffers()
void SwapBuffersOn()
void SwapBuffersOff()

Turn on/off buffer swapping between images.

char *GetName()

Get name of rendering window

void SetFilename(char *)
char *GetFilename()

Set/Get the filename used for saving images. See the SaveImageAsPPM method.

virtual void SaveImageAsPPM();

Save the current image as a PPM file.

virtual unsigned char *GetPixelData(int x,int y,int x2,int y2,int front) = 0;
virtual void SetPixelData(int x,int y,int x2,int y2,unsigned char *,int front) = 0;

Set/Get the pixel data of an image, transmitted as RGBRGBRGB. The front argument indicates if the front buffer should be used or the back buffer. It is the caller's responsibility to delete the resulting array. It is very important to realize that the memory in this array is organized from the bottom of the window to the top. The origin of the screen is in the lower left corner. The y axis increases as you go up the screen. So the storage of pixels is from left to right and from bottom to top.

int GetAAFrames()
void SetAAFrames(int)

Set the number of frames for doing antialiasing. The default is zero. Typically five or six will yield reasonable results without taking too long.

int GetFDFrames()
void SetFDFrames(int)

Set the number of frames for doing focal depth. The default is zero. Depending on how your scene is organized, you can get away with as few as four frames for focal depth or you might need thirty. One thing to note is that if you are using focal depth frames, then you will not need many (if any) frames for antialiasing.

int GetSubFrames()
void SetSubFrames(int)

Set the number of sub frames for doing motion blur. The default is zero. Once this is set greater than one, you will no longer see a new frame for every Render(). If you set this to five, you will need to do five Render() invocations before seeing the result. This isn't very impressive unless something is changing between the Renders.

vtkRenderWindow

void SetDesiredUpdateRate(float);
float GetDesiredUpdateRate()

Set/Get the desired update rate. This is used with the vtkLODActor class. When using level of detail actors you need to specify what update rate you require. The LODActors then will pick the correct resolution to meet your desired update rate in frames per second. A value of zero indicates that they can use all the time they want to.

vtkRenderWindow()

Construct an instance of vtkRenderWindow with its screen size set to 300x300, borders turned on, positioned at (0,0), double buffering turned on.

void Render()

Ask each renderer owned by this RenderWindow to render its image and synchronize this process.

void DoAARender()

Handle rendering any antialiased frames.

void DoFDRender()

Handle rendering any focal depth frames.

void DoStereoRender()

Handle rendering the two different views for stereo rendering.

void AddRenderers(vtkRenderer *ren)

Add a renderer to the list of renderers.

void RemoveRenderers(vtkRenderer *ren)

Remove a renderer from the list of renderers.

void StereoUpdate(void)

Update the system, if needed, to support stereo rendering. For some stereo methods, subclasses might need to switch some hardware settings here.

void StereoMidpoint(void)

Handles work required between the left and right eye renders.

void StereoRenderComplete(void)

Handles work required, once both views have been rendered when using stereo rendering.

int GetRemapWindow(void)

This method indicates if a StereoOn/Off will require the window to be remapped. Some types of stereo rendering require a new window to be created.

vtkRenderWindowInteractor

NAME

vtkRenderWindowInteractor - provide event driven interface to rendering window

CLASS HIERARCHY

class vtkRenderWindowInteractor : public vtkObject

EVENT BINDINGS

Specific devices have different camera bindings. The bindings are on both mouse events as well as keyboard presses. See vtkXRenderWindowInteractor and vtkWin32RenderWindowInteractor for specific information.

SEE ALSO

vtkXRenderWindowInteractor vtkWin32RenderWindowInteractor vtkPicker

SUMMARY

void SetRenderWindow(vtkRenderWindow*)
void SetRenderWindow(vtkRenderWindow&)
vtkRenderWindow *GetRenderWindow()
Set/Get the rendering window being controlled by this object.

void SetLightFollowCamera(int)
int GetLightFollowCamera()
void LightFollowCameraOn()
void LightFollowCameraOff()
Turn on/off the automatic repositioning of lights as the camera moves.

void SetDesiredUpdateRate(float)
float GetDesiredUpdateRate()
Set/Get the desired update rate. This is used by vtkLODActors to tell them how quickly they need to render. This update is in effect only when the camera is being rotated, or zoomed. When the interactor is still, the StillUpdateRate is used instead. A value of zero indicates that the update rate is unimportant (i.e. take as long as you want).

void SetStillUpdateRate(float)
float GetStillUpdateRate()
Set/Get the desired update rate when movement has stopped. See the SetDesiredUpdateRate method.

int GetInitialized()
See whether interactor has been initialized yet.

void FindPokedCamera(int,int);
void FindPokedRenderer(int,int);
When an event occurs, we must determine which Renderer the event occurred within, since one RenderWindow may contain multiple renderers. We also need to know what camera to operate on. This is just the ActiveCamera of the poked renderer.

vtkRenderWindowInteractor

vtkPicker *GetPicker()
Get the object used to perform pick operations.

virtual vtkPicker *CreateDefaultPicker();
Create default picker. Used to create one when none is specified.

vtkRenderWindowInteractor()
Construct object so that light follows camera motion.

void HighlightActor(vtkActor *actor)
When pick action successfully selects actor, this method highlights the actor appropriately. Currently this is done by placing a bounding box around the actor.

void SetStartPickMethod(void (*f)(void *), void *arg)
Specify a method to be executed prior to the pick operation.

void SetEndPickMethod(void (*f)(void *), void *arg)
Specify a method to be executed after the pick operation.

void SetPicker(vtkPicker *picker)
Set the object used to perform pick operations. You can use this to control what type of data is picked.

void SetUserMethod(void (*f)(void *), void *arg)
Set the user method. This method is invoked on a <u> keypress.

void SetUserMethodArgDelete(void (*f)(void *))
Called when a void* argument is being discarded. Lets the user free it.

void SetStartPickMethodArgDelete(void (*f)(void *))
Called when a void* argument is being discarded. Lets the user free it.

void SetEndPickMethodArgDelete(void (*f)(void *))
Called when a void* argument is being discarded. Lets the user free it.

vtkRenderer

NAME

vtkRenderer - abstract specification for renderers

CLASS HIERARCHY

class vtkRenderer : public vtkObject

DESCRIPTION

vtkRenderer provides an abstract specification for renderers. A renderer is an object that controls the rendering process for objects. Rendering is the process of converting geometry, a specification for lights, and a camera view into an image. vtkRenderer also performs coordinate transformation between world coordinates, view coordinates (the computer graphics rendering coordinate system), and display coordinates (the actual screen coordinates on the display device).

SEE ALSO

vtkRenderWindow vtkActor vtkCamera vtkLight

SUMMARY

void SetBackground(float, float, float)
void SetBackground(float *)
float *GetBackground()
void GetBackground(float data[3])
> Set/Get the background color of the rendering screen using an rgb color specification.

void SetAspect(float, float)
void SetAspect(float *)
float *GetAspect()
void GetAspect(float data[2])
> Set the aspect ratio of the rendered image. This is computed automatically and should not be set by the user.

void SetAmbient(float, float, float)
void SetAmbient(float *)
float *GetAmbient()
void GetAmbient(float data[3])
> Set the intensity of ambient lighting.

void SetBackLight(int)
int   GetBackLight()
void BackLightOn()
void BackLightOff()
> Turn on/off whether objects are lit from behind with another light. If backlighting is on, for every light that is created, a second opposing light is created to backlight the object.

vtkRenderer

void SetAllocatedRenderTime(float)
float GetAllocatedRenderTime()
>Set/Get the amount of time this renderer is allowed to spend rendering its scene. Zero indicates an infinite amount of time. This is used by vtkLODActors.

virtual void Render() = 0;
>Create an image. Subclasses of vtkRenderer must implement this method.

virtual vtkGeometryPrimitive *GetPrimitive(char *) = 0;
>Get a device specific geometry representation. vtkMapper and its subclasses need to get device specific GeometryPrimitives to render their polygons, lines, triangle strips and vertices. This method, which must be supplied by all subclasses of vtkRenderer, takes a string indicating what type of primitive to create.

virtual int UpdateActors(void) = 0;
>Ask all actors to build and draw themselves.

virtual int UpdateCameras(void) = 0;
>Ask the active camera to do whatever it needs to do. This method returns one if there was an active camera and it was on. It returns zero otherwise.

virtual int UpdateLights(void) = 0;
>Ask all lights to load themselves into rendering pipeline. This method will return the actual number of lights that were on.

void SetDisplayPoint(float, float, float)
void SetDisplayPoint(float *)
float *GetDisplayPoint()
void GetDisplayPoint(float data[3])
>Set/get a point location in display (or screen) coordinates. The lower left corner of the window is the origin and y increases as you go up the screen.

void SetViewPoint(float, float, float)
void SetViewPoint(float *)
float *GetViewPoint()
void GetViewPoint(float data[3])
>Specify a point location in view coordinates. The origin is in the middle of the viewport and it extends from -1 to 1 in all three dimensions.

void SetWorldPoint(float, float, float, float)
void SetWorldPoint(float *)
float *GetWorldPoint()
void GetWorldPoint(float data[4])
>Specify a point location in world coordinates. This method takes homogeneous coordinates.

void SetViewport(float, float, float, float)
void SetViewport(float *)
float *GetViewport()
void GetViewport(float data[4])
>Specify the viewport for the renderer to draw in the rendering window. Coordinates are expressed as (xmin,ymin,xmax,ymax), where each coordinate is 0 <= coordinate <= 1.0.

vtkLightCollection *GetLights()
>Get the list of lights for this renderer.

vtkRenderer

vtkActorCollection *GetActors()
Get the list of actors for this renderer.

void DisplayToWorld()
Convert display (or screen) coordinates to world coordinates.

void WorldToDisplay()
Convert world point coordinates to display (or screen) coordinates.

vtkRenderer()
Create a vtkRenderer with a black background, a white ambient light, backlighting turned on, a viewport of (0,0,1,1).

void SetActiveCamera(vtkCamera *cam)
Specify the camera to use for this renderer.

vtkCamera *GetActiveCamera()
Get the current camera.

void SetVolumeRenderer(vtkVolumeRenderer *vol)
Specify a volume renderer to use. If this is set, then volume rendering will be done. It isn't a very good volume renderer, but it works.

vtkVolumeRenderer *GetVolumeRenderer()
Get the volume renderer.

void AddLights(vtkLight *light)
Add a light to the list of lights.

void AddActors(vtkActor *actor)
Add an actor to the list of actors.

void RemoveLights(vtkLight *light)
Remove a light from the list of lights.

void RemoveActors(vtkActor *actor)
Remove an actor from the list of actors.

void DoLights()
Process the list of lights during the rendering process. If no lights are currently on or defined, then one will be generated automatically and placed at the same location and direction as the active camera.

void DoCameras()
Process the list of cameras during the rendering process. If a camera hasn't been specified, then one is created and correctly positioned.

void DoActors()
Process the list of actors during the rendering process.

void ResetCamera()
Automatically set up the camera based on the visible actors. The camera will reposition itself to view the center point of the actors, and move along its initial view plane normal (i.e., vector defined from camera position to focal point), so that all of the actors can be seen.

vtkRenderer

void ResetCamera(float bounds[6])

Automatically set up the camera based on a specified bounding box (xmin,xmax, ymin,ymax, zmin,zmax). Camera will reposition itself so that its focal point is the center of the bounding box, and adjust its distance and position to preserve its initial view plane normal (i.e., vector defined from camera position to focal point). Note: is the view plane is parallel to the view up axis, the view up axis will be reset to one of the three coordinate axes.

void SetRenderWindow(vtkRenderWindow *renwin)

Specify the rendering window in which to draw. This is automatically set when the renderer is created by MakeRenderer. The user probably shouldn't ever need to call this method.

void DisplayToView()

Convert display coordinates to view coordinates.

void ViewToDisplay()

Convert view coordinates to display coordinates.

void ViewToWorld()

Convert view point coordinates to world coordinates.

void WorldToView()

Convert world point coordinates to view coordinates.

float *GetCenter()

Return the center of this renderer in display coordinates.

int IsInViewport(int x,int y)

Is a given display point in this renderer's viewport.

void SetStartRenderMethod(void (*f)(void *), void *arg)

Specify a function to be called before rendering process begins. Function will be called with argument provided.

void SetStartRenderMethodArgDelete(void (*f)(void *))

Set the arg delete method. This is used to free user memory.

void SetEndRenderMethodArgDelete(void (*f)(void *))

Set the arg delete method. This is used to free user memory.

void SetEndRenderMethod(void (*f)(void *), void *arg)

Specify a function to be called when rendering process completes. Function will be called with argument provided.

vtkRendererCollection

NAME

vtkRendererCollection - a list of renderers

CLASS HIERARCHY

class vtkRendererCollection : public vtkCollection

DESCRIPTION

vtkRendererCollection represents and provides methods to manipulate a list of renderers (i.e., vtkRenderer and subclasses). The list is unsorted and duplicate entries are not prevented.

SEE ALSO

vtkRenderer vtkCollection

SUMMARY

void AddItem(vtkRenderer *a)
Add a renderer to the list.

void RemoveItem(vtkRenderer *a)
Remove a renderer from the list.

int IsItemPresent(vtkRenderer *a)
Determine whether a particular renderer is present. Returns its position in the list.

vtkRenderer *GetNextItem()
Get the next renderer in the list. Return NULL when at the end of the list.

void Render()
Forward the Render() method to each renderer in the list.

vtkRendererSource

NAME

vtkRendererSource - take a renderer into the pipeline

CLASS HIERARCHY

class vtkRendererSource : public vtkStructuredPointsSource

DESCRIPTION

vtkRendererSource is a source object that gets its input from a renderer and converts it to structured points. This can then be used in a visualization pipeline. You must explicitly send a Modify() to this object to get it to reload its data from the renderer.

SEE ALSO

vtkRenderer vtkStructuredPoints

SUMMARY

void SetInput(vtkRenderer*)
void SetInput(vtkRenderer&)
Indicates what renderer to get the pixel data from.

vtkRenderer *GetInput()
Returns which renderer is being used as the source for the pixel data.

vtkRibbonFilter

NAME

vtkRibbonFilter - create oriented ribbons from lines defined in polygonal dataset

CLASS HIERARCHY

class vtkRibbonFilter : public vtkPolyToPolyFilter

DESCRIPTION

vtkRibbonFilter is a filter to create oriented ribbons from lines defined in polygonal dataset. The orientation of the ribbon is along the line segments and perpendicular to "projected" line normals. Projected line normals are the original line normals projected to be perpendicular to the local line segment. An offset angle can be specified to rotate the ribbon with respect to the normal.

The input line must not have duplicate points, or normals at points that are parallel to the incoming/outgoing line segments. (Duplicate points can be removed with vtkCleanPolyData.)

SEE ALSO

vtkTubeFilter

SUMMARY

void SetWidth(float)
float GetWidth()
> Set the "half" width of the ribbon. If the width is allowed to vary, this is the minimum width.

void SetAngle(float)
float GetAngle()
> Set the offset angle of the ribbon from the line normal.

void SetVaryWidth(int)
int GetVaryWidth()
void VaryWidthOn()
void VaryWidthOff()
> Turn on/off the variation of ribbon width with scalar value.

void SetWidthFactor(float)
float GetWidthFactor()
> Set the maximum ribbon width in terms of a multiple of the minimum width.

vtkRibbonFilter()
> Construct ribbon so that width is 0.1, the width does not vary with scalar values, and the width factor is 2.0.

vtkRotationalExtrusionFilter

NAME

vtkRotationalExtrusionFilter - sweep polygonal data creating "skirt" from free edges and lines, and lines from vertices

CLASS HIERARCHY

class vtkRotationalExtrusionFilter : public vtkPolyToPolyFilter

DESCRIPTION

vtkRotationalExtrusionFilter is a modelling filter. It takes polygonal data as input and generates polygonal data on output. The input dataset is swept around the z-axis to create new polygonal primitives. These primitives form a "skirt" or swept surface. For example, sweeping a line results in a cylindrical shell, and sweeping a circle creates a torus.

There are a number of control parameters for this filter. You can control whether the sweep of a 2D object (i.e., polygon or triangle strip) is capped with the generating geometry via the "Capping" instance variable. Also, you can control the angle of rotation, and whether translation along the z-axis is performed along with the rotation. (Translation is useful for creating "springs".) You also can adjust the radius of the generating geometry using the "DeltaRotation" instance variable.

The skirt is generated by locating certain topological features. Free edges (edges of polygons or triangle strips only used by one polygon or triangle strips) generate surfaces. This is true also of lines or polylines. Vertices generate lines.

This filter can be used to model axisymmetric objects like cylinders, bottles, and wine glasses; or translational/rotational symmetric objects like springs or corkscrews.

CAVEATS

If the object sweeps 360 degrees, radius does not vary, and the object does not translate, capping is not performed. This is because the cap is unnecessary.

Some polygonal objects have no free edges (e.g., sphere). When swept, this will result in two separate surfaces if capping is on, or no surface if capping is off.

SEE ALSO

vtkLinearExtrusionFilter

SUMMARY

void SetResolution(int)
int GetResolution()
Set/Get resolution of sweep operation. Resolution controls the number of intermediate node points.

vtkRotationalExtrusionFilter

void **SetCapping(int)**
int **GetCapping()**
void **CappingOn()**
void **CappingOff()**
> Turn on/off the capping of the skirt.

void **SetAngle(float)**
float **GetAngle()**
> Set/Get angle of rotation.

void **SetTranslation(float)**
float **GetTranslation()**
> Set/Get total amount of translation along the z-axis.

void **SetDeltaRadius(float)**
float **GetDeltaRadius()**
> Set/Get change in radius during sweep process.

vtkRotationalExtrusionFilter()
> Create object with capping on, angle of 360 degrees, resolution = 12, and no translation along z-axis. vector (0,0,1), and point (0,0,0).

vtkSTLReader

NAME

vtkSTLReader - read ASCII or binary stereo lithography files

CLASS HIERARCHY

class vtkSTLReader : public vtkPolySource

DESCRIPTION

vtkSTLReader is a source object that reads ASCII or binary stereo lithography files (.stl files). The filename must be specified to vtkSTLReader. The object automatically detects whether the file is ASCII or binary.

.stl files are quite inefficient, and duplicate vertex definitions. By setting the Merging boolean you can control wether the point data is merged after reading. Merging is performed by default, however, merging requires a large amount of temporary storage since a 3D hash table must be constructed.

CAVEATS

Binary files written on one system may not be readable on other systems. vtkSTLWriter uses VAX or PC byte ordering and swaps bytes on other systems.

SUMMARY

void SetFilename(char *)
char *GetFilename()

Specify file name of stereo lithography file.

void SetMerging(int)
int   GetMerging()
void MergingOn()
void MergingOff()

Turn on/off merging of points/triangles.

void CreateDefaultLocator();

Create default locator. Used to create one when none is specified.

vtkSTLReader()

Construct object with merging set to true.

void SetLocator(vtkLocator *locator)

Specify a spatial locator for merging points. By default an instance of vtkMergePoints is used.

vtkSTLWriter

NAME

vtkSTLWriter - write stereo lithography files

CLASS HIERARCHY

class vtkSTLWriter : public vtkWriter

DESCRIPTION

vtkSTLWriter writes stereo lithography (.stl) files in either ASCII or binary form.

CAVEATS

Binary files written on one system may not be readable on other systems. vtkSTLWriter uses VAX or PC byte ordering and swaps bytes on other systems.

SUMMARY

void SetFilename(char *)
char *GetFilename()
Specify the name of the file to write.

void SetFileType(int)
int GetFileType()
Specify type of file to write (ascii or binary).

void SetInput(vtkPolyData *input)
Specify the input data or filter.

vtkSampleFunction

NAME

vtkSampleFunction - sample an implicit function over a structured point set

CLASS HIERARCHY

class vtkSampleFunction : public vtkStructuredPointsSource

DESCRIPTION

vtkSampleFunction is a source object that evaluates an implicit function and normals at each point in a vtkStructuredPointSet. The user can specify the sample dimensions and location in space to perform the sampling. To create closed surfaces (in conjunction with the vtkContourFilter), capping can be turned on to set a particular value on the boundaries of the sample space.

SEE ALSO

vtkImplicitModeller

SUMMARY

void SetImplicitFunction(vtkImplicitFunction*)
void SetImplicitFunction(vtkImplicitFunction&)
vtkImplicitFunction *GetImplicitFunction()
    Specify the implicit function to use to generate data.

void SetModelBounds(float data[6])
void SetModelBounds(float *)
float *GetModelBounds()
void GetModelBounds(float data[6])
    Specify the region in space over which the sampling occurs.

void SetCapping(int)
int   GetCapping()
void CappingOn()
void CappingOff()
    Turn on/off capping. If capping is on, then the outer boundaries of the structured point set are set to cap value. This can be used to insure surfaces are closed.

void SetCapValue(float)
float GetCapValue()
    Set the cap value.

void SetComputeNormals(int)
int   GetComputeNormals()
void ComputeNormalsOn()
void ComputeNormalsOff()
    Turn on/off the computation of normals.

vtkSampleFunction()
    Construct with ModelBounds=(-1,1,-1,1,-1,1), SampleDimensions=(50,50,50), Capping turned off, and normal generation on.

vtkSampleFunction

void SetSampleDimensions(int i, int j, int k)
Specify the dimensions of the data on which to sample.

void SetSampleDimensions(int dim[3])
Specify the dimensions of the data on which to sample.

void SetModelBounds(float xmin, float xmax, float ymin,
                        float ymax, float zmin, float zmax)
Specify the region in space over which the sampling occurs.

vtkScalars

NAME

vtkScalars - abstract interface to array of scalar data

CLASS HIERARCHY

class vtkScalars : public vtkRefCount

DESCRIPTION

vtkScalars provides an abstract interface to an array of scalar data. The data model for vtkScalars is an array accessible by point id. The subclasses of vtkScalars are concrete data types (float, int, etc.) that implement the interface of vtkScalars.

Scalars typically provide a single value per point. However, there are types of scalars that have multiple values per point (e.g., vtkPixmap or vtkAPixmap that provide three and four values per point, respectively). These are used when reading data in rgb and RGBA form (e.g., images and volumes).

Because of the close relationship between scalars and colors, scalars also maintain an internal lookup table. If provided, this table is used to map scalars into colors, rather than the lookup table that the vtkMapper objects are associated with.

SUMMARY

virtual vtkScalars *MakeObject(int sze, int ext=1000) = 0;
    Create a copy of this object.

virtual char *GetDataType() = 0;
    Return data type. One of "bit", "unsigned char", "short", "int", "float", or "double".

virtual char *GetScalarType()
    Return the type of scalar. Want to differentiate between single-valued scalars and multiple-valued (e.g., "color" scalars). Returns either "SingleValued" or "ColorScalar".

virtual int GetNumberOfValuesPerScalar()
    Return the number of values per scalar. Should range between (1,4).

virtual int GetNumberOfScalars() = 0;
    Return number of scalars in this object.

virtual float GetScalar(int id) = 0;
    Return a float scalar value for a particular point id.

virtual void SetScalar(int id, float s) = 0;
    Insert scalar into array. No range checking performed (fast!).

virtual void InsertScalar(int id, float s) = 0;
    Insert scalar into array. Range checking performed and memory allocated as necessary.

virtual int InsertNextScalar(float s) = 0;
    Insert scalar into next available slot. Returns point id of slot.

vtkScalars

virtual void Squeeze() = 0;
Reclaim any extra memory.

virtual void GetScalars(vtkIdList& ptIds, vtkFloatScalars& fs);
Get the scalar values for the point ids specified.

virtual void CreateDefaultLookupTable();
Create default lookup table. Generally used to create one when none is available.

void GetScalars(vtkIdList& ptId, vtkFloatScalars& fs)
Given a list of pt ids, return an array of scalar values.

void ComputeRange()
Determine (rmin,rmax) range of scalar values.

float *GetRange()
Return the range of scalar values. Data returned as pointer to float array of length 2.

void GetRange(float range[2])
Return the range of scalar values. Range copied into array provided.

vtkShepardMethod

NAME

vtkShepardMethod - sample unstructured points onto structured points using the method of Shepard

CLASS HIERARCHY

class vtkShepardMethod : public vtkDataSetToStructuredPointsFilter

DESCRIPTION

vtkShepardMethod is a filter used to visualize unstructured point data using Shepard's method. The method works by resampling the unstructured points onto a structured points set. The influence functions are described as "inverse distance weighted". Once the structured points are computed, the usual visualization techniques can be used visualize the structured points.

CAVEATS

The input to this filter is any dataset type. This filter can be used to resample any form of data, i.e., the input data need not be unstructured.

The bounds of the data (i.e., the sample space) is automatically computed if not set by the user.

If you use a maximum distance less than 1.0, some output points may never receive a contribution. The final value of these points can be specified with the "NullValue" instance variable.

SUMMARY

int   *GetSampleDimensions()
void GetSampleDimensions(int data[3])
Specify i-j-k dimensions on which to sample input points.

void SetMaximumDistance(float)
float GetMaximumDistance()
Specify influence distance of each input point. This distance is a fraction of the length of the diagonal of the sample space. Thus, values of 1.0 will cause each input point to influence all points in the structured point dataset. Values less than 1.0 can improve performance significantly.

void SetModelBounds(float data[6])
void SetModelBounds(float *)
float *GetModelBounds()
void GetModelBounds(float data[6])
void SetModelBounds(float xmin, float xmax, float ymin, float ymax,
float zmin, float zmax);
Specify the position in space to perform the sampling.

void SetNullValue(float)
float GetNullValue()
Set the Null value for output points not receiving a contribution from the input points.

vtkShepardMethod

vtkShepardMethod()
Construct with sample dimensions=(50,50,50) and so that model bounds are automatically computed from input. Null value for each unvisited output point is 0.0. Maximum distance is 0.25.

float **ComputeModelBounds(float origin[3], float ar[3])**
Compute ModelBounds from input geometry.

void **SetSampleDimensions(int i, int j, int k)**
Set the i-j-k dimensions on which to sample the distance function.

void **SetSampleDimensions(int dim[3])**
Set the i-j-k dimensions on which to sample the distance function.

vtkShortArray

NAME

vtkShortArray - dynamic, self-adjusting short integer array

CLASS HIERARCHY

class vtkShortArray : public vtkObject

DESCRIPTION

vtkShortArray is an array of short integer numbers. It provides methods for insertion and retrieval of integer values, and will automatically resize itself to hold new data.

SUMMARY

short GetValue(const int id)
Get the data at a particular index.

short *GetPtr(const int id)
Get the address of a particular data index.

short *WritePtr(const int id, const int number)
Get the address of a particular data index. Make sure data is allocated for the number of items requested. Set MaxId according to the number of data values requested.

vtkShortArray& InsertValue(const int id, const short i)
Insert data at a specified position in the array.

int   InsertNextValue(const short i)
Insert data at the end of the array. Return its location in the array.

short& operator[](const int i)
Does insert or get (depending on location on lhs or rhs of statement). Does not do automatic resizing - user's responsibility to range check.

void Squeeze()
Resize object to just fit data requirement. Reclaims extra memory.

int   GetSize()
Get the allocated size of the object in terms of number of data items.

int   GetMaxId()
Returning the maximum index of data inserted so far.

short *GetArray()
Get the pointer to the array. Useful for interfacing to C or FORTRAN routines.

void Reset()
Reuse the memory allocated by this object. Objects appears like no data has been previously inserted.

int   Allocate(const int sz, const int ext)
Allocate memory for this array. Delete old storage if present.

void Initialize()
Release storage and reset array to initial state.

vtkShortArray

vtkShortArray(const int sz, const int ext)
Construct with specified storage size and extend value.

vtkShortArray(const vtkShortArray& sa)
Construct array from another array. Copy each element of other array.

vtkShortArray& operator=(const vtkShortArray& sa)
Deep copy of another array.

void operator+=(const vtkShortArray& sa)
Append one array onto the end of this array.

vtkShortScalars

NAME

vtkShortScalars - short integer representation of scalar data

CLASS HIERARCHY

class vtkShortScalars : public vtkScalars

DESCRIPTION

vtkShortScalars is a concrete implementation of vtkScalars. Scalars are represented using short integer values.

SUMMARY

short *GetPtr(const int id)

Get pointer to array of data starting at data position "id".

short *WritePtr(const int id, const int number)

Get pointer to data array. Useful for direct writes of data. MaxId is bumped by number (and memory allocated if necessary). Id is the location you wish to write into; number is the number of scalars to write. Use the method WrotePtr() to mark completion of write.

void WrotePtr()

Terminate direct write of data. Although dummy routine now, reserved for future use.

vtkShortScalars& operator=(const vtkShortScalars& ss)

Deep copy of scalars.

vtkShrinkFilter

NAME

vtkShrinkFilter - shrink cells composing an arbitrary data set

CLASS HIERARCHY

class vtkShrinkFilter : public vtkDataSetToUnstructuredGridFilter

DESCRIPTION

vtkShrinkFilter shrinks cells composing an arbitrary data set towards their centroid. The centroid of a cell is computed as the average position of the cell points. Shrinking results in disconnecting the cells from one another. The output of this filter is of general dataset type vtkUnstructuredGrid.

CAVEATS

It is possible to turn cells inside out or cause self intersection in special cases.

SEE ALSO

vtkShrinkPolyData

SUMMARY

void SetShrinkFactor(float)
Set the fraction of shrink for each cell.

float GetShrinkFactor()
Get the fraction of shrink for each cell.

vtkShrinkPolyData

NAME

vtkShrinkPolyData - shrink cells composing PolyData

CLASS HIERARCHY

class vtkShrinkPolyData : public vtkPolyToPolyFilter

DESCRIPTION

vtkShrinkPolyData shrinks cells composing a polygonal dataset (e.g., vertices, lines, polygons, and triangle strips) towards their centroid. The centroid of a cell is computed as the average position of the cell points. Shrinking results in disconnecting the cells from one another. The output dataset type of this filter is polygonal data.

CAVEATS

It is possible to turn cells inside out or cause self intersection in special cases.

SEE ALSO

vtkShrinkFilter

SUMMARY

void SetShrinkFactor(float)
Set the fraction of shrink for each cell.

float GetShrinkFactor()
Get the fraction of shrink for each cell.

vtkSliceCubes

NAME

vtkSliceCubes - generate isosurface(s) from volume four slices at a time

CLASS HIERARCHY

class vtkSliceCubes : public vtkObject

DESCRIPTION

vtkSliceCubes is a special version of the marching cubes filter. Instead of ingesting an entire volume at once it processes only four slices at a time. This way, it can generate isosurfaces from huge volumes. Also, the output of this object is written to a marching cubes triangle file. That way, output triangles do not need to be held in memory.

To use vtkSliceCubes you must specify an instance of vtkVolume16Reader to read the data. Set this object up with the proper file prefix, image range, data origin, data dimensions, header size, and swap bytes flag. The vtkSliceCubes object will then take over and read slices as necessary. You also will need to specify the name of an output marching cubes triangle file.

CAVEATS

This process object is both a source and mapper (i.e., it reads and writes data to a file). This is different than the other marching cubes objects (and most process objects in the system). It's specialized to handle very large data.

This object only extracts a single isosurface. This compares with the other contouring objects in vtk that generate multiple surfaces.

To read the output file use vtkMCubesReader.

SEE ALSO

vtkMarchingCubes vtkContourFilter vtkMCubesReader vtkDividingCubes

SUMMARY

void SetReader(vtkVolume16Reader*)
void SetReader(vtkVolume16Reader&)
vtkVolume16Reader *GetReader()
    Set/get object to read slices.

void SetFilename(char *)
char *GetFilename()
    Specify file name of marching cubes output file.

void SetValue(short)
short GetValue()
    Set/get isosurface contour value.

vtkSliceCubes

void SetLimitsFilename(char *)
char *GetLimitsFilename()
  Specify file name of marching cubes limits file. The limits file speeds up
  subsequent reading of output triangle file.

vtkSliceCubes()
  Construct with NULL reader, output filename specification, and limits filename.

void Update()
  Method causes object to read slices and generate isosurface.

vtkSource

NAME

vtkSource - abstract class specifies interface for visualization network source (or objects that generate output data)

CLASS HIERARCHY

class vtkSource : public vtkObject

DESCRIPTION

vtkSource is an abstract object that specifies behavior and interface of source objects. Source objects are objects that begin visualization pipeline. Sources include readers (read data from file or communications port) and procedural sources (generate data programmatically). vtkSource objects are also objects that generate output data. In this sense vtkSource is used as a superclass to vtkFilter.

Concrete subclasses of vtkSource must define Update() and Execute() methods. The public method Update() invokes network execution and will bring the network up-to-date. The protected Execute() method actually does the work of data creation/generation. The difference between the two methods is that Update() implements input consistency checks and modified time comparisons and then invokes the Execute(), which is an implementation of a particular algorithm.

vtkSource provides a mechanism for invoking the methods StartMethod() and EndMethod() before and after object execution (via Execute()). These are convenience methods you can use for any purpose (e.g., debugging info, highlighting/notifying user interface, etc.) These methods accept a single void* pointer that can be used to send data to the methods. It is also possible to specify a function to delete the argument via StartMethodArgDelete and EndMethodArgDelete.

An important feature of subclasses of vtkSource is that it is possible to control the memory-management model (i.e., retain output versus delete output data). If enabled the ReleaseDataFlag enables the deletion of the output data once the downstream process object finishes processing the data (please see text).

SUMMARY

virtual void Update();
> Bring object up-to-date before execution. Update() checks modified time against last execution time, and re-executes object if necessary.

virtual void SetReleaseDataFlag(int);
virtual int GetReleaseDataFlag();
void   ReleaseDataFlagOn()
void   ReleaseDataFlagOff()
> Turn on/off flag to control whether this object's data is released after being used by a source.

virtual int GetDataReleased();
virtual void SetDataReleased(int flag);
> Set/Get flag indicating whether data has been released since last execution. Used during update method to determine whether to execute or not.

vtkSource

void SetStartMethod(void (*f)(void *), void *arg)
Specify function to be called before object executes.

void SetEndMethod(void (*f)(void *), void *arg)
Specify function to be called after object executes.

void SetStartMethodArgDelete(void (*f)(void *))
Set the arg delete method. This is used to free user memory.

void SetEndMethodArgDelete(void (*f)(void *))
Set the arg delete method. This is used to free user memory.

vtkSphere

NAME

vtkSphere - implicit function for a sphere

CLASS HIERARCHY

class vtkSphere : public vtkImplicitFunction

DESCRIPTION

vtkSphere computes the implicit function and/or gradient for a sphere. vtkSphere is a concrete implementation of vtkImplicitFunction.

vtkSphereSource

NAME

vtkSphereSource - create a sphere centered at the origin

CLASS HIERARCHY

class vtkSphereSource : public vtkPolySource

DESCRIPTION

vtkSphereSource creates a polygonal sphere of specified radius centered at the origin. The resolution (polygonal discretization) in both the latitude (phi) and longitude (theta) directions can be specified. It also is possible to create partial spheres by specifying maximum phi and theta angles.

DEFINES

VTK_MAX_SPHERE_RESOLUTION 1024

SUMMARY

void SetRadius(float)
float GetRadius()

Set radius of sphere.

void SetThetaResolution(int)
int GetThetaResolution()

Set the number of points in the longitude direction.

void SetPhiResolution(int)
int GetPhiResolution()

Set the number of points in the latitude direction.

void SetTheta(float)
float GetTheta()

Set the maximum longitude angle.

void SetPhi(float)
float GetPhi()

Set the maximum latitude angle (0 is at north pole).

vtkSphereSource(int res)

Construct sphere with radius=0.5 and default resolution 8 in both Phi and Theta directions.

vtkStack

NAME

vtkStack - create and manipulate lists of objects

CLASS HIERARCHY

class vtkStack : public vtkObject

DESCRIPTION

vtkStack is a general object for creating and manipulating lists of objects. vtkStack also serves as a base class for lists of specific types of objects.

SUMMARY

vtkStack()
Construct with empty stack.

void Push(vtkObject *a)
Add an object to the top of the stack. Does not prevent duplicate entries.

vtkObject *Pop()
Remove an object from the top of the list.

vtkObject *GetTop()
Return the number of objects in the stack.

int   GetNumberOfItems()
Return the number of objects in the stack.

vtkStreamLine

NAME

vtkStreamLine - generate streamline in arbitrary dataset

CLASS HIERARCHY

class vtkStreamLine : public vtkStreamer

DESCRIPTION

vtkStreamLine is a filter that generates a streamline for an arbitrary dataset. A streamline is a line that is everywhere tangent to the vector field. Scalar values also are calculated along the streamline and can be used to color the line. Streamlines are calculated by integrating from a starting point through the vector field. Integration can be performed forward in time (see where the line goes), backward in time (see where the line came from), or in both directions. It also is possible to compute vorticity along the streamline. Vorticity is the projection (i.e., dot product) of the flow rotation on the velocity vector, i.e., the rotation of flow around the streamline.

vtkStreamLine defines the instance variable StepLength. This parameter controls the length of the line segments used to define the streamline. The streamline(s) will consist of one (or more) polylines with line segment lengths of size StepLength. Smaller values reduce in more line primitives but smoother streamlines. The StepLength instance variable is defined in terms of time (i.e., the distance that the particle travels in the specified time period). Thus, the line segments will be smaller in areas of low velocity and larger in regions of high velocity. (NOTE: This is different than the IntegrationStepLength defined by the superclass vtkStreamer. IntegrationStepLength is used to control integration step size and is expressed as a fraction of the cell length.) The StepLength instance variable is important because subclasses of vtkStreamLine (e.g., vtkDashedStreamLine) depend on this value to build their representation.

SEE ALSO

vtkStreamer vtkDashedStreamLine vtkStreamPoints

SUMMARY

void SetStepLength(float)
float GetStepLength()

Specify the length of a line segment. The length is expressed in terms of elapsed time. Smaller values result in smoother appearing streamlines, but greater numbers of line primitives.

vtkStreamLine()

Construct object with step size set to 1.0.

vtkStreamPoints

NAME

vtkStreamPoints - generate points along streamer separated by constant time increment

CLASS HIERARCHY

class vtkStreamPoints : public vtkStreamer

DESCRIPTION

vtkStreamPoints is a filter that generates points along a streamer. The points are separated by a constant time increment. The resulting visual effect (especially when coupled with vtkGlyph3D) is an indication of particle speed.

SEE ALSO

vtkStreamer vtkStreamLine vtkDashedStreamLine

SUMMARY

void SetTimeIncrement(float)
float GetTimeIncrement()
Specify the separation of points in terms of absolute time.

vtkStreamPoints()
Construct object with time increment set to 1.0.

NAME

vtkStreamer - abstract object implements integration of massless particle through vector field

CLASS HIERARCHY

class vtkStreamer : public vtkDataSetToPolyFilter

DESCRIPTION

vtkStreamer is a filter that integrates a massless particle through a vector field. The integration is performed using second order Runge-Kutta method. vtkStreamer often serves as a base class for other classes that perform numerical integration through a vector field (e.g., vtkStreamLine).

Note that vtkStreamer can integrate both forward and backward in time, or in both directions. The length of the streamer time is controlled by specifying an elapsed time. (The elapsed time is the time each particle travels.) Otherwise, the integration terminates after exiting the dataset or if the particle speed is reduced to a value less than the terminal speed.

vtkStreamer integrates through any type of dataset. Thus, if the dataset contains 2D cells such as polygons or triangles, the integration is constrained to lie on the surface defined by the 2D cells.

The starting point of streamers may be defined in three different ways. Starting from global x-y-z "position" allows you to start a single streamer at a specified x-y-z coordinate. Starting from "location" allows you to start at a specified cell, subId, and parametric coordinate. Finally, you may specify a source object to start multiple streamers. If you start streamers using a source object, for each point in the source that is inside the dataset a streamer is created.

vtkStreamer implements the integration process in the Integrate() method. Because vtkStreamer does not implement the Execute() method that its superclass (i.e., Filter) requires, it is an abstract class. Its subclasses implement the execute method and use the Integrate() method, and then build their own representation of the integration path (i.e., lines, dashed lines, points, etc.).

SEE ALSO

vtkStreamLine vtkDashedStreamLine vtkStreamPoints

DEFINES

VTK_INTEGRATE_FORWARD 0
VTK_INTEGRATE_BACKWARD 1
VTK_INTEGRATE_BOTH_DIRECTIONS 2
VTK_START_FROM_POSITION 0
VTK_START_FROM_LOCATION 1

vtkStreamer

SUMMARY

void SetSource(vtkDataSet*)
void SetSource(vtkDataSet&)
vtkDataSet *GetSource()
Specify the source object used to generate starting points.

void SetMaximumPropagationTime(float)
float GetMaximumPropagationTime()
Specify the maximum length of the Streamer expressed in elapsed time.

void SetIntegrationDirection(int)
VTK_INTEGRATE_FORWARD,VTK_INTEGRATE_BOTH_DIRECTIONS);
int GetIntegrationDirection()
Specify the direction in which to integrate the Streamer.

void SetIntegrationStepLength(float)
float GetIntegrationStepLength()
Specify a nominal integration step size (expressed as a fraction of the size of each cell).

void SetSpeedScalars(int)
int GetSpeedScalars()
void SpeedScalarsOn()
void SpeedScalarsOff()
Turn on/off the creation of scalar data from velocity magnitude. If off, and input dataset has scalars, input dataset scalars are used.

void SetTerminalSpeed(float)
float GetTerminalSpeed()
Set/get terminal speed (i.e., speed is velocity magnitude). Terminal speed is speed at which streamer will terminate propagation.

void SetVorticity(int)
int GetVorticity()
void VorticityOn()
void VorticityOff()
Turn on/off the computation of vorticity. Vorticity is an indication of the rotation of the flow. In combination with vtkStreamLine and vtkTubeFilter can be used to create rotated tubes.

vtkStreamer()
Construct object to start from position (0,0,0); integrate forward; terminal speed 0.0; vorticity computation off; integrations step length 0.2; and maximum propagation time 100.0.

void SetStartLocation(int cellId, int subId, float pcoords[3])
Specify the start of the streamline in the cell coordinate system. That is, cellId and subId (if composite cell), and parametric coordinates.

void SetStartLocation(int cellId, int subId, float r, float s, float t)
Specify the start of the streamline in the cell coordinate system. That is, cellId and subId (if composite cell), and parametric coordinates.

int GetStartLocation(int& subId, float pcoords[3])
Get the starting location of the streamline in the cell coordinate system.

vtkStreamer

void SetStartPosition(float x[3])
Specify the start of the streamline in the global coordinate system. Search must be performed to find initial cell to start integration from.

void SetStartPosition(float x, float y, float z)
Specify the start of the streamline in the global coordinate system. Search must be performed to find initial cell to start integration from.

float *GetStartPosition()
Get the start position in global x-y-z coordinates.

void Update()
Override update method because execution can branch two ways (Input and Source).

vtkStripper

NAME

vtkStripper - create triangle strips

CLASS HIERARCHY

class vtkStripper : public vtkPolyToPolyFilter

DESCRIPTION

vtkStripper is a filter that generates triangle strips from input polygons and triangle strips. Input polygons are assumed to be triangles. (Use vtkTriangleFilter to triangulate non-triangular polygons.) The filter will also pass through vertices and lines, if requested.

SUMMARY

void SetMaximumStripLength(int)
int   GetMaximumStripLength()
Specify the maximum number of triangles in a triangle strip.

void PassVertsOn()
void PassVertsOff()
void SetPassVerts(int)
int   GetPassVerts()
Turn on/off passing of vertices through to output.

void PassLinesOn()
void PassLinesOff()
void SetPassLines(int)
int   GetPassLines()
Turn on/off passing of lines through to output.

vtkStripper()
Construct object with vertex and line passing turned on.

vtkStructuredData

NAME

vtkStructuredData - abstract class for topologically regular data

CLASS HIERARCHY

class vtkStructuredData : public vtkLWObject

DESCRIPTION

vtkStructuredData is an abstract class that specifies an interface for topologically regular data. Regular data is data that can be accessed in rectangular fashion using an i-j-k index. A finite difference grid, a volume, or a pixmap are all considered regular.

DEFINES

```
VTK_SINGLE_POINT 0
VTK_X_LINE 1
VTK_Y_LINE 2
VTK_Z_LINE 3
VTK_XY_PLANE 4
VTK_YZ_PLANE 5
VTK_XZ_PLANE 6
VTK_XYZ_GRID 7
```

SUMMARY

int   IsPointVisible(int ptId)
Return non-zero value if specified point is visible.

int   GetDataDimension()
Return the topological dimension of the data (e.g., 0, 1, 2, or 3D).

void SetDimensions(int i, int j, int k)
Set the i-j-k dimensions of the data.

void BlankingOn()
Turn on data blanking. Data blanking is the ability to turn off portions of the grid when displaying or operating on it. Some data (like finite difference data) routinely turns off data to simulate solid obstacles.

void BlankingOff()
Turn off data blanking.

void BlankPoint(int ptId)
Turn off a particular data point.

void UnBlankPoint(int ptId)
Turn on a particular data point.

vtkStructuredGrid

NAME

vtkStructuredGrid - topologically regular array of data

CLASS HIERARCHY

class vtkStructuredGrid : public vtkPointSet, public vtkStructuredData

DESCRIPTION

vtkStructuredGrid is a data object that is a concrete implementation of vtkDataSet. vtkStructuredGrid represents a geometric structure that is a topologically regular array of points. The topology is that of a cube that has been subdivided into a regular array of smaller cubes. Each point/cell can be addressed with i-j-k indices. Examples include finite difference grids.

SUMMARY

void CopyStructure(vtkDataSet *ds)
Copy the geometric and topological structure of an input structured grid.

vtkStructuredGridFilter

NAME

vtkStructuredGridFilter - filter that takes vtkStructuredGrid as input

CLASS HIERARCHY

class vtkStructuredGridFilter : public vtkFilter

DESCRIPTION

vtkStructuredGridFilter is a filter that takes a single vtkStructuredGrid object as input.

SUMMARY

void SetInput(vtkStructuredGrid *input)
Specify the input Grid or filter.

vtkStructuredGridGeometryFilter

NAME

vtkStructuredGridGeometryFilter - extract geometry for structured grid

CLASS HIERARCHY

class vtkStructuredGridGeometryFilter : public vtkStructuredGridToPolyFilter

DESCRIPTION

vtkStructuredGridGeometryFilter is a filter that extracts geometry from a structured grid. By specifying appropriate i-j-k indices, it is possible to extract a point, a curve, a surface, or a "volume". Depending upon the type of data, the curve and surface may be curved or planar. The volume is actually a (n x m x o) region of points.

The extent specification is zero-offset. That is, the first k-plane in a 50x50x50 structured grid is given by (0,49, 0,49, 0,0).

CAVEATS

If you don't know the dimensions of the input dataset, you can use a large number to specify extent (the number will be clamped appropriately). For example, if the dataset dimensions are 50x50x50, and you want a fifth k-plane, you can use the extents (0,100, 0,100, 4,4). The 100 will automatically be clamped to 49.

SEE ALSO

vtkGeometryFilter vtkStructuredPointsFilter

SUMMARY

int   *GetExtent()
void GetExtent(int data[6])

Get the extent in topological coordinate range (imin,imax, jmin,jmax, kmin,kmax).

vtkStructuredGridGeometryFilter()

Construct with initial extent (0,100, 0,100, 0,0) (i.e., a k-plane).

void SetExtent(int iMin, int iMax, int jMin, int jMax,
**   int kMin, int kMax)**

Specify (imin,imax, jmin,jmax, kmin,kmax) indices.

void SetExtent(int *extent)

Specify (imin,imax, jmin,jmax, kmin,kmax) indices in array form.

vtkStructuredGridOutlineFilter

NAME

vtkStructuredGridOutlineFilter - create wireframe outline for structured grid

CLASS HIERARCHY

class vtkStructuredGridOutlineFilter : public vtkStructuredGridToPolyFilter

DESCRIPTION

vtkStructuredGridOutlineFilter is a filter that generates a wireframe outline of a structured grid (vtkStructuredGrid). Structured data is topologically a cube, so the outline will have 12 "edges".

vtkStructuredGridReader

NAME

vtkStructuredGridReader - read **vtk** structured grid data file

CLASS HIERARCHY

class vtkStructuredGridReader : public vtkStructuredGridSource

DESCRIPTION

vtkStructuredGridReader is a source object that reads ASCII or binary structured grid data files in **vtk** format. See text for format details.

CAVEATS

Binary files written on one system may not be readable on other systems.

SUMMARY

void SetFilename(char *name)
Specify file name of **vtk** structured grid data file to read.

int GetFileType()
Get the type of file (VTK_ASCII or VTK_BINARY).

void SetScalarsName(char *name)
Set the name of the scalar data to extract. If not specified, first scalar data encountered is extracted.

void SetVectorsName(char *name)
Set the name of the vector data to extract. If not specified, first vector data encountered is extracted.

void SetTensorsName(char *name)
Set the name of the tensor data to extract. If not specified, first tensor data encountered is extracted.

void SetNormalsName(char *name)
Set the name of the normal data to extract. If not specified, first normal data encountered is extracted.

void SetTCoordsName(char *name)
Set the name of the texture coordinate data to extract. If not specified, first texture coordinate data encountered is extracted.

void SetLookupTableName(char *name)
Set the name of the lookup table data to extract. If not specified, uses lookup table named by scalar. Otherwise, this specification supersedes.

vtkStructuredGridSource

NAME

vtkStructuredGridSource - Abstract class whose subclasses generates structured grid data

CLASS HIERARCHY

class vtkStructuredGridSource : public vtkSource

DESCRIPTION

vtkStructuredGridSource is an abstract class whose subclasses generate structured grid data.

SUMMARY

vtkStructuredGrid *GetOutput()
  Get the output of this source.

vtkStructuredGridToPolyFilter

NAME

vtkStructuredGridToPolyFilter - abstract filter class

CLASS HIERARCHY

class vtkStructuredGridToPolyFilter : public vtkStructuredGridFilter

DESCRIPTION

vtkStructuredGridToPolyFilter is a filter whose subclasses take as input structured grid datasets and generate polygonal data on output.

SUMMARY

vtkPolyData *GetOutput()
Get the output of this filter.

vtkStructuredGridWriter

NAME

vtkStructuredGridWriter - write **vtk** structured grid data file

CLASS HIERARCHY

class vtkStructuredGridWriter : public vtkDataWriter

DESCRIPTION

vtkStructuredGridWriter is a source object that writes ASCII or binary structured grid data files in **vtk** format. See text for format details.

CAVEATS

Binary files written on one system may not be readable on other systems.

SUMMARY

void   SetInput(vtkStructuredGrid *input)
Specify the input data or filter.

vtkStructuredPoints

NAME

vtkStructuredPoints - topologically and geometrically regular array of data

CLASS HIERARCHY

class vtkStructuredPoints : public vtkDataSet, public vtkStructuredData

DESCRIPTION

vtkStructuredPoints is a data object that is a concrete implementation of vtkDataSet. vtkStructuredPoints represents a geometric structure that is a topological and geometrical regular array of points. Examples include volumes (voxel data) and pixmaps.

SUMMARY

```
void  SetAspectRatio(float, float, float)
void  SetAspectRatio(float *)
float *GetAspectRatio()
void  GetAspectRatio(float data[3])
```

Set the aspect ratio of the cubical cells that compose the structured point set.

```
void  SetOrigin(float, float, float)
void  SetOrigin(float *)
float *GetOrigin()
void  GetOrigin(float data[3])
```

Set the origin of the data. The origin plus aspect ratio determine the position in space of the structured points.

void CopyStructure(vtkDataSet *ds)

Copy the geometric and topological structure of an input structured points object.

void GetVoxelGradient(int i, int j, int k, vtkScalars *s, vtkFloatVectors& g)

Given structured coordinates (i,j,k) for a voxel cell, compute the eight gradient values for the voxel corners. The order in which the gradient vectors are arranged corresponds to the ordering of the voxel points. Gradient vector is computed by central differences (except on edges of volume where forward difference is used). The scalars s are the scalars from which the gradient is to be computed. This method will treat only 3D structured point datasets (i.e., volumes).

void GetPointGradient(int i,int j,int k, vtkScalars *s, float g[3])

Given structured coordinates (i,j,k) for a point in a structured point dataset, compute the gradient vector from the scalar data at that point. The scalars s are the scalars from which the gradient is to be computed. This method will treat structured point datasets of any dimension.

vtkStructuredPointsCollection

NAME

vtkStructuredPointsCollection - maintain a list of structured points data objects

CLASS HIERARCHY

class vtkStructuredPointsCollection : public vtkCollection

DESCRIPTION

vtkStructuredPointsCollection is an object that creates and manipulates lists of structured points datasets.

SEE ALSO

vtkCollection

SUMMARY

void AddItem(vtkStructuredPoints *ds)
Add a vtkStructuredPoints to the list.

void RemoveItem(vtkStructuredPoints *ds)
Remove a vtkStructuredPoints from the list.

int IsItemPresent(vtkStructuredPoints *ds)
Determine whether a particular tkStructuredPoints is present. Returns its position in the list.

vtkStructuredPoints *GetNextItem()
Get the next item in the collection. NULL is returned if the collection is exhausted.

vtkStructuredPointsFilter

NAME

vtkStructuredPointsFilter - filter that takes vtkStructuredPoints as input

CLASS HIERARCHY

class vtkStructuredPointsFilter : public vtkFilter

DESCRIPTION

vtkStructuredPointsFilter is a filter that takes a single vtkStructuredPoints data object as input.

SUMMARY

void SetInput(vtkStructuredPoints *input)
Specify the input data or filter.

vtkStructuredPointsGeometryFilter

NAME

vtkStructuredPointsGeometryFilter - extract geometry for structured points

CLASS HIERARCHY

class vtkStructuredPointsGeometryFilter :
public vtkStructuredPointsToPolyDataFilter

DESCRIPTION

vtkStructuredPointsGeometryFilter is a filter that extracts geometry from a structured points dataset. By specifying appropriate i-j-k indices (via the "Extent" instance variable), it is possible to extract a point, a line, a plane (i.e., image), or a "volume" from dataset. (Since the output is of type polydata, the volume is actually a (n x m x o) region of points.)

The extent specification is zero-offset. That is, the first k-plane in a 50x50x50 volume is given by (0,49, 0,49, 0,0).

CAVEATS

If you don't know the dimensions of the input dataset, you can use a large number to specify extent (the number will be clamped appropriately). For example, if the dataset dimensions are 50x50x50, and you want a the fifth k-plane, you can use the extents (0,100, 0,100, 4,4). The 100 will automatically be clamped to 49.

SEE ALSO

vtkGeometryFilter vtkStructuredGridFilter

SUMMARY

vtkStructuredPointsGeometryFilter()
Construct with initial extent (0,100, 0,100, 0,0) (i.e., a plane).

void SetExtent(int *extent)
Specify (imin,imax, jmin,jmax, kmin,kmax) indices.

vtkStructuredPointsReader

NAME

vtkStructuredPointsReader - read **vtk** structured points data file

CLASS HIERARCHY

class vtkStructuredPointsReader : public vtkStructuredPointsSource

DESCRIPTION

vtkStructuredPointsReader is a source object that reads ASCII or binary structured points data files in **vtk** format. See text for format details.

CAVEATS

Binary files written on one system may not be readable on other systems.

SUMMARY

void SetFilename(char *name)
Specify file name of **vtk** structured points file to read.

int   GetFileType()
Get the type of file (VTK_ASCII or VTK_BINARY)

void SetScalarsName(char *name)
Set the name of the scalar data to extract. If not specified, first scalar data encountered is extracted.

void SetVectorsName(char *name)
Set the name of the vector data to extract. If not specified, first vector data encountered is extracted.

void SetTensorsName(char *name)
Set the name of the tensor data to extract. If not specified, first tensor data encountered is extracted.

void SetNormalsName(char *name)
Set the name of the normal data to extract. If not specified, first normal data encountered is extracted.

void SetTCoordsName(char *name)
Set the name of the texture coordinate data to extract. If not specified, first texture coordinate data encountered is extracted.

void SetLookupTableName(char *name)
Set the name of the lookup table data to extract. If not specified, uses lookup table named by scalar. Otherwise, this specification supersedes.

vtkStructuredPointsSource

NAME

vtkStructuredPointsSource - abstract class whose subclasses generate structured points data

CLASS HIERARCHY

class vtkStructuredPointsSource : public vtkSource

DESCRIPTION

vtkStructuredPointsSource is an abstract class whose subclasses generate vtkStructuredPoints data.

SUMMARY

vtkStructuredPoints *GetOutput()
Get the output of this source.

vtkStructuredPointsToImageFilter

NAME

vtkStructuredPointsToImageFilter - convert structured points to image type

CLASS HIERARCHY

class vtkStructuredPointsToImageFilter : public vtkStructuredPointsFilter

DESCRIPTION

vtkStructuredPointsToImageFilter is a filter whose subclasses take on input structured points and specifically generate structured points with float scalars on output.

SUMMARY

vtkImage *GetOutput()
Get the output of this filter.

vtkStructuredPointsToPolyDataFilter

NAME

vtkStructuredPointsToPolyDataFilter - abstract filter class

CLASS HIERARCHY

class vtkStructuredPointsToPolyDataFilter : public vtkStructuredPointsFilter

DESCRIPTION

vtkStructuredPointsToPolyDataFilter is an abstract filter class whose subclasses take on input structured points and generate polygonal data on output.

SUMMARY

vtkPolyData *GetOutput()
Get the output of this filter.

vtkStructuredPointsToStructuredPointsFilter

NAME

vtkStructuredPointsToStructuredPointsFilter - abstract filter class

CLASS HIERARCHY

**class vtkStructuredPointsToStructuredPointsFilter :
public vtkStructuredPointsFilter**

DESCRIPTION

vtkStructuredPointsToStructuredPointsFilter is an abstract filter class whose subclasses take on input structured points and generate structured points on output.

SUMMARY

vtkStructuredPoints *GetOutput()
Get the output of this filter.

vtkStructuredPointsWriter

NAME

vtkStructuredPointsWriter - write **vtk** structured points data file

CLASS HIERARCHY

class vtkStructuredPointsWriter : public vtkDataWriter

DESCRIPTION

vtkStructuredPointsWriter is a source object that writes ASCII or binary structured points data in **vtk** file format. See text for format details.

CAVEATS

Binary files written on one system may not be writable on other systems.

SUMMARY

void SetInput(vtkStructuredPoints *input)
Specify the input data or filter.

vtkSweptSurface

NAME

vtkSweptSurface - given a path and input geometry generate an (implicit) representation of a swept surface

CLASS HIERARCHY

class vtkSweptSurface : public vtkStructuredPointsToStructuredPointsFilter

DESCRIPTION

vtkSweptSurface is a filter that is used to create a surface defined by moving a part along a path. In this implementation, the path is defined as a list of transformation matrices (vtkTransform), and the part geometry is implicitly defined using a volume (i.e., distance scalars in structured point dataset). The input to the filter is the geometry (i.e., a structured point dataset) and the output is a structured point dataset (i.e., an implicit representation of the swept surface). If you wish to generate a polygonal representation of swept surface you will have to use a contouring filter (e.g., vtkContourFilter). (You may also wish to use vtkDecimate to reduce mesh size.)

The swept surface algorithm can be summarized as follows. A geometry (i.e. the input) is swept along a path (list of transforms). At each point on the path the input is re-sampled into a volume using a union operation. (Union means that the minimum scalar value is retained - minimum distance value for example.) At the end, an implicit representation of the swept surface is defined.

SEE ALSO

vtkImplicitModeller vtkContourFilter vtkDecimate

SUMMARY

```
void  SetSampleDimensions(int, int, int)
void  SetSampleDimensions(int *)
int   *GetSampleDimensions()
void  GetSampleDimensions(int data[3])
```
Specify i-j-k dimensions to sample input with. The higher the resolution the lower the error but the greater the processing time.

```
void  SetTransforms( vtkTransformCollection*)
void  SetTransforms( vtkTransformCollection& )
      vtkTransformCollection *GetTransforms()
```
Specify a path (i.e., list of transforms) that the input moves along. At least two transforms must be used to define a path.

```
void  SetFillValue(float)
float GetFillValue()
```
Voxels are initialized to this value. By default a large floating point value is used, since the scalar values are assumed to be a distance function.

```
void  SetNumberOfInterpolationSteps(int)
int   GetNumberOfInterpolationSteps()
```
Value specifies/controls interpolation between the nodes (i.e., transforms) defining the path. A positive value indicates the number of steps to take between

transforms (i.e., interpolation is performed). A negative value indicates that no interpolation to be performed, that is, only the points defined at each transform are used (interpolation not performed). A zero value indicates that automatic interpolation is to be performed, that is, interpolation is computed so that potential errors fall below the error bounds defined in the text. By default, automatic computation is performed (Interpolation = 0).

void	**SetMaximumNumberOfInterpolationSteps(int)**
int	**GetMaximumNumberOfInterpolationSteps()**

Set/get the maximum number of interpolation steps to take. This is useful if you are limited in computation time or just know that the number of computed steps should not exceed a certain value.

void	**SetCapping(int)**
int	**GetCapping()**
void	**CappingOn()**
void	**CappingOff()**

The outer boundary of the sampling volume can be capped (i.e., assigned fill value). This will "close" the implicit model if the geometry approaches close to or passes through the boundary of the volume (i.e., defined by ModelBounds instance variable). Capping turns on/off this capability. By default capping is on.

void	**SetModelBounds(float data[6])**
void	**SetModelBounds(float *)**
float	***GetModelBounds()**
void	**GetModelBounds(float data[6])**
void	**SetModelBounds(float xmin, float xmax, float ymin, float ymax,**
float	**zmin, float zmax);**

Define the volume (in world coordinates) in which the sampling is to occur. Make sure that the volume is large enough to accommodate the motion of the geometry along the path. If the model bounds are set to all zero values, the model bounds will be computed automatically from the input geometry and path.

vtkSweptSurface()

Construct object with SampleDimensions = (50,50,50), FillValue = VTK_LARGE_FLOAT, ModelBounds=(0,0,0,0,0,0) (i.e, bounds will be computed automatically), and Capping turned on.

vtkTCoords

NAME

vtkTCoords - abstract interface to texture coordinates

CLASS HIERARCHY

class vtkTCoords : public vtkRefCount

DESCRIPTION

vtkTCoords provides an abstract interface to 2D or 3D texture coordinates. Texture coordinates are 2D (s,t) or 3D (r,s,t) parametric values that map geometry into regular 2D or 3D arrays of color and/or transparency values. During rendering the array are mapped onto the geometry for fast image detailing. The subclasses of vtkTCoords are concrete data types (float, int, etc.) that implement the interface of vtkTCoords.

SUMMARY

virtual vtkTCoords *MakeObject(int sze, int d=2, int ext=1000) = 0;
Create a copy of this object.

virtual char *GetDataType() = 0;
Return data type. One of "bit", "unsigned char", "short", "int", "float", or "double".

virtual int GetNumberOfTCoords() = 0;
Return number of texture coordinates in array.

virtual float *GetTCoord(int id) = 0;
Return a float texture coordinate tc[2/3] for a particular point id.

virtual void GetTCoord(int id, float tc[3]);
Copy float texture coordinates into user provided array tc[2/3] for specified point id.

virtual void SetTCoord(int id, float *tc) = 0;
Insert texture coordinate into object. No range checking performed (fast!).

virtual void InsertTCoord(int id, float *tc) = 0;
void InsertTCoord(int id, float tc1, float tc2, float tc3);
Insert texture coordinate into object. Range checking performed and memory allocated as necessary.

virtual int InsertNextTCoord(float *tc) = 0;
int InsertNextTCoord(float tc1, float tc2, float tc3);
Insert texture coordinate into next available slot. Returns point id of slot.

virtual void Squeeze() = 0;
Reclaim any extra memory.

void InsertTCoord(int id, float tc1, float tc2, float tc3)
Insert texture coordinate into position indicated. Although up to three texture components may be specified (i.e., tc1, tc2, tc3), if the texture coordinates are less than 3 dimensions the extra components will be ignored.

vtkTCoords

int InsertNextTCoord(float tc1, float tc2, float tc3)
Insert texture coordinate into position indicated. Although up to three texture components may be specified (i.e., tc1, tc2, tc3), if the texture coordinates are less than 3 dimensions, the extra components will be ignored.

vtkTCoords(int dim)
Construct object whose texture coordinates are of specified dimension.

void GetTCoords(vtkIdList& ptId, vtkFloatTCoords& ftc)
Given a list of pt ids, return an array of texture coordinates.

vtkTensor

NAME

vtkTensor - supporting class to enable assignment and referencing of tensors

CLASS HIERARCHY

class vtkTensor

DESCRIPTION

vtkTensor is a floating point representation of an nxn tensor. vtkTensor provides methods for assignment and reference of tensor components. It does it in such a way as to minimize data copying.

CAVEATS

vtkTensor performs its operations using pointer reference. You are responsible for supplying data storage (if necessary) if local copies of data are being made.

DEFINES

VTK_TENSOR_MAXDIM 3

SUMMARY

vtkTensor(int dim)
Construct tensor initially pointing to internal storage.

void SetDimension(int dim)
Set the dimensions of the tensor.

int   GetDimension()
Get the dimensions of the tensor.

void Initialize()
Initialize tensor components to 0.0.

float GetComponent(int i, int j)
Get the tensor component (i,j).

void SetComponent(int i, int j, float v)
Set the value of the tensor component (i,j).

void AddComponent(int i, int j, float v)
Add to the value of the tensor component at location (i,j).

void operator=(float *t)
Assign tensors to a float array. Float array must be sized Dimension*Dimension.

void operator=(vtkTensor &t)
Assign tensor to another tensor.

float *GetColumn(int j)
Return column vector from tensor. (Assumes 2D matrix form.) 0-offset.

vtkTensorGlyph

NAME

vtkTensorGlyph - scale and orient glyph according to tensor eigenvalues and eigenvectors

CLASS HIERARCHY

class vtkTensorGlyph : public vtkDataSetToPolyFilter

DESCRIPTION

vtkTensorGlyph is a filter that copies a geometric representation (specified as polygonal data) to every input point. The geometric representation, or glyph, can be scaled and/or rotated according to the tensor at the input point. Scaling and rotation is controlled by the eigenvalues/eigenvectors of the tensor as follows. For each tensor, the eigenvalues (and associated eigenvectors) are sorted to determine the major, medium, and minor eigenvalues/eigenvectors. The major eigenvalue scales the glyph in the x-direction, the medium in the y-direction, and the minor in the z-direction. Then, the glyph is rotated so that the glyph's local x-axis lies along the major eigenvector, y-axis along the medium eigenvector, and z-axis along the minor.

A scale factor is provided to control the amount of scaling. Also, you can turn off scaling completely if desired. The boolean variable ClampScaling controls the maximum scaling (in conjunction with MaxScaleFactor.) This is useful in certain applications where singularities or large order of magnitude differences exist in the eigenvalues.

Another instance variable, ExtractEigenvalues, has been provided to control extraction of eigenvalues/eigenvectors. If this boolean is false, then eigenvalues/eigenvectors are not extracted, and the columns of the tensor are taken as the eigenvectors (norm of column is eigenvalue). This allows additional capability over the vtkGlyph3D object. That is, the glyph can be oriented in three directions instead of one.

SEE ALSO

vtkGlyph3D vtkPointLoad vtkHyperStreamline

SUMMARY

```
void  SetSource(vtkPolyData*)
void  SetSource(vtkPolyData& )
vtkPolyData *GetSource()
```
Specify the geometry to copy to each point.

```
void  SetScaling(int)
int    GetScaling()
void  ScalingOn()
void  ScalingOff()
```
Turn on/off scaling of glyph with eigenvalues.

vtkTensorGlyph

void SetScaleFactor(float)
float GetScaleFactor()
Specify scale factor to scale object by. (Scale factor always affects output even if scaling is off.)

void SetExtractEigenvalues(int)
void ExtractEigenvaluesOn()
void ExtractEigenvaluesOff()
int GetExtractEigenvalues()
Turn on/off extraction of eigenvalues from tensor.

void SetColorGlyphs(int)
int GetColorGlyphs()
void ColorGlyphsOn()
void ColorGlyphsOff()
Turn on/off coloring of glyph with input scalar data. If false, or input scalar data not present, then the scalars from the source object are passed through the filter.

void SetClampScaling(int)
int GetClampScaling()
void ClampScalingOn()
void ClampScalingOff()
Turn on/off scalar clamping. If scalar clamping is on, the ivar MaxScaleFactor is used to control the maximum scale factor. (This is useful to prevent uncontrolled scaling near singularities.)

void SetMaxScaleFactor(float)
float GetMaxScaleFactor()
Set/Get the maximum allowable scale factor. This value is compared to the combination of the scale factor times the eigenvalue. If less, the scale factor is reset to the MaxScaleFactor. The boolean ClampScaling has to be "on" for this to work.

void Update()
Override update method because execution can branch two ways (Input and Source).

vtkTensors

NAME

vtkTensors - abstract interface to tensors

CLASS HIERARCHY

class vtkTensors : public vtkRefCount

DESCRIPTION

vtkTensors provides an abstract interface to n-dimensional tensors. The data model for vtkTensors is a list of arrays of nxn tensor matrices accessible by point id. The subclasses of vtkTensors are concrete data types (float, int, etc.) that implement the interface of vtkTensors.

SUMMARY

virtual vtkTensors *MakeObject(int sze, int d=3, int ext=1000) = 0;
   Create a copy of this object.

virtual char *GetDataType() = 0;
   Return data type. One of "bit", "unsigned char", "short", "int", "float", or "double".

virtual int GetNumberOfTensors() = 0;
   Return number of tensors in array.

virtual vtkTensor *GetTensor(int id) = 0;
   Return a float tensor t[dim*dim] for a particular point id.

virtual void GetTensor(int id, vtkTensor& t);
   Copy float tensor into user provided tensor for specified point id.

virtual void SetTensor(int id, vtkTensor *t) = 0;
   Insert tensor into object. No range checking performed (fast!).

virtual void InsertTensor(int id, vtkTensor *t) = 0;
void InsertTensor(int id, float t11, float t12, float t13,
float t21, float t22, float t23,
float t31, float t32, float t33);
   Insert tensor into object. Range checking performed and memory allocated as necessary.

virtual int InsertNextTensor(vtkTensor *t) = 0;
int   InsertNextTensor(float t11, float t12, float t13,
float t21, float t22, float t23,
float t31, float t32, float t33);
   Insert tensor into next available slot. Returns point id of slot.

virtual void Squeeze() = 0;
   Reclaim any extra memory.

void GetTensors(vtkIdList& ptId, vtkFloatTensors& ft)
   Given a list of pt ids, return an array of tensors.

vtkTetra

NAME

vtkTetra - a 3D cell that represents a tetrahedron

CLASS HIERARCHY

class vtkTetra : public vtkCell

DESCRIPTION

vtkTetra is a concrete implementation of vtkCell to represent a 3D tetrahedron.

SUMMARY

vtkTetra(const vtkTetra& t)
Deep copy of cell.

NAME

vtkTextSource - create polygonal text

CLASS HIERARCHY

class vtkTextSource : public vtkPolySource

DESCRIPTION

vtkTextSource converts a text string into polygons. This way you can insert text into your renderings. It uses the 9x15 font from X Windows. You can specify if you want the background to be drawn or not.

SUMMARY

void SetText(char *)
char *GetText()
Set/Get the text to be drawn.

void SetBacking(int)
int GetBacking()
void BackingOn()
void BackingOff()
Controls whether or not a background is drawn with the text.

vtkTextSource()
Construct text object with no string set and backing enabled.

vtkTexture

NAME

vtkTexture - handles properties associated with a texture map

CLASS HIERARCHY

class vtkTexture : public vtkObject

DESCRIPTION

vtkTexture is an object that handles loading and binding of texture maps. It obtains its data from an input structured points dataset type. Thus you can create visualization pipelines to read, process, and construct textures. Note that textures will only work if texture coordinates are also defined, and if the rendering system supports texture.

Instances of vtkTexture are associated with actors via the actor's SetTexture() method. Actors can share texture maps (this is encouraged to save memory resources.)

CAVEATS

Currently only 2D texture maps are supported, even though the data pipeline supports 1,2, and 3D texture coordinates.

Some renderers such as OpenGL require that the texture map dimensions are a power of two in each direction. Other renderers may have similar (ridiculous) restrictions, so please be careful out there...

SEE ALSO

vtkActor vtkRenderer vtkTextureDevice

SUMMARY

virtual void Render(vtkRenderer *ren);
Renders a texture map. It first checks the object's modified time to make sure the texture maps Input is valid, then it invokes the Load() method.

virtual void Load(vtkRenderer *ren);
Abstract interface to renderer. Each concrete subclass of vtkTextureDevice will load its data into graphics system in response to this method invocation. An instance of vtkTextureDevice will automatically be created.

int   GetRepeat()
void   SetRepeat(int)
void   RepeatOn()
void   RepeatOff()
Turn on/off the repetition of the texture map when the texture coords extend beyond the [0,1] range.

int   GetInterpolate()
void   SetInterpolate(int)
void   InterpolateOn()
void   InterpolateOff()
Turn on/off linear interpolation of the texture map when rendering.

vtkTexture

void SetInput(vtkStructuredPoints*)
void SetInput(vtkStructuredPoints&)
vtkStructuredPoints *GetInput()
> Specify the data for the texture map.

vtkTexture()
> Construct object and initialize.

vtkTextureDevice

NAME

vtkTextureDevice - abstract definition of a hardware dependent texture

CLASS HIERARCHY

class vtkTextureDevice : public vtkObject

DESCRIPTION

vtkTextureDevice is the superclass of the hardware dependent textures such as vtkOglrTexture and vtkSbrTexture. This object is typically created automatically by a vtkTexture object when it renders. The user should never see this class.

SEE ALSO

vtkTexture

SUMMARY

virtual void Load(vtkTexture *txt, vtkRenderer *ren) = 0;
This is the only method that the subclasses must supply.

vtkTextureMapToBox

NAME

vtkTextureMapToBox - generate 3D texture coordinates by mapping points into bounding box

CLASS HIERARCHY

class vtkTextureMapToBox : public vtkDataSetToDataSetFilter

DESCRIPTION

vtkTextureMapToBox is a filter that generates 3D texture coordinates by mapping input dataset points onto a bounding box. The bounding box can either be user specified or generated automatically. If the box is generated automatically, all points will lie inside of it. If a point lies outside the bounding box (only for manual box specification), its generated texture coordinate will be clamped into the r-s-t texture coordinate range.

SUMMARY

void SetRRange(float, float)
void SetRRange(float *)
float *GetRRange()
void GetRRange(float data[2])
> Specify r-coordinate range for texture r-s-t coordinate triplet.

void SetSRange(float, float)
void SetSRange(float *)
float *GetSRange()
void GetSRange(float data[2])
> Specify s-coordinate range for texture r-s-t coordinate triplet.

void SetTRange(float, float)
void SetTRange(float *)
float *GetTRange()
void GetTRange(float data[2])
> Specify t-coordinate range for texture r-s-t coordinate triplet.

void SetAutomaticBoxGeneration(int)
int GetAutomaticBoxGeneration()
void AutomaticBoxGenerationOn()
void AutomaticBoxGenerationOff()
> Turn on/off automatic bounding box generation.

vtkTextureMapToBox()
> Construct with r-s-t range=(0,1) and automatic box generation turned on.

void SetBox(float xmin, float xmax, float ymin, float ymax,
float zmin, float zmax)
> Specify the bounding box to map into.

vtkTextureMapToPlane

NAME

vtkTextureMapToPlane - generate texture coordinates by mapping points to plane

CLASS HIERARCHY

class vtkTextureMapToPlane : public vtkDataSetToDataSetFilter

DESCRIPTION

vtkTextureMapToPlane is a filter that generates 2D texture coordinates by mapping input dataset points onto a plane. The plane can either be user specified or generated automatically. (A least squares method is used to generate the plane.)

SUMMARY

void SetNormal(float, float, float)
void SetNormal(float *)
float *GetNormal()
void GetNormal(float data[3])
　　　Specify plane normal.

void SetSRange(float, float)
void SetSRange(float *)
float *GetSRange()
void GetSRange(float data[2])
　　　Specify s-coordinate range for texture s-t coordinate pair.

void SetTRange(float, float)
void SetTRange(float *)
float *GetTRange()
void GetTRange(float data[2])
　　　Specify t-coordinate range for texture s-t coordinate pair.

void SetAutomaticPlaneGeneration(int)
int   GetAutomaticPlaneGeneration()
void AutomaticPlaneGenerationOn()
void AutomaticPlaneGenerationOff()
　　　Turn on/off automatic plane generation.

vtkTextureMapToPlane()
　　　Construct with s,t range=(0,1) and automatic plane generation turned on.

vtkThreshold

NAME

vtkThreshold - extracts cells where scalar value of every point in cell satisfies threshold criterion

CLASS HIERARCHY

class vtkThreshold : public vtkDataSetToUnstructuredGridFilter

DESCRIPTION

vtkThreshold is a filter that extracts cells from any dataset type that satisfy a threshold criterion. A cell satisfies the criterion if the scalar value of every point satisfies the criterion. The criterion can take three forms: 1) greater than a particular value; 2) less than a particular value; or 3) between two values. The output of this filter is an unstructured grid.

SEE ALSO

vtkThresholdPoints vtkThresholdTextureCoords

SUMMARY

void ThresholdByLower(float lower)
Criterion is cells whose scalars are less than lower threshold.

void ThresholdByUpper(float upper)
Criterion is cells whose scalars are less than upper threshold.

void ThresholdBetween(float lower, float upper)
Criterion is cells whose scalars are between lower and upper thresholds.

vtkThresholdPoints

NAME

vtkThresholdPoints - extracts points whose scalar value satisfies threshold criterion

CLASS HIERARCHY

class vtkThresholdPoints : public vtkDataSetToPolyFilter

DESCRIPTION

vtkThresholdPoints is a filter that extracts points from a dataset that satisfy a threshold criterion. The criterion can take three forms: 1) greater than a particular value; 2) less than a particular value; and 3) between a particular value. The output of the filter is polygonal data.

SEE ALSO

vtkThreshold

SUMMARY

void   ThresholdByLower(float lower)
Criterion is cells whose scalars are less than lower threshold.

void   ThresholdByUpper(float upper)
Criterion is cells whose scalars are less than upper threshold.

void   ThresholdBetween(float lower, float upper)
Criterion is cells whose scalars are between lower and upper thresholds.

vtkThresholdTextureCoords

NAME

vtkThresholdTextureCoords - compute 1D, 2D, or 3D texture coordinates based on scalar threshold

CLASS HIERARCHY

class vtkThresholdTextureCoords : public vtkDataSetToDataSetFilter

DESCRIPTION

vtkThresholdTextureCoords is a filter that generates texture coordinates for any input dataset type given a threshold criterion. The criterion can take three forms: 1) greater than a particular value (ThresholdByUpper()); 2) less than a particular value (ThresholdByLower()); or 3) between two values (ThresholdBetween(). If the threshold criterion is satisfied, the "in" texture coordinate will be set (this can be specified by the user). If the threshold criterion is not satisfied the "out" is set.

CAVEATS

There is a texture map - texThres.vtk - that can be used in conjunction with this filter. This map defines a "transparent" region for texture coordinates $0<=r<0.5$, and an opaque full intensity map for texture coordinates $0.5<r<=1.0$. There is a small transition region for r=0.5.

SEE ALSO

vtkThreshold vtkThresholdPoints

SUMMARY

void SetTextureDimension(int)
int GetTextureDimension()
Set the desired dimension of the texture map.

void SetInTextureCoord(float, float, float)
void SetInTextureCoord(float *)
float *GetInTextureCoord()
void GetInTextureCoord(float data[3])
Set the texture coordinate value for point satisfying threshold criterion.

void SetOutTextureCoord(float, float, float)
void SetOutTextureCoord(float *)
float *GetOutTextureCoord()
void GetOutTextureCoord(float data[3])
Set the texture coordinate value for point NOT satisfying threshold criterion.

void ThresholdByLower(float lower)
Criterion is cells whose scalars are less than lower threshold.

void ThresholdByUpper(float upper)
Criterion is cells whose scalars are less than upper threshold.

void ThresholdBetween(float lower, float upper)
Criterion is cells whose scalars are between lower and upper thresholds.

vtkTimeStamp

NAME

vtkTimeStamp - record modification and/or execution time

CLASS HIERARCHY

class vtkTimeStamp

DESCRIPTION

vtkTimeStamp records a unique time when the method Modified() is executed. This time is guaranteed to be monotonically increasing. Classes use this object to record modified and/or execution time. There is built in support for the binary < and > comparison operators between two vtkTimeStamp objects.

SUMMARY

void Modified()

Set this objects time to the current time. The current time is just a monotonically increasing unsigned long integer. It is possible for this number to wrap around back to zero. This should only happen for processes that have been running for a very long time, or if constantly changing objects within the program. When this does occur, the typical consequence should be that some filters will update themselves when really they don't need to.

unsigned long int GetMTime()

Return this object's Modified time.

vtkTransform

NAME

vtkTransform - a general matrix transformation class

CLASS HIERARCHY

class vtkTransform : public vtkObject

DESCRIPTION

vtkTransform maintains a stack of 4x4 transformation matrices. A variety of methods are provided to manipulate the translation, scale, and rotation components of the matrix. Methods operate on the matrix at the top of the stack. Many objects, such as vtkActor and vtkCamera , use this class for performing their matrix operations. It is very important to realize that this class performs all of its operations in a right handed coordinate system with right handed rotations. Some other graphics libraries use left handed coordinate systems and rotations.

CAVEATS

By default the initial matrix is the identity matrix.

SEE ALSO

vtkMatrix4x4 vtkTransformCollection vtkTransformFilter vtkTransformPolyFilter

EXAMPLES

XFormSph.cc

SUMMARY

vtkTransform ()
Constructs a transform and sets the following defaults preMultiplyFlag = 1 stackSize = 10. It then creates an identity matrix as the top matrix on the stack.

vtkTransform (const vtkTransform& t)
Copy constructor. Creates an instance of vtkTransform and then copies its instance variables from the values in t.

void Pop ()
Deletes the transformation on the top of the stack and sets the top to the next transformation on the stack.

void PostMultiply ()
Sets the internal state of the transform to post multiply. All subsequent matrix operations will occur after those already represented in the current transformation matrix.

void PreMultiply ()
Sets the internal state of the transform to pre multiply. All subsequent matrix operations will occur before those already represented in the current transformation matrix.

void Push ()
Pushes the current transformation matrix onto the transformation stack.

vtkTransform

void RotateX (float angle)
Creates an x rotation matrix and concatenates it with the current transformation matrix. The angle is specified in degrees.

void RotateY (float angle)
Creates a y rotation matrix and concatenates it with the current transformation matrix. The angle is specified in degrees. Creates a y rotation matrix and concatenates it with the current transformation matrix.

void RotateZ (float angle)
Creates a z rotation matrix and concatenates it with the current transformation matrix. The angle is specified in degrees. Creates a z rotation matrix and concatenates it with the current transformation matrix.

void RotateWXYZ (float angle, float x, float y, float z)
Creates a matrix that rotates angle degrees about an axis through the origin and x, y, z. It then concatenates this matrix with the current transformation matrix.

void Scale (float x, float y, float z)
Scales the current transformation matrix in the x, y and z directions. A scale factor of zero will automatically be replaced with one.

void Translate (float x, float y, float z)
Translate the current transformation matrix by the vector {x, y, z}.

void GetTranspose (vtkMatrix4x4& (transpose))
Obtain the transpose of the current transformation matrix.

void Inverse ()
Invert the current transformation matrix.

void GetInverse (vtkMatrix4x4& inverse)
Return the inverse of the current transformation matrix.

void GetOrientation(float& rx, float& ry, float &rz)
Get the x, y, z orientation angles from the transformation matrix.

float *GetOrientation ()
Get the x, y, z orientation angles from the transformation matrix as an array of three floating point values.

void GetPosition (float & x,float & y,float & z)
Return the x, y, z positions from the current transformation matrix. This is simply returning the translation component of the 4x4 matrix.

float *GetPosition()
Return the position from the current transformation matrix as an array of three floating point numbers. This is simply returning the translation component of the 4x4 matrix.

void GetScale (float& x, float& y, float& z)
Return the x, y, z scale factors of the current transformation matrix.

float *GetScale()
Return the x, y, z scale factors of the current transformation matrix as an array of three float numbers.

vtkTransform

vtkMatrix4x4 & GetMatrix ()

Returns the current transformation matrix.

void SetMatrix(vtkMatrix4x4& m)

Set the current matrix directly.

void Identity ()

Creates an identity matrix and makes it the current transformation matrix.

void Concatenate (vtkMatrix4x4 & matrix)

Concatenates the input matrix with the current transformation matrix. The resulting matrix becomes the new current transformation matrix. The setting of the PreMultiply flag determines whether the matrix is PreConcatenated or PostConcatenated.

void Multiply4x4 (vtkMatrix4x4 & a, vtkMatrix4x4 & b, vtkMatrix4x4 & c)

Multiplies matrices a and b and stores the result in c.

void Transpose ()

Transposes the current transformation matrix.

void GetMatrix (vtkMatrix4x4 & ctm)

Returns the current transformation matrix.

float *GetPoint()

Returns the result of multiplying the currently set Point by the current transformation matrix. Point is expressed in homogeneous coordinates. The setting of the PreMultiplyFlag will determine if the Point is Pre or Post multiplied.

void MultiplyPoints(vtkPoints *inPts, vtkPoints *outPts)

Multiplies a list of points (inPts) by the current transformation matrix. Transformed points are appended to the output list (outPts).

void MultiplyVectors(vtkVectors *inVectors, vtkVectors *outVectors)

Multiplies a list of vectors (inVectors) by the current transformation matrix. The transformed vectors are appended to the output list (outVectors). This is a special multiplication, since these are vectors. It multiplies vectors by the transposed inverse of the matrix, ignoring the translational components.

void MultiplyNormals(vtkNormals *inNormals, vtkNormals *outNormals)

Multiplies a list of normals (inNormals) by the current transformation matrix. The transformed normals are then appended to the output list (outNormals). This is a special multiplication, since these are normals. It multiplies the normals by the transposed inverse of the matrix, ignoring the translational components.

vtkTransformCollection

NAME

vtkTransformCollection - maintain a list of transforms

CLASS HIERARCHY

class vtkTransformCollection : public vtkCollection

DESCRIPTION

vtkTransformCollection is an object that creates and manipulates lists of objects of type vtkTransform.

SEE ALSO

vtkCollection vtkTransform

SUMMARY

void AddItem(vtkTransform *t)
Add a Transform to the list.

void RemoveItem(vtkTransform *t)
Remove a Transform from the list.

int   IsItemPresent(vtkTransform *t)
Determine whether a particular Transform is present. Returns its position in the list.

vtkTransform *GetNextItem()
Get the next Transform in the list. Return NULL when the end of the list is reached.

vtkTransformFilter

NAME

vtkTransformFilter - transform points and associated normals and vectors

CLASS HIERARCHY

class vtkTransformFilter : public vtkPointSetToPointSetFilter

DESCRIPTION

vtkTransformFilter is a filter to transform point coordinates, and associated point normals and vectors. Other point data is passed through the filter.

An alternative method of transformation is to use vtkActor's methods to scale, rotate, and translate objects. The difference between the two methods is that vtkActor's transformation simply effects where objects are rendered (via the graphics pipeline), whereas vtkTransformFilter actually modifies point coordinates in the visualization pipeline. This is necessary for some objects (e.g., vtkProbeFilter) that require point coordinates as input.

SEE ALSO

vtkTransform vtkTransformPolyFilter vtkActor

EXAMPLES

XFormSph.cc

SUMMARY

void SetTransform(vtkTransform*)
void SetTransform(vtkTransform&)
vtkTransform *GetTransform()
    Specify the transform object used to transform points.

vtkTransformPolyFilter

NAME

vtkTransformPolyFilter - transform points and associated normals and vectors for polygonal dataset

CLASS HIERARCHY

class vtkTransformPolyFilter : public vtkPolyToPolyFilter

DESCRIPTION

vtkTransformPolyFilter is a filter to transform point coordinates and associated point normals and vectors. Other point data is passed through the filter. This filter is specialized for polygonal data. See vtkTransformFilter for more general data.

An alternative method of transformation is to use vtkActors methods to scale, rotate, and translate objects. The difference between the two methods is that vtkActor's transformation simply effects where objects are rendered (via the graphics pipeline), whereas vtkTransformPolyFilter actually modifies point coordinates in the visualization pipeline. This is necessary for some objects (e.g., vtkProbeFilter) that require point coordinates as input.

SEE ALSO

vtkTransform vtkTransformFilter vtkActor

SUMMARY

void SetTransform(vtkTransform*)
void SetTransform(vtkTransform&)
vtkTransform *GetTransform()
    Specify the transform object used to transform points.

vtkTransformStructuredPoints

NAME

vtkTransformStructuredPoints - transform (and resample) vtkStructuredPoints

CLASS HIERARCHY

class vtkTransformStructuredPoints :
public vtkStructuredPointsToStructuredPointsFilter

DESCRIPTION

vtkTransformStructuredPoints is a filter that samples an input structured point set with a "transformed" structured point set. The sampling process occurs as follows: each output point (or voxel) is transformed according to a user specified transformation object. The point is used to sample the input. If the point does not fall inside the input structured point set, then the point is assigned a fill value (user specified). Otherwise, tri-linear interpolation is used to assign the value.

SUMMARY

void SetSampleDimensions(int, int, int)
void SetSampleDimensions(int *)
int   *GetSampleDimensions()
void GetSampleDimensions(int data[3])
Specify i-j-k dimensions to sample input with.

void SetFillValue(float)
float GetFillValue()
All voxels not within input structured point set are assigned this value.

void SetTransform(vtkTransform*)
void SetTransform(vtkTransform&)
vtkTransform *GetTransform()
Specify object to transform output voxels prior to sampling.

vtkTransformStructuredPoints()
Construct object to use input dimensions as sample dimensions, and to compute bounds automatically from input. Fill value is set to large positive integer.

void SetModelBounds(float *bounds)
Define pre-transformed size of structured point set.

vtkTriangle

NAME

vtkTriangle - a cell that represents a triangle

CLASS HIERARCHY

class vtkTriangle : public vtkCell

DESCRIPTION

vtkTriangle is a concrete implementation of vtkCell to represent a triangle located in 3-space.

SUMMARY

void   TriangleCenter(float p1[3], float p2[3], float p3[3],
Compute the center of the triangle.

float   TriangleArea(float p1[3], float p2[3], float p3[3])
Compute the area of a triangle in 3D.

vtkTriangle(const vtkTriangle& t)
Deep copy of cell.

vtkTriangleFilter

NAME

vtkTriangleFilter - create triangle polygons from input polygons and triangle strips

CLASS HIERARCHY

class vtkTriangleFilter : public vtkPolyToPolyFilter

DESCRIPTION

vtkTriangleFilter generates triangles from input polygons and triangle strips. The filter also will pass through vertices and lines, if requested.

SUMMARY

void	**PassVertsOn()**
void	**PassVertsOff()**
void	**SetPassVerts(int)**
int	**GetPassVerts()**

Turn on/off passing vertices through filter.

void	**PassLinesOn()**
void	**PassLinesOff()**
void	**SetPassLines(int)**
int	**GetPassLines()**

Turn on/off passing lines through filter.

vtkTriangleStrip

NAME

vtkTriangleStrip - a cell that represents a triangle strip

CLASS HIERARCHY

class vtkTriangleStrip : public vtkCell

DESCRIPTION

vtkTriangleStrip is a concrete implementation of vtkCell to represent a 2D triangle strip. A triangle strip is a compact representation of triangles connected edge to edge in strip fashion. The connectivity of a triangle strip is three points defining an initial triangle, then for each additional triangle, a single point that, combined with the previous two points, defines the next triangle.

SUMMARY

vtkTriangleStrip(const vtkTriangleStrip& ts)
Deep copy of cell.

vtkTubeFilter

NAME

vtkTubeFilter - filter that generates tubes around lines

CLASS HIERARCHY

class vtkTubeFilter : public vtkPolyToPolyFilter

DESCRIPTION

vtkTubeFilter is a filter that generates a tube around each input line. The tubes are made up of triangle strips and rotate around the tube with the rotation of the line normals. (If no normals are present, they are computed automatically.) The radius of the tube can be set to vary with scalar or vector value. If the radius varies with scalar value the radius is linearly adjusted. If the radius varies with vector value, a mass flux preserving variation is used. The number of sides for the tube also can be specified.

CAVEATS

The number of tube sides must be greater than 3. If you wish to use fewer sides (i.e., a ribbon), use vtkRibbonFilter.

The input line must not have duplicate points, or normals at points that are parallel to the incoming/outgoing line segments. (Duplicate points can be removed with vtkCleanPolyData.)

SEE ALSO

vtkRibbonFilter

DEFINES

VTK_VARY_RADIUS_OFF 0
VTK_VARY_RADIUS_BY_SCALAR 1
VTK_VARY_RADIUS_BY_VECTOR 2

SUMMARY

void SetRadius(float)
float GetRadius()
Set the minimum tube radius (minimum because the tube radius may vary).

void SetVaryRadius(int)
VTK_VARY_RADIUS_OFF,VTK_VARY_RADIUS_BY_VECTOR);
int GetVaryRadius()
Turn on/off the variation of tube radius with scalar value.

void SetNumberOfSides(int)
int GetNumberOfSides()
Set the number of sides for the tube. At a minimum, number of sides is 3.

void SetRadiusFactor(float)
float GetRadiusFactor()
Set the maximum tube radius in terms of a multiple of the minimum radius.

vtkTubeFilter

vtkTubeFilter()
Construct object with radius 0.5, radius variation turned off, the number of sides set to 3, and radius factor of 10.

vtkUnsignedCharArray

NAME

vtkUnsignedCharArray - dynamic, self-adjusting unsigned character array

CLASS HIERARCHY

class vtkUnsignedCharArray : public vtkObject

DESCRIPTION

vtkUnsignedCharArray is an array of unsigned character values. It provides methods for insertion and retrieval of characters, and will automatically resize itself to hold new data.

SUMMARY

unsigned char GetValue(const int id)
Get the data at a particular index.

unsigned char *GetPtr(const int id)
Get the address of a particular data index.

unsigned char *WritePtr(const int id, const int number)
Get the address of a particular data index. Make sure data is allocated for the number of items requested. Set MaxId according to the number of data values requested.

vtkUnsignedCharArray& InsertValue(const int id, const unsigned char c)
Insert data at a specified position in the array.

int   InsertNextValue(const unsigned char c)
Insert data at the end of the array. Return its location in the array.

unsigned char& operator[](const int i)
Does insert or get (depending on location on lhs or rhs of statement). Does not do automatic resizing - user's responsibility to range check.

void Squeeze()
Resize object to just fit data requirement. Reclaims extra memory.

int   GetSize()
Get the allocated size of the object in terms of number of data items.

int   GetMaxId()
Returning the maximum index of data inserted so far.

void Reset()
Reuse the memory allocated by this object. Objects appears like no data has been previously inserted.

int   Allocate(const int sz, const int ext)
Allocate memory for this array. Delete old storage if present.

void Initialize()
Release storage and reset array to initial state.

vtkUnsignedCharArray

vtkUnsignedCharArray(const int sz, const int ext)
Construct with specified storage size and extend value.

vtkUnsignedCharArray(const vtkUnsignedCharArray& ia)
Construct array from another array. Copy each element of other array.

vtkUnsignedCharArray& operator=(const vtkUnsignedCharArray& ia)
Deep copy of another array.

void operator+=(const vtkUnsignedCharArray& ia)
Append one array onto the end of this array.

vtkUnsignedCharScalars

NAME

vtkUnsignedCharScalars - unsigned char representation of scalar data

CLASS HIERARCHY

class vtkUnsignedCharScalars : public vtkScalars

DESCRIPTION

vtkUnsignedCharScalars is a concrete implementation of vtkScalars. Scalars are represented using char values.

SUMMARY

unsigned char *GetPtr(const int id)

Get pointer to array of data starting at data position "id".

unsigned char *WritePtr(const int id, const int number)

Get pointer to data array. Useful for direct writes of data. MaxId is bumped by number (and memory allocated if necessary). Id is the location you wish to write into; number is the number of scalars to write. Use the method WrotePtr() to mark completion of write.

void WrotePtr()

Terminate direct write of data. Although dummy routine now, reserved for future use.

vtkUnsignedCharScalars& operator=(const vtkUnsignedCharScalars& cs)

Deep copy of scalars.

vtkUnstructuredGrid

NAME

vtkUnstructuredGrid - dataset represents arbitrary combinations of all possible cell types

CLASS HIERARCHY

class vtkUnstructuredGrid : public vtkPointSet

DESCRIPTION

vtkUnstructuredGrid is a data object that is a concrete implementation of vtkDataSet. vtkUnstructuredGrid represents any combinations of any cell types. This includes 0D (e.g., points), 1D (e.g., lines, polylines), 2D (e.g., triangles, polygons), and 3D (e.g., hexahedron, tetrahedron).

SUMMARY

void Allocate (int numCells, int extSize)
Allocate memory space for data insertion. Execute this method before inserting any cells into object.

vtkUnstructuredGrid(const vtkUnstructuredGrid& ug) :
vtkPointSet(ug)
Shallow construction of object.

void CopyStructure(vtkDataSet *ds)
Copy the geometric and topological structure of an input unstructured grid.

int InsertNextCell(int type, vtkIdList& ptIds)
Insert/create cell in object by type and list of point ids defining cell topology.

int InsertNextCell(int type, int npts, int *pts)
Insert/create cell in object by type and list of point ids defining cell topology.

vtkUnstructuredGridFilter

NAME

vtkUnstructuredGridFilter - filter that takes an unstructured grid as input

CLASS HIERARCHY

class vtkUnstructuredGridFilter : public vtkFilter

DESCRIPTION

vtkUnstructuredGridFilter is a filter that takes a single unstructured grid data object as input.

SUMMARY

void SetInput(vtkUnstructuredGrid *input)
Specify the input data or filter.

vtkUnstructuredGridReader

NAME

vtkUnstructuredGridReader - read **vtk** unstructured grid data file

CLASS HIERARCHY

class vtkUnstructuredGridReader : public vtkUnstructuredGridSource

DESCRIPTION

vtkUnstructuredGridReader is a source object that reads ASCII or binary unstructured grid data files in **vtk** format. See text for format details.

CAVEATS

Binary files written on one system may not be readable on other systems.

SUMMARY

void SetFilename(char *name)
Specify file name of **vtk** unstructured grid data file to read.

int   GetFileType()
Get the type of file (VTK_ASCII or VTK_BINARY)

void SetScalarsName(char *name)
Set the name of the scalar data to extract. If not specified, first scalar data encountered is extracted.

void SetVectorsName(char *name)
Set the name of the vector data to extract. If not specified, first vector data encountered is extracted.

void SetTensorsName(char *name)
Set the name of the tensor data to extract. If not specified, first tensor data encountered is extracted.

void SetNormalsName(char *name)
Set the name of the normal data to extract. If not specified, first normal data encountered is extracted.

void SetTCoordsName(char *name)
Set the name of the texture coordinate data to extract. If not specified, first texture coordinate data encountered is extracted.

void SetLookupTableName(char *name)
Set the name of the lookup table data to extract. If not specified, uses lookup table named by scalar. Otherwise, this specification supersedes.

vtkUnstructuredGridSource

NAME

vtkUnstructuredGridSource - abstract class whose subclasses generate unstructured grid data

CLASS HIERARCHY

class vtkUnstructuredGridSource : public vtkSource

DESCRIPTION

vtkUnstructuredGridSource is an abstract class whose subclasses generate unstructured grid data.

SUMMARY

vtkUnstructuredGrid *GetOutput()
Get the output of this source.

vtkUnstructuredGridWriter

NAME

vtkUnstructuredGridWriter - write **vtk** unstructured grid data file

CLASS HIERARCHY

class vtkUnstructuredGridWriter : public vtkDataWriter

DESCRIPTION

vtkUnstructuredGridWriter is a source object that writes ASCII or binary unstructured grid data files in **vtk** format. See text for format details.

CAVEATS

Binary files written on one system may not be readable on other systems.

SUMMARY

void SetInput(vtkUnstructuredGrid *input)
Specify the input data or filter.

vtkUserDefined

NAME

vtkUserDefined - interface to user defined data

CLASS HIERARCHY

class vtkUserDefined : public vtkRefCount

DESCRIPTION

vtkUserDefined provides an abstract interface to user defined data. User defined data are manipulated using void* pointers. These pointers are accessed via point id, so information can be represented on a per vertex basis.

SUMMARY

virtual void* Interpolate(float *weights)
Interpolate user defined data. Method must be supplied by user. Return value must be non-static void* pointer to data.

vtkUserDefined& operator=(const vtkUserDefined& ud)
Deep copy of UserDefined data.

void GetUserDefined(vtkIdList& ptId, vtkUserDefined& ud)
Given a list of pt ids, return an array of point coordinates.

vtkVectorDot

NAME

vtkVectorDot - generate scalars from dot product of vectors and normals (e.g., show displacement plot)

CLASS HIERARCHY

class vtkVectorDot : public vtkDataSetToDataSetFilter

DESCRIPTION

vtkVectorDot is a filter to generate scalar values from a dataset. The scalar value at a point is created by computing the dot product between the normal and vector at that point. Combined with the appropriate color map, this can show nodal lines/mode shapes of vibration, or a displacement plot.

SUMMARY

void SetScalarRange(float, float)
void SetScalarRange(float *)
Specify range to map scalars into.

float *GetScalarRange()
void GetScalarRange(float data[2])
Get the range that scalars map into.

vtkVectorDot()
Construct object with scalar range is (-1,1).

vtkVectorNorm

NAME

vtkVectorNorm - generate scalars from Euclidean norm of vectors

CLASS HIERARCHY

class vtkVectorNorm : public vtkDataSetToDataSetFilter

DESCRIPTION

vtkVectorNorm is a filter that generates scalar values by computing euclidean norm of vector triplets. Scalars can be normalized $0<=s<=1$ if desired.

SUMMARY

void	**SetNormalize(int)**
int	**GetNormalize()**
void	**NormalizeOn()**
void	**NormalizeOff()**

Specify whether to normalize scalar values.

vtkVectorNorm()

Construct with normalize flag off.

vtkVectorTopology

NAME

vtkVectorTopology - mark points where the vector field vanishes (singularities exist).

CLASS HIERARCHY

class vtkVectorTopology : public vtkDataSetToPolyFilter

DESCRIPTION

vtkVectorTopology is a filter that marks points where the vector field vanishes. At these points various important flow features are found, including regions of circulation, separation, etc. The region around these areas are good places to start streamlines. (The vector field vanishes in cells where the x-y-z vector components each pass through zero.)

The output of this filter is a set of vertices. These vertices mark the vector field singularities. You can use an object like vtkGlyph3D to place markers at these points, or use the vertices to initiate streamlines.

The Distance instance variable controls the accuracy of placement of the vertices. Smaller values result in greater execution times.

The input to this filter is any dataset type. The position of the vertices is found by sampling the cell in parametric space. Sampling is repeated until the Distance criterion is satisfied.

SEE ALSO

vtkGlyph3D vtkStreamLine

SUMMARY

void SetDistance(float)
float GetDistance()
Specify distance from singularity to generate point.

vtkVectorTopology()
Construct object with distance 0.1.

vtkVectors

NAME

vtkVectors - abstract interface to 3D vectors

CLASS HIERARCHY

class vtkVectors : public vtkRefCount

DESCRIPTION

vtkVectors provides an abstract interface to 3D vectors. The data model for vtkVectors is an array of vx-vy-vz triplets accessible by point id. The subclasses of vtkVectors are concrete data types (float, int, etc.) that implement the interface of vtkVectors.

SUMMARY

virtual vtkVectors *MakeObject(int sze, int ext=1000) = 0;
Create a copy of this object.

virtual char *GetDataType() = 0;
Return data type. One of "bit", "unsigned char", "short", "int", "float", or "double".

virtual int GetNumberOfVectors() = 0;
Return number of vectors in array.

virtual float *GetVector(int id) = 0;
Return a pointer to a float vector v[3] for a specific point id.

virtual void GetVector(int id, float v[3]);
Copy vector components into user provided array v[3] for specified point id.

virtual void SetVector(int id, float v[3]) = 0;
Insert vector into object. No range checking performed (fast!).

virtual void InsertVector(int id, float v[3]) = 0;
void InsertVector(int id, float vx, float vy, float vz);
Insert vector into object. Range checking performed and memory allocated as necessary.

virtual int InsertNextVector(float v[3]) = 0;
int   InsertNextVector(float vx, float vy, float vz);
Insert vector into next available slot. Returns point id of slot.

virtual void Squeeze() = 0;
Reclaim any extra memory.

void InsertVector(int id, float vx, float vy, float vz)
Insert vector into position indicated.

int   InsertNextVector(float vx, float vy, float vz)
Insert vector into position indicated.

void GetVectors(vtkIdList& ptId, vtkFloatVectors& fp)
Given a list of pt ids, return an array of vectors.

vtkVectors

void ComputeMaxNorm()
Compute the largest norm for these vectors.

float GetMaxNorm()
Return the maximum norm for these vectors.

vtkVertex

NAME

vtkVertex - a cell that represents a 3D point

CLASS HIERARCHY

class vtkVertex : public vtkCell

DESCRIPTION

vtkVertex is a concrete implementation of vtkCell to represent a 3D point.

SUMMARY

vtkVertex(const vtkVertex& p)
Deep copy of cell.

vtkVoidArray

NAME

vtkVoidArray - dynamic, self-adjusting array of void* pointers

CLASS HIERARCHY

class vtkVoidArray : public vtkObject

DESCRIPTION

vtkVoidArray is an array of pointers to void. It provides methods for insertion and retrieval of these pointers values, and will automatically resize itself to hold new data.

SUMMARY

void* GetValue(const int id)
Get the data at a particular index.

void GetPtr(const int id)**
Get the address of a particular data index.

void WritePtr(const int id, const int number)**
Get the address of a particular data index. Make sure data is allocated for the number of items requested. Set MaxId according to the number of data values requested.

vtkVoidArray& InsertValue(const int id, void* p)
Insert data at a specified position in the array.

int   InsertNextValue(void* p)
Insert data at the end of the array. Return its location in the array.

void* &operator[](const int i)
Does insert or get (depending on location on lhs or rhs of statement). Does not do automatic resizing - user's responsibility to range check.

void Squeeze()
Resize object to just fit data requirement. Reclaims extra memory.

int   GetSize()
Get the allocated size of the object in terms of number of data items.

int   GetMaxId()
Returning the maximum index of data inserted so far.

void Reset()
Reuse the memory allocated by this object. Objects appears like no data has been previously inserted.

int   Allocate(const int sz, const int ext)
Allocate memory for this array. Delete old storage if present.

void Initialize()
Release storage and reset array to initial state.

vtkVoidArray(const int sz, const int ext)
Construct with specified storage and extend value.

vtkVoidArray

vtkVoidArray(const vtkVoidArray& fa)
Construct array from another array. Copy each element of other array.

vtkVoidArray& operator=(const vtkVoidArray& fa)
Deep copy of another array.

void operator+=(const vtkVoidArray& fa)
Append one array onto the end of this array.

vtkVolume

NAME

vtkVolume - a volumetric entity in a rendered image

CLASS HIERARCHY

class vtkVolume : public vtkObject

DESCRIPTION

vtkVolume is used to represent a volume entity in a rendering scene. It handles functions related to the volume's position, orientation, and scaling. It combines these instance variables into one matrix as follows: [x y z 1] = [x y z 1] Translate(-origin) Scale(scale) Rot(y) Rot(x) Rot (z) Trans(origin) Trans(position).

SEE ALSO

vtkActor vtkVolumeCollection vtkVolumeRenderer

SUMMARY

void SetInput(vtkStructuredPoints*)
void SetInput(vtkStructuredPoints&)
This is the method that is used to connect a volume to the end of a visualization pipeline.

vtkStructuredPoints *GetInput()
Returns the Input that this volume is getting its data from.

void SetLookupTable(vtkLookupTable *lut);
void SetLookupTable(vtkLookupTable& lut)
vtkLookupTable *GetLookupTable();
Set/Get the Look Up Table for this volume.

virtual void CreateDefaultLookupTable();
Create a default lookup table. Generally used to create one when one wasn't specified by the user.

void SetScalarRange(float, float)
void SetScalarRange(float *)
float *GetScalarRange()
void GetScalarRange(float data[2])
Specify range in terms of (smin,smax) through which to map scalars into lookup table.

float *GetPosition()
void GetPosition(float data[3])
void SetPosition(float, float, float)
void SetPosition(float *)
void AddPosition(float deltaPosition[3]);
void AddPosition(float deltaX,float deltaY,float deltaZ);
Set/Get/Add the position of the volume.

float *GetOrigin()
void GetOrigin(float data[3])

vtkVolume

void SetOrigin(float, float, float)
void SetOrigin(float *)

Set/Get the origin of the volume. This is the point about which all rotations take place.

float *GetScale()
void GetScale(float data[3])
void SetScale(float, float, float)
void SetScale(float *)

Set/Get the scale of the volume. Scaling in performed independently on the X,Y and Z axis. Any scale values that are zero will be automatically converted to one.

int   GetVisibility()
void SetVisibility(int)
void VisibilityOn()
void VisibilityOff()

Set/Get the visibility of the volume. Visibility is like a light switch for volumes. Use it to turn them on or off.

int   GetPickable()
void SetPickable(int)
void PickableOn()
void PickableOff()

Set/Get the pickable instance variable. This determines if the volume can be picked (typically using the mouse). Also see dragable.

int   GetDragable()
void SetDragable(int)
void DragableOn()
void DragableOff()

Set/Get the value of the dragable instance variable. This determines if a volume, once picked, can be dragged (translated) through space. This is typically done through an interactive mouse interface. This does not affect methods such as SetPosition.

void Render();

Builds the lookuptable and Input.

vtkVolume()

Creates a Volume with the following defaults: origin(0,0,0) position=(0,0,0) scale=(1,1,1) visibility=1 pickable=1 dragable=1 orientation=(0,0,0).

void SetLookupTable(vtkLookupTable *lut)

Specify a lookup table for the volume to use.

void Render()

This causes the volume to be rendered. It in turn will build the volume's lookuptable.

void SetOrientation (float x,float y,float z)

Sets the orientation of the volume. Orientation is specified as X,Y and Z rotations in that order, but they are performed as RotateZ, RotateX, and finally RotateY.

vtkVolume

float *GetOrientation ()
Returns the orientation of the volume as s vector of X,Y and Z rotation. The ordering in which these rotations must be done to generate the same matrix is RotateZ, RotateX, and finally RotateY. See also SetOrientation.

void AddOrientation (float a1,float a2,float a3)
Add to the current orientation. See SetOrientation and GetOrientation for more details.

void RotateX (float angle)
Rotate the volume in degrees about the X axis using the right hand rule.

void RotateY (float angle)
Rotate the volume in degrees about the Y axis using the right hand rule.

void RotateZ (float angle)
Rotate the volume in degrees about the Z axis using the right hand rule.

void RotateWXYZ (float degree, float x, float y, float z)
Rotate the volume in degrees about an arbitrary axis specified by the last three arguments.

void GetMatrix(vtkMatrix4x4& result)
Copy the volume's composite 4x4 matrix into the matrix provided.

vtkMatrix4x4& GetMatrix()
Return a reference to the volume's 4x4 composite matrix.

float *GetBounds()
Get the bounds for this volume as (Xmin,Xmax,Ymin,Ymax,Zmin,Zmax).

float *GetXRange()
Get the volume's x range in world coordinates.

float *GetYRange()
Get the volume's y range in world coordinates.

float *GetZRange()
Get the volume's z range in world coordinates.

vtkVolume16Reader

NAME

vtkVolume16Reader - read 16 bit image files

CLASS HIERARCHY

class vtkVolume16Reader : public vtkStructuredPointsSource

DESCRIPTION

vtkVolume16Reader is a source object that reads 16 bit image files.

Volume16Reader creates structured point datasets. The dimension of the dataset depends upon the number of files read. Reading a single file results in a 2D image, while reading more than one file results in a 3D volume.

File names are created using FilePattern and FilePrefix as follows: sprintf (filename, FilePattern, FilePrefix, number); where number is in the range ImageRange[0] to ImageRange[1]. If ImageRange[1] <= ImageRange[0], then slice number ImageRange[0] is read. Thus to read an image set ImageRange[0] = ImageRange[1] = slice number. The default behavior is to read a single file (i.e., image slice 1).

The DataMask instance variable is used to read data files with imbedded connectivity or segmentation information. For example, some data has the high order bit set to indicate connected surface. The DataMask allows you to select this data. Other important ivars include HeaderSize, which allows you to skip over initial info, and SwapBytes, which turns on/off byte swapping.

SEE ALSO

vtkSliceCubes vtkMarchingCubes

SUMMARY

void SetFilePrefix(char *)
char *GetFilePrefix()
    Specify file prefix for the image file(s).

void SetFilePattern(char *)
char *GetFilePattern()
    Set the sprintf format to use to build filename from FilePrefix and number.

void SetImageRange(int, int)
void SetImageRange(int *)
int *GetImageRange()
void GetImageRange(int data[2])
    Set the range of files to read.

void SetDataAspectRatio(float, float, float)
void SetDataAspectRatio(float *)
float *GetDataAspectRatio()
void GetDataAspectRatio(float data[3])
    Specify an aspect ratio for the data.

vtkVolume16Reader

void   SetDataOrigin(float, float, float)
void   SetDataOrigin(float *)
float *GetDataOrigin()
void   GetDataOrigin(float data[3])
  Specify the origin for the data.

void   SetDataDimensions(int, int)
void   SetDataDimensions(int *)
int   *GetDataDimensions()
void   GetDataDimensions(int data[2])
  Specify the dimensions for the data.

void   SetDataMask(short)
short GetDataMask()
  Specify a mask used to eliminate data in the data file (e.g., connectivity bits).

void   SetHeaderSize(int)
int   GetHeaderSize()
  Specify the number of bytes to seek over at start of image.

void   SetSwapBytes(int)
int   GetSwapBytes()
void   SwapBytesOn()
void   SwapBytesOff()
  Turn on/off byte swapping.

vtkVolume16Reader()
  Construct object with NULL file prefix; file pattern "%s.%d"; image range set
  to(1,1); data origin (0,0,0); data aspect ratio (1,1,1); no data mask; header size 0;
  and byte swapping turned off.

vtkShortScalars *ReadImage(int sliceNumber, int dim[2])
  Read a slice of volume data.

vtkShortScalars *ReadVolume(int first, int last, int dim[2])
  Read a volume of data.

vtkVolumeCollection

NAME

vtkVolumeCollection - a list of volumes

CLASS HIERARCHY

class vtkVolumeCollection : public vtkCollection

DESCRIPTION

vtkVolumeCollection represents and provides methods to manipulate a list of volumes (i.e., vtkVolume and subclasses). The list is unsorted and duplicate entries are not prevented.

SEE ALSO

vtkCollection vtkVolume

SUMMARY

void AddItem(vtkVolume *a)
Add a volume to the list.

void RemoveItem(vtkVolume *a)
Remove a volume from the list.

int IsItemPresent(vtkVolume *a)
Determine whether a particular volume is present. Returns its position in the list.

vtkVolume *GetNextItem()
Get the next volume in the list. Return NULL when the end of the list is reached.

vtkVolumeRenderer

NAME

vtkVolumeRenderer - renders volumetric data

CLASS HIERARCHY

class vtkVolumeRenderer : public vtkObject

DESCRIPTION

vtkVolumeRenderer handles volume data much like the vtkRenderer handles polygonal data. A vtkVolumeRenderer renders its image during the normal rendering cycle, after the renderer has rendered its surfaces, but before any doublebuffer switching is done. Many of the attributes this object requires for rendering are obtained from the renderer, which invokes its Render() method. This object must be associated with a renderer in order to work.

SEE ALSO

vtkRenderer vtkVolume

SUMMARY

virtual void Render(vtkRenderer *);

Render its volumes to create a composite image.

float GetStepSize()
void SetStepSize(float)

Set/Get the ray step size in world coordinates. The step size you select will make a big difference in the required rendering time and possibly the results as well. A larger step size will render more quickly. Too large of a step size will result in under sampling your volumes, yielding less accurate results.

vtkVolumeCollection *GetVolumes()

Get the list of volumes for this renderer.

vtkVolumeRenderer()

Create an instance of a vtkVolumeRenderer with its step size to one.

void Render(vtkRenderer *ren)

Main routine to do the volume rendering.

void CalcRayValues(vtkRenderer *ren, float Vecs[6][3],
**   int *size,int *steps)**

Calculates six vectors from the camera, renderer, and volume information. These six vectors can be combined to determine the start and end world coordinate points for the rays to be cast.

void Composite(float *rays,int steps, int numRays,
**   unsigned char *resultColor)**

Composite the traced rays into a resulting pixel color.

vtkVolumeRenderer

void TraceOneRay(float p1World[4],float p2World[4],
    vtkVolume *vol,
    int steps, float *resultRay)
Traces one ray through one volume.

void AddVolume(vtkVolume *actor)
Add a volume to the list of volumes.

void RemoveVolume(vtkVolume *actor)
Remove a volume from the list of volumes.

vtkVoxel

NAME

vtkVoxel - a cell that represents a 3D orthogonal parallelepiped

CLASS HIERARCHY

class vtkVoxel : public vtkCell

DESCRIPTION

vtkVoxel is a concrete implementation of vtkCell to represent a 3D orthogonal parallelepiped. Unlike vtkHexahedron, vtkVoxel has interior angles of 90 degrees, and sides are parallel to coordinate axes. This results in large increases in computational performance.

SUMMARY

vtkVoxel(const vtkVoxel& b)
    Deep copy of cell.

NAME

vtkVoxelModeller - convert an arbitrary dataset to a voxel representation

CLASS HIERARCHY

class vtkVoxelModeller : public vtkDataSetToStructuredPointsFilter

DESCRIPTION

vtkVoxelModeller is a filter that converts an arbitrary data set to a structured point (i.e., voxel) representation. It is very similar to vtkImplicitModeller, except that it doesn't record distance, it records occupancy. As such, it stores its results in the more compact form of 0/1 bits.

SEE ALSO

vtkBitScalars vtkImplicitModeller

SUMMARY

void SetMaximumDistance(float)
float GetMaximumDistance()
Specify distance away from surface of input geometry to sample. Smaller values make large increases in performance.

vtkVoxelModeller()
Construct an instance of vtkVoxelModeller with its sample dimensions set to (50,50,50), and so that the model bounds are automatically computed from its input. The maximum distance is set to examine the whole grid. This could be made much faster, and probably will be in the future.

void SetModelBounds(float *bounds)
Specify the position in space to perform the voxelization.

float ComputeModelBounds(float origin[3], float ar[3])
Compute the ModelBounds based on the input geometry.

void SetSampleDimensions(int i, int j, int k)
Set the i-j-k dimensions on which to sample the distance function.

vtkVoxelReader

NAME

vtkVoxelReader - read a binary 0/1 bit voxel file

CLASS HIERARCHY

class vtkVoxelReader : public vtkStructuredPointsSource

DESCRIPTION

vtkVoxelReader reads a binary 0/1 bit voxel file. File is written by vtkVoxelModeller.

SUMMARY

void SetFilename(char *)
char *GetFilename()
Set the name of the file to read.

vtkVoxelWriter

NAME

vtkVoxelWriter - write out 0/1 voxel data from vtkVoxelModeller

CLASS HIERARCHY

class vtkVoxelWriter : public vtkWriter

DESCRIPTION

vtkVoxelWriter writes a binary 0/1 voxel file. vtkVoxelWriter writes only structured points data.

SUMMARY

void SetFilename(char *)
char *GetFilename()
    Specify name of file to write.

void SetInput(vtkStructuredPoints *input)
    Specify the input data or filter.

void WriteData()
    Write voxel data out.

vtkWarpScalar

NAME

vtkWarpScalar - deform geometry with scalar data

CLASS HIERARCHY

class vtkWarpScalar : public vtkPointSetToPointSetFilter

DESCRIPTION

vtkWarpScalar is a filter that modifies point coordinates by moving points along point normals by the scalar amount times the scale factor. Useful for creating carpet or x-y-z plots.

If normals are not present in data, the Normal instance variable will be used as the direction along which to warp the geometry. If normals are present but you would like to use the Normal instance variable, set the UseNormal boolean to true.

If XYPlane boolean is set true, then the z-value is considered to be a scalar value (still scaled by scale factor), and the displacement is along the z-axis. If scalars are also present, these are copied through and can be used to color the surface.

SUMMARY

void SetScaleFactor(float)
float GetScaleFactor()

Specify value to scale displacement.

void SetUseNormal(int)
int   GetUseNormal()
void UseNormalOn()
void UseNormalOff()

Turn on/off use of user specified normal. If on, data normals will be ignored and instance variable Normal will be used instead.

void SetNormal(float, float, float)
void SetNormal(float *)
float *GetNormal()
void GetNormal(float data[3])

Normal (i.e., direction) along which to warp geometry. Only used if UseNormal boolean set to true or no normals available in data.

void SetXYPlane(int)
int   GetXYPlane()
void XYPlaneOn()
void XYPlaneOff()

Turn on/off flag specifying that input data is x-y plane. If x-y plane, then the z value is used to warp the surface in the z-axis direction (times the scale factor) and scalars are used to color the surface.

vtkWarpTo

NAME

vtkWarpTo - deform geometry by warping towards a point

CLASS HIERARCHY

class vtkWarpTo : public vtkPointSetToPointSetFilter

DESCRIPTION

vtkWarpTo is a filter that modifies point coordinates by moving the points towards a user specified position.

SUMMARY

void SetScaleFactor(float)
float GetScaleFactor()
    Set/Get the value to scale displacement.

float *GetPosition()
void GetPosition(float data[3])
void SetPosition(float, float, float)
void SetPosition(float *)
    Set/Get the position to warp towards.

void SetAbsolute(int)
int   GetAbsolute()
void AbsoluteOn()
void AbsoluteOff()
    Set/Get the Absolute ivar. Turning Absolute on causes scale factor of the new position to be one unit away from Position.

vtkWarpVector

NAME

vtkWarpVector - deform geometry with vector data

CLASS HIERARCHY

class vtkWarpVector : public vtkPointSetToPointSetFilter

DESCRIPTION

vtkWarpVector is a filter that modifies point coordinates by moving points along vector times the scale factor. Useful for showing flow profiles or mechanical deformation.

SUMMARY

void SetScaleFactor(float)
float GetScaleFactor()
      Specify value to scale displacement.

vtkWriter

NAME

vtkWriter - abstract class to write data to file(s)

CLASS HIERARCHY

class vtkWriter : public vtkObject

DESCRIPTION

vtkWriter is an abstract class for mapper objects that write their data to disk (or into a communications port). All writers respond to Write() method. This method insures that there is input and input is up to date.

vtkWriter provides the convenience methods StartWrite() and EndWrite(). These methods are executed before and after execution of the Write() method. You can also specify arguments to these methods.

CAVEATS

Every subclass of vtkWriter must implement a WriteData() method. Most likely will have to create SetInput() method as well.

DEFINES

VTK_ASCII 1
VTK_BINARY 2

SUMMARY

vtkWriter()
Construct with no start and end write methods or arguments.

void Write()
Write data to output. Method executes subclasses WriteData() method, as well as StartWrite() and EndWrite() methods.

void Update()
Convenient alias for Write() method.

void SetStartWrite(void (*f)(void *), void *arg)
Specify a function to be called before data is written. Function will be called with argument provided.

void SetStartWriteArgDelete(void (*f)(void *))
Set the arg delete method. This is used to free user memory.

void SetEndWriteArgDelete(void (*f)(void *))
Set the arg delete method. This is used to free user memory.

void SetEndWrite(void (*f)(void *), void *arg)
Specify a function to be called after data is written. Function will be called with argument provided.

vtkXRenderWindow

NAME

vtkXRenderWindow - a rendering window for the X Window system

CLASS HIERARCHY

class vtkXRenderWindow : public vtkRenderWindow

DESCRIPTION

vtkXRenderWindow is a subclass of the abstract class vtkRenderWindow. vtkXRenderer interfaces to the X Window system and provides some methods that are common to any vtkRenderingWindow subclass that renders under X Windows. The vtkXRenderWindowInteractor makes heavy use of these common methods.

SEE ALSO

vtkRenderWindow vtkXRenderWindowInteractor

SUMMARY

int *GetScreenSize()
Get the size of the screen in pixels

int *GetSize(void)
Get the current size of the window in pixels.

int *GetPosition(void)
Get the position in screen coordinates (pixels) of the window.

Display *GetDisplayId()
Get this RenderWindow's X display id.

Window GetWindowId()
Get this RenderWindow's X window id.

void SetWindowId(Window arg)
Set this RenderWindow's X window id to a pre-existing window.

void SetNextWindowId(Window arg)
Specify the X window id to use if a WindowRemap is done.

void SetDisplayId(Display *arg)
Set the X display id for this RenderWindow to use to a pre-existing X display id.

vtkRenderWindowInteractor *MakeRenderWindowInteractor()
Create an interactor that will work with this renderer. Since all subclasses of this class will be running on machines that are running X Windows. The correct vtkRenderWindowInteractor is the vtkXRenderWindowInteractor. So it creates one, type casts it and returns it.

vtkXRenderWindowInteractor

NAME

vtkXRenderWindowInteractor - an X event driven interface for a RenderWindow

CLASS HIERARCHY

class vtkXRenderWindowInteractor : public vtkRenderWindowInteractor

DESCRIPTION

vtkXRenderWindowInteractor is a convenience object that provides event bindings to common graphics functions. For example, camera zoom-in/zoom-out, azimuth, and roll. It is one of the window system specific subclasses of vtkRenderWindowInteractor.

SEE ALSO

vtkRenderWindowInteractor vtkXRenderWindow

EVENT BINDINGS

Mouse bindings: Button 1 - rotate, Button 2 - pan, Button 3 - zoom. The distance from the center of the renderer viewport determines how quickly to rotate, pan and zoom. Keystrokes: r - reset camera view   w - turn all actors wireframe   s - turn all actors surface   u - execute user defined function   p - pick actor under mouse pointer (if pickable)   3 - toggle in/out of 3D mode (if supported by renderer)   e - exit

SUMMARY

vtkXRenderWindowInteractor()
Construct an instance so that the light follows the camera motion.

void   SetWidget(Widget foo)
Specify the Xt widget to use for interaction. This method is one of a couple steps that are required for setting up a RenderWindowInteractor as a widget inside of another user interface. You do not need to use this method if the RenderWindow will be a stand-alone window. This is only used when you want the RenderWindow to be a subwindow within a larger user interface. In that case, you must tell the RenderWindow what X display id to use, and then ask the RenderWindow what depth, visual and colormap it wants. Then you must create an Xt TopLevelShell with those settings. Then you can create the rest of your user interface as a child of the TopLevelShell you created. Eventually, you will create a drawing area or some other widget to serve as the rendering window. You must use the SetWidget method to tell this Interactor about that widget. It's X and it's not terribly easy, but it looks cool.

void   Start()
This will start up the X event loop and never return. If you call this method it will loop processing X events until the application is exited.

void   Initialize(XtAppContext app)
Initializes the event handlers using an XtAppContext that you have provided. This assumes that you want to own the event loop.

vtkXRenderWindowInteractor

void Initialize()
Initializes the event handlers without an XtAppContext. This is good for when you don't have a user interface but you still want to have mouse interaction.

void SetupNewWindow(int Stereo)
Setup a new window before a WindowRemap

void FinishSettingUpNewWindow()
Finish setting up a new window after the WindowRemap.

Glossary

API. An acronym for application programmer's interface.

Abstract Class. A class that provides methods and data members for the express purpose of deriving subclasses. Such objects are used to define a common interface and attributes for their subclasses.

Abstraction. A mental process that extracts the essential form or unifying properties of a concept.

Alpha. A specification of opacity (or transparency). An alpha value of one indicates that the object is opaque. An alpha value of zero indicates that the object is completely transparent.

Ambient Lighting. The background lighting of unlit surfaces.

Animation. A sequence of images displayed in rapid succession. The images may vary due to changes in geometry, color, lighting, camera position, or other graphics parameters. Animations are used to display the variation of one or more variables.

Antialiasing. The process of reducing aliasing artifacts. These artifacts typically result from undersampling the data. A common use of antialiasing is to draw straight lines that don't have the jagged edges found in many systems without antialiasing.

Azimuth. A rotation of a camera about the vertical (or view up) axis.

Attribute. A named member of a class that captures some characteristic of the class. Attributes have a name, a data type, and a data value. This is the same as a data member or instance variable.

Base Class. A superclass in C++.

Boolean Texture. A texture map consisting of distinct regions used to "cut" or accentuate features of data. For example, a texture map may consist of regions of zero opacity.When such a texture is mapped onto the surface of an object, portions of its interior becomes visible. Generally used in conjunction with a quadric (or other implicit function) to generate texture coordinates.

C++. A compiled programming language with roots in the C programming language. C++ is an extension of C that incorporates object-oriented principles.

CT (Computed Tomography). A data acquisition technique based on X-rays. Data is acquired in a 3D volume as a series of slice planes (i.e., a grid of n^2 points).

Cell. The atoms of visualization datasets. Cells define a topology (e.g., polygon, triangle) in terms of a list of point coordinates.

Cell Attributes. Dataset attributes associated with a cell.

Class. An object that defines the characteristics of a subset of objects. Typically it defines methods and data members. All objects instantiated from a class share that class's methods and data members.

Clipping Plane. A plane that restricts the rendering or processing of data. Front and back clipping planes are commonly used to restrict the rendering of primitives to those lying between the two planes.

Color Mapping. A scalar visualization technique that maps scalar values into color. Generally used to display the variation of data on a surface or through a volume.

Compiled System. A compiled system requires that a program be compiled (or translated into a lower level language) before it is executed. Contrast with *interpreted systems*.

Composite Cell. A cell consisting of one or more primary cells.

Concrete Class. A class that can be instantiated. Typically abstract classes are not instantiated but concrete classes are.

Connectivity. A technique to extract connected cells. Cells are connected when they share common features such as points, edges, or faces.

Contouring. A scalar visualization technique that creates lines (in 2D) or surfaces (in 3D) representing a constant scalar value across a scalar field. Contour lines are called isovalue lines or isolines. Contour surfaces are called isovalue surfaces or isosurfaces.

Constructor. A class method that is invoked when an instance of that class is created. Typically the constructor sets any default values and allocates any memory that the instance needs. See also *destructor*.

Critical Points. Locations in a vector field where the local vector magnitude goes to zero and the direction becomes undefined.

Cutting. A visualization technique to slice through or cut data. The cutting surface is typically described with an implicit function, and data attributes are mapped onto the cut surface. See also *boolean texture*.

Dataset. The general term used to describe visualization data. Datasets consist of structure (geometry and topology) and dataset attributes (scalars, vectors, tensors, etc.).

Dataset Attributes. The information associated with the structure of a dataset. This can be scalars, vectors, tensors, normals, texture coordinates, or user defined data.

Data Extraction. The process of selecting a portion of data based on characteristics of the data. These characteristics may be based on geometric or topological constraints or constraints on data attribute values.

Data Flow Diagram. A diagram that shows the information flow and operations on that information as it moves throughout a program or process.

Data Object. An object that is an abstraction of data. For example, a patient's file in a hospital could be a data object. Typical visualization objects include structured grids and volumes. See also *process object*.

Data Member. A named member of a class that captures some characteristic of the class. Data members have a name, a data type, and a data value. This is the same as an attribute or instance variable.

Data Visualization. The process of transforming data into sensory stimuli, usually visual images. Data visualization is a general term, encompassing data from engineering and science, as well as information from business, finance, sociology, geography, information management, and other fields. Data visualization also includes elements of data analysis, such as statistical analysis. Contrast with *scientific visualization* and *information visualization*.

Decimation. A type of polygon reduction technique that deletes points in a polygonal mesh that satisfy a co-planar or co-linear condition, and replaces the resulting hole with a new triangulation.

Delaunay Triangulation. A triangulation that satisfies the Delaunay circumsphere criterion. This criterion states that a circumsphere of each simplex in the triangulation contains only the points defining the simplex.

Delegation. The process of assigning an object to handle the execution of another object's methods. Sometimes it is said that one object forwards certain methods to another object for execution.

Demand-driven. A method of visualization pipeline update where the update occurs only when data is requested, and occurs only in the portion of the network required to generate the data.

Derived Class. A class that is more specific or complete than its superclass. The derived class, which is also known as the subclass, inherits all the members of its superclass. Usually a derived class adds new functionality or fills in what was defined by its superclass. See also *subclass*.

Destructor. A class method that is invoked when an instance of that class is deleted. Typically the destructor frees memory that the instance was using. See also *constructor*.

Device Mapper. A mapper that interfaces data to a graphics library or subsystem.

Diffuse Lighting. Reflected light from a matte surface. Diffuse lighting is a function of the relative angle between the incoming light and surface normal of the object.

Displacement Plots. A vector visualization technique that shows the displacement of the surface of an object. The method generates scalar values by computing the dot product between the surface normal and vector displacement of the surface. The scalars are visualized using color mapping.

Display Coordinate System. A coordinate system that is the result of mapping the view coordinate system onto the display hardware.

Divergence. In numerical computation: the tendency of computation to move away from the solution. In fluid flow: the rapid motion of fluid particles away from one another.

Dividing Cubes. A contour algorithm that represents isosurfaces as a dense cloud of points.

Dolly. A camera operation that moves the camera position towards (*dolly in*) or away (*dolly out*) from the camera focal point.

Double Buffering. A display technique that is used to display animations more smoothly. It consists of using two buffers in the rendering process. While one buffer is being displayed, the next frame in the animation is being drawn on the other buffer. Once the drawing is complete the two buffers are swapped and the new image is displayed.

Dynamic Memory Model. A data flow network that does not retain intermediate results as it executes. Each time the network executes it must recompute any data required as input to another process object. A dynamic memory model reduces system memory requirements, but places greater demands on computational requirements.

Dynamic Model. A description of a system concerned with synchronizing events and objects.

Effective Stress. A mathematical combination of the normal and shear stress components that provide a measure of the stress at a point. Effective stress is a scalar value, while stress is represented with a tensor value. See *stress*.

Eigenfields. Vector fields defined by the eigenvectors of a tensor.

Eigenvalue. A characteristic value of a matrix. Eigenvalues often correspond to physical phenomena, such as frequency of vibration or magnitude of principal components of stress.

Eigenvector. A vector associated with each eigenvalue. The eigenvector spans the space of the matrix. Eigenvectors are orthogonal to one another. Eigenvectors often correspond to physical phenomena, such as mode shapes of vibration.

Elevation. A rotation of a camera about the horizontal axis.

Entity. Something within a system that has identity. Chairs, airplanes, and cameras are things that correspond to physical entities in the real world. A database and isosurface algorithm are examples of non-physical entities.

Event-driven. A method of visualization pipeline update where updates occur when an event affects the pipeline, e.g., when an object instance variable is set or modified. See also *demand-driven*.

Execution. The process of updating a visualization network.

Explicit Execution. Controlling network updates by performing explicit dependency analysis.

Fan-in. The flow of multiple pieces of data into a single filter.

Fan-out. The flow of data from an filter's output to other objects.

Feature Angle. The angle between surface normal vectors, e.g., the angle between the normal vectors on two adjacent polygons.

Filter. A process object that takes at least one input and generates at least one output.

Finite Element Method (FEM). A numerical technique for the solution of partial differential equations. FEM is based on discretizing a domain into elements (and nodes) and constructing basis (or interpolation) functions across the elements. From these functions a system of linear equations is generated and solved on the computer. Typical applications include stress, heat transfer, and vibration analysis.

Finite Difference Method. A numerical technique for the solution of partial differential equations (PDE's). Finite difference methods replace the PDE's with truncated Taylor series approximations. This results in a system of equations that is solved on a computer. Typical applications include fluid flow, combustion, and heat transfer.

Flat Shading. A shading technique where the lighting equation for a geometric primitive is calculated once, and then used to fill in the entire area of the primitive. This is also known as faceted shading. See also *gouraud shading* and *phong shading*.

Functional Model. The description of a system based on what it does.

Generalization. The abstraction of a subset of classes to a common superclass. Generalization extracts the common members or methods from a group of classes to create a common superclass. See also *specialization* and *inheritance*.

Geometry. Used generally to mean the characteristic position, shape, and topology of an object. Used specifically (in tandem with topology) to mean the position and shape of an object.

Glyph. A general visualization technique used to represent data using a meaningful shape or pictorial representation. Each glyph is generally a function of its input data and may change size, orientation, and shape; or modify graphics properties in response to changes in input.

Gouraud Shading. A shading technique that applies the lighting equations for a geometric primitive at each vertex. The resulting colors are then interpolated over the areas between the vertices. See also *flat shading* and *Phong shading*.

Hedgehog. A vector visualization technique that represents vector direction and magnitude with oriented lines.

Height Field. A set of altitude or height samples in a rectangular grid. Height fields are typically used to represent terrain.

Hexahedron. A type of primary 3D cell. The hexahedron looks like a "brick". It has six faces, twelve edges, and eight vertices. The faces of the hexahedron are not necessarily planar.

Homogeneous Coordinates. An alternate coordinate representation that provides more flexibility than traditional Cartesian coordinates. This includes perspective transformation and combined translation, scaling, and rotation.

Hyperstreamline. A tensor visualization technique. Hyperstreamlines are created by treating the eigenvectors as three separate vectors. The maximum eigenvalue/eigenvector is used as a vector field in which particle integration is performed (like streamlines). The other two vectors control the cross-sectional shape of an ellipse that is swept along the integration path. See also *streampolygon*.

Image-Order Techniques. Rendering techniques that determine for each pixel in the image plane which data samples contribute to it. Image-order techniques are implemented using ray casting. Contrast with *object-order techniques*.

Implicit Execution. Controlling network updates by distributing network dependency throughout the visualization process objects. Each process object requests that its input be updated before it executes. This results in a recursive update/execution process throughout the network.

Implicit Function. A mathematical function of the form $F(x, y, z) = c$, where c is a constant.

Implicit Modelling. A modelling technique that represents geometry as a scalar field. Usually the scalar is a distance function or implicit function distributed through a volume.

Information Visualization. The process of transforming information into sensory stimuli, usually visual images. Information visualization is used to describe the process of visualizing data without structure, such as information on the world wide web; or abstract data structures, like computer file systems or documents. Contrast with *scientific visualization* and *data visualization*.

Inheritance. A process where the attributes and methods of a superclass are bestowed upon all subclasses derived from that superclass. It is said that the subclasses inherit their superclasses' methods and attributes.

Instance. An object that is defined by a class and used by a program or application. There may be many instances of a specific class.

Instance Variable. A named member of a class that captures some characteristic of the class. Instance variables have a name, a data type, and a data value. The phrase, instance variable, is often abbreviated as ivar. This is the same as an attribute or data member.

Intensity. The light energy transferred per unit time across a unit plane perpendicular to the light rays.

Interpolate. Estimate a value of a function at a point p, given known function values and points that bracket p.

Interpolation Functions. Functions continuous in value and derivatives used to interpolate data from known points and function values. Cells use interpolation functions to compute data values interior to or on the boundary of the cell.

Interpreted System. An interpreted system can execute programs without going through a separate compilation stage. Interpreted systems often allow the user to interact and modify the program as it is running. Contrast with *compiled systems*.

Irregular Data. Data in which the relationship of one data item to the other data items in the dataset is arbitrary. Irregular data is also known as unstructured data.

Isosurface. A surface representing a constant valued scalar function. See *contouring*.

Isovalue. The scalar value used to generate an isosurface.

Jacobian. A matrix that relates one coordinate system to another.

Line. A cell defined by two points.

MRI (Magnetic Resonance Imaging). A data acquisition technique based on measuring variation in magnetic field in response to radio-wave pulses. The data is acquired in a 3D region as a series of slice planes (i.e., a grid of n^2 points).

Mapper. A process object that terminates the visualization network. It maps input data into graphics libraries (or other devices) or writes data to disk (or communication device).

Manifold Topology. A domain is manifold at a point p in a topological space of dimension n if the neighborhood around p is homeomorphic to a n-dimensional sphere. Homeomorphic means that the mapping is one-to-one without tearing (i.e., like mapping a rubber sheet from a square to a disk). We generally refer to an object's topology as manifold if every point in the object is manifold. Contrast with *non-manifold topology*.

Marching Cubes. A contouring algorithm to create surfaces of constant scalar value in 3D. Marching cubes is described for volume datasets, but has been extended to datasets consisting of other cell types.

Member Function. A member function is a function or transformation that can be applied to an object. It is the functional equivalent to a data member. Member functions define the behavior of an object. Methods, operations, and member functions are essentially the same.

Method. A function or transformation that can be applied to an object. Methods define the behavior of an object. Methods, operations, and member functions are essentially the same.

Modal Lines. Lines on the surface of a vibrating object that separate regions of positive and negative displacement.

Mode Shape. The motion of an object vibrating at a natural frequency. See also *eigenvalues* and *eigenvectors*.

Model Coordinate System. The coordinate system that a model or geometric entity is defined in. There may be many different model coordinate systems defined for one scene.

Motion blur. An artifact of the shutter speed of a camera. Since the camera's shutter stays open for a finite amount of time, changes in the scene that occur during that time can result in blurring of the resulting image.

Morph. A progressive transformation of one object into another. Generally used to transform images (2D morphing) and in some cases geometry (3D morphing).

Multiple Input. Process objects that accept more than one input.

Multiple Output. Process objects that generate more than one output.

Multi-Dimensional Visualization. Visualizing data of four or more variables. Generally requires a mapping of many dimensions into three or fewer dimensions so that standard visualization techniques can be applied.

Non-Manifold Topology. Topology that is not manifold. Examples include polygonal meshes, where an edge is used by more than two polygons, or polygons connected to each other at their vertices (i.e., do not share an edge). Contrast with *manifold topology.*

Normal. A unit vector that indicates perpendicular direction to a surface. Normals are a common type of data attribute.

Object. An abstraction that models the state and behavior of entities in a system. Instances and classes are both objects.

Object Model. The description of a system in terms of the components that make up the system, including the relationship of the components one to another.

Object-Order Techniques. Rendering techniques that project object data (e.g., polygons or voxels) onto the image plane. Example techniques include ordered compositing and splatting.

Object-Oriented. A software development technique that uses objects to represent the state and behavior of entities in a system.

Octree Decomposition. A technique to decompose a cubical region of three-dimensional space into smaller cubes. The cubes, or octants, are related in tree fashion. The root octant is the cubical region. Each octant may have eight children created by dividing the parent in half in the x, y, and z directions.

OMT. *Object Modelling Technique*. An object-oriented design technique that models software systems with object, dynamic, and functional diagrams.

Operation. A function or transformation that can be applied to an object. Operations define the behavior of an object. Methods and member functions implement operations.

Overloading. Having multiple methods with the same name. Some methods are overloaded because there are different versions of the same method. These differences are based on argument types, while the underlying algorithm remains the same. Contrast with *polymorphic*.

Painter's Algorithm. An object-order rendering technique that sorts rendering primitives from back to front and then draws them.

Parametric Coordinates. A coordinate system natural to the geometry of a geometric object. For example, a line may be described by the single coordinate s even though the line may lie in three or higher dimensions.

Parallel Projection. A mapping of world coordinates into view coordinates that preserves all parallel lines. In a parallel projection an object will appear the same size regardless of how far away it is from the viewer. This is equivalent to having a center of projection that is infinitely far away. Contrast with *perspective projection*.

Particle Trace. The trajectory that particles trace over time in fluid flow. Particle traces are everywhere tangent to the velocity field. Unlike streamlines, particle lines are time-dependent.

Pathline. The trajectory that a particle follows in fluid flow.

Perspective Projection. A mapping of world coordinates into view coordinates that roughly approximates a camera lens. Specifically, the center of projection must be a finite distance from the view plane. As a result closer, objects will appear larger than distant objects. Contrast with *parallel projection*.

Phong Shading. A shading technique that applies the lighting equations for a geometric primitive at each pixel. See also *flat shading* and *Gouraud shading*.

Pitch. A rotation of a camera's position about the horizontal axis, centered at its viewpoint. See also *yaw* and *roll*. Contrast with *elevation*.

Pixel. Short for picture element. Constant valued elements in an image. In **vtk**, a two-dimensional cell defined by an ordered list of four points.

Point. A geometric specification of position in 3D space.

Point Attributes. Data attributes associates with the points of a dataset.

Polygon. A cell consisting of three or more co-planar points defining a polygon. The polygon can be concave but without imbedded loops.

Polygonal Data. A dataset type consisting of arbitrary combinations of vertices, poly-vertices, lines, poly-lines, polygons, and triangle strips. Polygonal data is an intermediate data form that can be easily rendered by graphics libraries, and yet can represent many types of visualization data.

Polygon Reduction. A family of techniques to reduce the size of large polygonal meshes. The goal is to reduce the number of polygons, while preserving a "good" approximation to the original geometry. In most techniques topology is preserved as well.

Poly-Line. A composite cell consisting of one or more lines.

Polymorphic. Having many forms. Some methods are polymorphic because the same method in different classes may implement a different algorithm. The semantics of the method are typically the same, even though the implementation may differ. Contrast with *overloading*.

Poly-Vertex. A composite cell consisting of one or more vertices.

Primary Cell. An cell that is not defined in terms of other cells.

Probing. Also known as sampling or resampling. A data selection technique that selects data at a set of points.

Process Object. A visualization object that is an abstraction of a process or algorithm. For example, the isosurfacing algorithm marching cubes is implemented as a process object. See also *data object*.

Properties. A general term used to describe the rendered properties of an actor. This includes lighting terms such as ambient, diffuse, and specular coefficients; color and opacity; shading techniques such as flat and Gouraud; and the actor's geometric representation (wireframe, points, or surface).

Quadric. A function of the form
$$f(x, y, z) = a_0 x^2 + a_1 y^2 + a_2 z^2 + a_3 xy + a_4 yz + a_5 xz + a_6 x + a_7 y + a_8 z + a_9.$$ The quadric equation can represent many useful 3D objects such as spheres, ellipsoids, cylinders, and cones.

Quadrilateral (Quad). A type of primary 2D cell. The quadrilateral is four sided with four vertices. The quadrilateral must be convex.

Reader. A source object that reads a file or files and produces a data object.

Reference Counting. A memory management technique used to reduce memory requirements. Portions of memory (in this case objects) may be referenced by more than one other object. The referenced object keeps a count of references to it. If the count returns to zero, the object deletes itself, returning memory back to the system. This technique avoids making copies of memory.

Region of Interest. A portion of a dataset that the user is interested in visualizing. Sometimes abbreviated ROI.

Regular Data. Data in which one data item is related (either geometrically or topologically) to other data items. Also referred to as structured data.

Rendering. The process of converting object geometry (i.e., geometric primitives), object properties, and a specification of lights and camera into an image. The primitives may take many forms including surface primitives (points, lines, polygons, splines), implicit functions, or volumes.

Resonant Frequency. A frequency at which an object vibrates.

Roll. A rotation of a camera about its direction of projection. See also *azimuth*, *elevation*, *pitch,* and *yaw.*

Sampling. Selective acquisition or sampling of data, usually at a regular interval. See also *probing*.

Scalar. A single value or function value. May also be used to represent a field of such values.

Scalar Range. The minimum and maximum scalar values of a scalar field.

Scalar Generation. Creating scalar values from other data such as vectors or tensors. One example is computing vector norm.

Scientific Visualization. The process of transforming data into sensory stimuli, usually visual images. Generally used to denote the application of visualization to the sciences and engineering. Contrast with *data visualization* and *information visualization.*

Searching. The process of locating data. Usually the search is based on spatial criteria such as position or being inside a cell.

Simplex. The convex combination of n independent vectors in n-space forms a n-dimensional simplex. Points, lines, triangles, and tetrahedra are examples of simplices in 0D, 1D, 2D, and 3D.

Source. A process object that produces at least one output. Contrast with *filter.*

Specialization. The creation of subclasses that are more refined or specialized than their superclass. See also *generalization* and *inheritance.*

Specular Lighting. Reflected lighting from a shiny surface. Specular lighting is a function of the relative angle between the incoming light, the surface normal of the object, and the view angle of the observer.

Splatting. A method to distribute data values across a region. The distribution functions are often based on Gaussian functions.

State Diagram. A diagram that relates states and events. Used to describe behavior in a software system.

Static Memory Model. A data flow network that retains intermediate results as it executes. A static memory model minimizes computational requirements, but places greater demands on memory requirements.

Strain. A non-dimensional quantity expressed as the ratio of the displacement of an object to its length (normal strain), or angular displacement (shear strain). Strain is a tensor quantity. See also *stress*.

Stress. A measure of force per unit area. Normal stress is stress normal to a given surface, and is either compressive (a negative value) or tensile (a positive value). Shear stress acts tangentially to a given surface. Stress is related to strain through the linear proportionality constants E (the modulus of elasticity), ν (Poisson's ratio), and G (modulus of elasticity in shear). Stress is a tensor quantity. See also *strain*.

Streakline. The set of particles that have previously passed through a particular point.

Streamline. Curves that are everywhere tangent to the velocity field. A streamline satisfies the integral curve $\frac{d}{ds}\vec{x} = \vec{v}(x, t')$ at some time t'.

Streampolygon. A vector and tensor visualization technique that represents flow with tubes that have polygonal cross-sections. The method is based on integrating through the vector field and then sweeping a regular polygon along the streamline. The radius, number of sides, shape, and rotation of the polygon are allowed to change in response to data values. See also *hyperstreamline*.

Streamribbon. A vector visualization technique that represents vectors with ribbons that are everywhere tangent to the vector field

Streamsurface. A surface that is everywhere tangent to a vector field. Can be approximated by generating a series of streamlines along a curve and connecting the lines with a surface.

Streamwise Vorticity. A measure of the rotation of flow around a streamline.

Structured Data. Data in which one data item is related (either geometrically or topologically) to other data items. Also referred to as regular data.

Structured Grid. A dataset whose structure is topologically regular, but whose geometry is irregular. Geometry is explicit and topology is implicit. Typically structured grids consist of hexahedral cells.

Structured Points. A dataset whose structure is both geometrically and topologically regular. Both geometry and topology are implicit. A 3D structured point dataset is known as a volume. A 2D structured point dataset is known as a pixmap.

Subclass. A class that is more specific or complete than its superclass. The subclass, which is also known as the derived class, inherits all the members of its superclass. Usually a subclass will add some new functionality or fill in what was defined by its superclass. See also *derived class*.

Subsampling. Sampling data at a resolution at less than final display resolution.

Superclass. A class from which other classes are derived. See also *base class*.

Surface Rendering. Rendering techniques based on geometric surface primitives such as points, lines, polygons, and splines. Contrast with *volume rendering*.

Swept Surface. The surface that an object creates as it is swept through space.

Swept Volume. The volume enclosed by a swept surface.

Tcl. An interpreted language developed by John Ousterhout in the early 1980s.

Tk. An graphical user interface toolkit based on Tcl.

Tensor. A mathematical generalization of vectors and matrices. A tensor of rank k can be considered a k-dimensional table. Tensor visualization algorithms treat 3×3 real symmetric matrix tensors (rank 2 tensors).

Tensor Ellipsoid. A type of glyph used to visualize tensors. The major, medium, and minor eigenvalues of a 3×3 tensor define an ellipsoid. The eigenvalues are used to scale along the axes.

Tetrahedron. A 3D primary cell that is a simplex with four triangular faces, six edges, and four vertices.

Texture Animation. Rapid application of texture maps to visualize data. A useful example maps a 1D texture map of varying intensity along a set of lines to simulate particle flow.

Texture Coordinate. Specification of position within texture map. Texture coordinates are used to map data from Cartesian system into 2D or 3D texture map.

Texture Map. A specification of object properties in a canonical region. These properties are most often intensity, color, and alpha, or combinations of these. The region is typically a structured array of data in a pixmap (2D) or in a volume (3D).

Texture Mapping. A rendering technique to add detail to objects without requiring extensive geometric modelling. One common example is to paste a picture on the surface of an object.

Texture Thresholding. Using texture mapping to display selected data. Often makes use of alpha opacity to conceal regions of minimal interest.

Thresholding. A data selection technique that selects data that lies within a range of data. Typically scalar thresholding selects data whose scalar values meet a scalar criterion.

Topology. A subset of the information about the structure of a dataset. Topology is a set of properties invariant under certain geometric transformation, such as scaling, rotation, and translation.

Topological Dimension. The dimension or number of parametric coordinates required to address the domain of an object. For example, a line in 3D space is of topological dimension one because the line can be parametrized with a single parameter.

Transformation Matrix. A 4×4 matrix of values used to control the position, orientation, and scale of objects.

Triangle Strip. A composite 2D cell consisting of triangles. The triangle strip is an efficient representation scheme for triangles where $n + 2$ points can represent n triangles.

Triangle. A primary 2D cell. The triangle is a simplex with three edges and three vertices.

Triangular Irregular Network (TIN). An unstructured triangulation consisting of triangles. Often used to represent terrain data.

Triangulation. A set of non-intersecting simplices sharing common vertices, edges, and/or faces.

Type Converter. A type of filter used to convert from one dataset type to another.

Type Checking. The process of enforcing compatibility between objects.

Uniform Grid. A synonym for structured points.

Unstructured Data. Data in which one data item is unrelated (either geometrically or topologically) to other data items. Also referred to as irregular data.

Unstructured Grid. A general dataset form consisting of arbitrary combinations of cells and points. Both the geometry and topology are explicitly defined.

Unstructured Points. A dataset consisting of vertex cells that are positioned irregularly in space, with no implicit or explicit topology.

User Defined Data. A data attribute beyond the typical data attributes scalars, vectors, tensor, normals, and texture coordinates. Typically a function of visualization application.

Visualization. The process of converting data to images (or other sensory stimuli). Alternatively, the end result of the visualization process.

Vector. A specification of direction and magnitude. Vectors can be used to describe fluid velocity, structural displacement, or object motion.

Vector Field Topology. Vector fields are characterized by regions flow diverges, converges, and/or rotates. The relationship of these regions one to another is the topology of the flow.

Vertex. A primary 0D cell. Is sometimes used synonymously with point or node.

View Coordinate System. The projection of the world coordinate system into the camera's viewing frustrum.

Visualization Network. A series of process objects and data objects joined together into a dataflow network.

Volume. A regular array of points in 3D space. Volumes are often defined as a series of 2D images arranged along the z-axis.

Volume Rendering. The process of directly viewing volume data without converting the data to intermediate surface primitives. Contrast with *surface rendering*.

Vorticity. A measure of the rotation of fluid flow.

Voxel. Short for volume element. In **vtk**, a primary three-dimensional cell with six faces. Each face is perpendicular to one of the coordinate axes.

Warping. A scalar and vector visualization technique that distorts an object to magnify the effects of data value. Warping may be used on vector data to display displacement or velocity, or on scalar data to show relative scalar values.

World Coordinate System. A three dimensional Cartesian coordinate system in which the main elements of a rendering scene are positioned.

Writer. A type of mapper object that writes data to disk or other I/O device.

Yaw. A rotation of a camera's position about the vertical axis, centered at its viewpoint. See also *pitch* and *roll*. Contrast with *azimuth*.

Z-Buffer. Memory that contains the depth (along the view plane normal) of a corresponding element in a frame buffer.

Z-Buffering. A technique for performing hidden line (point, surface) removal by keeping track of the current depth, or *z* value for each pixel. These values are stored in the *z*-buffer.

Zoom. A camera operation that changes the field of view of the camera. Contrast with *dolly*.

Index